HOW OFTEN WOULD I HAVE GATHERED YOU

STORIES FROM THE OLD TESTAMENT
AND RELATED SOURCES
FOR LATTER-DAY SAINTS

HOW OFTEN WOULD I HAVE GATHERED YOU

STORIES FROM THE OLD TESTAMENT
AND RELATED SOURCES
FOR LATTER-DAY SAINTS

as told by

Val D. Greenwood

Illustrations by

Owen Richardson

Edenwood Press

P.O. Box 1194

Riverton, UT 84065

Printed in the United States of America on acid-free paper.

How Often Would I Have Gathered You: Stories from the Old Testament and Related Sources for Latter-Day Saints

Designed by Jana Rade, design@american-book.com

Library of Congress Cataloging-in-Publication Data

Greenwood, Val D.
 How often would I have gathered you : stories from the Old Testament and related sources for Latter-day Saints / as told by Val D. Greenwood ; illustrations by Owen Richardson.
    p. cm.
 Includes bibliographical references and index.
 ISBN-13: 978-0-9826017-0-9
 ISBN-10: 0-9826017-0-0
 1. Bible stories, English--O.T. 2. Book of Mormon stories. I. Title.
 BS550.3.G74 2007
 221.9'505--dc22

                    2006033536

Special Sales

These books are available at special discounts for bulk purchases. Special editions, including personalized covers, excerpts of existing books, and corporate imprints, can be created in large quantities for special needs. For more information e-mail val@valgreenwood.com.

DEDICATION

To Peggy and Patty:
Peggy, my first wife,
who has gone on ahead of me,
and Patty, my present wife,
who now blesses my life with her love.

"A virtuous woman is a crown to her husband" (Proverbs 12:4).

FOREWORD

I love stories in the Old Testament. However to get the full and accurate story perfectly in my mind I have to do quite a bit of work—work that I do not always do. Recently, in my private scripture study I've been reading the stories of Abraham, Isaac, and Jacob. Because I already know, or at least once knew, the many stories of these remarkable Patriarchs, I am able to go right to the Bible and have the thrill of having these real-life stories unfold before my eyes. But, for that to happen, it surely helps to know the stories before I start to read.

If you're like me and would like to have somebody give you some help on both the familiar and unfamiliar stories of the Old Testament, then this book is for you. Val Greenwood does just that. He's done a lot of research to bring these accounts to life. Now you and I can open his book and read with clarity all the facts, feelings, and lessons of the stories in this vitally important record.

Once you and I have in our minds and hearts the vital framework that Val has provided, then we can go right to the Old Testament and read with clarity the marvelous words of that sacred book. On the other hand, if we go to the Bible first, it's a bit difficult unless you're quite a gifted scholar. Plus, Val puts it all in historical perspective, and gives magnificent insights into the stories. I feel this book is going to be a great treasure for those who want to know more about the Old Testament. And that's all of us—both the teachers and the learners.

As I read many of the stories I found myself thinking, "Oh yes! Now I remember how that goes." It was quite a revelation to me to read the stories again and fix them in my mind. But more than that, Val goes into some stories that I've really never understood and makes them perfectly clear. I know, at least in part, something of each of these stories, but Val gives me *the rest of the story.*

I have known, respected, and loved Val for many years. His mind and heart have made him a valuable resource to family history and temple work. His book on family history research in the United States is a classic. Now, with this book, he has written an equally meaningful book on another vital subject. Thanks, Val Greenwood.

George D. Durrant

PREFACE

During 2002, while reading the Old Testament as part of the Church's four-year scripture-study schedule, I was impressed that it would be very helpful to members of the Church if the wonderful stories from that great book of scripture were available in a simple, straightforward style consistent with the Latter-day Saint perspective. As this impression persisted, I felt inspired to undertake the project myself. And I can truthfully say that it has been a marvelous and exciting adventure.

Before I began writing, I thought there might be perhaps fifty or sixty good stories, but before I was through, I had written 229 stories, and I know that several more could have been found. Someone will surely ask why this or that story was not included, just as some will ask why some stories *were* included. In response to the latter question, I can only answer that every story was included because it is part of the Old Testament mosaic and provides important historical perspective, and not necessarily because of its inspirational or spiritual value. I trust that the overall effect of this collection of stories will be both inspirational and educational.

My stories are based on the King James Version of the Bible. And, insofar as possible, they are arranged in chronological sequence, beginning with the Grand Council in Heaven and continuing down through the return of the Jews from their Babylonian captivity and the rebuilding of the temple and Jerusalem. Some of the books of the Old Testament—notably the literary writings and the books of the prophets—are not included in the scope of these stories merely because they do not contain stories.

During the writing process, I was blessed with abundant inspiration. I received critical and profound insights important to the various stories from unexpected sources. It was amazing how the project unfolded and progressed.

Most of the stories are quite short (with some notable exceptions, such as the stories of Job and Esther). In some cases, such as with the life of Samson, I took what could have been one very long story and created two or three shorter ones. I have made every effort to keep the stories simple, straightforward, and free from fictionalizing and embellishment. I have also tried to tell each story as the scriptures tell it while, at the same time, eliminating redundancy and cumbersome (and sometimes sordid) details. I have also chosen not to draw any morals or lessons from the stories, but rather to let them speak for themselves.

Where appropriate, the stories contain dialogue, seeking to be faithful to the scriptural message while carefully using modern expressions rather than the cryptic language of the seventeenth-century King James Version translators. The old-style pronouns (*thee, thy, thou,* and *thine*) relating to people are replaced with modern equivalents. However, the old-style pronouns have been retained and capitalized when they relate to Deity. Along with these, I have also retained the old-style verbs (*wilt, shalt, canst, dost, goest, sayest, couldest,* etc.) to match the pronouns. After careful and agonizing deliberation, I chose *not* to capitalize the pronouns *he, him,* and *his* as they relate to Deity, for I discovered early on that trying to do so was very confusing. No disrespect is intended.

Because the King James translators replaced the name Jehovah with "the LORD" (with LORD in small caps, as you see here), I have chosen, in most cases, to reinsert the name of Jehovah into my stories. One exception (and there are some others) was in the phrase "the house of the LORD" in reference to the temple. I kept this wording because the usage is so familiar. In some cases (such as in the Ten Commandments) this usage may seem strange to you, but I think you will also find it enlightening.

Because many people struggle with the pronunciation of biblical names and places, a pronunciation guide (with suggested pronunciations) is included in the back of the book. Maps are also included to help provide perspective. Two indexes are also included: a name index and a subject index. I believe these indexes enhance the value of the book as a reference source.

Where various weights and measures are included in a story, I have given metric equivalents (mostly in footnote references) for the benefit of readers outside the United States.

One area of interpretation that I did not attempt to deal with relates to numbers. When large numbers—especially as they concern the sizes of armies or populations—are found in the Old Testament, they should be viewed with some skepticism. Though the numbers used in these stories are exactly as they appear in the scriptures, you should remember that there was a tendency among many Old Testament writers to greatly exaggerate.

I have used footnotes extensively in these stories. Though many of these notes are not essential to the understanding of a story, I have tried to provide insights and salient background information. Because the individual stories were intended to stand on their own, the same footnotes (or similar variations) are repeated in several stories; there are also many footnote cross-references to related stories.

To enhance understanding, I have—in addition to the King James text—relied heavily on the study helps contained in the Latter-day Saint editions of the scriptures, including footnote references, the Bible Dictionary, and the Joseph Smith Translation. I have also used the modern scriptures (Book of Mormon, Doctrine and Covenants, and Pearl of Great Price) to provide additional understanding and insight, where applicable. Some of the stories were taken entirely from these other scriptures—such as the stories relating to the Grand Council in Heaven, the council at Adam-ondi-Ahman, Moses' vision on the mountain, etc.

I wish I could say that these stories are perfect, but I cannot. Unfortunately, the biblical record is not always clear. There are cases where the record is incomplete and many pertinent facts are missing so that the events seem illogical. But I have full confidence that at some future time, when our understanding is perfected and the full story is known, the truth will be clear and enlightening. In the meantime, I have attempted to fill a few such gaps.

Another source of possible imperfection in my stories is the case where separate accounts of an event were included in the writings of more than one Old Testament writer. Because some of these duplicate accounts differ in their details, I have made interpretative decisions in order to write the stories. However, I have tried, in most cases, to give footnote explanations for my interpretations. I have also tried to explain my reasoning (in the footnotes) when my conclusions differ from traditional interpretations. Wherever my interpretations may prove to be inaccurate, I take full responsibility, as I do for everything else you find here.

I do not intend that this book should replace or upstage the scriptures in any way. I hope, rather, that these stories will introduce the Old Testament, enhance the scriptural experience, and help you gain greater appreciation for the Old Testament canon. Where many of our friends of other faiths consider much of the Old Testament to be myth, the Latter-day Saints hold a different view. We believe that the Old Testament accounts are essentially literal and accurate, insofar as they are translated correctly (Articles of Faith 8).

I am grateful to all who have offered encouragement, insight, and help. They kept me on track and provided the impetus for me to complete it. Thomas G. Chapman, director of the LDS Institute of Religion in Santa Barbara, California (now in Boston, Massachusetts), was one who offered continual encouragement. Two other men who had an influence on the project (though they did not know it) were S. Michael Wilcox and Richard Neitzel Holzapfel. Each gave me many significant insights as I attended their Old Testament classes. Dana Pike provided useful information about pagan deities.

I express appreciation to Brad Burgon, the editor assigned by American Book Publishing to work with me in pulling everything together. His careful scrutiny and helpful suggestions have added much value to the book. I also appreciate the painstaking efforts of Bonnie Schenck Darrington, my copy editor, for urging me to clarify some important issues, and Jana Rade for a magnificent book cover design. I would also be remiss if I did not thank Net Ministries for granting permission for me to use their phonetic system in my pronunciation guide, to Abigdon Press for allowing me to use their Old Testament maps, and to Owen Richardson for his illustrations.

I have special appreciation for the two women in my life—both of whom have been English teachers. My first wife, Peggy, before her passing in 2003, read most of an early draft and offered valuable suggestions. My present wife, Patty, read and offered suggestions on a later draft.

And lastly, I am grateful to you, the reader, for your willingness to look at another view. I hope you will find it refreshing and the effort rewarding.

TABLE OF CONTENTS

III. Jacob and Joseph

IV From Egypt to Sinai

V.   **Through the Wilderness and Into Canaan**

VIII. David and Solomon: The House of Judah on the Throne

IX. Divided Israel (Part I): Two Separate Kingdoms

X.   **Divided Israel (Part II): Good Kings, Bad Kings, and the Threat of Captivity**

XI. Judah's Captivity: The Prophecies, the Siege, and the Reality

XII.   The Captivity of Judah, the Return, and Beyond

ILLUSTRATIONS

Maps

INTRODUCTION

Most people would probably not tell you that the Old Testament is their favorite book of scripture. And many would say they find it difficult to read and understand. In fact, the Old Testament is not read as often as other scriptures; and books relating to it gather dust on bookstore shelves. The Latter-day Saints, however, do keep coming back to the Old Testament every four years—when prompted to do so by Church curriculum.

Most of us, in addition to finding the Old Testament complex and difficult to understand, are also confused by its message. We are impressed that God may have acted too harshly as he dealt with his children—quite differently, we think, from the way the Savior taught in the New Testament.

Indeed, it is true that God did act harshly on many occasions as he dealt with his chosen people—a stiff-necked people with a penchant for turning their backs on him and worshipping false gods. But, though he was harsh at times in meting out his justice, he gave his people the opportunity to repent time after time after time; and he promised them deliverance if they would but heed him and keep their covenants. The people of Israel did not become God's holy people because they were perfect, for certainly they were not. They were his chosen people because they were more righteous (or perhaps less wicked) than their neighbors and because of God's promises to their fathers Abraham, Isaac, and Jacob (see Deuteronomy 9:4–6).

Many stories in this book are accounts of miraculous deliverance. And, in spite of all the unfaithfulness and infidelity on the part of Jehovah's chosen people, he repeatedly promised them that in the last days they will inherit eternal blessings and that he will gather them from the four corners of the earth—when they will truly be his people and he will be their God (see, for example, Ezekiel 11:20, 14:11; Zechariah 8:8).

It is important for the student of the gospel to remember that the Old Testament gospel is the same as the New Testament gospel and the same as the latter-day gospel. It was taught from the days of Father Adam, and even before the foundations of this earth were laid. The principles of the gospel are eternal, unchanging principles.

The Old Testament is brimming with wonderful stories—some inspiring and some not so inspiring—but the primary message of the Old Testament is of the then-future mortal mission of our Savior, who is identified thirty-four times in the Old Testament as "the Holy One of Israel." And it is quite clear from the Old Testament record that Jehovah himself, the God of the Old Testament, is also the Holy One of Israel.

Though the Old Testament contains many accounts of harsh punishment being meted out for disobedience, a second great message of the Old Testament is of Jehovah's love for his chosen people. That very message is the basis for the title of this book (not stated in the Old Testament in those exact words, but rather in Doctrine and Covenants 43:24).

I hope that as you read these stories you will gain a greater understanding of and appreciation for the Old Testament and for the love that God has for his children—a love that is deeper and more abiding than we as mortals can comprehend.

I

THE COUNCIL, THE CREATION, THE FALL, AND THE EARLY PATRIARCHS

1–WHOM SHALL I SEND?

(Moses 4; Abraham 3; Revelation 5)

Long ago, before our earth was created, we lived with God, our Father in Heaven; we were his spirit children. As he stood in our midst, he looked at the greatest and most noble spirits among us and said, "I will make these my rulers." Jehovah, God's firstborn son in the spirit, was one of these. Jehovah was the greatest of God's children because he was like God. Others of those great and noble spirit children were Abraham, Moses, Jeremiah, and the prophets of all dispensations.

God called his spirit children together in a Grand Council; all of us were there. In that council, he explained his plan for saving his children—his plan of salvation. One part of the plan was to create an earth where his spirit children could be born and gain physical bodies—bodies like his own. Life on this earth would be called mortality. In mortality we would have experiences to help us develop our faith, overcome our weaknesses, and learn to serve each other.

God explained to us that he would give us our agency. This meant that we would have the right to obey his laws and receive his blessings. He said that if we used our agency wisely—acting in truth and righteousness and keeping the covenants that we would make with him—we could become like him and return to live with him. "I will prove you by your mortal experience," he said, "to see if you will do all things that I command you. And, if you keep my commandments, I will add glory upon your heads forever."

We liked God's plan and shouted for joy when we heard it.

Our Father explained that there were two great obstacles to be overcome as part of his plan—physical death and spiritual death. Because we would all become mortal and have corruptible bodies, we would suffer physical death, the separation of our spirits from those bodies that we needed to be like him.

The other obstacle, spiritual death, would come as a result of our sins, he said. Because all mortals would be imperfect and thus make some bad choices in the use of our agency, we would be unable to live again with our perfect Father, thus being spiritually dead.

To overcome these obstacles, God's plan required that there be a Savior—someone completely without sin. This sinless person, because of his perfection, would have power to overcome both physical and spiritual death for us by giving his life as an infinite and eternal sacrifice. As a result of this great sacrifice, the sins of all those who would repent and be obedient to God's plan would be paid for. This victory over sin and imperfection would overcome spiritual death for those who would accept it.

Then, after incomprehensible suffering as he laid down his life as a sacrifice for our sins, this sinless being would break the bands of physical death by rising from the grave in glorious resurrection. His resurrection would overcome physical death and enable the bodies and spirits of all mankind to be reunited forever.

God the Father himself was the only one fully qualified to make such a sacrifice—to give his life as an infinite and eternal sacrifice for mankind. Because he was the only infinite, eternal, and perfect being, the plan would require God's own death and resurrection in our behalf. But that was a problem. Because the Father was already perfect and had a glorified immortal body, he could neither die nor be resurrected. A substitute was needed to stand in his place.[1]

This substitute would need to be someone else who was without sin; someone whom God could name as his authorized representative; someone to whom he could give power to lay down his life for our sins and power to take it up again, breaking the bands of death. With this in mind, our Father in Heaven asked the question in the council: "Whom shall I send?"

Two of God's greatest spirit children stepped forward in response to that question and offered to go. Each said he was willing to stand in God's place and be our Savior. The first to volunteer was Jehovah, God's firstborn son. Though he understood the high price he would have to pay, he said, "Father, here am I, send me. Thy will be done and the glory be Thine forever."

The other great spirit son who offered to be our Savior was Lucifer.[2] "Send me," said Lucifer. "I will be Thy son. And I will redeem all mankind so that not one soul shall be lost."

Though Lucifer's objectives sounded noble, he had his own agenda. "In order for me to be the savior of mankind," he said, "the plan will need some major changes." Lucifer first explained that our agency—our right to obey God's laws and receive his blessings—would have to be taken from us so that we could be forced to be saved.

Besides wanting to take away man's agency, Lucifer also wanted God's own glory for himself. "Surely I will do it;" he said. "Wherefore, give me Thine honor."

---

[1] The idea of the Savior acting as a substitute for the Father in completing the Atonement was borrowed from Allen J. Fletcher, "Facsimile No. 1: Principles and Reflections," *Two Articles on the Facsimiles of the Book of Abraham,* 2nd ed. [Sterling, Alberta, Canada: the author, 1999].

[2] The name Lucifer means "bearer of light" or "morning star."

Because God did not like the changes that Lucifer demanded, and because he knew that those changes could never succeed, he chose Jehovah to be our Savior and become the Son of God in the flesh. Jehovah was chosen because he was so much like God, because he completely supported God's plan, and because he was the only one with the ability to live a perfect life. He was, in fact, the one who had been chosen from the beginning because he was the only one of God's spirit children qualified to serve as God's substitute and to be our Savior. And consequently God said, "I will send the first."

When our Father in Heaven chose Jehovah to become our Savior and overcome the obstacles to man's salvation, he made Jehovah a member of the presidency of the heavens—a member of the Godhead. He gave Jehovah power to have life in himself,[3] which was total power over life and death. By this power Jehovah was able to either give his life or keep it. And, after giving his life, he also had power to take it up again. When all mankind had lost their lives, he would have power to restore them once again to life and thus become "the Resurrection and the Life."[4]

Lucifer—angry because his proposal was rejected and he was denied God's power—rebelled against Heavenly Father and Jehovah. He led those who would follow him in a fierce battle. In that battle, Lucifer and his disciples were defeated by Jehovah's great power and cast down to the earth where Lucifer became Satan or the devil. He and his followers are on the earth today—still as spirits—providing the opposition and temptations necessary to make man's agency effective and thus enable man to prove himself. These evil spirits are trying with all their might to thwart God's plan by blinding and leading captive those who choose not to hear God's voice.

2—A HOME FOR HIS CHILDREN
(Genesis 1–2; Moses 2–3; Abraham 4–5)

The earth we live on was created in six days or six periods of time, but we do not know exactly how long those time periods were. The scriptures say, however, that one day to God is like a thousand years to man. Whatever their length, we know that the days of creation were a great deal longer than any days that we can imagine.

The scriptures describe only the physical creation of the earth, but the spirit of every plant and every animal, as well as the spirit of every person, was created before it was placed upon the earth. The scriptures give no details of this spirit creation, so we know little about it. We know only that all things were created in the spirit before they were created naturally upon the face of the earth. We also know that all mankind are spirit children of God himself and that he is literally our Father in Heaven.

It may be more correct to say that the earth was organized than to say it was created, for it was not created out of nothing. We are told that the earth was made from materials that were available in space, but we are not told how this was done. Heavenly Father was in charge, but others helped with the work of creation, under the direction of God's firstborn and Beloved Son, Jehovah.[5] Not only did Jehovah act for God in the creation, but he was also chosen in the Grand Council to come to the earth as a man, acting in God's place, to be our Savior.[6]

This earth is only one of God's worlds, for he has many of them. The scriptures say that he has created worlds without number, all of them through his Beloved Son. As part of the creation of this earth, he also created the heavens or the sky and the atmosphere above the earth.

---

[3] See John 5:26.
[4] See John Taylor, *Mediation and Atonement* (Salt Lake City: Deseret News Co., 1882), 135-136.

---

[5] Jehovah and Yahweh are modern translations of the four consonants in the Hebrew name that was variously identified in ancient scriptures as JHVH, JHWH, YHVH, or YHWH. The name was considered too sacred to be spoken aloud, and the word "Adonai" (which means Lord) was substituted when it was spoken. Based on this principle, the translators of the King James Bible used the name Jehovah very rarely; in most cases they used the term "the LORD" (in small capital letters) instead. A quick look at the Old Testament will show that this usage was extensive.
[6] See story "1—Whom Shall I Send?"

On the first day of the creative process, God brought forth light and then divided the light from the darkness. "Let there be light," he said, and there was light.

On the second day, God created a firmament and called the firmament heaven. He also divided the waters under heaven from the waters above heaven.

On the third day, he gathered all the waters under the heavens together in one place and caused the dry land to appear. He called the waters sea and the dry land earth. He also caused grass, herbs, and trees to grow on the land. Each of these produced seeds to bring forth other plants of its same kind.

On the fourth day of creation, God placed the lights in the heavens to divide the day from the night and provide light to the earth. There were two great lights. The greater light, the sun, was set in the heavens to rule the day. The lesser light, the moon, was set to rule the night. God also set the stars in the heavens.

On the fifth day, God created all the creatures in the sea, including fish and great whales. He also created fowls and birds of every kind. And he commanded these birds and sea creatures to multiply and to each bring forth its own kind.

On the sixth day, God made beasts and cattle of every kind, as well as creeping things. He also created man and gave him dominion over all other living things. All of God's creations were important to him, but man was God's most important creation because man was God's child.

All things that God created and placed on this earth, including man, were created physically, but they were not in the same state in which we know them because they were not subject to death—they were not mortal. They were in a spiritual condition—so called because they were not yet mortal and could not die. Because they were no longer just spirit, but not yet mortal, we say that they were in a spiritual state.

God commanded the man whom he created to multiply and to fill[7] the earth. This was the first commandment that he gave.

On the seventh day, after the creation of the earth and the heavens was finished, God rested and was refreshed.[8] And he blessed the seventh day and made it a holy day.

God was pleased with the earth that he had made. He knew it would be a wonderful home for his children.

---

[7] The word *fill* is used here rather than *replenish* because it is more correct. Elder Joseph Fielding Smith gave the following explanation: "Why the translators of the King James Version of the Bible used the word *replenish* may not be clearly known, but it is not the word used in other translations and is not the correct meaning of the Hebrew word from which the translation was originally taken. It is true that the Prophet Joseph Smith followed the King James Version in the use of this word, perhaps because it had obtained common usage among the English-speaking peoples. *Replenish*, however, is incorrectly used in the King James translation. The Hebrew verb is Mole... meaning fill, to fill, or make full. (*Hebrew Lexicon* by Joshua W. Gibbs, A.M., p. 120.) This word *Mole* is the same word which is translated fill in Genesis 1:22, in the King James Bible, wherein reference is made to the fish, fowl, and beasts of the earth: 'And God blessed them, saying, Be fruitful, and multiply, and fill the waters in the seas, and let fowl multiply in the earth.'" (Joseph Fielding Smith, *Answers to Gospel Questions*, 5 vols. [Salt Lake City: Deseret Book Co., 1957–1966], 1:207.)

[8] See Exodus 23:12

3

3—WERE IT NOT FOR OUR TRANSGRESSION

(Genesis 2–3; Moses 3–4, 6)

After God created the first man, he gave him the breath of life and named him Adam. Then God planted a beautiful garden in a place called Eden and put Adam in the garden.

The garden was filled with trees, and the trees bore much fruit. Among those many trees were two of special significance, the tree of life and the tree of knowledge of good and evil. God instructed Adam to take care of the garden and told him that he could eat the fruit of every tree, all except that fruit which came from the tree of knowledge of good and evil. He said to Adam, "You will surely die in the day you eat the fruit of that tree."

God understood that it was not good for man to be alone, so he created a woman to be Adam's wife. Adam named the woman Eve, and Adam and Eve lived together in the Garden. Adam understood that man was not complete without woman and that Eve, as his wife, was part of him. He said, "I now know that she is bone of my bones and flesh of my flesh. She shall be called woman because she was taken out of man, and the two of us together shall be one flesh."

Adam and Eve enjoyed their lives in the garden and were kept busy caring for it. They were also busy naming the animals. God told them that whatever they called an animal, that would be its name.[9]

While they lived there in the Garden of Eden, Adam and Eve were privileged to walk and talk with God. And, though both of them were naked, they did not know it. And though they had their agency—the right to obey God's laws and receive his blessings—they were innocent. They knew neither good nor evil, joy nor sorrow, pleasure nor pain. Also, as long as Adam and Eve were in the Garden of Eden, they could have no children. And their bodies—though physical—were spiritual rather than mortal, so they could not die.

By and by the serpent in the garden disrupted the idyllic lives of Adam and Eve. Satan put it into the serpent's heart to trick Eve into eating the fruit of the tree of knowledge of good and evil, contrary to God's commandment. Satan mistakenly believed that if Adam and Eve would eat the fruit, God's plan for saving his

---

[9] The Book of Moses (Moses 3:19–20) has Adam naming the animals before Eve is created. The Book of Abraham (Abraham 5:19–21), however, says that the animals were named after Eve's creation.

children would fail and the earth could not fulfill the purpose of its creation. Satan did not understand that Adam and Eve needed to eat the fruit of the tree before the plan for the salvation of God's children could become fully effective.

Adam and Eve are tempted by Satan

The serpent deceived Eve by telling her that she would *not* die if she ate the fruit of the tree. "You will be as God," he said, "knowing good and evil." He told her that the fruit was delicious and that it would make her wise like the Gods. Being thus tempted, Eve became curious. She longed to eat the fruit—and she soon did so. And not only did Eve eat the fruit, she gave some to Adam and he ate it also. Adam protested at first, but he knew that he must also eat the fruit if he and Eve were to remain together.

Eating the forbidden fruit changed the nature of Adam and Eve from spiritual to natural or mortal. Knowing good and evil, they now understood that they were naked. The very act of eating the fruit changed everything. Not only were Adam and Eve changed in nature from spiritual to mortal, but everything on the earth underwent that same change. The Fall was complete.

To cover their bodies, they sewed fig leaves together and made aprons. And when they heard the voice of God in the garden, they hid among the trees.

God called to Adam and asked him why he was hiding and if he had eaten the fruit. Adam was quick to blame Eve. "The woman Thou gavest me and commanded to remain with me,"[10] he said, "she gave me some of the fruit and I ate it."

God then spoke to Eve. "What have you done?" he asked her.

"The serpent beguiled me," replied Eve. "He gave me some of the fruit and I ate it."

Angered by Eve's answer, God spoke to the serpent. "Because you have done this," he said, "you shall be cursed above the cattle and above every beast of the field. You shall go upon your belly and eat the dust of the earth all the days of your life."

God also told Satan that he would put a spirit of enmity, or ill will, between the serpent and the woman's child. "You will have power to bruise the man's heel," he said to the serpent, "but the seed of the woman shall crush your head."

God then spoke once more to Eve. "I will greatly multiply your sorrow and your conception," he said. "You will bring forth children in sorrow, your desire will be to your husband, and your husband shall rule over you."

Then, speaking to Adam, God said, "Because you hearkened to the voice of your wife and ate the forbidden fruit, the ground will be cursed for your sake. You will eat of it in sorrow all the days of your life. It shall bring forth thorns and thistles, and you shall eat the herb of the field. By the sweat of your face you shall eat your bread until you return to the ground—for you shall surely die."

Jehovah then spoke saying, "The man has become as one of us for he now knows good and evil. And now, so that he does not eat also of the tree of life and live in his sins forever, I will send him out of the garden to till the earth."

Jehovah made coats of animal skins to clothe Adam and Eve and sent them out of the garden. He then placed cherubim[11] and a flaming sword at the east of the garden to keep Adam and Eve from eating the fruit of the tree of life.

Adam and Eve—now mortal—were subject to all the trials and problems of mortality, but they remained faithful to God. They tilled the ground as they were commanded and they began to have children.

When Adam and Eve called upon God, they heard the voice of Jehovah from inside the garden but they were shut out of his presence. He commanded them to worship him and to offer up the firstlings of their flocks as a sacrifice to him, but he did not tell them why. An angel later explained to them the reason for these sacrifices. "Your sacrifices," said the angel, "are in similitude of the great sacrifice that will be made by the Only Begotten Son of God, who is full of grace and truth."

Jehovah taught Adam and Eve that, although they had fallen and become mortal, they could still be saved through his great plan of salvation. And Adam, being filled with the Holy Ghost, praised God. "Because of my transgression," he said, "my eyes have been opened. In this life I shall have joy, and again in my flesh I shall see God."

Eve also rejoiced because of the fall. Said she, "Were it not for our transgression we never should have had children. We never should have known good and evil or the joy of our redemption. And we never could attain the eternal life that God gives to the obedient."

Adam and Eve were baptized by the power of the Holy Ghost, and God forgave them of their transgression in the Garden of Eden.

---

[10] This commandment for Adam and Eve to stay together (as stated in Moses 4:18) is not often noted, but it is just as significant as the other commandments that they were given. And, like the commandments to multiply and fill the earth (see footnote 7) and to subdue it, this commandment relates also to us and to our marriages.

[11] A cherub is a heavenly creature, the exact form of which is unknown. The plural is *cherubim*.

4–BECAUSE OF MY BROTHER'S FLOCKS

(Genesis 4; Moses 5–6)

Adam and Eve were blessed to have a large family, and they taught their children the gospel. Many of their children, however, did not obey the gospel teachings. For Satan came among them, claiming to be the Son of God and telling them not to believe the teachings of their parents. Many of Adam and Eve's children loved Satan more than they loved God and began, as the scriptures say, to be carnal, sensual, and devilish.

After many years, Eve had a son whom she called Cain.[12] She was very happy because she thought this son would surely be a man of God. Cain, however, proved to be a disappointment for he rejected God and the teachings of his parents. Cain, like his brothers and sisters before him, loved Satan more than he loved God and was quick to do whatever Satan asked.

Later, Eve had another son whom she named Abel.[13] Abel loved God and obeyed him; he also obeyed his parents. Abel became a sheep farmer and had many flocks.

Satan commanded Cain, who farmed the land, to offer a sacrifice to Jehovah of the fruits of his ground. Though Cain was reluctant, he made the offering after a long time had passed. Cain's offering, however, was not accepted by Jehovah because it was inspired by Satan and not by faith and because it was not a blood sacrifice as Jehovah had commanded.

When Jehovah accepted Abel's animal offering, Cain became jealous of his brother. He was angry because his offering was rejected while that of Abel had been accepted. He felt that his offering was as good as Abel's and that Jehovah was playing favorites.

Satan knew the feelings of Cain's heart, and he was pleased.

Jehovah spoke to Cain and asked him why he was upset. "If you do well," said Jehovah, "you will be accepted. But if you do not do well, sin lies at the door and Satan desires to have you. Except you repent and keep my commandments, I will deliver you up to Satan, and you will rule over him. You will become the father of lies and will be called Perdition,[14] for you were known as such before this world was." Jehovah went on to warn Cain that future peoples, when they saw wickedness among them, would say that it began with Cain, because Cain rejected the counsel of God.

Cain was offended and he became even more angry. And because he refused to listen to Jehovah's voice, Adam and Eve suffered great heartache. They mourned for their son because they loved him.

While Cain was still upset, Satan came to him and asked him to swear an oath of secrecy. He also asked Cain to have his wicked brothers swear that same oath so that Adam would not know of it. "If you will do this," Satan promised, "I will deliver Abel into your hands, along with everything that he owns." This was all done in secret, and Cain felt evil satisfaction because of the secret oath that would allow him to murder his brother for gain.

One day while Cain and Abel were together in the field, Cain rose up and slew his younger brother. He rejoiced in his murderous deed, "For," said he, "I am now free, and my brother's flocks are mine."

Cain was not left much time to gloat. When he returned from the field that day, Jehovah came and spoke to him again. "Where is your brother Abel?" asked Jehovah.

"I do not know," Cain lied in response. "Am I my brother's keeper?"

Then Jehovah said, "What have you done, Cain? Abel's blood cries to me from the ground, and the earth that has opened her mouth to receive your brother's blood shall curse you. From this time forth, the ground will not yield to you in its strength, and you shall be a fugitive and vagabond in the earth."

"Such a punishment is too hard for me to bear," cried Cain. "Satan tempted me because of my brother's flocks—and I was angry when you accepted Abel's offering but rejected mine. If you drive me out now, I fear that whoever finds me will kill me because of my sins."

"Whoever slays you," answered Jehovah, "shall receive of my vengeance sevenfold."

Jehovah then put a mark upon Cain so that no one would slay him. Then Cain went to dwell in the land of Nod with his wife and many of his brothers. And, from that time forth, he was shut out of Jehovah's presence.

Though Adam and Eve mourned for both Cain and Abel, they were soon blessed to receive another son in place of the martyred Abel—a son whom they named Seth.[15] Seth looked exactly like father Adam, except for the difference in their ages. He obeyed God and, as his brother Abel had done before him, offered an acceptable sacrifice to Jehovah.

---

[12] The name *Cain* means "possession."

[13] The name *Abel* means "breath" or "vapor," probably because of the shortness of his life.

[14] The title *Perdition* means "to give ruin."

---

[15] The name Seth means "compensation" or "substitute."

5–CAIN'S LEGACY
(Genesis 4; Moses 5)

When Jehovah set a mark upon Cain so that no one would kill him, Cain went with his wife to live in the land of Nod on the east side of Eden. There in Nod with his wife, who was the daughter of one of his brothers, Cain had a son whom they named Enoch. And the city that Cain built he called the city of Enoch, after his son.[16]

As time passed Enoch had a son whom he named Irad, as well as other sons and daughters. Irad had a son whom he named Mehujael, as well as other sons and daughters. Mehujael had a son whom he named Methusael, as well as other sons and daughters. And Methusael had a son whom he named Lamech.

Lamech had two wives—Adah and Zillah—and Adah bore two sons. Adah's son Jabal was father of those who dwell in tents and keep cattle. His brother Jubal was the father of musicians, those who handle the harp and the organ.

Zillah had two children, a son and a daughter. She named her son Tubal-cain, and he was an instructor of those who were artisans with brass and iron. Her daughter she called Naamah.

One day Lamech called his wives to him and told them that he had killed a man. "I have slain a man to my wounding," he said, "and a young man to my hurt. If our father Cain shall be avenged sevenfold for killing his brother, surely I shall be avenged seventy-and-sevenfold." But Lamech did not tell his wives the man's name.

Lamech had made a covenant with Satan just as Cain had done before him and, because of that covenant, he became known as Master Mahan. He was master of that same great secret that Satan had administered unto Cain.

Then, when Irad, Lamech's great-grandfather, began to tell Cain's secret among the sons of Adam, Lamech slew him also—not to get gain as Cain had when he slew Abel—but for the sake of the oath and to preserve his secret. For, from the days of Cain there was a secret alliance among the sons of men, and they were caught up in perversions and works of darkness.

Because of this secret alliance or secret combination (as it was called), Jehovah cursed Lamech, all his family, and all others who had covenanted with Satan. But the curse did not prevent their abominable works from being spread among the sons of men.

Lamech also had other problems. Because he had revealed the secret to his wives and they had rebelled against him and revealed it, Lamech was despised and cast out. He was forced to live in exile for fear of being slain because he had broken his pledge to preserve the secret. And because Lamech's wives rebelled against him and declared his secret abroad without compassion, the daughters of men, from that time forth, did not speak these secret things.

As works of darkness prevailed among the people, God was angry with the wicked and cursed the earth with a sore curse. Yea, he was angry with all the sons of men whom he had created for they refused to hearken to his voice or to believe on his Only Begotten Son who had been prepared from the foundation of the world.

---

[16] Neither Cain's son Enoch, nor the city of Enoch which was named after him, should be confused with the Enoch who was a third great-grandson of Seth (see story "6–The Mountains Will Flee Before You"). The city that Seth's descendant built was called the City of Zion but is also referred to as the City of Enoch.

6—THE MOUNTAINS WILL FLEE BEFORE YOU

(Moses 6–7)

Enoch, Adam's fourth great-grandson, was a very righteous man. He was ordained to the Melchizedek Priesthood by Adam when he was twenty-five years old[17] and was taught all the ways of God by his father, Jared. Though Enoch was born into a family line of righteous men and women, the people who lived around him did not obey God's prophets and were very wicked.

One day as Enoch was going about his business, he heard the voice of Jehovah speaking to him. "I am angry with this people," Jehovah told Enoch, "because they have hardened their hearts, denied God, and sought their own counsel." Jehovah then proceeded to call Enoch to preach the gospel to these wicked people and call them to repentance.

Enoch was confused when he heard these words because he felt incapable of doing what Jehovah had called him to do. Bowing to the earth, he asked why he had been chosen. "The people will not listen to me because I am very young," he said. "I am also slow of speech and the people hate me."

"If you will open your mouth," responded Jehovah, "I will give you the words to speak. The Holy Spirit will be with you and will give you great power. Mountains will flee before you and rivers will turn from their courses."

Jehovah proceeded to show Enoch many wonderful things, unknown to other men, and Enoch became well known throughout the land as a seer because of these marvelous visions.

Because Enoch loved God, he went among the people to warn them for their wickedness and to call them to repentance. His message, however, was less than popular with the people. In fact, poor Enoch offended everyone. But, though the people were offended, they still came to hear him. It seemed such a strange thing to them to hear a man preach the word of God.

Enoch taught the people that a Savior, God's Only Begotten Son, would someday come into the world to die for the sins of all those who would accept him. And though most people did not believe what Enoch told them, they were afraid to harm him because God was obviously with him. Enoch's power was so great that, when he preached, the people trembled and could not stand in his presence.

Enoch told the people about his experiences on Mount Simeon, when Jehovah stood before him and talked to him face-to-face. He told them how he had seen many generations of the world in vision, including their wars and their destruction.

As time went by, the righteous separated themselves from the wicked. And just as the wicked hated Enoch, the righteous were attracted to him. They followed him, obeyed his teachings, and became the people of God. And when the armies of the wicked came to war against the people of God, Enoch led his people to victory in battle. So great was Enoch's faith that when he spoke the word of God, the earth trembled, the mountains fled before him, and the rivers ran out of their courses, just as Jehovah had promised.

A curse came upon those who fought against Enoch and the people of God. They began to fight among themselves while, at the same time, the people of God lived in righteousness and peace.

When Enoch built a city for his righteous followers, Jehovah came and lived with them. Jehovah blessed his people and called them Zion because they were of one heart and one mind and had no poor among them.

After the City of Zion prospered for 365 years in righteousness, while nearly everyone else was wicked, Jehovah took the city and all who lived there up into heaven. They were translated.[18] And with the City of Zion gone from the earth, the power of Satan was rampant upon all the face of the land.

Jehovah, however, did not give up on his wicked children. He sent angels to preach to them and bear testimony of the Father and the Son. And when the Holy Ghost fell upon those who believed the words of the angels, they too were translated and caught up into the City of Zion.

---

[17] See Doctrine and Covenants 107:47.

[18] Translated beings do not become immortal, but are given power over death. When the purpose of their translation is fulfilled, they will die—or, in most cases—be changed from mortality to immortality (i.e., resurrected) in the twinkling of an eye. The best description of a translated body is found in 3 Nephi 28:37. This description relates to the three Nephite disciples who were to remain upon the earth as translated beings until the Second Coming of the Savior. The scripture says that they could "not suffer pain nor sorrow,... that Satan could have no power over them, that he could not tempt them; and they were sanctified in the flesh, that they were holy, and that the powers of earth could not hold them."

7—A PRINCE OVER THEM FOREVER

(Doctrine and Covenants 107, 116; Daniel 7)

Adam lived for 960 years after he and Eve became mortal and were expelled from the Garden of Eden. He was privileged to see many generations of his family.

Three years before Adam's death, when he was bowed down with age, he called his righteous descendants together in a beautiful green valley called Adam-ondi-Ahman.[19] Among the many thousands who came in response to Adam's call were his faithful descendants Seth, Enos, Cainan, Mahalaleel, Jared, Enoch, Methuselah, and Lamech—all high priests.

After Adam had addressed his descendants at the council of Adam-ondi-Ahman and had given them his last blessing, the people rose up and blessed him. They honored him as Michael, the archangel, who had played an important part in the premortal worlds.

Because Adam was righteous and obeyed the voice of Jehovah, Jehovah also appeared at the council and blessed him. In his blessing, Jehovah declared to Adam, "I have set you to be at the head, many nations shall come out of you, and you are a prince over them forever."

When Adam had received Jehovah's blessing, he was filled with the Holy Ghost. He stood and foretold all things that mankind would experience down to the latest generations of the earth. All of these prophecies of Adam were written in the book of Enoch and will someday be available to us.

The council at Adam-ondi-Ahman was a great and marvelous gathering of Adam's seed, unlike any other that has ever been held. But it has been promised that Adam, the Ancient of Days, will visit his righteous people again before the Savior's Second Coming. He will attend another great council at Adam-ondi-Ahman, and the Savior will also be present. There in that great council, Adam will deliver to our Savior all the keys he holds as the father of the peoples of the earth.

---

[19] According to a revelation given to the Prophet Joseph Smith on May 19, 1838, the valley of Adam-ondi-Ahman is located in what is now Daviess County, Missouri (see Doctrine and Covenants, section 116). There are many diverse opinions about the meaning of the name, but it seems to mean "the valley where God talked to Adam."

8—THE GREAT FLOOD

(Genesis 6–9 [including JST]; Moses 8)

Noah was a great-grandson of Enoch.[20] He and his sons—Shem, Ham, and Japheth—were righteous men; they lived by God's teachings and God loved them.

At the time Noah lived, because the earth was filled with so much wickedness and violence, the righteous were being translated[21] and taken into heaven to join with Enoch and the people of the City of Zion.

The very thoughts of the people of Noah's time were evil in God's sight. Young men and women of faithful families were marrying unbelievers and were being led away from their faith. Jehovah mourned the wickedness of the people and vowed that if they did not repent they would be destroyed. "My Spirit," he said, "will not always strive with man. If they do not repent, I will send a flood upon them."

Noah and his sons preached the gospel to the people and warned them of the impending flood but, when no one would listen, Jehovah commanded Noah to build a giant boat called an ark. The ark, Jehovah said, would save the lives of Noah and his family—him, his three sons, his wife, and his sons' wives—when the floodwaters came to cover the earth.

Because Noah had never built an ark before, Jehovah gave him careful instructions. The ark was to be 450 feet (137.16 meters) long and 75 feet (22.86 meters) wide. It was to be 45 feet (13.72 meters) high (three stories), and was to be watertight. There would also be one window and a door in the side of the ark.

---

[20] Noah was the ninth generation from Adam and the first of his direct family line born after Adam's death. Lamech, Noah's father, was 182 years old when Noah was born, and Noah was but ten years old when his grandfather Methuselah ordained him to the priesthood (see Doctrine and Covenants 107:52).

[21] Translated beings do not become immortal, but are given power over death. When the purpose of their translation is fulfilled, they will die—or, in most cases—be changed from mortality to immortality (i.e., resurrected) in the twinkling of an eye. The best description of a translated body is found in 3 Nephi 28:37–39. This description relates to the three Nephite disciples who were to remain upon the earth as translated beings until the Second Coming of the Savior but, no doubt, relates to all translated beings. The scripture says that they could "not suffer pain nor sorrow, … that Satan could have no power over them, that he could not tempt them; and they were sanctified in the flesh, that they were holy, and that the powers of earth could not hold them."

When the ark was finished, Jehovah commanded Noah to take two of every kind of animal—a male and a female—inside. This was to include birds, cattle, creeping things, and wild beasts—every living thing that breathes through its nostrils. However, he was to take seven of every clean animal and clean bird. He was also commanded to take sufficient food for both his family and the animals.

Noah and his sons worked hard and did as Jehovah commanded them. But it must have looked strange to their unrepentant neighbors when they saw Noah's massive ark sitting on dry ground with no water in sight.

One day Jehovah spoke to Noah telling him that the time had finally come to enter the ark. "Beginning in seven days," Jehovah said, "I will make it rain upon the earth for forty days and forty nights. Every living thing will be destroyed." Noah again did all that Jehovah commanded him. He and his family entered the ark and brought in the animals. When the animals had all been brought on board, two-by-two, male and female, Jehovah shut them in.

In the 600th year of Noah's life, on the seventeenth day of the second month—after the seven days had passed—the rain began to fall in torrents as the clouds of heaven were opened. Soon the water began to rise and the fountains of the great deep were broken up.

The floodwaters rose and the ark began to float and toss about on top of the water. Water soon covered all the land, all the high hills, and then all the mountains. Every living creature that breathed through its nostrils, except for those saved in the ark, was destroyed. After forty days and forty nights of torrential rain, water covered everything. And after the rain finally stopped, water still covered the land for many days.

Remembering Noah and his family in the ark, Jehovah caused the winds to blow across the water, and the water level slowly began to fall. When the ark finally came to rest on the mountains of Ararat on the seventeenth day of the seventh month, Noah and his family were still locked safely inside. Nearly three months later, on the tenth day of the tenth month, the tops of the mountains could be seen.

After another forty days, Noah opened the window of the ark and sent out a raven. The raven did not return but flew back and forth above the ark until the waters dried up. Noah also sent out a dove but, when the dove found no place to land, she returned to the shelter of the ark.

When seven days more had passed, Noah released the dove a second time. This time, the dove returned in the evening with an olive leaf in her mouth. Noah and his family now had assurance that the waters were dry-ing up. And, after seven days more, the dove went out again never to return.

On the first day of year 601, Noah and his sons removed the covering from the ark and saw that the land was dry. Then on the twenty-seventh day of the second month—more than a year after the rains began—Jehovah commanded Noah and his family to release the animals and leave the ark.

Once Noah and his family had left the ark, he built an altar and gave thanks to God. On that altar, he made a burnt offering of one of every clean beast and every clean bird that he had preserved.

When Noah's offering was complete, Jehovah spoke to him and blessed him. He commanded Noah and his sons to multiply and to replenish the earth. Jehovah gave them power over the animals, the fowls of the air, and the fishes of the sea. They were commanded to use these for food, along with the green herb. Jehovah warned them, however, that the blood of animals should not be shed unless the meat was required for food.

Noah pleaded with Jehovah that he would never again curse the ground for the sake of mankind and that he would never again destroy all the living from off the earth. In response to Noah's pleading, Jehovah made a covenant that he would never again destroy the earth by flood. Jehovah also set the rainbow in the clouds of heaven as a token of the covenant he made with Enoch many years before—that when men will faithfully keep the commandments of God, the City of Zion[22] will return to the earth.[23]

---

[22] The account of the City of Zion being taken into heaven is told in story "6–The Mountains Shall Flee before You."

[23] It has been widely understood that the rainbow was set in the heavens as a token from God that he would never again send a flood to destroy the inhabitants of the earth. However, the Joseph Smith Translation (see JST Genesis 9:21–25) makes it clear that the rainbow was a token of the covenant Jehovah made with Enoch relative to the return of the City of Zion. Though Jehovah did indeed promise that he would never again destroy the earth's inhabitants with water, the rainbow was not a token of that promise.

9—A TOWER AND A CITY CALLED BABEL

(Genesis 10–11; Ether)

A tower was built to reach to heaven

Many years had passed since the great Flood of Noah's time, and, as the people multiplied upon the land, they migrated from the east to the land of Shinar.[24] All the people spoke the same language and were able to communicate freely. Their leader, a man named Nimrod, was a grandson of Ham, Noah's son. Nimrod was known as a mighty hunter.

The people built cities and had everything they wanted but, for many of them, the things that were important had little to do with God. Because they remembered that God had once destroyed the peoples of the earth with a great flood, they determined to build a city and a tower whose top would reach to the heavens, where no flood could ever reach them. They called their city Babel. It was a very wicked city and its future name, Babylon, has been used in the scriptures to describe both wicked cities and wicked peoples.

As the people united their labors in the construction of their city and tower, Jehovah came down to see their work, and he was angered by what he saw. Because of the wickedness of the people and their lack of faith in him, he said, "Because these people all speak the same language and are united in their purpose, nothing is impossible to them. I will confuse their language so they cannot understand one another, and they will scatter over all the face of the earth."

When the languages were confused and a man could no longer understand the speech and language of another, their unity was disrupted and their work on the tower soon halted. They scattered to many places and built many cities. Never again did man seek to build a tower that would reach to the heavens.

Living in the city of Babel at the time of the tower was a righteous man named Jared, as well as Jared's righteous brother.[25] The brother of Jared was a large and mighty man who was dearly loved by Jehovah because of his righteousness. When Jared observed that the language of many had been confounded so they could not communicate, he asked his brother to plead with Jehovah to turn away his anger and not confound their language. In response to the pleadings of the brother of Jared, Jehovah preserved the language of the two brothers, their families, their friends, and their friends' families.

Jehovah smiled with favor upon this little group of people and led them northward out of the land of Shinar. He told them, "I will go before you into a land that is choice above all the lands of the earth. There I will bless you and your seed and raise up a great nation unto me. There shall be no greater nation than that which I will raise up from your seed."

Jehovah led this righteous little band in the wilderness for many years, and then guided them in the construction of eight barges, which were watertight like Noah's ark. With these barges, they were able to cross the great sea to another land. Their voyage took them nearly a year.

The descendants of Jared, his brother, and their friends became a mighty people, still speaking the language of their fathers. When they were righteous they prospered in the land of promise that Jehovah had given them—the American continents. When they were wicked, they brought war and captivity upon themselves—and finally their own destruction.

---

[24] Shinar was in the lower plain between the Tigris and Euphrates rivers in the area where the country of Iraq is now located. Shinar is said to be the original name for the area that later came to be known as Babylonia.

[25] It is reported that the Prophet Joseph Smith gave the name Mahonri Moriancumer to a son of Reynolds Cahoon and then told them that this was the name of the Brother of Jared. This report came from one of Brother Cahoon's children who said he overheard the conversation as a young child. It is more likely that the Brother of Jared had only one name—like everyone else of that time period—and that this name was Moriancumer, the same name that the Jaredites gave to their encampment on the seashore, as reported in Ether 2:13 (see Sydney B. Sperry, *Book of Mormon Compendium*, [Salt Lake City: Bookcraft, 1968], 465).

II

ABRAHAM AND ISAAC

10—SAVED BY GOD'S POWER
(Genesis 11; Abraham 1–2)

About 200 years after the Tower of Babel,[26] a young man named Abram—a descendant of Shem—lived with his family in a place called Ur, among a people who were known as Chaldeans.[27] Included in Abram's family were his father Terah, his brothers Nahor and Haran, and his wife Sarai.

The Egyptians had great influence among the Chaldeans, and many of the people, including Abram's father and most of his family, worshipped the false Egyptian gods. Abram, however, because of his righteousness, did not turn to idolatry. Rather, he sought to have the blessings of God in his life. He wanted to hold the true priesthood that had been held by his ancestors. Abram was blessed for his righteousness and was ordained to the priesthood by Melchizedek, the great high priest.[28]

As part of their worship of Egyptian gods, the people of Ur offered their children as sacrifices. Those most likely to be offered were the ones who refused to worship the Egyptian gods. Because many in Abram's family were not happy with him, he was identified as one whose life would be sacrificed in such an offering.

When he was forcibly placed on the sacrificial altar and the Egyptian priest lifted his hand to take Abram's life, he prayed earnestly for deliverance. As Abram prayed, he was filled with a vision of God and an angel stood beside him. The angel untied the ropes that bound him, destroyed the altar, and smote the officiating priest so that he died.

God then spoke to Abram saying, "Behold, my name is Jehovah. I have heard your prayers and have come to deliver you. I will take you away from your father's house and from your family into a strange land. I will lead you by the hand and my power will be over you. And through your ministry, Abram, my name will be known in the earth forever, for I am your God."

"You will be like Noah," Jehovah continued, "for your life will be saved by God's power and you will become the father of many nations."

Abram is bound and ready to be sacrificed

Following Abram's narrow escape from death on the Egyptian altar, a great famine swept the land of Chaldea and Abram's family suffered greatly. His brother Haran died from the famine, and his father Terah suffered until he repented of both his desire to take Abram's life and his worship of false gods.

As the famine reached its peak, Jehovah spoke to Abram and told him that the time had come for him to leave Ur and go to a land that would be shown him. So, Abram left Ur, taking with him Sarai and Haran's son Lot, and traveled to a place that they named Haran after Abram's late brother. Here they settled, and here Terah, who had followed him, found them. They lived in Haran for many years, and, when the famine abated, Terah returned to his worship of false gods. He eventually died at Haran.

---

[26] The account of the Tower of Babel and the confusion of tongues that took place there is told in story "9–A Tower and a City Called Babel."

[27] Ur of the Chaldees has traditionally been identified with what is now the city of Mugheir in southern Mesopotamia, located on the Euphrates River about 150 miles (241.4. kilometers) north of the Persian Gulf. However, more recent evidence suggests that Ur may have been a place now called Urfa in south central Turkey, a place much closer to Haran (see Hugh Nibley, *Abraham in Egypt* [Salt Lake City: Deseret Book Co. 1981], 68–69).

[28] See Doctrine and Covenants 84:14.

11–LOT CHOOSES SODOM

(Genesis 12–13; Abraham 2)

After Abram and Lot had lived for many years in Haran, the land they had named for Abram's brother, Jehovah appeared in answer to Abram's prayers and told him to take Lot and go to the land of Canaan. "You will be a minister to bear God's name in a strange land," Jehovah declared to Abram, "and I will give this land to you and to your seed forever if they will obey my voice."

Abram left Haran as Jehovah commanded him, taking his wife Sarai, his nephew Lot, the people they had converted in Haran, and all the substance that they had gained there. Journeying southward toward the land of Canaan, they dwelt in tents along the way. But travel was difficult because there was a famine in the land.

When the travelers arrived at a place called Jershon, Abram built an altar and prayed to Jehovah that the famine would be turned away from his father's house so that they would not perish. When they reached Moreh, within the borders of Canaan, Abram felt uneasy because he did not know what to expect in that unfamiliar land. When he offered another sacrifice and prayed for guidance, Jehovah appeared in answer to his prayer and said, "Behold, I will give this land to your seed."

As Abram and Lot moved slowly through the land, they worshipped God and built many altars. One of these they built on a mountain east of Beth-el. This was a place to which Abram and Lot would later return when the famine had passed. But, for fear of perishing from starvation, they determined to go into Egypt for the time being, where they lived for many years.[29]

Abram and Lot prospered in Egypt and both accumulated large herds and much wealth. But when the famine had passed, they returned to that mountain east of Beth-el where they had once built a holy altar. Though the land yielded its abundance, Abram and Lot soon learned that it could not support the vast herds of both men, and this became a source of conflict among their herdsmen, as well as among the Canaanites who lived in the area.

As the situation became more difficult, Abram called Lot to him and said, "There should not be strife between us, or between our herdsmen, for we are brothers. Because the whole land lies before us, it seems prudent for us to separate ourselves. So I will let you choose. If you take the left hand, I will go to the right; or if you choose to go to the right hand, I will go to the left."

Considering Abram's generous offer, Lot looked up from his place on the mountain and surveyed the surrounding lands. He beheld that the fertile plains to the east were well watered, even as it were the Lord's garden or the land of Egypt. Lot was pleased with what he saw, and he chose the plains of the Jordan as the place where he would live. Separating his flocks from those of Abram, he and his family journeyed eastward, while Abram remained on the mountain. Lot settled among the cities of the plains and pitched his tent near the city of Sodom.[30]

As Abram stood upon the mountain after Lot's departure, Jehovah spoke to him. "Lift up your eyes," said Jehovah to Abram, "and look northward from the place where you stand; then look southward, and eastward, and westward. I will give you all the land that you can see—to you and to your seed forever. I will also make your seed as the dust of the earth, so that if a man can number the particles of the earth, your seed shall also be numbered. Arise now, Abram, and walk through the length and breadth of the land; for this land will all be yours."

Once Abram had viewed the lands that Jehovah had promised him, he removed his dwelling place to the plain of Mamre in Hebron. There he built an altar to Jehovah and offered sacrifices.

---

[29] There are two other stories that fit within the time sequence of this account and give more detail about the covenants God made with Abram and the experiences of Abram in Egypt. These stories are entitled "12–In You and in Your Seed" and "13–Abram and Lot Go to Egypt." They are presented as separate stories because of their significance in the scriptural account.

[30] It is believed by many that the fertile plains that Lot chose lay to the south of the Dead Sea and that the land they occupied is now partially covered by the waters of that sea. The area has been associated with the fertile Vale of Siddim (see Werner Keller, *The Bible as History: What Archaeology Reveals about Scripture*, 2nd rev. ed. [New York: William Morrow and Co. Inc., 1981], 90-91).

12–IN YOU AND IN YOUR SEED

(Genesis 12; Abraham 2)

In addition to the promises that Jehovah made to Abram concerning a land of inheritance for his descendants, he also made other significant promises to him and his seed. Many years earlier, when Jehovah first called Abram, he promised that he would give the land of Canaan to him and his seed as an everlasting possession. He also called Abram as a minister to bear God's name in that land.

As Abram left Haran and first set his feet upon the land that Jehovah had promised him, Jehovah spoke to him again. "I am the Lord your God," he said. "My name is Jehovah, and I know the end from the beginning. I dwell in the heavens, and the earth is my footstool. I stretch my hand over the sea, and it obeys my voice. I cause the wind and the fire to be my chariot. I say to the mountains, 'Depart hence,' and they are taken away in an instant by the whirlwind.

"My hand shall be over you, Abram, and will make of you a great nation. I will bless you above measure and make your name great among all nations.

"You will be a blessing unto your seed, and they will bear this ministry and priesthood unto all nations. Indeed, all nations will be blessed through your name, for as many as receive this gospel shall be called after your name and be counted as your seed. And they shall rise up and bless you as their father.

"I will bless those who bless you and curse those who curse you. And in you and your seed—that is, in your priesthood—all families of the earth shall be blessed, even with the blessings of the gospel, which are the blessings of salvation and eternal life. And I give you this promise, Abram, that the right to this priesthood will continue in you and in your seed—that is, in the literal seed of your body."

Jehovah then promised Abram that all who would be righteous and obey the gospel and the commandments of God would be counted as his seed forever and would carry the gospel message to the whole world.

Jehovah also preserved the records of Abram's fathers in Abram's hands and told him that the records were of great worth because they contained knowledge of the beginning of the creation of the earth, the planets, and the stars, as these things were made known to the fathers.

Because Abram was righteous, even in the face of great opposition, God loved him dearly and blessed him for his faithfulness.

13–ABRAM AND LOT GO TO EGYPT

(Genesis 12; Abraham 3)

Abram and Lot suffered much because of the famine in the land of Canaan after leaving Haran. For fear of perishing from starvation, they decided to go into Egypt. As they journeyed southward, Jehovah appeared to Abram and taught him many things that he wanted Abram to teach the Egyptians.

Abram introduces Sarai as his sister

When Abram lived in Ur of Chaldees, Jehovah had given him a Urim and Thummim,[31] which Abram was able to use to communicate with Jehovah and to see into the heavens. As he viewed the heavens, he saw many great stars, including the star nearest to the throne of God, which was greater than all the others. Jehovah spoke to Abram through the Urim and Thummim and told him that the stars he saw were the governing stars. He said that the greatest star was called Kolob and that Kolob ruled over all the others. Jehovah told Abram

---

[31] According to *Bible Dictionary*, LDS-KJV, s.v. "Urim and Thummim," the words *Urim* and *Thummim* mean "lights" and "perfections." The two together constitute one instrument through which a prophet can receive revelation or by which he can translate languages, just as the Prophet Joseph Smith used the Urim and Thummim to translate the ancient Book of Mormon manuscript.

that, according to the times and seasons of Kolob, one revolution was a day, just as it is on the earth. "But one day on Kolob," he said, "is the same as a thousand years of this earth's time. And the time on Kolob is God's time."

Jehovah showed Abram all of the worlds that he had organized. The number of them was so great that he could not see the end of them. "Your seed," said Jehovah, "will be as these stars in number. If you can count their number, so shall you number my seed."

Through the Urim and Thummim, Abram saw all of the intelligences that God had organized before the world was. "You, Abram," said Jehovah, "were one of the noble and great ones whom I chose to be his rulers."

Abram was shown the Grand Council in Heaven where Jehovah, God's firstborn spirit son, was chosen to be the Savior of the world. He also saw Lucifer or Satan being cast out of heaven when he rebelled against God's plan. He was then shown the creation of the earth and everything that would happen on this earth from the beginning until the end of it.

As Abram prepared to enter Egypt, Jehovah gave him some instructions that you and I might think strange. "Your wife Sarai," he said to Abram, "is a woman very fair to look upon. When the Egyptians see her they will say, 'She is his wife,' and they will then kill you and save her. However, if she tells them she is your sister, you shall both live."

Abram told Sarai all that Jehovah had told him, and they did as they were counseled. When the Egyptian princes saw Sarai, believing her to be Abram's sister, they spared both of their lives and took Sarai into the Pharaoh's house. Abram, at the same time, was given great honors by the Pharaoh and was able to teach the Egyptians the important things that Jehovah had prepared him to teach.

The Pharaoh was pleased with Sarai because of her beauty, and he pleaded with Abram because of her, offering many gifts if Abram would give Sarai to him to become his wife. But, though Abram declined, Jehovah brought great plagues upon the Pharaoh and his house because of Sarai.

The Pharaoh became very angry when he finally learned that Sarai was Abram's wife. "Look at the trouble you have caused me," he said to Abram, accusing him. "Why did you tell me she is your sister and not your wife? Do you not know that I might have taken her as my wife? You must take her now and leave my country."

The Egyptian Pharaoh commanded his servants concerning Abram, and they sent him away from their country with his wife, his nephew Lot, and all their belongings.

14–THE RESCUE OF LOT
(Genesis 14)

After Abram and Lot were well settled in their own places—Abram on the plains of Mamre and Lot on the fertile plains of the Jordan—there was a war involving the cities on the plains of the Jordan. The war extended to the city of Sodom, where Lot lived, and lasted for many years.[32] As the war progressed, the kings of Sodom and Gomorrah were defeated in a battle near the Dead Sea by people from the east under the leadership of several kings, chief of whom was Chedorlaomer, the king of Elam. Though there were some who escaped the battle and fled to the mountains, Lot and several others were taken captive. One of those who escaped came to Abram on the plain of Mamre and told him of Lot's plight.

When Abram learned that Lot had been captured, he armed 318 of his own trained servants and three of his young Amorite neighbors. Then Abram and his little army followed the outlaws north to Hobah, near Damascus, where he engaged them in battle. Abram and his servants were successful in overpowering the kings and their army and freeing the captives.[33] They then returned to Sodom with Lot and the other captives, also bringing with them the spoils of the battle.

Upon their arrival in Sodom, they were met by Melchizedek, the great high priest and king of Salem.[34] Being God's high priest, Melchizedek administered bread and wine to those present. He then blessed

---

[32] The cities on the plain of Jordan are identified in the scriptures as Sodom, Gomorrah, Admah, Zeboiim, and Bela (later renamed Zoar by Lot). For twelve years these five cities—known historically as the cities of the Vale of Siddim—and their kings had paid tribute to King Chedorlaomer. In the thirteenth year, when they rebelled, Chedorlaomer sought the help of three other kings and waged war against the rebels. In the ensuing battle, the kings of the five cities were defeated and their lands were ravaged. King Chedorlaomer has been identified with Khudur-Lagamar of the ancient inscriptions. The name means "servant of [the goddess] Lagamar" (see Werner Keller, *The Bible as History: What Archaeology Reveals about Scripture*, 2nd rev. ed. [New York: William Morrow and Co. Inc., 1981], 86).

[33] Many who have written about this battle waged by Abram to rescue his nephew Lot have called it the battle of the kings.

[34] This was not the first meeting of Abram and Melchizedek. Abram's ordination to the priesthood (see Doctrine and Covenants 84:14) was likely much earlier than this.

Abram saying, "Blessed be Abram of the Most High God. And blessed be the Most High God, possessor of heaven and earth, who has delivered your enemies into your hands."

Because Melchizedek, as the high priest, was the keeper of God's storehouse, Abram paid tithing to him, delivering up everything that God had given him beyond his need.

Because he had been so soundly defeated himself, the king of Sodom rejoiced to learn of Abram's success against the kings from the east. When he saw that Abram had rescued all the captives and had also brought back spoils from the battle, he said to Abram, "I will take the people you have brought back, but you may keep the goods for yourself."

Abram declined the king's offer. "I will take no reward," he replied, "not even the thread of a shoe latchet. I will give all the spoils to you. For if I were to take these things, you would claim that you have made me rich." Abram asked only that the three young Amorites who went with him to battle be given a fair share of the goods as their reward.

15—THE BIRTH OF ISHMAEL
(Genesis 15–16)

Abram was beginning to worry. Jehovah had promised him a great posterity, yet he was getting to be an old man and still had no children. And he had little hope of children because his wife Sarai was barren.

When a child was born in Abram's household—the son of his steward, Eliezer—Abram wondered if this child would become his heir. But Jehovah spoke to him and said, "This child shall not be your heir, Abram. Your heir shall be your own seed." And again Jehovah showed him the stars of heaven and renewed his promise that Abram's seed would be as numerous as those stars. Then he said to Abram, "Know of a surety that your seed will be strangers in a land that is not theirs. They shall serve the people of that land and be afflicted by them for 400 years. But I will judge that land and your seed shall come out of her with great substance."

Abram's wife Sarai was also concerned that Jehovah's promise had not been fulfilled because of her inability to have children. As she contemplated the problem, she devised a plan that would make Abram a father. She would give her Egyptian handmaid, Hagar, to Abram as a concubine, or second wife.[35] With the plan firm in her mind, Sarai said to Abram, "Because the Lord has kept me from having children, go in unto my maid that perhaps I may obtain children through her." Abram was not convinced, but after ten more years had passed and he still had no children, he heeded

---

[35] The main difference between a wife and a concubine was probably the fact that a concubine could be rejected or cast aside without a bill of divorcement, while a wife could not. There was no difference between the children of a wife and those of a concubine, and the latter were a supplementary family to the former. The names of the concubines' children are listed in the patriarchal genealogies, and their position and provision depend on their father's will. The state of concubinage was provided for by the law of Moses and certainly also preceded that law. A concubine would generally be either (1) a Hebrew girl bought from her father, (2) a Gentile captive taken in war, (3) a foreign slave who had been bought, or (4) a Canaanite woman, bond or free. The rights of the first two were protected by the law (Exodus 21:7; Deuteronomy 21:10–14), but the third was unrecognized and the fourth prohibited. Some free Hebrew women also became concubines (see William Smith, *Dictionary of the Bible*, GospeLink, CD-ROM, s.v. "concubine").

Sarai's voice and took Hagar to be his wife because God commanded him to do so.[36]

Sarai's plan did not work as nicely as she had thought it might. For, once Hagar had conceived, she began to despise Sarai and to treat her badly. This, of course, upset Sarai and she complained to Abram. "I have given my maid into your bosom," Sarai lamented, "and when she saw that she conceived, she began to hate me."

Abram assured Sarai that she was free to do with Hagar whatever seemed best to her, but when Sarai began to treat her harshly, Hagar fled into the wilderness.

An angel found Hagar by a well on the way to Shur and confronted her. "Hagar, Sarai's maid," said the angel, "where did you come from and where are you going?"

"I am running away from the face of my mistress Sarai," answered Hagar.

"If you will return to your mistress and submit yourself to her," the angel said, "I will multiply your seed exceedingly. Your seed shall not be numbered because of the greatness of their number. You shall bear a son and shall call him Ishmael,[37] because God has heard your afflictions. Your son shall be a wild man; his hand shall be against every man, and every man's hand against him. But he shall dwell in the presence of all his brethren."

When the angel departed, Hagar obediently returned to the house of Abram, where she bore him a son whom she named Ishmael. Abram was eighty-six years old when Ishmael was born.

16—A CHANGED NAME AND A PROMISED SON
(Genesis 17–18)

When Abram was ninety-nine years old, Jehovah appeared to him again. "Walk before me and be perfect," Jehovah commanded him. "I will make my covenant between me and you and will multiply you greatly. And your name shall no longer be Abram, but Abraham, for I will make you a father of many nations.[38] You will be very fruitful; I will make nations of you and kings shall come out of you."

Jehovah continued: "I will establish my covenant between me and you and your seed after you as an everlasting covenant. I will give the land of Canaan to you and your seed forever as an everlasting possession—as long as they keep my covenant—and I will be their God.

"And this is the token of the covenant between us, which you and your seed shall keep: every man-child among you shall be circumcised in his foreskin when he is eight days old. For my covenant shall be in your flesh as an everlasting covenant."

Then Jehovah spoke to Abraham concerning his wife. "You shall no longer call your wife Sarai," he said, "but she shall now be called Sarah.[39] I will bless her and give you a son of her. She shall be the mother of nations and kings shall descend from her."

When Abraham heard Jehovah's words, he fell on his face and rejoiced. Yet such a thing seemed impossible to him, and he said in his heart, "How can a child be born of him that is 100 years old, and how shall Sarah have a child when she is ninety?"

Then Abraham, still doubting that he and Sarah could produce children in their old age and thinking also of his love for his son Ishmael, said to Jehovah, "Oh, that Ishmael might live before Thee." For, indeed, Abraham was satisfied to have Ishmael as his heir and content to have God's covenant fulfilled through him. During those thirteen years that had passed since Ishmael's birth, Abraham had considered Ishmael to be the son of the covenant. But this was not God's plan.

Jehovah spoke again. "Sarah shall bear you a son and you shall name him Isaac,"[40] he said. "As for Ishmael, because I know how much you love him, I have blessed him also and will make him fruitful. He shall beget twelve princes and become a great nation. But though Ishmael will be great, my covenant will be es-

---

[36] Genesis does not say that God commanded Abram to take Hagar as a wife, but that fact is made quite clear in Doctrine and Covenants 132:34 and 65.

[37] The name Ishmael means "God hears."

[38] The name Abraham means "father of a multitude."

[39] The name Sarah means "princess."

[40] The name Isaac means "laughter."

tablished through Isaac, the son that Sarah will bear unto you at this same time next year."

When Jehovah had departed, Abraham followed his instructions carefully. He took his son Ishmael and every male of his household and circumcised them in their foreskins. Abraham was also circumcised that day as a token of his covenant with Jehovah. But Abraham did not tell Sarah of Jehovah's promise to give them a son in their old age.

Then, as Abraham sat in the door of his tent in the heat of the day, he looked up and saw three holy men—one of whom was Jehovah himself—approaching. Leaping to his feet, Abraham ran and bowed deeply before them. Urging them to stay and rest by his tree, he offered water to wash their feet. When he offered to prepare food for them before they departed, the men agreed.

Abraham asked Sarah to prepare some cakes while he killed a fat calf for his guests. He then gave the calf to one of his servants to dress, and the meal was soon prepared and set before the three holy travelers.

When they had eaten and Abraham and the men stood under the tree, Jehovah spoke. "Where is Sarah, your wife?" he asked.

"She is in the tent," replied Abraham.

Then Jehovah spoke again saying, "You shall both become fertile, as if you were in the prime of your lives, and Sarah will have a son."

Sarah, who was sitting in the tent door behind them, overheard the man's promise. She was completely surprised by what she heard because she was not aware of the message Jehovah had previously delivered to her husband. Because this information came as such a great shock to her, she laughed. "Shall I have the pleasure of a son after I am old—Abraham being old also?" she asked herself.

Upon hearing Sarah's laughter, Jehovah asked Abraham, "Why did Sarah laugh and why does she doubt that she can have a child when she is old? Is anything too hard for the Lord? At the appointed time you shall both become fertile as in the prime of your lives, and Sarah shall bear a son."

Even Sarah had come to accept the idea that Ishmael was Abraham's promised heir, and she was frightened by the words of the holy man. His words were more than she could comprehend and she denied that she had laughed.

17—FOR THE SAKE OF TEN
(Genesis 18–19)

After their visit with Abraham, Jehovah and his two companions arose and looked toward Sodom and the plains of Jordan where Lot had gone to live. "We must go there," they said.

As they started on their journey, Abraham walked with them to show the way. As they walked, they told Abraham of the fate in store for the wicked city of Sodom. "Because the sins of Sodom and Gomorrah are great," they said, "we are going there now to see if they are ripe for destruction."

When they reached the point where Abraham would turn back, he took courage and stood before them in the road. "Will the righteous be destroyed along with the wicked?" Abraham asked. "If there are fifty righteous people in the city, can it not be spared? For surely God would not slay the righteous with the wicked."

The answer came: "If fifty righteous are found in Sodom, the city will be spared for their sake."

Abraham had second thoughts. "I know I am not worthy to speak," he said boldly, "but what if there should be five less than fifty? Would the city be destroyed for lack of five?"

"If there are forty and five righteous, it will not be destroyed."

Abraham thought on this reply and then spoke yet again: "What if only forty righteous are found?"

"It will not be destroyed for forty's sake."

Abraham was persistent; perhaps there were not as many righteous people there as he had thought. "Please don't be angry if I speak more," he said, "but what if only thirty are found?"

"The city will not be destroyed if we find thirty righteous there."

"And what if there are only twenty?" he asked.

"Sodom will not be destroyed for twenty's sake."

"Do not be angry with me and I will speak just one more time," said Abraham, "but what if only ten righteous people are found in the city?"

"It will not be destroyed if there are ten righteous people," answered Jehovah. Then he and his companions continued on their way to Sodom as Abraham returned to his tent and to his wife.

Lot was sitting at the city gate as Jehovah his and angelic companions approached the city of Sodom. When he saw them, he rose and bowed to the ground before them. But when Lot invited his visitors to stay at his house and rest for the night before continuing their journey; they declined his invitation. "We will stay in the street," they said. But when Lot pressed them further, they agreed to spend the night with him.

Things became unpleasant during that night when the men of Sodom surrounded Lot's house, issuing many threats and demanding the involvement of Lot's guests in the vile homosexual sins for which the city of Sodom is remembered. When Lot resisted, his own life became endangered. He was spared, however, when his guests rescued him from the angry mob by pulling him into the house and shutting the door. The three holy messengers then caused blindness to come upon the mischief-makers so that they were unable to find the door. The plight of Lot and his family was now serious and their safety was in jeopardy.

The holy visitors instructed Lot to gather his family and to promptly leave the city. They said that Sodom and all who lived there were about to be destroyed for their wickedness. Ten righteous people could not be found there.

Lot went out hastily into the night to find his sons-in-law. "We must leave Sodom at once," he told them, "for Jehovah is about to destroy it." But the young men, thinking that Lot was mocking them, refused to heed his warning, and Lot returned to his home discouraged.

Before morning arrived, Lot's holy visitors spoke to him again—this time with extreme urgency. "Hurry!" they pleaded. "If you do not take your wife and your unmarried daughters and leave at once, you will all be destroyed with the wicked!"

When Lot and his family delayed, Jehovah and his companions took their hands, led them out of the city, and told them to run for their lives. "Do not look back!" they warned, "and do not stay here on the plain! You must flee to the mountains or be consumed with the city."

"I know you have spared my life," said Lot as they passed a little city, "but I cannot make it to the mountains. If I have found grace in your sight, let us stop at this place, and everything will be fine." The holy visitors agreed that, for Lot's sake, they would not destroy that little city. And Lot called the city Zoar.[41]

The sun had already risen when Lot and his family arrived at Zoar. And Jehovah caused fire and brimstone to rain from the heavens that morning on the cities of the plains.[42] He destroyed the cities, all the people who lived there, and everything that grew there.

Lot's wife did not heed the warning of the holy visitors, however. She looked back toward the burning cities and became a pillar of salt.

Lot and his two unmarried daughters soon left Zoar and went to live in a cave in the mountains. And through his daughters, Lot became the father of the Moabites and Ammonites.

---

[41] The name Zoar means "little thing."

[42] The cities on the plain of Jordan, as identified in Genesis 14, were Sodom, Gomorrah, Admah, Zeboiim, and Bela (which was renamed Zoar by Lot and was not destroyed).

18–A MAN OF GREAT INFLUENCE

(Genesis 20)

After the destruction of Sodom,[43] Abraham left his home on the plains of Mamre and journeyed among the Philistines. His journey took him southward to Gerar where Abimelech was king. Abraham took his wife Sarah with him and told Abimelech that she was his sister, just as he had told the Egyptians earlier.[44]

When Abimelech took Sarah into his own house, Jehovah warned him in a dream that she was Abraham's wife and that he would die if he touched her. Abimelech was stunned. "Will you slay an innocent nation?" Abimelech pleaded. "I have brought her here in innocence! The man told me she was his sister, and she also said it was true."

"Because I know that you brought her into your house in the integrity of your heart," said Jehovah to Abimelech, "I have kept you from sinning against me. However, you must now restore her to her husband. This man is a prophet and will pray for you, but, if you do not restore her to him, you and all your house shall die."

When Abimelech arose in the morning, he quickly called his servants and told them his dream. And when they heard it, they were all afraid. Abimelech then called for Abraham to come before him. "What have you done to me?" he asked. "Why did you tell me this woman was your sister?"

"I told you she was my sister," replied Abraham, "because I did not believe that you and your people had reverence for God. My fear was that you would slay me for my wife's sake."[45]

Abraham continued: "In truth, she is my sister as well as my wife. We are children of the same father but of different mothers.[46] Many years ago when we left our father's house, I asked her to show me this one kindness and to tell the people at every place that we would go that I am her brother so that I may live."

Abimelech gave Abraham and Sarah many gifts and invited them to remain and live in Gerar. And to Sarah he spoke emphatically: "I gave your brother a thousand pieces of silver, and you need not worry about him being killed because of you. He is a man of great influence, and no one will look at you while he is with you. He is as a covering over the eyes of all those who would desire to have you."

When Abimelech took Sarah into his house, Jehovah caused that the women of Abimelech's household would become barren and unable to bear children. But they were all healed when Abraham prayed for them.

---

[43] See story "17–For the Sake of Ten."

[44] See story "13–Abram and Lot Go to Egypt."

[45] It seems strange that the beauty of a ninety-year-old woman would be such that men would kill her husband in order to marry her. This story is likely out of sequence.

[46] It is generally believed that Sarah was the daughter of Haran and the sister of Lot, thus being Abraham's niece. He could properly say that both he and Sarah were seed of the same father—Terah—because there was no distinction in the Hebrew language between direct ancestors (or descendants) of different generations. Whatever the generation—father, grandfather, great-grandfather, etc.—they were all the same.

19—HEARKEN TO THE VOICE OF SARAH

(Genesis 21)

Jehovah remembered Sarah as he had promised and opened her womb.[47] She conceived in her old age and, at the set time that Jehovah had told Abraham, Sarah bore a son. Abraham called his son Isaac[48] and, when Isaac was eight days old, Abraham circumcised him according to his covenant.

Sarah said, "God has made me laugh[49] so that all who hear me may laugh with me. No one thought that I would have children, yet I have borne Abraham a son in his old age." As Isaac grew, Abraham and Sarah loved him. And they held a great feast in Isaac's honor on the day he was weaned.

Isaac and Ishmael, the son of Sarah's bondswoman Hagar, were growing up together, but when Sarah saw Ishmael mocking her son, she was offended. She demanded that Abraham send Hagar and her son away. "The son of the bondswoman will not be heir with my son," she told Abraham. "You must send them away."

This dispute between Sarah and Hagar caused great sadness for Abraham because of the great love he had for both of his sons. But, as Abraham pondered on a solution to his dilemma, Jehovah spoke to him saying, "Do not be grieved because of Ishmael and Hagar. You must hearken to the voice of Sarah because my covenant with you will be fulfilled through Isaac. However, because Ishmael is your son, I will also make him a great nation."

Though this answer did not resolve all of Abraham's concerns, he rose early in the morning and prepared to send Hagar and Ishmael away. When he had given them bread and a bottle[50] of water, he bade them good-bye.

Feeling totally rejected, Hagar and her young son wandered in the wilderness of Beersheba until their water was gone. Then Hagar, discouraged because she thought her hope was also gone, put Ishmael under a shrub, went off a short distance, and sat on the ground.

"Let me not see the death of my child," Hagar pleaded with God. And she lifted up her voice and wept.

God, however, heard the young child's voice and sent an angel to minister to Hagar's needs. "What ails you, Hagar?" queried the angel. "You must not be afraid, for God has heard the lad's voice. Arise now! Lift him up and hold him in your hand, for he will be a great nation." Then Hagar's eyes were opened to see a well, and she went there to fill her bottle and give her son water to drink.

Ishmael was not only spared from death, but God was with him. He grew up in the wilderness of Paran where he became a skillful archer and, when he came of age, his mother took him a wife out of the land of Egypt.

---

[47] See story "17–For the Sake of Ten" to read of Jehovah's promise to Sarah that she would bear a son in her old age.

[48] The name Isaac means "laughter."

[49] The Hebrew root word used here was *tzachak*. It means both "to laugh" and "to rejoice," so there is a double meaning suggested.

[50] A bottle might be better called a water skin. Bottles were the skins of animals and were used as containers for both water and wine.

20—THE SON WHOM YOU LOVE

(Genesis 22)

The years passed quickly after Isaac's birth, and he grew into a fine and faithful young man. He was the light of his parents' life, and they loved him dearly.

One day Jehovah decided that he must test his servant Abraham. "Take Isaac, the son whom you love," Jehovah instructed Abraham, "and go up into the land of Moriah. There you will offer Isaac as a burnt offering upon a mountain that I will show you."

Abraham prepares to offer Isaac as a sacrifice

Abraham was deeply troubled by Jehovah's request, for he did not understand how the covenants that Jehovah had made with him could ever be fulfilled if Isaac were to die without having children himself. But Abraham obeyed Jehovah's command. He rose early the next morning, saddled his beast of burden, and prepared for his journey to the land of Moriah. Only Abraham knew the purpose of this journey. After carefully tying the wood for his burnt offering onto the back of his ass, Abraham began the dreaded trip. Only Isaac and two young servants went with him.

On the third day of their travels, Abraham looked up and saw in the distance the place about which Jehovah had told him. Though the journey had been long and hard, it was still ending too soon. "Stay here with the ass," he said to the servants, "while Isaac and I go up on the mountain to worship. We will return shortly." Taking the wood he had brought for the offering, he

laid it on Isaac's back. And Abraham walked beside his son, carrying the fire and the knife.

Isaac had great faith in his father, but he was troubled because they had brought no animal for the sacrifice. They had walked but a short distance when Isaac raised the question that troubled him. "I see that we have fire and wood for the offering," he said, "but where is the lamb?"

"My son," responded Abraham, grasping for an answer that would satisfy Isaac, "God will provide himself with a lamb for our offering."

Abraham and Isaac continued together on their trek up the mountain. And when they came to the place about which God had told him, Abraham built an altar and carefully laid the wood upon it. When this was done, he bound Isaac with cords and laid the young man on top of the wood. Then poor Abraham, mustering all of his inner strength, stretched forth the knife to slay his covenant son according to Jehovah's commandment. Before the deed could be done, however, an angel spoke: "Abraham! Abraham!"

Abraham stopped. "Here am I!" he responded.

"Do not lay your hand upon the young man, nor do anything to hurt him," said the angel. "Your sacrifice is sufficient. You have proven yourself before God and have shown that you would not withhold from him even your only son."

As Abraham looked up from his place at the side of the altar, he saw a ram caught by its horns in the thicket behind him. Then, taking the ram, he offered it as a burnt offering instead of his son Isaac. And Abraham called the place Jehovah-jireh.[51]

The angel spoke again to Abraham, speaking now as if he were Jehovah himself. Said he, "Because you have done what I commanded you and have not withheld your son, I will bless you. In multiplying, I will multiply your seed as the stars of heaven and as the sand upon the seashore. Your seed shall possess the gates of their enemies. And in your seed all nations of the earth will be blessed because you have obeyed the voice of God."

With the ordeal now behind them, Abraham and Isaac returned from the mountain to the place where their servants waited. And they returned together to their home in Beersheba.

---

[51] Jehovah-jireh means "God will provide."

21—THIS THING IS OF JEHOVAH

(Genesis 23–24)

Sarah had passed away and was buried in a cave that Abraham purchased at Hebron in the land of Canaan. Abraham was now very old and, because he lived among the Canaanites, he feared that his forty-year-old son Isaac might marry a Canaanite woman.[52] One day he summoned his faithful eldest servant and said to him, "Put your hand under my hand[53] and swear an oath by the God of Heaven that you will not allow Isaac to take a wife from among the Canaanites. Instead, I want you to go to the country where my family lives and find a wife for him there."

The servant replied, "Your request is good, but if no woman will come back here with me, shall I take Isaac into that land?"

"No," replied Abraham. "You must never take him there. I know that God will send his angel before you, and you will be blessed to find a wife for Isaac and bring her back. Nevertheless, if the woman will not willingly return with you, you shall be free from your oath."

After this explanation, the servant put his hand beneath Abraham's hand and swore the oath that Abraham had requested of him.

The old servant prepared carefully for his journey, then set out for Padan-aram, the land where Abraham's brother Nahor had settled. He took many gifts with him, including ten of Abraham's camels laden with gold and silver. He also took other servants with him to assist. As the old servant and his party came to the city of Nahor in the land between the two rivers, he made his camels kneel near a well at evening time, when the women of the city came to draw water.

Feeling uneasy about the task before him—the servant prayed to Jehovah for help. "O Jehovah, God of my master Abraham," he pleaded, "send me good speed this day and show kindness unto Abraham. As the daughters of the city come to draw water, let it be that the maiden to whom I say, 'Let down your pitcher that I may drink,' may reply, 'Drink, and I will give your camels water also.' May the maiden who so says be the one who should marry Isaac, and I will surely know that Thou hast shown kindness unto Abraham."

Before the servant's prayer was finished, Rebekah, the daughter of Bethuel and granddaughter of Nahor, Abraham's brother, came and went down the small incline to the well. When she had filled her pitcher and come back up, the servant—impressed by the young woman's beauty—ran to her and said, "Let me drink a little water from your pitcher."

"Drink, my lord," replied Rebekah. Then, taking the pitcher from her shoulder, she gave him water. When the servant had finished drinking, Rebekah said, "Sir, I will also draw water for your camels." She quickly returned to the well to draw water for the camels, pouring it into the adjacent trough. Seeing all this transpire just as he had prayed, the servant was elated. "Is this not the answer to my prayers?" he thought.

In his excitement, the servant gave Rebekah precious gifts for her kindness. Then he asked her, "Who is your father, and is there room in your father's house for my men and I to lodge?"

"I am the daughter of Bethuel," she answered. "And Bethuel is the son that Milcah bore to Nahor. Also, we have both straw and food, as well as room for you and those who are with you to lodge."

The servant bowed in gratitude. "Blessed be Jehovah, the God of my master Abraham," he said. "He has led me to the house of Abraham's brethren." And Rebekah hurried back to the city to tell her family.

When Rebekah's brother Laban heard her account, he ran to the well to meet the old servant. "Come into the city," he said. "Why are you still standing here? I have prepared our house to receive you, as well as room for your camels."

When Abraham's servant arrived at the house, Laban tended to the camels. He also washed the servant's feet and the feet of those who were with him. But when Laban and Bethuel set food before him, the servant would not eat. "I cannot eat before I tell you my errand," he said.

"Speak on," said Laban.

The servant proceeded to explain his mission. "I am the servant of your kinsman Abraham, whom Jehovah has blessed with great wealth," he said. "His wife Sarah bore him a son in her old age, and Abraham has given his son all that he has. And now my master has made me swear an oath that I would not allow his son to marry a daughter of the Canaanites, but has sent me here to choose his son a wife from among the daughters of his own kindred. Abraham promised to release me from my oath, however, if the woman will not return with me."

---

[52] The Canaanites were the primary inhabitants of the land where Abraham lived. Their lineage was through Canaan, the son of Ham. Abraham objected to a Canaanite as a wife for Isaac because the Canaanites were unbelievers who worshipped false gods.

[53] This wording comes from the Joseph Smith Translation of the Bible. The King James Translation says that the servant was requested by Abraham to put his hand under Abraham's thigh.

The servant then told how he prayed at the well and how Rebekah served him in answer to his prayer. He told also of how he had bowed to worship Jehovah when he learned whose child she was. "And now," he said, "I must know if you will deal kindly with my master. If not, tell me now that I may depart in peace."

When Laban and Bethuel had heard the servant's story, they were deeply touched. "This thing is of Jehovah," they said. "We cannot speak unto you either good or bad, but there is Rebekah. Take her and go. Let her be your master's son's wife as Jehovah has spoken."

The servant was overjoyed at this reply and bowed to the earth to praise Jehovah. Then he and his men brought in gold, silver, and other precious gifts for Rebekah. He also gave precious gifts to Rebekah's brother Laban and to her mother.

The servant and his traveling party rose early the next morning and prepared to depart for home, but Rebekah's mother and brother pleaded with them to let her stay for ten more days before taking her away from them forever.

"Please do not hinder me in my mission," pleaded the servant. "Seeing that Jehovah has prospered my way, let me go now that I may return to my master."

"Call for Rebekah and let her settle the matter," they said. And when Rebekah came, they asked her, "Will you tarry here a few more days or will you go with this man now?"

"I will go now," she answered.

As Rebekah left her family behind, they blessed her, saying, "You are our sister and you shall be the mother of thousands of millions. Your seed will possess the gates of those that hate them."

Rebekah arose with her servants and followed Abraham's servant. Riding on camels, they made their journey back to the land of Canaan. The little party traveled rapidly and did not stop along the way. All were anxious to reach the land of Canaan where Rebekah would become the wife of her kinsman Isaac—a man whom she had never met.

Isaac was in the field at dusk when he looked up and saw the camels coming, and he went out to meet them. Rebekah looked up also when she saw Isaac coming toward them. "Who is that man walking to meet us?" she asked Abraham's servant.

"That man is my master Isaac," replied the servant, "the man who will be your husband." Hearing this, Rebekah covered her face with a veil and, when Isaac drew near, she got down from the camel.

The servant told Isaac all that had happened and how God had answered his prayers in the household of Bethuel.

Isaac was pleased with Rebekah and brought her into the tent that had belonged to his late mother Sarah. Rebekah became Isaac's wife, and he loved her dearly.

22—ABRAHAM IS GATHERED TO HIS PEOPLE

(Genesis 25)

After the death of Sarah, Abraham took Keturah to be his wife. Keturah bore him six sons, whom he named Zimran, Jokshan, Medan, Midian, Ishbak, and Shuah. These sons of Abraham were like their brother Ishmael, for they were not heirs to the covenant blessings. To them Abraham gave many gifts, but then he sent them away from Isaac, into the east country. All that Abraham had he gave to Isaac the son of Sarah because of the covenant.

When Abraham was 165 years old, he died and was buried by his sons Isaac and Ishmael in the same cave at Hebron that he had purchased for the burial of Sarah. And, as the scriptures say, "Abraham was gathered to his people."

23—THE ELDER SHALL SERVE THE YOUNGER

(Genesis 25)

Isaac was 40 years old when he married Rebekah. He loved her with all his heart, but Rebekah, like Isaac's own mother, was barren and could have no children. This posed a problem because Jehovah's covenant with Abraham—that he would have posterity beyond number—was supposed to be fulfilled through Isaac. Yet here was Isaac, now sixty years old and still without children.

When Isaac pleaded with Jehovah in Rebekah's behalf, Jehovah heard his prayers: Rebekah was able to conceive. When she felt struggling within her womb, she prayed, asking Jehovah why it was so, and he answered her saying, "Two nations are in your womb, and two kinds of people will come out of you. One people shall be stronger than the other, and the elder shall serve the younger."

When Rebekah's time came, she gave birth to twin sons as Jehovah had promised. The firstborn came out red and had much hair. And the second, when he was born, took hold of his brother's heel. Isaac and Rebekah named their sons Esau[54] and Jacob.[55]

The boys, growing up together in the household of Isaac and Rebekah, were rivals from the beginning. They had little in common because they had different personalities and different interests. Esau loved to hunt and was good at it. He spent most of his time in the hunting fields. Jacob, on the other hand, had simple tastes and liked to be at home with his mother. Isaac was partial to Esau because he liked to eat his venison, but Rebekah was partial to Jacob. She remembered what Jehovah had told her before her twins were born about the elder serving the younger.

When Esau came one day from the fields, weary and faint for want of food, Jacob had just made some red pottage, or lentil soup, that smelled very good to Esau. "Feed me some of that red pottage, for I am faint," he pleaded with his brother.

Jacob, taking advantage of his brother's hunger, answered, "I will give you my pottage for your birthright." Jacob was well aware that the eldest son was entitled to the birthright by law.

"I am about to die," said Esau, "and my birthright is of no value to me if I am dead." So, at Jacob's urging,

---

[54] Esau means "hairy."
[55] Jacob means "supplanter or one who supersedes another by deception."

Esau swore an oath to trade his birthright for his fill of red lentil soup.

Esau ate the soup that Jacob gave him and went his way, despising the birthright he had so cheaply sold.

24–A MAN OF PATIENCE
(Genesis 26)

Because of a severe famine in the land of Canaan, Isaac went down to Gerar, in the land of the Philistines, to escape. His father Abraham had lived there before him and had dug many wells. Though Isaac had thought to go to Egypt, Jehovah told him to stay in the land that had been promised to his father. "If you will stay in this land," said Jehovah, "I will be with you and bless you. I will give all these countries to you and your seed, and I will perform the oath that I swore unto your father. Your seed shall multiply as the stars of heaven, and all the nations of the earth shall be blessed in your seed, because Abraham obeyed my voice and kept my statutes."

When he came to Gerar, Isaac told King Abimelech and the people of the city that Rebekah was his sister.[56] He did not tell them that Rebekah was his wife because of Rebekah's beauty. He was afraid that the men of Gerar would kill him for her. However, when Abimelech finally learned that Rebekah was Isaac's wife, he rebuked Isaac severely. He also sent out a warning to his people saying, "I will put to death anyone who touches this man or his wife."

Isaac's crops were bounteous that year in Gerar and brought forth a hundredfold. He grew great in the land, prospering in his flocks as well as his crops. But Isaac's prosperity caused the Philistines to envy him. In their envy, they filled with dirt the wells that had been dug years earlier by his father Abraham. Even King Abimelech, who had once treated Isaac with great kindness, was now filled with envy. "Go away from among us," he told Isaac, "for you are much mightier than we are."

Isaac patiently left his prosperous land in the city of Gerar and pitched his tent in the nearby valley of the same name, where he once again dug the wells of Abraham. Isaac's servants also dug a new well of running water in the valley, but the herdsmen of Gerar contended with Isaac's herdsmen over the water. Because of the contention Isaac called his new well Esek, which means "strife," and, seeking to be at peace with his neighbors, he soon abandoned the new well and had his servants dig another. This did not solve Isaac's problem, however. The people of Gerar fought with

---

[56] Whether this is the same King Abimelech that Abraham had dealings with in Genesis 20, is not known. It is possible that this is a retelling of the same story. The details are very similar (see story "18–A Man of Great Influence").

him over this well also and claimed that the water belonged to them. Isaac called this well Sitnah, which means "opposition."

Isaac, once again exercising great patience, moved to a new location and dug yet another well. This seemed to satisfy his tormentors and things went well for a while. There was no strife over this new well, and Isaac called it Rehoboth, which means "broad open places." Isaac was convinced that he had finally found a place where there would be no contention over the wells and the water. "Now God has made room for us," he said, "and we shall be fruitful in the land."

Isaac had hoped for too much, however, and the complainers soon came to contend with him. Wishing to avoid further problems, he arose once again and moved his flocks. This time he moved out of the land of the Philistines to new pastures further to the southeast. He believed that this was the only way he would ever have peace with these people. On Isaac's first night in the new place, Jehovah appeared to him and said, "I am the God of your father Abraham. You need not fear, for I am with you. I will bless you and multiply your seed for the sake of my servant Abraham." With this assurance Isaac built an altar and called upon the name of Jehovah, and his servants began digging another well.

Isaac had been in his new place for only a short time when he received a surprise visit from King Abimelech. Abimelech did not come alone. He came into Isaac's camp with the captain of his army and another friend. "Why have you come here," asked Isaac, "seeing that you hate me and have driven me from your country?"

The men replied, "When we saw that God was with you, we said, 'Let us go and make an oath and a covenant between Isaac and us.' So we have now come. We ask only that you agree to do us no harm, for we have done no harm to you and have sent you away from our country in peace." They seemed to forget all the ill will that the people of Gerar had shown to Isaac and the trouble they had caused him because of his water and his wells. Isaac, however, was a patient man and not one to hold grudges. He graciously made a feast for his visitors, and they ate and drank together. The next morning they all rose early and swore their oaths of peace to each other. Then Isaac sent his guests away with his blessings.

When Abimelech and his friends had departed, Isaac's servants informed him that they had found water in their new well. So, Isaac, because of the oath he had made with Abimelech, called the well Shebah and the city Beersheba.[57]

---

[57] Shebah means "oath," and Beersheba means "well of the oath."

III

JACOB AND JOSEPH

25—JACOB RECEIVES THE BLESSING
(Genesis 26–28)

When Isaac's son Esau was forty years old, he took Judith and Bashemath, who were both daughters of the Hittites, to be his wives. These marriages to unbelievers were the cause of much grief to Isaac and Rebekah, but they still loved him and they kept a close relationship with their son.

As time passed and Isaac grew old, he became blind. One day he called Esau to him and said, "I am growing old, my son, and I do not know how long I shall live. Before I die, however, I want you to go into the field and slay some venison to make me some savory meat. When I have eaten the meat, I will give you a blessing because you are my eldest son."

Esau's mother, Rebekah, heard the exchange between Isaac and Esau and, when Esau had gone to the field, she told Esau's twin brother Jacob what she had heard. "Now, my son," she told him, "it is important for you to do just as I tell you. Go out to the flock and bring me two young goats that I may prepare the savory meat that your father loves. You will then take the meat to him that he may eat it and give his blessing to you instead of Esau."

Jacob protested. "My brother is a hairy man, and I am not," he said. "When my father feels my skin, I will seem to him as a deceiver and will bring a curse upon me instead of a blessing."

"If there is a curse, it shall be upon me, my son," answered Rebekah. "Just obey me and bring me the two kids." So Jacob went and did as his mother said. When he brought the young goats, she prepared the savory meat. She then took some of Esau's best clothes and put them on Jacob. She also put the skins of the young goats on Jacob's hands and neck and sent him to his father with bread and meat.

"Who is there?" asked Isaac as Jacob came into his tent.

"It is I, Esau, your firstborn," Jacob lied. "I have done as you asked. Arise and eat my venison so that you can give me a blessing."

"How did you find it so quickly?" asked Isaac.

"Because your God Jehovah brought it to me."

Something still seemed amiss to Isaac. "Come near to me, my son, that I may feel whether you are Esau," he said. And Jacob went near so his father could feel him. "Your voice sounds like Jacob's voice," said Isaac, "but your hands are surely the hands of Esau."

But again he asked, "Are you my son Esau?"

And again Jacob answered that he was.

"Good," said Isaac. "Bring the meat that I may eat it and bless you." So Jacob took the meat to Isaac and he ate it. Jacob also gave his father wine, and he drank it.

Isaac had one more test for his visitor. "Come here and kiss me, my son," he said. And when Jacob came forward to kiss his father, Isaac smelled his clothing.

Finally Isaac was satisfied that this man was his eldest son. "You have the smell of the field," he said, "even the smell of Esau."

When Isaac had finished eating, he laid his hands on Jacob's head—thinking him to be Esau—and gave him the blessing that he had planned to give to his brother. "God give you of the dew of heaven," he said, "of the fatness of the earth, and plenty of grain and wine. Let people serve you and nations bow down to you. Be lord over your brethren and let your mother's sons bow down to you. Cursed be everyone that curses you and blessed be everyone that blesses you."

No sooner was the blessing finished and Jacob was gone from Isaac's presence, than Esau arrived with the savory meat he had prepared for his father. As he entered his father's tent, he said, "Arise, my father, and eat my savory meat so that you will be able to give me the blessing that you promised."

Isaac was greatly puzzled. "Who are you?" he asked.

"Your firstborn son, Esau," came the reply.

Isaac began to tremble. "Who?" he asked again. "Where is he that has already brought me venison, which I ate before you came, and whom I have already blessed?"

Esau was heartsick, and he cried out with bitterness, "Bless me also, my father!"

"I cannot," replied Isaac. "Your brother has deceived me, and I have given your blessing to him."

"Is he not rightly named Jacob?" asked Esau. "For he has supplanted me twice.[58] First he took away my birthright, and now he has taken away my blessing. O my father, do you not still have a blessing for me?"

Isaac answered, "Behold, my son, the blessing has been given. I have made your brother your lord, and all his brethren I have given to him for servants. With grain and wine I have sustained him, and what is there left now for you?"

Esau wept bitterly. "Do you not have even one blessing for me, Father?" he cried. "Oh, please bless me also."

So, as they wept together, Isaac laid his hands upon Esau's head and gave him this blessing: "Behold, your dwelling place shall be the fatness of the earth, and the dew of heaven from above. By your sword shall you

---

[58] The name Jacob means "supplanter or one who supersedes another by deception."

live, and you shall serve your brother. But when you have dominion, you shall break his yoke from off your neck."

Esau could not be consoled. He hated Jacob because of the blessing, and he said in his heart, "When my father is dead, I will slay my brother."

When these thoughts of Esau were made known to Rebekah, she proposed to send her youngest son away to live with her brother Laban. "When your brother's anger is turned away and he forgets what you have done to him," she told Jacob, "I will send word for you to return."

To carry out her plan to save her youngest son, Rebekah went to Isaac and told him that she feared that Jacob would take a wife from the daughters of the Hittites. And so Isaac called Jacob to him, blessed him, and sent him away to Padan-aram to seek a wife from among the daughters of Rebekah's brother Laban.

26–A LADDER THAT REACHES TO HEAVEN
(Genesis 28)

Isaac counseled his son Jacob that it was not God's will for him to seek a wife among the Canaanites. And, following Rebekah's suggestion, he told Isaac to go to the house of Laban, Rebekah's brother, to seek a suitable wife.

Before Jacob began his journey, Isaac gave him a blessing. "May God bless you and make you fruitful," he said. "May he multiply you that you become a multitude of people. May he give the blessings of Abraham to you and your seed, that you may inherit this land wherein you are now a stranger—even this land that God gave to Abraham."

Leaving Beersheba, Jacob traveled north toward Haran in the land of Padan-aram. And when the sun went down one night, he found a place where he could sleep. Taking a stone from the ground for his pillow, he lay down to sleep. And while he slept, he dreamed.

In Jacob's dream, he saw a ladder set upon the earth, the top of which reached to heaven. The angels of God were going up and down the ladder, and Jehovah stood at the top. Jehovah spoke to Jacob. "I am the God of your father Abraham," he said. "I am also the God of Isaac. I will give the land whereon you are lying to you and to your seed after you. Your seed will be numbered as the dust of the earth. They will spread abroad to the west, to the east, to the north, and to the south. For in you and in your seed shall all nations of the earth be blessed. Behold, I am with you and will keep you safe in all places that you go and bring you again into this land. Yea, I will not leave you until I have done that which I have told you."

When Jacob awoke from his dream his heart was filled with fear. "Surely Jehovah is in this place and I did not know it," he said. "What a fearful[59] place this is! For this is surely the house of God and the gate of heaven."

When Jacob arose the next morning, he took the stone that he had used for his pillow, set it up for a pil-

---

[59] I have used the word *fearful* in this story instead of *dreadful* as it appears in KJV. The Hebrew word that appears in the text is *yare' (YAH-ray)*. The word appears multiple times in the Hebrew scriptures and was usually translated as *fear* or some other word relating to *fear* (see "The King James Bible with Strong's Dictionary," *The HTML Bible* [2004], <http://www.sacrednamebible.com/kjvstrongs/index2.htm >).

lar, and anointed the top of it with oil. The place had been called Luz, but Jacob renamed it Beth-el, which means "house of God."

Jacob, kneeling at his newly erected pillar, humbled himself and made a vow to Jehovah. "If Thou wilt be with me and will keep me in the way that I am going," he said, "and if Thou wilt give me bread to eat and clothes to wear so that I may come again to my father's house in peace, then shalt Thou, Jehovah, be my God. This stone, which I have set up for a pillar and anointed with oil, shall be Thine house and, of everything that Thou dost give me, I will return one tenth to Thee."

And when Jacob had finished praying, he continued on his journey toward Padan-aram to the house of his uncle Laban.

27—THE YOUNGER DAUGHTER
(Genesis 29)

As Jacob entered Padan-aram[60] in search of his mother's family, he saw three flocks of sheep by a well. He noticed that those who tended the sheep kept a large stone over the mouth of the well, which they removed only to water their flocks, and when the flocks were watered, the stone was carefully replaced. Jacob drew near to the herdsmen and asked, "Where do you live?"

"We are from Haran," was their reply.

Jacob was excited now. "Do you know Laban, the grandson of Nahor?"[61] he asked.

"We know him."

"Is he well?"

"He is well," they replied and, pointing to an approaching flock of sheep, they said, "Behold, Laban's daughter Rachel is coming now with her father's sheep." This was more good fortune than Jacob had hoped for. And when Rachel came to the well, he rolled away the stone and watered her sheep.

Jacob, overjoyed to see his cousin Rachel, kissed her and wept. He told her that he was Rebekah's son and that he had come to her land seeking her father Laban. Upon hearing this news, Rachel left her flocks and ran immediately to tell her father.

When Laban received the news that Jacob was at the well, he ran to meet him, rejoicing that Rebekah's son had come to Haran. After making Jacob feel welcome, Laban took him to his house. "You are my bone and my

---

[60] Padan-aram, which means the tableland of Aram, was in the area between the upper parts of the Tigris and the Euphrates rivers. It was later known as Mesopotamia (which means "between two rivers) and is now partly in Turkey, partly in Syria, and partly in Iraq. In some places, the scriptures (Genesis 25:19 and 31:24) refer to Laban, the man who became Jacob's father-in-law, as "Laban the Syrian." Aram was a very large area that included many peoples. It was named for Aram, the son of Seth. The Aramaic language originated in this area (see William Smith, *Dictionary of the Bible*, *GospeLink*, CD-ROM, s.v. "Padan," and *Bible Dictionary*, LDS-KJV, s.v. "Padan").

[61] The scripture (Genesis 29:5) calls Laban the *son* of Nahor rather than his grandson. It should be remembered that kinship terms in Hebrew did not distinguish between generations. A direct ancestor of any generation was called a father or a mother, and a direct descendant of any generation was referred to as a son or a daughter.

flesh," he said, "and it is good to have you here. You are welcome to stay."

Jacob meets Rachael at the well in Padan-aram

When Jacob had been in Laban's house for a month, Laban said to him, "Because we are brothers, it is not right that you should labor for me without pay. Please tell me what wages you would have me pay you."

As Jacob considered his wages, he thought of Laban's daughters, Leah and Rachel. Leah had tender, weepy eyes, but Rachel was beautiful and well favored. Jacob loved Rachel and wanted her for his wife. So he said to Laban, "I will serve you seven years for the hand of your younger daughter Rachel."

Laban agreed. "I accept your offer," he replied. "It is surely better that I give Rachel to you than to another man." So Jacob served Laban seven years for Rachel's hand, and the time seemed to him as but a few days because of his love for her.

When the seven years were passed, Jacob said to Laban, "My agreement with you to serve seven years for Rachel is fulfilled. Give her to me now that she may be my wife." So Laban called together the people of Haran and held a great feast in honor of the marriage. But in the evening, when he should have brought Rachel for Jacob, he brought Leah instead. But because she was veiled, Jacob did not realize that Laban gave him the wrong daughter.

In the morning when he discovered that Laban had given him Leah instead of Rachel, he was angry. He pressed Laban. "What have you done to me, Laban?" he asked angrily. "I served seven years for Rachel, but you have given me Leah. Why have you cheated me of what I labored for and was rightfully mine?"

Laban had a ready answer. "In my country," he explained, "the younger daughter may not marry before the firstborn. However, if you will serve me seven years more, you shall also have Rachel."

So Jacob served Laban another seven years, and Laban gave him Rachel also.

When his daughters became Jacob's wives, Laban gave each a handmaid. To Leah he gave Zilpah, and to Rachel he gave Bilhah.

28—ONE MAN'S FAMILY

(Genesis 30)

After completing fourteen years of service to his uncle Laban in payment for his two wives, Jacob felt at home in Haran. And because he had received no word from his mother to tell him it was safe to return to Beersheba,[62] he decided to remain in Haran in the service of his father-in-law. While Jacob served her father, Jacob's wife Leah bore him four sons—Reuben, Simeon, Levi, and Judah.[63] Rachel, however, had no children and she envied her sister. She said to Jacob, "Give me children, Jacob, or I shall die."

Rachel's complaints made Jacob angry, and he said to her, "It is not my fault that you have no children. Am I in God's place to withhold children from you?"

Because Rachel wanted children so badly, she gave her handmaid Bilhah to Jacob to be his wife, and when Bilhah had a son, Rachel was elated. "God has judged me," she said, "but he has also heard my voice and given me a son." And she named Bilhah's son Dan.[64] And Rachel rejoiced again when Bilhah bore a second son, and she named that son Naphtali.[65]

As time passed and Leah realized that she was having no more children, she too gave her handmaid to be Jacob's wife; and Zilpah bore Jacob two sons. Leah rejoiced in Zilpah's sons. "I am happy," she said, "for the daughters will call me blessed." Zilpah's sons were named Gad and Asher.[66]

Leah was later blessed to bear two more sons and a daughter herself. Her sons she named Issachar and Zebulun,[67] and her daughter she named Dinah.[68] She rejoiced greatly in these three children, believing that God had given them to her because she had given her handmaid to be her husband's wife.

After several years, God also remembered Rachel. She was blessed to conceive and bear a son—a son whom she named Joseph.[69] When Joseph was born, Rachel was more than delighted. And now that she had borne one son, she said she felt that God would also bless her with another.

---

[62] See story "25—Jacob Receives the Blessing." In that story Rebekah told Jacob that she would let him know when it was safe for him to return home.

[63] Reuben means "behold, a son," Simeon means "heard," Levi means "joined," and Judah means "praised" or "celebrated."

[64] Dan means "vindicated" or "judged."

[65] Naphtali means "my wrestling."

[66] Gad means "good fortune" and Asher means "happy" or "blessed."

[67] Issachar means "reward" and Zebulun means "exalt me" or "honor me."

[68] Dinah means "judged" or "acquitted."

[69] The name Joseph is associated with two Hebrew root words: *yasaph*, which means "to add," and *asaph*, which means "to take away" or "to gather." These meanings are significant in the context of Joseph's life and his mission (see footnote 24a of Genesis 30 [LDS-KJV]).

29–JACOB'S PROSPERITY
(Genesis 30, 31)

Though Jacob felt at home in Haran with his wives and family, he began to be restless. He had served his father-in-law Laban faithfully for many years, and now he felt it was time to return to his own people and to his own land—the land that Jehovah had promised him as an eternal inheritance. After Rachel's son Joseph was born, Jacob went to Laban and said, "Send me away that I may return to my own country. Give me my wives and my children, for whom I have served you these many years, and let me go. For you know that I have served you well."

Laban was reluctant to let Jacob leave. He knew he had prospered and become wealthy while Jacob had managed his flocks. "If I have found favor in your sight," he said to Jacob, "stay here. I know that Jehovah has blessed me because of you. You need only tell me what wages will be required for you to stay, and I will pay whatever you ask."

Jacob thought carefully about Laban's offer and then said, "You know how your flocks have prospered under my care. When I came you had but few; now you have many. However, it is now time for me to also provide for my own family."

"What do you want me to give you?" asked Laban.

"I will stay and care for your flocks," Jacob answered, "if you will do this one thing for me. I will take from among your flocks today all the speckled, spotted, and brown sheep and all the ringstreaked and speckled goats. These will be my wages. And from this time on my righteousness will answer for me. If ever a sheep that is not speckled, spotted, or brown or a goat that is not speckled or spotted is found with my flocks instead of yours, it shall be counted as stolen."

Laban gave verbal assent to the terms that Jacob had stated. But that same day, he went against his word and removed from his flocks every brown sheep, every he-goat that was ringstreaked and spotted, and every she-goat that was speckled, spotted, or that had some white on it. These he delivered to his sons, who separated them from the remaining flocks by three days' journey.

Jacob did not complain about what Laban had done but stayed and tended the flocks that remained, and he dealt fairly with his father-in-law. As time went by, however, an interesting thing happened. When the flocks conceived and bore their young, almost all of them were ringstreaked, spotted, speckled, or brown, and thus belonged to Jacob. When Laban observed what was happening, he changed Jacob's wages to give him only the spotted animals. Then he changed them to give only the speckled ones, and finally to give only those that were ringstreaked. But no matter how Laban changed Jacob's wages, most of the animals bore their young only with those markings that would belong to Jacob.

And so it went. No matter how Laban set Jacob's wages, Jacob's herds grew and prospered more than his own. And in just a few short years, Jacob became a prosperous and wealthy man with many sheep and goats, as well as servants, camels, and asses.

30—A COVENANT OF PEACE

(Genesis 31)

As Jacob prospered in Laban's service, his relationship with Laban became increasingly more difficult. Laban's sons complained that Jacob had taken away their father's wealth and that he had gained his own wealth and glory at the expense of their father. It was also easy for Jacob to see that Laban himself did not look upon him with the same favor that he once had. As the atmosphere became more strained, Jehovah spoke to Jacob and commanded him to return to Canaan. "Return to your family and to the land of your fathers," said Jehovah, "and I will be with you."

Jacob called to him his wives Rachel and Leah and said, "Your father's countenance is not favorable toward me as it once was, but the God of my fathers has been with me. I have served your father with my might. And though he has dealt unfairly with me and changed my wages ten times, God has not let him hurt me. If your father said, 'The speckled animals will be your wages,' all the animals bore speckled lambs. And if he said 'The ringstreaked shall be your wages,' they all bore ringstreaked lambs. When the ewes and she-goats conceived, I saw in a dream that all of the rams that bred them were ringstreaked, speckled, and gray.

"An angel has told me that God has taken away your father's cattle and given them to me because your father dealt unfairly with me. And the angel also said that it is now time for me to return to the land of my fathers."

Much to Jacob's relief, both Rachel and Leah agreed with him. "Our father has been unfair to us also," they said. "We have been left as strangers in his house with no inheritance, for he has sold us and consumed our money. The riches that God took from our father and gave to you belonged to us and to our children. We agree with you, Jacob, and whatever God has said to you, you must do it."

Knowing now that he had the support of his wives, Jacob gathered his family and all his possessions and prepared to depart for the land of Canaan. When Jacob and his family departed from Haran, he gave no word to Laban, for Laban had gone to shear his sheep. And as they left, Rachel secretly took with her the idols that her father worshipped.

On the third day after Jacob's departure, Laban was told that he and his family were gone. Being greatly upset, Laban took his brethren and set out in pursuit, but it was seven days before Laban caught up with Jacob and his company at Mount Gilead.

The night before Laban entered Jacob's camp, he had a dream. And in his dream, God said to him, "Take heed that you speak neither good nor bad to Jacob."

There was tension on both sides as Laban and his brethren entered Jacob's camp the next day. Everyone—including Laban—was very cautious.

"What have you done?" Laban asked Jacob. "Why have you stolen away without telling me—carrying away my daughters as captives taken with the sword? If you had told me you were leaving, I would have held a great celebration. But you left without even allowing me to kiss my children good-bye.

"Your hasty departure was very foolish, for I have power to do you great harm and I came prepared to do so. Last night, however, the God of your fathers spoke to me in a dream and said that I should speak neither good nor bad to you. Nevertheless, my son, I am greatly insulted that you left without notice and that you have also stolen my gods."

Jacob bristled at Laban's accusations and replied, "I left without telling you because I feared you would take your daughters from me by force. However, where your idols are concerned, we do not have them. If you find them here with my family, the person who has them shall be put to death." Jacob did not know that Rachel had stolen her father's idols.

Laban searched the tents of Jacob, Leah, and the two handmaids without finding his idols, for Rachel—the guilty party—had hidden them in her camel's furniture. When Laban entered Rachel's tent to search, she was sitting on them. "Do not be displeased, my father, because I am unable to rise before you," she said, "for the custom of women is upon me." And Laban searched Rachel's tent without finding his idols.

Jacob was now even more upset by Laban's search of his goods when nothing was found. "What is my sin," Jacob demanded, "that you have so hotly pursued me and have now searched through my property? If you have found anything that belongs to you, set it here before our brethren that they may judge between us."

Jacob went on: "I have served you for twenty years. Your ewes and she-goats have not cast their young, and I have not eaten the rams of your flock. When they were torn by beasts, I bore the loss myself. I served you in all kinds of weather and have lost much sleep in your service.

"I served fourteen years for your two daughters and six years for my flocks. And, during those six years, you changed my wages ten times. If the God of my fathers had not been with me, you would have sent me away empty. But, because he has seen my afflictions and my labors in your behalf, he rebuked you last night."

Laban, becoming defensive at Jacob's accusations, snapped back, "But these are my daughters, these are my children, and these are my flocks. All that you can see here is mine, and what can I do now to these my daughters and their children?"

Then Laban's mood softened. "Come," he said, "let us make a covenant of peace as a witness between us to settle our dispute."

Jacob also softened his stance when he heard Laban's offer to make a covenant of peace. He took a stone and set it up for a pillar. Then he asked all those who were present to gather stones and put them in a heap. Laban called the heap of stones Jegarsahadutha,[70] but Jacob called it Galeed.[71] Then Laban said, "This heap of stones is a witness between us this day and its name shall be called Galeed and Mizpah,[72] for the Lord will watch between us when we are absent from each other. If you afflict my daughters or take other wives, no man will be with us, as God is witness between us. This heap and this pillar now stand as witnesses that I will not pass beyond this pillar to do you harm. Let the God of Abraham, the God of Nahor, and the God of their father Terah judge between us."

In response, Jacob swore an oath by his father Isaac and offered sacrifices upon Mount Gilead. Then he called together all who were present that they might eat.

Laban and his brethren arose early the next morning. And when he had kissed his daughters and his grandchildren good-bye and had blessed them, Laban returned to his home in Haran.

---

[70] Jegarsahadutha means "the heap of witness" in Aramaic.

[71] Galeed means "the heap of witness" in Hebrew. This is not the same as Mount Gilead, upon which they were encamped.

[72] Mizpah means "the lookout point." The scriptures, in various places, use both Mizpah and Mizpeh. There is more than one location with this name.

31—FACE-TO-FACE
(Genesis 32, 35)

Jacob continued on his journey back to the land of Canaan after twenty years at Haran in the land of Padan-aram. And as he traveled, the angels of God met him. When he saw them, he said, "This place is God's camp," and he called the place Mahanaim.[73] From there, Jacob sent messengers into Edom to tell his brother Esau that he was finally coming home.

As Jacob continued on his way, he went off one night by himself, after sending his family across the river Jabbok. And as the night progressed, Jacob lay down to rest. There was no rest for him, however, for an angel of God[74] came and wrestled with Jacob throughout the night. Jacob was unable to overpower the angel, but when Jacob reached down and touched the hollow of his (i.e., Jacob's) thigh, he discovered that it was out of joint.

"Let me go," the angel said, "for the day is breaking."

"I will not let you go unless you will give me a blessing," answered Jacob.

"What is your name?" the angel asked in response.

"Jacob."

Then the angel said, "You shall no longer be Jacob, but shall be called Israel.[75] As a prince you have persevered with both God and men and have prevailed."

"Will you also tell me your name?" Jacob then asked the angel.

---

[73] Mahanaim means "two hosts" or "two camps," referring, it seems, to the camp of God and the camp of Jacob.

[74] According to Dr. Hugh Nibley, the translation in the King James Bible is incorrect here and that it was not an angel, but Jehovah himself, who was present and wrestled with Jacob. (Hugh Nibley, *Teachings of the Book of Mormon,* semester 2 (transcript of lectures presented to an Honors Book of Mormon class at Brigham Young University, Provo, Utah, 1988–90), 412.) Many years later when Jacob was blessing his two grandsons in Egypt, he called upon "The angel which redeemed me from all evil," to bless the lads (Genesis 48:16 and story "40—Blessings with Crossed Hands").

[75] The name Israel has two possible meanings—both significant. One meaning of the name is "He perseveres (with) God." The other meaning is "Let God prevail" (see footnote 28b of Genesis 32 [LDS-KJV]). Though God changed Jacob's name to Israel, he is rarely identified by that name in the scriptures. More frequently, the name was used as a collective title for Jacob's descendants.

"Why do you ask my name?" answered the angel. "I am El Shaddai.[76] You will be fruitful and will multiply; a nation and a company of nations will come out of you. Kings will spring from your loins, and I will also give to you and your seed after you the land that I gave to Abraham and Isaac."

Jacob called the place of his wrestle Peniel.[77] "For," said he, "I have seen God face-to-face and my life is preserved."

The sun was rising as Jacob departed from Peniel to return to his family, and he limped upon his leg because of the tissue that had shrunk in the hollow of his thigh.

---

[76] El Shaddai, in Hebrew, is "God Almighty." Jehovah was frequently identified by this name to the Patriarchs (see Genesis 17:1; 28:3; 43:14; 48:3; and 49:25).

[77] Peniel means "the face of God." There is some confusion in the biblical record about this event, which happened as Jacob was coming out of Padan-aram. Part of what is reported in Genesis 32 as taking place at Peniel is reported in Genesis 35 as taking place at Bethel. There seems to be something missing from the record. If the record were more complete, it might also be easier to explain why it was that either Jehovah or an angel would wrestle with Jacob.

32–THE REUNION
(Genesis 32–33)

During Jacob's journey from Padan-aram back to the land of Canaan, he sent messengers to Mount Seir[78] in the land of Edom to tell his brother Esau of his coming. "Thus shall you speak to my brother," he told the messengers. "Your servant Jacob sends this message: I have dwelt with Laban, our uncle, these many years. I have oxen, asses, flocks, menservants, and womenservants. And I send now to tell you of my coming, that I may find mercy in your sight."

When the messengers returned from delivering Jacob's message, they told him, "Your brother Esau is coming to meet us with 400 men."

Jacob did not consider this to be good news. Though twenty years had passed since he and Esau had seen each other, the last he knew was that Esau planned to kill him, as soon as their father was dead, because Jacob had deceitfully taken away both his birthright and his blessing.[79]

Because of his fear of Esau, Jacob divided his party into two groups. "If Esau comes and destroys one company," he reasoned, "the other shall escape."

Jacob prayed with all his heart. "O Jehovah, God of my fathers Abraham and Isaac," he pleaded, "I am returning to this country and to my family because Thou hast told me to do so. Thou didst tell me that it would be well with me here. I know I am not worthy of the least of Thy mercies or of the truths that Thou hast shown me, but I pray that Thou wilt deliver me from the hands of Esau—for I fear that he is coming to smite me and the mothers of my children.

"Remember, O Lord Jehovah, that Thou hast promised to do me good and to make my seed as the sand of the sea, which cannot be numbered for multitude." And though Jacob prayed fervently, he had little hope that Jehovah's promise could ever be fulfilled.

When Jacob stopped for the night, he separated out part of his flock as a gift for Esau that perhaps he might be pacified. The gift included 200 she-goats, twenty he-goats, 200 ewes, twenty rams, thirty camels that were kept for milking, the young of those camels, forty cows, ten bulls, twenty she-asses, and ten foals—a very generous gift.

As Jacob put these gift animals in the charge of his servants, he instructed them, "You go on ahead of the

---

[78] Mount Seir was located to the south and east of the Dead Sea.

[79] These events are recounted in stories "23–The Elder Shall Serve the Younger" and "25–Jacob Receives the Blessing."

company with this gift, putting a space between us. Then, when Esau meets you and asks who you are and whose animals these are, tell him, 'These are a gift sent by your servant Jacob to my lord Esau. And Jacob is coming behind us.'" Jacob reasoned that if Esau would accept the gift that he offered, he might also accept him.

As Jacob and his company were traveling the next day, he looked up and beheld Esau coming with his 400 men. Seeing them, he feared for his family and separated his wives and children from himself. Bilhah and Zilpah, the two handmaidens, and their children he put in front, then Leah and her children. Rachel, with her son Joseph, he put in the rear. He then went out ahead of them and bowed to the ground seven times as he approached his brother.

But—miracle of miracles—Esau came running to meet him. The two men then embraced and wept together.

Esau was startled as he looked up and saw the four women and their twelve children. "Whose are all these?" he asked.

"These," answered Jacob, "are the children that God has graciously given me." Bilhah, Zilpah, and their children then came and bowed before Esau, then Leah and her children, and finally Rachel and Joseph.

"What is the meaning of the herd of animals that I met on the way?" asked Esau.

"They are a gift for you, my brother," said Jacob, "to find mercy in your sight."

"I have enough, my brother. Keep what you have for yourself."

"Oh, no!" replied Jacob. "You must take them. If I have found favor with you, please receive my gift. I cannot tell you what a blessing it is to see your face and to know that you are pleased with me. Why, to see your face again is as though I have seen the face of God. Please take this gift as a blessing from me, for God has dealt kindly with me and has given me great abundance."

And, after some urging, Esau accepted his brother's gift.

"Let us travel together," suggested Esau.

"That would please me," answered Jacob, "but my children are tender and my flocks and herds are with young. If we drive them too far in one day, all the flock would die. Please go on ahead, and I will follow you to Seir at a speed suitable for my children and my animals."

Esau agreed. "But though I go ahead," he said, "I will leave some of my men to help you." So Esau returned that day to his home in Mount Seir.

Jacob and his company followed and, after a brief stop at Mount Seir, took their journey to a place that he named Succoth,[80] on the borders of Egypt. There Jacob built a house and booths for his flocks. He then went north and bought land on the beautiful plain of Shechem, where he built an altar to God and named it El-elohe-Israel.[81]

---

[80] Succoth means "booths."

[81] This means "El [God] is the God of Israel." In Hebrew, the word *El* signifies strength and is used to identify the Divine Being. It is used as a root in many Hebrew words.

33—IN DEFENSE OF DINAH'S HONOR

(Genesis 34)

While Jacob and his family were living on the plain of Shechem, Jacob and Leah's daughter, Dinah, went out to socialize with the other young women of the land. A young man named Shechem, the prince of the land, saw Dinah and was greatly infatuated with her. He treated her with great kindness but then took her to his house where he had sexual relations with her. Shechem wanted to have Dinah as his wife and requested that his father Hamor obtain Jacob's consent for the union.

When Dinah failed to return home, word got back to Jacob that Shechem had defiled his daughter.

The air was filled with tension when Hamor and Shechem came to Jacob's tent to ask for Dinah's hand. While they were talking with Jacob, his sons came in from the fields and joined the discussion. When Dinah's brothers learned what had happened, they were furious.

Hamor talked to them saying, "The soul of my son Shechem longs to have Dinah. I pray that you will give her to him to be his wife. Because we are your neighbors, it would be good for your family to enter into marriages with my people—give your daughters to us and take our daughters unto you. You can dwell among us, and the whole land will be before you. You will be able to dwell here, trade freely in the land, and increase your possessions."

After Hamor had finished speaking, Shechem spoke in his own behalf. "If I can find favor in your eyes," he said to Jacob and his sons, "I will give whatever you ask to have Dinah as my wife. I will provide a dowry and gifts of whatever you ask if you will but give your consent."

Jacob's sons discussed Shechem's offer among themselves, being very angry because of what Shechem had done to their sister. They agreed upon a plan of deceit to respond to him; then they gave their reply. "We cannot give our dear sister to one who is uncircumcised," they said, "for that would bring us dishonor. However, we will consent to your marriage to our sister if every male of your city will be circumcised as we are. Then we will give our daughters to you in marriage, you may take our daughters, and we will be as one people. However, if you will not be circumcised, we will take our sister and leave your country."

Hamor and Shechem were pleased by this answer, and Shechem agreed to all that was requested because of his love for Dinah. When they left Jacob's tent, they went to the gate of their city, where Shechem told the men of his agreement with Jacob's sons. "These men are peaceable with us," he said. "We can let them dwell in our land and trade here. The land is large enough for them and us. And they have agreed that we may take their daughters to wife and they will take our daughters."

Shechem continued: "But there is one more thing. They will not agree to dwell among us and be one with us unless every male among us is circumcised. It is a small price for us to pay, for their cattle and all their substance shall be ours."

The men of the city agreed to do as Hamor and Shechem requested, and all were circumcised that day.

On the third day, when the men of Shechem were most sore from their circumcisions, Dinah's brothers carried out their dishonorable plan. Simeon and Levi took their swords, went into the city, and killed every man. They took Dinah out of Shechem's house and killed both Shechem and Hamor. They took as spoils all the sheep, oxen, and asses of the city, the crops of their fields, and all their wealth. They also took the women and children captive and took spoils of all that was in their houses.

When Jacob learned of the destruction that Simeon and Levi had wrought in the city of Shechem, he was both angry and afraid. He said to them, "Your shameful deeds have caused great problems for me. You have made me stink among all the people of this land. And because I am but few in numbers, they will unite against me and kill me. Both I and my household shall surely be destroyed."

Simeon and Levi, unrepentant, answered their father, "Would you have us allow Shechem to deal with our sister as if she were a harlot?"

34—THE LAST SON
(Genesis 35)

Following the destruction that Simeon and Levi had visited upon the city of Shechem, Jehovah commanded Jacob to go to Beth-el and build an altar. But Jacob was concerned because many of his household had been accumulating idols for worship. He gathered everyone around him and said, "The time has come for you to put away the strange gods that are among you, to change your garments, and to be clean before God. When your false gods are destroyed, let us go to Beth-el, where I have been commanded to build an altar to Jehovah, even that God who answered me in the day of my distress and was with me on my journey."

When the people had gathered up their idols and brought them to Jacob, he buried them under an oak tree on the plain of Shechem. Then, as Jacob and his company prepared to leave the plain of Shechem, Jehovah put terror into the hearts of the people in the cities round about. They were afraid to pursue Jacob and his sons as they departed.

Jacob and his household traveled south from Shechem to Luz, which Jacob had renamed Beth-el when he dreamed of a ladder going up into heaven.[82] There Jacob built an altar, as he had been commanded, and called the place El-Beth-el[83] because Jehovah appeared to him there when he fled from his brother Esau.

Jacob set up a stone pillar in the place where he talked with Jehovah and poured a drink offering of strong wine upon the pillar. He also anointed the pillar with oil.

Leaving Beth-el, Jacob and his party traveled the short distance to Bethlehem, which was called Ephrath. When they were nearly there, his beloved wife Rachel bore him another son, but the labor was too hard and Rachel died in childbirth. Before her death, however, she named her son Benoni.[84] Jacob, however, called him Benjamin.[85]

When Jacob had buried his beloved Rachel along the way to Bethlehem[86] and had set a stone pillar to mark her grave, he and his party resumed their journey to the plain of Mamre, the city of Arbah (which later became Hebron), where his forefathers had lived. Isaac, in fact, was still living there. At the age of 180, Isaac's health was not good, and he had been blind for many years.

Isaac died shortly after Jacob's arrival, and, as the scripture says, "He was gathered unto his people, being old and full of years." Jacob and Esau buried their father in the cave that Abraham had bought for Sarah's burial many years before. Isaac's wife Rebekah and his parents, Abraham and Sarah, were all buried in that same cave.

---

[82] See story "26—A Ladder That Reaches to Heaven."

[83] El-Beth-el means "God is the house of God."

[84] Benoni means "Son of my sorrow" or "Son of my strength."

[85] Benjamin means "Son of the right hand."

[86] In 1 Samuel 10:2, Rachel's burial place is identified as Zelzah. Zelzah is not mentioned anywhere else in the scriptures.

35—SOLD INTO EGYPT
(Genesis 37)

Jacob was living at Mamre when his young son Joseph was seventeen years old. Joseph and his older brothers were in charge of their father's flocks and tended them in the field. The brothers were jealous of Joseph because he was their father's favorite. And when Jacob gave Joseph a beautiful coat of many colors,[87] the brothers' jealousy turned to bitterness and they treated him badly.

Joseph was a dreamer, and his dreams offended his brothers when he told them. "I dreamed," he said, "that our family was in the field binding grain into sheaves. As we did so, the sheaf that I bound stood upright, and your sheaves all stood around it and bowed down before it."

This dream only served to increase his brothers' jealousy, and they said to him, "Do you think you are better than we are and that you will reign over us?" The idea that Joseph could even dream of such a thing was repulsive to them, and the feelings they had against their younger brother turned from jealousy to hatred.

Then Joseph had another dream that he told to his family. "Behold," he said, "I have dreamed that the sun and the moon and the eleven stars all bowed down to the earth before me."

Jacob rebuked Joseph for telling such a dream. "What kind of a dream is this?" he asked. "Shall your mother and I and your eleven brothers bow down to the earth before you? That is a very selfish dream." Joseph's brothers hated him even more, and Jacob was troubled about what Joseph had told them.

Joseph's older brothers had gone to tend their father's flocks on the plains of Shechem, the place where Simeon and Levi had killed Shechem and all the men of his city when Shechem had defiled their sister Dinah.[88] One day Jacob called Joseph to him and said, "Go down to your brothers at Shechem, see if all is well, and bring word back to me."

Joseph went to Shechem but did not find his brothers there. When a man saw him wandering in the field, he asked Joseph what he was looking for. "I have come to find my brothers," answered Joseph. "Do you know where they are feeding their flocks?"

"I heard them say they were going to Dothan," replied the man. And Joseph went on to Dothan where he found his brothers with their flocks.

As Joseph's brothers saw him coming afar off, they said to one another, "Behold, the dreamer is coming," and they discussed a plan to kill him: "Let us slay our brother and cast his body into a pit," they schemed. "We can tell our father that some evil beast has devoured him, then we will see what becomes of his dreams."

Reuben, however, had compassion on young Joseph. "Let us not kill him," countered Reuben, "but let us only cast him into a pit in the wilderness." Reuben said this with the idea that he would go back later to deliver Joseph and return him to his father.

And so it was that when Joseph came to the place where his brothers were, they stripped him of his beautiful coat and put him into an empty pit.

Later, when they sat to eat, they saw a company of Ishmaelite traders coming from Gilead on their way to Egypt. As they watched the traders pass, Judah observed, "Rather than slay our younger brother and conceal his blood, let us sell him to these Ishmaelites. That would be better than killing one of our own flesh." When his brothers had agreed on the plan, they pulled young Joseph from the pit and sold him for twenty pieces of silver.[89]

Reuben, who had planned to return Joseph to his father, was not with his brothers when Joseph was sold to the traders. When he later returned to the pit and saw that Joseph was gone, he tore his clothes and ran quickly to tell his brothers. "What shall we do?" he cried. "Joseph is gone! What will we tell our father?"

When the brothers told Reuben what they had done, they began to discuss a strategy for telling Jacob. And, as they viewed the matter, they were left with few choices. When they agreed that they could not tell their father that they had sold Joseph to a company of traders on their way to Egypt, they took his beautiful coat and tore it to shreds. They then dipped the remnants of the coat in kid's blood and took it to their father. "We found this coat," they told him. "Is it the coat you gave your son?"

---

[87] The term that is interpreted as "many colors" in the Bible may have another meaning. It does mean *many colors* in the Septuagint (the Greek translation of the Old Testament), but in Hebrew it means that the coat had *long sleeves.*

[88] See story "33—In Defense of Dinah's Honor."

---

[89] There is some disagreement about who actually sold Joseph to the Ishmaelites, his brothers or the Midianite merchants mentioned in Genesis 37:28. In that verse it seems clear that it was the Midianites that made the sale, but in the Book of Mormon (Alma 10:3) and in Genesis 45:4, we are told that it was Joseph's brothers. Whether or not Joseph's brothers actually sold him, they certainly had the intent and would have done so had someone else not done it first.

Jacob immediately recognized the tattered coat as the one he had given to Joseph. "Surely my son has been eaten by some beast," cried Jacob. Then he tore his clothes, put sackcloth about his loins, and mourned for many days. When Jacob's family tried to console him, he would not be comforted. And as he wept, he said, "I shall go down to my grave mourning for this great loss."

The Ishmaelite traders,[90] in the meantime, carried Joseph into Egypt, where they sold him to Potiphar, a high officer in Pharaoh's court and captain of the guard.

36–JUDAH'S FOLLY
(Genesis 38)

Judah, the fourth son of Jacob and Leah, was married to a Canaanite woman, who bore him three sons, and he named them Er, Onan, and Shelah. As a wife for his son Er, Judah chose Tamar. Er, however, was a wicked man and Jehovah slew him.

Now, it was according to custom that if a man died leaving a widow, the dead man's next brother would marry the widow and raise up seed to the brother who had died.[91] Thus, Judah said to Onan, "Go and marry your brother's wife and raise up seed to him."

Onan was well aware that any children born to him and Tamar would be counted as the seed of Er. And though he married Tamar, he refused to give children to his brother Er and Jehovah slew him also.

With his two eldest sons dead, Judah said to Tamar, "Go live in your father's house until Shelah, my youngest son, is grown. Then, unless he should die also, he will marry you." Thus, Tamar went to live in her father's house and wore the clothing of her widowhood.

Years passed and Shelah came of age, but Judah neglected to have him take Tamar to wife. Judah's own wife also died and the time of his mourning was passed.

One day Judah went with his friend Hirah to shear his sheep at Timnath, and Tamar learned that he was going. When she became aware that her father-in-law was going to Timnath, Tamar put off her widow's garments, covered her face with a veil, and sat in an open place along the way. When Judah saw her sitting there, he did not recognize her but—because of the veil—thought she was a harlot. Judah went in and asked to lie with her, but she stopped him and asked, "First tell me what you will give me."

"I will send you a kid from my flock," he promised.

"Will you give me a pledge till you send it?

"What pledge do you want?" asked Judah.

"Your signet ring, your bracelets, and that staff in your hand," she replied. And Judah gave them to her.

Tamar conceived that day and was thus with child by Judah, her father-in-law. Then she returned to her father's house and donned again her widow's clothing.

By the hand of his friend Hirah, Judah sent back the kid that he had promised, but Hirah could find no harlot. Returning without accomplishing his mission, he told Judah. "I cannot find her, and the men of the place say there was no harlot there."

---

[90] There is some confusion in the scriptural text, for it says in Genesis 37:36 that Joseph was sold to Potiphar by *Midianite* traders (see also footnote 89 and the discussion about who sold Joseph).

[91] This custom was well established by the time of Judah and later became part of the law of Moses (see Deuteronomy 25:5–6).

Judah became greatly concerned when the harlot could not be found. He feared that he would be shamed in the matter because the woman had not received what he had pledged to her and because she had his signet, his bracelets, and his staff.

When three months had passed and Judah was informed that Tamar was with child, he was enraged to think that she should become pregnant when she was not married. What shame she was bringing to his family! "Bring her forth," he demanded, "and let her be burned!"

When Tamar was brought for the burning, she sent a message to Judah saying, "By him to whom this signet, bracelets, and staff belong am I with child." And when Judah saw those things, that they were his, he wept. "She has been more righteous than I," he wailed, "for I failed to give Shelah to be her husband."

Judah spared Tamar's life and, when the time came for her delivery, she bore twin sons. During the labor, one of the babies put out his hand from the womb and the midwife tied a scarlet thread on the wrist. "This one came out first," she said. But the babe drew back his hand, and the other child was born before him. The firstborn was given the name Pharez, and his brother was named Zarah. And the line of Pharez became the royal lineage nearly 700 years later when David came to the throne of Israel. And Jesus himself was born through that same lineage in the meridian of time.

37—MY MASTER TRUSTS ME
(Genesis 39)

Jehovah poured out bounteous blessings on Joseph in Egypt. Everything he did seemed to improve his position. The traders had sold him to Potiphar, an officer of the king and captain of the guard, and Joseph proved to be a faithful servant. He was completely loyal to his master and honest to the nth degree. Potiphar saw that Jehovah was with Joseph and caused him to prosper in all that he did, and, before much time had passed, he came to trust Joseph so completely that he made him overseer of his house and all of his property.

God blessed Potiphar's property because of Joseph and he became a wealthy man. So complete was his trust that he no longer kept track of what he owned or what dealings Joseph had with it. Joseph was the ideal servant, faithful in every way. He was not only trustworthy, but he was also skillful in his management of Potiphar's goods. He had also grown into a strong and handsome young man.

Joseph had complete freedom in Potiphar's house and was able to come and go as he pleased. There was not any thing or any place off limits to him. As time passed, however, a problem developed. Potiphar's wife was attracted to this handsome young Hebrew and tried repeatedly to tempt him to have an intimate relationship with her. But Joseph always refused.

"My master trusts me," Joseph told the woman. "He knows none of my doings with his house and his property because of that trust. There is no one in Potiphar's house greater than I am, and he has kept nothing from me except for you—because you are his wife. How then could I do this great wickedness and sin against both my master and my God?"

Potiphar's wife was not satisfied with Joseph's answer. His refusal only made her want him more, and she continued day after day, seeking to tempt Joseph to lie with her.

One day when Joseph went into the house to conduct his business, the woman tried again to tempt him. Because none of the men of the house were present, she thought she could surely convince him. Taking hold of Joseph's coat, she said, "Come now, Joseph, and lie with me. You and I are the only ones here, and no one else will ever know."

Joseph resisted the woman's advances without hesitation. He did not waiver for a moment but fled from the house. Unfortunately, however, his coat remained behind in the woman's hands.

Rejected by Joseph, Potiphar's wife sought bitter revenge. She called loudly for the men of the house to come quickly. "Look!" she cried. "Our master has brought in a Hebrew to mock us. He came in to lie with me, but my screams frightened him away. He fled when I screamed—but see, he has left his coat."

The woman kept Joseph's coat with her until Potiphar returned; then she rehearsed for her husband the same lying tale that she had told the other men. Joseph's righteousness and his loyalty to Potiphar counted for nothing when the woman told her twisted tale. Potiphar believed his wife—for he had only Joseph's word against hers. In his anger, Potiphar cast Joseph into the prison, where the king's prisoners were held captive.

Things looked very bad for Joseph. From all outward appearances, his loyalty and righteousness had turned to his disadvantage.

38—RULER OVER ALL EGYPT
(Genesis 39–41)

Jehovah did not forget his servant Joseph. Joseph had been faithful, and Jehovah continued to bless him, even while he was confined in the Pharaoh's prison. Because Joseph found favor with the keeper of the prison, he was made overseer and placed in charge of the other prisoners.

One day the Pharaoh's chief butler and chief baker offended their master and were cast into prison, and the captain of the guard put them in Joseph's care. After they had been in prison for some time, both men had dreams on the same night. Their dreams troubled them because they did not understand them. And when Joseph came in and saw that they were very sad, he asked the cause of their distress.

"We have dreamed dreams," they replied, "and there is no one to interpret them for us."

"Do not such interpretations belong to God?" Joseph answered them. "Tell me your dreams."

The chief butler told his dream first. "I saw a vine," he said, "and on the vine were three branches. The vine budded, its blossoms shot forth, and the clusters of blossoms brought forth ripe grapes. I also saw that Pharaoh's cup was in my hand, and I took the grapes, pressed them into the cup, and gave it to Pharaoh."

"This is the interpretation of your dream," said Joseph. "The three branches are three days. Within three days Pharaoh will lift up your head and restore you to your place as his butler. You will then deliver Pharaoh's cup into his hand as you did before."

When Joseph had given the interpretation of the butler's dream, he pleaded with the man, "Please remember me when you are restored to your post. Show your kindness by mentioning me to Pharaoh, that he might bring me out of this prison. For I was stolen out of the land of the Hebrews and I have done nothing to deserve this dungeon."

Then the chief baker, because of the favorable interpretation of the butler's dream, told Joseph his dream also. "In my dream," he said, "I had three white baskets on my head. All manner of bakery goods for the Pharaoh were in the top basket, but the birds came and ate them from the basket."

"This is the interpretation," said Joseph. "The three baskets are three days. Within three days the Pharaoh will lift up your head from you. He will hang you on a tree, and the birds will eat your flesh."

And so it was that on the third day, which was Pharaoh's birthday, he gave a great feast for all his servants and brought both the chief butler and the chief baker out of the prison. The butler was restored to his former post and delivered the cup into Pharaoh's hand, as Joseph had said, and the chief baker was hanged.

The butler, caught up in his own affairs, forgot about Joseph and his request to be remembered to Pharaoh, thus Joseph remained in prison without guilt.

When two more years had passed, Pharaoh had a dream. He dreamed that he stood by a river and seven fat cows came up out of the river and grazed in a meadow. Then he saw seven cows of very poor flesh come up out of the river and eat the fat cows.

The dream troubled Pharaoh and awakened him. When he finally went back to sleep, he dreamed again. In his second dream he saw seven large and full heads of grain[92] growing on one stalk. Then seven lean and withered heads—blasted by the east wind—sprang up after them. The seven lean heads of grain then devoured the seven fat ones.

Pharaoh called for all the magicians and wise men of Egypt that they might interpret his dreams, but none could tell him their meaning. It was then that the chief butler remembered Joseph and how Joseph had interpreted his dream in prison, and he remembered Joseph to the Pharaoh.

"I remember," he said, "that two years ago you were angry with me and cast me into prison, both me and your chief baker. While in prison, when we both had dreams on the same night, a young Hebrew man, a servant to the captain of the guard, who was in prison with us, interpreted our dreams. Each dream was fulfilled according to this man's interpretation; I was restored to my office and the baker was hanged." When Pharaoh heard this report, he sent instructions for Joseph to be brought from the prison at once.

Joseph, clean-shaven and dressed in clean clothing, was brought quickly before the king, and the king wasted no time in making his desires known. "I have dreamed a dream," he told Joseph, "and no one can interpret it. I have been told that you can understand dreams and give their interpretations. Is this true?"

"There is no such a power in me," answered Joseph, "but God shall give Pharaoh an answer of peace."

When Pharaoh heard this he related both of his dreams, telling Joseph about both the fat and the lean cows and the fat and the lean heads of grain. Once the dreams had been told, Joseph said, "Both of your dreams are the same. The seven fat cows are seven years, and the seven fat heads of grain are those same seven years. The seven lean cows and the seven empty heads of grain both represent seven years of famine.

"God has shown the Pharaoh what he is about to do. There will be seven years of great plenty throughout Egypt, but those years of plenty will be followed by seven years of famine. The years of plenty will be forgotten as famine consumes the land. Because the famine will be sore, the dream was shown to you twice. God has established this thing, and he will shortly bring it to pass."

Joseph continued: "The Pharaoh should choose a wise and discreet man and set him over the land so that preparations can be made. Let this man appoint officers to lay up in store during the seven plenteous years. Let them gather the food of those good years and lay it up in store against the famine, lest Egypt perish."

The Pharaoh was pleased and impressed with what Joseph had suggested, and he said to him, "Because God has shown all these things to you, there in no other man so discreet and wise as you are. I will set you over all Egypt, and all my people shall be ruled according to your word. Only I, in my throne, will be greater than you." Then the Pharaoh took off his ring and put it on Joseph's hand. He dressed him in the finest clothing and put a gold chain about his neck. And, from that day forward, Joseph rode in the second chariot and ruled over all of Egypt.

Pharaoh changed Joseph's name to Zaphnath-paaneah[93] and gave him Asenath to be his wife.[94] Asenath was the daughter of Potipherah, the priest of On.[95]

---

[92] The scripture says "ears of corn" rather than "heads of grain" as stated in this story. The "ears of corn" usage was based on the understanding of the KJV translators who had no knowledge of what Americans call corn today; corn, or maize, is a product of the Western Hemisphere. In British English, *corn* is another word for *grain*.

[93] In Hebrew, this name given to Joseph by Pharaoh is interpreted as "revealer of a secret." However, the name must have been Egyptian and has been explained from the Coptic as meaning "preserver of the age" (see William Smith, *Dictionary of the Bible*, GospeLink, CD-ROM, s.v. "Zaphnath-paaneah"). Both meanings are significant.

[94] It is generally understood that the rulers of Egypt, as well as the religious leaders, at the time of Joseph were a Semitic people known as the Hyksos, or the shepherd kings, who had conquered the native Egyptians prior to the time of Abraham. Asenath would likely have been of this race. However, the important thing is not Asenath's race but the fact that she was converted to the religion of her husband Joseph and was obedient to the commandments of God.

[95] On means "city of the sun." It was a town of lower (or northern) Egypt. In Jeremiah 43:13 it is called Beth-shemesh, but it is better known under its Greek name

Joseph was thirty years old when he became the ruler of Egypt. And, as the ruler, he was able to faithfully carry out his plan, gathering and storing grain throughout the seven plenteous years. The land produced in great abundance, and Joseph gathered grain in abundance beyond reckoning. Great stores were laid up in every city of Egypt.

Joseph is made ruler over all Egypt

When the seven years of plenty had passed, according to Pharaoh's dream, severe drought and famine followed; and all the world came to Egypt to buy grain.

Heliopolis. It lay east of the Pelusiac branch of the Nile, just below the delta, and about twenty miles (32.2 kilometers) northeast of Memphis (see William Smith, *Dictionary of the Bible*, *GospeLink*, CD-ROM, s.v. "On").

39—ISRAEL GOES INTO EGYPT

(Genesis 41–47)

The seven years of prosperity in Egypt passed, but, under Joseph's direction, great storehouses in every city were filled with grain. And even as the famine foreseen in Pharaoh's dream came to the land, there was still plenty to eat. When the people became hungry and cried to the Pharaoh for bread, he sent them to Joseph. And Joseph opened his storehouses and sold grain. And the famine was very sore.

When the famine spread into other countries, the storehouses of Egypt became widely known, and the entire world came to Egypt to buy grain. When Jacob learned that there was grain in Egypt, he sent his sons from Canaan to Egypt to buy food for their families. However, he did not send his youngest son Benjamin because he feared for the young man's safety. Jacob believed that his son Joseph was dead, and it would have broken his heart if anything happened to Benjamin.

When the ten brothers arrived in Egypt, they bowed their faces to the ground before the governor of the land, not recognizing that the governor was their brother Joseph. They had no such thought because they believed that Joseph must surely be dead. Joseph, however, recognized his brothers when he first saw them. But he gave no sign that he knew who they were. "Where have you come from?" he inquired.

"We have come from the land of Canaan to buy food," they answered, again bowing to the ground. And Joseph remembered the dream of his youth when the grain sheaves of his brothers had bowed before his own.[96]

"You are spies!" he accused them. "You have come to see the nakedness of our land."

"We have come only to buy food for our families," they answered. "We are not spies but honest men."

When Joseph pressed his brothers further, they told him that they were twelve brothers, the sons of one man. "Our youngest brother," they said, "is at home with our father and one other is dead."

Joseph ordered that his brothers be locked in a house for three days, after which he went to them again. "I still think you are spies," he said, "so you must prove to me otherwise. If you do what I say, you will be allowed to live, for I am a God-fearing man. For you to prove your innocence, one of you shall remain here, a prisoner in this house, while the rest carry grain to your

[96] See story "35 Sold Into Egypt."

families. You must then return with your youngest brother, or the one I keep as a prisoner shall die." The brothers, who had little choice in the matter, nodded their agreement to Joseph's terms.

Greatly upset by Joseph's request, the brothers talked among themselves in Hebrew, thinking that the governor could not understand, for he spoke to them only through an interpreter. "This terrible distress has come upon us because of what we did to our brother Joseph," they said.

"That's right," agreed Reuben. "Though I told you to leave him alone, you would not hear me, and now our blood is required for his." When Joseph heard their anguish, he turned away from them and wept.

When Joseph turned back, he took Simeon and bound him before the others. "This is the man who shall remain here," he said.

Joseph then commanded that when his brothers' sacks were filled with grain, the money they paid for it should be put into the mouths of their sacks. He then gave them provisions for their journey and sent them away.

When the sons of Jacob arrived home, they recounted to their father all that had happened in Egypt. They told how Simeon was being held as a prisoner and how they had promised to bring Benjamin back in return for Simeon's life.

When they emptied their grain, they found the money they had paid for it in the mouths of their sacks, and both they and their father feared what might happen if they returned to Egypt. "You have bereaved me of my children," Jacob lamented. "Joseph and Simeon are both dead, and now you would also take Benjamin. All these things are against me, and Benjamin shall not go!"

"Please, Father," pleaded Reuben. "You *must* allow him to go. If I fail to return him to you, you may kill my two sons. If you will put Benjamin into my hands, I promise to bring him back."

"He shall not go!" repeated Jacob. "His brother is dead, and he is the only son of his mother. If mischief should befall Benjamin, it would bring my gray hairs down to the grave with sorrow."

Time passed and the grain brought from Egypt was almost gone. With starvation staring him in the face, Jacob began to soften. He said to his sons, "You must go back to Egypt and get more grain."

"The man in Egypt said that we will not see his face unless we bring our brother with us," Judah reminded him. "If you will send Benjamin with us, we will go and buy food. If you will not send him, we cannot go."

Jacob felt betrayed and trapped. "Why did you tell this man you had a brother?" he asked.

"Because he asked about our family," replied Judah. "He asked if our father was yet alive and if we had a brother. If we had known he would require us to bring our brother, we would not have told him. But if you will not send the lad with us now, we shall all die— you, and us, and our children—for lack of food."

Jacob reluctantly relented. "If this must be," he said, "take your brother and go. But you must take gifts for this man of Egypt. And you must also take double the money required for the grain to repay what you found in your sacks." So the ten sons of Jacob, with their money and their gifts, returned to Egypt to redeem their brother Simeon and to buy more grain.

When the sons of Jacob arrived in Egypt and Joseph saw Benjamin with his brothers, he commanded his servants to take them to his house and prepare a feast. "These men will dine with me today," he said.

The brothers were afraid when they were taken to Joseph's house. They feared that—because of the money they had found in their sacks—they would be made slaves and their animals would be taken. They told the steward of Joseph's house about the money in their sacks and that they had brought it with them again. Sensing their anxiety, the steward said, "Peace be to you. I had your money. It must have been your God who gave you treasure in your sacks." And he brought Simeon out to join them.

Joseph's servants gave the brothers water, washed their feet, fed their animals, and prepared them to eat with Joseph. But while they were being prepared, their only thoughts were about giving the governor their gifts. They were filled with fear and they wished to risk no offense.

When Joseph finally arrived, he asked his brothers, "Is your father well, the old man of whom you spoke? Is he yet alive?"

"Your servant our father is in good health," they assured him. And they all bowed with deep respect.

Joseph's eyes then fell on Benjamin, his own mother's other son, and he asked, "Is this the younger brother of whom you spoke?" Then, speaking directly to Benjamin, he said, "God be gracious unto you, my son." Then Joseph left quickly, for he was unable to hold back his tears of joy for his brother. He went to his chamber and wept until he was able to control his emotions. He then washed his face and returned to his brothers.

When Joseph had dined with his eleven brothers, he had his steward again fill their sacks with grain and put their money in the mouths of their sacks. Then he said to his steward, "In the sack of the youngest put also my silver cup." It was done as Joseph said, and in the morning the sons of Jacob began their journey back to Canaan.

51

When the brothers had traveled but a short distance from the city, Joseph sent his servants to catch them with his silver cup, telling his steward the words that he should speak.

Joseph's servants soon overtook the eleven brothers. "Why have you rewarded our master evil for good," asked the steward, "in that you have taken his silver cup—that cup from which he both drinks and tells the future?"

The brothers were stunned. "How can your lord accuse us of stealing his cup?" they asked. "If we were honest enough to bring back the money that we found in our sacks, why would we steal silver or gold from your master's house?" They were certain that none of them had taken the governor's cup. "If the cup is found with one of us," they said, "let that one die. And the rest of us will be your master's bondsmen."

"Not so," the steward responded, according to Joseph's instructions. "Our master has said that he who has stolen the cup shall be his servant and the rest of you shall be blameless." So each brother, beginning with the eldest, opened his sack to be searched—and the cup was found with Benjamin.

What a shock this was! How could such a thing be possible? Remembering their father's concern for Benjamin's life, the brothers tore their clothes in despair. They returned to Joseph's house with the servants and fell before him on the ground.

"What is this you have done?" demanded Joseph. "Did you not know that a man such as I can tell the future?"

"God knows we are guilty," replied Judah, "and there is nothing more we can say. We will all be your servants for this great sin."

"Such cannot be," replied Joseph. "God forbid that any should be my servant except the man with whom the cup was found. The rest of you must return to your father."

Then Judah came near to Joseph and spoke in hushed tones. "Do not be angry with me," he said, "but I must speak to you privately. I know that you are even as Pharaoh himself." Then, in privacy, Judah continued: "You asked about our father and our brother, and we told you that our father is an old man and our brother is the child of his old age. This boy's brother is dead, and he is the only surviving child of his mother.

"Our father loves this young man dearly, and I have sworn an oath to our father that I will bring him back. If the lad does not return, our father will surely die. I was able to persuade our father to let the young man come here only because you said we could not see your face again unless he came. If he does not return, I must bear the blame forever. I urge you now to let me be your servant in his place and let him return to our father."

Joseph, deeply touched, could control his emotions no longer. He stood before his brothers and wept. Then he sent away all others who were there that he might make himself known. "I am Joseph!" he told them. "I am your brother whom you sold into Egypt." And he wept so loudly that the Egyptians and all the house of Pharaoh heard it.

"Grieve no longer nor be angry with yourselves because you sold me," he said. "Jehovah sent me into Egypt that I might preserve life. Though there has been famine in the land for two years already, it will last for five years more. Jehovah sent me here before you to save your lives and the lives of your posterity by a great deliverance. He has made me a father to Pharaoh, the lord of Pharaoh's house, and a ruler over all of Egypt."

Joseph continued: "You must go to our father and tell him that God has made me lord of Egypt. Tell him that if he will come to Egypt, he may dwell in the land of Goshen with his children, his children's children, his flocks, his herds, and all that he has. And I will nurture him through these five years of famine lest he come to poverty. Go quickly now and bring our father down." Joseph then fell on Benjamin's neck and wept. They kissed each other, and the others wept with them.

When Pharaoh learned of the coming of Joseph's brothers, he said to Joseph, "Tell your brothers to bring your father and their families and come into Egypt. I will give them the good of Egypt and they shall eat the fat of the land." He then commanded that they take wagons with them to bring back their wives and children.

Joseph gave his brothers provisions for their trip and gave each a change of clothing. But to Benjamin he gave five changes of clothing and 300 pieces of silver. To his father he sent ten asses laden with the good things of Egypt and ten she-asses laden with grain, bread, and meat for his use on the way.

Bearing the bounty of Egypt, Jacob's sons returned to their father in Canaan. They told him the words of Joseph and all that had happened to them. When they told him that Joseph was governor of Egypt, his heart fainted and he would not believe them. When he saw the wagons and the gifts, however, his heart revived. "It is enough!" he exclaimed. "I will go to Egypt to see my son Joseph before I die."

In preparation for the journey—still having some doubts—Jacob went to Beersheba where he offered sacrifices to Jehovah. While he was there at Beersheba, Jehovah spoke to him in a night vision, telling him that he should not be afraid to go to Egypt. "Fear not," said Jehovah, "for I will make you a great nation in Egypt. I will go with you there and will also bring you up again, and Joseph shall put his hand upon your eyes."

So Jacob rose up from Beersheba and went into Egypt with his sons, their families, their flocks, and all of their possessions. And sixty-six people went down to Egypt on the wagons that Pharaoh had sent.

Judah went ahead to direct them into the land of Goshen, and Joseph came up to meet them. When he saw his father, he fell on his neck and wept. "Let me now die," cried Jacob, "for I have seen your face and you are yet alive."

When Jacob and his family were settled in Goshen, Joseph took his father and five of his brothers to meet Pharaoh, and Jacob gave Pharaoh a blessing. Then, because Pharaoh loved Joseph, he gave Joseph's family the best of the land of Egypt.

40–BLESSINGS WITH CROSSED HANDS
(Genesis 47– 48)

When Jacob and his family had been in Egypt for seventeen years, Jacob's eyes grew dim. He was now 147 years old, and he knew that his life must soon end. In preparation for the time when he would die, Jacob called his son Joseph to him one day and made him swear an oath that when he was dead, Joseph would carry his body back to Canaan to be buried with his fathers. He knew he would die in Egypt, but he did not want to be buried there.

Joseph had two sons who were born to him by his wife Asenath. The eldest was named Manasseh and the other Ephraim. These young men had never met their grandfather. Thus, when Jacob became sick and it appeared that this illness might be his last, Joseph brought his sons to their grandfather for a blessing.

Jacob learned that Joseph was coming, but he did not know he was bringing his sons. When he learned of the impending visit, he was strengthened and sat up on the side of his bed. Though unable to see, he heard Joseph enter. "Joseph," he said, "Jehovah appeared to me when I was at Luz in Canaan.[97] He told me that I would be fruitful and that he would make me a multitude of people. He also told me that he would give the land of Canaan unto my seed after me as an everlasting possession."

Jacob continued: "Your sons, Ephraim and Manasseh, who were born before I came into Egypt, I now claim as my own sons, just as I claim Reuben and Simeon. If you have any other children, they will be yours and will be called after your name, but these two are mine and will receive their inheritance from me."

As Jacob talked to Joseph, he realized that two young men were there with him. "Who are these who are with you?" asked Jacob.

"These are Manasseh and Ephraim, the sons whom God has given me in this place," answered Joseph.

"Bring them here to me that I may bless them," said Jacob. And as he drew the young men near to him, he kissed and embraced them both. Then to Joseph he said, "I thought I would never again see your face, but now God has also shown me your children."

---

[97] It was at Luz, on his way to Padan-aram that Jacob dreamed of a ladder going up into heaven. He saw Jehovah at the top of the ladder and received instructions from him. It was after this experience that Jacob renamed the place Beth-el (see story "26–A Ladder That Reaches to Heaven").

Joseph placed Manasseh at Jacob's right hand—for he was the eldest—and Ephraim at the left to receive a blessing from their grandfather. But as the young men came to him, Jacob crossed his hands, putting the right hand on Ephraim's head and the left on Manasseh's.

He gave them this blessing: "O God, before whom my fathers Abraham and Isaac did walk and who fed me all my life unto this day—yea, even the angel who redeemed me from all evil—bless these lads and let my name be named upon them, as well as the names of my fathers Abraham and Isaac. Let them grow into a multitude in the midst of the earth."

As Jacob paused in his blessing, Joseph noticed the placement of his father's hands. When he saw that Jacob's right hand was on Ephraim's head, he was displeased. He lifted his father's hands to move the right hand to Manasseh and said to Jacob, "You have erred, my father, for this is the firstborn. Put your right hand on him."

Jacob refused. "I know, my son," he replied firmly. "Though Manasseh will become a great people, his younger brother will be greater than he. The seed of the younger shall become a multitude of nations."

Then Jacob continued his blessing. "In the two of you shall all Israel be blessed," he said, "and they shall say, 'May God make us as Ephraim and Manasseh.'"

When Jacob's blessing upon his grandsons was completed and he had set Ephraim before Manasseh, he said to Joseph, "I am going to die, but God will be with you and bring you unto the land of your fathers. And, through these sons of yours whom I have taken as my own, I have given you an inheritance above the inheritance of your brothers in the land that God has given us."

41—JACOB'S PASSING
(Genesis 49–50)

After Jacob had claimed his grandsons, Ephraim and Manasseh, as his own sons and had given them his blessing, he called together the twelve sons born to his four wives that he might also bless each of them. "Come," he said, "that I may tell you what will happen to your descendants in the last days." And Jacob sat upon his bed and blessed his sons, each in the order of his age, from Reuben to Benjamin.

"Reuben," said Jacob, "you are my firstborn, my might, and the beginning of my strength—excellent in dignity and power. You are unstable as water and shall not excel.

"Simeon and Levi, you are brothers with instruments of cruelty in your dwelling places. On my honor, my soul would have no fellowship with your secret works, for you slew a man in your anger. Cursed be your anger for it was fierce, and your wrath for it was cruel. I will divide you in Jacob and scatter you throughout Israel.

"And you, Judah, are the one whom your brothers shall praise. Your hand shall be in the neck of your enemies and your father's children shall bow down before you. You are a lion's whelp and have gone up from the prey. And when you lie down as an old lion, there is no one to rouse you up. The scepter shall not depart from you, Judah, nor the lawgiver from between your feet, until Shiloh shall come and the people shall gather unto you. You shall wash your garments in the blood of grapes. Your eyes shall be red with wine and your teeth white with milk.

"Zebulun, you shall dwell at the haven of the sea and be a refuge for ships, with a border that reaches to Zidon.[98]

"Issachar, you are a strong ass lying down between two burdens. When you saw that rest was good and that the land was pleasant, you bowed your shoulder to bear your burdens and became a servant and a payer of tribute.

"Dan, you shall judge your people as one of the tribes of Israel. You, Dan, shall be a serpent by the path to bite the horse's heels and cause the riders to fall backwards.

"A troop shall overcome you, Gad, but you shall prevail and overcome at the last.

"The bread of Asher shall be fat, and you, Asher, shall yield royal dainties.

---

[98] Zidon is Sidon, the chief city of Phoenicia (or Zidonia).

"You, Naphtali, are a young deer that is let loose; you give goodly words.

"You, Joseph, are a fruitful bough by a well, whose branches run over the wall. The archers have grieved you sorely and have shot at you because they hate you. But your bow remains strong and your arms are strengthened by the hands of the mighty God of Jacob (through whose lineage shall come the shepherd and stone of Israel—even the Messiah). You will be strengthened by the God of your father, who will help you and who will bless you with the blessings of heaven above, the blessings of the deep that lie beneath, and the blessings of the breast and the womb. And the blessings of your father have prevailed above the blessings of my progenitors unto the utmost bounds of the everlasting hills. These are the blessings that shall be upon the crown of Joseph's head—even the head of him who was separated from his brothers.

"And you, Benjamin, shall ravin and seek plunder as a wolf. You shall devour the prey in the morning and divide the spoils at night."[99]

---

[99] It would be interesting if we could identify the fulfillment of all the blessings that Jacob pronounced upon his twelve sons. Though the fulfillment of some of those blessings is clear, others are not—perhaps because the tribes are lost. However, let's look at what is known:

- Reuben — Specific fulfillment unknown.
- Simeon and Levi — The combined blessing of these two sons of Leah refers to the incident, told in story "33—In Defense of Dinah's Honor," where these brothers slew all the men of Shechem. The part about scattering them throughout Israel was fulfilled in Levi's call to assist the priesthood and their dispersal throughout Israel without an inheritance of land.
- Judah — The fulfillment of Judah's blessing is well known. His descendants sat on the throne of Israel and the Savior was born through his lineage.
- Zebulun — The inheritance of Zebulun in Canaan reached to the Mediterranean Sea in one place and had a small

When his blessings upon his sons were complete, the Patriarch Jacob made his sons swear an oath that they would not bury him Egypt. "When I am gathered to my people," he said, "bury me in the cave at Hebron, where my wife Leah, my parents, and my grandparents are all buried." Then Jacob, gathering his feet into the bed, lay down, and died.

Joseph wept sorely at the passing of his father, for he loved him dearly. He commanded the Egyptian physicians to embalm his father's body, and the Egyptians mourned for Jacob for seventy days. And once the days of mourning were past, Joseph requested Pharaoh's permission to go up and bury him at Hebron in the land of Canaan. "My father made me swear that I would bury him in the grave that he dug for himself at Hebron on the plain of Mamre," Joseph said to Pharaoh. "Let me go and bury him, then I will return."

Pharaoh was sympathetic to Joseph's request. "Go and bury your father as he made you promise," he said.

So Jacob's family went up from Egypt to Hebron. They went up with both chariots and horsemen in a very large company to bury Jacob with his fathers. In addition to Jacob's own family—except the small children, who did not go—the burial party included all of Pharaoh's servants, the elders of Pharaoh's house, and

---

common area of border with Sidon.
- Issachar — Specific fulfillment unknown.
- Dan — One possible fulfillment of Dan's blessing is in the appointment of the Nazarite Samson as a Judge in Israel and the inroads that Samson made against the tyranny of the Philistines.
- Gad — Specific fulfillment unknown.
- Asher — Specific fulfillment unknown.
- Naphtali — Specific fulfillment unknown.
- Joseph — The fulfillment of Joseph's blessing is also well known, as some of his descendants (as told in the Book of Mormon) were led by the Lord, as branches going over the wall, to the Western Hemisphere, where they were greatly blessed in the land of the everlasting hills.
- Benjamin — Specific fulfillment unknown.

55

the elders of Egypt. And when the burial was completed, they all returned to Egypt.

Now that their father was buried, Joseph's brothers were afraid that he would seek revenge because they had sold him into Egypt. They sent a messenger to Joseph to remind him that Jacob had requested that he forgive them for what they had done. Then Joseph's older brothers came and fell down before him, pledging to be his servants if only he would forgive them.

Joseph wept when he heard his brothers' pleadings. "Fear not," he said to them. "I do not presume to take the place of God. Though you thought to do me evil, God used you to do good and to bring to pass things as they are today. It is because you sold me that this people are now alive. You must not fear me for I will not harm you, but I will nurture both you and your children." And Joseph comforted his brothers, speaking to them with great kindness.

42—A CHOICE SEER

(Genesis 50 [especially JST]; 2 Nephi 3)

Joseph lived in Egypt the rest of his days, dying there when he was 110 years old. He saw the children of his sons Ephraim and Manasseh to the third generation. As the time came for his passing, Joseph said to his brethren, "I am going to die and go unto my fathers, but God will be with you in the days of your affliction."

Joseph continued: "I have obtained a promise from Jehovah that he will raise up a righteous branch from the fruit of my loins. He has also promised me that he will raise up unto this his people whom he has named Israel, a prophet to deliver them out of Egypt in the days of their bondage. That prophet will bring our seed out of this land and take them to the land that Jehovah gave by oath to Abraham, Isaac, and Jacob.

"After Israel has been brought out of Egypt, they will be scattered again, and a branch of my seed will be broken off and carried to a far country. Nevertheless, that branch will be remembered in the covenants of God when the Messiah comes. For he will appear to them in the spirit of power and will bring them out of darkness into the light.

"The seer who will deliver our seed out of Egypt shall be called Moses, and by this name he shall know that he is of the house of Israel, for he shall be nursed by the king's daughter and shall be called her son.

"The Lord has promised me that he will preserve our seed forever. He said to me, 'I will raise up Moses, and a rod will be in his hand. He will gather my people and lead them as a flock, and he will smite the waters of the Red Sea with his rod. He will not speak many words, but I will make a spokesman for him, whose name will be Aaron. Moses will have judgment and will write my words, and I will write my law unto him with the finger of my hand.

"Jehovah has also told me that he will raise up a choice seer unto the fruit of my loins in the last days who shall be highly esteemed by them. Jehovah will command this seer to do a work for the fruit of my loins, for he shall also be of the fruit of my loins. He shall bring my seed to know the covenants that were made with our fathers and shall be great in God's eyes. For he will do God's work and will be great like unto Moses."

"This latter-day seer," Joseph said, "will be made strong in his weaknesses in the day that God brings his work forth among my people. And to him will God give power to bring forth his word unto my seed—not in the bringing forth of his word only, but also in convincing them of God's word that has already gone forth among them. For two records shall be kept; the fruit of my loins shall write and the fruit of the loins of Judah shall write. And in the latter days the two records shall grow together to confound false doctrines, lay down contentions, and establish peace among the fruit of my loins. These two records will also bring my seed to a knowledge of their fathers and of God's covenants.

"God will restore the house of Israel in the latter days, for he has promised to remember my seed from generation to generation, and those who seek to destroy this latter-day seer will be confounded. His name will be Joseph, and Joseph will also be his father's name. He shall be like me, for that which God brings forth by his hand will bring God's people to salvation."

Then Joseph said to his brethren, "God will surely visit you and bring you out of Egypt, and he will give you the land that he promised unto Abraham, Isaac, and Jacob."

Then Joseph made his brethren swear that, when the time came that God delivered them out of Egypt to the land of their inheritance, they would take his bones with them. So when Joseph died, his body was embalmed and kept from burial, awaiting the time when his people would carry his coffin up with them to lay it in the sepulcher of his fathers.

43—THE FAITHFULNESS OF JOB
(Job 1–42)

There lived in the land of Uz,[100] in the time of the Patriarchs, a righteous man named Job.[101] Job had seven sons and three daughters and was blessed with an abundance of material goods. He had 7,000 sheep, 3,000 camels, 500 yoke of oxen, 500 she-asses, and a large and beautiful home. He was the greatest of all the men of the East. Job's children were given to feasting and revelry, but Job prayed for them and made burnt offerings for them daily for fear that they might have cursed God in their hearts.

Now there was a day when the sons of God came to present themselves before Jehovah, and Satan was among those who came. "Where have you come from?" Jehovah asked Satan.

"From going to and fro in the earth and from walking up and down in it," was Satan's reply.

"Have you considered my servant Job," Jehovah inquired, "that there is none other like him in all the earth? He is a perfect and upright man who has reverence for God and avoids evil."

"It appears to me," said Satan, "that Job reverences God for good reasons, for Thou hast given him everything that he desires and placed a hedge around all that he owns. If Thou didst put forth Thy hand to take away all that Job has, he would curse Thee to Thy face."[102]

Then Jehovah said to Satan, "I will put all that he has within your power. But you may not put your hand upon his person."

So Satan went forth to take away Job possessions. When Job's children were feasting at the home of the eldest son, a great wind caused the house to fall and

---

[100] Uz is believed to have been east of Palestine and north of Edom. It was a land occupied by descendants of Shem.

[101] Job appears to have lived in the days of the Patriarchs because he was able to offer sacrifices in his own behalf rather than having the priest offer them.

[102] In many respects, all of us are like Job and will face whatever challenges mortality gives to us. One writer makes this observation: "Satan is shown here in his role of testing Job, as he may test every earthbound soul. Because the narrative of Job is a particular example of the general predicament of man, any of us may relate Job's experiences to the tests and trials we have in life." (Ellis T. Rasmussen, *A Latter-day Saint Commentary on the Old Testament* [Salt Lake City: Deseret Book Co., 1993], 394.)

they were all killed. Job's oxen and asses were stolen by a troop of marauding Sabeans. A fire burned up his sheep, and the Chaldeans stole his camels. And, in each case, all the servants who tended the animals were slain—except one who escaped to bear the sad news back to Job.

When Job received word that all he had, including his family, had been taken away, he tore his clothing, shaved his head, fell upon the ground, and worshipped God. "I came naked from my mother's womb," he lamented, "and naked shall I return again to God. The Lord Jehovah has given, and he has also taken away. Blessed be the name of Jehovah."

As Satan once more presented himself before Jehovah, Jehovah again asked him, "Have you considered my servant Job, that there is none other like him in all the earth? He is a perfect and upright man who has reverence for God and eschews evil. Although you have moved to destroy him without a cause, Job has remained faithful."

Satan was not yet convinced. "A man will give all that he has for his life," he said. "If Thou would put forth Thy hand to touch Job's bones and flesh, he would curse Thee to Thy face."

"He is in your hands," replied Jehovah, "but save his life."

As Satan went forth, he caused Job to be afflicted with sore boils from the soles of his feet to the crown of his head, and Job suffered much. He used a piece of broken pottery[103] to scrape his skin as he sat among the ashes. Not only was he covered with sore boils, but he was also unable to sleep. And, when he did sleep, he had terrible nightmares.

Job's wife rebuked him. "How can you suffer so and still remain true?" she asked him. "Curse God and die!" When all that he had was lost, not even Job's wife would stand by him.

"You speak as a foolish women," replied Job. "Shall we receive good from the hand of God and not be willing also to receive evil?" And still Job did not sin before God.

When Job's three friends—Eliphaz, Bildad, and Zophar—heard of his misfortune, they came to console him, desiring to mourn with him and offer comfort. Each tore his clothing, covered his head with dust, and wept. Seven days and seven nights they sat with Job, but no one spoke because of Job's great suffering.

Finally Job broke the silence. "Let the day perish wherein I was born," he said, "and the night wherein it was said that I was conceived. Why did I not die in the womb? Though I now long for death, it does not come."

Eliphaz sought to respond to Job's complaints. "I cannot restrain myself from speaking," he said. "It appears to me that your troubles are of your own making, for a man does not perish when he is innocent. Those who plow iniquity and sow wickedness always reap the same and are consumed by the breath of God's nostrils. As you are no doubt guilty of great sin, you would do well to seek God and commit your cause to him. For he can do marvelous things. Do not despise God's chastening, Job, for happy is the man whom he corrects."

Job answered, "One who is afflicted should receive pity from his friends, yet you have offered none. I did not ask you to bring me gifts or to deliver me from the hands of the mighty, but if you will teach me to understand how I have erred, I will hold my tongue. And if I have sinned, why does God not pardon my transgressions and take away my iniquity?"

Bildad spoke next, also reproving Job. "How long will you speak such things?" he asked. "The judgments of God are not perverse. If you were pure and upright, he would make your habitation prosperous. For he will neither cast away a perfect man nor help the evil-doer."

"How should a man be just before God?" asked Job. "I shall ask him to show me why he oppresses me and why he despises the works of my hands. If I am wicked, woe unto me, yet if I am righteous—as I think I am—I still cannot lift up my head and my afflictions increase. I am confused."

Zophar spoke next. "How can a man who is so full of talk be justified?" he asked. "You have said that your doctrine is pure and that you are clean. But if God would open his mouth and speak against you, he would show you the secrets of his wisdom. And you would know that he has punished you less than you deserve. The thing for you to do is to repent and put off your iniquity."

"I have understanding as well as you do," answered Job. "The soul of every living thing and the breath of all mankind are in the hands of God, yet I know that he gives and he takes away as he will. You would display greater wisdom if you held your peace, left me alone to speak to God, and let come upon me what will. Though God may slay me, yet will I trust in him, for he is my salvation."

Then Job, more earnest than ever, pleaded with Jehovah. "I ask now that Thou wouldst do just two things for me," he said. "First withdraw Thy hand from me so that Thy dread does not also make me afraid. And second, make me to know my transgressions and my sins."

"Your mouth betrays your iniquity," responded Eliphaz. "You have chosen the tongue of the crafty, and your own lips testify against you."

---

[103] The word used in the scripture is "potsherd," meaning the shard of a pot, or a pot shard.

"I have heard many vain things from you," answered Job, "and I wonder if your vain words will ever end. For all of you are miserable comforters. I know that if you were in my place, I could also heap up words against you and shake my head at you. But I would not do it. Rather, I would strengthen you and console you in your grief. Yet God has delivered me into the hand of the ungodly and turned me over to the wicked. He has also taken me by my neck and shaken me to pieces. My face is foul from weeping and the shadow of death is on my eyelids, but not for any injustice that I have done—for my heart is pure. Though my friends scorn me, my witness is in heaven, my record is on high, and my eyes pour out tears unto God."

"Why are we counted as vile beasts in your sight?" asked Bildad. "We tell you only of the wretched state of the wicked and those who do not know God."

"Your problem," cried Job, "is that you persecute me as if you were God and are not satisfied with the state of my suffering. Oh that my words were printed in a book and graven forever in a rock with an iron pen! For I know that my redeemer lives, and that he shall stand upon the earth at the latter day. And though my skin worms destroy this body, yet in my flesh shall I see God. And I shall see him for myself. I shall behold him with my own eyes—and not another—though my reins[104] are consumed within me."

"I am compelled to answer you," said Zophar. "It has been known from the beginning of the earth that the triumph of the wicked is short and the joy of the hypocrite is for but a moment. Though the excellence of the wicked mounts up to the heavens and his head reaches to the clouds, he shall perish forever. The heavens shall reveal his iniquity and the earth shall rise up against him. The increase of his house will depart, and his goods shall flow away in the day of wrath."

"Hear my speech and let this be your consolation," said Job. "I know the devices that you wrongfully imagine against me, but you are deceived in your judgments. I know that the wicked are often mighty in power, their children established and safe, and their houses free from fear. Though they spend their days in wealth, they go down to the grave in a moment. The rich and the poor, the righteous and the wicked, shall all lie down alike in the dust. But the wicked are reserved for the day of destruction and shall be brought forth in the day of wrath."

Then Eliphaz answered with false accusation. "We know, Job, that your wickedness is great," he said. "You have taken pledges from your brother for nothing and have stripped the naked of their clothing. You have not given water to the weary and have withheld your bread from the hungry. You have sent widows away empty and broken the arms of the fatherless. It is because of these deeds that snares are around you and sudden fear troubles you. However, if you will repent of your sins and return to God, you shall be built up and again lay up much treasure. He shall answer your prayers again and save you."

"Even though my complaint is bitter, the stroke that is laid upon me is heavier than my groaning," replied Job. "Oh that I knew where I might find God, that I might come to his seat. I go forward but he is not there, and I go backward and do not find him. I go also to the left hand and to the right, but he hides himself that I cannot see him. Yet I know that when he has tried me, I shall come forth as gold because my foot has held his steps and I have not gone back from the commandments of his lips. I hold fast to my righteousness because reverence for God is wisdom and departure from evil is understanding. Yet look at me now. They who are younger than I hold me in derision—even those who are the children of fools and of base men. I am now their song and their byword. They abhor me and spit in my face."

Then, in the agony of his soul, Job cried out to God once more. "I cry unto Thee and Thou dost not hear me. I stand up and Thou dost not regard me. I have wept for those who were in trouble, and my soul has grieved for the poor. If I have not given freely to those in need—the widows, the orphans and the poor—let my arm fall from my shoulder blade and be broken from the bone. If I have made gold my hope or have rejoiced in wealth, if I have rejoiced in the destruction of those who have hated me, or if I have done any other evil thing or sought to cover my sins, I would like to know. Oh how I wish that Thou wouldst answer me."

Job's three friends gave up and ceased to answer him because they thought he appeared too righteous in his own eyes. There was, however, a young man named Elihu who was now stirred up to speak. Elihu was angry with Job because he thought Job justified himself rather than God. But Elihu was also angry with Eliphaz, Bildad, and Zophar—Job's supposed friends—because they condemned Job for faults that they could never identify. "I was afraid to speak before," he said, "because of my respect for your age. But there is a spirit in man and the inspiration of the Almighty gives him understanding. Great men are not always wise. Neither do

---

[104] The reins are the kidneys (having the same root as "renal"). In the sense the word is used here, the reins were considered to be the center of a person's desires and affections and reflected his or her innermost feelings. In the Psalms and in the writings of Jeremiah, the *reins* and the *heart* are often mentioned together.

the aged always understand judgment. Therefore, hearken to me as I give my opinion. You have spoken many words, but none of you has convinced Job of his wickedness or answered his questions.

"I pray that you, Job, will also hearken to my words, for I speak in the uprightness of my heart. You have endured great suffering, though you say that you are without sin. In this you are not just, for God is greater than man. He deals justly with man, and though he may cause man to suffer, he is gracious and will provide a ransom to deliver man from the pit.

"One would not tell a king that he was wicked or a prince that he was ungodly. How much less should a man tell God that he has treated him poorly. For God's eyes are upon man and no sin is hidden from him. All are alike unto God—the weak and the mighty. He prospers those who obey him and serve him. But those who do not obey perish and die without knowledge.

"God controls all nature and uses the forces of nature to judge the people, both to bless and to correct them. But, O Job, stand still and consider the wondrous works of God. Men cannot understand his ways, for he is excellent in power and judgment. And, in his justice, he will not afflict a man more than that man can bear."

When Elihu had finished his speaking, the voice of Jehovah came to Job out of the whirlwind and said, "Who are you, O man, to darken counsel by words without knowledge? Gird up your loins now like a man, Job, for I will ask questions and expect you to answer."

Jehovah's questions came rapidly: "Where were you when I laid the foundations of the earth? Declare if you have understanding. And, if you know, who laid the dimensions of it? Or who has stretched the line upon it? Where are the foundations of the earth fastened? Or who laid the cornerstone when the morning stars sang together and the sons of God shouted for joy? Or who shut up the sea with doors when it broke forth as if coming from the womb, when it made the clouds its clothing and thick darkness its swathing band? Who made the place for the sea and set limits beyond which its proud waves cannot stray? Have you commanded the morning or caused daybreak to know his place, to take hold of the ends of the earth so that the wicked may be shaken out of it?"

Jehovah continued, asking many difficult questions of Job—questions designed to show God's hand in the grand design of all things, but certainly beyond the scope of Job's knowledge and experience. Jehovah's questions removed all doubt from Job's mind that man does not begin to comprehend the ways of God. Then Jehovah said to Job, "Shall the man who contends with God instruct him? Let that man answer who would reprove God."

"I am guilty," replied Job. "I am indeed a vile man. I have spoken once—perhaps twice—but I will go no further."

"Gird up your loins now like a man," said Jehovah out of the whirlwind, "and I will ask you more questions. Would you condemn me in order to make yourself righteous? Do you have an arm like God's? Or can you thunder with a voice like God's? If you are able to do the works of God and to show forth great wonders, then I will also concede that you are able to save yourself with your own right hand."

"I know that Thou canst do all things," answered Job, "and that no thought can be withheld from Thee. I cannot answer your questions, for they are things too wonderful for me. But hear me, I pray, and I will speak. And I will ask that Thou declare the answers to me."

Then Jehovah spoke to Eliphaz. "My wrath is kindled against you, Eliphaz," he said, "and against your two friends. Because you have spoken of me falsely, go to my servant Job and offer a burnt offering unto me. Ask Job to pray for you—for I will accept his prayers—lest I deal with you for your false speaking." And Eliphaz, Bildad, and Zophar did as Jehovah commanded them.

Once Job had prayed for his friends, Jehovah ended his suffering and blessed him with twice as much as he had before. Thus, Job's latter end was more blessed than his beginning, for he had 14,000 sheep, 6,000 camels, 1,000 yoke of oxen, and 1,000 she-asses. He was also blessed with seven more sons and three more daughters. And of Job's three daughters—Jemima, Kezia, and Keren-happuch—it was said that there were no other women in the land as fair as they. After this Job lived 140 years and saw his grandchildren unto the fourth generation.

IV

FROM EGYPT TO SINAI

44—THE SON OF PHARAOH'S DAUGHTER

(Exodus 1–2)

Jacob's descendants prospered in Egypt and became a mighty people. But, as time passed, the greatness of Joseph and how he had saved Egypt from famine were forgotten. The Hebrews—as the children of Israel were called—were no longer highly favored but were feared by the Egyptians because of their numbers. The Pharaoh said to his people, "Behold, the Hebrews are more numerous and mightier than we are. We must deal wisely with them lest they multiply more and become a threat to us. If there should be war, they could unite with our enemies, fight against us, and free themselves."

It was decided that the Hebrew people could be best controlled if taskmasters were placed over them to inflict heavy burdens and enforce their labors. The people of Israel were put in bondage to build treasure cities for the Pharaoh.[105] The work was strenuous and the lives of the people were bitter with hard labor.

Though the children of Israel were carefully controlled by their taskmasters, they continued to multiply and the king sought other means to curtail their growth. He spoke to the two midwives who delivered the Hebrew babies, saying, "When you deliver their babies, if the child is a boy you shall kill him, but if a daughter you shall let her live."

But the midwives feared God and did not do as the Pharaoh commanded. When he asked them why they disobeyed him, they replied, "It is because the Hebrew women are more vigorous than the Egyptian women. Their babies are delivered before we arrive." Because the midwives rejected Pharaoh's counsel and preserved the babies' lives, Jehovah blessed them and gave them children of their own. The Hebrews, in the meantime, continued to prosper and to multiply.

Pharaoh, still seeking for a way to control the Hebrew population, changed his instructions. He commanded that every son born to a Hebrew mother should be thrown into the River Nile. This commandment, as you can imagine, was the source of great sorrow to the Hebrews.

Now, there was at this time a man among the Hebrew people named Amram, a grandson of Levi. He was married to his father's sister, Jochebed.[106] Some time after the Pharaoh's deadly decree, Jochebed bore a son. Because she loved her son and despised the Pharaoh's decree, she could not throw him into the river. Rather, she hid him carefully in her house for three months following his birth.

When Jochebed could no longer conceal the child safely in her house, she made a basket from bulrushes, covered it with mud and tar, and set it afloat among the reeds at the river's edge with the baby inside. Then she set her daughter Miriam to watch from a distance to see what would happen.

When the daughter of Pharaoh came to bathe in the river, she and her maidens walked along the riverbank and saw the basket floating among the reeds. She sent one of her maids to retrieve the basket and was greatly surprised to find a baby inside—a crying baby. The princess's heart was filled with feelings of great tenderness for the baby and she wanted to keep him, though she recognized that he was a Hebrew child.

As the princess pondered her dilemma, Miriam came forward and asked, "Shall I go and find one of the Hebrew women who can nurse the child for you?"

"Go," said the princess. And Miriam ran and called Jochebed, the child's own mother.

When Jochebed came, the princess said, "Take this child and nurse him for me, and I will pay you for your service." So Jochebed took the child to her home, nursed him, and prepared him to be a son to Pharaoh's daughter.

Time passed, the child grew, and Jochebed took him to Pharaoh's daughter. The child became her son, and she called him Moses[107] because she drew him out of the water. The boy was schooled in Pharaoh's court and had every advantage of the royal household, yet he knew who he was because he had spent his early childhood in the nurture of his Hebrew mother.

---

[105] The cities of Pithom and Rameses are mentioned. Rameses is spelled *Raamses* in Exodus 1.

[106] See Exodus 6:20.

---

[107] In Egyptian, the name Moses means "to draw out." In Hebrew, it means "to beget a child."

45–FROM PRINCE TO SHEPHERD

(Exodus 2)

Although Moses was schooled in Pharaoh's household, he knew that he was a Hebrew, and the Hebrews also knew it. Life was good for him and he enjoyed every benefit of the royal household, but when he had grown to manhood, he saw the heavy burdens that Pharaoh and the Egyptians had placed upon his people and became concerned for them. One day as he walked among the Hebrews in their work camps, he saw an Egyptian taskmaster beating one of his Hebrew brethren. After looking around to be sure no one was watching, Moses killed the surly Egyptian and hid his body in the sand.

In the work camps the following day, when Moses saw one Hebrew beating another, he said to the one who was in the wrong, "Why do you fight against one of your own brethren?"

The man's reply to Moses was shocking. "Who made you a prince and judge over us?" the man asked with disdain. "Do you intend to kill me as you did that Egyptian yesterday?"

When Moses heard this, he knew he was no longer safe in Egypt and he began to fear for his life. He knew that someone had seen him kill the Egyptian and that, when the word got out, he would pay with his own life.

It was just as he had feared. When the Pharaoh learned that Moses had killed an Egyptian, he sought Moses' life. Thus Moses, having no other choice than to flee, left Egypt immediately and went to Midian, the land where the descendants of Lot, Abraham's nephew, had settled hundreds of years earlier.

Once in Midian, Moses sat down by a well to rest. And, as he sat there, he watched as seven young women came to water their father's flocks. He saw that when they drew water and poured it in the trough, other shepherds drove their flocks away. Touched by the plight of these young women, Moses helped them resist the other shepherds and then watered their flocks for them.

When the girls returned to their father Jethro,[108] the high priest of Midian, he asked how it was that they had come so early from their chores. "An Egyptian delivered us from the hands of the other shepherds," they replied with excitement, "and also drew water for our flocks."

"Where is this Egyptian now?" queried Jethro. "Why have you left the man who did you such a good turn? Go call him to eat bread with us."

Thus Moses was brought into the household of Jethro. This was his introduction to the family, but his relationship with them would last much longer. Moses felt safe in Midian and was content to dwell there. He lived there for many years and tended Jethro's sheep in the wilderness. Because of his fondness for Moses, Jethro gave his daughter Zipporah to be Moses' wife and also ordained the young Hebrew to the holy priesthood.[109]

During the years that Moses tended Jethro's sheep in Midian, the old Pharaoh of Egypt died. The burdens that the Egyptians placed upon the Hebrews, however, were not lightened. Their burdens were oppressive, and the people sighed under the weight of their bondage. In that day God heard the cries of his chosen people and remembered his covenant with Abraham, Isaac, and Jacob. He remembered his promise to bring them out of Egypt to inherit the land of Canaan, the land that was promised to their fathers.

---

[108] In the second chapter of Exodus and elsewhere, Jethro's name is given as Reuel. In other places, he is also called Raguel (see Numbers 10:29).

[109] See Doctrine and Covenants 84:6.

46—I HAVE SEEN THE AFFLICTIONS OF MY PEOPLE

(Exodus 3–4)

Moses was content to keep the flocks of his father-in-law, Jethro. His work was pleasant and his worries few. The life of a shepherd agreed with him, and he was content to spend the rest of his life in Midian. As a shepherd working for his father-in-law, he felt much less pressure than he had as a prince in Pharaoh's court. But this was not to last.

One day as Moses tended Jethro's flocks in the desert of Mount Horeb,[110] an event occurred that would cause a significant change in his life. He saw a bush on fire, but, as he observed the bush, he saw that it was never consumed though the fire burned continuously. When he stopped to watch, the voice of Jehovah called to him from the bush, "Moses, Moses."

"Here am I," answered Moses.

"Do not come near the bush," said Jehovah. "Take off your shoes, for the ground on which you stand is holy ground. I am the God of your fathers—the God of Abraham, Isaac, and Jacob." And Moses hid his face because he was afraid to look upon God.

Jehovah continued: "I have seen the afflictions of my people in Egypt and I know their sorrows, for I have heard their cries for relief. I have now come to deliver them from the hand of the Egyptians and to bring them to a good land, even a land that flows with milk and honey. I am come to bring them to the land that I promised unto their fathers forever, and I will send you to Pharaoh that you may bring my people out of Egypt."

Moses was shocked. How could *he* possibly deliver the children of Israel from Egypt? "Who am I," he asked, "that I should go to Pharaoh or lead Israel out of Egypt?"

"I will be with you in this," answered Jehovah. "And this will be the sign to show that I have sent you: when you have brought my people out of Egypt, you shall return to worship me upon this same mountain."

Then Moses, still overwhelmed with self-doubt, said, "If I go to the children of Israel and tell them that the God of their fathers has sent me, they will ask me, 'What is his name?' What shall I tell them then?"

And Jehovah said to Moses, "I AM THAT I AM. Thus shall you say to the children of Israel: 'I AM has sent me—even Jehovah,[111] the God of your fathers, the God of Abraham, Isaac, and Jacob. He has sent me to you.' Thus shall I be remembered forever, and this is my memorial unto all generations."

Moses kneels before the burning bush

Jehovah continued: "You shall gather the elders of Israel and tell them that Jehovah has appeared to you because he has seen their suffering. Tell them I am ready to deliver them from the afflictions of Egypt unto a land that flows with milk and honey. The elders will listen to you and shall go with you to the king of Egypt. And you will tell him that Jehovah, the God of the Hebrews, has met with you and that you desire to go three days' journey into the wilderness and make a sacrifice unto him.

"I know, however, that the king will deny your request. But when he does so, I will stretch forth my hand and smite Egypt with all my wonders. Then he will let you go. And when the time comes that you go, I will give you favor in the sight of the Egyptians that you will not go empty. Every woman of Israel shall borrow fine clothing and jewels of gold and silver from her neighbors. They will put these upon their children, and the Egyptians will be left empty."

Moses was still in shock, and certainly not convinced. "The children of Israel will not listen to me," he countered. "They will not believe that Thou hast appeared unto me." Moses was not easily convinced.

"What is that in your hand?" asked Jehovah.

"My rod."

---

[110] Mount Horeb is another name for Mount Sinai.

[111] Jehovah (JHVH) is "the Unchangeable," "the Eternal I Am."

"Cast it upon the ground." And when Moses cast his rod upon the ground, it turned into a serpent and Moses fled from before it.

"Pick it up by the tail," Jehovah instructed Moses. And when Moses did so, it once again became a rod in his hand. "When the people see what you do with your rod, they will not doubt that I have sent you."

Then Jehovah said to Moses, "Put your hand into your bosom." Moses did so. And when he pulled it out, it was leprous and white as snow. "Put your hand into your bosom again," said Jehovah. Again Moses obeyed and, when he drew it out, it was as healthy as his other flesh.

"If the people will not believe you and refuse to hearken to the first sign, they will believe the second," said Jehovah. "However, if they believe neither sign, take water from the river and pour it upon the dry ground. The water will become blood upon the ground."

Moses was still reluctant. "I am slow of speech," he argued. "I have a slow tongue."

"Is it not I who made man's mouth?" asked Jehovah. "I will be your mouth and teach you what to say."

"Oh, my Lord," pleaded Moses, "send someone to help me."

Jehovah was becoming impatient because of Moses' continued reluctance. "Is not Aaron the Levite your brother?" he asked. "I will send him to speak for you. You shall speak and put words into his mouth, and I will be with your mouth and with his mouth to teach you both what to do. Aaron will be to you instead of a mouth, you will be to him instead of God, and you shall take your rod in your hand to do signs. Aaron is on his way here to meet you now, and when you see him, he will be glad in his heart."

It was enough. Moses was finally convinced, and he agreed that he would go back to Egypt and do what Jehovah had called him to do.

47—THIS IS MY WORK AND MY GLORY
(Moses 1)

After Moses' call by Jehovah, he was caught up into a high mountain where he saw God face to face and talked to him.[112] And the glory of God was upon Moses so that he could endure God's presence.[113]

There on the mountain, while Moses was within the influence of God's glory, God spoke to him saying, "Behold, I am the Lord God Almighty, and Endless is my name, for I am without beginning of days or end of years. And is that not endless? You are my son, Moses, and I will show you the workmanship of my hands. Nevertheless, I cannot show it all because my works and my words are endless. No one can behold all of my works without seeing all of my glory, and no one can behold all of my glory and remain in the flesh. I show you these things, Moses my son, because I have a work for you to do.

"You, Moses, are in the likeness of my Only Begotten Son, who is and shall be the Savior because he is full of grace and truth. There is no God besides me, and all things are present with me for I know them all. And now this one thing I will show you because you are in the world."

God then showed Moses a vision of the world. He saw all of it—even to the ends thereof—and all of the people who belong to this world. And Moses marveled greatly.

When the vision was ended and God withdrew, Moses was left to himself. He fell to the earth and lay there for many hours before he regained his strength. When he finally came to himself, he thought about all he had seen, and he said, "Now I know that man is nothing, which thing I had never before supposed. I have beheld God with my own eyes—not my natural eyes but my spiritual eyes. If my natural eyes had seen him I would have withered and died, but because his

---

[112] We do not know when Moses had the experiences recounted in this story, but, from the context of the scriptural account, it is certain that it was sometime after the burning bush incident (see Moses 1:17) and before he parted the Red Sea and led Israel out of Egypt (see Moses 1:25–26).

[113] It was Jehovah, the God of the Old Testament and the premortal Jesus Christ, who talked to Moses on the mount. However, by the authority that his Father had given him, Jehovah—God the Son—spoke to Moses as if he were God the Father.

glory was upon me and I was transfigured[114] I could see his face and live."

When Moses had spoken these words, Satan came before him, pretending to be God, to tempt him. "Moses, son of man," said Satan, "worship me."

Moses was troubled by this request, for he could sense that something was wrong. God had called him a son of God, but this being called him a son of man. Moses looked at the being who was standing before him and asked, "Who are *you*? Behold, I am a son of God, in the likeness of his Only Begotten Son. I could not look upon God without his glory being upon me. But where is *your* glory? For I can see you with my natural eyes. Your glory appears to be darkness, and I can judge between you and God."

Moses had recognized Satan for who he was and thus continued his challenge: "When God called to me from the burning bush he commanded that I should pray in the name of his Only Begotten Son and worship only him. And I shall not cease to call upon him, for I have other things to ask him. I am able to judge between him and you because I have experienced his glory. Depart hence, Satan, and seek to deceive me no more!"

Satan became livid at Moses' rebuke. He cried out with a loud voice and raged about upon the earth. "I am the Only Begotten!" he shouted. "Worship me!"

In the face of this terrible display, Moses was filled with fear, but he received strength when he called upon God. "The only God I will worship," Moses cried, "is the God of glory!"

Satan trembled, the earth shook, and Moses saw the bitterness of hell. Then he called upon God and commanded Satan to depart. "In the name of the Only Begotten," he said, "depart hence, Satan!" Then Satan cried out with a loud voice—with much weeping, wailing, and gnashing of teeth—and departed from Moses' presence.

When Satan was gone, Moses was filled with the Holy Ghost and called again upon God. Once more he beheld God's glory and heard God's voice declaring, "Blessed are you, Moses, for I, the Almighty, have chosen you. You shall be stronger than many waters, for the waters shall obey you as if you were God. You shall deliver Israel from bondage, and I shall be with you till the end of your days."

As God spoke to Moses, another great vision opened before him—more grand and glorious than that which he had beheld before. Through the Spirit of God, Moses beheld the whole earth, even to its tiniest particle. Through the power of the Spirit, he also saw the peoples of the earth, and there was not one soul that he did not see. He beheld that they were numberless, even as the sands of the seashore. Moses was also shown many other worlds and their inhabitants. And when he saw them, he said, "Tell me why these things are and by what power they are created."

And God answered, "I have made these worlds for my own purpose, for here is wisdom and the wisdom remains in me. By the word of my power I created them, which word is my Only Begotten Son, who is full of grace and truth. I have created worlds without number, all for my own purpose, and I made them all by the power of my Only Begotten. But though there are many worlds, Moses, I give to you an account of only this world and its people.

"Many worlds have passed away by the word of my power, but there are also many that now stand. They are innumerable unto man, but all things are numbered unto me, for they are mine and I know them."

"O God, be merciful unto me," cried Moses, "and tell me about this earth and its people—also about the heavens—and I will be content."

"The heavens are many, and they cannot be numbered unto man," said God. "But they are numbered unto me, for they are mine. And as one earth and its heavens pass away, even so another comes; and there is no end to either my works or my words. For behold, this is my work and my glory: to bring to pass the immortality and eternal life of man.

"And now, Moses my son, as I speak to you concerning this earth, write the things that I speak. Then, in a day when the people place no value upon my words and remove them from the book that you will write, I will raise up a prophet like unto you to give my words once again to the children of men, even to as many as will believe."

---

[114] When one is transfigured, his body is temporarily changed to a glorified state that enables his body to be in the presence of God without being consumed or destroyed.

48—LET MY PEOPLE GO
(Exodus 4–6)

Once Moses was convinced that he could do the work that Jehovah had called him to do, he went to his father-in-law Jethro and sought permission to return to Egypt. "Let me go to my brethren," he said, "to see if they are still alive."

Jethro was agreeable to Moses' request. "Go in peace," he said.

As Moses prepared for the journey, Jehovah appeared to him again to reassure him that it was safe for him to return to Egypt. "All those who sought your life in Egypt are now dead," said Jehovah. But he also told Moses some things that were cause for concern. "When you return to Egypt," said Jehovah, "you must do before Pharaoh all of those wonders that I have shown you. And though I will bless you in this, Pharaoh will harden his heart and will not let Israel go. When he refuses, however, you must tell him that Israel is my firstborn son. Say to him, 'Let my son go that he may serve me. And if you refuse, I will slay your son, even your firstborn.'"

Moses took his wife Zipporah and his sons Gershom and Eliezer and set off for Egypt with his rod in his hand. At the same time Moses was leaving Midian, Jehovah sent Aaron out into the wilderness to meet him. The two men met at Mount Horeb where Jehovah had spoken to Moses from the burning bush. Aaron rejoiced to see his brother. And when he had kissed him, Moses rehearsed to Aaron all that Jehovah had told him and the signs that he had been commanded to perform.

Once Moses and Aaron were in Egypt, they called together the elders of Israel. Aaron then shared with them all that Moses had told him, and Moses showed his signs[115] in the sight of all the people. The people believed Moses and Aaron, and when they heard that God knew of their afflictions, they bowed their heads and praised him.

Leaving their meeting with the people of Israel, Moses and Aaron took the elders of Israel with them and went to speak to Pharaoh, as Jehovah had commanded. Standing before Pharaoh, they said, "Thus says Jehovah, the God of Israel, 'Let my people go that they may hold a feast unto me in the wilderness.'"

---

[115] The signs included turning Moses' rod into a serpent, putting his hand into his bosom and drawing it out leprous, and pouring water from the river upon dry ground and turning it into blood (see story "46–I Have Seen the Afflictions of My People").

But Pharaoh was only irritated at this request. "Who is Jehovah that I should obey his voice?" he asked. "I do not know Jehovah, and I will not let Israel go."

Then Moses and Aaron said, "The God of the Hebrews has met with us. He asks only that you let us go three days' journey into the desert to make a sacrifice to him, lest he fall upon us with pestilence or the sword."

"Why do you seek to interfere with the work that your people have been given?" replied the king. "Get back to your labors." And that same day Pharaoh commanded the Egyptian taskmasters that they should no longer provide straw for the Hebrews to make bricks. "They must now gather the straw themselves," he said, "but their quota of bricks shall not be lessened. It appears that the Hebrews do not have enough work to keep them busy, for they are crying for me to let them go into the desert to make a sacrifice to their God. Perhaps if I give them more work, they will have less time to think about such vain things."

As Pharaoh's order was enforced, the burden became severe upon the Hebrew workers. They could have managed if there had been straw for them to gather, but there was none. The people scoured the land for stubble wherever they could find it, and when their production quotas were not met, the Egyptian taskmasters beat the Hebrew officers for their failure.

Feeling the great injustice of their situation, the Hebrew officers complained to Pharaoh—but Pharaoh was unmoved. "This was done because you are idle," said Pharaoh. "If you had enough work, you would not be seeking to go into the desert to make a sacrifice to your God. Now get back to work!"

The Hebrew officers knew they were in trouble. They could plainly see that there was no way, without the straw, to do what Pharaoh had ordered them to do. As they left Pharaoh's house, greatly upset, they met Moses and Aaron and confronted them. "May Jehovah look upon you and judge you for what you have done to us," they shouted. "You have caused us to be hated by Pharaoh and his servants, even to take swords in their hands to slay us."

Things were not working out as Moses had envisioned, and in his frustration he called once more upon Jehovah. "Why, O Lord," he pleaded, "hast Thou done such a disservice to this people? In fact, why didst Thou send me here? Since the time that I spoke to Pharaoh in Thy name, he has done only evil to this people, and Thou hast not delivered them."

Jehovah spoke in response. "Now you will see what I will do to Pharaoh," he said. "For with a strong hand he will let my people go, and with a strong hand he will drive them out of this land. I am the Lord God Almighty. I am Jehovah, and by that name was I known unto your fathers. I established my covenant with them and gave them the land of Canaan—the land where they lived but were yet strangers. I have also heard the groanings of the children of Israel because of their cruel bondage, and I have remembered my covenant.

"Wherefore, Moses, tell this people that I will bring them out from under the burdens of the Egyptians. I will redeem them with a stretched-out arm and with great judgments. I will take them to be my people, and I will be their God. They shall know that I am Jehovah and that I will bring them unto the land that I swore to give to their fathers. And I will give that land to them as an inheritance forever."

Moses felt somewhat encouraged by this message, but when he told the children of Israel what Jehovah had said, they did not believe him because of the spiritual anguish they were suffering and the cruel bondage in which they were being held.

Again Jehovah spoke to Moses with the same message: "Return to Pharaoh," he said, "and tell him to let my people go."

Moses, in his bitter discouragement, questioned Jehovah's instructions. "Not even my own people will hear me," he said. "Why should Pharaoh listen to a man of such slow speech?"

Moses was deeply troubled. On one hand, Jehovah was telling him to persist in his request to Pharaoh to let Israel go, while on the other hand everything he did turned out wrong. The circumstances of the children of Israel were now much worse than they had ever been before he came to help them.

49—THE PLAGUES OF GOD
(Exodus 7–11)

Things were going badly for Moses—worse than he had ever imagined. Only his faith in God and his devotion to his mission kept him from giving up. The situation seemed to only get worse for the children of Israel. "I am a man with a slow tongue," he told Jehovah. "Why should Pharaoh listen to me?"

"I have sent you to be a prophet to Pharaoh," replied Jehovah, "and Aaron shall be your spokesman. You shall speak to Aaron all that I command you, and Aaron shall speak to Pharaoh. However, you must understand that when you ask that he allow the children of Israel to depart out of the land, he will still harden his heart. When his heart is hardened, you will multiply my signs and wonders and I will cause great judgments to come upon Egypt. But when I stretch forth my hand and bring Israel out from among them, the Egyptians shall know that I am Jehovah. When Pharaoh asks you to show him a miracle, tell Aaron to cast down his rod before him, and it will become a serpent."

Moses and Aaron went again to Pharaoh as Jehovah had directed them. When Aaron cast down his rod and it became a serpent, Pharaoh's magicians also cast down their rods with the same result. Aaron's rod swallowed the rods of the magicians, but Pharaoh hardened his heart and refused once more to let Israel go.

Jehovah sent Moses and Aaron again to Pharaoh, meeting him in the morning on the banks of the Nile. Jehovah told them to smite the river with Aaron's rod and turn the water into blood if Pharaoh still refused to let Israel go. They did as Jehovah commanded, and when Pharaoh rejected their request, Aaron struck the water with his rod and the water turned to blood. The fish died, the river stank, and no one could drink the water. But when Pharaoh's magicians also turned water into blood, Pharaoh again hardened his heart. When seven days had passed, the Egyptians dug about the riverbanks in search of drinking water, for the Nile still flowed with blood.

Jehovah again spoke to Moses. "Go to Pharaoh," he said. "Tell him to let my people go that they may serve me. If he still refuses, tell him I will smite his borders with frogs. They will come up out of the river into his house, into his bedchamber, and onto his bed. They will also come into the houses of all the people, even into their ovens and kneading troughs." And when Pharaoh refused to let the people go, Aaron stretched his rod over the waters and frogs come up upon all Egypt. But Pharaoh's magicians also brought up frogs from the waters.

Pharaoh asked Moses and Aaron to entreat Jehovah to take away the frogs. "If he will do so," Pharaoh promised, "your people may go to make their sacrifice."

"Tell me this," responded Moses. "When do you want the frogs removed?"

"Tomorrow," was Pharaoh's reply.

"It shall be done according to your word," said Moses, "that you may know there is none like unto Jehovah. The frogs on the land and in your houses shall die, but they shall remain in the river."

Moses cried to Jehovah, and Jehovah answered his prayers. Dead frogs were everywhere. They were gathered in great heaps upon the land, and the land stank. But when Pharaoh saw that there was relief, he hardened his heart and did not keep his promise to let Israel go.

Then Jehovah said to Moses, "Tell Aaron to stretch forth his rod and smite the dust of the earth that it may turn to lice." Aaron did so, and the dust of the earth became lice. When Pharaoh's magicians could not bring forth lice, they said to Pharaoh, "This is surely the finger of God." But Pharaoh's heart was hardened and he paid them no heed.

Jehovah directed Moses to arise early in the morning and ask Pharaoh again to let the people go and serve their God. "If you do not let them go," said Moses, "Jehovah will send swarms of flies. The houses of all Egypt shall be filled with flies, and the ground shall be covered with them." Then Moses added, "Tomorrow when the flies come to Egypt, there will be no flies in Goshen where the people of Israel dwell, that you may know Jehovah is God."

The flies came as promised—dreadful swarms of them—filling Pharaoh's house and polluted the whole land. Pharaoh called for Moses and Aaron, seeking a compromise. "Make your sacrifice to Jehovah in the land of Goshen," he suggested.

"You know we cannot offer sacrifices in Egypt," replied Moses, "for the things we offer offend the Egyptians. They would stone us. We must go three days' journey into the wilderness to make our sacrifice as Jehovah has commanded."

"I will let you go," said Pharaoh, "if you go only a short distance. Ask your God Jehovah if that is acceptable."

Moses responded, "I will ask Jehovah that the swarms of flies may depart tomorrow, but you must deal with us honestly and let us do what Jehovah requires." Moses petitioned Jehovah to remove the flies on the morrow, and they were removed—but Pharaoh hardened his heart and would not let Israel go.

Jehovah spoke to Moses again: "Go to Pharaoh and say, 'Thus says Jehovah, the God of the Hebrews: let my people go that they may serve me, or my hand will be upon all the flocks and herds of Egypt. They will die from a terrible plague, while the cattle of Israel live.'" Then Jehovah gave Moses a time for the plague if Pharaoh should resist. "Tomorrow," he said, "shall this plague be."

Jehovah did as he promised. The animals of the Egyptians died, but not those of the Israelites. And when Pharaoh saw that the Israelites' cattle did not die, his heart was hardened again and he declined to let them go.

Jehovah then told Moses and Aaron to take handfuls of ashes and throw them into the air in Pharaoh's sight. "These ashes will be fine dust throughout Egypt," he said, "causing festering boils with blisters on all the people and all the animals that the ashes touch."

When Moses and Aaron scattered the ashes, the people and animals of Egypt were covered with boils. The magicians were unable to stand before Moses because of their boils, but again Pharaoh's heart was hardened so that he refused to hearken.

Once more Jehovah spoke to Moses and instructed him to stand before Pharaoh and ask him to let Israel go that they might serve him. He told Moses to tell Pharaoh, "Thus says Jehovah: I will now send all my plagues upon your heart, your servants, and your people, that you may know that there is none like me in all the earth. I will smite you and your people with pestilence, and you shall be cut off from the earth. I have let you remain only to show my power and so that my name may be declared throughout the earth.

"About this time tomorrow I will send a grievous hailstorm, such a storm as has never been in Egypt. Before the storm comes, however, you must gather your cattle and all that are in the field, for the hail will kill every man or beast that is found there." When Moses and Aaron had delivered their warning, the people of Egypt who had regard for Jehovah gathered their servants and cattle into their houses, but most of the people gave no heed.

When Moses stretched forth his rod toward heaven, Jehovah sent thunder and hail. There was fire mingled with the hail, and all that were in the field died. The hail smote every herb of the field and broke every tree. Only in Goshen was there no hail.

As the storm continued, Pharaoh called for Moses and Aaron. "I have sinned," he admitted. "Jehovah is righteous and I am wicked. I have had enough. Entreat Jehovah that there be no more thunderings and hail, and I will let his people go."

Moses responded, "As soon as I am outside the city, I will raise my hands to Jehovah and the thunder and the hail will cease. By this you may know that the earth is Jehovah's, though I know that you and your servants will not yet fear him."

When Moses went out of the city and raised his hands, the storm ceased. But when Pharaoh saw that the storm was over he hardened his heart.

Jehovah said to Moses, "Go again to Pharaoh and I will show such signs before him that you may tell your sons and your grandsons what things I have wrought in Egypt."

Moses and Aaron dutifully went again before Pharaoh and asked, "How long will you refuse to humble yourself before Jehovah? If you still refuse to let this people go, he will bring locusts into your coasts tomorrow. They shall cover the earth and will eat what is left from the hail. They will eat every tree and fill every house." Then Moses and Aaron turned and left Pharaoh's presence.

When they had gone, Pharaoh's servants pleaded before him to relent. "How long shall this man be a snare to us?" they asked. "Let his people go to serve their God. Can you not see that Egypt is being destroyed because of your hard heart?"

Moses and Aaron were then brought back, and Pharaoh spoke. "I agree to let you go to serve your God," he said, "but first tell me who will go with you."

"We will all go," said Moses, "our old and our young, our sons and our daughters, our flocks and our herds. For we must hold a feast to Jehovah."

"If I let everyone go, I think that you will be up to some mischief," replied Pharaoh. "Let just your men go and serve your God." And Moses and Aaron were driven from Pharaoh's presence.

"Stretch forth your rod over the land," said Jehovah to Moses, "that the locusts may come." And as Moses stretched out his rod, an east wind began to blow. It blew upon Egypt all that day and all that night, and in the morning the wind brought the locusts. They covered the face of the land and everything that grew was swept away in their path.

Pharaoh called again for Moses and Aaron. "I have sinned against your God and against you," he confessed. "Forgive my sin and entreat Jehovah to take away this death." And, at Moses' entreaty, the wind blew from the west, casting the locusts into the Red Sea. But Pharaoh again hardened his heart and would not let Israel go.

Then Jehovah said to Moses, "Stretch forth your hands toward heaven that there may be darkness over the land—even darkness that can be felt." And as Moses stretched forth his hands, a thick darkness covered all Egypt for three days—such a darkness that people could not see each other or leave their homes—but the children of Israel had light in their houses in Goshen.

"Go!" said Pharaoh to Moses and Aaron. "Go and serve your God! I have decided that you may take your little ones with you, but you cannot take your flocks and herds."

Moses knew this was unacceptable and he held his ground. "Our animals must go," he said, "that we may have animals to offer as sacrifices. We must take them all because we do not know which ones we will offer until we are there." But again Pharaoh refused.

"Get out of my sight!" Pharaoh shouted at Moses. "For in the day you see my face again, you shall die!"

"You have spoken well," said Moses as he turned to leave. "I will see your face no more."

50–THE LAST PLAGUE AND THE PASSOVER

(Exodus 11–12)

Egypt lay in ruin from the plagues that Jehovah had sent upon the land by the hands of Moses and Aaron in response to Pharaoh's hard heart. But Israel was still in bondage. It seemed as if Pharaoh's hard heart would never relent and he would never let Israel go, in spite of Jehovah's promise. But Jehovah spoke again to Moses saying, "I will bring yet one more plague upon this land. After this plague, Pharaoh will not only let Israel go to worship me, he will request that you never return."

Jehovah continued: "Because of what I will do, this month will become the beginning of months for my people. From this time forward, this will be the first month of the year. Now, however, you must listen carefully and have the people do exactly as I tell you. On the tenth day of this month, every man who stands at the head of a family shall take a male lamb or male goat of the first year, one without blemish or spot, set it aside and maintain it until the fourteenth day—one animal to a house. But if a family is too small to eat a lamb, that family shall join with another.

"On the fourteenth day, each family shall kill its lamb in the evening and save its blood in a basin. Then they shall take a bunch of hyssop,[116] dip the hyssop in the lamb's blood, and strike it upon the two sideposts and on the lintel, or upper post, of the door to the house where the lamb will be eaten. They shall then roast the lamb with fire and eat its flesh that night with unleavened bread and bitter herbs. It is to be roasted with its head, legs, and edible inner parts and no bones shall be broken. All of the meat must be eaten that night in that same house, and if any remains in the morning, it shall be burned. They must eat the lamb in haste, with their girdles about their loins, their shoes upon their feet, and their staves in their hands, for this is Jehovah's Passover."

Jehovah's instructions continued: "On that same night I will pass through the land of Egypt to destroy all firstborn of both man and beast,[117] executing judgment against all the gods of Egypt. The blood on your doorposts will be a token to me of where the children of Israel are, and wherever I see the blood of the lamb, I will pass over that house and not destroy its firstborn.

"This day of Passover will be a memorial for Israel forever. It shall be kept as a feast to Jehovah at this same time each year throughout the generations. Seven days of unleavened bread shall be kept. On the first day all leaven shall be removed from your houses; and anyone who eats leavened bread during those seven days shall be cut off from Israel. There shall be a holy meeting on the first day and another on the seventh, and no work shall be done on those days, except to prepare food. Israel shall observe this feast forever in remembrance of this day on which I brought them as an army out of Egypt."

When Moses and Aaron received these instructions from Jehovah, they called the elders of Israel together and told them concerning the killing, roasting, and eating of the lamb. They explained how the blood should be struck on the doorposts and the importance of not leaving the house until morning. "For," said they, "Jehovah will pass through Egypt to smite the Egyptians; but when he sees the blood upon a doorpost, he will not suffer the destroyer to come into that house." And the people of Israel went and did as Moses and Aaron commanded them.

The plagues had taken a mighty toll. Moses was now well known throughout Egypt, and all the people now listened when he spoke. And Moses said to the people of Egypt (for Jehovah had so instructed him), "Jehovah will go through the midst of this land on the fourteenth day about midnight and all the firstborn of Egypt will die—from the firstborn of Pharaoh to the firstborn of the maidservant behind the mill. The firstborn of your beasts will die also. There will be a great cry throughout Egypt, such as there has never been before or shall ever be again. But against the children of Israel there shall not even a dog move his tongue. And by this you may know how Jehovah puts a difference between the Egyptians and the children of Israel. Then shall the people of Egypt bow before me and say, 'Please leave our land—both you and your people.' And after this we will go out."

---

[116] The plant that was called hyssop in the Bible is not known. Some believe that it was marjoram, while others believe that caper is more likely (see William Smith, *Dictionary of the Bible*, *GospeLink*, CD-ROM, s.v. "hyssop").

[117] The KJV scriptural passage reads firstborn, but it not conclusive from the Hebrew word involved whether this included all firstborn, both male and female, or if it was limited to firstborn males only. A persuasive argument can be made for the latter. The Hebrew word *bkowr (behk-OR)*, which was used here, has been translated both ways. Related scriptures, such as those in which Jehovah said that the firstborn males belonged to him following the preservation of the firstborn of Israel (e.g., Exodus 13:12), provide some evidence that it may have been only the firstborn males that were slain.

And so it came to pass, at midnight on the fourteenth day of the first month, Jehovah smote all the firstborn of Egypt, both man and beast, that they died. And Pharaoh rose up in the night—he, all his servants, and all the Egyptians. There was great weeping in Egypt that night, for the tragedy of death fell on every Egyptian house.

Pharaoh, in the agony of his soul, called Moses and Aaron to him in the night and said, "Rise up and get out of Egypt, both you and your people. Go and serve your God as you have said, and take also your flocks and your herds. Begone from Egypt, and do not return."

The Egyptians were eager to have the Israelites out of their land. "Go now," they said, "or we shall all be dead!"

As Israel prepared to depart, Jehovah spoke again to Moses. "Tell the women of Israel to borrow jewels of silver and gold from their Egyptian neighbors," he said. And thus Jehovah fulfilled his earlier promise,[118] giving the Israelites favor with the Egyptians that they gave them their jewels as well as other things needed for their sojourn in the wilderness.

51—STAND STILL AND SEE THE SALVATION OF JEHOVAH
(Exodus 12–14)

The time had finally come; Jehovah's promise was fulfilled. The Egyptian Pharaoh had not only allowed the children of Israel to leave Egypt, but also insisted that they not return. Israel was on the move.

Seventy souls of the family of Jacob had come down into Egypt during the great famine 430 years before. Now 600,000[119] men of Israel and their families were leaving, plus and a large number of non-Israelites whose ethnic identities are unknown to us. And, as they left, they took with them the bones of Joseph, as their oath had been sworn, that he might be buried with his fathers.[120]

As the great exodus commenced, Jehovah spoke to Moses saying, "Because I caused the destroying angel to pass over the firstborn of Israel when all the firstborn of Egypt were smitten, the firstborn males of Israel shall be sanctified unto me, both man and beast, for they are mine. When you come into the land of the Canaanites, I will give you that land, as I swore to your fathers. There you shall sacrifice unto me the firstborn males of all your animals. But the firstlings of the ass shall be redeemed by sacrificing a lamb, and the firstborn of man shall you also redeem with a lamb."

Moses taught these things to his people, then he said to them: "Remember this day in which you came out of bondage in Egypt, for the strength of Jehovah's hand has brought you out. And when he shall bring you to the land that he swore to your fathers to give you— even a land that flows with milk and honey—you shall keep forever the service of the unleavened bread in remembrance of what he did today. Seven days shall you eat unleavened bread, and on the seventh day you shall make a feast to Jehovah."

Jehovah forbade the children of Israel to depart from Egypt through the land of the Philistines, though the way was shorter, for he feared that they would be-

---

[118] This promise is given in story "46—I Have Seen the Afflictions of My People."

[119] It is not clear exactly how many Israelites actually left Egypt at this time. Though the scripture says there were 600,000 men, plus women and children, exaggerations were not uncommon in the Old Testament record.

[120] See story "42—A Choice Seer." That story tells of Joseph's request to have his bones taken back to Canaan for burial when Israel returned to inherit the land that was promised to their fathers. The eventual burial of Joseph's bones in the promised land is told in story "78—A Land for Which You Did Not Labor."

come involved in a war and desire to return to Egypt. Instead, he led them southward toward the Red Sea—going before them by day in a pillar of a cloud and by night in a pillar of fire. And Jehovah spoke to Moses and told him to make camp for his people between Migdol and the Red Sea.[121]

Pharaoh was still predictable. When he realized that Israel had actually fled into the wilderness, he again hardened his heart. He and his servants began to regret that they had let the children of Israel go out of their service. In haste Pharaoh prepared his chariot and took his people with him. Six hundred chariots and all his army went in pursuit of the children of Israel and found them encamped by the Red Sea. "They are entangled in the land," said Pharaoh, "trapped between the wilderness and the sea and have no way of escape."

When the children of Israel saw the vast Egyptian army descending upon them, they were afraid and began to cry to Jehovah. They said to Moses, "Did you bring us out here to die in the wilderness because there were no graves in Egypt? Why did you not listen to us when we told you to leave us alone to serve the Egyptians? That would surely have been better than dying here in the desert."

"Fear not!" said Moses. "Stand still and see the salvation of Jehovah that he will show you today. For the Egyptians whom you see today, you shall see no more forever. Yea, if you will hold your peace, Jehovah will fight for you."

---

[121] Modern scripture (see 1 Nephi 4:2, 17:26–27; Helaman 8:11; and Doctrine and Covenants 8:3) and the New Testament (Acts 7:37 and Hebrews 11:29) offer verification that it was indeed the Red Sea that Moses parted, even though the map shows that the Israel's travels during their exodus from Egypt are believed to have been farther to the north. There is little question about the reality of the miracle, in spite of what some commentators have written, but there is some question about the actual scene of the event. From what we know, it is likely that the passage of the children of Israel through the Red Sea was near the far northern end of the Gulf of Suez. One writer points out that there are often strong northwesterly winds in that area that "occasionally...drive the water at the northern extremity of the Gulf back so far that it is possible to wade across" (see Werner Keller, *The Bible as History: What Archaeology Reveals about Scripture*, 2nd rev. ed. [New York: William Morrow and Co. Inc., 1981], 126). Note that the scriptural account of the miracle speaks of an east wind—the kind of wind that is more typical of Palestine—but Jehovah can certainly cause the wind to blow from whatever direction he chooses.

And Jehovah said to Moses, "Why do you stand there crying to me? Speak to the children of Israel that they go forward. Lift up your rod and stretch out your hand over the water to divide it, and the children of Israel will go through the sea on dry ground. The hearts of the Egyptians shall be hardened that they will follow you into the sea, and then will I bring honor to myself because of Pharaoh, his army, his chariots, and his horsemen. They shall know that I am Jehovah."

The pillar of the cloud that had gone before the camp of Israel now went behind them and stood between the Egyptian army and the camp of Israel. It was a cloud of darkness to the Egyptians by night, but gave light to the camp of Israel.

When Moses had stretched forth his hand over the sea, the waters were driven back by a strong east wind all that night and made a path of dry land through the sea. Great walls of water billowed up on either side as the entire camp of Israel passed through the sea on dry ground.

In the morning Jehovah troubled the Egyptians as he looked at them through the pillar of fire and cloud, and many began to be afraid. "Let us flee from the face of Israel," they cried, "for the Lord Jehovah is fighting for them." But, in the hardness of his heart, Pharaoh urged them to follow the hosts of Israel into that pathway through the sea—even all of Pharaoh's horses, his horsemen, and his chariots.

With Israel now safely on the other side of the sea, Moses stretched forth his hand again and the waters returned as they had been before. And as the walls of water gave way and began to tumble, the Egyptians, who were now in the sea, turned to escape—but it was too late. Not one of them was spared.

Thus, Jehovah saved his people from the Egyptians, and all Israel saw the Egyptians lying dead on the seashore. And, seeing this great miracle that Jehovah had wrought that day in their behalf, the children of Israel believed in Jehovah and in his servant Moses.

52–THE BREAD THAT JEHOVAH HAS GIVEN YOU

(Exodus 15–17)

There was great rejoicing in Israel's camp because of their miraculous delivery from Egypt. The people prayed in gratitude and sang praises to Jehovah. The women of Israel—led by Moses' sister Miriam—played their timbrels[122] and danced in thanksgiving. They felt deeply indebted to Jehovah for saving their lives. Not only had he saved their lives, but he had also delivered them from their terrible bondage. And now they were on their way back to inherit the land Jehovah had promised to their fathers—a land flowing with milk and honey. Things could not get much better than this.

But the mood soon changed. As the camp of Israel traveled away from the Red Sea three days into the Wilderness of Shur, they ran out of water. When they came to Marah,[123] they made camp because they found water there. But when the water proved to be bitter and undrinkable, the people immediately began to murmur. "What shall we drink?" they cried to Moses. And when Moses took the problem to Jehovah, he was shown a tree which, when its wood was placed in the water, made the water sweet.

Then Jehovah made a covenant with the people of Israel. Through Moses he said to them, "If you will diligently hearken to my voice and do that which is right in my sight—giving ear to my commandments and keeping my statutes—I will bless you that none of the diseases of the Egyptians will come upon you."

From Marah, the camp of Israel moved to Elim where there were twelve wells of water and seventy palm trees. Life was good again.

But again the good feelings would not last. As the camp moved from Elim into the Wilderness of Sin, between Elim and Sinai, the people became unhappy with their food. And the whole congregation once more murmured against Moses and Aaron. "Would to God we had died in Egypt," they said. "There we at least had all the meat and bread we could eat. But you have brought us into this wilderness to kill us with hunger."

Then Jehovah said to Moses, "In the evening I will give you meat and in the morning I will rain bread from heaven upon you. The people shall gather a certain portion of the bread each day, and by this I will test them to see if they will obey me. On the sixth day, however, they shall gather a double portion so they will have no need to gather on the seventh day."

And Moses and Aaron said to the children of Israel, "In the evening you will know that Jehovah has brought you out of Egypt, and in the morning you will see his glory, for he has heard your murmurings. He will give you flesh to eat in the evening, and in the morning he will give you bread until you are full."

When evening came, flocks of quail came into the camp and there was meat to eat. In the morning, the hosts of Israel were covered with dew. And when the dew was gone, small round morsels—about the size of the hoarfrost[124]—covered the ground in its place. When the children of Israel saw it, they said to each other, "This is manna," because they knew not what else to call it. It was white like coriander seed and tasted like wafers made with honey.

"This manna is the bread that Jehovah has given you," Moses told them, "and this is what he has commanded you concerning its use: each man shall gather manna according to the amount that he and his family can eat. As all families eat differently, some will gather more than others, but no one shall gather more than is needed for one day."

Some did not listen to Moses and gathered too much. When it sat overnight, however, it stank and was full of worms in the morning. But when the people of Israel did what Moses told them, all had enough, and the excess upon the ground melted in the heat of the sun. On the sixth day, each man gathered a double portion and laid it away for the Sabbath, and it did not stink or have worms. On the seventh day there was no manna upon the ground, and those who went out to gather came back empty.

When Jehovah saw that some went out to gather manna on the Sabbath, he said to Moses, "How long will this people refuse to obey my laws? I have given you bread for two days on the sixth day so that every man may rest on the Sabbath." So the children of Israel hearkened to the voice of Jehovah and rested on the seventh day, and Jehovah provided manna continually for the children of Israel in the wilderness until they entered the promised land.

From the Wilderness of Sin, the camp of Israel moved to Rephidim where again they murmured because there was no water. "Why have you brought us out of Egypt?" they whined. "To kill us with thirst? We are beginning to wonder if Jehovah is with us or not."

As the murmuring became worse, Moses said to Jehovah, "What shall I do for this people, for they are almost ready to stone me?"

---

[122] A timbrel is an ancient type of tambourine or hand drum.

[123] The word Marah means "bitterness."

---

[124] Hoarfrost is the white icy crystals that form when the moisture in the air condenses on a freezing surface.

"Go before them," said Jehovah. "Take the elders of Israel with you and the rod you used to smite the Red Sea. I will stand before you on the rock of Horeb and, when you strike the rock, water will come out of it that they may drink."

Moses went up unto the rock of Horeb as Jehovah commanded him and there, in the sight of the elders, he struck the rock with his rod and water came out.

Moses called the place Massah and Meribah[125] because the children of Israel murmured and because they tempted Jehovah.

53–AS LONG AS HIS HANDS WERE RAISED
(Exodus 17; Deuteronomy 25)

While the children of Israel were at Rephidim, the Amalekites came against them to battle. The attack was of the most cowardly sort because it was against the feeble and weary at the rear of the company. When Moses saw what was happening, he spoke to Joshua, his servant or minister, and told him to choose an army from the men of Israel and to fight thc Amalekites. "You will fight them tomorrow," he said to Joshua. "And as you fight, I will stand on top of yonder hill with my rod in my hands."

The next day, Joshua took his chosen army to fight the people of Amalek, while Moses, Aaron, and Hur climbed to the top of the hill. As the battle ensued, Moses held up his hands, holding the rod high above his head. As long as his hands were raised, Israel prevailed, but when his hands dropped down, Amalek gained the advantage.

Because Moses' hands were heavy and the battle was long, he was unable to continue to hold them above his head. So Aaron and Hur found a rock for him to sit on. With Moses seated on the rock, Aaron and Hur were able to stand, one on either side of him, and hold up his hands.

Aaron and Hur hold up Moses' arms

With the help of Aaron and Hur, Moses' hands were steady until sundown, and Joshua's army subdued the Amalekites with the edge of the sword.

When the battle was over, Jehovah said to Moses, "So that you will remember what happened here, write about this battle in a book and read it to Joshua. For when the time comes that you possess the promised land, I will destroy all memory of Amalek."

---

[125] Massah means "testing" or "trying," and Meribah mcans "strife" or "complaint."

Moses built an altar to commemorate Israel's battle against the Amalekites and called his altar Jehovah-nissi,[126] because Jehovah had sworn an oath that he would have warfare against Amalek from generation to generation.

54—THE TASK IS TOO GREAT FOR ONE MAN
(Exodus 18)

Life had been stressful for Moses' family in Egypt during the time of the plagues, with Moses being the focus of the conflict between the Egyptians and the children of Israel. So, while Moses was struggling with Pharaoh for the freedom of the Israelites, his wife Zipporah and his sons, Gershom[127] and Eliezer,[128] returned to Midian to live with Zipporah's father, Jethro the high priest.

When Jethro heard all that God had done for Moses in bringing the children of Israel out of Egyptian bondage, he sent word to Moses that he was coming to meet him in the wilderness, bringing Zipporah, Gershom, and Eliezer with him. Moses was excited, and when he saw his family coming, he went out to meet them, bowing before Jethro and kissing him.

When they were comfortably settled in Moses' tent, Moses related to Jethro all that Jehovah had done to Pharaoh and the Egyptians for the sake of Israel. He also told of the hardships they had suffered in the wilderness and how Jehovah had delivered them.

Jethro rejoiced for the blessings of Jehovah upon Israel and said, "Blessed be the Lord Jehovah, who has delivered you out of Pharaoh's hand and delivered this people from the Egyptians. Now I know that Jehovah is greater than all other gods." Then Jethro made a burnt offering and sacrifice to Jehovah.

The following day Moses sat to hear the problems of the people and to judge them. Jethro watched as the people stood by Moses from morning till evening awaiting his judgments. When he saw all that Moses did for the people, he asked him, "What is this thing that you do for the people? Why do you sit alone to judge them? And why must the people stand waiting from morning till evening for your judgments?"

"I do this," Moses replied, "because the people come to me to inquire of God. When there is a problem, they come to me and I judge between one and another and make known the laws and statutes of God."

"What you do is not good," replied Jethro. "You will surely be worn out, both you and these people, for the task is too great for one man. If you will hearken to my counsel, God will be with you. Because you represent these people before God, that you may bring their causes unto him, it is expected that you will teach them

---

[126] Which means "Jehovah is my banner."

[127] The name Gershom means "a sojourner there."

[128] The name Eliezer means "God of help."

the laws and ordinances. Indeed, you must show them the way they must walk and the works they must do.

"But you need others to help you rule—able men who fear God, love truth, and hate covetousness. Choose such men and place them over the people to be rulers of thousands, rulers of hundreds, rulers of fifties, and rulers of tens; and let these men judge the people. When there are hard cases, they will bring these to you; but they can judge the small matters. Thus, it will be easier for you because they will share your burden. This will be a blessing both to you and to the people, for they will no longer have to wait all day for their problems to be heard."

Moses hearkened to the words of Jethro and did all that he said. He chose able men from among the people and made them rulers of thousands, rulers of hundreds, rulers of fifties, and rulers of tens. And these men judged the people at all seasons. The hard cases they brought to Moses, and the small matters they judged themselves. And Jethro returned to his home in Midian.

55—GOD IS COME TO PROVE YOU

(Exodus 19–23, Deuteronomy 5)

Fifty days after the children of Israel came out of Egypt, they moved from Rephidim into the Sinai desert. Once they had made their camp at the base of that great mountain where Moses had encountered the burning bush and had been called as a prophet, Jehovah called Moses to come up onto the mount. There he spoke to Moses saying, "Give this message to the children of Israel: you have seen what I did unto the Egyptians and how I carried you on eagles' wings and brought you unto myself. Now, if you will obey my voice and keep the covenant that I made with your fathers, you will become a peculiar treasure to me above all other people. Yea, you who have been slaves and servants in Egypt shall be a kingdom of priests and a holy nation."

As Moses returned to the camp, he called together the elders of Israel and told them what Jehovah had said. The people were deeply moved and responded in one voice saying, "We will do all that Jehovah has commanded us." And Moses took this report back to Jehovah on the mountain.

When Jehovah heard Moses' report, he said, "Go back now and sanctify this people today and tomorrow. Then have them wash their clothes so that on the third day, when I come down on the mountain in the view of the people, they will be ready to meet me. Set bounds for them so they do not touch the mountain or come up into it. For whoever touches the mountain, whether man or beast, must be stoned to death. Only when they hear the trumpet sounding from the mountain shall they come up."

At Moses' direction, the children of Israel prepared for that day when Jehovah was to appear to them. They washed their clothing and kept themselves from all worldly pursuits, that they might make themselves holy.

On the morning of the third day there was thunder and lightening. A thick cloud hung over the mountain and there was a great noise like the blast of a trumpet. When the blast was heard in the camp, the people began to tremble. Moses then led them to the base of the mountain where that day they were to meet Jehovah.

As the people stood waiting, the mountain shook as if by an earthquake. The entire mountain was covered with smoke—ascending like the smoke of a furnace—because Jehovah had come down upon the mountain. When the sound of the trumpet became louder, Moses spoke to Jehovah and Jehovah summoned him to go up to the top of the mountain.

When Moses had ascended to the top of the mount, Jehovah told him to return to his people. "You must warn the priests and the people once more that they must not come onto the mountain," said Jehovah. "And when you have warned them, return to me here with your brother Aaron."

Moses returned to his people at the base of the mountain and gave them the warning that Jehovah had requested, and they hearkened to all the words that Moses spoke. Then Moses and Aaron went back to the top of the mountain to hear what Jehovah would tell them.

When Moses and Aaron reached the top of the mountain, Jehovah spoke so that all Israel could hear. "I am Jehovah your God who brought you out of Egypt and out of the house of bondage," he said, his voice thundering from the mountain. He then gave them Ten Commandments and wrote them with his finger on tablets of stone:

"You shall have no other gods before me.

"You shall not make unto yourself any graven image, or any likeness of any thing that is in heaven above or in the earth beneath, or in the water that is under the earth.

"You shall not take the name of Jehovah your God in vain.

"Remember the Sabbath day to keep it holy.

"Honor your father and your mother, that your days may be long upon the land which Jehovah your God has given you.

"You shall not kill.

"You shall not commit adultery.

"You shall not steal.

"You shall not bear false witness against your neighbor.

"You shall not covet your neighbor's house, your neighbor's wife, or anything that belongs to your neighbor."

As the people watched fearfully from their waiting place at the base of the mountain, they saw lightning and smoke on the mountain. And when they heard the thundering voice and the noise of the trumpet, they removed from the base of the mountain and stood afar off. When Moses and Aaron finally returned, the people said to them, "Speak to us and we will hear you, but please do not let God speak to us, lest we die."

"Do not be afraid," said Moses. "God is come to prove you, that his fear may be before your faces and that you do not sin."

Moses' words of assurance did little to diminish the people's fears. They chose to keep a safe distance, but Moses returned to the mountain, drawing near to the thick darkness where Jehovah was. As he did so, Jehovah spoke again. "Thus shall you say to the children of Israel: because you have seen that I have talked to you from heaven, you shall make no gods of silver or gold in association with me. But you shall build an altar that you may sacrifice burnt offerings thereon unto me. In all places where I record my name I will come unto you and bless you. The altar you build shall not be made of cut stones, for it will be polluted if you lift up your tools upon it. Neither shall you make steps to go up to it, but shall go up by way of a ramp."

There upon Mount Sinai, Jehovah outlined for Moses various laws by which Israel was to be governed. He also designated three feast days to be kept each year. "Three times each year shall you keep a feast unto me," he said. "You shall keep the feast of the unleavened bread, the feast of harvest—the firstfruits of your labors which you have sown in the field—and the feast of ingathering, which is in the end of the year when you have gathered in your labors from the field.[129] At these three times all the males of Israel shall present themselves before me.

"If the children of Israel will do all of these things that I speak, I will send my angel before them to keep them in the way and bring them to the place that I have prepared for them. But they must give heed to the angel, for my name is in him, and they must obey his voice. If they provoke him, he will not pardon their transgressions. But if they obey the angel's voice and do all that I speak, I will be an enemy unto their enemies and an adversary unto their adversaries."

Jehovah told Moses of the land that Israel would inherit and explained how he would remove the present inhabitants from the land. Said he, "I will send my fear before you and destroy all those people to whom you come. Your enemies will turn their backs and flee before you. I will also send hornets to drive them from the land. But I will not drive them out in one year, lest the land become desolate and the beasts of the field multiply there. Little by little will I drive them out before you until you are increased and can inherit the land.

"I will set your boundaries from the Red Sea to the sea of the Philistines, and from the desert to the Euphrates River. And as I deliver the inhabitants into your hands, you shall drive them out before you."

Then Jehovah, understanding the problems that would later beset the children of Israel in the promised land, gave Moses a solemn warning: "Israel must make no covenants with the people of the land or with the gods of those people. And they must not allow the people of the land to live among them, lest they make my

---

[129] These three feasts came to be known in Israel as the Feast of the Passover, the Feast of Weeks, and the Feast of Tabernacles.

people sin against me. For if Israel serves their gods, it will surely be a snare unto them."

56—COME UP INTO THE MOUNTAIN
(Exodus 24−31)

The children of Israel were greatly blessed as they camped in the desert of Sinai. Jehovah had spoken to Moses and they had heard his voice from the mountain, though they had not seen him. Jehovah had also renewed the covenant he had made with their fathers to go before them into the promised land. They were humbled by all they had experienced and were more determined than ever to keep God's commandments. And, to help them do so, Moses received instructions from Jehovah and wrote all that he was told so that he might teach it to them.

Moses rose early in the morning and built an altar with twelve pillars to represent the tribes of Israel. He offered sacrifices upon the altar and read to the people the words that he had written. And when the people heard what Moses read, they responded in one voice saying, "We will obey all of Jehovah's words."

Moses was pleased by the people's response, and he sprinkled blood from the sacrifices upon them to sanctify them. "This," he said, "is the blood of the covenant that Jehovah made with you because of your promises."

Then the voice of Jehovah spoke again to Moses. "Come up toward the mountain," he said, "and bring Aaron, Nadab, Abihu,[130] and seventy of the elders of Israel with you. These will worship me from afar off, but Moses shall come into the mountain." As Moses and those who had been designated neared the mountain, they were privileged to see Jehovah. And under his feet they beheld a paved work of sapphire stone. The vision was as clear to them as the very heavens, but Jehovah did not lay his hands upon the elders of Israel.

"Come up into the mountain," Jehovah said to Moses, "and I will give you tables of stone. I will give you a law and commandments that you may teach to this people."

"Wait here until I return," Moses told the elders. "If problems arise while I am gone, bring them to Aaron and Hur." Then Moses took his servant or minister, Joshua, and the two men went part way up the mountain.

A cloud covered the mountain and the glory of Jehovah was upon it for six days. On the seventh day, Jehovah called to Moses from out of the cloud. Moses left Joshua to wait where he was and went on alone, climbing to the top of the mountain, where he remained for forty days and forty nights. From the camp of Israel,

---

[130] Nadab and Abihu were two of Aaron's four sons.

the glory of Jehovah appeared as if it were a devouring fire on top of Mount Sinai.

There on Mount Sinai, Jehovah told Moses that he wanted the children of Israel to make an offering to him of their gold, silver, brass, fine linens, goats' hair, dyed animal skins, acacia wood,[131] oil, spices, and precious stones. These things would all be used to build a portable tabernacle or temple for Israel to carry with them in the wilderness. Jehovah gave Moses detailed instructions for the tabernacle and its furnishings and showed him exactly how they should be built.[132] He told Moses that two men in Israel's camp—Bezaleel of the tribe of Judah and Aholiab of the tribe of Dan—had been prepared as artisans to build and furnish the tabernacle.

"You shall put the ark of the covenant in this tabernacle to preserve the testimony that I shall give you," said Jehovah. He explained that the ark of the covenant was to be made from acacia wood overlaid with gold. It. would be two and one-half cubits long, one and one-half cubits wide, and one-half cubit high.[133] There would be a gold crown on top and two golden rings on each side so it could be carried with golden staves. A mercy seat—a golden slab of the same size—would provide a covering for the ark. And at each end of the mercy seat would be a golden cherub,[134] the two cherubim facing each other. This mercy seat was to be the place where God's glory would be revealed and would be regarded as God's throne.

_____

[131] Acacia wood was also known as shittim wood because it came from the area of Shittim, which lay east of the Jordan, opposite Jericho.

[132] The instructions were given in great detail, which will not be considered here. Suffice it to say that the tabernacle itself was to be thirty cubits (forty-five feet or 13.7 meters) long and ten cubits (fifteen feet or 4.57 meters) wide. It was to be covered by a tent that was forty cubits (sixty feet or 18.3 meters) long and twenty-five cubits (37.5 feet or 11.4 meters) wide and was to stand in a court that was 100 cubits (150 feet or 45.7 meters) long and fifty cubits (seventy-five feet or 22.9 meters) wide.

[133] A cubit was considered to be the length of a man's forearm, from the elbow to the tip of the middle finger, or about eighteen inches. Thus, 2.5 cubits would be about three feet, nine inches (1.14 meters), and 1.5 cubits would be about two feet, three inches (sixty-eight centimeters). Ten cubits would be about fifteen feet (4.57 meters).

[134] A cherub is a heavenly creature, the exact form of which is unknown. The plural form is *cherubim*. There is an interesting description of cherubim in Ezekiel 10 that may, or may not, be relevant.

The tabernacle itself would be thirty cubits long and ten cubits wide, made of ten curtains of fine linen. Gold-overlaid boards would support the curtains. Inside the tabernacle would be four pillars of gold-overlaid acacia wood and a veil of blue, purple, and scarlet hanging from the pillars. The ark and the mercy seat would be kept behind the veil in an area ten cubits square called the holy of holies or the most holy place. On a small altar of incense in front of the veil would be a lamp that would burn constantly. On the south side[135] of the altar of incense would be golden oil cups;[136] and on the north side would be a table for showbread.[137] This area of the tabernacle would be called the holy place.

As a covering over the tabernacle, there was to be a tent of rams' skins dyed red, with badgers' skins on top of them. The tent would be forty cubits long.

A court 100 cubits long and fifty cubits wide would surround the tent, and the walls of the court would be five cubits high. Inside the court and in front of the tent, would be an altar of acacia wood, overlaid with brass, five cubits square and three cubits high.

Jehovah instructed Moses that Aaron and his four sons—Nadab, Abihu, Eleazar, and Ithamar—were to officiate as priests for Israel in the tabernacle and keep the tabernacle in order. Moses was shown how to make the sacred clothing that the priests would wear to perform their priestly duties—the breastplate, the ephod, the robes, the broidered coat, the miter, and the girdle. "You shall put this sacred clothing on Aaron and on his sons with him," said Jehovah, "and you shall anoint them and sanctify them that they may minister in the priest's office."

Then Jehovah said to Moses, "When the tabernacle is built, you will bring Aaron to the door of the tabernacle and wash him with water, put the sacred clothing on him, and pour the holy anointing oil on his head. The holy garments of Aaron shall belong to his sons after him, and they too shall be anointed and consecrated in them. The office of priest will belong to them and to their seed forever."

Jehovah specified certain rites, sacrifices, and offerings to be made by Aaron and his sons in fulfillment of their office. "When they do as I have directed them," he

_____

[135] The tabernacle was always to be erected so that it faced east.

[136] The scripture (Exodus 25:31) says candlestick, but they had no candles. They burned olive oil in cup-like receptacles, using cloth for wicks.

[137] Showbread consisted of unleavened wafers that were used by the priest in performing the rites of the tabernacle and, later, the temple. The King James Version of the Bible uses the archaic spelling of "shewbread."

said, "the tabernacle and the altar will be sanctified by my glory (or my presence). Yea, the children of Israel shall know that I brought them out of Egypt that I might dwell among them. I am Jehovah their God."

Jehovah reminded Moses of the importance of the Sabbath day. "Everyone who defiles the Sabbath," he said, "or who does work on that day shall surely be put to death. The Sabbath has been given as a perpetual covenant and sign between me and the children of Israel, for in six days I made heaven and earth and I rested on the seventh."

When Jehovah had finished his instructions, he gave Moses two tablets of stone upon which he had written with his finger. These stone tablets contained the testimony of Jehovah's covenants with his people.

57—FORGOTTEN COVENANTS AND A GOLDEN CALF

(Exodus 32–33; Deuteronomy 9)

When Moses was so long upon the mountain,[138] the children of Israel became impatient. Many of them feared that Moses was dead and would never return. Even Aaron and Hur, whom Moses had left in charge of Aaron's sons and the seventy elders at the base of the mountain, had apparently grown weary of waiting and returned to the main camp. Forty days was a long time.

Fearing they had been left in the wilderness without a prophet, the children of Israel quickly let their fears become more important than their covenants. They came to Aaron and said, "Because we do not know what has become of the man Moses who brought us out of Egypt, you must make gods to go before us in the wilderness." It is hard to believe that these were the same people who, just days before, had made a solemn covenant to obey every word that Jehovah had spoken to them through Moses.[139]

Aaron, apparently having some of the same fears as the people, yielded to their will. "Break off your wives' golden earrings and bring them to me," he told them. "I will make gods for you to follow."

Thinking it could calm their unrest, Aaron took their earrings and fashioned a golden calf like the ones the people had known in Egypt. Said he, "These are your gods, O Israel, which brought you out of the land of Egypt."

Aaron next built an altar and placed it before the golden image. Then he made a very unusual announcement: "Tomorrow," he said, "we will make a feast to Jehovah." It seems that Aaron had convinced himself that the golden calf, around which the children of Israel were to hold their riotous feast, was only a representation of Jehovah, when in reality the people had traded their wealth for a false god.

The children of Israel rose early the next morning and made burnt offerings on the altar before the golden

---

[138] As indicated in story, "56—Come Up into the Mountain," Moses was six days on the mountain before going to the top and was then at the top of the mountain for forty days and forty nights conversing with Jehovah.

[139] The children of Israel had made this covenant of obedience with Jehovah twice since they came into the wilderness of Sinai (see stories "55—God Has Come to Prove You" and "56—Come Up into the Mountain").

calf. They sat down to eat and drink, and then rose up to frolic and make merry.

Meanwhile on Sinai, Jehovah spoke to Moses. "Make haste and go down," he said, "for your people have corrupted themselves. They have made a molten calf and offered sacrifices to it. They say it is the god that brought them out of Egypt. My wrath has waxed hot against this ungrateful and stiffnecked people. Surely I will destroy them and make a greater and mightier nation than they."

Moses was frightened. He pleaded before Jehovah. "Do not let Thine anger wax hot against these people that Thou didst bring out of Egypt with great power," he pleaded. "If Thou wilt destroy them now, it will be said that Thou didst bring them out of Egypt only to slay them in the wilderness. But if Thou wilt turn away Thine anger from them, they will surely repent of the evil they have done. Remember Thy covenant with Abraham, Isaac, and Jacob, to multiply their seed as the stars of heaven, and to give the land that Thou didst speak of unto their seed forever. If that covenant means anything, Thou canst not now destroy this people."

"If they will repent," answered Jehovah, "I will spare their lives and turn away my anger. But you must execute judgment this day against all those who will not repent. If not, I will do all that I have thought to do."

Moses descended quickly from the mountain, carrying the two stone tablets of testimony that Jehovah had written with his finger. And he brought Joshua with him. When the two men came near to the camp of Israel and Joshua heard the revelry and shouting of the people, he said, "The noise of war is in the camp." Then, after listening more closely, he reconsidered his assessment. "This is not the voice of those who cry for mastery, nor the voice of those who are overcome," he said. "It is the noise of singing."

As Moses and Joshua came closer, they saw the golden calf and observed the dancing and merrymaking of the people. Becoming very angry, Moses threw down the stone tablets, breaking them on the ground. Then, entering the camp, he took the calf, burned it, and ground the residue into fine powder. When he had sprinkled the powder in the brook that flowed from the mountain, he made the people drink it.

"What did these people do to you that you have brought such a great sin upon them?" Moses asked Aaron.

"Do not let Jehovah be upset by this," answered Aaron, choosing his words carefully. "You know that these people are set on mischief. They said to me, 'Make us gods to go before us, for we know not what has become of Moses.' And I told them that whoever had gold should break it off and bring it to me. Then, when they had brought their gold, I cast it in the fire and this calf was formed from it."

Aaron's story did not merit Moses' reply. He turned and walked away, going directly to the gate of the camp as the people gathered to hear him. There Moses addressed the people. "Who is on Jehovah's side?" he cried. "Let him come forward!" Then, when all the sons of Levi came forward, Moses said to them, "Take your swords in your hands and go in and out of every gate of this camp slaying those who do not repent of this great evil." And that day there were about 3,000 men slain by the sons of Levi.

Moses charged those who remained to rededicate themselves to Jehovah. "If you will have God's forgiveness," he said, "every man must bestow a blessing upon his son and upon his brother this day."

Jehovah was angry with the children of Israel because they had so quickly turned aside from the truths he had given them to the worship of idols, and Moses feared greatly for his people lest Jehovah should destroy them in his anger. He returned to Mount Sinai, where he fasted another forty days and forty nights, pleading with Jehovah to forgive the great sin of Israel. "If Thou canst not forgive this people, said Moses to Jehovah, "Blot me out of the book that Thou hast written."

"I will not blot you out of my book," answered Jehovah, "but I will blot out those who have sinned against me. Go now and lead this people into the land that I have promised them. But, because they have worshipped the golden calf and are a stiffnecked people, I will not go up in their midst to the promised land, lest I become angry and destroy them. Nevertheless, I will send my angel before them to drive out the inhabitants of the land."

58—A LESSER LAW
(Exodus 34; Deuteronomy 10)

With the incident of the golden calf now behind them, Israel was greatly humbled, though they still lacked spiritual stability.[140] They needed the law of God to govern them, but the tablets of stone upon which Jehovah had written the Law with his finger had been dashed to pieces when Moses saw the golden calf.

Jehovah spoke again to Moses, saying, "Hew out two new stones like the ones that were broken, and I will write the words of my law upon them, as I did upon the others, that you may put them in the ark of the covenant. But the Law that I will write shall be different from that which I wrote before. Because of their sin, I will not give this people the words of the everlasting covenant of my holy priesthood. My holy order[141] and its ordinances shall not be among them.

"I will give this people a law of carnal—or worldly—commandments, and not a spiritual law. Because they are not ready to have my presence among them, I have sworn that they shall not enter into my rest while in the wilderness—which rest is the fullness of my glory (or my presence). Therefore, prepare the stone tablets and come up in the morning to present yourself before me on the holy mount."

Moses hewed the stone tablets as he was commanded, and in the morning he took them up into the mountain. There, on top of Mount Sinai, Jehovah said to Moses, "I am Jehovah, the Lord God, merciful and gracious, long-suffering, abundant in goodness and truth. I keep mercy for thousands, and though I forgive iniquity, transgression, and sin, that will not clear the unrepentant. And I visit the iniquity of the fathers upon the children, and upon the children's children, unto the third and fourth generations."

Moses bowed to the earth and worshipped. "If I have found grace in Thy sight, O Lord," he said, "let my Lord be in the midst of Israel in the wilderness, though they are a stiffnecked people. Pardon our iniquity and our sin and choose us as Thine inheritance."

"I will make this covenant with you," answered Jehovah. "Before all the people of Israel I will do marvels such as have not been done in all the earth. And all the people around you shall see my works. If Israel will observe my commandments, I will drive out the inhabitants of the land that I will give unto you. Israel must not make alliances with the inhabitants of that land, for such will be a snare to them.

"They must destroy the altars, break down the images, and destroy everything that relates to the pagan cults of the people in that land. They must worship no other gods, for the Lord, whose name is Jehovah, is a jealous God. They must not take the daughters of the land to be their sons' wives, lest their sons go after other gods. And they must not make them molten gods.

"They must keep the feast of the unleavened bread in remembrance of their coming out of Egypt. And all of their firstborn, man and beast, are mine and shall be sacrificed unto me. However, the firstborn of the ass shall either be redeemed with a lamb or its neck shall be broken. Also, the firstborn of the sons of Israel shall be redeemed with a lamb. They shall also keep the feast of weeks and the feast of ingathering, for I require every covenant male among you to appear before me three times each year. If Israel will do this, I will cast out nations before them, I will enlarge their borders, and no man shall desire their land."

During those forty days and forty nights that Moses was with Jehovah on the mountain, he neither ate nor drank. And Jehovah wrote his Ten Commandments and his covenant with Israel on the newly hewn tablets of stone.

When Moses descended from the mountain his face shone with a brilliant whiteness and the people were afraid to come near him. But, when he called to them, Aaron and the leaders of the congregation came near to be taught.

After Moses had taught their leaders, all of the children of Israel gathered to receive the commandments that Jehovah had given him on Mount Sinai. And because of the brilliance of Moses' face, he covered it with a veil while he talked with them.

---

[140] Note that Exodus 33 and the chapters that follow it, to the end of Exodus, appear to be out of sequence. Chapter 33 speaks of the tabernacle as already being built, but it was not begun until chapter 35. The sequence of these stories reflects what seems to be the correct sequence of the events.

[141] The holy order spoken of was the Melchizedek Priesthood. The Book of Mormon also uses this title to refer to the higher priesthood.

59—THE TABERNACLE

(Exodus 35–40; Leviticus 8)

After Moses had taught the children of Israel the Law that Jehovah had given him on the mountain, he told them about the tabernacle that he had been commanded to build. He also told them that Jehovah had asked the children of Israel to donate the fine and precious materials required for the project.

The people were excited when they heard it. They went quickly to their tents and brought back their offerings for the work. They brought precious gifts, according to the materials that were required, each one as the Spirit moved his heart.

Moses called two men—Bezaleel of the tribe of Judah and Aholiab of the tribe of Dan—to direct the building of the tabernacle. Jehovah had prepared these men, both of them skilled artisans, to build his holy house. Other men with wisdom and skill were also called, and the work proceeded according to the pattern that Jehovah had shown to Moses.

The people of Israel were more than generous. Precious offerings were brought in great abundance. Finally the workers spoke to Moses and told him that the people had given much more material than was needed. So Moses sent a notice throughout the camp that no more offerings were required.

When the tabernacle and the ark of the covenant were completed according to Jehovah's instructions, the workers prepared the sacred clothing to be worn by Aaron and his sons as they served in the priest's office. When Moses saw that the work was finished and that it was good, he pronounced his blessings upon those who had done it.

Then Jehovah spoke to Moses saying, "Assemble this tabernacle on the first day of the month, put the ark of the covenant into it, and cover the ark with the veil."

Jehovah explained the placement of the furnishings within the tabernacle, and gave further instructions concerning the priests. "Put the holy garments on Aaron," he said, "then anoint him and sanctify him that he may minister in the priest's office. Also bring his sons, clothe them with coats, and anoint them just as you anoint their father, that they also may serve as priests. Their anointings will be for an everlasting priesthood throughout their generations." And Moses did as Jehovah commanded him.

When the tabernacle and the ark of the covenant were ready, Moses, Aaron, and Aaron's sons washed their hands and feet at the laver[142] between the tent and the altar. Having washed, they erected the walls to create the outer court.

When everything had been done according to Jehovah's instructions, Moses took the anointing oil that had been prepared and anointed the tabernacle. He anointed the furnishings, the vessels, and all the implements that were in the tabernacle. He also offered sacrifices and burnt offerings to Jehovah as he had been commanded. To sanctify Aaron and his sons, Moses sprinkled them and their sacred clothing with the anointing oil and the blood from the sacrifices. Then he instructed them to remain in the tabernacle for seven days to complete their consecration.

When all of these things were accomplished, a cloud covered the tent of the congregation and Jehovah's glory filled the tabernacle. The cloud was upon the tabernacle by day, and fire was upon it by night, in the sight of all the children of Israel. And thus it remained throughout their travels in the wilderness.

When the cloud was taken up from the tabernacle, the children of Israel went forward on their journey. And when the cloud rested on the tabernacle, the people rested.

---

[142] A laver is a large washbasin.

60—MY PRESENCE SHALL GO WITH YOU

(Exodus 33; Leviticus 9; Numbers 2; Deuteronomy 9)

The tabernacle was built according to the pattern Jehovah had shown to Moses on Mount Sinai. And when Israel was encamped, the tabernacle was set up in the center of the camp, while the tribes—with their tents afar off—surrounded it. Every tent was set up with its door facing the tabernacle. On the East were Judah, Issachar, and Zebulun; on the South Reuben, Simeon, and Gad; on the West Ephraim, Manasseh, and Benjamin; and on the North Dan, Asher, and Naphtali. The tribe of Levi set their tents in the midst of the camp, closer to the tabernacle. Moses called it the tabernacle of the congregation or the tent of meeting, and everyone who sought Jehovah went out to the tabernacle.

When Moses entered the tabernacle, the cloudy pillar descended and stood at the door, and Jehovah talked to Moses face-to-face, as a man talks to his friend. And when the people saw the cloudy pillar, they bowed down and worshipped at the doors of their tents.

Moses pleaded with Jehovah to forgive his people of their sins and go with them into the wilderness. "I have been commanded to lead this people to the land that Thou hast promised them," said Moses, "but Thou hast not yet shown who will go with me. Thou hast also said that I would know Thee by name and would have grace in Thy sight. If I have truly found grace in Thy sight, make it known to me if the people of Israel are Thy people. We will surely know that these are Thy people if Thou wilt go with us. For, if so, we will be a special people, a people separated from all other peoples of the earth. But if Thy presence will not go with us into the wilderness, please do not lead us forth out of this place."

When Jehovah had heard Moses' petition, he relented from his earlier stance. "My presence shall go with you," he answered Moses, "and I will give you rest. Because you have found grace in my sight and I know you by name, I will do what you have asked."

Then Moses became bolder. "Show me Thy glory, O Lord," he requested.

"I will make all my goodness pass before you," Jehovah answered, "and I will proclaim my name before you, but I will be gracious to whom I will be gracious and I will show mercy to whom I will show mercy. I will not allow you to see my face at this time," he said, "lest my anger be kindled against you also and I destroy both you and your people. None of the people of Israel shall see me at this time for they are sinful, and no sinful man has seen my face at any time. Neither can a sinful man see my face and live."

Then Jehovah, showing great love for his prophet, said to Moses, "There is a place where you shall stand on a rock and, while my glory passes by you, I will put you in the cleft of the rock and cover you with my hand. Then I shall take away my hand and you shall see my back, but you shall not see my face as you have at other times. For I am angry with my people Israel."

Though Jehovah was angry with them, the children of Israel were privileged to see more manifestations of his power. On the eighth day, Moses called Aaron and his sons and commanded them to prepare a burnt offering for the sins of the people. "For," Moses said to the people, "Jehovah will appear to you today."

While the children of Israel stood by and watched, Aaron prepared the burnt offering on the altar as Moses gave him directions. When the offering was prepared, Aaron lifted his hand toward the people, and Moses and Aaron went inside the tabernacle. When they came out, they blessed the people. Then—as all Israel watched in great wonderment—fire came down from heaven and consumed the burnt offering that lay upon the altar. When the people saw it, they shouted and fell on their faces.

61–THE LEVITES
SHALL BE MINE

(Leviticus 6, 10; Numbers 3, 18; Deuteronomy 10)

Jehovah instructed Moses that the fire upon the altar in the outer court of the tabernacle was never to be extinguished.[143] And Aaron and his sons were assigned to provide fuel for the flame and tend it as part of their priestly service. No sacrifice was to be offered to Jehovah except in this fire. And no incense was to be burned by the priest unless the fire came from this altar. Fire from any other source was considered "strange fire" and was unacceptable to God.

Aaron's sons, Nadab and Abihu, apparently did not understand the importance of this instruction. And when they lit their censers, or incense burners, with strange fire, fire came down from heaven and slew them. Thus, at the cost of the lives of two of Jehovah's priests, the difference between the holy and the unholy, between the clean and the unclean, became very clear.

Because Nadab and Abihu had no children, Aaron, Eleazar, and Ithamar were left alone to minister in the priest's office. Their assigned tasks were many and exacting, and there was much required of them—much more than they could ever do by themselves. It would be impossible for them to do what was required when the tabernacle had to be moved with the camp.

When the need for more help in the priest's office became evident, Jehovah spoke to Moses, saying, "Bring the tribe of Levi and present them to Aaron the priest, that they may help him. They shall care for the tabernacle and assist with the details of the priest's office. They shall keep your charge and the charge of all the tabernacle, but if they come near to the vessels of the sanctuary or to the altar, either they or you shall die.

"The entire tribe of Levi will I give to Aaron, and they shall wait on him in the priest's office. They shall take charge of the tabernacle only, but responsibility for the sanctuary and the altar is charged to you and your sons. Any other person who comes near to these things shall be put to death."

Jehovah continued: "I have chosen the Levites from among the children of Israel instead of the firstborn, and they shall be mine. They are mine because the firstborn are mine, both man and beast, and I sanctified them unto myself on the day that I smote the firstborn in the land of Egypt."

Jehovah commanded Moses to count the males of Levi from one month old and upward. They were all counted; the descendants of Gershon numbered 7,500, the descendants of Kohath numbered 8,600, and the descendants of Merari numbered 6,200. Each family of Levi's three sons was given specific assignments as directed by Jehovah.[144]

According to instructions given by Jehovah, the Levites were brought before the congregation of Israel, where they were cleansed and purified. They washed their clothes, shaved their bodies, and Aaron offered a young bullock as a sin offering for them.

Jehovah explained that the descendants of Levi were to have no inheritance of land with the other tribes in the promised land. Levi's inheritance, instead, was to be Jehovah or service to Jehovah, and the tithes of the children of Israel were to provide their support. However, only those Levites between thirty and fifty years of age would serve actively in the tabernacle.[145]

When the camp of Israel moved and it became necessary to move the tabernacle, Aaron and his sons were charged to cover all of the holy things and to prepare them to be moved by the Levites. Jehovah did not want the Levites to touch that which was holy and die.

---

[143] This instruction about the perpetual fire on the altar is in Leviticus 6:12–13. This obviously posed some difficulties when the tabernacle was disassembled and moved from one place to another. It appears that someone (some of the Levites) had to transport the fire.

[144] The three men named here—Gershon, Kohath, and Merari—were the three sons of Levi and thus the nominal heads of the Levites. Kohath was the ancestor of Moses and Aaron. All of the priests, as descendants of Aaron, were Kohath's descendants. Also, Kohath's other descendants, the Kohathites, had superior standing among the Levites.

[145] Some scriptures (see Numbers 8:24) say the Levites were to serve in the tabernacle from age 25 to 50.

V

THROUGH THE WILDERNESS

AND INTO CANAAN

62–THE BURDEN OF AN UNGRATEFUL PEOPLE

(Numbers 10–11)

The children of Israel had camped for several months in the wilderness near Mount Sinai and were anxious to resume their journey toward the promised land. At Jehovah's direction, Moses made two silver trumpets to help him communicate with the people. Aaron's sons, Eleazar and Ithamar, were to be the trumpeters.

When both trumpets were blown, the people assembled at the door of the tabernacle. If only one call was sounded, the princes, or heads of thousands, assembled. The trumpets were used to signal many things. They signaled when and how the camp was to move as they began each journey, and they signaled when they were to go to war. The trumpets were also blown as a remembrance before God on feast days, at the start of each new month, and over all burnt offerings and sacrifices.

On the twentieth day of the second month of the second year after Israel came out of Egypt, the pillar of the cloud rose from the tabernacle, according to the sign that Jehovah had given,[146] and the children of Israel began their journey. They traveled in a northeasterly direction, following the cloud. The Levites led the way, bearing the ark of the covenant and the tabernacle. The tribes in their order, each with its own standard bearer, followed.

After three days' journey, the cloud rested and the tabernacle was set up. But because of the murmurings of the people, fire was sent by Jehovah and consumed many of those in the outward parts of the camp. Moses called the place Taberah[147] because the fire of Jehovah burned among them.

The people complained to Moses because they were hungry for meat. "We remember the fish that we ate in abundance in Egypt," they said, "the cucumbers, melons, leeks, onions, and garlic, also. But here we have nothing but manna."

Jehovah was angry because of the ungrateful murmurings of the people, and Moses was frustrated. He went to Jehovah in prayer. "Why hast Thou placed the burden of these ungrateful people on me?" he asked. "What have I done to find such disfavor in Thy sight? Did I beget these people that Thou didst say to me 'Carry them in your bosom and nurse them as a sucking child'? I cannot provide meat for them, and I can no longer bear this burden alone. If I have found favor with Thee, O Lord, kill me now and deliver me from this misery."

Jehovah had compassion for Moses, but not enough to kill him. He felt that there was a better solution to Moses' problems. He commanded Moses to gather seventy of the elders of Israel at the tabernacle, where he would give them responsibility to stand with Moses in governing the people. "I will come down and talk with you there," said Jehovah. "And I will take the Spirit that is in you and put it in them that they may share this burden with you."

Jehovah spoke also concerning the desire of the people for meat. "Tell them to sanctify themselves against the morrow," he said. "Because their weeping has come up into my ears, I will give them meat to eat. They shall not have meat for one day only, nor for two, nor for five, nor even for ten or twenty days—but they shall eat meat for a month. Because they have questioned why I brought them out of Egypt, they shall eat meat until it comes out their nostrils and is repulsive to them."

Moses was puzzled and concerned. "Where will meat come from to feed them for a month?" he asked. "There are 600,000 men in Israel's camp. Shall we slay all our flocks to feed them? Or shall the fish of the sea be gathered together for them?"

"Has my hand waxed short?" asked Jehovah. "Watch and see how my word is fulfilled!"

Moses went to the people and told them all that Jehovah had said. Then he gathered the seventy elders to the tabernacle. As the elders were seated there around the tabernacle, Jehovah came down in a cloud and spoke to them. As he had promised, Jehovah took of the Spirit that was in Moses and bestowed it on them. And when it rested upon them, they prophesied without ceasing.

Though two of the leading elders of the people, Eldad and Medad, had not gone out to the tabernacle with the others, the Spirit rested on them in the camp and they prophesied to the people. Some of the people became concerned because of this prophesying and sent two young men out to the tabernacle to tell Moses. When the matter had been told, Joshua, who was Moses' servant or minister, said, "Moses, my lord, you must forbid these men from prophesying."

But Moses saw the matter differently. He replied, "Do you envy Eldad and Medad for my sake, Joshua? I would to God that all of Jehovah's people were prophets and that he would put his Spirit upon all of them."

In further fulfillment of what he had told Moses, Jehovah sent a wind that brought quail from the sea, letting them fall round about Israel's camp. There were so

---

[146] See story "59–The Tabernacle."

[147] The name Taberah means "burning."

many quail that they were two cubits deep[148] and extended beyond the camp about a day's journey in every direction. The children of Israel were excited and began to gather quail. Many gathered quail all that day, all that night, and all the next day. Those who gathered least gathered ten homers[149] and spread them throughout the camp.

The greed of the people was too much for Jehovah. While the quail flesh was still unchewed between their teeth, Jehovah's anger was kindled against them and they were stricken with a great plague. And the place was named Kibroth-hattaavah[150] because the people who lusted were buried there.

The pillar of the cloud next rose from the tabernacle and led Israel's camp from Kibroth-hattaavah to Hazeroth, where they stayed for a short season.

63—WHAT KIND OF PROPHET?
(Numbers 12)

Life in the wilderness was not easy, and it was difficult for the children of Israel to focus on the blessings they received rather than on their difficulties and challenges. Criticism and murmuring seemed to be contagious. When one person complained, others joined in the carping. Not only did the average Israelite have problems, but also those in prominent positions sometimes complained. This was, after all, not the land flowing with milk and honey that they had been promised. And Moses, although greatly blessed by Jehovah, was a very humble man and did not always stand up for himself. He was, as the scripture says, meek above all men on the earth.[151]

While Israel was encamped at Hazeroth, Aaron and Miriam, Moses' brother and sister, raised their voices against him. They spoke against Moses openly among the people because he married an Ethiopian woman—a choice they questioned. "What kind of prophet would make such a choice?" they asked. "Are not the things we say just as good as what Moses says? Has Jehovah spoken to Israel only through Moses? Has he not also spoken through us?" And one complaint led to another.

When Jehovah heard these complaints, he spoke suddenly to all three—Moses, Aaron, and Miriam—telling them to leave the camp and go to the tabernacle. As they went out, Jehovah came down in the pillar of the cloud and stood in the tabernacle door. When he called to Aaron and Miriam, both came forth. "Hear now my words," said Jehovah. "If there is a prophet among the people, I will make myself known to him in a vision and will speak to him in a dream. There are many such prophets. But my servant Moses, who is faithful in all my house, is like no other prophet. I speak to him openly, even mouth to mouth, and not in dark speeches. And when I speak to him, he beholds my likeness. Why then," Jehovah asked in anger, "did you not fear to speak out against my servant Moses?" Jehovah's fierce anger had indeed been kindled in Moses' behalf.

When Jehovah had departed with the cloud, Miriam's skin became leprous and white as snow. When Aaron saw it, he said to Moses, "Alas, my lord, do not charge this sin to us. I know we have done foolishly and have sinned, but this is more than we can

---

[148] That would be about thirty-six inches (0.9144 meters) deep.

[149] A homer is about 6.5 U.S. bushels (about 230 liters) (see *Bible Dictionary*, LDS-KJV, s.v. "Weights and Measures").

[150] The name Kibroth-hattaavah means "graves of lust."

[151] This is an interesting commentary on Moses' meekness, but we should remember that Moses was the author (see Numbers 12:3).

bear. Let Miriam not be as one who is dead, like one who is leprous from her mother's womb."

And Moses, having compassion for Miriam although she had spoken against him, cried to Jehovah in his sister's behalf: "Heal her, O God, I beseech Thee!"

Jehovah answered in response to Moses' pleadings. "If Miriam's father had spit in her face, she would be ashamed for seven days," said Jehovah. "Should she not bear as much shame for this? Let her be shut out from the camp seven days, and then be received again."

So Miriam was cast out of the camp for seven days while Israel remained at Hazeroth. She was then brought back, healed of her leprosy. When she returned, the camp of Israel moved from Hazeroth, going northward, to pitch their tents in the Wilderness of Paran.

64—FORTY YEARS FOR FORTY DAYS

(Numbers 13−14; Deuteronomy 1)

While Israel was encamped at Kadesh in the Wilderness of Paran, not far from the borders of the promised land, Jehovah instructed Moses to send spies into Canaan to learn what challenges they would face when they entered the land. Twelve leaders of the people were sent, one from each tribe. Israel had already been two years in the wilderness and they looked forward to the end of this ordeal.

"Go and see what the land is like," said Moses. "See also what the people are like—whether they are strong or weak, many or few. See whether the land is good, and whether there is wood in the land. See what their cities are like and whether the people dwell in tents or in strongholds. Bring back also some fruit of the land for us to see."

The spies went as Moses directed, observing the land and its peoples for forty days. When they returned, they brought grapes, pomegranates, and figs with them. Once back in the camp of Israel at Kadesh, they came before the people and showed the fruit that they had found. "We went into the land where you sent us," they reported, "and surely it flows with milk and honey. However, we have bad news; the people who dwell there are very strong. They live in great walled cities, and the land is covered with people—the Amalekites in the south; the Hittites, Jebusites, and Amorites in the mountains; and the Canaanites by the sea and in the coasts of Jordan. We do not have the strength to go up against these people, for they are stronger than we are."

The report of the spies was less than optimistic and great murmurings stirred throughout the crowd. But not all the spies agreed with this report. Caleb, the spy from the tribe of Judah, rose and stilled the people. "Let us go up and possess the land at once," he said. "We are able to overcome it."

"No, no!" cried the other spies. "The people we saw are men of great stature. We also saw giants—the sons of Anak—in the land, and we are in size to them as grasshoppers are to us."

When the people of Israel heard this, they lifted their voices and cried. There was great weeping throughout the night, and there began to be murmuring once more against Moses and Aaron. "Would to God that we had died in Egypt," they complained, "or that we had died in the wilderness! Why has Jehovah brought us here to fall by the sword and that our wives and children should be prey? Let us go back to Egypt."

Moses and Aaron fell on their faces before the people, and two of the spies, Joshua from the tribe of Ephraim and Caleb from the tribe of Judah, rent their clothing. These two cried out to the children of Israel saying, "The land that we passed through is exceedingly good; it flows with milk and honey. If Jehovah delights in us, he will bring us into the land and give it to us, for so he has promised. We must not fear the people of the land, for Jehovah is with us and not with them."

The people became as an unruly mob. Because of the great fear planted in their hearts by the ten spies, they became angry with Joshua and Caleb and called for them to be stoned.

Then suddenly, in the midst of the confusion, the glory of Jehovah appeared before them as a pillar of a cloud in the tabernacle. "How long will this people provoke me?" Jehovah asked Moses. "How long will it be before they believe me and believe the signs that I have shown them? I will smite them with pestilence and disinherit them. For surely I can make of you a greater and a mightier nation than they."

"Do not destroy them," Moses pleaded. "For the Egyptians will hear of it and tell it to the inhabitants of the land. They have been told that Thou art among this people, that Thou art seen face-to-face, that Thy cloud stands over them, and that Thou goest before them—by day in a pillar of a cloud and by night in a pillar of fire. If Thou shouldst destroy this people now, those nations will say that Thou didst slay them in the wilderness because Thou couldst not bring them into the land that Thou didst promise to them.

"Therefore, forgive the iniquity of this people according to the greatness of Thy mercy, O Jehovah, and as Thou hast forgiven them from Egypt until now."

"I will forgive as you have asked," replied Jehovah to Moses, "for as I live, all the earth shall be filled with my glory. But, because this people has failed to hearken to my voice, they shall never see the land that I promised to their fathers. They shall all die in the wilderness—all who are twenty years old and upward—because they murmured against me. Only Caleb and Joshua shall come into the land. Yea, I will bring my servant Caleb into the promised land and his seed shall possess it because he had another spirit with him and has followed me fully.

"It is those who are now children that I will bring into the land, but they shall wander in the wilderness for forty years, until their fathers are dead. This people shall surely know of my displeasure, for as the spies were forty days in the land, Israel shall be one year in the wilderness for each of those days."

When Moses told these things to the people, they mourned greatly. They arose early in the morning and went to the top of the mountain where they pleaded with Jehovah to forgive them and let them enter the land, but their pleadings were in vain. Moses said to them, "Why do you break the commandments of God? You cannot go into the land because Jehovah is no longer with you. Because you turned away from him, he has also turned away from you. And if you go up into the land now, you will fall by the sword."

In spite of Moses' warnings, many people left the camp, still determined to enter the promised land, but neither the ark of the covenant nor Moses left the camp. Those who went were attacked by the inhabitants of the land and many were slain. The survivors returned weeping, but Jehovah did not hearken to their cries. And the ten spies who brought the evil report to the children of Israel died of a plague.

65—THE PRIESTHOOD
AND THE PLAGUE
(Numbers 16–17)

Complaints were common among the children of Israel while they were in the wilderness. It seems that everyone had something to complain about. Even if there were no real problems, the people were able to imagine some. And some of those imagined problems led the people to rebellion.

One day 250 men of Israel came to Moses and Aaron complaining because they were not allowed to minister in the priest's office. A Levite named Korah led the group, along with two men from the tribe of Reuben named Dathan and Abiram. "These men take too much on yourselves," they said, speaking of Aaron and the priests. "All the men of Israel are holy and Jehovah is among them, yet those who have been called as priests think they are better than the congregation."

Moses fell on his face when he heard the complaint. He could not believe that they would oppose the men whom God had chosen to bear the priesthood. Then to the company Moses said, "Jehovah will show you whom he has chosen. He will show you who is holy and will cause those whom he has chosen to come near to him."

Then Moses spoke directly to Korah, the Levite who was in charge. "Why are you not satisfied with the honor that Jehovah has given you?" Moses asked him. "Does it seem a small thing to you that God has separated the Levites from the rest of Israel to serve in the tabernacle and minister to the congregation? He has honored you to bring you near to him, yet you seek to have the priesthood also. And what has Aaron done that you also murmur against him?"

Moses did not wait for Korah's response but spoke to the entire group of rebels. "This is what you should do," he said, "to see whom Jehovah has chosen: come here tomorrow, each of you with a censer, and put fire and incense into it before Jehovah. Then the man whom Jehovah shall choose, that man shall be holy."

The next day, each man of Korah's group came with his censer in hand to the tabernacle with Moses and Aaron. Each put fire into his censer and laid incense on the fire. When all were gathered at the tabernacle door, the voice of Jehovah spoke to Moses and Aaron. "Separate yourselves from this congregation," said Jehovah, "that I may consume them in a moment."

When Moses and Aaron heard Jehovah's command they were stunned. "Shall one man sin and Thou be angry with the whole congregation?" they asked.

"Tell those who have come only to watch to move away from the tents of Korah, Dathan, and Abiram," replied Jehovah. "And tell them to touch nothing that belongs to these three wicked men, or they will be destroyed."

When Moses repeated Jehovah's instructions, the people moved back, while Korah, Dathan and Abiram stood with their families in the doors of their tents. Then Moses said, "This is how you shall know that Jehovah has sent me to do the mighty works that I have done. If the earth opens up and swallows these men, you may know that Jehovah has sent me and that these men have offended him."

As Moses finished speaking, the earth opened and swallowed the three men—they, their families, their tents, and all their goods. Then fire came down from heaven and burned the 250 men who offered incense.

At Moses' instruction, Eleazar the priest gathered the censers of those who were burned and made from them broad plates to cover the altar. These plates were to remind the children of Israel that no man not of Aaron's seed had authority to offer incense before Jehovah.

The following day, complaints arose among the people because of what happened to Korah and his followers. "You have killed the people of Jehovah," they said to Moses and Aaron.

"Will these complaints have no end?" thought Moses.

As Moses and Aaron went out to the tabernacle, Jehovah spoke to them again. "Separate yourselves from this wayward people," he said, "that I may consume them; and Moses and Aaron fell again upon their faces. That day 14,700 of the children of Israel died of the plague.

When the plague had passed, Jehovah told Moses that he would give the children of Israel a sign to show whom he had chosen to bear his the priesthood and officiate in the priest's office. "Have the head of each tribe bring you a rod," said Jehovah, "with each man's name on the rod that he brings. Aaron's name shall be on the rod for the tribe of Levi. When you have all the rods, lay them together in the tabernacle, and the rod of the man whom I have chosen to bear my priesthood shall bloom."

When Moses explained Jehovah's test to the people, they agreed to it. The heads of the twelve tribes brought their rods, wrote their names on them, and gave them to Moses. When all the rods had been brought, Moses put them in the tabernacle.

The following day when the people were gathered to see the result of the test, Moses retrieved the twelve rods from the tabernacle. And all the people beheld, to their amazement, that Aaron's rod had not only budded and bloomed but had also yielded almonds.

Then Jehovah instructed Moses to keep Aaron's rod in the ark of the covenant as a remembrance against the rebels, that all might know Jehovah's will concerning the priesthood.

66–SPEAK TO THE ROCK
(Numbers 20)

Israel had moved from the Wilderness of Paran to the Wilderness of Zin, but there was no water for them either to drink or to water their flocks. This was another chance for the people to find fault with Moses, and they took advantage of that opportunity. Their complaints were not new, for Moses had heard them all before. "Why have you brought us into this wilderness?" they whined. "That we and our cattle may die here? You have brought us out of Egypt to this terrible place where there are no seeds, nor figs, nor vines, nor pomegranates. Neither is there water for us to drink."

And once more Moses and Aaron took the complaints of the people to Jehovah. Leaving the assembly of Israel, they went to the door of the tabernacle, where they prostrated themselves upon the ground and pleaded with Jehovah in Israel's behalf.

"Take the rod that I have given you and go with Aaron and the assembly of Israel to the rock," Jehovah said to Moses. "There you shall speak to the rock before their eyes and bring forth water out of the rock that they and their animals may drink."

Moses took his rod from the tabernacle and went with Aaron and the people to the rock that Jehovah had identified. Then, as the congregation watched and listened, Moses spoke. "Hear now, you rebels," he said with great drama and untypical arrogance. "Must we fetch water out of this rock for you?" And then Moses struck the rock twice with his rod, causing water to flow in abundance.

The children of Israel were satisfied, but Jehovah was offended by what Moses and Aaron had done. When he spoke to them again, his message was sobering. "Because you did not obey me," said Jehovah, "and struck the rock with your rod instead of speaking to it, as I commanded you—and because you sought to take the glory to yourselves instead of giving it to me—you shall not bring this people into the promised land. I will call these waters the waters of Meribah[152] because the children of Israel strove with me and I was sanctified in them."

When the children of Israel were prepared to move again, the people of Edom[153] refused to let them pass through their lands but came out to battle against them.

---

[152] The name Meribah means "contention" or "strife."
[153] The people of Edom were the descendants of Esau, Jacob's brother. The close blood relationship between Israel and Edom, however, did not keep them from fighting with each other, even as they still do today.

Thus Moses changed his course and led Israel to Mount Hor. There at Mount Hor, Jehovah spoke to Moses concerning Aaron. "As I have told you before," said Jehovah, "because Aaron rebelled against my word at the waters of Meribah, he shall not enter into the promised land. You must now take him and Eleazar his son up onto Mount Hor. There you will remove the sacred clothing of the priest's office from Aaron and put it on Eleazar. Then Aaron will die and be gathered to his people."

Moses did as Jehovah had commanded him, going up onto Mount Hor with Aaron and Eleazar in the sight of all the people. There on top of the mountain, Moses removed the sacred clothing of the priest's office from his brother Aaron and put it on Aaron's son Eleazar. After this was done, Aaron died and was gathered to his people. When Moses and Eleazar had buried Aaron's body, they returned from the mountain to the camp of Israel, and the children of Israel mourned for Aaron thirty days.

67—THE BRASS SERPENT
(Numbers 21, Deuteronomy 29, Helaman 8)

Moses and the brass serpent on a stick

As the children of Israel traveled in the wilderness, Jehovah protected them and gave them victory against all who came against them in battle. Because Jehovah was with them, they were reputed as mighty warriors among all of the people round about. While they were still in the area of Mount Hor, they were attacked by the Canaanites, whom Jehovah delivered into their hands.

Besides being protected from their enemies, Israel was blessed in many other ways. Jehovah provided the food for them to eat, he made their clothing strong so that it did not wear out, and he made their feet that they did not swell.[154]

Following their victory over the Canaanites, the people of Israel traveled southward, going as far as the Red Sea[155] in order to avoid the land of Edom. The way was long and hard, and as the people grew very discouraged, they began to murmur once again against Jehovah and against Moses for bringing them out of Egypt. "We have come to loathe this light bread that you have given us to eat," they said.

When Jehovah tired of the complaints and murmurings of the people, he sent poisonous serpents into their camp. Many people died from the bites of the serpents, but the plague of the serpents also caused many to repent. They came to Moses saying, "We have sinned, for

---

[154] See Deuteronomy 8:4. This was truly an amazing thing. The scripture does not say that the clothing of the children grew with them, but that is certainly possible. With all the miracles that Israel experienced on a daily basis, it is amazing that they complained so much.
[155] This would have been the northern tip of the Gulf of Aqaba.

we have spoken against Jehovah and against you. Pray for us that Jehovah may take away these serpents."

And Moses prayed for the people.

In answer to Moses' prayers, Jehovah said, "Make a fiery serpent of brass and put it on a pole. Then, if the one who has been bitten will look upon the brass serpent, that person shall live."

Moses made a serpent of brass and put it on a pole before the people as Jehovah commanded him. And, as he did so, he testified that the serpent was a symbol of the Son of God who was to come. "As those who look upon this serpent shall live," said Moses, "as many as will look upon the Son of God with faith shall also live, even that they might have eternal life."

And it happened as Jehovah had said. If those who had been bitten would look upon the brass serpent that Moses had made, they did not die. But because this was such a simple thing, many—not believing that it would work—died because they refused to look.

68—THE CURSE OF BALAAM
(Numbers 21–24)

When the Amorites made war against the children of Israel rather than let them pass peacefully through their lands, Israel subdued them and occupied their cities. Israel also, in the process of defending themselves, defeated other peoples and possessed their lands. Jehovah was with the armies of Israel, and those who sought to subdue them had great reason to fear.

Thus, when Israel set up camp on the plains of Moab, Balak, king of the Moabites, was terrified. Israel's army was vast, and Balak knew what Israel had done to the Amorites. To the elders of Midian, his allies, he said, "Shall this company lick up all that are round about us, as an ox licks up the grass of the field?"

Because of his great fear of the children of Israel, Balak sent messengers to Pethor near the Euphrates River to find a prophet named Balaam.[156] "Behold," said Balak's message, "a people who have come out from Egypt cover the face of the earth and are now in my country. Come now and curse this people. For I know that he whom you bless is blessed and he whom you curse is cursed. These people are too mighty for me, but, if you will curse them, I might be able to drive them from my land."

"Lodge with me tonight," Balaam told the messengers. "I will give you an answer in the morning as Jehovah shall speak to me."

That night Jehovah spoke to Balaam and said, "Do not go with these men and do not curse the people about whom these men report, for they are a blessed people."

In the morning, Balaam spoke to the messengers. "Return to your own land," he said, "for Jehovah will not let me go with you." So the messengers returned to Balak and reported that Balaam had refused to come.

Balak did not give up. He sent other messengers to Balaam and promised him great honors and rewards if he would come and curse Israel. But Balaam answered: "Though Balak should give me his house full of silver and gold, I cannot do more or less than what Jehovah has told me. However, lodge here tonight that I may ask Jehovah again if I should go."

Balaam sought Jehovah a second time for an answer he had already received. This time Jehovah spoke to him and said, "You may go with these men if you wish but must speak only those words that I tell you." Ba-

---

[156] Balaam, it appears, was a false prophet. He is referred to in Joshua 13:22 as a soothsayer. He was slain by the armies of Israel in their campaign to free the lands east of the Jordan (see Numbers 31:8).

laam thought much about the rewards that were offered him and how they might improve his life. And though he knew from his earlier experience that Jehovah did not want him to go to Moab, he decided to go anyway. So Balaam arose the next day and went with the messengers, riding upon his ass.

Jehovah was angry with Balaam. He knew that he was going to Moab only because of the honors and rewards that were promised, and he sent an angel with a drawn sword to block Balaam's way. When Balaam's ass saw the angel—which Balaam could not see—she turned out into the field, and Balaam struck her to correct her course. The angel, however, stood in the way again at a place where there were walls on both sides. When the ass saw the angel she ran into the wall, crushing Balaam's foot. He struck her again.

Now the angel stood in a narrow place where they could not pass, and when the ass saw him this third time, she fell down. Balaam, in his anger, struck her again with his staff. Then Jehovah opened the ass's mouth and she spoke to Balaam. "Why have you struck me these three times?" she asked.

"Because you have mocked me," answered Balaam. "If I had my sword, I would kill you now."

"Am I not your ass?" she said. "You have ridden me since you first owned me, and have I ever been disloyal to you?"

"You have not," answered Balaam.

Then Jehovah opened Balaam's eyes to see the angel standing in the way with his sword drawn. Balaam, stunned, bowed his head, and fell to the earth. "Why have you stuck your beast three times?" asked the angel. "I came to stop you because the way you are going is wicked. If your ass had not seen me and turned three times, you would now be dead. She has saved your life."

"I have sinned," cried Balaam, "and if my going displeases you, I will now turn back."

"Go now," said the angel. "But you must speak only that which God speaks to you." So, Balaam continued on to Moab.

Balak came out to meet Balaam and said to him, "Why did you not come when I first bid you? Am I not able to give you honor?"

"The past does not matter," answered Balaam. "I am here now, but I have power to say only that which God puts into my mouth."

The next day Balak took Balaam to a place on the mountain where they could look out over the camp of Israel. "Build me seven altars," said Balaam, "and bring seven bullocks and seven rams." And, when the animals were brought, Balaam offered a bullock and a ram on each altar. He then said to Balak, "Stay here and I will go see what Jehovah tells me." And Balaam went up to a high place where Jehovah met him and taught him.

When Balaam returned he said to Balak, "You have brought me from the mountains of the east to curse Jacob and defy Israel, but I cannot curse what God has not cursed and I cannot defy what God has not defied. I saw this people of Jacob from the tops of the hills, and I know that they shall dwell alone and shall not be reckoned among the nations."

Balak was stunned. "What have you done to me?" he asked. "I brought you to curse my enemies and you have blessed them."

Then Balak took Balaam to a second place for a different view of Israel's camp, and again asked Balaam to curse them. Seven rams and seven bullocks were offered as before, and Balaam went up to meet Jehovah while Balak waited. When Balaam returned he said, "Rise up, Balak, and hear! God is not a man that he should lie, nor the son of man that he should repent. That which he speaks he shall make good. He has commanded me to bless these people, and I cannot reverse it. He said that he has not beheld iniquity in Jacob nor seen perverseness in Israel. He brought Israel out of Egypt and has given him the strength of a wild ox. There is no curse against this people."

"If what you say is true," said Balak, "then neither curse them nor bless them."

"I cannot," said Balaam, "for that which Jehovah speaks I must do."

Balak and Balaam went to a third high place where they built altars and offered sacrifices as before. Then Balaam turned his face and looked toward the wilderness. As he saw Israel in their tents, the Spirit of God came upon him and he was caught up in a vision. When the vision ended he said to Balak, "He who has heard the word of Jehovah and who has seen a vision says this to you: how goodly are the tents of Jacob and the dwellings of Israel! God has brought Israel out of Egypt and given them the strength of a wild ox. They shall devour the nations of their enemies, break their bones, and pierce them with arrows. They lie down as a great lion, and who shall stir them up? Blessed is he that blesses Israel, and cursed is he that curses them."

Balak was now very angry. "I brought you here to curse my enemies," he shouted, "but you have blessed them three times. Though I had thought to give you great honor, Jehovah has kept that honor from you."

Then Balaam replied, "I told your messengers that, though you would give me your house full of silver and gold, I could not go beyond Jehovah's commandment. For what Jehovah says, that must I speak. And now, before I return to my own people, I will tell you what Israel will do in the latter days."

Balaam then prophesied that, among other things, the Messiah would be born—at some future time—through Jacob's lineage. Then Balaam, son of Beor, returned to his home in Pethor, and Balak also went to his home.

69—HE WAS ZEALOUS FOR HIS GOD

(Numbers 25)

While the children of Israel dwelt at Shittim,[157] they developed a close relationship with their Moabite neighbors, but that close relationship led to problems. The men of Israel were enticed by the Moabites to worship the false god, Baal-peor.[158] They began to participate in fertility rites—being invited to the pagan sacrifices—and to commit adultery with the daughters of Moab.

As more people became involved in these awful sins of adultery and idolatry promoted by those who worshipped fertility gods, Jehovah spoke to Moses saying, "Take the leaders of the people and hang them up before me, facing the sun, that my fierce anger may be turned away."[159]

Moses instructed the judges of Israel that they must slay those men who had joined in the worship of Baal-peor. But, in addition to this, Jehovah caused a plague to come among them,[160] taking the lives of 24,000. This was not a joyful time in Israel's camp. There was great bitterness and weeping—and also much repentance—as the judgments of Jehovah came upon the people.

---

[157] Shittim was east of the Jordan, opposite Jericho. It was also known as Acacia. This was the last dwelling place of Israel before they were brought across Jordan into the promised land.

[158] Baal (plural form Baalim), the storm and fertility god, was symbolic of the male generative principle in nature. Baal worship was most common among the Zidonians or Phoenicians, but it seems that Baal's name (which means "lord") was used broadly in the Old Testament to refer to all heathen or foreign gods. When a scripture compounds a term such as "peor" with the name of Baal, the second word of the compound relates to some attribute of Baal, the place or manner of his worship, or something that a place possesses (see *Bible Dictionary*, LDS-KJV, s.v. "Baal"). The word "peor," which appears here, relates to a mountain peak by that name in the area. Baal-peor actually means "lord of the opening," that is, the opening for others to join in the worship. There is little doubt, from the context of this story, that this form of Baal worship involved immoral rites.

[159] The scriptures give no information about how this instruction was carried out.

[160] It is not clear from the scripture here, but the plague mentioned may not have been a disease but rather a slaying of the transgressors by the sword.

100

In the midst of these difficult times, one of the princes from the tribe of Simeon—a man named Zimri—brought a Midianite woman into the camp and took her to his tent.[161] And this he did openly in the sight of all the congregation of Israel as they wept before the door of the tabernacle.

When Phinehas, the son of Eleazar the priest, saw Zimri's bold disobedience, he rose from the congregation, took a javelin in his hand, and followed the disobedient couple into the tent. Once inside, he thrust both of them through with the javelin—and the plague was stopped.

Jehovah then spoke to Moses. "Phinehas has turned away my anger from the children of Israel, that I did not consume them in my jealousy," he said. "Tell him that I give him my covenant of peace. He and his seed after him shall have the covenant of an everlasting priesthood because he was zealous for his God and made an atonement for the children of Israel."

70—PREPARATION FOR THE PROMISED LAND
(Numbers 26–36)

The children of Israel had been a long time in the wilderness. Many nations had come against them in battle, but Jehovah had blessed them that they might prevail. He had remembered the covenants he had made with their fathers and was prepared to fulfill those covenants when the conditions were satisfied.

As Israel dwelt on the plains of Moab near Jordan, Jehovah spoke to Moses and Eleazar the priest and requested that they count the people. "Take the sum of all the congregation of Israel, from twenty years old and upward, who are able to go to war," he said. "Count them as you did at Sinai when the people first came out of Egypt."

Moses and Eleazar counted the men of Israel according to their tribes, and the total number was 601,730. They also counted the descendants of Levi, for their number was not included with the others. And there were 23,000 Levite males above the age of one month. Because forty years had passed since they came out of Egypt, this numbering of the people had special significance. For among those that were numbered, there was not one man—save Moses, Caleb, and Joshua—who was over twenty when the count was taken at Sinai.[162]

Jehovah promised that each tribe of Israel would receive an inheritance of land appropriate to its size, though the land that each received would be decided by casting lots. The tribe of Levi was to receive no inheritance of land, but the other tribes were commanded to give Levi forty-eight cities, together with the open fields around them. Six of these cities were to be cities of refuge to which a person who had accidentally taken the life of another might flee for safety.

Jehovah warned Moses of the importance of driving out those who now possessed the land and destroying all trappings and traces of these peoples' pagan religions. "For, if you do not drive them out," he said, "those who remain will become as pricks in your eyes and thorns in your sides. They will vex you in the land, and I will do to you as I thought to do to them."

"Go up into the mountains of Abarim," Jehovah said to Moses, "and see the land that I will give to the children of Israel. When you have seen it, you shall be

---

[161] It is interesting that the woman is a Midianite rather than a Moabite. Perhaps Zimri rationalized that Jehovah was displeased only by Israel's immoral acts with the Moabites and that it was all right to be immoral with a Midianite.

[162] The scriptures do not say so, but it appears from the record that Eleazar the priest, Aaron's son, may also have been part of this select group of men enumerated at Sinai who were still living.

gathered to your people, as was Aaron your brother. You—as Aaron—shall not enter that land because you disobeyed me in Kadesh at the waters of Meribah and did not sanctify me in the eyes of the people."[163]

Realizing now that his time among the people was short, Moses said to Jehovah, "Let Jehovah choose a man to lead this congregation, that they be not as sheep without a shepherd."

And Jehovah answered, "Take Joshua,[164] the son of Nun, a man in whom is the Spirit of God, to stand in your place. Present him before Eleazar and the congregation and give him a charge in their sight. Give him some of your power, that the children of Israel will obey him. He shall stand before Eleazar and ask counsel as revealed through the Urim and Thummim, and at the word of Joshua the people will go in and come out, even all this congregation. You shall also encourage him and strengthen him, for he is the one who shall lead this people over Jordan to inherit the land."

Moses did as Jehovah commanded and set Joshua before Eleazar and the congregation. As he laid his hands on Joshua's head, he gave him the holy priesthood, charged him to seek the counsel of the priest, and gave encouragement to strengthen him in his calling.

---

[163] See story "66—Speak to the Rock."

[164] The Hebrew name *Joshua* is the same name as the Greek name *Jesus*. The name means "Jehovah is [his] help." The prophet Joshua was certainly a type of the Savior who later came bearing the same name.

71—MOSES' FAREWELL
(Deuteronomy 1–34)

As Moses neared the end of his life and the children of Israel were encamped on the plains of Moab, poised to enter the promised land, he preached three great sermons, reminding his people of Jehovah's covenants with them and of the great blessings they had received. He recounted much of the history of Israel's forty years in the wilderness to show how the hand of Jehovah was evident in their lives. But Moses primarily used these sermons to clarify the Law that Jehovah had given to govern them. These sermons are recorded in the book of Deuteronomy, which means "repetition of the law."

Moses reminded Israel why Jehovah had promised them the land of Canaan and why they were his chosen people. "You were not chosen for your righteousness," he told them, "nor for the uprightness of your hearts, for you are a stiffnecked people. You were chosen because of the wickedness of the nations who now dwell in the land and because of the covenant that Jehovah made with your fathers, Abraham, Isaac, and Jacob."

Moses taught the people the importance of loving God and teaching their children to love God. "Hear, O Israel," he said. "The Lord Jehovah is one God, and you shall love him with all your heart, with all your soul, and with all your might. These words shall be always in your heart, and you shall teach them to your children. You shall talk of them when you sit in your houses, when you walk by the way, when you lie down, and when you rise up."

Moses taught the children of Israel the things that would be most important for them to understand in order to prosper in the land of promise. Said he, "Jehovah requires nothing of you but to fear him, to walk in all his ways, to love him, to serve him, and to keep the commandments and statutes that he has given you."

He went on: "Behold, the heavens are Jehovah's and the earth also, together with all that is in them. Yet he delighted to love your fathers, and he chose their seed above all other peoples. You must, therefore, purify your hearts and be no more stiffnecked, for your God Jehovah is God of gods, and Lord of lords. He is a great and mighty God, who neither regards persons nor takes bribes. He deals justly with the fatherless and the widow. He loves the stranger and gives him food and raiment. And you too are commanded to love strangers, for you were strangers in the land of Egypt."

Moses gave a prophetic warning and prophecy to the children of Israel concerning kings and the problems that would beset Israel if they ever chose to have kings. "When you have come into the land that Jehovah your God will give you," said Moses, "and you shall say, 'Set a king over us like other nations,' then you shall set a king over you whom Jehovah will choose from among your brethren. And that king who is chosen must not multiply horses unto himself or cause the people to return to Egypt to multiply horses. Neither shall your king multiply wives unto himself, that his heart be not turned away. And he shall not multiply unto himself silver and gold.[165] Yea, the king you choose should read the Law and keep all the words of the Law and the statutes, that his heart be not lifted up above his brethren and that he turn not aside from the commandments."

Moses also prophesied of the future coming of the Savior. He said, "The Lord Jehovah will raise up unto you a prophet from among your brethren who is like me. He shall speak the words that God commands him to speak, and you shall hearken to him. And whoever will not hearken to the words that he will speak, will be called to account for his disobedience."

Moses taught the people the fruits of obedience. Said he, "If you will hearken to the voice of Jehovah and observe the commandments, he will set you above all nations. He will establish you as a holy people, and all the peoples of the earth will call you by his name and will be afraid of you. He will open to you his good treasure. He will open the heavens to give rain to your land in season and will bless all the works of your hands. He will not fail you nor forsake you."

When these messages were delivered, Jehovah called for Moses and Joshua to come to the tabernacle where he warned them that the people of Israel would go astray after false gods, break their covenants, forsake Jehovah, and blame Jehovah for the evils that would come upon them. Then Jehovah charged Joshua, "Be strong and of a good courage, Joshua, for you shall bring Israel into the land that I swore to give them, and I will be with you."

Moses and Joshua then called the elders of Israel together and Moses addressed them. "I know that after my death you will corrupt yourselves and turn aside from the way that I have commanded you," he told them. "And evil will befall you because you will do evil in the sight of Jehovah."

That same day Jehovah spoke again and told Moses to go up to Mount Nebo in the mountains of Abarim and look out over the promised land. "You shall die there on the mount," said Jehovah, "and be gathered unto your people."

Moses knew that his time was now very short. But before going to the mountain, he called the children of Israel together one last time and pronounced a blessing upon each tribe. It was with deep regret that he was now leaving them behind. Though they had caused him much heartache, he loved them dearly.

As Moses came to the top of the mountain and looked out across the land, Jehovah said to him, "This is the land that I swore to Abraham, Isaac, and Jacob that I would give to their seed. I have caused you to see it, but you shall not go over." Then, there on the mountain, Jehovah took Moses into heaven without tasting death,[166] just as he had taken the people of Enoch many years before.

When Israel had mourned for Moses thirty days, Joshua the son of Nun became their leader, for Moses had so ordained him. But there was never another prophet in Israel like unto Moses, the man whom Jehovah knew face to face.

---

[165] These three warnings: not to multiply horses (i.e., not to build up military power), not to multiply wives, and not to multiply silver and gold were in fact the very things that brought about the downfall of King Solomon (see story "142−Because You Have Broken My Covenant"). Moses' warning about kings also relates to the circumstances described in story "97−That We Might Be Like Other Nations," where the people pleaded with the prophet Samuel to replace their judges with a king so that they could be like other nations.

[166] The Old Testament does not actually say that Moses was translated, or taken into heaven without tasting death. Deuteronomy 34:5–6 says that "the LORD [Jehovah]" buried him in a valley in the land of Moab, and that, "no man knoweth his sepulchre unto this day." The Book of Mormon, however (Alma 45:19), says that "the Lord took Moses unto himself", which suggests that he was translated. It is also generally understood—based on the fact that Moses and Elijah (called Elias in the New Testament) appeared on the Mount of Transfiguration with Jesus (see Matthew 17 and Mark 9) to bestow priesthood keys on Peter, James, and John—that Moses was also translated. This bestowal of priesthood authority would have been impossible without a physical body. Moses and Elijah also restored those same priesthood keys to Joseph Smith and Oliver Cowdery in the Kirtland Temple on April 3, 1836 (see Doctrine and Covenants 110).

72—JEHOVAH HAS GIVEN YOU THIS LAND

(Joshua 1–2)

After Moses' passing, Jehovah spoke to Joshua, the man chosen to be Moses' successor. "Rise up, Joshua," he said, "and take this people over Jordan into the land that I will give them. For I will give this people every place upon which the soles of your feet shall tread. Your borders shall be from the wilderness of Lebanon, to the River Euphrates, to the great sea.

Jehovah continued his charge to Joshua: "There will be no man superior to you as long as you live. As I was with Moses, so will I be with you, but you must be strong and courageous and keep the Law that Moses gave you. If you will do this, your way shall be prosperous and you will inherit this land that I swore to give to your fathers."

Joshua sent out word to the children of Israel to prepare to cross the Jordan and inherit the land within three days. "We will do as you command us," they answered. "We will go wherever you send us. For as we hearkened to Moses, so will we hearken to you and put to death any who do not obey your words."

Joshua, who had been a spy himself forty years earlier,[167] sent two spies to Jericho in the land of Canaan to see what they could learn about the city and its people. Once in Jericho, they lodged at the house of Rahab the harlot.[168]

---

[167] See story "64–Forty Years for Forty Days" where the story is told of Joshua being a faithful spy from the tribe of Ephraim two years after Israel came out of Egypt.

[168] It is possible that Rahab was not a harlot. The Hebrew word for harlot is "zonah." This word has the same root as "mazon," which means "food." Thus, a possible translation might be "woman of food," or "innkeeper." It is true that ancient inns did keep harlots, but it did not necessarily follow that one who kept an inn was a harlot (see Victor Ludlow, *Unlocking the Old Testament* [Salt Lake City: Deseret Book Co., 1981], 55 [citing Adam Clarke, *Clarke's Bible Commentary* (New York: Abingdon Press, n.d.) 2:11]). What may be more important, however, is the fact that even harlots can show faith in God and repent. There can be no doubt that God blessed Rahab because of her good works. It would be logical to assume that the spies might go to an inn and mingle with the guests as they sought information about the land and the state of the peoples' minds.

When the king of Jericho heard that there were Israelite spies at Rahab's house, he sent men requesting that Rahab turn the spies over to him. But Rahab, who had hid the spies among some stocks of flax on her roof, told the king's agents, "The men you seek were here, but I did not know who they were. However, when it was dark—about the time of the closing of the city gate—they left. If you go quickly you will surely overtake them."

After the king's men were gone, Rahab went to the roof and talked with the spies. "I know that Jehovah has given you this land," she said, "and all the people are afraid. We have heard how Jehovah dried up the Red Sea when you came out of Egypt and how you destroyed the Amorites on the other side of the Jordan. When we heard these things, we were filled with great fear, for Jehovah is God both in the heavens above and on the earth beneath." Then Rahab pleaded with them to spare her life and the lives of her father's household when Israel came to possess the land.

"We will save you and your father's house," they assured her, "if you do not disclose our business. When Jehovah has given us the land, we will deal kindly and truly with you." It was agreed that Rahab would use a line of scarlet string to mark her window in the city wall. "But, if any of your family leaves your house, their blood will be on their own heads," said the spies. "However, if they remain with you in the house and any hand comes upon them, their blood will be on our heads. Nevertheless, if you tell our secret, we will not be bound by this agreement."

"It shall be according to your words," responded Rahab. And when she let them down from her window by a cord, she warned them to hide in the mountains for three days until their pursuers returned to the city.

Rahab bound the scarlet string in her window, and—after seeing how and where she had bound it—the spies went to the mountains, where they waited. Then, after three days, they descended the mountain and returned to Joshua and the children of Israel with their report. "Truly," they said, "Jehovah has delivered this land into our hands. The inhabitants of the country are all faint because of us."

73—JEHOVAH WILL DO WONDERS AMONG YOU

(Joshua 3–4)

The forty years that Jehovah had given the children of Israel to remain in the desert had now passed, and the time had come for them to cross the Jordan and inhabit the land that Jehovah had promised to their faithful fathers. When the camp of Israel had moved from Shittim to the river, the leaders went through the camp giving their final instructions. "When you see the priests move forward bearing the ark of the covenant," they said, "then shall you leave your places and follow it. But you must keep 2,000 cubits[169] between you and the ark so that you can clearly see the way that you should go."

Then Joshua gathered the people and said to them, "Sanctify yourselves, for tomorrow Jehovah will do wonders among you."

Finally, as the new day dawned, Joshua gave the signal for the priests to lift up the ark of the covenant and move forward toward the river.

Joshua had not proven himself as a leader, neither was it obvious to the people—though they had sworn to follow him—whether he would be able to call upon the powers of heaven to bless them as Moses had done. Thus, Jehovah spoke to Joshua to give him courage and ease his concerns. "This day will I begin to magnify you in the sight of all Israel," said Jehovah, "that they may know that I am with you as I was with Moses. You shall command the priests that bear the ark to go to the brink of the Jordan and to stand still in the water. When their feet shall rest in the water, the river shall be cut off from upstream and stand up in a heap, and the children of Israel shall pass through on dry land."

Jehovah continued his instruction to Joshua: "Choose twelve men from among you, one from each tribe, that each may take a stone from the midst of the river and carry it upon his shoulder to the place where you will camp tonight."

When Joshua had heard this, he called to the people. "Come here, Israel," he cried, "and hear the words of Jehovah. For by this shall you know that the living God is among you and that he will drive out the inhabitants of this land before you. When the feet of the priests who bear the ark enter the river, the waters of Jordan shall be cut off and you shall cross over on dry land."

Joshua next instructed one man from each tribe to carry a stone. "Pass over Jordan before the ark of God, every man with his stone," he told them. "These stones will be a sign among you so that you may tell your children how the waters were cut off before the ark of the covenant and the children of Israel came over Jordan on dry land."

The twelve men carried the stones on their shoulders to the place where they had determined to camp. And Joshua also set up twelve stones in the river, in the place where the priests had stood.

The priests who bore the ark of the covenant stood in the midst of the river until all the children of Israel had crossed. Then, when all were safely across, the priests carried the ark of the covenant through the river. And when their feet came out of the riverbed, the water came back and the river returned as it had been before.

That night as the children of Israel camped on the west side of the Jordan near the borders of Jericho, the twelve river stones were set up as a memorial. That pile of stones was to stand as a witness to all peoples of the earth that Jehovah had dried up the river before them and the host of Israel had crossed on dry land.

Through the events of that day, Joshua was magnified in the eyes of all Israel, and they revered him all the days of his life as they had revered Moses before him.

---

[169] That would be about 1,000 yards (914.4 meters).

74—THE CAPTAIN OF JEHOVAH'S ARMY
(Joshua 5)

The people of the land of Canaan were afraid when they heard that Jehovah had dried up the waters of Jordan for the children of Israel to cross. They did not understand either the power of Jehovah or his love for Israel, but their fear would make the task of subduing them much easier.

The children of Israel, however, remained in their camp. They had much to do before they would begin to make war on the land. First, Jehovah commanded that all males be circumcised, for none had been circumcised since their fathers came out of Egypt. When this was done, Jehovah said to Joshua, "This day have I rolled away the shame that came upon Israel in Egypt." And Israel named the place of their camp Gilgal.[170]

While the children of Israel were encamped at Gilgal, they kept the Passover on the fourteenth day of the first month. And on that feast day they ate the grain of the land from the previous year. From that day forward, the manna that Jehovah had provided for their food in the desert ceased, and they ate the fruit of the land.

One day when Joshua ventured out of the camp and came near to the city of Jericho, he looked up and beheld a man standing before him with a drawn sword. He confronted the man, asking, "Are you for us or for our enemies?"

"No," replied the man, "I am captain of Jehovah's army."

Upon learning the man's identity, Joshua fell to the earth, worshipping him. "What instruction would my lord give to his servant?" he asked.

"Take off your shoes," replied the man, "for the place where you now stand is holy."

And Joshua did so.

---

[170] The name Gilgal means "wheel" or "rolling."

75—THE FALL OF JERICHO
(Joshua 6)

No city was more afraid of the children of Israel than Jericho.[171] With Israel encamped on their doorstep at nearby Gilgal, the gates of Jericho were sealed tight and no one either went in or came out. Although the city was fortified with high walls, Joshua knew that Israel would prevail against it because Jehovah was on their side. And Joshua was even more encouraged when Jehovah spoke to him saying, "I have given Jericho into your hands—the city, its king, and its mighty men of valor."

Then Jehovah told Joshua how the battle was to be waged. "Have your men of war march around the outside of the city wall once each day for six days," he said. "The ark of the covenant shall go with them and before the ark shall go seven priests blowing trumpets of rams' horns. On the seventh day you shall march around the city seven times with the priests blowing on their trumpets. Then, when they blow a long blast on their trumpets and the people all shout with a great shout, the city walls shall fall before you and the army of Israel shall enter the city and take it."

Joshua summoned the priests and said to them, "Take up the ark of the covenant to march around Jericho, and let seven priests with seven trumpets of rams' horns march before you." Then he said to the men of Israel, "March together around the city wall, with those who are armed going before the trumpeters and the ark of God."

When Joshua had given his instructions, the armed men of Israel began their march around the city, followed by seven priests blowing on trumpets of rams' horns,[172] by the ark of the covenant, and then by the rest of Israel's men.

Joshua commanded the people to march with silent voices. "You shall not make any sound with your

---

[171] Jericho, which is 400 feet (121.9 meters) below sea level, lies five miles (8 kilometers) west of the Jordan and seven miles (11.3 kilometers) northwest of the Dead Sea. It was the most important city on the Jordan plain and the key to the Israelite invasion. It was the most strongly fortified city in the land.

[172] Most accounts written about the taking of Jericho have the priests blowing their trumpets of rams' horns only on the seventh time around the city on the seventh day. However, the scripture seems clear (Joshua 6:13) that the trumpets were blown constantly throughout the march on all seven days. Such trumpets were (and are) called shofars.

voices," he said, "until I shall tell you to shout on the seventh day."

The hosts of Israel march around Jericho

Joshua also pointedly warned the children of Israel that they were to take no spoils of the battle when they entered the city, because Jehovah had forbidden it. "The silver and gold and the vessels of brass and iron are consecrated to Jehovah and shall come into his treasury of the tabernacle," said Joshua. "But you must keep yourself from the accursed thing.[173] If you take anything that is accursed, you will bring a curse upon Israel's camp."

So the company—the armed men, the seven priests blowing trumpets of rams' horns, the priests bearing the ark of the covenant, and the remainder of Israel's army—went forth to march once around the city wall and then returned to their camp. Then each day for five more days this procedure was repeated, with Israel marching once around the city—their voices silent but seven trumpets of rams' horns blowing before the ark of the covenant.

Then came the fateful seventh day. The children of Israel rose at dawn and compassed the city seven times. And on the seventh time, when the priests blew a long blast on their trumpets, Joshua gave his command. "Shout!" he cried, "for Jehovah has given you the city!"

And when the people of Israel gave a great shout, the walls of Jericho tumbled to the ground. Then, as they had been instructed, the army of Israel turned and went over the rubble into the city, taking the city and

destroying every creature, both man and beast, except for Rahab and her family. For Joshua had sent the two spies whom Rahab had hidden[174] to bring her and her family out.

Jericho was burned that day and everything within the city was destroyed—except the gold, the silver, and the vessels of brass and iron, which were put in the treasury of the tabernacle. Then Joshua charged the children of Israel with an oath, saying, "Cursed will be the man who rises up to rebuild this city. He shall lay the foundation at the cost of his firstborn and shall set up the gates at the cost of his youngest son."[175]

Jehovah was with Joshua, and Joshua's fame spread throughout the land. Those who inhabited the land realized now more than ever that they had great cause to fear.

---

[173] An accursed thing was anything that the people had been forbidden to take.

[174] See story "72–Jehovah Has Given You This Land" for the account of Rahab hiding the spies.

[175] For the eventual fulfillment of Joshua's prophecy about the rebuilding of Jericho, see story "151–The Curse of Jericho Fulfilled."

76—THE PRICE OF DISOBEDIENCE

(Joshua 7–8)

After the destruction of Jericho, Joshua sent scouts to Ai, a small city east of Beth-el, to view the country and determine Israel's chances for success in battle. The men returned filled with confidence. "Do not let all the people go up," they said. "Two or three thousand men should be enough to destroy Ai, for their people are few."

Three thousand men were chosen and sent to the battle. But they were greatly distressed when the men of Ai killed thirty-six of their number and drove the rest away.

The hearts of the children of Israel were melted and became as water, and poor Joshua was beside himself. He tore his clothes and fell on his face before the ark of the covenant, praying there until evening. And all of the elders of Israel put dust upon their heads.

"Alas, O Jehovah," cried Joshua, "why hast Thou brought this people over Jordan to deliver us into the hands of the Amorites? It would have been better for us if we had been content to dwell on the other side of the river! What shall I say now when the people of Israel turn their backs and flee from their enemies? When the inhabitants of this land hear of our defeat at Ai, they will surely unite themselves and surround us. And when they cut off our name from the earth, what wilt Thou do then for Thy great name?"

"Get up!" Jehovah commanded Joshua. "Why are you lying on your face? Israel fell before her enemies because someone broke the covenant that I commanded them and took the accursed thing at Jericho. The guilty man has stolen and has spoken falsely, and he put that which he has taken among his own things. Tell the people of Israel to sanctify themselves because of the accursed thing that is among them. They will be unable to stand against their enemies until it is taken away."

Jehovah continued: "Tomorrow shall the people come before you tribe by tribe, each tribe family by family, each family household by household, and each household man by man. And when the man is found who has the accursed thing, he shall be burned with fire—he and all that he has—because he broke my covenant and did this foolish thing."

Joshua arose in the morning and summoned the children of Israel to come before him tribe by tribe and family by family, with Judah coming first. And when a man of Judah named Achan, the son of Carmi, came before Joshua, Joshua discerned that Achan was the guilty man. "My son," said Joshua to Achan, "I pray, give glory to Jehovah, the God of Israel, and confess what you have done. Do not hide it from me."

"I have sinned!" cried Achan. "Indeed, I have sinned against Jehovah, the God of Israel, for when I saw among the spoils a goodly Babylonish garment, 200 shekels of silver, and a wedge of gold, I took them. They are hidden in the earth in the midst of my tent with the silver underneath."

When messengers brought back the forbidden items from their hiding place in Achan's tent, the men of Israel took Achan outside their camp—together with his family and all that he had—where they stoned them and burned them with fire.

The anger of Jehovah was turned away from Israel by the death of Achan that day, and Israel was able to take the city of Ai by ambush. And they did to Ai as they had done to Jericho.

When Ai was destroyed, Joshua built an altar of unhewn stones on Mount Ebal and the priests offered a peace offering to Jehovah. Then Joshua wrote the law of Moses upon the stones of the altar in the presence of the children of Israel and read them all the words of the law—the blessings and the curses—even all that was written in the book.

77—FROM A VERY FAR COUNTRY

(Joshua 9)

As the children of Israel remained encamped at Gilgal, preparing for their campaign through the country, their fame spread throughout the land. The peoples of the land began to be concerned about what Israel might do to them. And to address these concerns, they began to combine their armies into one great united force.

Knowing that Israel's objective was to destroy all of the peoples of the land, the men of the city of Gibeon devised a plan that they thought might deceive the children of Israel and preserve their own lives. Dressing themselves in old clothing and worn-out shoes, they took old bottles[176] and dry and moldy bread, then loaded their beasts with old empty sacks and went as a caravan to Israel's camp at Gilgal. They looked—from all appearances—as if they had traveled a great distance.

"We have come from a far country," they said to Joshua and the princes of Israel, "and are here to make a league with you that we might be your servants."

"Where are you from?" asked Joshua.

In order to carry out their deception, the men avoided specifics. "We have come from a very far country," they said, "because of the name of Jehovah, your God. We have heard of his fame and all that he did in Egypt, and have also heard what he did to the Amorites.

"The people of our country have sent us to meet you and to be your servants. This bread, which you now see dry and moldy before you, we took hot from our houses. These bottles of wine, which are now old and torn, were new when we left home. And our clothes and our shoes are now old and worn from this long journey." The story was well dramatized and very convincing.

Joshua was so convinced of the truth of the men's story that he did not seek Jehovah's counsel. He made peace with the men of Gibeon and gave them food. He also made an agreement with them to let them live, and the princes of Israel swore a covenant.

Three days later the children of Israel learned the truth. These "road-weary" travelers were their neighbors from Gibeon and lived just three days' journey from Gilgal. Upon making this discovery, the army of Israel journeyed to their cities–Gibeon, Chephirah, Beeroth, and Kirjath-jearim—but they did not attack the cities because of the agreement and covenant they had made. And all the congregation of Israel murmured against the princes who had sworn a covenant not to destroy these people.

"Because we have sworn to them by Jehovah, the God of Israel," said the princes, "we cannot touch them or the wrath of God will be upon us. However, we will make them our bondsmen. They shall chop wood and draw water for the congregation of Israel forever. None of them shall be freed."

The people of Gibeon explained to Joshua what they had done and why they did it. "We have done this thing," they said, "because we were told how Jehovah commanded Moses to give this land to the children of Israel and to destroy all the peoples of the land. We were afraid for our lives."

So Joshua made the Gibeonites servants to the children of Israel.

---

[176] The bottles referred to could more appropriately be called water skins. They were the skins of animals used by travelers to carry water or wine. New wine was put into new bottles that were still pliable. During the aging process, the wine would expand and stretch the skins so that they could not be used again for that purpose. Thus, old bottles would be water skins that had been used before and were probably hardened and cracked.

78—A LAND FOR WHICH YOU DID NOT LABOR

(Joshua 10–24)

The children of Israel did all that Jehovah commanded them. As they marched through the land of Canaan, they made no leagues or alliances with the people who lived there, except with the Gibeonites.[177] And they were able to overcome and destroy the peoples of the land because Jehovah was with them. Great miracles were wrought during this process. Great stones fell from heaven upon their enemies at Beth-horon,[178] and the sun and moon stood still in the sky as they fought the Amorites in the valley of Ajalon. In all, the children of Israel had conquered thirty-one kings in the land that lay west of the Jordan. But there were still many parts of the land and many peoples that were not yet conquered.

Jehovah told Joshua the names of the peoples who were yet to be conquered and promised to drive them out. "But," he said, "though these peoples of the land are still here, the time has come for you to divide the land as an inheritance among the nine and one-half tribes."[179]

The inheritances of the various tribes were determined by casting lots, and each tribe received its portion based on the size of the tribe. As the inheritances were being laid out, Caleb, who was now eighty-five years old, came to Joshua, seeking to receive the personal inheritance that Moses had promised him forty-five years before.[180]

Caleb said to Joshua, "Moses swore that the land whereon my feet did tread when I espied this land should be my inheritance and the inheritance of my children forever. And though forty-five years have passed since Moses sent me, Jehovah has kept me alive and I am as strong today as I was then, both to go out and to come in. Give me this mountain and, if Jehovah will be with me, I will drive out the people who live there, even the giants—the children of Anak."

Because Caleb followed Jehovah unconditionally, Joshua blessed him and gave him the city of Hebron for his inheritance. Hebron, the location of the tomb Abraham bought for his family long years before, lay within the boundaries of the land belonging to Judah—the very tribe for which Caleb had been a spy.

Jehovah gave the children of Israel all the land that he had promised to their fathers, and they possessed the land and dwelt there. And Jehovah gave them rest according to all that he promised to their fathers. He delivered their enemies into their hands, and the good things that he had promised to the house of Israel did not fail. The tabernacle, with the ark of the covenant, was set up at Shiloh, within the inheritance of Ephraim, and Shiloh became the religious center of the nation.

When the children of Israel had taken all the land that they could readily take, those soldiers from the tribes that had received their inheritance east of the Jordan returned home to their families. And as they went, they built a monument on the east bank of the river to remind future generations that those who lived east of the Jordan were also part of Israel, though separated from the other tribes.

Time passed and Joshua grew old. And in his advanced years he called the children of Israel together to instruct them. "You have seen all that Jehovah has done to those nations that fought against you," said Joshua, "for he has fought your battles for you. You must now courageously keep and do all that is written in the book of the law of Moses and not turn aside. You must not go among the peoples who remain among you in this land nor mention the names of their gods. You must never swear by their gods, serve those gods, or bow down before them; but you must cleave to Jehovah as you have done until this day. Should you cleave to the remnants of these other nations and make marriages with their sons and daughters, they will be as snares and traps to you, as scourges in your sides, and as thorns in your eyes until you perish from the land."

Joshua explained to the people how those of old—including Terah, Abraham's father—had served other gods. He related to them how Jehovah had blessed Abraham, Isaac, and Jacob, and how he had called Moses and Aaron to lead captive Israel out of Egypt. He reminded the people of Israel's forty years in the wilderness and how, with Jehovah's help, they were brought into the promised land and overcame the peoples who lived there. Then he said, "Jehovah has given you a land for which you did not labor and cities that

---

[177] The account of the Gibeonites is given in story "77—From a Very Far Country."

[178] It appears from the scripture (Joshua 10:11) that the stones that fell from heaven on the Amorites were hailstones, and more people died that day from the hailstones than were slain by the sword.

[179] Moses had already given two and one-half tribes—Reuben, Gad, and half of Manasseh—their inheritances in the lands taken from the Amorites and the people of Bashan east of the Jordan. This distribution of inheritances east of the Jordan is recorded in Numbers 31 and 32 and in Deuteronomy 2 and 3, but the story is not told in this book.

[180] Story "64—Forty Years for Forty Days," gives the account of Caleb's faithfulness and Moses' promise to him.

you did not build, yet you dwell in them. He has also given you vineyards and oliveyards that you did not plant but do eat."

"Now, therefore," Joshua continued, "you must fear Jehovah and serve him in sincerity and truth. You must serve Jehovah and put away the strange gods that your fathers served both on the other side of the flood[181] and in Egypt. But, if it seems evil to you to serve Jehovah, you must choose this day whom you will serve—whether it be the false gods that your fathers served on the other side of the flood or the gods of the Amorites in whose land you dwell—but as for me and my house, we will serve Jehovah."

The people responded to Joshua's challenge, as with one voice, that they too would serve Jehovah. And

Joshua made a covenant with them that day and wrote the words of the covenant in the book of the Law of God. He also took a great stone and set it under an oak tree at Shechem saying, "This stone shall be a witness unto us, for it has heard the words that Jehovah has spoken to us. It shall be a witness unto you, lest you deny your God."

And also at Shechem, the children of Israel buried the bones of Joseph that they had brought with them out of Egypt.[182]

Israel served Jehovah faithfully during all the days of Joshua, and they continued to serve him all the days of those elders who had lived in Joshua's time, and they remembered what Jehovah had done for Israel.

---

[181] It is apparent, from the examples Joshua gave that he was not speaking of the great Flood in the days of Noah. Some authorities say that what Joshua called "the flood" was the Euphrates River, thus referring to the gods worshipped by Abraham's forebears east of the Euphrates (see Werner Keller, *The Bible as History: What Archaeology Reveals about Scripture,* 2nd rev. ed. [New York: William Morrow and Co. Inc., 1981], 41).

[182] See story "42–A Choice Seer" where the story is told of how Joseph's brethren had covenanted to carry his bones with them out of Egypt and back to Canaan when they returned to inherit the promised land. There is no explanation of why Joseph was buried at Shechem rather than at Hebron in the tomb of his fathers. Perhaps the place of the family burial place was no longer known after so many years.

VI

THE REIGN OF THE JUDGES

79—A MESSAGE FOR YOU FROM GOD

(Judges 3)

After the death of Joshua, the children of Israel were ruled for 450 years[183] by men and women called judges. Those who served as judges in Israel, though they acted as civil authorities, often earned that right because of their military prowess. Those who remembered Joshua were faithful and devoted to Jehovah, but after that generation had passed on, the people forgot Jehovah and began to worship the false gods of the unbelievers in their midst—the Philistines, the Canaanites, the Amorites, the Zidonians, and the Hivites. And, in addition, many of the children of Israel served Baal[184] and Ashtoreth.[185] They also ignored the counsel given by Jehovah through both Moses and Joshua that they were not to intermarry with other peoples.

Because Jehovah was displeased with the wickedness of his covenant people, he allowed oppressors from other nations to bring them into bondage. They were in bondage to Mesopotamia for eight years before Jehovah responded to their pleadings and raised up Othniel, a son of Caleb's brother, to judge them and lead them in defeating the Mesopotamians. After forty years of peace, Othniel died.

When Israel again became wicked, Jehovah strengthened Moab—through alliances with the peoples of Ammon and Amalek—and Israel served in bondage to King Eglon of Moab for eighteen years.

As the Moabite oppression caused the children of Israel to begin to repent, Jehovah raised up Ehud, a left-handed man from the tribe of Benjamin, to be their deliverer. To accomplish the delivery of his people, Ehud devised a plan to deliver a gift from the children of Israel to King Eglon. Before going to the king to deliver his gift, Ehud hid a long, two-edged dagger beneath his clothing on his right thigh. When his gift was brought into Eglon's house, Ehud sent away those who came to help carry it. And when he said to King Eglon, "I have a secret message for you, O King," Eglon also sent away those who served him—leaving Ehud and Eglon alone in the king's upper chamber.

As Ehud bowed deeply and came near to the king, he said, "I have a message for you from God." And as King Eglon arose from his seat, Ehud pulled the hidden dagger from his right thigh with his left hand and thrust it deep into Eglon's belly. Because Eglon was a very fat man, the handle of the dagger went into him after the blade, and the fat closed upon the blade so that it could not be pulled out.

His sinister mission accomplished, Ehud fled from the king's chamber, locking the doors behind him and leaving Eglon alone and dead on the floor. When Eglon's servants returned, they saw the doors locked and thought their master had locked them to take a nap. But when they finally got a key and entered the chamber, they found the body of their dead king.

In the meantime, Ehud had escaped to Seirath.[186] When he came there, he blew his trumpet on Mount Ephraim and led the children of Israel down from the mountain. "Follow me!" he cried, "for Jehovah has delivered the Moabites into our hands." Following Ehud, the people of Israel took over the fords on the Jordan so that no one could cross. And, with their escape route blocked, 10,000 Moabite warriors fell that day before Ehud and the children of Israel. There were none who escaped.

And after their deliverance from the Moabites, the children of Israel had rest for eighty years.

---

[183] See Acts 13:20. Some say, however, that the reign of the judges was much shorter—perhaps closer to 200 years.

[184] Baal (plural form Baalim), the storm and fertility god, was symbolic of the male generative principle in nature. Baal worship was most common among the Zidonians or Phoenicians, but it seems that Baal's name (which means "lord") was used broadly in the Old Testament to refer to all heathen or foreign gods.

[185] Ashtoreth (meaning "a star") was the principal female deity of the Phoenicians. She was called Ishtar by the Assyrians and Astarte by the Greeks and Romans. Some ancient writers identified her with the moon, though Ishtar and Astarte have both been identified with the planet Venus.

[186] Seirath was a locality somewhere in the territory belonging to Ephraim. Nothing more is known of it. Some have suggested that it was the same as Mount Seir, but such does not appear likely.

80—THE MAN WHOM YOU SEEK

(Judges 4)

Because of the unrighteousness of the children of Israel, Jehovah brought them into bondage under the Canaanites. Jabin was king of Canaan and Sisera was captain of the Canaanite army. After twenty years of oppression at the hands of Sisera and his 900 iron chariots, the people of Israel began to repent and cry to Jehovah for relief.

The judge of Israel at that time was a prophetess named Deborah who lived between Ramah and Beth-el in Mount Ephraim. When Jehovah gave Deborah reason to believe that Israel could prevail over Canaan, she called Barak out of the tribe of Naphtali and asked him to lead an army in battle against Sisera. "Jehovah has told me that if 10,000 men of Israel will go to Mount Tabor," Deborah said to Barak, "he will draw Sisera with his army and chariots to them and deliver them into Israel's hands at the River Kishon."

Barak was not excited about Deborah's request. "However," he said to her, "if you will go with me, I will go." Barak believed that she would decline to participate in such an adventure, but he was wrong.

"I will surely go with you," responded Deborah. "The journey, however, will not be for your honor, because Jehovah will sell Sisera into the hands of a woman."

Deborah went with Barak to Kedesh,[187] where they recruited 10,000 men from the tribes of Zebulun and Naphtali. Then, according to Deborah's instructions, they marched with their army to Mount Tabor.

When Heber the Kenite,[188] who was encamped nearby, saw Barak's army leave Kedesh, he reported to Sisera that the army of Israel had gone to Mount Tabor. Delighted by this information, Sisera gathered all those under his command, together with his 900 iron chariots, and went to meet the army of Barak at the River Kishon.

As Sisera's hosts approached, Deborah saw them coming. "Arise!" she called to Barak, "for this is the day that Jehovah will deliver Sisera into your hands."

As the battle raged, Jehovah caused the army of Sisera to panic and flee before the men of Israel. Barak and his forces pursued them eagerly and fell upon them until there was not one Canaanite left standing. But Sisera had not fallen in the battle. In the confusion he had left his chariot and fled on foot from the field of battle.

Sisera came in his flight to the tent of Jael, the wife of Heber the Kenite. He felt safe there because there was peace between the Canaanites and Heber the Kenite. When Jael saw him coming, she went out to meet him. "Turn in here, my lord, and fear not," she said to Sisera. "You will be safe here." And when Sisera came into Jael's tent, she laid him on the floor and covered him with a rug.

"Give me a little water to drink," Sisera said to Jael, "for I am thirsty." But instead of water, she gave him milk—then she covered him again with her rug.

Sisera spoke to Jael from under his covering, giving her instructions to ensure his safety. "Stand at the door of your tent," he said, "so that if any man comes and asks if I am here, you can tell him no."

Sisera fell asleep quickly in his warm hiding place, for he was weary from the battle and from his flight. And as he slept, Jael took a tent nail and a hammer in her hands and went to him quietly. Then, with the hammer, she drove the tent nail deep into his temple, through his head, and into the ground beneath. Sisera was a dead man.

As Barak later came by in pursuit of Sisera, Jael saw him and went out to meet him. "Come," she said to Barak, "and I will show you the man whom you seek." And when Barak came into Jael's tent, he beheld Sisera lying dead with the tent nail in his temple.

Jehovah subdued the Canaanites that day, and the children of Israel prevailed against Jabin, king of Canaan. Israel was again free from bondage and had rest for forty years.

---

[187] Kedesh was located in the northern part of Palestine in the territory belonging to Naphtali. It was about thirty-one miles (forty-eight kilometers) north of Mount Tabor. Deborah's home, between Ramah and Beth-el, was approximately fifty miles (eighty kilometers) south of Mount Tabor.

[188] The Kenites are thought to be descendants of Abraham through his wife Keturah. They were a tribe of the Midianites.

81–THE SWORD OF JEHOVAH AND OF GIDEON

(Judges 6–8)

To punish Israel for embracing the gods of the Amorites, Jehovah had caused the people of Midian to descend upon them in great hordes and overrun the land, bringing with them their flocks and their herds. The invading Midianites destroyed the crops of the Israelites, leaving the land desolate; and they drove the people from their homes. In their poverty, the children of Israel, cried to Jehovah for deliverance, and Jehovah sent a prophet to call them to repentance. "Jehovah has blessed you," said the prophet, "and has brought you out of Egypt. He has delivered you from those who oppressed you and has driven them out and given you their land. He gave you warning that you should not serve the gods of the Amorites in whose land you dwell, but you have not obeyed his voice."

The condemnation was harsh.

One day while a young man named Gideon from the tribe of Manasseh was threshing wheat in his father's winepress at Ophrah,[189] in order to hide it from the Midianites, an angel appeared to him. "Jehovah is with you, Gideon," said the angel, "and you are a mighty man of valor." Gideon did not perceive that his visitor was an angel.

"If Jehovah is with us," answered Gideon with a hint of bitterness, "why has such misfortune befallen us, and where are those miracles about which our fathers have spoken? For Jehovah has delivered us to the Midianites."

"If you will go out against the Midianites in your might, you can save Israel," the angel said to Gideon, "because Jehovah has sent you."

"How could I ever save Israel?" asked Gideon. "My family is poor in Manasseh, and I am the least in my father's house."

"Surely Jehovah will be with you," replied the angel, "and you shall smite the Midianites as if they were but one man."

"I do not understand all of this," responded Gideon, "but if I have found grace in your sight, show me a sign that I might know the truth of what you say. First, however, let me give you a gift. Stay here until I return."

"I will stay," replied the angel.

Gideon prepared leavened cakes and the meat of a young goat and brought them to the angel, along with the broth from the meat. When the angel saw the food, he said, "Take the meat and cakes and lay them upon this rock, then pour the broth on top." Gideon was puzzled by this strange request, but he did as he was directed.

When the angel touched the meat and cakes on the rock with the end of his staff, fire rose up from the rock and consumed them. Then the angel departed.

Gideon, then understanding that he had been conversing with an angel, exclaimed, "Alas, O Lord Jehovah! I have seen Thine angel face-to-face." And Gideon built an altar at the place where the angel appeared and called it Jehovah-shalom.[190]

That same night Jehovah spoke to Gideon and commanded him to tear down his father's altar to Baal and to cut down the grove of the fertility gods, or Asherah, nearby.[191] He commanded Gideon further to use the wood from the grove as fuel for an offering to Jehovah on a new altar he was to build for that purpose. Gideon took ten of his servants and did as Jehovah commanded him. But he went at night because he feared his father's household and the men of the city.

When the men came in the morning and saw that the altar of Baal had been cast down, the grove cut down, and a sacrifice offered on a new altar, they asked who caused the destruction. The answer came back: "Gideon, the son of Joash!"

When the men threatened to kill Gideon, his father Joash intervened. "Will you plead for Baal?" he asked them. "Will you save him? He that will plead for Baal, let him be put to death while it is still morning. If Baal be a god, let him plead for himself." The men were pacified, and Joash called his son Gideon Jerubbaal.[192]

---

[189] Ophrah was a small village in the tribe of Benjamin.

[190] Jehovah-shalom means "Jehovah the God of peace." Gideon apparently chose this name in honor of the angel and his salutation of peace.

[191] Baal (plural form Baalim), the storm and fertility god, was symbolic of the male generative principle in nature. Baal worship was most common among the Zidonians or Phoenicians, but it seems that Baal's name (which means "lord") was used broadly in the Old Testament to refer to all heathen or foreign gods. Asherah, as named here, is probably incorrect. The Zidonian goddess who was the principal consort of Baal, was actually Ashtoreth (plural form Ashtaroth) or Astarte. Though the goddess Asherah is mentioned in various places in the Old Testament, her Hebrew name was usually translated as "groves" in the King James Version. There seems to be no doubt about Asherah being part of Baal worship or about her being symbolic of female fertility, but she and Ashtoreth were not the same goddess, as many once believed them to be.

[192] Jerubbaal means "he that strives with Baal."

When the vast Midianite armies pitched their tents in the valley of Jezreel, Gideon thought about what the angel had told him. As he thought, the Spirit of God moved upon him and he blew his trumpet to gather the people. He then sent messengers throughout the tribes of Manasseh, Asher, Zebulun, and Naphtali, and the men of Israel rallied to his cause.

Gideon, still having doubts about himself in the role of a conqueror, asked Jehovah for a sign. "I will put a woolen fleece on the ground," he said, "and if Thou wilt save Israel by my hand, let the dew of the night be only on the fleece and the earth around it be dry in the morning." And when Gideon arose in the morning, it was so. He wrung a bowlful of water from the fleece.

Gideon was still hesitant and uncertain. "Do not be angry," he pleaded with Jehovah, "but I need one more test. Let the fleece be dry and the dew fall on the earth around it." And the next morning, it was as Gideon had asked.

While Gideon's army—32,000 strong—was encamped on Mount Gilead preparing to battle the Midianites, Jehovah spoke again to Gideon. "The people who are with you are too many for me to give the Midianites into your hands," he said. "If you go to battle with so many, Israel will vaunt themselves against me and claim they have delivered themselves from the Midianites. Send those to their homes who are fearful of battle." And, when this instruction was given, 22,000 men left Gideon's ranks and returned to their homes.

Jehovah spoke again to Gideon. "Your people are still too many," he said. "Bring your men down to the water and I will try them there. When the men drink, set by themselves those who lap the water from their hands with their tongues. Set also by themselves, in another group, those who bow down upon their knees to drink." And from the 10,000 men who remained, Jehovah chose those 300 men who lapped the water from their hands like dogs. Said he, "By these men will I deliver the Midianites into your hands. Send the others home."

As the darkness of evening fell upon the camp, Jehovah said to Gideon, "Go down to the army of the Midianites; for I have delivered them into your hands. However, if you fear to go to battle now, take your servant Phurah and go down and listen to what they say. Once you have heard them, your hands will be strengthened for battle."

The soldiers of the Midianites and their allies were so vast that they could not be numbered, but Gideon and Phurah crept down to their camp in the darkness and listened, as Jehovah had instructed. As they listened, they heard one man tell another of his dream: "I dreamed," he said, "that a barley cake fell among the army of Midian. The cake hit a tent, and the tent fell flat upon the ground."

The second man answered, interpreting the dream. "That barley cake is the sword of Gideon, the son of Joash," he said, "for God has delivered Midian and all its hosts into Gideon's hands."

When Gideon and Phurah heard the dream and its interpretation, they offered a prayer of thanks and returned to their men. "Arise!" cried Gideon, "for Jehovah has delivered the Midianites into your hands."

Gideon divided his 300 soldiers into three groups and gave each man a trumpet and a pitcher with a lamp inside. Then he said to them, "Whatever I do, you must do also. We will go down to the camp, one group of us on each side. Then, when I blow my trumpet and break my pitcher, you must do the same. Then you must shout, 'The sword of Jehovah and of Gideon!'"

When Gideon and those 100 men who were with him came to the Midianite camp, they blew their trumpets and broke their pitchers to reveal the lamps. Then the other two companies also blew their trumpets and broke their pitchers. And they all cried out as with one voice, "The sword of Jehovah and of Gideon!"

As this little army of 300 all stood in their places and blew their trumpets, the hosts of Midian fled into the night. Then Jehovah set the sword of every man of the Midianites against his fellow, and they slew one another in their retreat.

As the Midianites fled, the men of Israel rallied from Naphtali, from Asher, and from Manasseh to pursue them. And Gideon sent messengers throughout Mount Ephraim saying, "Come down against the Midianites and take control of the waters of Jordan and Beth-barah before they do." And as the men of Ephraim took control of the waters, they slew two Midianite princes in the process and took their heads to Gideon.

The battle continued until Midian was subdued before the children of Israel. And the country was at peace for forty years in the days that Gideon was judge of Israel.

The people loved Gideon. They asked him to be their king and his son to succeed him, but Gideon declined their request. "I will not rule over you," said Gideon, "and neither will my son. For Jehovah shall be your ruler."

82—THE WICKEDNESS OF ABIMELECH

(Judges 9)

Gideon had many wives, and seventy sons were born to him. One son, whose name was Abimelech, was the son of a concubine[193] from the city of Shechem. Abimelech was an ambitious man and sought to be king of Israel after his father's death. He convinced his mother's family in Shechem that many advantages would come to them if he could be their king. "Consider," he said to them, "whether it is better to have all seventy of Gideon's sons reign over you or to have just one. It will also be good for you if I am that one, for I am your bone and flesh." And when his mother's family was convinced, they were able to convince the men of Shechem also.

The men of Shechem gave Abimelech money with which he hired a gang of outlaws to assist with his campaign for office. Their strategy for victory was simple. They went up to the house of Gideon and killed sixty-eight of Abimelech's sixty-nine brothers. Only Jotham, the youngest, was able to hide and escape. With the competition out of the way, the men of Shechem and the house of Millo[194] made Abimelech their king.

When the surviving brother Jotham heard that Abimelech was king in Shechem, he went there. Standing on top of Mount Gerizim, Jotham told the people of Shechem a parable:

"The trees decided that they would anoint a king," said Jotham. "When they petitioned the olive tree to be their king, he declined because of the honors that he already had. For his oil was used to honor both God and man. The fig tree also refused to become their king because he was unwilling to give up his sweetness and his good fruit. Likewise, the vine declined because the office would require him to give up his wine that was pleasing to both God and man."

Jotham's parable continued: "When no tree was found that was willing to serve as their king, all the trees went to the thistle and pleaded with him to be their king. The thistle agreed, but he told the trees that, if they anointed him king, they would have to put their whole trust in his shadow or he would bring forth fire to devour the cedars of Lebanon."

When Jotham had finished his parable, he said to the people of Shechem, "If you have acted truly and sincerely in making Abimelech your king, and if you have dealt fairly with Gideon's family and given them what they deserve, then you should rejoice in Abimelech and let him rejoice in you. If not, however, let fire come out from Abimelech and devour the men of Shechem and the house of Millo. And then let fire come out from the men of Shechem and the house of Millo also to devour Abimelech." Once Jotham's parable was told and his message of warning delivered, he fled for fear of his brother.

When Abimelech had reigned for just three years, Jehovah caused bad feelings between Abimelech and the men of Shechem because of the blood of Abimelech's brothers that had been spilt. As the bad feelings festered, a man named Gaal came to Shechem and won the confidence of the people. "Who is Abimelech that we should serve him?" Gaal asked the people of the city. "I would to God this people were under my hand, then I would remove Abimelech." And Gaal threw out a challenge for Abimelech to meet him in battle. This challenge, however, was not made to Abimelech's face.

Zebul, the ruler of the city, heard Gaal's boasting and went to tell Abimelech. He convinced Abimelech to take his armies outside the city and lie in wait through the night to attack Gaal's armies in the morning.

When Gaal came with Zebul to the city gate in the morning, Gaal saw Abimelech's armies rise up on the mountainside and move toward the city. And he said to Zebul, "Behold, there are people coming down from the tops of the mountains."

---

[193] The main difference between a wife and a concubine was probably the fact that a concubine could be rejected or cast aside without a bill of divorcement, while a wife could not. There was no difference between the children of a wife and those of a concubine, and the latter were a supplementary family to the former. The names of the concubines' children are listed in the patriarchal genealogies, and their position and provision depended on their father's will. The state of concubinage was provided for by the law of Moses and certainly also preceded that law. A concubine would generally be either (1) a Hebrew girl bought from her father, (2) a Gentile captive taken in war, (3) a foreign slave who had been bought, or (4) a Canaanite woman, bond or free. The rights of the first two were protected by the law (Exodus 21:7; Deuteronomy 21:10–14), but the third was unrecognized and the fourth prohibited. Some free Hebrew women also became concubines (William Smith, *Dictionary of the Bible, GospeLink*, CD-ROM, s.v. "concubine").

[194] Millo was apparently a castle near Shechem. It may be the tower of Shechem referred to later in this story.

"You are surely mistaken," replied Zebul, lying. "What you see are the shadows of the mountains as if they were men."

"Those are people coming," insisted Gaal. "Some are coming down by the middle of the land and others are coming along by the oak of the diviners."

Then Zebul said, "Those men who are coming are the armies of Abimelech. And where is your mouth now that asked, 'Who is Abimelech that we should serve him?' If these are the people that you hate, go out and fight them."

Gaal took Zebul's challenge and quickly gathered his forces. And, in the fierce battle that ensued, Abimelech's army defeated the men of Gaal, killing many and driving the rest back into the city.

The following day, when Abimelech heard that Zebul had driven Gaal and his followers out of the city, Abimelech's armies attacked both those who fled from Shechem and the city itself. All the people of Shechem were slain, and the soil was covered with salt to make it desolate. It seemed as if Abimelech had gone mad.

The men at the tower of Shechem quickly learned that their city had fallen to Abimelech and hid in the stronghold at the house of the god Baal-berith.[195] But when Abimelech discovered that they were at the stronghold, he took his armies into the field to cut tree branches, which they threw over the stronghold wall, then set the stronghold on fire. The resulting blaze consumed the house of Baal-berith and all who were inside.

Abimelech and his army went next to the city of Thebez, quickly capturing the city and driving the people to the city tower. But when Abimelech approached the door of the tower to set the tower on fire, a woman hiding there threw down a piece of millstone that broke Abimelech's skull. Mortally wounded, Abimelech called to his armorbearer and commanded that he kill him so it would not be said that he was slain by a woman. And the young man obediently thrust Abimelech through with his sword.

Thus, the curse pronounced in Jotham's parable was fulfilled. God destroyed Abimelech for the unjust slaying of his brothers. And he destroyed the men of She-

chem for the evil they had done in making Abimelech their king.

83—THE VICTORY AND THE VOW
(Judges 11)

Jephthah was the son of a harlot and had been expelled from his father Gilead's house by his brothers. However, because Jephthah was a mighty warrior, the elders of Gilead came seeking him at his home in Mizpeh[196] when the Ammonites invaded their land. They wanted Jephthah to be their captain.

Jephthah resented his brothers because they had treated his so poorly and he was suspicious of their motives for inviting him back. "Did you not hate me and expel me from my father's house?" he asked them. "Why do you come to me now when you are in distress?"

"We need you to be with us when we fight against the children of Ammon," they answered, "and to be head over all the people of Gilead."

"And if you bring me home again to fight against the children of Ammon, and Jehovah delivers them before me, shall I then be your head?" asked Jephthah.

"May Jehovah be witness between us," they replied, "if we do not do according to your words."

So Jephthah went with his brethren and was made captain over their armies. Seeking to avoid a war, if possible, he sent messengers to the king of the Ammonites asking why his people had come to war against Gilead.

The Ammonite king made his reply: "Because the children of Israel took away our land when they came out of Egypt—from Arnon, to Jabbok, and unto Jordan. We have now come to claim our land and take it back. If you will restore it to us, we will depart in peace." The Ammonites wanted all the land long since claimed by Israel east of the Jordan—the land that was occupied by the tribes of Reuben and Gad.

---

[195] When a term such as "berith" is compounded with the name of Baal in the scripture, the second word of the compound relates to some attribute of Baal, the place or manner of his worship, or something that a place possesses (see *Bible Dictionary*, LDS-KJV, s.v. "Baal"). The Hebrew term "berith" is synonymous with "law and commandment" (Charles D. Tate, Jr., and Monte S. Nyman, *Alma, the Testimony of the Word* [Provo, Utah: BYU Religious Studies Center, 1992], 225).

[196] This Mizpeh on the east side of the Jordan does not appear to be the same Mizpeh (Mizpah) where Jacob and his father-in-law Laban erected a heap of stones and made a covenant of peace (see story "30—A Covenant of Peace"). And it is certainly a different place than the Mizpeh (Mizpah) located in Benjamin, about four miles (6.4 kilometers) northwest of Jerusalem, that later became a rallying place where Israel gathered in times of emergency (see, for example, stories "96—Samuel's Victory over the Philistines" and "98—Jehovah Has Anointed You").

Jephthah's response to the Ammonite king was pointed. He explained carefully and in great detail how Israel had come to possess the land in question. "Israel did not take this land from Moab or from the children of Ammon," he said. "When this people came out of Egypt and camped at Kadesh, Moses sent messengers to the king of Edom seeking permission to pass through his land peacefully. But the king of Edom denied Moses' request, and Israel retraced their steps in the wilderness to pass on the east side of Edom and Moab. They camped on the other side of Arnon but did not venture within the borders of Moab.

"Then, when Moses sent messengers to King Sihon of the Amorites seeking permission to pass peacefully through his land, Sihon came out to battle against Israel because he did not trust them. In that battle, Jehovah delivered Sihon and his people into the hands of Israel, and Israel's victory over the Amorites gave Israel possession of all the land in question, from Arnon to Jabbok and from the wilderness even unto Jordan."

Then Jephthah asked, "Seeing that the Lord Jehovah took this land from the Amorites and gave it to his people Israel, should we now give it to the Ammonites after 300 years? If you had any claim to this land, why did you not seek to recover it before now? Israel has not sinned against you, and you do us wrong to war against us now. Let Jehovah judge this day between Israel and the children of Ammon."

The logic of Jephthah's explanation was not sufficient to dissuade the king of the Ammonites from his misguided objective. He was determined to have the land.

When Jephthah's best effort to solve the problem without bloodshed failed, the Spirit of Jehovah came upon him and he marched with his army through all of Israel's land east of the Jordan until he came to the borders of Ammon. And, as he did so, he made a solemn vow to Jehovah: "If Thou wilt deliver the children of Ammon into my hands, then whatever comes forth from my house to meet me when I return from this war, shall be Thine. I will offer it to Thee as a burnt offering."

Jephthah and his army prevailed decisively over the Ammonites, for Jehovah delivered the children of Ammon into his hands. The Ammonites were smitten with great destruction through twenty of their cities and were completely subdued before Jephthah's army.

When the victory had been won, Jephthah returned to his home at Mizpeh. And as he came to his house, his daughter—his only child—ran out from the house to welcome him. When Jephthah saw her coming, he tore his clothes and cried, "Alas, my daughter! You have brought me very low, for I have opened my mouth to Jehovah and cannot take back my vow!"

"My father," replied the girl, "if you have opened your mouth to Jehovah, do to me according to what you said. For Jehovah has surely taken vengeance on the children of Ammon for you. Let this thing be done, but let me live for two more months that I may go up and down upon the mountains and bewail the fact that I shall never marry."

"Go," said Jephthah.

And, at the end of two months, Jephthah's daughter returned to her father, who offered her as a burnt offering to Jehovah according to his vow. And it became a custom that the daughters of Israel went to Mizpeh four days each year to lament the daughter of Jephthah the Gileadite.

84—SHIBBOLETH
(Judges 12)

The men of Ephraim were upset with Jephthah because he had led the army of Gilead in battle against the Ammonites without inviting Ephraim to join their forces. To show their displeasure, the men of Ephraim gathered an army and went across the Jordan to confront Jephthah in Mizpeh.[197]

"Because you went to fight against the children of Ammon and did not call us to go with you," they complained, "we have come now to burn your house with fire."

"I *did* call you to help us," Jephthah reminded them, "but my people were in a great battle with the children of Ammon, and it was necessary for us to act quickly. When you did not come to deliver us, I took my life in my own hands and went to battle without you; and the Lord delivered the Ammonites into my hands. And so I ask you—because I do not understand—why have you come here now to fight against me?"

When the Ephraimites were not satisfied with Jephthah's explanation and mounted their assault, Jephthah gathered the men of Gilead to defend themselves. Seeking to gain some advantage, he sent his men to block the fords across the Jordan so that the men of Ephraim could not escape.

"Question all those who come to cross the river," Jephthah instructed his men. "Ask each one who comes if he is of Ephraim. Then, if a man answers no, ask him to say 'shibboleth.'" For Jephthah knew that the people of Ephraim could not pronounce the word, but would say "shibboleth" instead."[198]

Thus it was that every man who said "sibboleth" instead of "shibboleth" was considered to be an Ephraimite and was slain. And that day 42,000 Ephraimites were slain by Jephthah's men at the passages across the Jordan.

---

[197] See footnote 196 in story "83—The Victory and the Vow."

[198] The Hebrew word *shibboleth* means "stream." It has significance here only because the "sh" pronunciation appears to have been peculiar to the Israelites dwelling east of the Jordan. Any word beginning with "sh" would have produced the same result.

85—HE SHALL BEGIN TO DELIVER ISRAEL
(Judges 13)

Because the children of Israel had strayed from the ways of Jehovah, they were held in bondage to the Philistines for forty years. Life was not easy for them, and most of the people could not remember when they did not suffer from the oppression of their Philistine neighbors.

At Zorah, in the tribe of Dan, lived a man named Manoah whose wife was barren. One day an angel appeared to Manoah's wife—though she did not know he was an angel—and told her that she would bear a son. He gave Manoah's wife exacting instructions. "Drink no wine or strong drink and eat no unclean thing," he told her. "And though you are barren, you shall conceive and bear a son. No razor shall be allowed to come upon the child's head, for he shall be a Nazarite[199] unto God from the womb and shall begin to deliver Israel from the hands of the Philistines."

The woman, in her excitement, went to her husband and told him of her visitor and his message. "A man of God came to me," she said, "and his countenance was terrible like an angel of God. I did not ask him where he came from and he did not tell me his name, but he said that I would conceive and bear a son. He then told me that because my son will be a Nazarite from the womb unto the day of his death, I am to drink no wine or strong drink and eat no unclean thing."

Hearing his wife's account, Manoah prayed, saying, "O Jehovah, let the man of God who came to my wife come to us again and teach us what we shall do unto this child who shall be born."

In answer to Manoah's prayer, the angel came again to the woman as she sat in the field. But again Manoah was not with her, and she went quickly to bring him back. When Manoah arrived in the field he saw the man; but neither he nor his wife yet realized that he was an angel. Manoah asked the man if he was the one who brought the earlier message to his wife. When he had been reassured, Manoah asked, "When your words come to pass, how shall we train this child and how shall we treat him?"

"Of all that I said unto the woman, let her beware," replied the angel. "She must eat nothing that comes

---

[199] The word Nazarite means "separate" or "set apart." The vows of a Nazarite might be either for a short period or lifelong. The person who took those vows was bound to abstain from wine, from contact with the dead, and from any cutting of the hair.

from the vine, neither drink wine or strong drink or eat any unclean thing."

As the angel prepared to depart, Manoah pleaded with him to stay longer. "Let us detain you until we have prepared a kid for you to eat," he said.

"Though you detain me," said the angel, "I will not eat. However, if you choose to make a burnt offering, you must offer it to Jehovah."

"You must tell us your name," said Manoah, "so that when your sayings come to pass, we may honor you."

"Do not ask my name," replied the angel, "for it is secret."

So Manoah went and prepared a kid for a sacrifice, together with a meat offering,[200] and presented his offering to Jehovah upon a rock. And when the flame from Manoah's offering went up from the altar, the angel ascended in the flame while Manoah and his wife stood watching. They did not see him again, but they now knew that the man was an angel.

When Manoah realized that an angel had visited them, he became concerned and said to his wife, "We shall surely die because we have seen God."

"Oh, not so," replied his wife. "For if Jehovah were pleased to kill us, he would not have received the burnt offering and meat offering at our hands. Neither would he have shown us all these things or told us such things as these."

Time passed and the woman bore the son that the angel had promised. She called her son Samson,[201] and, as the child grew, Jehovah blessed him and the Spirit of Jehovah began to move upon him.

---

[200] Meat offerings are described in some detail in Leviticus 2. They could more properly be called meal offerings and were not always exactly alike. Usually they consisted of unleavened cakes or wafers made with fine flour and oil or of wafers anointed with oil.

[201] The name Samson means "like the sun."

86–SAMSON, THE BANE OF THE PHILISTINES

(Judges 14–15)

Because of what the angel had told Samson's parents before his birth, they had great hopes for him. As a Nazarite, he would certainly be a righteous man, devoted to Jehovah. And was not their son to deliver Israel from the Philistines?

As it turned out, Samson did become an instrument of Jehovah against the Philistines, but he did not always make wise choices. When he fell in love with a Philistine woman at Timnath and asked his father to get the woman for him as a wife, his parents were deeply hurt. "His father asked, "Are there no women among the daughters of Israel, that you must take a wife of the uncircumcised Philistines?"

But Samson replied, "Get her for me, for she pleases me."

Samson's parents were not pleased by their son's choice because they did not realize that Jehovah's hand was in Samson's wedding plans. The events that arose as a result of this marriage, however, would create the rift between Israel and the Philistines that Jehovah desired.

One day when Samson went to Timnath, a young lion attacked him. But Samson was filled with the Spirit of Jehovah and killed the lion with his bare hands. Later, when he returned to the place, he found that bees had taken over the lion's carcass and filled it with honey. Samson took some of the honey in his hands and ate it. He also took some to share with his parents, but he did not tell them where he got the honey.

Samson's father asked for the hand of the Philistine woman in his son's behalf, and Samson married her. During the seven-day wedding feast, which was held according to Philistine custom, the bride's family brought thirty Philistine men from the city to be Samson's companions. When the men were come, Samson said to them, "Let me give you a riddle. If you can tell me its meaning during the seven days of this feast, I will give each of you a linen tunic and a change of clothing. But if you cannot tell its meaning, then each of you shall give me a tunic and a change of clothing."

They were now curious. "Give us your riddle," they urged.

And Samson gave them this riddle: "Out of the eater came forth meat, and out of the strong came forth sweetness."

Samson's companions, being unable to solve his riddle, went to the bride on the seventh day and asked her to entice Samson to tell her the answer so she could tell it to them. "If you do not do it, we will burn your father's house," they threatened. "After all, have you called us to this feast to take away our possessions?"

Samson's bride wept before him and pestered him for the answer to his riddle and, when he tired of her weeping, he told her the answer—which she promptly told to the men.

The men then came to Samson and said, "What is sweeter than honey, and what is stronger than a lion?"

When Samson realized that his wife had betrayed his trust, he was very angry. "If you had not plowed with my heifer, you would not have found out my riddle," he said to his companions.

Leaving the feast hurriedly, Samson went to Ashkelon where he killed thirty Philistine men and took from them the thirty changes of clothing to pay his debt. Afterwards, he returned to his father's house in Zorah, leaving his wife at Timnath with her father. And while Samson was at Zorah, his wife's father gave her to one of those thirty men who had been his companions at the marriage feast.

Later, when Samson returned to Timnath for his wife, her father would not let him go in to her. "I thought you hated her," said the father, "and I gave her to your companion. Is not her younger sister fairer than she? Take her instead."

The father's insult did not set well with Samson and he sought revenge against the Philistines. Catching 300 foxes, he tied each pair of foxes tail to tail, and put a firebrand between their two tails. When the brands were set on fire, Samson let the foxes go into the Philistine grain fields, burning both the shocks and the standing grain—as well as their adjoining vineyards and olive trees.

The Philistines soon learned who was responsible for the fires. "Samson, the son-in-law of the Timnite has done this," they were told, "because the Timnite took away his wife and gave her to his companion." So the Philistines went to Timnath and burned the father's house.

But Samson was not pleased that the Philistines would burn the house of his father-in-law for something he had done. "Though what you have done may appear to benefit me," he told the Philistines, "yet will I take revenge." And after he had smitten them with a great slaughter, Samson went to dwell in the top of the rock Etam in the land of Judah.

Because of the sore losses that Samson had inflicted upon the Philistines, they marched to war against the tribe of Judah and made their camp at Lehi. The men of Judah were not pleased. "Why have you come to war against us?" they asked.

"We have come to bind Samson," the Philistines answered, "and to do to him as he has done to us."

Anxious to avoid war with the Philistines, 3,000 men of Judah went to Samson on Etam and said, "Do you not know that the Philistines are our rulers? What is this that you have done to us?"

"I have done to them only as they did to me," answered Samson.

"We have come to bind you," said the men of Judah, "and deliver you into the hands of the Philistines."

"I will go with you," replied Samson. "Only swear to me that you will not fall upon me yourselves."

"We will bind you fast and deliver you to the Philistines," said the men of Judah, "but we will not kill you." And they bound him with two new cords and delivered him to the Philistines at Lehi.

When Samson came to the Philistine camp at Lehi and heard their shouts against him, the Spirit of Jehovah moved upon him. The cords that bound him became as flax in the fire, and the bands were loosed from his hands. He found the jawbone of an ass, took it up, and with it slew 1,000 men.

After this great feat, Samson became faint with thirst and called upon Jehovah for water: "Thou hast given me this great deliverance," he prayed, "and shall I now die of thirst and fall into the hands of the uncircumcised?"

In answer to Samson's prayer, Jehovah caused water to flow from a hollow place in the rock of Lehi that he might drink.[202]

This great slaughter of the Philistines, wrought by Jehovah through the hand of Samson the Nazarite, elevated Samson to the position of judge in Israel, and he judged Israel for twenty years. This, however, was not the end of Samson's troubles, for the yoke of the Philistines was not yet fully broken.

---

[202] The word Lehi means "jawbone," so it is likely that the water came from the rock at Lehi, as this story states, rather than from the hollow in the jawbone itself, as the scripture seems to suggest (Judges 15:19).

87—TELL ME THE SOURCE OF YOUR STRENGTH

(Judges 16)

Though Samson, the judge of Israel, had great physical strength and was greatly blessed by Jehovah, he did not have great moral strength. And though he frequently gave in to his baser instincts and offended Jehovah, he continued to be a thorn in the sides of the Philistines. When he went to Gaza to see a harlot, the Philistines waited for him at the city gates, thinking to slay him. But when Samson came out at midnight, he carried away the gates.

Then Samson fell in love again—this time with a Philistine woman named Delilah in the valley of Sorek. Delilah's feelings for Samson, however, were apparently not the same as his, for she bargained with the lords of the Philistines against him. She agreed that she would entice Samson to tell her the source of his strength and the means by which the Philistines might prevail against him. In return, the lords of the Philistines agreed to pay her well—1,100 pieces of silver from each of them—if she succeeded.

Delilah wasted little time. "Tell me the source of your strength," she pleaded with Samson, "and how you might be bound."

"If they bind me with seven fresh sinews from a slain animal," answered Samson, "I shall be weak and shall be as any other man." Then the lords of the Philistines brought her seven new, moist animal sinews, and Delilah bound Samson as he slept. Meanwhile, the Philistines lay in wait in Samson's bedchamber.

"Arise, Samson!" cried Delilah. "The Philistines are upon you!" But he awoke and burst the sinews as if they were threads in the fire. Samson fled untouched and the source of his strength remained unknown.

"You have mocked me and told me lies," said Delilah, "but now you must tell me the source of your strength and how you might be bound."

And he said to her, "If I am bound fast with new ropes that have never been used, then I shall be weak and like any other man." So she bound him with new ropes as he slept.

"The Philistines are upon you, Samson!" cried Delilah. But those who lay in wait were again disappointed when Samson broke the ropes from his arms as if they were threads and fled from their presence.

Delilah tried him a third time. "Do not mock me, Samson," she begged. "Tell me the source of your strength and how you might be bound."

"If you weave the seven locks of my hair with the web of a loom, I will have no strength," Samson assured her. So she wove his locks with the web as he slept and fastened them with the pin of a weaver's beam.

"The Philistines are upon you, Samson!" she shouted again. But he awoke and went out as before, taking the pin and the web with him.

Delilah was beside herself. She was through using her charm to get the answer that she had agreed to deliver to the lords of the Philistines. More pressure was obviously needed, for she would not be lied to again. "How can you say you love me, Samson, when your heart is not with me? You have mocked me these three times and have not told me the source of your strength."

Delilah was unrelenting. Daily she pressed Samson for the answer until his soul was vexed unto death.

Samson finally reached his limit. "Perhaps," he thought to himself, "I can tell her that my strength comes from my hair." He knew that his hair had never been cut because of his vows as a Nazarite, and he believed that his hair was the source of his strength—but he had no proof.

And so he said to Delilah, "There has been no razor come upon my head in all my days, for I have been a Nazarite unto God from my birth. If I am shaven, my strength will depart from me, and I will be as weak as any other man."

Delilah entices Samson to tell her his secret

Delilah perceived that Samson had told her the truth, and she sent for the lords of the Philistines. "Come at once!" she urged, "for this time Samson has shown me all his heart." Then the lords of the Philistines came to her, bringing money to pay as they had bargained.

As Samson lay to rest, Delilah made him sleep with his head upon her knees. Then she called for a man to come and shave his seven locks. When the hair was gone, Delilah called to him as she had before, "Arise, Samson, for the Philistines are upon you!"

When Samson awoke, he was not aware that Jehovah had departed from him and that his strength was gone. And, though he thought he would go out as he had before, he was helpless before the Philistines who came to capture him. They took him, put out his eyes, and took him to Gaza, where they bound him with fetters of brass in the prison house.

This was a great victory for the Philistines, and they rejoiced in Samson's downfall. No longer was he a threat to their nation or to their dominion over Israel.

When the Philistines gathered to offer a great sacrifice to their god Dagon, they praised Dagon and said, "Our god has delivered our enemy and the man who destroyed our country into our hands." But no one seemed to notice that Samson's hair had begun to grow again, nor did they worry that his strength might return with his hair. As they celebrated, they called for Samson to be brought in from the prison that they might make sport of him.

As the blind judge of Israel was brought into the house of Dagon, he said to the lad who led him by the hand, "Let me feel the pillars that this house stands on, that I may lean upon them."

The people watched while Samson entertained them. Anything he did was entertaining, because he was no longer hurting them. About 3,000 people were gathered to enjoy this wonderful occasion.

Samson was completely humiliated, and he called upon Jehovah in his humility. "O Jehovah," he cried. "Remember me, I pray, and give me strength this one time only that I may be avenged of the Philistines for my eyes." Samson then took hold of the two middle pillars that held up the house of Dagon, one with his right hand and the other with his left. "Let me die with the Philistines," he said. And as he bowed with all his might against the pillars, they gave way. The house of Dagon fell, and those who were killed that day in its fall were more than Samson had slain in all his life.

88—MICAH AND THE DANITES
(Judges 17–18)

During the time that the judges ruled in Israel, every man in Israel did what was right in his own eyes because there was no king and no one to enforce the law. During this time there lived in Mount Ephraim a man named Micah who stole 1,100 shekels of silver from his mother. When he confessed his crime to her and returned the money, she said, "You are blessed of Jehovah, my son, for this is money that I dedicated to Jehovah for you, to make you a graven image.[203] So now I will restore it to you." She then took 200 shekels of the silver and had the founder make two idols from it—a graven image and a molten image—both of which Micah put in his house that he might worship them, along with the ephod[204] and teraphim[205] that he already had there.

Micah consecrated one of his sons to be his priest. Later, however, when an errant young Levite came to Micah's house from Bethlehem-judah, Micah offered him the priest's position for the yearly wages of a suit of clothing and ten shekels of silver. Micah was pleased with this arrangement and said, "Now I know that Jehovah will do me good because I have a Levite as my priest." This young man was not a Levite of ordinary lineage. He was Jonathan, the grandson of Moses through his son Gershom.

During this same period of time, the tribe of Dan was seeking a place to enlarge its inheritance. Though Dan had been given an inheritance during the time of Joshua, much of what they had been given was still in the hands of other well-established peoples. Thus five men were sent to the north as spies to find other lands where the people of Dan might settle. As these five

---

[203] Or carved image.

[204] The ephod was one of the items of sacred clothing worn by the priests. It is possible that the richly ornamented ephod had become an object of worship in Israel by this time, but it is more likely that the ephod referred to here was actually a graven image of some false god.

[205] Teraphim (plural of teraph) were domestic or household gods, perhaps in the size and shape of men, used for working magic. It has been said by some that to have teraphim was not to worship false gods but to worship the true God in a corrupt manner (see the discussion in *Bible Dictionary*, LDS-KJV, s.v. "Teraphim"). That seems to be a distinction without a difference.

men of Dan traveled though Mount Ephraim, they lodged overnight at Micah's house. While there, they recognized the young Levite and asked him, "Who brought you here and what are you doing in this place?"

"Micah has hired me to be his priest," replied Jonathan.

"If you are a priest," they said, "tell us whether the way we are going will be prosperous."

"Go in peace," Jonathan told them, pretending to speak with authority. "The way you have chosen is approved of Jehovah."

The five Danite spies departed and went north as far as Laish, where they encountered a people who lived very casually but who were quiet and secure in their circumstances. These people lived in relative isolation from other peoples and there was no outside trade. Also, there were no magistrates in the area who might cause problems. These people were Zidonians[206] but they were a long way from Zidonia. This looked to the Danite spies like the ideal place to expand their dominion.

When the spies returned to their brethren in the south, they recommended that the Danites go up against the people of Laish and take their land from them. "When you go," said the spies, "you will come to a good land—a place where there is no want of anything that is in the earth. The people are peaceful and there is no magistrate. You must go and possess this land, and, if you are not slothful, Jehovah will give it into your hands."

Because of this favorable report, 600 men of Dan were sent to lay claim to Laish and vanquish the present inhabitants. As they went, they (as the five spies before them) traveled through Mount Ephraim near Micah's house. The five spies, who were now the guides for the others, said to them, "In this house there are teraphim, an ephod, a graven image, and a molten image. It would be good for us to take these with us." Thus the group went to Michah's house and saluted Jonathan, the young Levite.

Then as the 600 men stood with their weapons drawn, the spies carried out Micah's idols. When Jonathan challenged them and asked what they were doing, they replied, "If you hold your peace, you may come with us to be our priest. For it is far better for you to be the priest to an entire tribe and family in Israel than to the house of just one man." The young Levite—being easily persuaded—agreed with the men of Dan and went with them.

When the Danite troop had traveled for some distance, Micah and his neighbors realized what had happened and set out after them. As they came near, the men of Dan turned and said to Micah, "What problem do you have that you have come after us with such a large company?"

Micah was angry. He could not believe they would ask such a question. "You have taken away both my gods and my priest so that I am left with nothing," he said. "How can you ask me what is wrong?"

The Danite leader answered Micah pointedly. "You would be wise to not let your voice be heard among us," he said calmly, "lest some angry fellows run upon you and you lose your life, as well as the lives of your household." Then, having made their point quite satisfactorily, the Danite troop turned and continued on its way to Laish. And Micah and his neighbors, seeing that the Danites were too strong for them to overpower, returned empty to their homes.

Thus the children of Dan, with their new priest and their new gods, traveled on to Laish, where they attacked the people and burned the city. When they rebuilt the city they named it Dan, and they set up their graven images and worshipped them for as long as the tabernacle of Israel was at Shiloh.

---

[206] Or Phoenicians.

89—THE DESOLATION OF BENJAMIN

(Judges 19–21)

A Levite who was returning to his home in Mount Ephraim from a visit to his father-in-law in Bethlehem-judah, stopped for the night in the city of Gibeah, which belonged to the tribe of Benjamin. His wife, who was with him, fell victim to some worthless men of Benjamin who raped her, abusing her throughout the night, and then left her dead. The Levite took his wife's body to his home in Mount Ephraim, where he cut it into twelve pieces, and sent one piece to each of the twelve tribes.

Because of the brutality of this crime, all Israel was incensed and came together to take vengeance upon the men of Benjamin. For all who saw the pieces of the woman's body said, "There has been no such deed done in Israel since we came out of Egypt."

As Israel came together, their leaders inquired of the Levite what had happened. "Tell us the cause of this wickedness," they said.

When the Levite told his story—how the men of Gibeah had forced his wife until she was dead—the people rose up as one and vowed they would not go home until Gibeah had paid for this terrible crime. Men were sent throughout Benjamin requesting that the guilty men be given up, but the people of Benjamin felt they were being picked on unjustly and refused to comply.

The people of the other tribes were so upset by this response that they made an oath to put to death the people of any city that did not join their war against Benjamin.

The battle that followed was fierce. After three days of fighting in which many thousands were slain on both sides and the city of Gibeah was burned, Israel prevailed and drove what was left of the Benjamite army into the wilderness to the rock of Rimmon.[207]

When four more months had passed, Israel attacked again, this time burning every Benjamite city and killing everyone who got in the way. The tribe of Benjamin was destroyed—except for those soldiers who had fled to the rock of Rimmon.

When the war was over, there was much sorrow in Israel because of Benjamin's destruction. The people came up to the tabernacle at Shiloh and wept bitterly. "O Jehovah, God of Israel," they cried, "why has this thing happened in Israel that there should now be one tribe lacking?"

Before going to battle, the men of Israel had sworn another oath besides their oath to kill all those who failed to fight against Benjamin. They had also sworn that they would not give their daughters to marry Benjamites. But now they were sorry for this oath, for it appeared that Israel would have one less tribe because of it.

When the children of Israel learned that the people from the city of Jabesh-gilead, in the tribe of Manasseh, had not gone to battle with them against Benjamin, the remaining tribes attacked the city and killed all of its inhabitants—because of their oath—sparing only those 400 young women of the city who had never married. These young women were given as wives to the surviving Benjamites. But there were still a few men of Benjamin left without wives.

"We must find wives for these others," said the leaders of Israel, "so that Benjamin is not destroyed." After much deliberation, the leaders agreed that those men of Benjamin who did not yet have wives should lie in wait in the vineyards near Shiloh and catch wives of the young women who came out to dance at the yearly feast. "And it shall be," they told the Benjamites, "that when the fathers and brothers of these young women complain, we will ask them to be favorable to you for our sakes because we killed your women in the war."

And the surviving men of Benjamin, according to the agreement, each took a wife—some from among the virgins of Jabesh-gilead and some from among the virgins who danced near Shiloh. They then returned to the land of their inheritance and repaired their burnt cities.

---

[207] This was a place in the wilderness of Benjamin.

90—THE LOYAL MOABITESS
(Ruth 1–4)

During a severe famine in the days of the judges, a man named Elimelech from the tribe of Judah went with his family from Bethlehem-judah to dwell in the land of Moab.[208] His family consisted of his wife Naomi and two sons, Chilion and Mahlon. But not too many years passed before Elimelech died and left Naomi a widow.

The two sons both married women of Moab. The wife of Chilion was named Orpah, and the wife of Mahlon was named Ruth. After ten years in Moab, Mahlon and Chilion also died, both without children, and the three widows—Naomi, Orpah, and Ruth—were left alone. So when Naomi heard that the famine in Israel had abated, she decided to return to her own people.

Naomi started her trek home to Bethlehem, accompanied by her two faithful daughters-in-law, but then thought it would be better for the younger women to remain in their own country. "You will be better off with your own mothers than with me," she told them, "and may Jehovah grant that you find husbands among your own people." Naomi kissed them and they all wept together, for they loved her as she loved them.

"No!" they said to her, "we will go with you to your people."

Then Naomi said, "Turn again, my daughters. There are no more sons in my womb that I can give you for husbands. Even if I had a husband tonight and could bear sons, would you wait for them to grow up?[209] No, my daughters, it grieves me deeply that the hand of Jehovah, has gone against me."

They all wept again; then Orpah kissed Naomi and returned to Moab. Ruth, however, would not go, though Naomi urged her. "Your sister-in-law has returned to her people and her gods," said Naomi. "It would be best for you to go, too."

"Do not request me to leave you or to return from following you," replied Ruth. "I will go wherever you go, and I will lodge wherever you lodge. Your people shall be my people, and your God shall be my God. I will die where you die, and there will I be buried. Jehovah do so to me, and more also, if anything but death should separate me from you." So Naomi and Ruth continued on to Bethlehem-judah together.

The people of Bethlehem-judah could not believe that Naomi had returned. "Is that you, Naomi?" they asked.

"Oh, please," she relied, "do not call me Naomi.[210] You must call me Mara,[211] for God has dealt bitterly with me. I went out full, but Jehovah has brought me home empty."

It was the season of the barley harvest when the two women arrived in Bethlehem-judah, and Ruth entreated Naomi to let her glean in the barley fields. For it was the law in Israel that those who reaped would not fully reap the corners of their fields but leave them to be gleaned by the poor and those who were strangers.[212] Naomi consented, and Ruth went to glean. By good fortune, but without prior planning, Ruth went to glean in the fields of Boaz, a wealthy kinsman of Naomi's late husband Elimelech. When Boaz saw Ruth, he asked his servant, "Who is this young woman?"

"She is the damsel who came from Moab with Naomi," the servant answered. "She came to me and requested to glean and gather after your reapers among the sheaves, and has continued from morning until now."

Then Boaz went to Ruth where she was gleaning in the field and said, "Do not go to glean in other fields, but stay close by my maidens. Watch the fields where they reap and follow them. And when you are thirsty, go to my water vessels and drink from them."

Ruth was overcome by Boaz's kindness. She bowed before him and asked, "Why have I found favor in your eyes that you would take note of me, though I am a stranger?"

"Because I have been told all that you do for your mother-in-law since the death of your husband," answered Boaz, "and how you have left the land of your birth to come unto a people you do not know. May Jehovah, the God of Israel, in whom you have come to trust, grant you a full reward for your work."

"Let me find favor in your sight, my lord," said Ruth, "for you have comforted me and have spoken to me in friendship, though I am not like one of your handmaidens."

Boaz took Ruth to eat with him at mealtime and gave her more than she could eat. And when she returned to her gleaning, Boaz commanded the young men to let her glean wherever she liked, even among the sheaves. "And, also," he said, "let some handfuls of grain fall on purpose for her to glean."

---

[208] The Moabites were closely related to the children of Israel, descendants of Abraham's nephew Lot.

[209] It was the law among the children of Israel that when a man died leaving a wife but no children, his next brother was to marry the widow and raise up children to the deceased brother (see Deuteronomy 5–6).

[210] The name Naomi means "pleasant."

[211] The name Mara means "bitter" or "very sad."

[212] See Leviticus 19:9.

When evening came and Ruth threshed out the grain she had gleaned, she had about an ephah of barley.[213] Returning to the city, she took some of the grain to Naomi. "Where did you glean today?" Naomi asked Ruth when she saw the bounty of her gleaning.

"The man in whose fields I gleaned is named Boaz," Ruth answered.

"May he be blessed of Jehovah," said Naomi, "for he has not ceased showing kindness to both the living and the dead. This man is near kin to us, one who has the right to redeem. It is good for you to go out with Boaz's maidens and not to other fields."

So from that day forward, Ruth stayed close to Boaz's maidens and gleaned in his fields until the end of both the barley harvest and the wheat harvest.

Then Naomi said to Ruth, "Boaz our kinsman will be winnowing the chaff from his barley tonight. Go to the threshing floor where he is working and do not let him see you. When he lies down to sleep, uncover his feet and lie down beside them, then he will tell you what to do."

When Boaz lay down at the end of the grain pile that night, Ruth came softly, uncovered his feet, and lay beside them. In the middle of the night, something seemed strange to Boaz and he awoke. When he turned, he saw a woman lying at his feet. "Who are you?" he asked.

"I am Ruth, your handmaid. Spread your skirt over me, for you are a near kinsman with the right to redeem me from my widowhood."

"You are blessed of Jehovah," said Boaz, "for you have shown more kindness in the latter end than in the beginning. And now, my daughter, fear not, for I will do for you all that you require. Though it is true that I am your late husband's near kinsman, there is another nearer than I am. Stay here tonight and in the morning I will perform my duty as your kinsman."

In the morning, Ruth arose while it was yet dark, and Boaz said to the others who were there, "Let it be known that a woman came into the threshing floor."

Then he said to Ruth, "Bring your cloak and hold it." And Boaz filled Ruth's cloak with six measures of barley, which she took back to Naomi.

"He gave me these six measures of barley," Ruth reported to Naomi, "for he said that I should not go empty to my mother-in-law." And she told Naomi all that Boaz had said.

"Sit still, my daughter, until you know how this matter turns out," said Naomi. "This man will not rest today until it is resolved."

Boaz went that day and waited at the city gate for the kinsman who was nearer to Ruth's husband than he. When the man came, Boaz bade him sit. Then he bade ten elders of the city to sit with them. To the kinsman he said, "Naomi, who has come recently from Moab, is selling a piece of land that belonged to our brother Elimelech. I am telling you this before the elders of our people so that you might redeem it if you wish. You are the nearest kin and have first right to redeem. But if you do not wish to do so, tell me, for my right is after yours."

And the man said, "I will redeem it."

Then Boaz continued: "When you buy this field from Naomi, you must also buy Ruth the Moabitess, the wife of the dead, to raise up seed unto her dead husband upon his inheritance."

When the kinsman heard these further details, he quickly changed his mind. "I cannot redeem it for myself, then," he said, "lest I mar my own inheritance. It is yours to redeem if you like."

Now the manner of doing such business in Israel was for a man to take off his shoe and give it to his neighbor as a testimony of their exchange. And Boaz took off his shoe and gave it to his kinsman. Then Boaz said to the ten elders and to all the people, "You are witnesses this day that I have bought all that was Elimelech's and all that was Chilion's and Mahlon's from Naomi. And Ruth the Moabitess, the wife of Mahlon, I have purchased to be my wife, to raise up the name of the dead upon his inheritance, that the name of Mahlon be not cut off from among his brethren."

Boaz took Ruth to be his wife, and she bore a son whom they named Obed. And this Obed was the father of Jesse, who was the father of King David. And the women of Bethlehem said to Naomi, "Blessed be Jehovah, for he has not left you without a kinsman. This grandson he has given you will restore your life and be nourishment to you in your old age. For your daughter-in-law, who loves you and who is better to you than seven sons, has borne him."

And Naomi laid the child in her bosom and became his nurse.

---

[213] An ephah would have been equal to about eight gallons (30.28 liters).

91—I AM LOANING HIM TO JEHOVAH

(1 Samuel 1–2)

In the days of the judges, there was a Levite from Ramah in Mount Ephraim named Elkanah[214] who went up to the house of the Lord at Shiloh with his family every year to offer sacrifices. Elkanah had two wives, Hannah and Peninnah. Peninnah had both sons and daughters, but Hannah was barren.

Elkanah loved Hannah, but she was unhappy with the lot that God had given her. Year after year she went up to Shiloh, but when Peninnah tormented her because she was childless, Hannah wept and was unable to eat. When Elkanah saw her weeping, he asked, "Why do you weep? Why do you not eat? And why is your heart so grieved because you have no children? Am I not better to you than ten sons?"

While at Shiloh, Hannah went to the temple[215] where she wept bitterly and poured out her heart to God. In her prayer she vowed that if God would give her a son, she would give that son to him all the days of his life. She vowed that her son would be dedicated to God with the lifelong vow of a Nazarite.[216]

Eli the priest was sitting by a post of the temple watching Hannah pray. As he observed her mouth, he saw that her lips moved but he could not hear her voice. Because of this, Eli thought Hannah was drunk. And after a while, he said to her, "How long will you be drunken? You must put away your wine."

"I am not drunk, my lord," answered Hannah, "but I am a woman of sorrowful spirit. I have drunk neither wine nor strong drink but have poured out my soul before God. Count me not worthless, for out of the abundance of my grief I have spoken to God."

"Go in peace then," said Eli. "And you will find grace in God's sight." So Hannah went her way and was no longer sad. The following day, Elkanah and his family rose early, worshiped at the temple, and then returned to their home in Ramah.

Hannah leaves her son Samuel in Eli's care

Once they were back at home in Ramah, Jehovah remembered Hannah and blessed her. She conceived and in due time bore a son whom she named Samuel[217] because she had asked Jehovah for him.

The next time Elkanah and his family went up to Shiloh to make their yearly sacrifice, Hannah did not go. "I will not go up again until the child is weaned," she told her husband. "Then I will take him with me that he may appear before Jehovah and abide there forever."

"Do what seems good to you," said Elkanah, "for you must keep your word to Jehovah."

When Samuel was weaned, Hannah took him with her to the house of the Lord. She also took three bullocks, an ephah of flour,[218] and a bottle[219] of wine. When a bullock had been killed, she took Samuel and gave him to Eli. "My lord," said Hannah to Eli, "as your soul lives, I am the woman who stood by you here, praying to Jehovah. It was for this child that I prayed, and Jehovah has given me that which I sought. I am now loaning him to Jehovah, and he shall be on loan to Jehovah for as long as he lives."

Hannah's heart rejoiced for the blessing Jehovah had given her, and Elkanah and his family returned to

---

[214] Elkanah was a descendant of Levi's son Kohath, as detailed in 1 Chronicles 6.

[215] The temple referred to here was the portable tabernacle that the children of Israel built in the wilderness at Sinai. It had remained in Shiloh since the time of Joshua.

[216] The word Nazarite means "separate" or "set apart." The vows of a Nazarite might be either for a short period or lifelong. The person who took those vows was bound to abstain from wine, from contact with the dead, and from any cutting of the hair.

[217] Samuel means "name of God."

[218] An ephah is about eight gallons (30.28 liters).

[219] A bottle might be better called a water skin. Bottles were the skins of animals and were used as containers for both water and wine.

their home in Ramah. Samuel, however, remained at the temple with Eli.

92—JEHOVAH CAN NO LONGER HONOR YOU
(1 Samuel 2)

Eli was a very old man and a revered judge in Israel. He also served as high priest in the house of the Lord at Shiloh,[220] and Eli's sons, Hophni and Phinehas, served as priests under their father. Though Eli's sons were qualified to be priests by their lineage, that was their only qualification. They were very wicked men and had no regard for the sacred nature of the priest's office. They stole from those who came to the tabernacle and enriched themselves from the sacrifices of the people—taking by force when the people did not give freely. Hophni and Phinehas were also immoral men, lying with the women who gathered at the door of the tabernacle. Jehovah was very displeased with them and also with Eli for allowing them to serve in the house of the Lord when they were unworthy.

When Eli became aware of his sons' unrighteous doings, he called them to account. "Why do you do such things?" he asked them. "For I hear of your evil doings from all the people. Your bad example not only degrades your high callings but also causes the people to sin. If one man sins against another, the judge will judge him, but if a man sins against God, who can plead his case before Jehovah?"

Hophni and Phinehas ignored their father's chastisement and continued unabated in their evil ways. And, though Eli knew better, he permitted his wicked sons to continue their service in the sacred work of the tabernacle in spite of their wickedness.

As the house of the Lord and the holy ordinances were brought to disgrace by these unrighteous priests, Jehovah sent a prophet to warn Eli of what would happen because he had failed to exclude his sons from the sacred work. Said the man of God to Eli, "Jehovah, the God of Israel, remembers the covenant he made with the house of your fathers, how he called you to walk before him forever. But, because you treat the offerings of the people with scorn and honor your sons more than you honor him, he can no longer keep his covenant. For those who honor Jehovah are honored by him, and those who despise him are lightly esteemed."

The man of God continued: "Jehovah can no longer honor you or your house, Eli. And the day will come when you will be cut off—both you and the arm of

---

[220] Eli descended from Aaron through Ithamar, Aaron's youngest son.

your father's house.[221] And the increase of your house shall all die in the flower of their age. Hophni and Phinehas shall both die in one day, and Jehovah will raise up a faithful priest in your place—one who will obey him and do what is in his heart and mind."

Though the prophet's message to Eli was clear, it had no effect. Eli feared his wicked sons more than he loved Jehovah. He still did nothing to restrain Hophni and Phinehas in their wickedness and preserve the sanctity of God's house.

---

[221] The ultimate fulfillment of this prophecy is told in the story "138—Justice for His Father's House," when King Solomon removed Abiathar from the priest's office.

93—SPEAK, LORD, FOR THY SERVANT HEARS THEE
(1 Samuel 2–3)

Because of his mother Hannah's promise to Jehovah, Samuel was left at the tabernacle in Shiloh where he served faithfully under the care and direction of Eli, the high priest and judge. Each year when the family came to offer sacrifices, Samuel's mother brought him a coat that she had made for him. Because Eli loved Samuel, he gave a blessing to Elkanah saying, "Jehovah will give you more seed of this woman because you have loaned your son to Jehovah." And so it was that Hannah was blessed to bear three sons and two daughters.

One night as young Samuel slept, Jehovah called to him. When Samuel heard the voice, he thought it was Eli who had called. "Here am I," he answered, and he ran to Eli. "Here am I, for you called me."

"I did not call, my son" answered Eli. "Go back to your bed." And Samuel returned to his bed.

When Jehovah called to Samuel a second time, Samuel again rose and went to Eli. "Here am I, for you called me," he said again.

But again Eli responded, "I did not call you, my son. Lie down again."

Jehovah called a third time, and again Samuel went to Eli. This time, however, Eli perceived that Jehovah had called the child, and he said to him, "This is what you should do, my son: go back to your bed, and if he calls again, say, 'Speak, Lord, for Thy servant hears Thee.'"

When Samuel had returned to his bed, Jehovah called to him the fourth time. "Samuel, Samuel," he said.

Samuel, when he heard Jehovah's call, remembered what Eli had said. And Samuel answered, "Speak, Lord, for Thy servant hears Thee."

Jehovah then spoke to the boy Samuel about the iniquity in the house of Eli. "Behold," he said, "that which I am about to do in Israel will cause the ears of all who hear it to tingle. For I will perform against Eli all those things that I have spoken to him concerning his household. And when I begin, I will also make an end. I have told Eli that I will judge his house forever because his sons made themselves vile and he did not restrain them. I have therefore sworn that the sins of Eli's house may not be purged with sacrifice or with burnt offerings."

Having heard Jehovah's message, Samuel was unable to sleep. He lay awake in his bed until morning, then went and opened the doors of the tabernacle. He was afraid that Eli would ask what Jehovah had told him in the night. And when Eli called him, Samuel's concerns were realized, for Eli raised the very issue that Samuel had feared. "Samuel, my son," said Eli. "What was it that Jehovah said to you? Do not hide it from me. God do so to you, and more also, if you hide from me what Jehovah said."

And Samuel, hiding nothing from Eli, told him all that Jehovah had spoken.

When Samuel had reported all of Jehovah's words, Eli responded, "It *is* Jehovah. He will do what seems good to him."

As the boy Samuel grew, Jehovah was with him. He forgot nothing that Jehovah had told him, and all of Israel—from Dan in the north to Beersheba in the south—knew that Samuel was called to be a prophet. It had been many years since Jehovah's voice had been heard in Israel, but now he had revealed himself to Samuel at Shiloh.

94—THE GLORY DEPARTS FROM ISRAEL
(1 Samuel 4)

The army of Israel had just returned from a battle against the Philistines in which they had been soundly defeated and had suffered the loss of about 4,000 men. The elders of Israel, troubled by the defeat, decided that Israel's army would be more successful in battle if the ark of the covenant were in the field with the troops. And thus it was that the elders sent to Shiloh asking that the ark, along with the mercy seat, be brought to the army's encampment at Ebenezer.

In response to the pleas of the elders, Eli's wicked sons, Hophni and Phinehas, removed the ark of the covenant from its place in the holy of holies and carried it to Ebenezer. When the ark came into the camp, all Israel rejoiced and shouted with such a great shout that the very earth rang. "Now Jehovah will surely be with us in battle!" they cried.

The Philistines, hearing the celebration in Israel's camp, wondered at the meaning of the great noise. When they learned that the ark of the covenant was in the camp of their enemies, they were genuinely frightened. "God is come into the camp of Israel!" they cried. "Woe unto us! There has never been such a thing before. Who now shall deliver us out of the hand of the mighty God who smote the Egyptians with great plagues in the wilderness?"

The Philistine leaders sought to bolster the courage of their men. "Be strong and fight like men, you Philistines," they said, "or we will become servants to the Hebrews as they have been to us." There was great alarm in the camp of the Philistines.

When the battle finally began, however, it soon became apparent that the fears of the Philistines were unjustified. The army of Israel was badly beaten that day and 30,000 footmen of Israel lay dead upon the ground. As the army of Israel fled in disarray, the Philistines captured the ark of the covenant, and Hophni and Phinehas—Eli's wicked sons—lay among the dead.

A soldier who escaped from the battle came to Shiloh that day to bring word of Israel's defeat. When the man came, Eli sat on a seat by the wayside watching, and his heart trembled for the ark of the covenant. He knew that it should not have left the tabernacle and that he had done nothing to stop it.

When the soldier told the people of Shiloh that the ark was lost to the Philistines, the whole city wept. When Eli heard the weeping he inquired for the reason, and the soldier was brought to him.

"I am the man who came from the army," the soldier told Eli, "and I fled this day for my life."

"What has happened?" asked Eli with grave concern.

"The news is not good," came the man's reply. "Israel has fled before the Philistines and there has been a great slaughter. Your sons Hophni and Phinehas are both dead, and the ark of God has been taken by our enemies."

The shock of this dire message was too much for the aged Eli.[222] Falling backwards off his seat, he broke his neck and died. The prophecy had been fulfilled. Eli, who had judged Israel for forty years, was now dead—along with his wicked sons.[223]

---

[222] The scripture says that Eli was ninety-eight years old and that he was "heavy."

[223] The prophecy that was told to Eli by an unnamed man of God is found in 1 Samuel 2:27–36, and is recounted briefly in the story "92–Jehovah Can No Longer Honor You." In actuality, the prophecy concerning the demise of Eli's family was not completely fulfilled until the days of Solomon (see story "138–Justice for His Father's Enemies").

95–THE ARK AMONG THE PHILISTINES
(1 Samuel 5–7)

When the Philistines routed the army of Israel, they took the ark of the covenant with them, as part of the spoils of the battle, and carried it to their city of Ashdod. Once in the city, they took the ark into the house of their stone god Dagon[224] and set it next to Dagon. When the people came the next morning, they saw that Dagon had fallen on his face before the ark and that the palms of both Dagon's hands had been cut off and were lying on the threshold. Only the stump of Dagon remained.

The day got worse as it continued, for the hand of Jehovah fell heavily upon Ashdod. The people were stricken with painful emerods[225] and many of them died. When the men of Ashdod saw what was happening to them, they cried, "The ark of the God of Israel must be removed from our city, for his hand is sore upon us and upon Dagon." And when the lords of the Philistines counseled together about what should be done with the ark, they decided to move it to Gath.

When the ark came to Gath, great destruction also came to that city. The men of Gath were also stricken with emerods in their secret parts and, in their misery, those who did not die sent the ark to Ekron.

When the ark of the covenant was brought into their city, the people of Ekron were afraid. They cried out to the lords of the Philistines, "The ark of the God of Israel has been brought to us to slay us. Send away this terrible ark and return it to its own place." The people of Ekron had good reason to be afraid, for there was deadly destruction throughout the city. Many died, and those who did not die were stricken with the emerods.

When the ark of the covenant had wrought destruction among the Philistines for seven months, it was decided that it must somehow be returned to the children of Israel. And the wise men of the Philistines were called to determine how this might be accomplished.

---

[224] Dagon was a god of the Philistines. Dagon means "fish," but it is not clear whether he was actually a fish god or a god of grain (which would be true if the translation were incorrect, as some scholars believe, and should have been *Dagan*). It was in the temple of Dagon in Gaza that Samson was killed.

[225] The scripture says that Jehovah "smote them with emerods." It is believed that emerods are probably a bad form of bleeding hemorrhoidal tumors (see William Smith, *Dictionary of the Bible*, GospeLink, CD-ROM, s.v. "emerods").

The wise men determined that they should make golden images of the emerods and of mice as a trespass offering and send them to Israel, along with ark.

Following the counsel of their wise men, the Philistines put the ark of the covenant on a new cart, along with their offerings of five golden mice and five golden emerods in a coffer next to it. They hitched two milk cows to the cart and set them on the road toward Israel and the town of Beth-shemesh.[226]

The cows followed the road straight to Beth-shemesh, lowing as they went, with the five lords of the Philistines walking behind. When the people of the town, who were laboring in the fields, looked up and saw the ark of the covenant coming toward them on the cart, they became very excited. The cows, meanwhile, turned into a field and stopped beside the great stone of Abel. The Levites lifted the ark and the coffer with the golden jewels from the cart, then used the wood of the cart to offer the cows as a burnt offering to Jehovah.

When many of the people of Beth-shemesh looked inside the ark, Jehovah smote them that they died.[227] Those who were left were frightened and dismayed. "Who is able to stand before the Lord Jehovah?" they asked. And they sent messengers to Kirjath-jearim[228] telling how the ark had been returned from the Philistines. "The Philistines have brought back the ark of God," they said. "Come down and get it."

So, the men of Kirjath-jearim carried the ark of the covenant from Beth-shemesh into their own city, putting it in the house of Abinadab, where it remained for twenty years. Abinadab's son Eleazar served as the priest, and Israel remained in bondage to the Philistines.

96—SAMUEL'S VICTORY OVER THE PHILISTINES
(1 Samuel 7)

Because the children of Israel were prone to worship false gods, Jehovah allowed the Philistines to dominate them, to even take away some of their land. The situation was not a happy one for of Israel, and the people lived in constant fear of their neighbors to the west. But Samuel promised the children of Israel that if they would put away their strange gods and return to Jehovah, Jehovah would deliver them from Philistine rule.

Israel responded as a body to Samuel's challenge. They forsook their worship of Baal[229] and Ashtoreth[230] and returned to the worship of Jehovah, serving him only. When the people had repented, Samuel called them to come together at Mizpeh[231] where he would pray for them. At Mizpeh they poured water on the ground before Jehovah and fasted all that day, seeking forgiveness for their sins.

When the lords of the Philistines learned that Israel was gathered at Mizpeh, they took their men of war and went to meet them in battle. The children of Israel were frightened when they saw the Philistine army approaching. "Do not cease to cry unto Jehovah for us," they pleaded with Samuel, "that he will save us from these Philistines." So Samuel continued to pray for them and offered a suckling lamb as a burnt offering in their behalf.

---

[226] Beth-shemesh was one of the towns on the northern border of Judah and was only about seven miles (11.3 kilometers) from Ekron.

[227] The people of Beth-shemesh were stricken because they disregarded the holiness and sanctity of the ark of the covenant. Even as Jehovah called all the descendants of Levi to assist the priests (the descendants of Aaron) in caring for the tabernacle and its sacred contents, he warned them that any except the priest who came near to the tabernacle, the vessels of the sanctuary, or the altar would die (see Numbers 17:13 and 18:3).

[228] Kirjath-jearim, like Beth-shemesh, was on the northern border of Judah, but lying more to the east.

[229] Baal (plural form Baalim), the storm and fertility god, was symbolic of the male generative principle in nature. Baal worship was most common among the Zidonians or Phoenicians, but it seems that Baal's name (which means "lord") was used broadly in the Old Testament to refer to all heathen and foreign gods.

[230] Ashtoreth (meaning "a star") was the principal female deity of the Phoenicians. She was called Ishtar by the Assyrians and Astarte by the Greeks and Romans. Some ancient writers identified her with the moon, though Ishtar and Astarte have both been identified with the planet Venus.

[231] This is not the same Mizpeh (Mizpah) where Jacob and his father-in-law Laban raised a heap of stones and made a covenant of peace (see story "30—A Covenant of Peace"). This Mizpeh was a city in Benjamin, located about four miles (6.4 kilometers) northwest of Jerusalem. Note that this is also a different place than the Mizpeh (Mizpah) where Jephthah lived (see story "83—The Victory and the Vow"). That Mizpeh was located east of the Jordan in Gilead.

As the Philistine army drew near, Jehovah caused a great thunderstorm that left them in a state of confusion. And, in the confusion of the storm, the Philistines were overcome and driven back by the army of Israel.

In his gratitude to Jehovah, Samuel erected a stone near Mizpeh and called it Ebenezer[232] because, he said, "Jehovah has helped us."

The Philistines were completely subdued at Mizpeh and did not return to do battle with Israel during all the days that Samuel served as judge of Israel. Those cities that the Philistines had taken from Israel were taken back—from Ekron[233] to Gath and all of the land between. And there was peace in the land once more.

---

[232] The name Ebenezer means "stone of help."

[233] Ekron was within the land that fell to the lot of Judah in Joshua's division of the land. It was later within the jurisdiction of Dan. However, it was a major Philistine stronghold and one those five towns belonging to the five lords of the Philistines. It was the northernmost of those towns and was in the lowlands. It was also one of the three cities where the Philistines took the ark of the covenant when it was captured from Israel (see story "95–The Ark among the Philistines").

VII

SAUL AND DAVID:

THE RISE AND FALL OF KING SAUL

97—THAT WE MIGHT BE LIKE OTHER NATIONS

(1 Samuel 8)

The children of Israel were unhappy with the rule of judges. To begin with, they were upset with Samuel's sons, Joel and Abiah, who had been appointed by Samuel as judges in Beersheba, for they were known to have taken bribes and had judged unrighteously. Israel had no complaints against Samuel himself, but he was getting old and would not be with them much longer.

The elders of Israel came to Samuel at his home in Ramah and said, "You are getting old, Samuel, and your sons do not walk in your ways. It is time for you to give us a king to govern Israel, that we might be like other nations."[234]

Samuel was deeply troubled by the people's request, but when he took the matter to Jehovah, Jehovah told him to hearken to the voice of the people. "Israel has not rejected you," he told Samuel. "They have rejected me. In fact, they have rejected me and have served other gods since the day I brought them out of Egypt. Give them what they ask, but, before you do, let them know what will happen to them when they are ruled by a king."

Responding to Jehovah's instructions, Samuel went to the people and told them all that Jehovah had said. Then he explained what would happen if a king were to rule over them. "This will be the manner of the king who will reign over you," he said. "He will take your sons for his own service—to drive his chariots, to be his horsemen, and some to run before his chariots. He will appoint some as captains over thousands and captains over fifties. He will have some to cultivate the ground for him and others to reap his harvest. And he will use them to make his instruments of war and his chariots. He will also take your daughters. They will be his perfumers and ointment makers, his cooks, and his bakers."

Samuel continued his list of reasons for avoiding the rule of a king, painting as bleak a picture as he knew how. "A king will take away your fields, your vineyards, and your oliveyards," said Samuel, "even the best of them, and give them to his servants. He will take your menservants, your maidservants, your best young men, and your asses, and put them all to work for his own purposes. He will also take a tenth of your sheep, and you shall be his servants. And when you will cry out to Jehovah in that day for relief because of the king that you have chosen, Jehovah will not hear you."

The people listened to Samuel arguments, but they were not convinced. This was not what they wanted to hear. "It does not matter what you say," they told Samuel. "We want a king to rule over us, that we might be like other nations. For a king will judge us and go before us to fight our battles."

Samuel was distressed because the people refused to believe him. But when he went back and told Jehovah, Jehovah told him to give the people what they wanted. "Hearken to the voice of the people and give them a king," he said. Then Samuel sent the people home.

---

[234] This request by the people of Israel is in direct fulfillment of the warning and prophecy given by Moses many hundreds of years before, as recorded in Deuteronomy 17:14 and ff. (see story "71—Moses' Farewell").

98−JEHOVAH HAS ANOINTED YOU

(1 Samuel 9−10)

The prophet Samuel had resigned himself to the idea that Israel was going to have a king. He did not like the idea, but he knew that the people would not be dissuaded. One day while Samuel was in the land of Zuph,[235] Jehovah spoke to him saying, "About this time tomorrow, I will send you a man from the land of Benjamin whom you shall anoint to be captain over Israel. He shall save Israel from the Philistines, for I have heard their cries for deliverance."

The next day two men came to Ramah seeking Samuel. One was a man named Saul from the tribe of Benjamin; the other was Saul's servant. They had been searching for the lost asses of Saul's father Kish for three days and, when the servant told Saul that there was a seer in the land, they decided to seek his counsel.

Taking a half-shekel of silver as a gift for the seer, the men ventured to Ramah to find him. As they entered the city gate, the first person the met was Samuel, who was on his way to the high place[236] to offer a sacrifice and to eat.

Saul was a choice, steadfast, and humble man. He was also handsome and impressive in his stature.[237] Most other men stood only to the height of Saul's shoulder. When Samuel saw Saul, Jehovah said to him, "Behold, Samuel, this is the man of whom I spoke! He shall reign over my people."

Saul and his servant, not knowing who Samuel was, approached him and asked, "Can you point us to the seer's house?"

"I am the seer," answered Samuel. "You must go ahead of me to the high place, and I will eat with you there today. But tomorrow I will let you go and will tell you all that is in your heart." Samuel then said, "As for your asses, have no more concern about them, for they have been found." Then, almost as an afterthought, he added, "Upon you and upon your father's house rests all the hope of Israel."

Saul could not believe what he had just heard, and he did not understand it. "Why do you speak to me this way?" he asked Samuel. "I am of Benjamin, the smallest tribe in Israel. And is not my family, the family of Matri,[238] the least of the families of Benjamin?"

Samuel did not answer Saul but took him and his servant to his dining area at the high place. There he seated them in the most prominent spot. Then Samuel said to his cook, "Bring this man the portion that I told you to set aside. He is the one for whom it was saved."

When they had eaten and returned to the city, Samuel visited with Saul and his servant upon the top of his house. After their visit, the three men began walking together toward the city gate, but Samuel desired to be alone with Saul. "Send your servant ahead," he said to Saul, "that I may speak to you the words of Jehovah."

When the Samuel and Saul were alone, Samuel poured a vial of oil on Saul's head. Then he kissed him and said, "Jehovah has anointed you to be captain over his inheritance."

Samuel then gave Saul some detailed instructions. He told him to go to Rachel's sepulcher at Zelzah[239] where he would meet two young men. "These men," said Samuel, "will tell you that your father's lost asses have been found, and that your father has stopped worrying for them and is now sorrowing for you.

"From Zelzah, go to the plain of Tabor, where you will meet three men on their way to Beth-el. One man will be carrying three kids, one three loaves of bread, and the third a bottle[240] of wine. These men will give you two loaves of their bread."

"Then," continued Samuel, "go to the hill of God where the garrison of the Philistines is located. At the city there you will meet a company of prophets coming down from the high place with a psaltery, a tabret, a pipe, and a harp, and they shall prophesy. The Spirit of Jehovah will also come upon you, and you will prophesy with them and be changed into a different man. When you see these signs, do whatever the occasion requires, for God is with you."

---

[235] Zuph was the Levite ancestor of Samuel.

[236] It was customary to build altars for worship on hilltops. These locations, known as high places, became local centers for worshipping Jehovah. Unfortunately many of these altars became desecrated and were used for the worship of false gods. Some, in fact, were created specifically for that purpose. After the temple was built in Jerusalem, there were periodic efforts made to eliminate all high places.

[237] The scripture speaks of Saul as a choice and goodly young man. It says, in fact, that "among the children of Israel there was not a goodlier person than he" (1 Samuel 9:2).

[238] Nothing is known about Matri or who he was. However, it was the family of Matri in the tribe of Benjamin to which Saul belonged.

[239] Zelzah is mentioned only this once in the scriptures. It is the place where Rachel died and was buried "in the way to Ephrath, which is Bethlehem" (see Genesis 35:19 and story "34−The Last Son").

[240] A bottle might more properly be called a water skin. It was an animal skin that was used by travelers and others to carry water and wine.

Samuel went on: "After this, go before me to Gilgal, and I will come to you there to offer burnt offerings and to sacrifice peace offerings. You must wait for me at Gilgal for seven days, then I will come and tell you what to do."[241] Then, when Saul turned his back to depart from Samuel, God gave Saul another heart.

As Saul followed Samuel's instructions, all the signs that Samuel had told to him were fulfilled. Then, when Saul came to the hill of God, a company of prophets met him and the Spirit of Jehovah came upon him. And when Saul prophesied, those who knew him were astonished. "What has come over the son of Kish?" they asked. "Is Saul also one of the prophets?"

When Saul came to the high place after he had prophesied, his uncle approached him and asked where he and his servant had been. "We went to seek my father's asses," replied Saul. "And when the asses could not be found, we went to see the prophet Samuel."

"And what did Samuel tell you?" asked Saul's uncle.

"He told us that the asses had been found," said Saul. But Saul said nothing to his uncle about what Samuel said concerning the kingdom.

Now that the prophet Samuel knew whom Jehovah had chosen to be king of Israel and the king had been anointed, he summoned all Israel to Mizpeh. Once they were gathered, Samuel said to them, "Thus sayeth Jehovah: 'I brought Israel out of Egypt and delivered you from the Egyptians. I have delivered you out of the hands of all kingdoms and from those who oppressed you. I have also delivered you from your adversities and tribulations. And now today, when you ask for a king to reign over you, you are rejecting me.'"

Samuel had the children of Israel divide themselves by tribes and gather near to him. When the tribes came near, he chose the tribe of Benjamin and set it apart from the others. Next Samuel chose from Benjamin the family of Matri; then from Matri he chose Saul the son of Kish. But when Samuel called for Saul to come forward, Saul could not be found in the multitude, for he had hidden himself.

When Saul's hiding place was discovered and he was brought before the congregation, Samuel said, "Look at the man whom Jehovah has chosen to be king of Israel. There is no other man like him among this people."

When the people heard this, Jehovah touched their hearts and they shouted, "May the king live long!"

Samuel then explained how the kingdom was to be set up and wrote it all down in a book. He then put the book in a safe place—hiding it up unto Jehovah—and sent the children of Israel to their homes.

When Saul returned to his home at Gibeah, a company of men went with him—men whose hearts Jehovah had touched. But there were some who objected to Saul being king. Seeking to sow discord, they asked, "How can this man save us?" But though these detractors despised Saul and brought him no gifts, he chose to ignore them.

The children of Israel, rejecting Jehovah as their king, now had the mortal king they had sought. And this king was indeed a man like no other.

---

[241] Certainly there are gaps in the scriptural account, and we are not told when this meeting at Gilgal between Saul and Samuel took place. An account of a similar meeting, however, is told in story "100—You Have Acted Very Foolishly." This event, however, occurred two years after Saul became king. It was unfortunate for Saul that he did not wait for Samuel's arrival.

99—VICTORY FOR KING SAUL

(1 Samuel 11–12)

In the days when Saul had newly been anointed king of Israel, the Ammonites, under the leadership of Nahash, invaded the land of Jabesh-gilead, which lay east of the Jordan. The people of Jabesh feared for their lives, and in their distress they went to Nahash and petitioned for peace. "Make a covenant with us that you will spare our lives," they urged, "and we will be your servants."

Nahash, however, wanted more than service. He wanted to humiliate Israel. "We will agree to your request on one condition," said Nahash. "We will save your lives and take you as servants if you will allow us to thrust out all of your right eyes as an insult and reproach upon Israel."

Though the people of Jabesh felt vulnerable and wanted to avoid war at all costs, the sight of their right eyes seemed a very high price to pay for peace. They answered Nahash: "Give us seven days to see if there is any man in Israel who will save us. If not, we will surrender and submit ourselves to your terms."

The people of Jabesh immediately sent messengers to Gibeah to find Saul, their new king. Because Saul was in the field tending his flocks, the messengers told their plight to the people of Gibeah. And when the people of Gibeah heard it, they lifted their voices and wept. When Saul returned from the field, he saw the people weeping and asked why. Then, as he listened carefully to the disturbing news, the Spirit of God moved upon him and his anger was kindled. Taking a yoke of oxen, Saul cut them into pieces, and sent messengers to carry the pieces throughout Israel and to say, "Whatever man does not come forth after Saul and Samuel to go against the Ammonites, it shall be done to him as to this ox."

The people of Israel responded to King Saul's request as one. They rejoiced to have a king who would lead them into battle. Some 330,000 men came forward to take up arms in defense of their brethren. "Tell the men of Jabesh-gilead," they said, "that by the time the sun is hot tomorrow they shall have our help."

The men of Jabesh-gilead rejoiced when they received this news. Planning a little subtlety of their own, they sent a message to Nahash. "We will come out to you tomorrow," the message said, "and you may do to us as it seems good to you."

And so it was that the next morning Saul, with the prophet Samuel at his side, came over Jordan with three companies of men and battled the Ammonites until the heat of the day. And those Ammonites who were not killed were scattered so that no two of them were left standing together.

With the Ammonites soundly defeated, the people of Israel said to Samuel, "Where are those men now who objected to Saul being king? Bring them to us that we may put them to death."

But Saul heard their plotting and intervened. "No man of Israel shall be put to death today," he said, "for Jehovah has wrought salvation in Israel."

Samuel, seeing this as an opportunity to strengthen the unity of Israel, said, "Come! Let us go to Gilgal and renew the kingdom." So all the people went with Samuel to Gilgal where they joined in anointing Saul their king. They also made sacrifices of peace offerings to Jehovah and held a great celebration. All Israel rejoiced because they now had a king to lead them into battle.

And Samuel said to the people, "If you will serve Jehovah, obey his voice, and not rebel against his commandments, then shall both you and your king continue to follow Jehovah. But stand now and see the great thing that Jehovah will do before your eyes. I will call upon Jehovah and he shall send thunder and rain that you may see the great wickedness you have done in asking for a king." Although Samuel had come to love Saul, he was still offended because Israel had demanded a king.

When Samuel called to Jehovah and Jehovah sent thunder and rain according to Samuel's promise, all the people became fearful because of the great storm. They pleaded with Samuel, "Pray for us that we do not die, for surely we have added this evil of asking for a king to our many sins."

"Fear not," Samuel answered them. "Though you have done this wickedness, you have not turned aside from following Jehovah. If you will now turn from vain things and serve him with all your hearts, he will not forsake you. He is pleased to make you his people."

Samuel continued: "I will teach you the good and right way and will not cease to pray for you. And all that Jehovah asks is for you to fear him, to serve him in truth with all your hearts, and to remember all that he has done for you. If, however, you still choose to do wickedly, both you and your king shall be consumed."

100—YOU HAVE ACTED VERY FOOLISHLY
(1 Samuel 13)

Saul was a popular king and well loved by his people. When he had reigned for two years he chose 3,000 men of Israel for his army. Two thousand were to fight directly under his command and 1,000 under his son Jonathan. Those troops under Jonathan's command attacked and overcame the Philistine garrison at Geba, and Saul proclaimed this great victory throughout all the land.

When the children of Israel heard that Saul's army had smitten the Philistines, they followed Saul to Gilgal. But when the Philistines learned that they were there, they too came—bringing them with 30,000 chariots, 6,000 horsemen, and an army as numerous as the sands of the seashore—and camped at Michmash. When the people saw the vast Philistine army, they were in great distress. Many fled from Gilgal and went to hide in caves and wherever else they thought might be safe. Many crossed the Jordan into Gilead, but Saul remained in Gilgal. Those who remained with him had great fear for their lives.

Saul was waiting in Gilgal for the prophet Samuel to come and offer sacrifices prior to going into battle. He waited at Gilgal for seven days as Samuel had requested, but, when Samuel failed to arrive, those who remained behind began to scatter also.

Because of Saul's fear of the mighty Philistine army encamped on his doorstep at Michmash, he became desperate. Why had Samuel not come? Something must be done, he thought; the Philistines would soon be upon them.

Saul, feeling he could wait no longer, requested that the burnt offering and the peace offerings that Samuel was going to offer be brought to him. Then, though he had no priesthood authority, Saul acted as if he were the priest and sacrificed the offerings to Jehovah.

No sooner had Saul finished his offerings than Samuel arrived, and Saul went out to meet him. Samuel sensed immediately that something was wrong. "What have you done?" he asked Saul.

Saul tried his best to explain: "Because I saw that the people were scattered from me and that you did not come within the appointed time—and because I saw the Philistines were amassing for war at Michmash—I became worried. I feared that the Philistines would come to battle before we had made supplication to Jehovah. With these concerns in mind, I forced myself to sacrifice the burnt offering."

Samuel was now very angry. "You have acted very foolishly!" he said to Saul. "You have failed to keep the commandments that Jehovah gave you! And now, because of this, you will pay a high price. Your descendants would have been established as kings in Israel forever, but now—because you have disobeyed Jehovah—your kingdom shall not continue after you. Jehovah has sought him out a man after his own heart to stand in your place and be captain over Israel."

Then Samuel departed from Gilgal.

101—VICTORY—AND NEARLY DEATH—FOR JONATHAN

(1 Samuel 14)

Saul's son Jonathan was both a mighty man of war and a man of great faith, and he brought glory to the cause of Israel in the continuing war against the Philistines. One day Jonathan said to his armorbearer, "Let us go over to the garrison of these uncircumcised Philistines. It may be that Jehovah will work in our behalf; for he is not limited as to whether he saves by many or by few."

"Do what is in your heart," answered the armorbearer, "for I am with you."

"This is the plan," explained Jonathan. "We will go over toward these men and make our presence known to them. If they tell us to stand still until they come to us, we will stay in our place and will not go to them. However, if they say for us to come to them, we will do so. That will be our sign that Jehovah has delivered them into our hands."

When the two men made their presence known to the Philistine garrison, the Philistines said, "Behold, the Hebrews have come out of their hiding places." And they called to Jonathan and the young man, "Come up to us and we will show you something."

"Follow me!" said Jonathan to his armorbearer, "for Jehovah has delivered the Philistines into the hands of Israel." And so it was that the two men went forward and began to slay with their swords every Philistine who came into their paths. When they had killed about twenty men, the earth began to tremble and the garrison trembled also.

Saul's watchman, who observed the garrison from the hill, could see something going on but he could not tell exactly what it was. He reported to Saul that the multitudes of Philistines were beginning to melt away and that they were beating one another down.

When Saul heard the watchman's report, he began to wonder who was fighting the Philistines. "Number our men," he ordered, "and see who is not here." And, when they did so, they discovered that Jonathan and his armorbearer were not accounted for.

Saul and those who were with him, sensing what had happened, immediately rushed to join the battle, and the Philistines began to flee in confusion. When the Hebrews in the Philistine army saw the success of their fellow Israelites, they also turned to be with Saul and Jonathan. Those Israelites who had been hiding also returned to join the fight. And Jehovah blessed the army of Israel that day that they prevailed against the Philistines.

Earlier in the day, some time after Jonathan had left his father's camp, Saul made his men take an oath that they would eat nothing before evening. Though many were now faint because of the battle, all were faithful to their oath. Jonathan, however, unaware of the oath, took some honeycomb on the end of his rod and ate it as the army passed through the woods.

One of the men, seeing Jonathan eating honey, said, "Your father strictly charged this people with an oath that any man who eats food this day will be cursed."

"My father has troubled the land," replied Jonathan. "Did you see how my eyes lit up when I tasted the honey? If this people had eaten freely of the spoils of their enemy today, I wonder how much greater our victory might have been."

When the men of Israel's army heard Jonathan's words, they flew upon the spoils of the battle, for they were hungry. They killed sheep, oxen, and cattle and began to eat them on the ground, with their blood.

Some others, who saw these men of Israel eating blood, went and reported it to Saul. "These people sin against Jehovah," they said, "because they are eating blood."

"They have transgressed!" cried Saul when he heard the report. "Roll a great stone upon me today! Tell these men to bring their animals to me that I might slay them properly. Then they may eat and not sin against Jehovah by eating blood." And Saul built an altar unto Jehovah and worshipped before it.

When Saul felt that the blood-eating problem had been resolved and that all was in order, he was eager to continue the battle. "Let us go down after the Philistines by night," he said, "and spoil them until morning, not leaving a man of them alive."

"We can go," answered Ahiah the priest, "but, before we do so, let us seek the counsel of God that we might follow it." But when Saul sought the counsel of Jehovah, he received no answer.

When it was determined that Israel would not go to battle against the Philistines again that night, Saul called the leaders of the army to counsel with him. He was troubled because so many had broken their oath not to eat that day, and he sought to learn who had caused the men to break that oath. "As Jehovah lives who saves Israel," said Saul, "even if the sin should be in my son Jonathan, the man who is responsible must surely die."

When no one would answer Saul's request for information, he decided that he would draw lots to identify the guilty party—and his lot fell upon Jonathan.

"Tell me what you have done," Saul demanded of his son.

146

"I tasted a little honey on the end of my rod," replied Jonathan, "and I am prepared to die."

"God do so to me and more also," said Saul. "You shall surely die for what you did."

But the people rose up in opposition and challenged Saul. "God forbid!" they cried, "that Jonathan, who has wrought this great victory in Israel, should die! As Jehovah lives, there shall not one hair of his head fall to the ground, for he has worked with God this day."

And Jonathan's life was spared that day because the will of the people prevailed over the will of the king. Later in Saul's life this could not have happened.

102−TO OBEY IS BETTER THAN SACRIFICE
(1 Samuel 15)

The prophet Samuel came to Saul and told him that Jehovah had commanded Israel to go to battle against the Amalekites. "Because Jehovah remembers what Amalek did to Israel in the wilderness when they came out of Egypt,"[242] Samuel explained to Saul, "he has now commanded that you smite the Amalekites to destroy them and all that they have. You must slay them all—man and woman, infant and suckling, ox and sheep, camel and ass."

In obedience to Samuel's instructions, Saul prepared his army, 210,000 strong, and marched against the Amalekites. When he came to the city of Amalek, he lay in wait in the valley and sent a warning to the Kenites to separate themselves from the Amalekites or be destroyed with them. For the Kenites showed kindness to the children of Israel when they came out of Egypt.[243]

When the Kenites were removed, Saul's army launched a mighty assault against the people of Amalek, smiting them from Havilah to Shur[244] and destroying every thing and every person before them—almost. They took Agag, king of the Amalekites, as a prisoner and also saved the best sheep and oxen, the fatlings, the lambs, and everything that was good.

Back in Ramah, Jehovah—seeing that Saul had failed to obey his instruction to destroy everything—spoke to Samuel saying, "I have set Saul up to be the king of Israel, but he has sinned and does not repent. He neither follows me nor keeps my commandments."

Samuel was grieved at Jehovah's message and cried unto him all that night. And in the morning he rose early and went out to meet Saul and the returning army. As Samuel went, however, he was unable to find Saul's army, for they were not on the road to Ramah. When he

---

[242] See story "53−As Long as His Hands Were Raised." At that time, Jehovah promised that, when Israel had possession of the promised land, he would "destroy the memory of Amalek" (see Exodus 17:14−16).

[243] The Kenites are thought to have been descendants of Abraham through his wife Keturah. They were a tribe of the Midianites.

[244] The location of Havilah is unknown, but Shur is near the eastern boundary of Egypt, probably near the head of the Red Sea. It was to the wilderness of Shur that Hagar went when she fled from Sarah (see story "15−The Birth of Ishmael").

147

inquired, he was told that Saul and his men had gone to Gilgal.

Samuel turned his course to follow Saul to Gilgal and soon found him. When Samuel found Saul, Saul said to him, "Blessed are you of Jehovah, Samuel. I have performed all that Jehovah commanded me."

Samuel was not impressed. "If you have done as Jehovah commanded," he asked, "what are this bleating of sheep and this lowing of oxen that I hear?"

"We brought these animals from the Amalekites," answered Saul. "The people spared the best of the sheep and oxen that we might sacrifice them to Jehovah. All the rest were destroyed."

Samuel was distraught. "Let me tell you what Jehovah told me last night," he said to Saul.

"Say on," responded Saul.

"He told me that when you were little in your own sight, he made you head of the tribes of Israel and anointed you to be their king because you obeyed him. But now it is not so. He charged you as king of Israel to go against the Amalekites and destroy them, but instead you flew upon the spoil and did evil in his sight. Why did you not obey Jehovah's voice?"

Saul was taken aback. "I *have* obeyed," he whined. "I went the way that Jehovah sent me and completely destroyed the Amalekites—but I brought back Agag, the king of Amalek. And my people took spoil of the sheep and oxen—the best of those things that were to be destroyed—that we might sacrifice them to Jehovah at Gilgal."

Saul's rationalizing stunned Samuel. How could such disregard for Jehovah's instructions be regarded as obedience? Measuring his words very carefully, Samuel posed another question to Saul: "Has Jehovah as great delight in burnt offerings and sacrifices as in obedience to his voice?"

Then, answering his own question, Samuel said, "Behold, to obey is better than sacrifice, and to hearken than the fat of rams. Rebellion is as the sin of witchcraft and stubbornness as iniquity and idolatry."

Saul was beginning to understand the seriousness of his disobedience. "I have sinned!" he confessed. "I have transgressed your words and Jehovah's commandment because I feared the people and obeyed them instead of him. Now, therefore, pardon my sin and return again with me that I may worship Jehovah."

"I cannot return with you, for you have rejected the word of Jehovah," answered Samuel, "and you have been rejected by Jehovah as king of Israel."

As Samuel turned to leave, Saul took hold of the skirt of his own mantle and tore it. Samuel responded to this act by saying, "Saul, as you have torn your mantle, so Jehovah has torn the kingdom of Israel from you today and given it to your neighbor who is better than you. Jehovah will neither lie nor repent, for he is not a man."

"Though I have sinned," cried Saul, "honor me before the elders of my people and before Israel. Return to me again that I may worship Jehovah." So Samuel, giving heed to Saul's pleadings, turned back to Saul, and Saul worshipped Jehovah.

Samuel still had some unfinished business. "Bring Agag, the king of the Amalekites, to me," he commanded. And when Agag was brought, Samuel said to him, "Agag, as your sword has made women childless, so shall your mother be childless." Then Samuel took a sword and killed Agag before Saul and all the army of Israel.

Samuel then returned to his home in Ramah and never again went to see Saul. But Samuel mourned for Saul because he loved him, and Jehovah regretted that he had ever made Saul king of Israel.

103—ARISE AND ANOINT HIM

(1 Samuel 16)

Samuel loved Saul and was greatly distressed when Saul was disobedient and Jehovah rejected him as king of Israel. Then Jehovah said to Samuel, "How long will you mourn because I have rejected Saul? Fill your horn with oil and go up to the house of Jesse in Bethlehem, for I have chosen a new king from among Jesse's sons."

Though Samuel loved Saul, he also feared him, and he said to Jehovah, "How can I go? If Saul hears of it, he will kill me."

"Take a calf with you," said Jehovah, "and tell the people you have come to offer a sacrifice. Then call Jesse to the sacrifice, and I will show you what to do. And you shall anoint unto me the man that I shall make known to you."

When Samuel came to Bethlehem, the elders of the town trembled at his coming and asked if he had come in peace. "I have come peaceably," answered Samuel. "I have come to offer a sacrifice to Jehovah. Sanctify yourselves and come with me."

Then Samuel sanctified Jesse and his sons and invited them to the sacrifice. When they had come, Samuel looked at Jesse's eldest son, Eliab, and said to himself, "Surely this man is Jehovah's anointed."

Then Jehovah taught Samuel an important lesson. "Jehovah does not see as men see," he said. "Men look at outward appearances, but Jehovah looks at men's hearts. Do not look upon this man's face or the height of his stature, for I have refused him."

Then Jesse called Abinadab, his second son, to pass before Samuel. And Samuel said, "He is not the man Jehovah has chosen." And when Jesse's third son Shammah came before Samuel, the answer was the same: "This is not the one."

When Jesse's seven sons had all passed before Samuel, he was puzzled for he knew that none of these men had been chosen by Jehovah to be king of Israel. This seemed very strange to Samuel because Jesse seemed to have no more sons. So, he asked Jesse, "Are these all of your sons? Jehovah has not chosen one of these."

"I have one more," replied Jesse. "My youngest son David is tending the sheep."

"Bring him to me," said Samuel, "for I shall not rest till I see him."

When David came in, Samuel saw that he was a handsome and radiant youth. And Jehovah said to Samuel, "Arise and anoint him king of Israel, for he is the man." And Samuel took his horn of oil and anointed young David, who was a descendant of Judah, in the midst of all his brothers.

104—LET DAVID STAY WITH ME

(1 Samuel 16)

Even as David had the Spirit of Jehovah upon him from the day Samuel anointed him to be king, that spirit departed from Saul and was replaced by an evil spirit. Saul's state of mind was troubling to his servants, and they said to him, "An evil spirit that is not from Jehovah is troubling you. Let us seek out a man with musical skill who can play the harp for you, and you shall be well."

"Yes, that is good," Saul agreed. "Find such a man and bring him to me."

Then one of Saul's servants said, "I know of such a man. David, the son of Jesse is skillful with the harp. He is also a mighty man of war and prudent in all things. He is a handsome man also, and Jehovah is with him." So, Saul sent messengers to Jesse at Bethlehem asking that David be sent to Gibeah to play for him.

The young man David came to Saul with gifts from his father and, as David stood before him, Saul loved him. Then Saul sent a message to Jesse saying, "Let David stay with me, for he has found favor with me."

And so it was that David, the man anointed by Samuel to become king of Israel in Saul's place, stayed with King Saul. He became Saul's armorbearer, and when the evil spirit troubled Saul, David played his harp to soothe him and the evil spirit departed.

105—DAVID vs. GOLIATH

(1 Samuel 17)

Israel was once again at war with the Philistines, and Saul had gone to lead his army. The war took the army of Israel to the mountains of Shochoh in the land belonging to Judah, and the men of Israel were encamped near the valley of Elah. As Israel's army stood on the mountain on one side of the valley, the Philistine army stood facing them on the mountain on the other side.

As the two armies stood poised for battle, a giant came out from the Philistine ranks and strutted across the valley toward the Israelites. This mountain of a man was Goliath of Gath. He stood six cubits and a span in height and wore a coat of armor that weighed 5,000 shekels of brass. His spear was like a weaver's beam and the head of it weighed 600 shekels of iron.[245] And this was not all of Goliath's protection; he also wore a large brass helmet on his head and additional armor to protect his neck and his legs.

This champion of the Philistines stood in the valley and cried out to the men of Israel: "Why have you come out in battle against us? I am a Philistine and you are servants of Saul. Choose a man from among you to come down and fight me. If your man kills me, the Philistines will be your servants, but if I prevail and kill him, Israel shall serve us. I defy you this day to give me a man so that we may fight."

The two armies fought daily, yet the massive Philistine came out into the valley morning and evening for forty days to torment the army of Israel. Goliath was greatly feared in Israel's camp, and no one dared to accept his haughty challenge.

David's three eldest brothers—Eliab, Abinadab, and Shammah—had followed Saul to the battle, but David was not there. He had left Saul's service and returned to his sheep.[246] One day, however, David's father Jesse sent him to take food and supplies to his brothers. David left his sheep in the care of another and went out to Israel's encampment where he greeted his brothers and gave them the supplies their father had sent. As David and his brothers talked, Goliath came out and

---

[245] According to those who are experts on weights and measures in Bible times, Goliath stood more than nine feet (2.74 meters) tall, had armor that weighed about 125 pounds (56.7 kilograms), and the head of his spear weighed about fifteen pounds (6.8 kilograms). (Daniel H. Ludlow, *A Companion to Your Study of the Old Testament*, [Salt Lake City: Deseret Book Co., 1981], 218.)

[246] For the account of David going into Saul's service, see story "104—Let David Stay with Me."

issued his dreaded challenge, and all the men of Israel fled from him because of their fear.

David, intrigued by this Philistine giant, questioned the men who stood by. "What shall be done for the man who kills this Philistine giant and takes away the reproach of Israel?" he asked.

"The king will give him great riches," the men answered. "He will also give the man his daughter and make his father's house free in Israel."

Then David, moved by the Spirit of God that was in him, said, "Who *is* this uncircumcised Philistine that he should defy the armies of the living God?" Because David was so full of the Spirit himself, he could not believe that there was no man in all of Israel's camp willing to accept Goliath's challenge.

David's brothers were embarrassed and angry when they heard how their younger brother talked. "Why did you come here?" asked Eliab. "And who is tending your sheep? I know your pride and the disobedience that is in your heart, and I think you came here only because you were curious to see the battle."

"What have I done now?" David asked his brother. "Is this not a just cause?" David then turned and continued questioning the other men, and they answered him as before.

When David's words were told to King Saul, Saul sent for him. And when David came to where Saul was, he said, "Let no man's heart fail him because of this uncircumcised Philistine. I will go and fight him."

"You cannot go against this man!" said Saul. "You are but a youth, and he is a man of war."

Then David explained to Saul how he had slain both a lion and a bear in defense of his father's sheep. Then he said, "This Philistine shall be as one of them, seeing he has defied the armies of the living God. The Lord Jehovah, who delivered me from the paws of both the lion and the bear, will also deliver me from this Philistine."

Saul recognized that David had the faith that he did not have himself. He also knew that there was no one else, including himself, willing to fight the Philistine. "Go then," he said, "and may Jehovah go with you."

Saul girded David in his own armor to prepare him for the battle. But David was uneasy, both because he was not accustomed to the armor and because Saul was a much larger man. "I cannot go with these," said David, "for I have not proved them." So he put off Saul's armor and departed out of his presence.

As young David took his staff in his hand, he chose five smooth stones from the brook. Putting the stones in his shepherd's bag and, with sling in hand, he descended the hill toward the haughty giant.

Goliath drew near, and the man who bore his shield came before him. When the Philistine champion saw young David, he mocked him, for David was but a fair-skinned youth. "Am I a dog?" shouted Goliath, "that you come to me with staves?"[247] And he cursed David by all the gods of the Philistines. "Come to me," he bellowed, "and I will give your flesh to the fowls of the air and to the beasts of the field!"

David accepts Goliath's challenge

Then David, filled with Spirit of God and with neither his confidence nor his faith shaken, called out to the giant Philistine, "You come to me with sword, spear, and shield, but I come to you in the name of Jehovah, the God of the armies of Israel, whom you have defied. This day will Jehovah deliver you into my hands and I will smite you and take your head from you."

David continued: "And I will give the carcasses of the army of the Philistines to the fowls of the air and the beasts of the field so that all the earth may know that there is a God in Israel. All this assembly shall know that Jehovah saves not with sword and spear. For this is his battle, and he will give you into my hands."

Then, as Goliath came near, David ran forward to meet him. He put his hand into his bag, drew out a stone, and hurled it at the giant with his sling. The stone struck hard in the Philistine's forehead, sinking deep into his skull. Then Goliath reeled and fell on his face to the earth.

As David had no sword of his own, he ran forward and stood upon the giant Philistine's body. As he drew Goliath's own sword from its sheath and cut off his head before both armies, the men of Israel and Judah arose and gave a mighty shout. And when the Philis-

---

247 Or thin sticks.

151

tines saw that their champion was dead, they fled in disarray before the army of Israel.

106—A VICTIM OF SAUL'S JEALOUSY
(1 Samuel 18–19)

After David's victory over Goliath,[248] King Saul took David into his house once again. He treated the young son of Jesse as one of his own family and gave him authority over his men of war. Wherever Saul went, David went also, and David gained great popularity in the eyes of the people. During David's stay in Saul's house, he and Saul's son Jonathan developed a fast friendship, and Jonathan had a great love for his friend David.

David behaved himself wisely before the king and acted with great humility, but his popularity with the people made Saul jealous. David was a great and fearless warrior, and when he returned victorious from a battle with the Philistines, the women of Israel came dancing and singing in the streets saying, "Saul has slain his thousands and David his ten thousands!"

Because of the people's display of preference for David, Saul began to look at him with suspicion. "David has the praise of the people," said Saul. "What more can he want now but my kingdom?" Samuel had told Saul very plainly that the kingdom was to be taken from him and given to another and, as David prospered, Saul had no doubt that David was that man.

When the evil spirit that had earlier vexed Saul returned to him, David came to play his harp, but Saul was not soothed. As David played, Saul cast a javelin at him, which David quickly dodged, and the javelin stuck in the wall.

Saul feared David because he knew that the Spirit of Jehovah was with David and not with him, and he became obsessed with David's destruction. He was sure that David would be destroyed if he could be placed at the forefront of the army, but David acted wisely and Jehovah preserved him. Then Saul became even more jealous because of the love that all Israel and Judah had for David.

As Saul plotted how he might destroy this son of Jesse, he called David to him and offered him the hand of his daughter. "Behold my eldest daughter Merab," said Saul. "I will give her to be your wife if you will valiantly fight Jehovah's battles." But Saul had no intention of giving David his daughter's hand. His secret desire was for David to be killed in battle.

When Saul offered David the hand of Merab, David replied, "Who am I, and who are my ancestors or my father's family in Israel that I should be the king's son-

---

[248] See story "105—David vs. Goliath."

152

in-law?" David was flattered by the offer, but Saul's insincerity became obvious when he gave Merab to another man. However, when Saul learned that his daughter Michal loved David, he was pleased. He thought he could use Michal as bait to bring the crushing hand of the Philistines upon his young nemesis. So, Saul plotted how he could offer David a second chance to be his son-in-law.

Saul instructed his servants to tell David secretly that the king and all his servants loved him and that he would surely become Saul's son-in-law. But when the servants told this to David, he expressed that he was unworthy of such an honor. "Does it seem a light thing to you to be the king's son-in-law?" David asked Saul's servants. "I am but a poor man and lightly esteemed."

Then, at Saul's instruction, the servants said to David, "The king seeks no dowry of you for Michal except that you slay 100 Philistines so that he may be avenged of his enemies." Saul thought David would surely be killed in such an attempt, but David was pleased by these words. He and his men went to battle against the Philistines and killed 200 men. When he brought proof to Saul that the men were dead, Saul kept his word and gave Michal to be David's wife.

King Saul knew that Jehovah was with David and that Michal loved him, but he was jealous of David because he perceived David as a threat to his throne and his power. With each passing day, Saul became even more jealous of David. And he feared David even more when he saw that he behaved himself more wisely than all of Saul's servants.

Saul became David's sworn enemy. But when he told his servants that they should kill David, Jonathan warned him of Saul's intent and told him to hide. "I will talk to my father concerning you," said Jonathan, "then tell you what I learn."

When Jonathan spoke to his father, he reminded him of all that David had done for him and that David's works were those of a true friend and not of an enemy. He also reminded Saul of how he had rejoiced when David killed the Philistine giant and saved Israel. "Why would you sin against innocent blood," he asked his father, "and slay David without a cause?" Saul was finally persuaded by Jonathan's pleadings and swore to him that David would not be harmed.

Jonathan returned to tell David of the king's change of heart and brought him back into Saul's house. But when the evil spirit returned to Saul and David played his harp to soothe him, Saul again cast a javelin to kill him. Once again, however, David escaped the king's wrath.

As David fled for his life to his own house, Saul's messengers followed him with instructions that they should watch through the night and then slay David in the morning. During the night, however, Michal let David down through a window to escape the assassins. When David was gone, Michal put a graven idol and a pillow in his bed to make it appear that David was still there. When Saul's men came in the morning to take David, Michal told them he was sick. And when David's illness was reported to Saul, he commanded his servants to bring David to him in his bed so that he could slay him himself. But when the men returned to David's house, they were disappointed to discover that David had escaped and that there was nothing in his bed but an idol and a pillow.

David, fleeing now for his life, went to Ramah to find the prophet Samuel, and the two of them went to dwell in Naioth.[249]

---

[249] The name Naioth means "habitations," and it was probably the huts or dwellings of a school of prophets over which Samuel presided. It was likely located at Ramah or nearby (William Smith, *Dictionary of the Bible*, *GospeLink*, CD-ROM, s.v. "Naioth").

153

107—TRUE FRIENDS

(1 Samuel 20)

From the first time Saul's son Jonathan met David, he was drawn to him and loved him as he loved his own soul. The two became fast friends, and Jonathan took his own clothes, even to his robe and his sword, and put them on David.

But, though the bond between Jonathan and David was strong, things did not go well between Saul and David. When David became popular with the people, Saul grew jealous and sought to destroy him. On several occasions, David had to flee from Saul to save his life. Jonathan and David's wife Michal seemed to be the only members of Saul's household who were not seeking to destroy David. Jonathan pleaded David's cause to his father on several occasions, and though Jonathan was successful in his pleadings, any good feelings that Saul had toward David were always short-lived.

When David left the prophet Samuel at Naioth, he returned to Gibeah and sought out his friend Jonathan. He thought Jonathan might know why Saul was trying to kill him. "What have I done," he asked Jonathan, "and what is my sin against your father that he seeks my life?"

Jonathan was surprised at David's question, for he was not aware of the extent of his father's wrath. "My father no longer seeks your life," replied Jonathan. "For he does nothing without telling me first. What you say cannot be true, for surely he would not hide such a thing from me."

"Perhaps because your father knows of your love for me, he would hide this matter from you," said David. "But as Jehovah lives, and as you live, there is but a step between me and death."

Jonathan was stunned and he wanted to help. "Whatever you ask of me," he vowed to his friend David, "I will do it." And the two men made a covenant of friendship before Jehovah.

The following day was the new moon, and though David was expected to dine with King Saul for three days,[250] he dared not show his face. "I will hide in the field until the third day," he told Jonathan. "If your father misses me, tell him that I asked your leave to go to

---

[250] Israel offered special sacrifices in connection with the new moon or the first day of each lunar month. It was, like the Sabbath, treated as a day of rest. It was also the occasion of state banquets. By Saul's time, these observances had expanded to three days. It was no doubt such banquets in the king's household that David was expected to attend.

Bethlehem for a family sacrifice. If he approves, then I will have peace. But if he is angry and is determined to do me harm, you must let me know, for we have covenanted before Jehovah."

David and Jonathan walked together in the field as Jonathan proposed a plan. "Come on the third day and hide yourself at the stone called Ezel," he said. "I will come with a lad and shoot three arrows, sending the lad to find them. If I tell him that the arrows are on this side of him, then my father will do you no harm and you may come out of hiding. However, if I tell the lad that the arrows are yet beyond him, you will know that my father seeks your life and that you must leave. But, whatever happens, David, Jehovah will be between us forever." And the two men swore again an oath of peace and friendship because of the great love they bore for each other.

When Saul came to eat on the new moon, he said nothing about David's absence. On the second day, however, he asked Jonathan, "Why did the son of Jesse not come to meat either yesterday or today?"

Jonathan gave the answer that David had told him. "David earnestly asked leave of me to go to Bethlehem for a family sacrifice," said Jonathan, "and he is unable to come to the king's table."

Saul became very angry at Jonathan's answer and shouted at him. "You son of the perverse rebellious woman," he roared. "Why have you chosen the son of Jesse before me? Can you not see that your choice is to your own harm? As long as David lives, your kingdom can never be established. Send now and bring him to me, for he must surely die! If you do not destroy David for your own sake, you should do it for the sake of the mother who bore you in nakedness."

"Why must David be slain?" asked Jonathan, trying to reason with his father. "What wrong has he done?" No man was a truer friend than Jonathan was to David. Unlike his father, Jonathan was not jealous of David, even though David would someday sit on the throne of Israel instead of him.

When Saul became so furious that he hurled a javelin at Jonathan, Jonathan could see the strength of his father's resolve. He left the table in anger, grieving for his dear friend who had been treated so shamefully by the king.

The next day, Jonathan went to the field at the appointed time, taking a small lad with him. "Run and find the arrows that I shoot," he said to the lad. And, as the lad ran, Jonathan shot three arrows over him and called, "The arrows are yet beyond you!"

When the lad had gathered the arrows, he returned—unaware of Jonathan's agreement with David. Then Jonathan gave his weapons to the boy and sent him back to the city. When the lad was gone, David arose from his hiding place and fell on his face to the ground. Then he and Jonathan fell upon each other, weeping together till they could weep no more.

"Go in peace," said Jonathan to David. "Your life is in grave danger here! But remember that we have sworn in the name of Jehovah that he will be between you and me and between your seed and my seed forever." Then David departed—once more fleeing for his life.

108—DAVID ON THE RUN
(1 Samuel 21–22)

David, in his flight from the vengeful wrath of King Saul, went to Nob[251] where he sought out Ahimelech the priest. "Why have you come here alone?" asked Ahimelech.

David did not want Ahimelech to know either that he was fleeing from Saul or that he was traveling by himself. "I am on secret business for the king," replied David. "I must tell no man why I am sent or where I have left those men who are with me."

When David saw that Saul's chief herdsman, Doeg the Edomite, was at Nob that day worshipping Jehovah, he felt uneasy, and he asked Ahimelech if he had either a spear or a sword that he could give him. "I left home in great haste because of the urgency of the king's business," David told Ahimelech, "and I brought no weapon with me." Ahimelech complied with David's request by giving him the sword of Goliath, which was kept there at Nob. Taking the sword with him, David left Nob and turned his face toward Gath, in the land of the Philistines. Once there he asked to see King Achish.

As the servants of Achish were taking David to their king, they talked among themselves about their visitor. "Is this not David, the king of the land?" they asked. Did the women not sing of him in their dances that Saul has slain his thousands and David his ten thousands?"

When David heard these words, he realized that it was not wise for him to be here, and he began to fear what Achish might do to him. To save himself he began to pretend that he was mad—scratching on the gates with his hands and letting his spittle run down onto his beard.

Much to David's relief, his charade of madness worked. When Achish saw how David was acting, he said, "This man is mad. Why have you brought him here? I have no need for madmen to be brought into my house!"

When David was turned away by Achish because of his feigned madness, he fled from Gath and hid in a cave in the limestone cliffs above Adullum.[252] Word of David's hiding place soon got out, and many people came to join him. These were mostly Israelites who were in distress or in debt or who were discontent with things as they were under the rule of Saul, and David soon had a supporting army of about 400 men.

---

[251] Nob was a city assigned to the Levites in the tribe of Benjamin. It was located near Jerusalem, though its exact location is unknown today.
[252] Adullum was a city in the lowlands of Judah.

When the prophet Gad advised David to leave his cave, he went with his followers to the forest of Hareth. In the meantime, however, Saul had also learned of David's whereabouts and set out to find him. Saul was angry with his servants because he believed that they all knew that Jonathan had sent David away to protect him. Saul also thought that his servants had more information about David's whereabouts than they were telling him. When he confronted his servants, Doeg the Edomite reported on his encounter with David at Nob. "I saw the son of Jesse coming to Nob, to Ahimilech the priest," said Doeg, "and Ahimilech inquired of Jehovah for him and gave him food. He also gave him the sword of Goliath the Philistine."

When Saul heard Doeg's report, he called Ahimelech and all the priests at Nob to come and give an account. He questioned Ahimelech carefully. "Why have you conspired with the son of Jesse against me?" he asked. "For I know that you gave him bread and a sword and that you inquired of Jehovah in his behalf, that he might rise up against me and lay in wait for me as he does this day."

Ahimelech, knowing that David would do Saul no harm, answered, "There is no one among all your servants more faithful to you than David, your son-in-law. He goes at your bidding and is honorable in your house. But did I inquire of God for him? I did not. And the king must not impute any mischief to me or any of my father's house, for we have no knowledge of the things of which you accuse this man."

Saul responded angrily: "Because your hand was with David, and because you knew when he fled and did not tell me, you shall die—you and all your father's house."

When Saul commanded his servants to slay the priests, they were stunned that he would go so far. They knew that Saul was mad and they refused to carry out his order. But when Saul gave the command to Doeg the Edomite, Doeg turned and slew eighty-five priests with his sword because they showed kindness to David. Then, at Saul's command, Doeg smote the city of Nob, killing every inhabitant with edge of his sword. The entire city was slain except Ahimelech's son Abiathar, who escaped to tell David of Saul's nefarious deed.

When David learned from Abiathar what had happened to the priests and the people of Nob, he blamed himself. "I knew that day," he lamented, "that Doeg would surely tell Saul. And now, because I did not stop him then, I have caused the death of your father's entire house. Stay here with me and fear not, for he that seeks my life seeks your life also. With me you shall be safe."

109—THE HUNTED SPARES THE HUNTER
(1 Samuel 23–24)

King Saul's madness and jealousy were a constant threat to David and his men. Whenever Saul became aware of their whereabouts, it became necessary for David and his followers to move. When their hiding place in the cliffs above Adullum[253] was compromised, Jehovah called David and his little troop to fight the Philistines who had attacked the city of Keilah.[254] David's army had now grown to 600, but this was still an insignificant number compared to the opposition. When his men expressed fear because of the smallness of their numbers, Jehovah promised David that he would give them victory over the Philistines—and he did so.

When word came to Saul that David was at Keilah, Saul was elated. "God has delivered the son of Jesse into my hands," he said, "for he has entered a city with gates and bars and is shut in." And Saul called his men to go down and lay siege to Keilah.

David, understanding the potential danger when he entered the city of Keilah, inquired of Jehovah: "Will Saul come down against Keilah?"

"He will come," answered Jehovah.

"Will the men of Keilah deliver me into Saul's hands?"

"They will."

So, with that warning, David and his men quickly left Keilah, each going wherever he could. As for David, he hid in the woods in the Wilderness of Ziph.[255] When Saul learned that David had escaped, he called off his siege of Keilah, but he did not give up the search.

While David was living in the woods, Saul's son Jonathan came to him to lend support. "Fear not," he told David. "My father shall not find you. You shall be king over Israel—with me next to you—and my father knows it." And before Jonathan returned to his home, he and David once more renewed before Jehovah their covenant of friendship.

The people of Ziph, who knew that David was hiding in their woods, sought out Saul and promised to deliver David to him. Saul thanked them and blessed them for their assistance, but—warning them of

---

[253] See story "108–David on the Run."
[254] Keilah was a city in the lowlands of Judah.
[255] Ziph was a city in the mountainous region of Judah between Mount Carmel and the city of Juttah. The wilderness was outside the city.

David's subtlety—sent them back to get better information. When they arrived back in Ziph, however, David and his men had already moved south to the Wilderness of Maon.[256]

Saul continued to stalk David, but just when David was finally surrounded, word came to Saul that the Philistines had invaded the land. Thus, Saul's plans to destroy his son-in-law were thwarted again as he was required to defend Israel against the Philistines.

With Saul and his army gone, David and his men moved again, seeking safety in the caves above Engedi.[257] But when Saul's battle with the Philistines was ended, he was informed that David had gone to Engedi and he renewed his pursuit with his own hand-picked army of 3,000 men.

As Saul's forces combed the mountains above Engedi in search of David, Saul came to some sheepfolds where there was a cave. Being tired, he went inside the cave to sleep. What Saul did not know was that David and his men were hiding in the innermost part of that same cave.

"Behold!" whispered David's men when they realized that the king was sleeping in their cave. "Is this not the day of which Jehovah spoke when he promised to deliver your enemy into your hands?" But David restrained his men; he would not let them lift their hands against Saul. Rather than kill Saul, David went to where Saul was sleeping and cut off the skirt of his robe and took it with him. But then, when David thought about what he had done, he became sick at heart. "God forbid that I should lift my hand to do this thing against my master, Jehovah's anointed," he said.

When King Saul awoke and left the cave, David followed and called after him, "My lord the king!"

Saul was stunned. He turned to see a man with his face bowed to the ground, kneeling before the cave. Saul bowed in return, not knowing who was there.

David spoke first. "Where did you hear that I seek your hurt?" he asked the king. "Today your eyes have seen how Jehovah delivered you into my hands in this cave, and though some of my men bade me kill you, I spared your life. I told them that I would not lift my hand against Jehovah's anointed."

David continued: "Look now and see that the skirt of your robe is in my hand, for I cut it off while you slept. Though I have committed no sin against you, yet you hunt me to take my life. Let Jehovah judge between us, plead my cause, and deliver me out of your hands."

"Is this the voice of my son David?" wept Saul. "You are more righteous than I, David, for you have rewarded the evil that I have done to you with good. You have dealt well with me, for Jehovah delivered me into your hands and you did not slay me. I know now that I am not your enemy, for no man will find his enemy and let him escape.

"May Jehovah reward you with good for what you have done to me this day. I know now that you shall surely be king of Israel and that the kingdom shall be established in your hand. Swear to me by Jehovah that, when you are king, you will not cut off my seed or destroy my name from out of my father's house."

David swore to Saul as he requested, and Saul returned to his home in Gibeah.

---

[256] Maon was a city in the mountain district of Judah. It is identified today with a large conical hill called Main about seven miles south of Hebron (see William Smith, *Dictionary of the Bible*, *GospeLink*, CD-ROM, s.v. "Maon").

[257] Engedi was a city in Judah about halfway down the western coast of the Dead Sea.

110—THE FOOLISHNESS OF NABAL

(1 Samuel 25)

After many years as both a judge in Israel and as God's prophet, Samuel died and was buried at his home in Ramah. All Israel mourned the death of this great man. Upon learning of Samuel's death, David left Engedi and went down to the wilderness of Paran where he and his men dwelt for some time. Then, being in need of provisions, they went north to Maon on the slopes of Mount Carmel.

Living at the pastures of Maon was a prosperous man named Nabal who had large herds of sheep and goats. David and his men had mingled with Nabal's servants as they tended his flocks in the wilderness and had provided a great deal of protection by their presence. Nabal was a descendant of Caleb the spy[258] and was a very disagreeable man.

When David came near to Maon and heard that Nabal was shearing his sheep, he sent ten young men to greet him in David's name. "Thus shall you say to him," David instructed. "May peace be upon both you and your house and upon all that you have. Your shepherds have been with us on the mountain but we did not hurt them and took nothing from them. We ask now that we may find favor in your sight and that you will provide food for us and our master David."

When the young men delivered David's message, Nabal showed his unpleasant nature. "Who is David? And what do I have to do with Jesse's son?" he asked. "Shall I take my bread, my water, and my meat that I have killed for my shearers and give it to men that I do not know?" Soundly rebuffed, the men returned to David and reported all that Nabal had said.

David was angry and insulted; and—because of the insult—he was about to do something that he would regret throughout his life. He commanded his men to arm themselves, and he took about 400 of them with him to go against Nabal, leaving the rest to guard their belongings. "Come!" said David to his men. "Though we have treated this man's goods with respect, he has returned evil for good. May God so do to my enemies—and more also—if one male that pertains to this man is still alive in the morning."

Nabal's wife Abigail was a woman of beauty and good understanding, quite the opposite of her churlish husband. So when Nabal rejected David's request for food, one of Nabal's servants, fearing what might happen next, went immediately to Abigail. "Behold," he said to her, "David sent messengers out of the wilderness to salute Nabal, but our master spoke to them with bitterness. These men are our friends because they respected our goods and provided safety for us while we were with them in the fields."

"Please consider what you might do now to help the situation," the servant pleaded to Abigail. "Evil will certainly come upon our master and all his household because this son of Belial[259] will allow no one to tell him anything."

Abigail was greatly worried by what she heard. She thought, however, that she might still have time to repair the damage that her thoughtless husband had done. She quickly took 200 loaves of bread, two bottles[260] of wine, five dressed sheep, five measures of parched grain, 100 clusters of raisins, and 200 fig cakes and loaded them on her asses. Then she said to the servants, "Go on ahead and I will follow you." She said nothing, however, to her husband Nabal.

As Abigail rode down and was concealed by the hill, she met David and his men coming up, bent on their mission of destruction. When she met David, she dismounted and fell down at his feet. "Let this iniquity of Nabal be upon me," she pleaded. "Please listen now to me and pay no heed to this man of Belial. Nabal[261] is his name and folly is in him, but if I had seen the young men whom you sent, they would have been treated with kindness.

"Now, therefore, because I have come, Jehovah has prevented you from shedding blood this day. I pray that your enemies and those who seek evil for you may be as Nabal. I pray also that this blessing may extend also to those who follow you. So if you will forgive my trespasses, Jehovah will bless you with posterity. For I know that you fight Jehovah's battles and that no evil is found in you."

Abigail went on in her praise of David, her words almost poetic: "Though a man has risen up to pursue you and to seek your soul, your soul shall be bound in the bundle of life with Jehovah your God, and the souls of your enemies shall he sling out as from the middle of

---

[258] For an account of Caleb's faithful service as a spy, see story "64—Forty Years for Forty Days." Moses promised Caleb that he would be allowed to enter the promised land and receive an inheritance. Story "78—A Land for Which You Did Not Labor" tells of Caleb receiving that inheritance.

[259] "Son of Belial" is a derisive term used many times in the scriptures. It simply means a worthless and lawless person.

[260] These bottles might more appropriately be called water skins. They were animal skins that were used by travelers and others to carry water and wine.

[261] The name Nabal means "fool."

a sling. When Jehovah has appointed you ruler over Israel, you will have no offense in your heart because you took no vengeance this day. And when Jehovah has thus dealt with you, I pray that you will also remember me."

"Blessed is Jehovah, God of Israel, who sent you to meet me," said David, "and blessed are you because you have kept me from shedding blood. For as God lives, except you had come, Nabal and all that he has would have been destroyed before morning."

Then David gratefully received Abigail's gifts and sent her away in peace. She had kept him from making a terrible mistake.

When Abigail arrived home, she found her husband Nabal holding a great feast. Because he was drunk, she told him nothing that night about what had happened. In the morning, however, Abigail told him of her meeting with David the night before and how his life had been spared. When Nabal heard it, his heart died within in him and he became as a stone. Ten days later he died.

"Blessed be Jehovah," said David when he learned of Nabal's death. "He has pleaded my cause and has turned Nabal's wickedness upon his own head."

David then sent messengers to Abigail, asking her to be his wife. And when David's servants came to her at Mount Carmel, she arose and bowed to the earth. In her humility she said, "Let me be only a servant to wash the feet of those who serve David." When Abigail came to David, however, she became his wife.

111—YOU SHALL DO GREAT THINGS
(1 Samuel 26)

Though Saul abandoned his pursuit of David for a short time after David had spared his life at Engedi,[262] it was not long before he was again on David's trail with his 3,000 handpicked warriors. When the people of Ziph reported that David and his 600-man army were living in the Wilderness of Ziph,[263] Saul went out after him and encamped on the hill of Hachilah. David saw the encampment on the hill and suspected that it was Saul—and his spies soon confirmed that David was right.

When David went to observe Saul's camp at closer range, he saw the place where Saul slept, as well as the sleeping place of Abner, Saul's captain. Saul lay in a trench with his men encamped around him.

When night came, David took his nephew Abishai[264] and crept into Saul's camp. They saw Saul sleeping in the barricade with his spear stuck in the ground near his head, while Abner and the people slept around him. When they saw Saul, Abishai said to David, "God has delivered Saul into your hands. Let me smite him to the earth with his spear."

"No!" replied David. "Who can lift his hand against Jehovah's anointed and be guiltless? As Jehovah lives, he will smite Saul. The day will come when Saul will die, or he shall perish in battle, but I shall not lift my hand against him. However, let us take his spear and his cruse[265] of water with us."

So, when David and Abishai had taken Saul's spear and his cruse of water, they left the camp. And no one in the camp knew they had been there, because Jehovah had caused a deep sleep to come upon them.

When the light of morning came, David stood afar off on a hill and cried out to Saul—then to Abner, "Will you not answer me, Abner?" he called.

---

[262] See story "109—The Hunted Spares the Hunter."
[263] Ziph was a city located in the mountainous region of Judah between Mount Carmel and the city of Juttah. The wilderness was outside the city. David had hidden in these woods before and was visited there by Jonathan, as told in story "109—The Hunted Spares the Hunter."
[264] Abishai was the eldest son of David's sister Zeruiah. He was a brother to Joab and Asahel (see also stories "117—King of Judah Only" and "118—Shall the Sword Devour Forever?").
[265] A cruse is a small vessel, perhaps made of pottery, for carrying water or oil.

"Who are you?" called Abner, "and why do you cry for the king?"

"You are a valiant man, Abner," cried David, still not identifying himself. "But though there is no other like you in all Israel, you have failed in your care of the king. Someone came into your camp last night to destroy him, and you did not know it. Your offense is worthy of death, Abner, for you have failed to keep Jehovah's anointed safe. Look at me now and see where the king's cruse of water is and the spear that stood by his head."

Saul, who was watching and listening to the exchange between David and Abner, recognized David's voice and called out, "Is that you, David, my son?"

"It is I, my lord," replied David. "And I ask that you tell me why you pursue me. If Jehovah has stirred you up against me, let him accept an offering. But if the children of men have stirred you up, may they be cursed before Jehovah, for they have driven me from abiding in the inheritance of Jehovah and told me to go serve other gods."

David continued, pleading, "Do not let my blood fall to the earth before the face of Jehovah, for the king of Israel has come out to seek a flea as one would arm himself to hunt a partridge in the mountains."

"I have sinned," cried Saul in reply. "Return, my son David, and I will seek to harm you no more because my soul was precious in your eyes this day. Yea, I have played the fool and have erred greatly."

"Let one of your young men come and fetch the king's spear!" called David. "And may Jehovah render his righteousness to every man. He delivered you into my hands this day, but I would not lift my hand against Jehovah's anointed. And, as your life is of great value to me today, so let my life have value in the eyes of Jehovah, that he may deliver me from tribulation."

"Blessed are you, my son David!" cried Saul. "You shall do great things and shall yet prevail." And Saul returned again to his own place.

112—DAVID AMONG THE PHILISTINES
(1 Samuel 27–28)

When David became convinced that Saul would someday destroy him if he remained in Israel, he determined to escape to the land of the Philistines. So, taking his army of 600 men and all their families with him, he went to Gath and dwelt there among the people. David's two wives—Ahinoam the Jezreelitess[266] and Abigail, Nabal's widow[267]—went with him.[268] And when Saul learned that David had fled to Gath, he ceased seeking him.

When David and his followers had been in Gath for a short while, he said to Achish the king, "If I have found grace in your eyes, give me a place to live in some town in your country. It is not right that I should live in the royal city with you."

So Achish gave Ziklag[269] to David and his followers, and they dwelt there—staying among the Philistines for sixteen months. David used Ziklag as his base of operations as he and his men fought against the nations to the south. And whenever David smote the land, he left no survivors, taking spoils of both goods and animals.

From what Achish was able to observe, he believed that David had made himself an enemy to the people of Israel and would never be able to return to them. And he wondered if David might agree to unite with the Philistines to fight against Saul's army. "Will you and your men go out to battle with me?" he asked.

David responded to Achish's question but avoided giving an answer. "Surely," he said, "you shall know what I can do."

And as the Philistines gathered their armies in preparation for battle with Israel, Achish made David his bodyguard.

---

[266] Jezreel was a city located in the land belonging to the tribe of Issachar.

[267] See story "110—The Foolishness of Nabal."

[268] Michal, the daughter of King Saul whom David had married earlier, had been given by her father to Phaltiel, the son of Laish.

[269] Ziklag was a city that had originally belonged to Judah but had been transferred to Simeon. At the time of Saul, however, it was in the hands of the Philistines.

113–LIGHT FROM A DARK SOURCE

(1 Samuel 28)

The man who started out with such great potential, the man of whom the scriptures say there was no one "goodlier" in all Israel,[270] was now just a shadow of his former self. Because of Saul's pride and his disobedience, the Spirit of Jehovah had withdrawn from him and he was left to himself. Even the great riches and honors that came to him as king of Israel offered no comfort. He was forever looking over his shoulder because of his fear of David, and now it appeared that David had joined forces with the Philistines. The Philistines and the Israelites were preparing to do battle with each other at Mount Gilboa, and Saul was a desperate and frightened man.

When Saul inquired of Jehovah, he received no answer, either by dreams, by the Urim and Thummim—which was in the hands of the priests—or by prophets. The prophet Samuel was dead, but long before Samuel's death, he had been commanded to cut off all communication with Saul.

In better times, Saul had banished from Israel all witches and wizards—those who possessed what were called familiar spirits[271]—because the law of Moses forbade them. Now, in a desperate state of mind, Saul disguised himself and went to Endor[272] because his servants told him there was a witch there. Going to the witch secretly by night, Saul said to her, "Divine up for me the man whose name I will tell you."

"I dare not," replied the witch, "for I fear you are laying a trap to take my life." Though she did not recognize her visitor, she knew that King Saul had forbidden all witches and wizards in the land.

"I swear," said Saul, "that no punishment will come to you because you do this thing." And he commanded her to bring up the word of the prophet Samuel.[273]

The woman proceeded. And when the spirit came to her that claimed to be Samuel, the woman cried out with alarm: "You have deceived me! You are Saul!"

"Do not be afraid," answered Saul. "What did you see?"

"I saw a god coming up out of the earth."

"What is his form?" asked Saul.

"There is an old man covered with a mantle."

And Saul, believing that the old man of whom the witch spoke was Samuel, bowed his face to the earth. Saul, however, did not see the spirit.[274]

"Why have you disturbed me?" the spirit asked Saul.

"I am sorely distressed," answered Saul. "The Philistines make war against me, and God has departed from me. He will not answer my prayers either by prophets or by dreams. I have, therefore, called you to tell me what to do."

Then the wretched spirit, still claiming to be Samuel, delivered a dire message: "Jehovah has done to you as he promised. Because you failed to execute his fierce wrath upon Amalek[275] as he commanded you, he has torn the kingdom out of your hands and given it to your neighbor David. Tomorrow Jehovah will deliver the army of Israel into the hands of the Philistines, and both you and your sons will be dead!"

When Saul heard this, he collapsed to the earth, frightened, demoralized, and faint from hunger. The woman offered him bread, but he would not eat. However, when urged also by his servants, Saul ate and then departed into the night to await fulfillment of the terrible prophecy.

---

[270] See 1 Samuel 9:2.

[271] Those who are said to seek after or embrace familiar spirits seek after revelation from sources that are not of God, especially from people or animals believed to be possessed by evil spirits.

[272] Endor was located in the territory of Issachar but was possessed by Manasseh (see Joshua 17:11). It was the scene of the great victory of Deborah and Barak over Sisera and the Canaanites as told in story "80–The Man Whom You Seek."

[273] In the King James Version of the Bible (1 Samuel 28:11) it is recorded that Saul told the witch to "bring me up Samuel." In the Joseph Smith Translation, however, he is reported to say, "Bring me up the word of Samuel," as shown here. Whatever he requested, it is apparent from the story that Saul never saw the spirit to whom he spoke.

[274] It would be absurd to believe that God, who had refused to communicate with Saul through legitimate channels, would send a valid revelation to him through a witch. One author has suggested that this may well have been "an apparition of the forces of evil that wished to bring about a formerly good man's destruction." (Ellis T. Rasmussen. *Latter-day Saint Commentary on the Old Testament* [Salt Lake City: Deseret Book Co., 1993], 251.)

[275] See story "102–To Obey Is Better than Sacrifice."

114—PROVIDENTIAL REHECTION

114—PROVIDENTIAL REJECTION

(1 Samuel 29–30)

As the armies of the Philistines gathered for war against Israel, David and his 600 men were in the rear of the Philistine army, along with Achish, preparing also to go to battle. However, when the Philistine princes saw David and his men, they had deep concerns. Confronting Achish, they demanded, "Why are these Hebrews here?"

Achish explained, "This man is David who was the servant of King Saul. He is now my servant and I have found no fault with him."

The Philistine princes were not convinced. They did not trust David and they were angry at Achish for bringing him there. "Send this man back to the place you have given him!" they demanded. "If he goes to battle with us, we fear that he will turn against us as an enemy. How could he better win back Saul's favor than to give him our heads? For is this not the man of whom Israel's women sang, 'Saul slew his thousands and David his ten thousands'?"

Achish had great admiration for David and was disappointed by the opposition, but he agreed to send David and his men back to Ziklag. "You are as good in my sight as an angel of God," Achish told David, "but the princes of my people will not let you go with us to battle. Now, therefore, arise early in the morning and return to your families."

Three days later, when David's little army arrived back at Ziklag, they discovered that their city had been burned by the Amalekites and that the women and children were all gone. The men wept until they had no more tears. David was severely distressed, but he took courage in Jehovah. Calling upon Abiathar the priest,[276] he used the ephod[277] to ask Jehovah if he and his men should go after the Amalekite raiders.

"Go after them," answered Jehovah, "and you shall overtake them and recover all."

Encouraged by this message, David took his 600 men and went in pursuit of the bandits. When they had traveled as far as the brook Besor, he left 200 men be-

hind with the supplies because they were too faint to cross the brook. Shortly afterwards, David and his men came upon a young man lying in a field. When they had fed and revived the young man, David asked him where he was from and who he was.

"I am from Egypt," replied the man, "the servant of an Amalekite. My master left me in the field three days ago because I fell sick. We invaded the land of the Philistines, the area belonging to Judah, and the south of Caleb. We also burned the city of Ziklag."

David knew now that he was on the right track, and he asked the man, "Can you lead us to this company of Amalekites?"

"Swear to me first that you will not kill me or deliver me into the hands of my master," said the young Egyptian, "and I will lead you to the company."

With the help of the young Egyptian, David and his men soon overtook the Amalekites. Their vast army was spread out upon the earth celebrating because of the great spoils they had taken from their victims. David and his 400 fearless soldiers fell upon them and smote them from twilight until the evening of the next day, and the Amalekite looters fell before them. All were slain except 400 men who escaped on camels.[278]

David's little army recovered their wives and families and all of the spoils that the Amalekites had taken from them. Nothing was lost. And, as they turned their faces back toward Ziklag, they took all the flocks and herds that the Amalekites had with them. "These are David's spoils," they said.

When the conquering heroes arrived back at the brook Besor, some of those who fought decided that none of the spoils of the battle should be shared with the men who stayed behind with their goods. "Give these men their wives and children that they may lead them away," said the greedy ones, "then let them depart."

David saw that what these men wanted was unjust. "You shall not do this, my brethren," he said. "Jehovah gave us these spoils when he preserved our lives and delivered the Amalekites into our hands. The share belonging to him who stayed with our goods shall be the same as the share of him who went to battle." And this became a law in Israel from that day forward.

And when David's company arrived back in Ziklag, he sent some of the spoils of his victory to the elders of Judah and some to various other places throughout Israel that he and his men had frequented.

---

[276] Abiathar was the son of Ahimelech and was the only survivor of the city of Nob when King Saul had all the priests and the people of the city slain because Ahimelech had helped David (see story "109–The Hunted Spares the Hunter").

[277] The ephod was an article of clothing worn by the priest, to which the breastplate was fastened. It is not clear how divine guidance was obtained through its use.

---

[278] This was apparently a sizable company of Amalekites if 400 escapees were coincidental. Keep in mind, however, that many of the Old Testament writers were prone to exaggerate numbers.

115–THE END OF KING SAUL

(1 Samuel 31; 1 Chronicles 10)

After much preparation on both sides, the armies of the Philistines and the Israelites came together in battle on Mount Gilboa.[279] The Philistines could not be contained, and many of Israel's army were slain; the rest were sent in full retreat. Three of Saul's sons—Jonathan, Abinadab, and Malchishua[280]—fell in the battle.[281]

The Philistine archers also hit Saul, and he was badly wounded. When he realized that he could not escape, Saul asked his armorbearer to kill him so that the Philistines could not claim that they took his life. "Thrust me through!" he commanded. When the man would not do it, Saul took his own sword and fell upon it.[282] And when the armorbearer saw that King Saul was dead, he also fell on his sword.

This was a sad day for Israel; they were beaten badly and their army was in disarray. When the people of Israel saw that Saul and his sons were dead and that the army was defeated, they abandoned their homes and their cities, leaving them to the Philistines.

When the Philistines came out the next day to strip the dead and take their spoils, they found the bodies of Saul and his sons on Mount Gilboa. They cut off Saul's head and took his armor, then they published the news of his death among all their people. Saul's head and his armor were put in the house of Ashtoreth[283] and the bodies of Saul and his sons were hung on the wall of Beth-shean.[284] The bodies were later retrieved through the valiant efforts of the men of Jabesh-gilead and taken to Jabesh where they were burned. Their bones were then buried beneath a tree at Jabesh, and the people fasted seven days.

---

[279] Mount Gilboa is west of the Jordan. It is the next mountain south of Mount Tabor, and Jezreel lies in the valley between the two mountains.

[280] The spelling used in this story for the name of this son of Saul is correct. The name was given in this scripture (2 Samuel 31:2) as Melchi-shua.

[281] Saul had four sons. His youngest son, Ishbosheth, was still living and—because of the support he had from Abner, the captain of Saul's army—Ishbosheth served briefly as king in his father's place (see story "117–The King of Judah Only").

[282] There is another version of how Saul died. It is presented in story "116–Your Own Mouth Testified against You." That version is based on a claim made by a young Amalekite (perhaps to win favor with David) that he killed Saul at Saul's request. But whether he did or not, David made him pay with his life for the deed.

[283] Ashtaroth, the plural name for the Phoenician fertility goddess, is given in the scripture. However, I have used the singular form, Ashtoreth, in this story. The Philistines worshiped her, along with Dagon. In 1 Chronicles 10:10, it says that Saul's head was placed in the temple of Dagon. Sadly, the worship of Ashtoreth was also common among the children of Israel.

[284] Beth-shean is called Beth-shan in this scripture. It is a city that belonged to Manasseh but lay within the limits of Issachar. It was in the valley of the Jordan about twelve miles (19.3 kilometers) south of the Sea of Galilee and four miles (6.4 kilometers) west of the river (see William Smith, *Dictionary of the Bible, GospeLink,* CD-ROM, s.v. "Beth-shean"). At this time the city was apparently under the control of the Philistines.

116–YOUR OWN MOUTH TESTIFIED AGAINST YOU

(2 Samuel 1)

When David had been back in Ziklag for just two days after the slaughter of the Amalekites,[285] word came to him of Saul's death and Israel's devastating defeat at the hands of the Philistines. The report was delivered by a young man who came into Ziklag with his clothes torn and his head covered with dirt. The man recognized David when he saw him and fell to the earth before him. "Where have you come from?" asked David.

"I have escaped from the camp of Israel's army," the young man replied.

And when David inquired about the war, the man said, "The people of Israel have fled from the battle and many of them are dead. Saul and his son Jonathan have both been slain."

David was shocked. He wanted more evidence. "How do you know that Saul and Jonathan are dead?" he asked.

Then the young man told the following story: "As I happened by chance upon Mount Gilboa, I saw Saul wounded and leaning upon his spear. Chariots and horsemen were pressing past him on all sides. When he looked behind him and saw me, he called me to him and asked who I was. I responded that I was an Amalekite. He then begged me to slay him because he was suffering great pain and anguish, yet was still alive. So I stood upon him and slew him because I was sure that he could not live after he had fallen. When he was dead, I took his crown and his bracelet and have now brought them here to you."[286]

David was beside himself. He could not believe what he had just been told. He and all those who were with him tore their clothing and wept. They fasted and mourned for King Saul, for his son Jonathan, and for the people of Israel for seven days. Then David pressed the young messenger for more information. "Where are you from?" he asked.

"I am a stranger," he answered. "An Amalekite."

Then David pinned the young stranger down. "How was it that you were not afraid to destroy Jehovah's anointed?" he asked. Then, without waiting for an answer to his question, David called one of his young men and commanded that the Amalekite be slain.

As the young man died, David said, "Your blood is upon your own head, for your own mouth testified against you when you said that you had slain Jehovah's anointed."

David sorrowed greatly over the deaths of Saul, his king, and Jonathan, his dear and faithful friend. "The beauty of Israel is slain upon the high places, and the mighty are fallen," he cried. "Do not tell of their deaths in Gath or Askelon, lest the daughters of the Philistines rejoice and the uncircumcised triumph. O, you mountains of Gilboa, let there be neither dew nor rain upon you, for there was the shield of Saul cast away as though he had not been anointed king. Saul and Jonathan were lovely and pleasant in their lives, and in their deaths they were not divided. They were swifter than eagles; they were stronger than lions.

"I am distressed for you, my brother Jonathan. You have been very pleasant to me, and your love towards me has been wonderful—exceeding even the love of women. How are the mighty fallen and the weapons of war destroyed?"

---

[285] See story "114–Providential Rejection."

[286] This account of Saul's death as told by the young man in this story differs from the account given in 1 Samuel 31 (see story "115–The End of King Saul"). Which, if either, account is correct is not clear, but it is possible that the young Amalekite made up his story in the belief that David would reward him for killing his enemy. If so, he was mistaken.

VIII

DAVID AND SOLOMON:

THE HOUSE OF JUDAH

ON THE THRONE

117−THE KING OF JUDAH ONLY

(2 Samuel 2−4)

When Saul was dead, David, knowing that he had been anointed by Samuel to be Israel's king, became concerned about what he should do next. Calling upon Jehovah in prayer, he asked, "Shall I go up into any of the cities of Judah?"

"Yes!" answered Jehovah. "Go up to Hebron."

In response to this instruction, David and his 600 men left Ziklag—together with their wives and families—and went to Hebron.

Once David was in Hebron, the men of Judah came and anointed him king of Judah, but David's challenges to the throne of Israel were not over. Abner, the man who had been captain of Saul's army, took Saul's youngest and only surviving son Ishbosheth[287] to Mahanaim[288] and made him king over the rest of Israel, both east and west of the Jordan. Ishbosheth was a righteous man but a weak king. He was king in name, but Abner managed the affairs of the kingdom.

There were continual wars between David's supporters in Judah and those forces led by Abner in support of Ishbosheth and the house of Saul. However, when Ishbosheth accused Abner of adultery with Rizpah, one of Saul's concubines,[289] Abner was angry and began to have second thoughts about supporting the young Benjamite. He told Ishbosheth that such accusations against his most loyal supporter might be sufficient to cause him to withdraw his support and give it to David.

Ishbosheth feared Abner and declined to respond to this threat. He let Abner send a message to David seeking to discuss the possibility of uniting their two kingdoms under David. "If you will make an alliance with me," said Abner's message to David, "my hand will be with you to bring all of Israel under your head."

"Very well," responded David. "I agree to make an alliance with you, but there is one thing that must be done before I join in any discussion. You will not see my face unless you first bring Saul's daughter Michal to me, for she was married to me at the price of 100 Philistines." So Ishbosheth took Michal from her husband Phaltiel, the son of Laish and delivered her to David,[290] with Phaltiel following behind weeping.

Once Michal was returned to David, David agreed to meet with Abner to discuss an alliance, and Abner came to Hebron in good faith to make peace. When he left Hebron to return to Mahanaim, however, he was cornered and slain by Joab, David's captain, and Joab's brother Abishai. They slew Abner because he had killed their brother Asahel in an earlier encounter. [291]

David was grieved by Abner's death. He followed Abner's bier and wept at his grave. And when David fasted until evening, it pleased the people, for they knew that David had no part in Abner's death. "A prince and a great man has fallen this day in Israel," said David to his servants. "May Jehovah reward those who have done this evil deed according to their wickedness."

When Ishbosheth learned of Abner's murder at Hebron, he, being troubled and frightened, retreated to his bed. And, as it turned out, Ishbosheth's fears were fully justified, for two of his own captains came and killed him in his bed at midday.

Thinking to win favor, Ishbosheth's assassins brought his head to David. "Behold the head of Ishbosheth," they boasted, "the man who sought your life. Jehovah has avenged you this day of Saul and his seed."

---

[287] The name Ishbosheth means "man of shame."

[288] Mahanaim was east of the Jordan in the territory belonging to thc tribe of Gad.

[289] The main difference between a wife and a concubine was probably the fact that a concubine could be rejected or cast aside without a bill of divorcement, while a wife could not. There was no difference between the children of a wife and those of a concubine, and the latter were a supplementary family to the former. The names of the concubines' children are listed in the patriarchal genealogies, and their position and provision depended on their father's will. The state of concubinage was provided for by the law of Moses and certainly also preceded that law. A concubine would generally be either (1) a Hebrew girl bought from her father, (2) a Gentile captive taken in war, (3) a foreign slave who had been bought, or (4) a Canaanite woman, bond or free. The rights of the first two were protected by the law (Exodus 21:7; Deuteronomy 21:10–14), but the third was unrecognized and the fourth prohibited. Some free Hebrew women also became concubines (William Smith, *Dictionary of the Bible*, *GospeLink*, CD-ROM, s.v. "concubine").

---

[290] Though Saul had given Michal to be David's wife, he later took her away from David and gave her to Phaltiel (1 Samuel 25:44).

[291] These two men, Joab and Abishai—together with their brother Asahel, whom Abner had slain—were the sons of David's sister Zeruiah. The account of the battle between David's men, led by Joab, and Abner and his men—including Abner's slaying of Asahel—is given in 2 Samuel 2:12–32 (see story "118−Shall the Sword Devour Forever?").

David was angered by what he saw and by what these traitors had done to their king. He wondered how they could possibly think they were doing him a favor. And he said to them, "When a man came and told me he had killed King Saul, thinking that he brought me good tidings and that I would reward him, I slew him. How much worse is it when wicked men have slain a righteous man in his own bed, as you have? Therefore, should I not also require your blood?"

At David's command, Ishbosheth's assassins were slain for their cowardly crime, and their bodies were hanged over the pool of Hebron. And Ishbosheth's head was buried in the sepulcher of Abner.

Two years had passed since Ishbosheth had been anointed king at Mahanaim. Now he was dead and all Israel anointed David to be their king.

118—SHALL THE SWORD DEVOUR FOREVER?
(2 Samuel 2)

While David was king over Judah in Hebron and Ishbosheth king over Israel in Mahanaim, their two captains, Joab and Abner, met at Gibeon, each with several young fighting men.

Joab and Abner sat down, one on either side of the pool of Gibeon, and the two men began to converse. "Let our young men arise and play together before us," suggested Abner. Both captains understood well that any skirmishes between their men would be much more than play, but Joab agreed to Abner's suggestion and twelve young men went out from each of their troops to play their games of war. The result was strange, for these young warriors apparently had all been taught the same method of warfare. Each man caught his counterpart from the other camp by his head and thrust his sword into the other's side. As these young warriors all fell, a great battle began between the remaining men of King David and the men of King Ishbosheth, with Joab and Abner leading the way. David's men prevailed over the men of Benjamin who fought for Abner, slaying 360 men while losing only nineteen of their own. But there is more to the story.

When the battle began, Joab's brother Asahel set his sights on Abner that he might take Abner's life. In his dogged determination, Asahel turned neither to the right nor the left from his pursuit of Ishbosheth's sturdy captain. And when Abner looked behind him, Asahel was there. Then Asahel asked him, "Are you Abner?"

"I am," replied Abner, "but if you value your life, I advise you to pursue one of the young men of Benjamin instead of me." But Asahel refused to turn back.

"Turn aside from following me," Abner warned again, "or I will smite you to the ground. And if I do so, how shall I hold up my face to your brother Joab?" But still Asahel refused to turn aside.

As Asahel came forward, Abner took the blunt end of his spear and pierced young Asahel beneath his fifth rib. The blow that Abner dealt was fierce, and the end of the spear went right through the young man and came out his back, causing Asahel to die on the spot.

As Asahel's body lay where it had fallen, all who came that way and saw it stood still, and the brothers of the fallen warrior, Joab and Abishai, set out to find Abner.

As Joab and Abishai came with their men at sundown to the hill Ammah, they found Abner and his men of Benjamin and Israel standing together as one troop at the top of the hill. The sight was formidable, but Asahel's brothers were not deterred.

When Abner saw the men of Judah coming, he called out to Joab. "Shall the sword devour forever, Joab?" Abner asked. "Do you not know that all of this will only end in bitterness? How long shall it be before you bid your people to return from pursuing us? Or we bid our men to return from pursuing you who are our brothers?"

Joab was touched by Abner's insight. He was convinced of the futility of the course he had chosen. "As God lives," he called to Abner, "if you had not spoken, my people would have come up against you in the morning." Then Joab blew his trumpet and his people stood still. They pursued no more after Abner and his men and returned that night to Hebron. But Joab and Abishai did not forget who killed their younger brother.[292]

119–THE ARK COMES TO THE CITY OF DAVID

(2 Samuel 5–6; 1 Chronicles 11, 13–15)

After the death of Saul's son Ishbosheth, all Israel came to Hebron and made David their king. He was a very successful king; the people loved him and served him willingly. Soon after David was anointed, his army conquered the fortress of the Jebusites and took their city—the city of Jerusalem. David loved Jerusalem and called it the City of David.[293] Then, with the help of Hiram, king of Tyre, who provided cedar wood and laborers, David made Jerusalem his capital and built a magnificent palace for himself in the city.

When the Philistines learned that David was king over all Israel, they sent their armies to defeat him, spreading themselves in the valley of Rephaim. But, because David loved Jehovah and sought him in all that he did, Jehovah was with him. David inquired of Jehovah concerning the Philistines. "Shall I go up to battle against them?" he asked. "Wilt Thou deliver them into my hands?"

"Go up!" answered Jehovah, "And I will deliver them." And because Jehovah was with David, he was able to defeat the Philistines and burn the idols that they worshipped as gods. When the Philistines came up to battle a second time, David again sought Jehovah's counsel and was able to defeat them from Geba to Gazer.[294]

One of David's greatest desires was for the ark of the covenant to be brought up to Jerusalem. Seeking to make that desire a reality, he gathered 30,000 of what he perceived to be the best men of Israel about him and

---

[292] The story of Joab's revenge for Asahel's death is told in story "117–The King of Judah Only."

[293] It is noteworthy that the New Testament, at the time of the Savior's birth, referred to Bethlehem as "the city of David" (see Luke 2:4 and 11). This was apparently because Bethlehem was David's birthplace and early home (see 1 Samuel 17:12). Bethlehem was the city of David's nativity, but in the Old Testament, after David conquered Jerusalem, Jerusalem was clearly identified as the City of David (see 2 Samuel 5:7 and 9).

[294] Geba was a small town in Benjamin about six miles (9.7 kilometers) north of Jerusalem. It was the site of the Philistine garrison that was smitten by Jonathan early in Saul's reign (see 1 Samuel 13:3 and story "101–Victory—and Nearly Death—for Jonathan"). Gazer is called Gezer in some other references. It is a city in the northeast area of Israel that was given to the Levites. However, it remained in the possession of the Philistines and had not been conquered.

went to fetch the ark from the house of Abinadab the priest at Kirjath-jearim,[295] where it had resided for twenty years.

The ark was placed upon a new cart, with Uzzah and Ahio, the sons of Abinadab the priest, driving the cart. Then David and all the house of Israel followed the cart and played musical instruments as the ark proceeded on its journey. When the ark came to Nachon's threshing floor, one of the oxen that pulled the cart stumbled and the ark shook. Uzzah, seeing the ark shake, reached out his hand to steady it and was struck dead for his error in judgment. For it was not the duty of man to steady the ark of God.

David was frightened and upset by Jehovah's harsh judgment on Uzzah, and he quickly lost his desire to take the ark of the covenant to Jerusalem. He directed instead that it be taken to the house of Obed-edom, the Gittite,[296] where it remained for three months and was the source of great blessings to Obed-edom and his household.

When David finally gained the courage to take the ark of the covenant the rest of the way to Jerusalem, he proceeded very carefully. After the ark had proceeded but six paces on its journey, the cart was stopped so that oxen and fatlings could be sacrificed to Jehovah. David wore a fine linen robe and a linen ephod and danced before Jehovah with all his might. And David's men brought the ark of the covenant to Jerusalem with shouting and the sound of the trumpet.

Once in Jerusalem, the ark of the covenant was placed in a tabernacle that David had prepared for it, and David had the priests make burnt offerings and peace offerings to Jehovah, and he blessed the people in the name of Jehovah.

120—LOVE TURNS TO HATE
(2 Samuel 6; 1 Chronicles 15)

Michal had loved David dearly and he had loved her. Though she had been taken away from David and given by her father to be the wife of another man, David still loved her. It was a glorious day in both of their lives when they were reunited.[297] But when David brought the ark of the covenant to Jerusalem and set it up in the tabernacle that he had prepared, David and Michal had a falling out.[298]

As Michal looked out of her window and beheld the holy procession coming into the city, she saw her husband, King David, leaping and dancing about as he led the procession, and she was embarrassed. And her feelings of embarrassment made her despise him in her heart.

When David finally returned to his house later that day, Michal came out to meet him. She wanted to make sure he knew just how she felt. "How glorious was the king of Israel today!" she said sarcastically, "who uncovered himself in the eyes of the handmaids of his servants as one of the vain fellows would uncover himself!"[299]

David was taken aback by Michal's rebuke, and his response was cutting. "I danced before Jehovah who chose me to be the king and ruler over his people instead of your father," he retorted. "Therefore did I play before Jehovah."

But David's antagonistic reply to Michal did not stop there. "I will yet be more vile," he shouted, "and will be base in my own sight. And if I choose to do so, I will also be base in the eyes of the maidservants of whom you have spoken. But yet they will have me in honor."

And, because of the combination of Michal's hatred for King David and David's pride, Michal, the daughter of Saul, had no children until the day of her death.[300]

---

[295] The scripture here (2 Samuel 6:4) says that the ark of the covenant was at "the house of Abinadab…at Gibeah." The word Gibeah means "hill," so we can assume that this refers to a hill in Kirjath-jearim. It is quite clear in 1 Samuel 7:1–2 that the ark was placed in "the house of Abinadab in the hill" and that it "abode in Kirjath-jearim" for twenty years.

[296] Obed-edom the Gittite was probably from the town of Gittaim in Benjamin.

[297] There is a brief discussion of this situation in story "117—The King of Judah Only."

[298] The account of David bringing the Ark up to Jerusalem is given in story "119—The Ark Comes to the City of David."

[299] It is not likely that David exposed his body to the point of indecency, but he must have exposed more than Michal thought was proper under the circumstances.

[300] The inference here is that it was David's decision that Michal have no children. It was the greatest reproach or embarrassment for a woman to be barren and have no children.

121–YOUR SON SHALL BUILD MY HOUSE
(2 Samuel 7; 1 Chronicles 17)

David loved Jehovah and was greatly blessed by him. He was blessed to prevail over Israel's enemies and there was peace throughout the land. One day as he sat in the beautiful palace he had built in Jerusalem, he said to the prophet Nathan who was there with him, "I am blessed to live in a house of cedar, but the ark of God still dwells in a tent."

Nathan was pleased by David's comment. He could tell that David was thinking about building a temple. "Go and do all that is in your heart," he replied, "for Jehovah is with you."

That night, however, Jehovah spoke to Nathan, giving him a different message. "Go to my servant David and tell him, thus says Jehovah: shall you build me a house to dwell in? I have not dwelt in any house since I brought the children of Israel out of Egypt, but have walked from tent to tent and from one tabernacle to another. But in all the places that I have walked with the children of Israel, I have asked none of the tribes of Israel why they have not built a house of cedar for me."

Jehovah continued his message to Nathan: "You shall also tell my servant David that I took him from the sheepfold and from following the sheep to make him a ruler over Israel. I have been with him wherever he has gone and have cut off his enemies. I have made his name great like the names of the great men of the earth. And I will appoint for my people Israel a place of their own that they shall move no more, and the children of wickedness shall afflict them no more.

"My servant David will not build my house himself but, when his days are fulfilled and he sleeps with his fathers, I will build David's house. I will set up David's son and will establish his kingdom. David's son shall build a house to my name, and I will establish his throne and his house forever. My mercy will not depart from David or from his son as it did from Saul, whom I put away before them. For the house and the kingdom of David will be established forever."

And Nathan went and spoke all of these words to David as Jehovah commanded him.

122–HONOR FOR THE HOUSE OF SAUL
(2 Samuel 9)

One day King David began to think about his friend Jonathan who had been killed in the fierce battle against the Philistines on Mount Gilboa.[301] These thoughts weighed heavily upon him because of his close friendship with Jonathan and the oath he had made not to cut off his kindness from Jonathan's house even after Jonathan was dead.[302] He also remembered King Saul's petition to him at Engedi that he would not cut off his seed or destroy his name.[303]

David called to him Ziba, a man who was a servant in Saul's house, and asked him, "Are there not any of Saul's house who are yet alive? For I desire to show the kindness of God to them."

"Jonathan has a son named Mephibosheth who is lame in both feet," answered Ziba. "He is in Machir's house at Lodebar."[304] And when David heard it, he requested that the young man be brought before him.

Mephibosheth was but five years old when his father Jonathan was killed in the war with the Philistines. When word came of his father's death, his nurse had taken him and fled. He was lame because he had fallen and injured himself in the haste of their flight.

When the young man was brought before King David, he bowed in deep respect. "Fear not," said David. "I will show kindness to you for the sake of your father and will restore to you all the lands that once belonged to your grandfather Saul."

Then David called Ziba, Saul's servant, to him again and said, "I have given all that pertained to Saul

---

[301] See story "115–The End of King Saul."

[302] The covenant that David swore to Jonathan is recorded in 1 Samuel 20:14–15 in the words of Jonathan. It was as follows: "And thou shalt not only while yet I live shew me the kindness of the LORD, that I die not; But also thou shalt not cut off thy kindness from my house for ever: no, not when the LORD hath cut off the enemies of David every one from the face of the earth." David also swore an oath to King Saul, at the time he spared Saul's life in the cave at Engedi that he would not cut off Saul's seed or destroy Saul's name out of his house (see story "109–The Hunted Spares the Hunter").

[303] See story "109–The Hunted Spares the Hunter."

[304] Lodebar is believed to have been located east of the Jordan near Mahanaim, the city where Ishbosheth was king of Israel. See story "117–The King of Judah Only" for a discussion of Ishbosheth's reign in Israel after the death of his father, King Saul.

and his house to this young man. You and your sons and your servants are to till the land for him and bring in the harvest, so that your master's son and his house may have food to eat."

"It shall be done as you have commanded," replied Ziba. And it was done well, for Ziba had fifteen sons and twenty servants.

"As for Mephibosheth," said David, "he shall eat at my table as if he were my own son."

123—DAVID AND THE TENTH COMMANDMENT

(2 Samuel 10–11)

David had made a gesture of kindness toward the king of the Ammonites, but when David's intent was misinterpreted and his servants were humiliated, war resulted. The Ammonites called upon Syria to assist them in the war, and David sent Joab to lead the army of Israel against the forces of Ammon and Syria. David, however, quite contrary to his usual custom, remained at home in Jerusalem.

One night in the heat of the summer, David rose from his bed and walked on the roof of his palace. From his vantage point on the roof, David could see a beautiful woman washing herself. When he inquired concerning the woman, his servants told him that her name was Bathsheba, and that she was the wife of one his thirty-seven most valiant and devoted soldiers, Uriah the Hittite.[305]

Though David had many wives of his own, he broke the tenth commandment by coveting Uriah's wife. He sent messengers to bring Bathsheba to his house. And once she was there, David was overcome by lust and lay with her. Then he sent her back to her home.

When a few weeks had passed and Bathsheba discovered she was with child, she sent a messenger to tell David. This was not good news for David, and he began to be concerned—not because he had sinned, but for fear of Bathsheba's husband and his own reputation. David, realizing that something must be done quickly, sent a request to Joab at the war's front, asking that Uriah be sent home to Jerusalem immediately.

When Uriah arrived, David met with him briefly, but he was evasive and talked about many things. He had no intention of telling Uriah what had happened. He asked instead about Joab, the morale of the army, and the progress of the war.

David had a devious plan. He believed that if Uriah got home soon enough, he would think that he was the father of Bathsheba's child. So he told Uriah to go home and wash himself. Then, when Uriah left him, David sent a gift of food to his house. Uriah, however, did not do as David told him. Instead of going home, he slept at the door of David's house with the servants.

---

[305] David's thirty-seven mighty men are named in both 2 Samuel 23:8–39 and 1 Chronicles 11:10–47. Uriah the Hittite is named in 2 Samuel 23:39 and 1 Chronicles 11:40. Though he was a Hittite, he was obviously a convert to the gospel and the law of Moses.

When David learned that Uriah had not gone home, he was frustrated. Seeing that his carefully laid plan was not working, he went to the servants' quarters to talk to Uriah. David spoke as if he had great concern for Uriah. "You have just returned from a long absence," he said. "Why did you not go home to your wife?" David's concern, however, was not for Uriah but for himself.

Uriah's response was evidence of his great loyalty to his king and his fellow soldiers. "The ark of the covenant and the armies of Israel and Judah are living in tents," replied Uriah. "And my lord Joab and his servants are encamped in the open fields. Considering this, would it be proper for me to go into my house to eat and drink and to lie with my wife? As you live and as your soul lives, I will not do this thing."

David hid his frustration, but he wanted to try one more time to get Uriah to go home to Bathsheba. "Remain here for one more day," said David, "then you may return to the war." So Uriah stayed in Jerusalem with David's servants all that day and the next.

In the evening of that second day, David called Uriah to eat and drink with him. He gave him too much to drink and made him drunk, but still Uriah did not go home to Bathsheba.

The next morning David wrote a letter to Joab, sealed it, and gave it to Uriah to deliver. David was desperate now. He had decided to do to Uriah what King Saul had long ago sought to do to him. His letter to Joab was short and to the point: "Place Uriah in the forefront of the hottest battle, then retire from him, that he may be smitten and die."

Joab was not totally obedient to what David asked him to do. He did not put Uriah at the forefront of a heated battle but instead set up an attack against a fortified city of the Ammonites where he knew there would be great danger. And he assigned Uriah to a place where he knew the valiant men would be. When the men of the city came out in response to the attack, they fought against Joab's men, taking many lives— including that of Uriah.

When the battle was done, Joab sent a message back to David to report on the status of the war. "The men of the city prevailed against us," he wrote. "When they came out into the field, we attacked them and drove them back to the gates of their city. But when we were near at the gates, those who shot from the wall caused the death of many of our men. And among the dead was your servant Uriah the Hittite."

David was pleased and relieved with the results of the battle and sent a response to Joab. "Do not be discouraged because of your defeat or for the loss of Uriah," he wrote, pretending to show regret, "for the sword will devour one man as well as another. What you must do now is make a stronger battle against the city and overthrow it."

When Bathsheba learned of her husband's death, she mourned his loss. But when the period of mourning was past, David sent for her. She became his wife and bore the son that was conceived by David's sin. And the thing that David had done displeased Jehovah.

124–THE EWE LAMB AND THE CURSE

(2 Samuel 12)

Jehovah was angry with King David, and he sent the prophet Nathan to David with a message. Nathan's message was delivered in the form of a simple story: "Two men lived in the same city, one rich and the other poor. The rich man had many flocks and herds, but the poor man had only one little ewe lamb that he had bought and raised. The lamb grew up together with the man's children. It ate his food and drank from his cup and was valued by him as his own daughter. One day a traveler came to the rich man's home, but when the rich man prepared food for the traveler, he spared his own flocks and dressed the poor man's lamb for the stranger."

Thinking that Nathan was telling him of something that had happened among the people of Israel, David was upset. "As Jehovah lives," he said to Nathan, "the man who has done this terrible deed must surely die! And he shall restore the lamb fourfold because he had no pity!"

Then Nathan said to David, "You are that man!"

David was stunned, but Nathan's message was not finished. He continued: "Thus says Jehovah, the God of Israel, to David: 'I anointed you king over Israel, and I delivered you out of the hands of Saul. I gave you your master's house and delivered wives into your bosom. I gave you both the house of Israel and the house of Judah. And, if all of these things were not enough, I would have given you whatever else you asked. Why, then, have you despised my commandments and done this evil in my sight? You have killed Uriah the Hittite with the sword of the Ammonites and have taken *his* wife to be *your* wife.

"Because you have despised me, David, the sword shall never depart from your house. And I will raise up evil against you out of your own house. I will take your wives before your eyes and give them to your neighbor, and he shall lie with them in the sight of the sun.[306] What you did, you did secretly; but I will do what I do in the sight of all Israel."

David knew that Nathan spoke the truth. "I have sinned against Jehovah," he confessed.

"Jehovah has not put away your sin, but you shall not die,"[307] continued Nathan. "You have given great occasion to Jehovah's enemies to blaspheme. And the child who was born because of your sin shall die."

After Nathan had departed, Bathsheba's child fell sick. David fasted and lay upon the ground, pleading with Jehovah for the child's life, but on the seventh day the child died.

The servants were afraid to tell David that the child was dead. "While the child was alive we spoke to him and he would not answer us," they said. "How then will he vex himself if we tell him the child is dead?" But when David saw the whisperings of his servants, he knew that the child had died. He arose from the earth, washed himself, put on clean clothes, and went to the tabernacle to worship. And when he had worshiped, he returned to his own house and ate.

David's servants were puzzled by his behavior. "Explain this to us," said the servants. "How is it that while the child was yet alive, you fasted and wept for him, but now he is dead, you rise and eat bread?"

"While the child was alive," said David, "I fasted and wept, praying that God would be gracious to me and spare his life. But now that he is dead, I have no reason to fast. I cannot bring him back. I shall go to him, but he cannot return here to me."

David comforted Bathsheba in the loss of her son, and Jehovah blessed them with another son in place of the first. They called their son Solomon, and Jehovah loved him. And Jehovah sent word through the prophet Nathan that the child should be named Jedidiah.[308]

---

[306] The fulfillment of this prophecy is given in 2 Samuel 16 and is told in story "129–The Rejection of Ahithophel."

[307] In other words, David was not punished immediately by death, but he was not to escape punishment.

[308] The name Solomon means "peaceable," and the name Jedidiah means "the darling of Jehovah." Solomon was apparently never called by this name Jedidiah. King David had many sons, but apparently only four by Bathsheba—Shimea, Shobab, Nathan, and Solomon (see 1 Chronicles 3:5). Nathan is the son of David who is mentioned in the Savior's lineage by Luke (Luke 3:31). In Matthew's account, however, Solomon is mentioned (Matthew 1:6).

125–ABSALOM'S REVENGE

(2 Samuel 13)

King David's eldest son Amnon was infatuated with David's daughter Tamar, his own half sister. He was filled with such lust for her that it made him ill. When he told his cousin Jonadab of his anguish over Tamar, Jonadab was quick to offer advice to his ailing cousin. "Lie down on your bed as if you are sick," he counseled. "Then, when your father comes to see you, ask him to let Tamar come and prepare food in your presence for you to eat."

So Amnon, feigning sickness, did as Jonadab suggested, and David sent Tamar to prepare food in Amnon's presence. Tamar made some cakes, which she baked in Amnon's presence, and put them before him. Amnon, however, refused to eat. He then dismissed all the men who were present and told Tamar to bring the cakes into his bedchamber where he would eat them from her hand. But when Tamar came into the privacy of Amnon's bedchamber, he took hold of her and said, "Come lie with me, my sister."

"Oh, no, my brother! Do not force me!" she cried. "Such a thing ought not to be done in Israel. You will cause me great shame, and you shall be thought one of the fools of Israel. If you must have me, speak to the king; for surely he will not withhold me from you."

Amnon would not be dissuaded and, being stronger than Tamar, he forced her to lie with him. Once Amnon had taken advantage of her, however, his heart was filled with contempt. The hate he now felt for Tamar was greater than the lust that had driven him to his immoral act. "Arise and be gone!" he shouted at her.

"You are crazy!" shouted Tamar. "Your evil in sending me away now is greater than the evil you did to lie with me." But Amnon would not hear her. He called his servant to put Tamar out and bar the door behind her.

Tamar, as one of the king's virgin daughters, wore a robe of many colors common to her station. But now, in her humiliation, she tore her robe, put ashes on head, and left Amnon's quarters in tears.

When King David learned what Amnon had done, he was furious. Tamar's brother Absalom was also angry with Amnon, but he was more subtle than his father. "Hold your peace," he said to her, "for Amnon is your brother." Absalom secretly hated Amnon for what he had done to his sister, but he did not tell her of the revenge that he was planning. So Tamar remained inconsolable in Absalom's house.

Two years passed without event. Then one day when Absalom had sheepshearers at his farm in the village of Baal-hazor, he invited his father and all his brothers to go there. King David opposed the idea and would not go himself but, after some persuasion from Absalom, agreed that his sons might go.

Absalom was now prepared to seek his revenge. "Watch Amnon," he said to his servants, "and observe when he is drunk. Then, when I tell you, you must kill him." At Absalom's signal, the servants fell upon Amnon and killed him. And when the rest of David's sons saw what happened to Amnon, they mounted their mules[309] and fled for Jerusalem.

Word soon came back to King David that Absalom had killed all of his brothers, and the news left David desolate. Both he and his servants tore their clothing, cast themselves upon the ground, and wept bitterly.

Jonadab soon arrived and set the record straight. "Do not suppose that all of your sons are slain," he said to David. "Only Amnon is dead. His death was planned by Absalom from the day Amnon forced his sister Tamar."

And as soon as Jonadab had finished speaking, the watchman pointed out a group of people coming up the hill behind them. "Behold!" said Jonadab, "your sons are coming now."

Once Absalom's revenge against Amnon was complete, he fled to the home of his grandfather Talmai, king of Geshur,[310] and lived there for three years.

David's anger against Amnon was put to rest with Amnon's death, and in his heart he longed to go to Absalom.

---

[309] The mule is a hybrid animal, the issue of a horse and an ass. Smaller than a horse, it is hardy and sure-footed and usually lives much longer. The Israelites, for reasons unknown to us, were forbidden from breeding mules, but sometimes they imported them. The mule became a symbol of royalty, and only kings and their family members rode them (see William Smith, *Dictionary of the Bible*, *GospeLink*, CD-ROM, s.v. "mule," and *Bible Dictionary*, LDS-KJV, s.v. "mule").

[310] Geshur was a small kingdom in Syria, east of the Sea of Chinnereth, or what we now know as the Sea of Galilee.

126−ABSALOM'S RETURN FROM EXILE

(2 Samuel 14)

Joab, the captain of King David's army, knew that David loved Absalom, and after three years of Absalom's absence from Jerusalem, he devised a plan to persuade King David to bring Absalom home from Geshur where he was in exile. Joab found a wise woman and sent her to David—posing as a widow—to tell a sad story about her only two sons, one of whom had killed the other. The story—which was fabricated by Joab—told how the woman's family demanded that the surviving son be slain for taking his brother's life. This was a problem, however, for if this son were slain, the widow's late husband would be left with no heir.

When David had heard the woman's story and had promised to intervene for the life of the surviving son, the woman reminded him of his own son who had slain his brother and lived in exile. Said she, "You speak as one who is at fault himself, because you have not brought home your own banished son. We must all die, but Jehovah has prepared a way that those who are banished need not be cast out." Then she thanked David profusely for what he had promised to do for her and her son.

When David had heard the woman's story and her advice concerning Absalom, he perceived the workings of Joab. Upon questioning, the woman admitted that all her words had been given her by Joab to convince David to bring Absalom home and save him from those who wanted revenge against him for the death of his brother Amnon. [311]

David relented. He sent Joab to Geshur to bring Absalom home to Jerusalem. But, though David agreed to bring his son back to Jerusalem, he was also very cautious. "Let Absalom return to his own house," he told Joab, "that I do not see his face."

After Absalom had been back in Jerusalem for two years and had still not been allowed to see his father, he sent for Joab to ask why David would not see him. Joab, however, would not come when he was summoned. So, after Absalom's second unanswered request to Joab, Absalom's servants set fire to Joab's barley fields. This brought Joab to him at once.

"I have asked you to come that I might send you to my father in my behalf," said Absalom to Joab. "Ask him why he brought me back from Geshur but will not see me, for it would have been better for me to stay there. Let me see the king, and then, if he finds iniquity in me, let him kill me."

When Joab went to King David in Absalom's behalf, David agreed to see his son. And when Absalom came before David, he bowed himself to the ground and David kissed him. The two were reconciled at last.

---

[311] This incident is told in story "125−Absalom's Revenge."

127—THE MAN WHO WOULD BE KING

(2 Samuel 15)

Absalom was a very handsome man. The scripture says that "in all Israel there was none to be so much praised as Absalom for his beauty." But Absalom was as cunning as he was handsome. Just as he had earlier devised a careful plan to kill his brother Amnon,[312] he now had a plan to take over his father David's throne as king of Israel. He prepared his chariots and horses and fifty men to run before him as he went throughout the kingdom. And when was not riding through the kingdom, he was standing beside the gate of Jerusalem conversed with the people.

When someone came to the king with a controversy, Absalom called the person aside and heard the matter himself. In each case he would tell the person that his case was good but, unfortunately, the king had no one who was authorized to hear such cases. Then he would say, "Oh that I were made judge of this land, then every man who had any suit or cause might come to me and I would do him justice!"

Absalom did everything possible to gain the favor of the people. He embraced everyone who came near to him and flattered the people until he won the hearts of all Israel.

When Absalom believed that the time was right for him to take the throne, he came to David and said, lying, "Let me go to Hebron and keep the vow that I made to Jehovah. When I was in Geshur in Syria, I vowed to him that if he would bring me again to Jerusalem I would serve him."

"Go in peace," answered David.

While Absalom was preparing for his journey to Hebron, he secretly sent spies throughout the tribes of Israel. These men were instructed to wait for the sound of the trumpet and then shout to the people, "Absalom reigns in Hebron!" However, most of the people— including the 200 men of Jerusalem that he took with him to Hebron—were not yet aware of Absalom's devious scheme.

When Absalom arrived in Hebron, he sent to Giloh[313] for Ahithophel. Ahithophel was David's counselor in the town of Giloh,[314] but he came to Hebron at Absalom's request to join in the conspiracy to overthrow David and take the throne.

When the conspiracy became evident, a messenger went to warn King David. "The hearts of the men of Israel are with Absalom," said the messenger, "and he seeks to be king."

This news alarmed David and he prepared to flee for his life. He also alerted his servants and all those who were with him in Jerusalem that they must also leave. "Arise and let us flee," he told them, "or we shall not escape from Absalom. If we do not go now, he will take us by surprise and smite the city with the edge of the sword."

Nearly everyone in the city of Jerusalem left. Zadok and Abiathar, the two high priests, and all of the Levites were numbered in the company. The ark of the covenant also went with them. Only ten women, David's concubines,[315] were left behind to look after the king's palace. David urged some whose lives would not be in danger to remain in Jerusalem, but all chose to go because of their love for their king and their loyalty to him.

After the company had crossed the brook Kidron, going east from Jerusalem, David instructed Zadok to take the ark of the covenant and return to Jerusalem. "If I find favor in Jehovah's eyes," David said, "he will bring me back to Jerusalem and will show me both the ark and his habitation. But if he has no delight in me, let him do to me as seems good to him."

Then David said to Abiathar, "You should return to the city with Zadok, and your two sons with you. I will

---

[312] See story "125—Absalom's Revenge."

[313] Giloh was a town in the mountainous part of Judah. Those who lived there were called Gilonites.

[314] Ahithophel was also the grandfather of David's wife Bathsheba and the father of Eliam, one of King David's thirty-seven mighty men. The name Ahithophel means "brother of folly."

[315] The main difference between a wife and a concubine was probably in the fact that a concubine could be rejected or cast aside without a bill of divorcement, while a wife could not. There was no difference between the children of a wife and those of a concubine, and the latter were a supplementary family to the former. The names of the concubines' children are listed in the patriarchal genealogies, and their position and provision depended on their father's will. The state of concubinage was provided for by the law of Moses and certainly also preceded that law. A concubine would generally be either (1) a Hebrew girl bought from her father, (2) a Gentile captive taken in war, (3) a foreign slave who had been bought, or (4) a Canaanite woman, bond or free. The rights of the first two were protected by the law (Exodus 21:7; Deuteronomy 21:10–14), but the third was unrecognized and the fourth prohibited. Some free Hebrew women also became concubines (see William Smith, *Dictionary of the Bible, GospeLink,* CD-ROM, s.v. "concubine").

tarry in the wilderness until you send word that I may safely return." Then Zadok, Abiathar, and their sons[316] returned to Jerusalem with the ark of the covenant, the ark being carried by the Levites.

As the exiles climbed the Mount of Olives, David took off his shoes and covered his head. And all those who were with him also covered their heads. They wept as they went. When someone told David that Ahithophel was one of Absalom's coconspirators, David prayed and said, "O Jehovah, turn Ahithophel's counsel into foolishness."

At the top of the mount, as they stopped to worship, David's dear friend Hushai met him with his coat torn and dirt upon his head. And David said to Hushai, "You must return to Jerusalem and tell Absalom that you have come to be his servant. Tell him that as you have served me, you will now serve him. Then, when he makes you his servant, you must defeat the counsel of Ahithophel. Also, whatever you learn from Absalom's house, tell it to Zadok and Abiathar, that they may send the information on to me."

And Hushai returned to Jerusalem to do as King David had counseled him.

128—THE FLIGHT FROM JERUSALEM
(2 Samuel 16)

As King David's company of fugitives made their way down the east slope of the Mount of Olives on their flight from Jerusalem, they were surprised to meet Ziba, the man who had been a servant in Saul's house and had, more recently, been assigned to care for the estate of Jonathan's lame son Mephibosheth.[317] Ziba came bearing gifts. He had with him two saddled asses, 100 loaves of bread, 100 bunches of raisins, 100 summer fruits, and a bottle[318] of wine.

"What is the meaning of all these gifts?" David asked Ziba.

"The asses are for the king's household to ride on," replied Ziba. "The summer fruit and bread are for the young men to eat, and the wine is to be drunk in the wilderness by those who are faint."

David was still puzzled by Ziba's gifts. "Where is Mephibosheth?" he asked.

"My master has stayed in Jerusalem," replied Ziba, "for he told me that today the house of Israel will restore the throne of his grandfather Saul to him." Though David had restored all Saul's property to Mephibosheth and had treated him as one of his own sons, it appeared—from Ziba's representations—that Mephibosheth still lived in hope that the kingdom of Israel would be restored to the house of Saul.[319]

David spoke to Ziba the sad truth. "You and your family," said David, "are all the kingdom that Mephibosheth shall have."

Ziba knew David was right. "I humbly beg of you then," he said, "that I may find grace in your sight."

When David and his party came to the village of Bahurim,[320] they received their second surprise from a man of the tribe of Benjamin. This man, whose name was Shimei, came out to curse David and throw stones

---

[316] Zadok's son was named Ahimaaz, and Abiathar's son was named Jonathan.

[317] See story "122—Honor for the House of Saul."

[318] A bottle as mentioned here could more appropriately be called a water skin. It was made from an animal skin and was used by travelers to carry water or wine.

[319] From what we learn later when David returned to Jerusalem, Ziba misrepresented the feelings of Mephibosheth when he came to King David with his gifts that day. He was apparently seeking to gain some advantage for himself. See story "131—David's Return from Exile" for Mephibosheth's side of the story.

[320] Bahurim was apparently located near the south border of Benjamin on the road that led from Jerusalem to the valley of the Jordan.

at him and his servants. Though Shimei's antics were certainly having an effect, he was frustrated because David was surrounded by the people and by his mighty men and could not be reached. "Come out! Come out! You bloody man!" cried Shimei. "Come out you man of Belial!"[321] Shimei's tirade against King David probably represented the feelings of many men in the tribe of Benjamin—feelings that no one else had the courage to express. For, after all, David had taken the throne of Israel from the tribe of Benjamin.

David's mighty men became upset by Shimei's display. David's nephew Abishai—Joab's younger brother—was particularly disturbed. "Why should this dead dog curse my lord the king?" he asked. "Let me go and take off his head."

"Come, come," responded David. "What have I to do with you? Let the man curse, for it was Jehovah who told him to curse me. Who then can ask him why he does so?"

David continued, speaking louder now so that all his servants could hear, and not just Abishai: "The son who came forth from my own bowels now seeks my life that he may be king. How much more justified is this Benjamite? Let him curse me, for Jehovah has bidden him. It may be that Jehovah will look on my afflictions and repay me with good for Shimei's cursing today."

And as David and his company of exiles went along their way, Shimei followed on the ridge beside them—all the while cursing, hurling stones at them, and throwing dust into the air. It was a stirring demonstration.

129—THE REJECTION OF AHITHOPHEL
(2 Samuel 16–17)

As King David and his supporters fled from Jerusalem to escape Absalom's murderous uprising, he sent his friend Hushai to be a spy against Absalom and to undermine whatever counsel Ahithophel might offer him. Ahithophel, Bathsheba's grandfather, had been one of David's trusted counselors but was now part of the conspiracy bent on making Absalom king of Israel. David did not know if his plan would work, but he felt it was worth trying.

When Absalom and Ahithophel came to Jerusalem, Hushai met them and bowed himself before them. "Let the king live! Let the king live!" he cried.

Absalom was flattered by Hushai's devotion, but he was suspicious because he knew of Hushai's loyalty to David. "Is this how you show kindness to your friend, King David?" asked Absalom. "Why did you not go with him?"

"My loyalty is not to your father," Hushai lied, "but to that man whom Jehovah and this people choose to be their king. As I have served in David's presence in the past, so will I now serve in the presence of his son."

Hushai's flattery won Absalom's heart, and he was accepted as one of Absalom's trusted servants. He was now in a position to complete his assigned mission and defeat the counsel of Ahithophel.

Absalom was eager to strengthen his position against David in any way he could, and he asked Ahithophel's counsel about how he might most effectively do so. When Ahithophel gave counsel to Absalom, he spoke as if his words were the very words of God. "Go in unto your father's concubines," said Ahithophel, "the ones that he has left here in Jerusalem to care for his house. By this all Israel will know that your father hates you, and this breach between you and your father will strengthen your hand with those who support you." So, Absalom and Ahithophel set up a tent on top of David's palace where Absalom went in and lay with his father's concubines so that all Israel could see him.[322]

Ahithophel also had a plan to destroy King David, and he explained his plan to Absalom. "Let me choose 12,000 men from among your followers and go after

---

[321] "Man (or son) of Belial" is a derisive term used many times in the scriptures. It simply means a worthless and lawless person.

[322] Absalom's overt immorality on top of the king's palace was in fulfillment of a prophecy made by Nathan after David had committed adultery with Bathsheba, the wife of Uriah the Hittite, and then had Uriah slain in battle (see story "124—The Ewe Lamb and the Curse").

David tonight," he urged. "We will overtake him when he is weary and weak-handed. He will be afraid, and all who are with him will flee. Thus, when he is left by himself, we will be able to kill him and deliver all the people to you. With their leader dead, they will be pleased to make you their king."

Though Absalom and the elders of Israel liked Ahithophel's proposal, they wanted another opinion. "Call Hushai," said Absalom, "and let us also hear what he says." So they brought in Hushai and told him Ahithophel's plan.

"Is this a good plan?" they asked Hushai. "Shall we do as Ahithophel suggests?"

Hushai was amazed at the simple brilliance of Ahithophel's plan and feared that David would be destroyed if it were carried out. But now he had his chance to overturn the counsel of Ahithophel.

"The counsel that Ahithophel has given is not good," Hushai told Absalom and the elders, "for you know that David and his men are mighty men. You also know that their souls are as bitter at this time as a she-bear robbed of her cubs. Also, because your father is a man of war, he will not lodge with the people but will hide somewhere in a pit. Thus, when Ahithophel comes against his people, the word will come to your father of the slaughter among the people, and he and his valiant men will rise up and destroy Ahithophel's army."

"Instead of going after David now," Hushai continued, "I think that you, Absalom, should gather all Israel—from Dan in the north to Beersheba in the south—and personally lead this great multitude to battle against your father. We shall come upon him as the dew that falls on the ground and, of him and those who are with him, there shall not one soul be left."

When Absalom and the men of Israel had heard Hushai's counsel, they said, "The counsel of Hushai is better than that of Ahithophel." Thus, Ahithophel's cunning counsel failed because Jehovah had so ordained, that evil might be brought upon Absalom.

Once Absalom had accepted Hushai's counsel, Hushai went quietly to Zadok and Abiathar, the priests, and told them of the plan so that King David might be warned as quickly as possible. And when Hushai's message was delivered to David by the priests' sons, Jonathan and Ahimaaz, his company crossed to the east side of the Jordan that night.

And Ahithophel, when he learned that Absalom had rejected his counsel, returned home to the city of Giloh, put his affairs in order, and hanged himself.

130—ABSALOM'S DEATH AND DAVID'S SORROW

(2 Samuel 18)

When David and his refugee camp had crossed the Jordan in their flight from Absalom, they went to Mahanaim, the city where Ishbosheth had ruled over Israel.[323] Absalom and the army of Israel—under the leadership of Amasa—were not far behind. Absalom chose Amasa, another of David's nephews, [324] to be captain of Israel's army because Joab had cast his lot with David. In preparation for war, Absalom and Amasa were encamped with the army of Israel in the land of Gilead.

The Ammonites, the Gileadites, and others in the area had great respect for David and, when they saw his plight, brought food and other supplies in order to assist.[325]

As the threat from Absalom increased, David numbered his men and set captains over thousands and over hundreds. Then he divided his army into three parts—one part under Joab, a second part under Joab's brother Abishai, and the third part under Ittai the Gittite.[326] Then David told the people, "I will also go to battle with you."

"No, no!" cried the people. "That would be unwise! It will be better for you to remain here in the city. If we should flee from them, they will not care about us. Not even if half of us die, will they care about us. You are the one they want and are worth 10,000 of us."

David knew they were right. "I will do what seems best to you," he said. And David stood at the city gate as his army went out of the city by hundreds and by thousands to fight against Absalom and the army of Israel.

In spite of all that Absalom had done, David still had great concern and love for his wayward son. "Deal

---

[323] For the account of Ishbosheth's short reign over Israel in opposition to David, see story "117—King of Judah Only."

[324] Amasa was the son of Ithra and David's sister Abigail (see 2 Samuel 17:25).

[325] Among those who showed great kindness to David and his company was a Gileadite named Barzillai. David's appreciation for Barzillai and his kindness are mentioned in story "137—Be Strong and Show Yourself a Man."

[326] The title Gittite means "belonging to Gath." This title, as used here, probably refers to the 600 men who came with David from Gath and Ziklag (see 2 Samuel 15:18).

gently with the young man Absalom," he told Joab, Abishai, and Ittai. And all the people heard this charge to David's captains.

David's army had prepared well and was able to prevail over Amasa and the army of Israel that day. As the battle scattered over the whole face of the country, 20,000 of Absalom's army of Israel were slain.

During the battle, the mule[327] on which Absalom was riding went under the bough of a great oak tree, and Absalom's head was caught in the tree. When the mule went out from under him, Absalom was left hanging in the tree.[328]

Absalom is snared by the branches of a tree

When one of Joab's men informed Joab that he saw Absalom hanging by his head in an oak tree, Joab became very excited. "Why did you not smite him to the ground?" Joab asked the man. "I would have given you ten shekels of silver and a girdle."[329]

The man was well aware of David's instructions to deal gently with Absalom, and the thought of smiting him had not crossed his mind. "Though I should receive 1,000 shekels of silver," he said, "I would not lift my hand against the king's son. For I know that the king charged you—together with Abishai and Ittai—that you should not touch Absalom. If I had smitten him I would have endangered my own life, for there is nothing hidden from the king. Why, I think that even you would have set yourself against me."

But the impetuous Joab had different ideas and had already made up his mind what he would do. He hated Absalom and had no regard for David's instructions concerning him. "I will not stay and listen to such talk," said Joab. And he took three darts and thrust them through Absalom's heart while he yet hung alive in the tree. Then the ten young men who bore Joab's armor circled around Absalom and killed him.

When Absalom was dead, Joab blew his trumpet to halt the attack against the army of Israel, and the army of Israel fled to their tents. Joab took Absalom's body down from the tree, cast it into a pit in the woods, and covered it with stones.

Then Ahimaaz, the son of Zadok the priest, said to Joab, "I will now run and tell the king that Jehovah has avenged him of his enemies."

"No!" said Joab. "You shall not bear such tidings to the king today. You will bear your tidings another day, for today the king's son is dead." Then Joab sent Cushi[330] to tell King David what Joab would have him know about the death of Absalom.

Ahimaaz persisted. "Let me go also," he said to Joab. "Let me run after Cushi."

"Why do you wish to go?" asked Joab. "You have no tidings ready."

"No matter," replied Ahimaaz. "Let me go anyway."

"Go then!" said Joab, finally relenting.

Ahimaaz ran to Mahanaim by a different way than Cushi and arrived before him. And as David sat between the two gates of the city, the watchman on the roof saw Ahimaaz coming. He could not tell who the

---

[327] The mule is a hybrid animal, the issue of a horse and an ass. Smaller than a horse, it is hardy and sure-footed and usually lives much longer. The Israelites, for reasons unknown to us, were forbidden from breeding mules, but sometimes they imported them. The mule became a symbol of royalty, and only kings and their family members rode them (see William Smith, *Dictionary of the Bible*, GospeLink, CD-ROM, s.v. "mule," and *Bible Dictionary*, LDS-KJV, s.v. "mule").

[328] It is possible that Absalom's hair became entangled in the branches of the tree. The scriptures tell us that he had lots of hair (see 2 Samuel 14:26).

[329] Girdles were highly prized in the Near East and were worn by both men and women. Some girdles were

very decorative and others quite plain; they could be made either of leather or linen. They were sometimes embroidered with silk and even gold thread. An ornate girdle might also be studded with various kinds of gemstones. It was an important part of a soldier's battle dress and provided a place for a sword or dagger. Girding up ones loins was an essential preparation for battle. (see William Smith, *Dictionary of the Bible*, GospeLink, CD-ROM, s.v. "girdle").

[330] Cushi was probably not the man's name. He was probably a Cushite, or Ethiopian.

messenger was, however, and he told the king what he saw.

"If the man is alone," said David, "there are tidings in his mouth."

As Ahimaaz drew near, the watchman looked and saw Cushi coming also. And when he told King David, David declared, "Surely this man also brings tidings."

"I think the first man runs like Ahimaaz, the son of Zadok the priest," said the watchman.

"Ahimaaz is a good man," replied David. "Surely he brings good tidings."

When Ahimaaz reached the city he called to David, "All is well!" and he fell to the earth before his king. "Blessed be Jehovah your God," said Ahimaaz, gasping for his breath, "for he has delivered up to us those men who lifted their hands against you."

When David heard this message, his first thoughts were for his rebellious son. "Is the young man Absalom safe?" he asked.

Ahimaaz tried to soften the blow. "When Joab sent me, I saw a great tumult," he answered, "but I could not tell what it was."

Then, as the other messenger drew near, David said to Ahimaaz, "Come, stand over here and wait." And Ahimaaz stood waiting by the side.

When Cushi arrived at the gate, he said to David, "Tidings, my lord the king. Jehovah has avenged you this day of those who rose up against you."

"Is the young man Absalom safe?" David asked Cushi, just as he had asked Ahimaaz before him.

"I would that all the king's enemies might be as that young man is," answered Cushi.

David was shaken by Cushi's reply. He now knew that his rebellious and ambitious son was dead. And he returned to his chamber above the gate where he wept bitterly for his son: "O my son Absalom, my son, my son Absalom!" he cried. "I would to God that I had died for you, O Absalom, my son, my son!"

131—DAVID'S RETURN FROM EXILE
(2 Samuel 19)

When Joab saw that the sorrow and weeping of King David for his fallen son Absalom were becoming a great burden to the people, he came to David and confronted him. "You have shamed the faces of the servants who saved your life," said Joab, "and you have also shamed the lives of your family. You act as if you love your enemies and hate your friends. And it seems to me that, if Absalom had lived and we had all died, you would be pleased."

Joab was not finished. "If you do not go now and speak to your servants," he said, "they will all leave you before the night is over, and the result of that will be worse than all the evil that has come upon you since your youth."

David could see that Joab was right. He knew that many had sacrificed a great deal to prevent Absalom from usurping the throne and that his sorrow for the loss of Absalom's life must not overshadow the service and love of his supporters.

David went to the city gate and spoke to his servants. And when he had spoken, all Israel and Judah pleaded for him to return to Jerusalem as their king. David agreed to go, but he made his nephew Amasa captain over the armies of Israel in Joab's place, because Joab had slain Absalom.

The trek back to Jerusalem was begun. And as David came to the Jordan, all the people of Judah came to Gilgal to meet him and invite him to return to Jerusalem and be their king once more. Among the first who met David and extended his welcome was Shimei, the Benjamite who had cursed him only days before.[331] Shimei's tone was much different now than it was at their previous encounter, and he asked forgiveness for his earlier conduct. "Do not charge me with iniquity," he pleaded with David, "and do not take to heart my perverse behavior on the day you came out of Jerusalem. I know that I have sinned, and am now the first to meet you as you return."

"Should not Shimei be put to death because he cursed Jehovah's anointed?" asked Abishai, picking up his earlier argument.

But David quickly jumped in to silence Abishai. "What have I to do with you, that you should be my adversary?" he asked Abishai. "No man shall be put to

---

[331] The account of Shimei's antics and his tirade against King David upon his departure from Jerusalem is found in story "128—The Flight from Jerusalem."

death in Israel today, for I know that I am king." Then David turned and said to Shimei, "You shall not die."

Mephibosheth, the lame son of Jonathan, also came out from Jerusalem to meet King David. He had neither dressed his feet, trimmed his beard, nor washed his clothes since David had fled. When David saw Mephibosheth, he spoke first. "Why did you not go with me?" David asked him.[332]

Mephibosheth was both angry and embarrassed. "My servant Ziba deceived me," he explained. "I told Ziba that I would saddle an ass because of my lameness and go with you. But instead, he took the ass and went to you and slandered me, thinking perhaps to gain some advantage. But you, my king, have been as an angel of God to me. For when my father's house was all but forgotten you set me among those who ate at your own table and gave me my father's land. I could ask no more than this."[333]

"Why do you speak any more of these matters?" asked David. "You and Ziba shall divide the land."

"Let Ziba take all of the land," replied Mephibosheth, "for the king has returned in peace to his own house."

There was a rivalry between Judah and the rest of Israel that became apparent with David's return to Jerusalem. Because the men of Judah accompanied David and his people as they returned, the men of Israel were offended. "Why," they asked David, "have our brethren of Judah stolen you from us and brought you over Jordan?"

But before David could respond to their question, the men of Judah responded: "We have been so attentive to the king because he is our near kin. Do not be angry with us, for we have not eaten food at the king's expense nor have we taken any gifts."

And the men of Israel answered, "We have more right than you because we have ten parts in the king because there are ten tribes of us. Why then did you despise us that you did not seek our advice before you brought King David home?"

Though David returned home to Jerusalem and was restored as king to all the house of Israel, the bad feelings between Judah and the rest of Israel would soon become the source of further trouble.

132—SHEBA THE BENJAMITE
(2 Samuel 20)

Some of the people from the tribe of Benjamin were still offended because the kingdom was taken from the house of Saul. One such Benjamite was Sheba, whom the scriptures refer to as a man of Belial.[334] Sheba was opposed to David and had significant support from those men of Israel who were still angry because Judah did not consult with them when they invited David to return to Jerusalem as their king.[335]

Sheba sounded a trumpet in Israel and declared, "We have no part in David, nor any inheritance in the son of Jesse. Every man to his tent, O Israel!" And, because they were offended, all of Israel except the tribe of Judah ceased to follow David that day and followed Sheba instead.

David was deeply concerned and was willing to do almost anything to preserve his kingdom as one. He called Amasa, the man whom he had made captain of his army in Joab's place, and told him to assemble the men of Judah within three days.

When three days had passed, however, and the men of Judah were not yet assembled, David turned to Abishai. "It appears that Sheba may do us more harm than did Absalom," he told Abishai. "Take Jehovah's servants and go after him, lest he obtain the fortified cities and escape." And all of David's mighty men went out from Jerusalem in pursuit of Sheba.

When David's mighty men reached the great stone in Gibeon, Amasa was at their head. But Joab, still smarting from his loss of position, slew Amasa with his sword during the pretense of a friendly greeting. When Amasa was dead, one of Joab's men cried out, "All those who favor Joab and are for David, let them follow Joab!" And all of David's mighty men followed Joab in pursuit of Sheba.

Sheba's trail led to the city of Abel Beth-maachah, in the far north of Israel, where he had taken refuge, and Joab and his men lay siege against the city. When they began to batter the city wall, a wise woman cried out from the city and asked Joab to come and speak to her. When she was assured that she was truly speaking to Joab, she said, "I am one of the peaceable and faithful in Israel, yet you seek to destroy both this city and a mother in Israel. Why would you swallow up the inheritance of Jehovah?"

---

[332] To understand why David asked this question of Mephibosheth, see story "128—The Flight from Jerusalem."

[333] See story "122—Honor for the House of Saul."

[334] "Man (or son) of Belial" is a derisive term used many times in the scriptures. It simply means a worthless and lawless person.

[335] See story "131—David's Return from Exile."

Joab was taken aback. "Far be it from me," he answered the woman, "that I should swallow up or destroy, but the matter is not as it appears. A man named Sheba who has lifted up his hand against the king is in your city. If you will deliver this man to us, we will depart in peace."

And the woman replied to Joab, "The man's head shall be thrown to you over the wall."

Then the woman, in her wisdom, went to all the people of the city and enlisted their support. They cornered Sheba, cut off his head, and threw it over the wall. And when Sheba's head came over the wall, Joab blew his trumpet and departed for Jerusalem with his men. David's kingdom was preserved.

133–RIZPAH'S FAITHFUL VIGIL
(2 Samuel 21)

A terrible famine came upon the land of Israel in the days of King David and lasted for three years. And as the famine persisted and became more devastating, David inquired of Jehovah the reason for this affliction. Responding to David's inquiry, Jehovah said, "The famine is for Saul and his bloody house because Saul was overzealous and slew the Gibeonites contrary to Israel's covenant."[336]

In an effort to regain Jehovah's favor and end the famine, David went to the surviving Gibeonites and inquired how he might repay them for what Saul had done. "What shall I do for you?" he asked, "and what will you require so that I can atone for this terrible deed and that you may bless the inheritance of Jehovah?"

The Gibeonites hedged. "We will have no silver or gold that belonged to Saul, nor to his house," they replied. "Neither do we ask that you kill any man in Israel."

"Whatever you ask of me," said David, "that will I do for you."

The answer of the Gibeonites was shocking: "The man who consumed our people and devised against us that we should be destroyed from the coasts of Israel— let seven of that man's sons (even that man whom Jehovah chose) be delivered unto us that we may hang them up unto Jehovah in Gibeah, Saul's own city."

Though King David was stunned by the Gibeonites' request, he agreed to it because of his promise. "I will give you the men you have requested," he promised.

As David sought for descendants of King Saul to fulfill his promise to the Gibeonites, he spared Jonathan's son Mephibosheth because of his oath with Jonathan, Saul's son and David's dear friend.[337] To satisfy the request, he chose two sons of Saul by his concubine

---

[336] The story of the Gibeonites is told in story "77–From a Very Far Country." The Gibeonites, who were actually Amorites, deceived Joshua and the children of Israel and tricked them into making a covenant with the people of Gibeon that they would not be destroyed. Though Israel had great resentment against the Gibeonites because of their deception, they kept their covenant and made the Gibeonites their servants. Unfortunately there is no scriptural reference to Saul's destruction of these people.

[337] The story that tells David's reason for sparing Mephibosheth is told in "122–Honor for the House of Saul."

Rizpah[338] and five sons of Merab, Saul's eldest daughter.[339] These seven men were delivered to the Gibeonites as requested. All were put to death together in the first days of the barley harvest, and their bodies were hanged together before Jehovah on the hill. And as the bodies hung on the hill, Rizpah, the mother of the two young men, came and spread sackcloth upon the nearby rock.

Rizpah stayed there upon the rock until the dry season was past and water fell upon them from the heavens. And by her faithful vigil, Rizpah kept the birds of the air away from the men's bodies during the day and the beasts of the field away from them during the night.

The people were touched by the faithfulness of Rizpah and told King David what she had done. And when David heard of it, he went to Jabesh-gilead to bring the bones of Saul and Jonathan back to the land of their fathers.[340]

When David returned from Jabesh with the bones of Saul and Jonathan, he put them with the bones of the seven slain men and they were all buried together in the sepulcher of Kish, Saul's father, in the land of Benjamin. And when all this was done, David pleaded again with Jehovah for an end to the terrible famine.

---

[338] The main difference between a wife and a concubine was probably the fact that a concubine could be rejected or cast aside without a bill of divorcement, while a wife could not. There was no difference between the children of a wife and those of a concubine, and the latter were a supplementary family to the former. The names of the concubines' children are listed in the patriarchal genealogies, and their position and provision depended on their father's will. The state of concubinage was provided for by the law of Moses and certainly also preceded that law. A concubine would generally be either (1) a Hebrew girl bought from her father, (2) a Gentile captive taken in war, (3) a foreign slave who had been bought, or (4) a Canaanite woman, bond or free. The rights of the first two were protected by the law (Exodus 21:7; Deuteronomy 21:10–14), but the third was unrecognized and the fourth prohibited. Some free Hebrew women also became concubines (see William Smith, *Dictionary of the Bible*, *GospeLink*, CD-ROM, s.v. "concubine").

[339] The scripture (2 Samuel 21:9) says that he took five sons of Michal, but that is an obvious error in the King James Bible. The man named in the scripture as father to those sons was Merab's husband. Also, David gave Michal no children (see 2 Samuel 6:23).

[340] See story "115—The End of King Saul" for an account of the deaths of Saul and Jonathan and how the men of Jabesh-gilead had stolen their bodies from the Philistines after they had been slain during the battle at Gilboa.

134–THAT WHICH COSTS ME NOTHING

(2 Samuel 24; 1 Chronicles 21)

When David yielded to the enticings of Satan to count the children of Israel, he sent Joab and his captains throughout the tribes to take the count. Though Joab did not like the idea because he feared that Jehovah would punish him, he did as David requested. And when the count was finished, 800,000 valiant men had been numbered in Israel and 500,000 in Judah.

When David realized that he had offended Jehovah by numbering the people, he prayed for forgiveness. "I have sinned greatly in what I have done," he confessed to Jehovah. "Forgive my iniquity."[341]

And the word of Jehovah came to the prophet Gad commanding him to go to David and tell him that he was going to punish Israel for what David had done.[342] David was given three options for his punishment. His first option was seven years of famine. His second was for David to flee before his enemies for three months. And the third was three days' of pestilence, or plague, in the land.

"Tell me what answer I shall give to him who sent me," said Gad.

David was troubled. This was not an easy choice because all three choices would be devastating. He had hoped for forgiveness rather than punishment. "Let me fall into the hands of Jehovah, for his mercies are great," he finally answered to Gad. "Let me not fall into the hands of men."

In response to David's answer, Jehovah sent a plague upon Israel for three days, taking the lives of 70,000 people. But when the destroying angel stretched forth his hand upon Jerusalem, Jehovah felt sorrow and said to the angel, "It is enough! Stay your hand."

David looked up and saw the angel with his sword drawn and stretched out over Jerusalem. And, when he saw the angel, he said, "I know that I have sinned, but what have these people done? Let your hand be against me and my father's house and not against the people."

Then Gad came to David again and told him to build an altar on the threshing floor of Araunah[343] the Jebusite,[344] and David took the priest with him and went to do as he was commanded. When Araunah met David coming, he bowed deeply and asked, "Why has my lord the king come here to me?"

"To buy your threshing floor and build an altar to Jehovah," answered David, "that the plague may cease from among the people."

"Take all that you see. Take and offer what seems good to you." said Araunah. "Take my oxen for your burnt sacrifice and the threshing instruments and ox yokes for your wood. And may Jehovah your God accept you."

David considered Araunah's offer, but he knew what had to be done if he were to be accepted by Jehovah. "I cannot take them," he said to Araunah, "but I will buy them from you at a fair price. I will not give an offering to Jehovah of that which costs me nothing."

David bought the threshing floor and the oxen for fifty shekels of silver. Then he built an altar and made his burnt offerings and peace offerings to Jehovah that the plague upon Israel might be stayed.[345] And Jehovah answered David by sending fire from heaven upon the altar.

---

[341] The scriptures do not make it clear why it was sinful for David to count the children of Israel. Perhaps it was because such an action amounted to trusting in the arm of flesh rather than trusting in Jehovah.

[342] This story is problematic because it has Jehovah punishing all of Israel for something that David did. There are probably other facts that are not available to us at present. The story is valuable, however, because of the lesson it teaches concerning sacrifice.

[343] In 2 Samuel 24 this man's name is given as Araunah, just as it is in this story. He is identified there as king of the Jebusites. In 1 Chronicles 21, however, he is called Ornan.

[344] Jebus was the earlier name for Jerusalem. Thus, a Jebusite was one of the previous inhabitants of the city or, as in this case, a descendant of those inhabitants.

[345] The site of David's altar was the same site upon which King Solomon later built the temple. There is also a tradition, expounded by Josephus and others, that the "Mount Moriah" of Chronicles is the same "mountain" in "the land of Moriah" in the book of Genesis (Genesis 22) where Abraham took Isaac to offer him as a sacrifice. Many scholars, however, doubt the accuracy of this tradition (see William Smith, *Dictionary of the Bible*, *GospeLink*, CD-ROM, s.v. "Moriah").

135—ALL THESE THINGS HAVE COME FROM THEE
(1 Chronicles 22, 28–29) [346]

Although Jehovah did not allow David to build a temple—but said that David's son would do so—David determined that he would do everything possible to prepare for the day when that temple would be built. He said to himself, "My son Solomon is young and tender, and the house that he is to build must be of great magnificence for it will be God's house and will have fame and glory throughout all nations. I will make special preparations for it."

When the right opportunity came, David explained to Solomon why he did not build the temple himself. "I had it in my mind to build a house to Jehovah and a place for the ark of the covenant to rest," he said, "but the word of Jehovah came to me and told me I should not build it. He told me that because I was a man of war and had shed much blood, it was not proper that I should build a house to his name, [347] but that my son would build it. Jehovah said that the name of the son who would build his house would be your name—Solomon—and that you would be a man of peace, having rest from your enemies in all your days. He said that he would consider you as his own son, and that he would be your father and establish the throne of your kingdom forever."

"Now," David continued, "may Jehovah be with you, Solomon. May he give you wisdom and understanding, and may he give you charge concerning Israel that you may keep his law. You must be strong, courageous, and have no fear, for he has said that you will prosper if you fulfill the statutes and judgments of the law of Moses."

Then David told Solomon of the preparations he had made for building the temple. "In my trouble I have prepared 100,000 talents of gold, a thousand thousand talents of silver, [348] and brass and iron beyond what I could measure," he said. "And though I have prepared excellent timber and stone, you may add to it." David also reminded Solomon that men with great skill were available to do every kind of work on the temple.

David also called together the princes of Israel and asked them to support Solomon in building the temple. "Because the enemies of Israel have been subdued," he told them, "you must now set your hearts and souls to seek Jehovah and to build his holy house—even a house where Israel can bring the ark of the covenant and the holy vessels of God. Jehovah chose Judah to be the ruler of Israel. From Judah he chose the house of my father. Then from among my father's sons, he chose me to be king over all Israel. And from all my sons—and he has given me many of them—he has chosen Solomon to reign after me and has told me that Solomon shall build his holy house."

Then David said to Solomon, "Come to know the God of your fathers and serve him with a perfect heart and a willing mind. For Jehovah searches all hearts and understands all the imaginations and thoughts of men. If you will seek him, you will surely find him. But if you forsake him, he will cast you off forever. Therefore, take heed, my son, for Jehovah has chosen you to build a house for his sanctuary. You must be strong and do it."

David gave Solomon all the plans for the temple, its furnishings, and the instruments of worship, for Jehovah had given these plans to David by the Spirit. He also taught Solomon how the priests and the Levites should be organized to do the work and the service of the temple.

Then David said to all those who were present, "My son Solomon is yet young and tender, but the work he has to do is great. For that which he shall build is not a palace for man but for God. I have prepared with all my might the things that will be needed and have given even of my own goods for this great work. Who then of you," he asked the leaders of Israel, "is willing to consecrate his service and his means to Jehovah?"

Each of the chief fathers and princes of Israel, the captains of thousands and of hundreds, and all those who were rulers of the king's work offered willingly to give their labor and substance for the temple. And they rejoiced because they had made an offering to Jehovah with perfect hearts.

---

[346] The incident referred to in 1 Chronicles 28–29 appears to be a different incident than the one recounted in 1 Chronicles 22. However, the two incidents have been combined in this story because the messages of the two are essentially the same.

[347] The message from Jehovah that is referred to here was delivered to David by the prophet Nathan and is recorded in 2 Samuel 7. An account is given in story "121–Your Son Shall Build My House."

[348] This is 1,000,000 talents of silver. A talent of silver was 3,000 shekels, or slightly more than 75.5 pounds (34.29 kilograms). A talent of gold was 10,000 shekels, or about 252 pounds (114.3 kilograms). These 1,000,000 talents of silver would weigh 75,600,000 pounds (34,291,555 kilograms), or 37,800 tons (33,750 long tons or 34,292 metric tons). The 100,000 talents of gold would weigh 25,200,000 pounds (11,430,518 kilograms), or 12,600 tons (11,250 long tons or 11,431 metric tons).

Then David prayed before the congregation and thanked Jehovah for his bounty. "We thank Thee, O Jehovah," he said, "and we praise Thy glorious name. But who am I and what are my people that we should be able to offer so willingly such vast treasure? All these things have come from Thee, and it is Thine own substance that we have given to Thee. We are all strangers and sojourners before Thee, as were our fathers. Our days on the earth are as a shadow and none will survive.

"I know also, O Jehovah, that Thou dost try men's hearts and have pleasure in their uprightness.

"Please give Solomon a perfect heart to keep Thy commandments, Thy testimonies, and Thy statutes, and to build this palace unto Thee."

Then all those who had gathered to hear David prayed and offered burnt offerings and sacrifices to Jehovah.

136—ADONIJAH'S AMBITION
(1 Kings 1)

David's son Adonijah was handsome like his older brother Absalom and desired—also like his brother—to be king of Israel. Though the leaders of Israel and those close to David knew that Jehovah had chosen Solomon to be David's successor, David said nothing to discourage Adonijah from his ambition.

Adonijah's mother Haggith supported him in his quest for the throne, and he also had the backing of his cousin Joab, the commander of Israel's army, and of Abiathar the priest.

When Adonijah called his brothers and all the men of Judah to come to a great feast, this raised serious concerns among some important people who were not invited, including the prophet Nathan; a mighty man named Benaiah, the son of Jehoiada; and Bathsheba's son Solomon.

Nathan, being aware of what was happening, went to see Bathsheba. "Have you not heard that Adonijah, the son of Haggith, reigns in Israel and David does not know it?" he asked her. "If this man is not challenged, both your life and Solomon's life are in danger."

Nathan counseled Bathsheba to go to the king and tell him that Adonijah was making himself king of Israel. "And while you are yet speaking to him," said Nathan, "I will come in and confirm your words."

Bathsheba went quickly to see King David and bowed before him. "You swore to me by Jehovah that my son Solomon would reign after you and sit upon your throne," she said to David. "And now, behold, Adonijah is reigning in Israel and you do not know it. He has slain oxen, fat cattle, and sheep for a great feast, and he has called to his feast all of your sons, Abiathar the priest, and Joab the captain of your army. But he did not call Solomon.

"And now, O King, the eyes of all Israel are upon you that you should tell them who will sit upon the throne of Israel after you. If you do not tell them now, Solomon and I shall be counted as offenders when you are dead."

While Bathsheba was yet speaking, the prophet Nathan came in as he had promised and bowed before David. "Have you said that Adonijah shall sit upon your throne and reign after you?" asked Nathan. "For he has gone down this day and has slain oxen, fat cattle, and sheep in abundance. He has called to his feast the king's sons, the captain of Israel's army, and Abiathar the priest, and as we speak they are eating and drinking before him and saying, 'May King Adonijah live long.' But neither I, nor Zadok the priest, nor Benaiah, nor

Solomon was invited. Have you given approval for Adonijah to be king and have not told me?"

David was now deeply concerned. This was not what he had wanted to happen. "As Jehovah lives who has redeemed my soul," he said to Bathsheba, "Solomon shall reign after me and sit upon my throne, even as I swore to you."

Then Bathsheba bowed before David and said, "Let my lord King David live forever."

"Call Benaiah and Zadok the priest to join us," said David to Nathan and Bathsheba, "for we must act quickly."

When they all came before him, David said, "Go down to Gihon.[349] Take Solomon with you and have him ride upon my mule.[350] Once in Gihon, let Zadok and Nathan anoint Solomon to be king over Israel. When he is anointed, blow the trumpet and shout, 'Let King Solomon live.' After this, bring him up to sit upon the throne, and he shall be king instead of me."

And so, accompanied by the king's servants,[351] Nathan, Zadok, Benaiah, and Solomon went to Gihon, as King David commanded them, with Solomon riding on King David's mule.

Zadok the priest carried the horn of oil from the tabernacle with them, and there at Gihon he and the prophet Nathan anointed Solomon to be king of Israel.

---

[349] All we know about Gihon is that it is a place very near Jerusalem. Its main claim to fame is that it is the place where Solomon was anointed king of Israel. Later on, King Hezekiah of Judah built a tunnel to carry water into the city of Jerusalem from the upper watercourse of Gihon (see story "184—Judah's Escape from Assyria's Grasp").

[350] The mule is a hybrid animal, the issue of a horse and an ass. Smaller than a horse, it is hardy and sure-footed and usually lives much longer. The Israelites, for reasons unknown to us, were forbidden from breeding mules, but sometimes they imported them. The mule became a symbol of royalty, and only kings and their family members rode them (see William Smith, *Dictionary of the Bible*, *GospeLink*, CD-ROM, s.v. "mule," and *Bible Dictionary*, LDS-KJV, s.v. "mule").

[351] The scripture (1 Kings 1:38) says that Nathan, Zadok, Benaiah, and Solomon took the Cherethites and the Pelethites with them to Gihon. The Cherethites and Pelethites were royal guards who served as couriers and executioners. They were probably Philistines. They went with David when he fled Jerusalem to escape Absalom (see 2 Samuel 15:18) and were also with David's mighty men when they went out in pursuit of Sheba (see 2 Samuel 20:23). They served under Benaiah's command, which accounts for the importance of Benaiah's presence on this occasion.

Once Solomon was anointed, they blew the trumpet and shouted, "Let King Solomon live!" And as they returned to Jerusalem, the people joined in the celebration; the noise was so great that it was heard everywhere.

Joab heard the noise of the trumpet and the shouting as Adonijah and his guests were finishing their feast. "What is this noise?" he asked. "Why is the city in an uproar?"

While Joab was yet speaking, Jonathan, Abiathar's son, came from the city and entered the room. "Come in," called Adonijah, "for you are a valiant man and must surely bring good tidings." And Adonijah asked Jonathan the reason for the uproar.

"Our lord, King David, has made Solomon king of Israel," Jonathan answered. "He sent Zadok, Nathan, and Benaiah to Gihon, with Solomon riding on David's mule, and Zadok and Nathan have anointed Solomon king. They have now returned to the city, and Solomon sits upon the throne. The noise of the people rejoicing is what you now hear."

Jonathan went on to tell how David's servants had blessed Solomon and asked God to make the name of Solomon greater that the name of David. He told also how David himself had said, "Blessed be Jehovah, God of Israel, who has given us one to sit on my throne this day and my own eyes have beheld it."

This was not good news for Adonijah and his guests. They knew that their conspiracy had failed. And, dispersing quickly from the feast, they went their various ways. Adonijah, now frightened and in fear for his life, went to the tabernacle, took hold of the horns of the altar, and prayed to Jehovah. "Let King Solomon swear to me that he will not slay me with the sword," he pleaded.

And when Solomon learned of Adonijah's prayer, he said, "If Adonijah will prove himself a worthy man, not one hair of his head shall fall to the earth. But if he is found to be wicked, he must die." Then Solomon sent a messenger to tell Adonijah to go home.

137–BE STRONG AND SHOW YOURSELF A MAN

(1 Kings 1, 2)

David knew that his son Solomon was the man Jehovah had chosen to succeed him as king of Israel. However, Solomon was still young and David had concern for him. As the time drew near when David thought he was going to die, he called Solomon to him and offered his advice. "As I must soon go the way of all the earth," he said, "you must be strong and show yourself a man. Keep the charge of Jehovah to walk in his ways that you may prosper in all that you do. For Jehovah has promised me that if my children will walk before him in truth, there shall always be a man of my seed upon Israel's throne."

David then talked to Solomon about some of his concerns. First he discussed his nephew Joab, the captain of Israel's army. Joab was a man who had little regard for human life and was reluctant to take counsel if it did not please him. "You know what Joab did to me," said David,[352] "and you know what he did to the two captains, Abner and Amasa,[353] whom he slew, shedding the blood of war in peace. He has shed the blood of war upon his girdle and in his shoes. Do according to your wisdom, Solomon, but you must not let Joab's gray head go down to the grave in peace."

David next spoke to Solomon concerning Barzillai the Gileadite who befriended him when he was in exile at Mahanaim. Barzillai provided food and supplies to David and his company when they were most needed. Then when David was returning to Jerusalem, Barzillai, though an old man, came to conduct David across the Jordan. David invited him to come up to Jerusalem at that time, but Barzillai declined because of his age and his fear of becoming a burden. "Show kindness to the sons of Barzillai," said David to Solomon. "Let them be among those who eat at your table, for they helped me when I fled because of your brother Absalom."[354]

David spoke also of Shimei, the Benjamite who cursed David and threw rocks at him at Bahurim when he was fleeing from Absalom. David had promised Shimei that he would spare his life and had kept Joab's brother Abishai from killing him, but David was not satisfied that justice had been served.[355] "Do not hold Shimei guiltless," he told Solomon. "You are a wise man and will know what you ought to do, but you must bring his gray head down to the grave with blood."

When King David had given these instructions to Solomon he died, having reigned in Israel for forty years. He was buried in Jerusalem, the City of David, and Solomon reigned in his stead.

---

[352] There were many issues between David and his nephew Joab, most of which were centered in Joab's tendency to place his own desires above the orders of his king. The chief problem was no doubt Joab's slaying of David's son Absalom (see story "130–Absalom's Death and David's Sorrow").

[353] The stories that tell of what Joab did to Abner and Amasa are "117–King of Judah Only" (Abner) and "132–Sheba the Benjamite" (Amasa). At the time Joab and his brother Abishai slew Abner, David said, "Let it rest on the head of Joab and on all his father's house; and let there not fail from the house of Joab one that hath an issue, or that is a leper, or that leaneth on a staff, or that falleth on the sword, or that lacketh bread" (2 Samuel 3:29).

[354] Barzillai's acts of kindness to King David and the exiles from Jerusalem are related in 2 Samuel 17:27–29 and 19:31–39. They are not mentioned specifically in any of these stories, except in footnote 325 of story "130–Absalom's Death and David's Sorrow."

[355] Shimei's attack on David and his plea for forgiveness are told in stories "128–The Flight from Jerusalem" and "131–David's Return from Exile."

138—JUSTICE FOR HIS FATHER'S ENEMIES
(1 Kings 1, 2)

When Solomon reigned as Israel's king, his brother Adonijah, who had conspired against him to take the throne, went to Bathsheba, Solomon's mother, to ask a favor. "As you know," Adonijah said to her, "the kingdom of Israel was mine and all Israel had set their faces on me that I should reign. However, the kingdom is now my brother's, for Jehovah gave it to him. And though I am now satisfied with that, I have one favor to ask of you."

"Say on," said Bathsheba.

"You must speak to Solomon for me," said Adonijah, "for I know he will not tell you no. Ask him to give me Abishag the Shunammite to be my wife."

When King David was old and his body could not generate sufficient heat, a beautiful young woman named Abishag from Shunem[356] in the tribe of Issachar was chosen to lie in his bosom and lend the heat of her body to give him warmth. King David dearly cherished Abishag, but he could not consummate a marriage with her because he was very old.[357] Now Adonijah wanted to take Abishag to be his wife, and Bathsheba gave her promise to Adonijah that she would to speak to Solomon in his behalf.

Bathsheba went to her son Solomon to ask Adonijah's petition, and she sat on his right hand. "I desire one small favor of you," she said to him. "Promise me you will not say no."

"I promise," said Solomon. "Ask on."

Her request startled Solomon. "Give Abishag the Shunammite to be the wife of Adonijah," she said.

When Solomon had recovered somewhat from the shock of his mother's request, he answered her with a question. "Why do you seek Abishag to be the wife of Adonijah?" he asked. "Why do you not also ask that I give him the kingdom—even to him, to Abithar the priest, and Joab the son of Zeruiah? For Adonijah *is* my elder brother. May God do so to me and more also, if Adonijah has not made this request at the cost of his life. As Jehovah lives, Adonijah shall be put to death this day." And King Solomon sent Benaiah[358] to slay Adonijah.[359]

Next on Solomon's list was Abiathar the priest. "Go to Anathoth[360] unto your own fields," he told Abiathar. "Though you are worthy of death, I will not slay you because you bore the ark of God before my father and suffered with him in all that he suffered." So, Solomon dismissed Abiathar from the priest's office, thus bringing final fulfillment to the promise that Jehovah spoke at Shiloh concerning the house of Eli.[361]

When word came to Joab that Abiathar the priest had been cast out, he also began to fear, for he too had favored Adonijah. He fled to the tabernacle and caught hold of the horns of the altar. When Solomon learned that Joab was in the tabernacle, he sent Benaiah to slay him. "You must slay him," said Solomon, "to take away from me and from my father the innocent blood that Joab has shed. Jehovah will return Joab's blood upon his own head for the deaths of Abner and Amasa, who were both better and more righteous men than he. Their blood shall be upon Joab and his seed and not on the house of David." So, in accordance with King Solomon's command, Benaiah fell upon Joab and slew him.

Solomon then made Benaiah captain of Israel's army in Joab's place, and he made Zadok priest in the place of Abiathar.

Solomon next sent a message to Shimei the Benjamite[362] that he should come and build a house in Jerusalem. "You shall dwell here in the house that you build," he told Shimei, "but you must not go out from the city. For on the day you cross the brook Kidron, you shall surely die and your blood will be on your own head." Shimei agreed and came to build a house and dwell in Jerusalem.

Three years later, when Solomon learned that Shimei had gone to Gath and back in pursuit of two

---

the Pelethites, those royal guards who served as couriers and executioners.

[359] Some may wonder why Solomon would be upset by this request from Adonijah. There can be no doubt that Solomon considered Abishag to be David's wife, although the marriage may not have been consummated. For a man to take his father's wife was strictly forbidden by the Law (see Deuteronomy 22:30).

[360] Anathoth was a priests' city in the tribe of Benjamin. It was near to Jerusalem.

[361] Story "92—Jehovah Can No Longer Honor You" tells of the prophecy that was made against Eli's house. For a full account of that prophecy, see 1 Samuel 2:27–36. The scriptures do not explain how King Solomon came to have authority over the priesthood.

[362] For information on Shimei's antics, see stories "128—The Flight from Jerusalem" and "131—David's Return from Exile."

---

[356] Shunem was located south of Mount Tabor and north of Jezreel.

[357] See 1 Kings 1:1–4.

[358] Benaiah was one of the king's mighty men. His specific assignment was to command the Cherethites and

run-away servants, he called for him and said, "Did you not swear by Jehovah that on the day you went out from Jerusalem and walked abroad, you would surely die? Why have you not kept your oath? You know all the wickedness that you did to my father David; Jehovah is now going to return that wickedness upon your head." And, at Solomon's command, Shimei was slain by Benaiah.

139—A WISE AND UNDERSTANDING HEART

(1 Kings 3)

Solomon was a good king and was obedient to the statutes of his father David. He loved Jehovah and sought to serve him. One day he went up to the high place[363] at Gibeon[364] to offer a great sacrifice to Jehovah because the house of the Lord had not yet been built.

While Solomon was in Gibeon, Jehovah appeared to him one night in a dream and asked, "What would you have me give you?"

Solomon answered carefully: "Thou didst show great mercy to my father David as he walked before Thee in truth, righteousness, and uprightness of heart. Thou didst also show him great kindness in giving him a son to sit on his throne, as I sit this day. And Thou hast made me king in the midst of Thy people who cannot be counted for the greatness of their number. I do not know how to lead them or how to go out or come in before them, for I am as a little child.[365]

"Give me, therefore, an understanding heart to judge Thy people, that I may discern between good and bad. For who is able to judge so great a people as these?"

Jehovah was pleased with Solomon's answer, and he said to him in his dream, "Because you have asked this thing of me, and have not asked for yourself either long life or riches, and have not asked for the lives of your enemies, I have done according to your words. I have given you a wise and an understanding heart. There has been none made king over Israel who is like you, and there shall be none arise after you among the kings of Israel who shall be like you."[366]

---

[363] When there was no temple in Israel, altars for worship and sacrifice were frequently built on hilltops. These high places, as they were called, became community centers for the worship of Jehovah. It appears that Solomon went to Gibeon to offer sacrifices because the altar was large and could accommodate large sacrifices. The scripture says that Gibeon was a "great high place" and that Solomon offered "a thousand burnt offerings" upon the altar.

[364] Gibeon was on a hill in the land belonging to Benjamin. It was about five miles (eight kilometers) north of Jerusalem.

[365] Note that the differences in this story from what is in the King James Bible are based on the Joseph Smith Translation.

[366] See footnote 365.

Jehovah continued: "I will also give you that for which you did not ask. I will give you both honor and riches, that there be none among Israel's kings who shall be like you in all your days. And if you will walk in my ways, to keep my statutes and my commandments, then I will lengthen your days. And you shall not walk in unrighteousness as did your father David."[367] Then Solomon awoke and knew that Jehovah had spoken to him in his dream.

140–DIVIDE THE LIVING CHILD IN TWO
(1 Kings 3)

Two women, both harlots, came before King Solomon, asking him to try their case and decide between them. The first explained her side of their dispute. "This woman and I dwell in the same house," she said. "I had a baby, and three days later she was also delivered of a child. However, when her baby died in the night because she laid on it, she rose from her bed while I was asleep, took my baby, and left her dead baby in my bosom. When I awoke in the morning to nurse my baby, he was dead, and—upon closer examination—I discovered that the dead baby in my arms was hers."

King Solomon orders the child to be cut in half

"Nay!" the second woman objected. "The living son is mine, and the dead is hers." And thus they argued before the king.

Solomon considered the case as he understood the information the women had given him. "Both of you say that the living child belongs to you," he said, "and that the dead one belongs to the other. Is this not so?"

"Yes!" they both agreed.

"Bring me a sword," said Solomon. And when the sword was delivered into his hand, he said, "Divide the living child in two and give half to each woman."

"Yes!" said the second woman. "It is fair to divide the child. Let it be neither mine nor hers."

[367] See footnote 365.

"No! Wait!" cried the woman whose son the living child was, her bowels yearning for her son. "Do not slay my child, but give him to her!"

Then King Solomon answered and said, "Do not slay the child but give him to her who would spare the child's life; she is the mother."

As Israel learned of the judgment that Solomon had made in this case, they saw that the wisdom of God was in him. And as King Solomon's fame spread throughout the earth, many people—even the kings of the earth—came to Jerusalem to hear his wisdom.[368]

141–THE HOLY TEMPLE
(1 Kings 4–8; 2 Chronicles 2–7)

It was in the fourth year of King Solomon's reign that work began on what was certainly his greatest accomplishment—the temple. The temple site was on Mount Moriah[369] in the same location as Araunah's threshing floor. This was the place where Jehovah, through Gad, commanded David to build an altar to stop the plague.[370] In the fourth year of Solomon's reign, when all the timber and stone for the temple were prepared,[371] construction began.

The temple was sixty cubits long and twenty cubits wide.[372] In reverence to the holy building, the stones and the timbers were all cut before they were brought to the temple site. There were no tools—neither hammer, nor ax, nor any tool of iron—heard in the temple during its construction.

Upon completion of the stone superstructure, Jehovah spoke to Solomon saying, "Concerning this house that you are building, if you will walk in my statutes, execute my judgments, and keep all my commandments, I will perform my word that I spoke unto your father David.[373] I will dwell among the children of Israel and not forsake my people."

The oracle of the temple, or the holy of holies, was twenty cubits long, twenty cubits wide, and twenty cu-

---

[368] This is a very unusual story because it is unlikely that any woman with a sound mind would consent to a baby being cut in half. One writer offered this insight: "In this famous illustration of Solomon's wisdom, it is surprising that his solution to the question worked out at all. Normally two women who both desired the same baby would *both* have objected to the crude suggestion that it be cut in two. His wisdom must have been in his insight to see that one would be brazen enough to consent. Naturally the true mother gave in rather than consent to the death of the child." (Ellis T. Rasmussen, *A Latter-day Saint Commentary on the Old Testament* [Salt Lake City: Deseret Book Co., 1993], 299.)

---

[369] See 2 Chronicles 3:1.

[370] See story "134–That Which Costs Me Nothing."

[371] King Hiram of Tyre, who had great affection and respect for David, assisted both David and Solomon in gathering materials for the temple, primarily the timbers of cedar and fir. Another man named Hiram (and also called Huram) who was a workman from Tyre was also sent to assist Solomon in the building if the temple. He has been omitted from this story to avoid confusion.

[372] That is, approximately ninety feet (27.43 meters) by thirty feet (9.14 meters), if we consider that a cubit is about eighteen inches (45.72 centimeters). Though this temple's dimensions were twice as long as, and its area four times greater than, the portable tabernacle the children of Israel built in the wilderness (thirty cubits long [forty-five feet or 13.7 meters] and ten cubits [fifteen feet or 4.57 meters] wide), it is certainly not large by today's standards. Its richly ornate furnishings and fine craftsmanship, however, made it distinctive.

[373] The "word" of which Jehovah spoke here, that he had given to David, is found in 2 Samuel 7:13. It was, essentially, that David's son would build the temple and that Jehovah would establish David's throne forever.

bits high[374]—a perfect cube. Its stone walls were paneled with cedar wood and overlaid with gold, and the floor was overlaid with gold. Inside the holy of holies were two cherubim of olive wood, overlaid with gold, each ten cubits tall.[375] They stood side by side, with their outstretched wings touching in the center of the room. The other outstretched wings of the two cherubim touched the north and south walls.[376]

On the porch of the temple were two large brass pillars. The one on the right he named Jachim (which means "he [God] shall establish"), and the one on the left he named Boaz (which means "in him [God] is strength"). There was also a large water basin (called a "molten sea"), 10 cubits from rim to rim,[377] resting on the backs of twelve brazen oxen. On each side of the temple, there were five small lavers, or basins, of bright brass standing on ornate bases.

Solomon made all the vessels that pertained to the temple itself—the altars, the tables, the oil cups,[378] the flowers, the lamps, the tongs, the bowls, the snuffers, the basins, the spoons, and the censers—of pure gold. The doors were also hung on golden hinges. Then Solomon took all of the materials that David had amassed for the temple—the silver, the gold, and the vessels—and put them among the treasures of the house of the Lord.

When the temple was finished and all was in readiness, Solomon brought together the leaders of Israel that the ark of the covenant might be brought into the place prepared for it in the holy of holies. The priests brought up the ark while Solomon, the elders of Israel, and the people sacrificed sheep and oxen beyond number. The ark of the covenant and the mercy seat were placed in the holy of holies beneath the wings of the ten-cubit cherubim.[379] The tabernacle that Israel built in the wilderness of Sinai was also brought into the temple. When the priests had placed the ark of the covenant inside and come out of the holy of holies, a cloud filled the temple so that they could not enter, for the glory of Jehovah was there.

King Solomon then spoke to Jehovah. "I have surely built Thee a house to dwell in," he said, "a settled place for Thee to abide in forever."

Then Solomon turned and said to the people, "Blessed be Jehovah, the God of Israel, who spoke unto David my father and has now fulfilled what he said. It was in David's heart to build a house to the name of Jehovah, but Jehovah told him that his son would build the temple instead. 'Though David shall not build my house,' Jehovah told my father, 'I will build the house of David. I will give him an eternal kingdom and the Messiah shall come through his loins.'

"I now sit on the throne of my father David and have built this house as Jehovah promised. And I have set therein a place for the ark, wherein is kept the covenant that Jehovah made with our fathers when he brought them out of Egypt."

Then Solomon stood before the altar of Jehovah in the presence of all the congregation of Israel, raised his hands toward heaven,[380] and offered a prayer of dedication upon the holy temple.[381] And when the prayer was finished, fire came down from heaven to consume the sacrifices and burnt offerings brought by the people. The glory of Jehovah filled the temple, and when the children of Israel saw how fire came from heaven and how the glory of Jehovah was upon the temple, they bowed their faces to the ground and worshipped.

The priests then offered sacrifices of 22,000 oxen and 120,000 sheep. As the sacrifices continued, Solomon held a great celebration, and all of Israel feasted with him for seven days. And after that feast was over, they feasted for seven days more. On the eighth day—the day following the end of the second feast—they held a solemn assembly. Then the people of Israel returned to their homes, rejoicing in the temple and in the goodness of Jehovah.

---

[374] About thirty feet (9.14 meters) by thirty feet (9.14 meters).

[375] About fifteen feet (4.57 meters) tall.

[376] The scriptures do not tell us which direction the cherubim faced or where within the room they were located. Josephus, however, tells us that their wings touched the north and south walls (see Flavius Josephus, *Antiquities of the Jews,* 8:3:3). The temple faced toward the east and the long dimension ran east and west.

[377] See footnote 375.

[378] The scriptures (1 Kings 7:49; 2 Chronicles 4:7, 20) say candlestick, but they had no candles. They burned olive oil in cup-like receptacles, using cloth for wicks.

[379] Note that the large cherubim in the holy of holies were in addition to the smaller cherubim on either end of the mercy seat.

[380] The act of raising one's hands to heaven is an act of complete surrender; here it is a sign that Solomon surrendered himself to Jehovah.

[381] Solomon's dedicatory prayer is recorded in 1 Kings 8:23–53 and in 2 Chronicles 6:14–42. We are not told where Solomon received the priesthood authority that authorized him to perform this temple dedication, but there is no doubt that he had it.

142–BECAUSE YOU HAVE BROKEN MY COVENANT

(1 Kings 11)

There was no other king like Solomon in the entire world. His great wisdom was legendary and rulers came from everywhere to partake. Those who came brought precious gifts, and Solomon's wealth became as great as his wisdom. Though he was a righteous man, his blessings were too much for him to endure and led him into paths of unrighteousness. Solomon took unto himself 700 wives and 300 concubines,[382] many of whom were not of Israel. In addition to a wife who was the daughter of the Pharaoh of Egypt, he also had wives who were Moabites, Ammonites, Edomites, Hittites, and Zidonians—those nations with whom Jehovah had commanded his people not to intermarry.

When Solomon became old, his wives turned him away from Jehovah to follow other gods. Though Jehovah had appeared to him twice, Solomon left the worship of Jehovah to follow after Ashtoreth,[383] the goddess of the Zidonians; Molech,[384] the god of the Am-monites; and Chemosh,[385] the god of the Moabites. He also built high places for the worship of these false gods.[386]

Jehovah was angry with Solomon and again commanded him that he not worship other gods. And, when Solomon failed to obey, Jehovah said to him, "Because you have broken my covenant and my statutes, I will rend your kingdom from you and give it to your servant.[387] However, for the sake of your father David, I will not do it during your life but during the days of your son. I will not tear away all of the kingdom, but will give one tribe to your son for the sake of David and the sake of Jerusalem, which I have chosen."[388]

Though the reign of King Solomon was peaceful, Jehovah stirred up adversaries against him because of his idolatry. Among these adversaries was a young man named Jeroboam, one of the king's own servants. Jeroboam, the son of a widow from Bethlehem, was one of Solomon's mighty men. Solomon trusted Jeroboam and, because he was of the tribe of Ephraim, Solomon gave him charge over the house of Joseph. Jeroboam had no complaints against the king, but one day as he went out from Jerusalem dressed in a new garment, he had an encounter and a discussion with the prophet Ahijah the Shilonite that changed everything.[389]

---

[382] The main difference between a wife and a concubine was probably the fact that a concubine could be rejected or cast aside without a bill of divorcement, while a wife could not. There was no difference between the children of a wife and those of a concubine, and the latter were a supplementary family to the former. The names of the concubines' children are listed in the patriarchal genealogies, and their position and provision depend on their father's will. The state of concubinage was provided for by the law of Moses and certainly also preceded that law. A concubine would generally be either (1) a Hebrew girl bought from her father, (2) a Gentile captive taken in war, (3) a foreign slave who had been bought, or (4) a Canaanite woman, bond or free. The rights of the first two were protected by the law (Exodus 21:7; Deuteronomy 21:10–14), but the third was unrecognized and the fourth prohibited. Some free Hebrew women also became concubines (see William Smith, *Dictionary of the Bible*, GospeLink, CD-ROM, s.v. "concubine").

[383] Ashtoreth was primarily the fertility goddess of the Phoenicians but was also worshipped by the Philistines, along with Dagon. Ashtaroth is the plural form of Ashtoreth.

[384] The fire god Molech, worshipped by the Ammonites, was essentially identical to the Moabitish Chemosh. Fire gods appear to have been common among the Canaanites, who worshipped the destructive element under an outward symbol with the most inhu-man rites. Human sacrifices were part of the ritual. Molech was called the "lord and master" of the Ammonites (William Smith, *Dictionary of the Bible*, GospeLink, CD-ROM, s.v. "Molech").

[385] Chemosh, like Molech, was a fire god (see footnote 384).

[386] Before the temple was built, the children of Israel set up community centers for worship on tops of hills. These were called high places. It became common, especially in the later years of both kingdoms, for high places to also be set up as places for the worship of false gods.

[387] King Solomon's downfall came because he failed to heed the Divine charge given by Moses and which is recorded in Deuteronomy 17:14–17. There Moses warned against the king of Israel multiplying horses, (i.e., building up military power), multiplying wives, and multiplying gold and silver (see story "71–Moses' Farewell").

[388] The language of the scriptures is interesting here. In some places they say that the seed of David and Solomon will be left to reign over just one tribe. In other places they say that there will be two tribes. Two tribes, Judah and Benjamin, were left, but they were as one and were called the kingdom of Judah.

[389] A Shilonite is a native or resident of the city of Shiloh.

When the two men were alone in a field, Ahijah took hold of Jeroboam's new garment, took it from him, and tore it into twelve pieces. "Take ten of these pieces," he told Jeroboam, "for Jehovah will rend the kingdom of Israel out of Solomon's hand and give ten tribes to you. But one tribe will remain for David's sake, and also the city of Jerusalem—the city that Jehovah has chosen out of all the tribes."

Ahijah continued: "Jehovah will do this because Solomon has forsaken him and worships false gods, and because his heart has become as David's heart. But because Solomon does not repent as David did, he cannot be forgiven. Solomon shall be king all the days of his life for the sake of David, but Jehovah will take the kingdom from the hands of Solomon's son and give it to you—even ten of the tribes. Solomon's son, however, will be left with one tribe so that David may always have a light before Jehovah in Jerusalem.

"If you will hearken to the commandments of God when you are king of Israel, and will walk in the ways of Jehovah as David did in the days that Jehovah blessed him, then Jehovah will also be with you. He will build you a sure house as he built a sure house for David. But remember that, though Jehovah will divide the kingdom for the transgressions of David and Solomon, that division will not last forever."

When word of Ahijah's prophecy came back to Solomon, he sought to take Jeroboam's life, but Jeroboam fled into Egypt and remained there for the rest of Solomon's life.

Solomon died after reigning for forty years in Israel. He, like his father, was buried in the City of David, and his son Rehoboam became king of all Israel in his place.

IX

DIVIDED ISRAEL (PART I):

TWO SEPARATE KINGDOMS

THE KINGS OF ISRAEL AND JUDAH*

King of Israel	King of Judah	Approx. Year (time served)	Scriptural References	Stories
	Rehoboam	953 BC (17 years)	1 Kings 12:1-24; 14:21-31 2 Chronicles 9:31–12:16	143–Israel Divided 145–Judah: Rehoboam's Kingdom
Jeroboam 1		953 BC (21 years)	1 Kings 12:25–14:20	143–Israel Divided 144–A Prophet Comes to Beth-el 146–The Fall of Jerobaom's House Foretold
	Abijam/ Abijah	936 BC (3 years)	1 Kings 15:1-8; 2 Chronicles 13	147–Righteous King Asa
	Asa	933 BC (41 years)	1 Kings 15:9-24; 2 Chronicles 14:1–16:14	147–Righteous King Asa 148–Prophecies Against Jeroboam and Baasha Fulfilled
Nadab		927 BC (2 years)	1 Kings 15:25-31	148–Prophecies Against Jeroboam and Baasha Fulfilled
Baasha		925 BC (24 years)	1 Kings 15:32–16:7	148–Prophecies Against Jeroboam and Baasha Fulfilled
Elah		901 BC (1 year)	1 Kings 16:8-14	148–Prophecies Against Jeroboam and Baasha Fulfilled
Zimri		900 BC (7 days)	1 Kings 16:15-20	148–Prophecies Against Jeroboam and Baasha Fulfilled 150–Greater Wickedness in Israel
Tibni & Omri		900 BC (5 years)	1 Kings 16-21-22	150–Greater Wickedness in Israel
Omri		904 BC (9 years)	1 Kings 16:23-28	150–Greater Wickedness in Israel
Ahab		895 BC (22 years)	1 Kings 16:29–22:40	150–Greater Wickedness in Israel 151–The Curse of Jericho Fulfilled 152–Your Barrel of Meal Shall Not Waste 153–Showdown at Mount Carmel 154–The Rains Return and Elijah Flees 155–A Still, Small Voice 156–King Ahab Defeats Syria 157–Naboth's Vineyard 158–King Ahab is Slain in Battle
	Jehoshaphat	891 BC (24 years)	1 Kings 22:41-50 2 Chronicles 17:1–20:37	149–The Righteous Reign of Jehoshaphat 158–King Ahab Slain in Battle 159–A Miraculous Victory for Judah 162–Moab Falls to Israel and Her Allies
Ahaziah		870 BC (2 years)	1 Kings 22:51–2 Kings 1:16	160–He Shall Not Come Down from His Bed

THE KINGS OF ISRAEL AND JUDAH*

King of Israel	King of Judah	Approx. Year (time served)	Scriptural References	Stories
	Jehoram/ Joram	869 BC (12 years)	2 Kings 8:16-24 2 Chronicles 21:1-20	171–The Wickedness of Jehoram
Joram/ Jehoram		867 BC (12 years)	2 Kings 1:17–8:15	161–I Have Seen the Chariot of Israel 162–Moab Falls to Israel and Her Allies 166–The Healing of Naaman 168–Elisha and the Blind Army 169–By This Time Tomorrow 172–The Beginning of the End for the House of Ahab
	Ahaziah	855 BC (1 year)	2 Kings 8:25-29 2 Chronicles 22:1-9	172–The Beginning of the End for the House of Ahab
Jehu		854 BC (27 years)	2 Kings 9:1–10:36	172–The Beginning of the End for the House of Ahab 173–Jehu's Sacrifice to Baal
	Athaliah	854 BC (6 years)	2 Kings 11:1-21 2 Chronicles 22:10–23:21	174–Farewell to Athaliah
	Joash/ Jehoash	848 BC (40 years)	2 Kings 11:1-21 2 Chronicles 24:1-27	174–Farewell to Atheliah 175–King Joash Forsakes Jehovah
Jehoahaz		834 BC (17 years)	2 Kings 13:1-9	176–The Arrow of Jehovah's Deliverance
Jehoash		818 BC (16 years)	2 Kings 13:10-25	176–The Arrow of Jehovah's Deliverance 177–Defeat on the Heals of Victory
	Amaziah	808 BC (29 years)	2 Kings 14:1-22 2 Chronicles 25:1-28	176–The Arrow of Jehovah's Deliverance 177–Defeat on the Heels of Victory
Jeroboam 2		803 BC (40 years)	2 Kings 14:23-29	178–Jeroboam's Success and Uzziah's Pride
	Uzziah/ Azariah	779 BC (41 years)	2 Kings 14:21-22; 15:1-7 2 Chronicles 26:1-23	178–Jeroboam's Success and Uzziah's Pride
Zachariah		764 BC 6 months)	2 Kings 15:8-12	180–The End of Israel is in Sight
Shallum		763 BC (1 month)	2 Kings 15:13-15	180–The End of Israel is in Sight
Menahem		763 BC (10 years)	2 Kings 15:16-22	180–The End of Israel is in Sight
Pekahiah		752 BC (2 years)	2 Kings 15:23-26	180–The End of Israel is in Sight
Pekah		750 BC (20 years)	2 Kings 15:27-71 Isaiah 7:1-9	180–The End of Israel is in Sight

THE KINGS OF ISRAEL AND JUDAH*

King of Israel	King of Judah	Approx. Year (time served)	Scriptural References	Stories
	Jotham	724 BC (16 years)	2 Kings 15:32-38 2 Chronicles 27:1-9	181−The Kings of Judah Forsake Jehovah
	Ahaz	708 BC (16 years)	2 Kings 16:1-20 2 Chronicles 28:1-27	181−The Kings of Judah Forsake Jehovah
Hoshea		731 BC (9 years)	2 Kings 17:1-23	182−Assyria's Victory and Israel's Captivity
	Hezekiah	715-686 BC (29 years)	2 Kings 18:1−20:21 2 Chronicles 29:1−32:33 Isaiah 36:1−39:8	183−The Renewal of Judah's Righteousness 184−Judah's Escape from Assyria's Grasp 185−Fifteen Additional Years 186−Judah's Captivity Prophesied 187−The Prophecy of a Sealed Book
	Manasseh	697-642 BC (55 years)	2 Kings 21:1-18 2 Chronicles 33:1-20	188−The Abominations of King Manasseh
	Amon	642-640 BC (2 years)	2 Kings 21:19-26 2 Chronicles 33:21-24	188−The Abominations of King Manasseh
	Josiah	640-609 BC (31 years)	2 Kings 22:1−23:30 2 Chronicles 33:25−35:27	189−King Josiah Fulfills the Prophecy
	Jchoahaz	609 BC (3 months)	2 Kings 23:31-33 2 Chronicles 36:1-4	195−The Burning of the Book
	Jehoiakim/ Eliakim	609-598 BC (11 years)	2 Kings 23:34−24:7 2 Chronicles 36:5-8	195−The Burning of the Book 197−Hananiah
	Jehoiachin	598-597 BC (3 months 10 days)	2 Kings 24:4-17 2 Chronicles 36:9-10	196−Judah on the Brink of Destruction
	Zedekiah/ Mattaniah	597-586 BC (11 years)	2 Kings 24:18−25:26 2 Chronicles 36:11-21	196−Judah on the Brink of Destruction 198−Jeremiah's Imprisonment

*There are some problems and inconsistencies with the information given in the scriptures concerning the time served by various kings and their relationships to the service of other kings. For example, one scripture says that King Uzziah (or Azariah) of Judah served for fifty-two years (2 Kings 15:2), while another says he served for forty-one years (2 Chronicles 26:3). One scripture says that King Jehoram of Judah began serving in the fifth year of King Joram of Israel, son of Ahab (2 Kings 8:16), while another says that King Joram of Israel began serving in the second year of King Jehoram of Judah, son of Jehoshaphat (2 Kings 1:17). Also, if one accepts the statements of length of service in every case, the years do not come out right and Israel and Judah get out of correlation with each other. Though the author has given the length of service for each (when stated in the scriptures), the numbers do not always agree. Thus, this table is useful only for a general overview, and the dates and service times are approximated and are not always consistent.

143–ISRAEL DIVIDED

(1 Kings 12; 2 Chronicles 10–11)

After Solomon was dead, all Israel went to Shechem[390] to make Rehoboam king in his father's place.[391] And Jeroboam, who had earlier fled to Egypt to escape execution by Solomon, heard of Solomon's death and came also.[392] As Rehoboam reveled in his new position, Jeroboam and all the congregation of Israel came to him with a challenging proposition. "Your father Solomon made our burden grievous," they said. "If you will lighten the yoke that your father put upon us, we will serve you."

Rehoboam could see there was cause for concern, and he wanted time to think about his answer; he did not want to make a mistake. "Come back to me in three days," said Rehoboam to the people, "and I shall tell you what I will do."

King Rehoboam consulted first with the elders who had served as advisers to his father. "How should I answer the people?" he asked.

"If you will be a true servant unto this people," the elders counseled, "tell them good words. Tell them that you will lighten their yoke. If you please the people and are kind to them, they will serve you forever."

But Rehoboam, not satisfied with the counsel of the elders, went to his friends—the young men who had grown up with him—and he put the same question to them. "What shall I tell these people who have asked me to lighten the yoke that my father has placed upon them?" he asked.

The young men had a much different point of view. "Tell the people that your little finger shall be thicker than your father's loins,"[393] they said to Rehoboam.

"Tell them that though the yoke your father placed upon them was heavy, you will add to their burden, and where your father chastised them with whips, you will chastise them with scorpions.[394] You must show them who is king and who has the authority."

When Jeroboam and the people returned to Rehoboam on the third day, as Rehoboam had requested, the young king talked to them roughly and answered their request according to the counsel of his young friends. He rejected an offer that his father would have gladly accepted and made it clear that the heavy burdens placed upon Israel by Solomon were to become even greater and harder to bear. This result, however, was from Jehovah so that Ahijah's prophecy to Jeroboam might be fulfilled.

When Israel saw that King Rehoboam had hardened his heart and would not hearken to them, they answered him, "What portion have we with the house of David? We have no inheritance in the son of Jesse. To your tents, O Israel, and leave David to his own house." Thus all the tribes of Israel—with the exception of Judah and Benjamin—followed Jeroboam.

When the people of Israel made Jeroboam their king, Rehoboam assembled an army of 180,000 hand-picked warriors to subdue these wayward subjects and bring them back. But before the battle could be launched, Jehovah sent Shemaiah the prophet to warn Rehoboam that his men must not go to fight against Israel. "Do not go up to fight against your brethren, the children of Israel," said Shemaiah. "You must all return to your houses, for this division of Israel is from Jehovah." And Rehoboam and his army were obedient to the words of the prophet.

Jeroboam set up his headquarters at Shechem[395] in Mount Ephraim, and he dwelt there. All was well and the new kingdom flourished but, as time passed, Jeroboam began to fear that his subjects might be enticed to return to the rule of Rehoboam and the house of David if they continued to go up to the temple in Jerusalem. "If they go up to Jerusalem to offer their sacrifices," he reasoned, "their hearts will surely return to Rehoboam and they will kill me."

After counseling with the leaders of his people, Jeroboam came up with what he felt was the perfect plan; he would provide opportunities for them to wor-

---

[390] Shechem lay in a beautiful sheltered valley between Mount Gerizin and Mount Ebal. It was located about thirty-four miles (54.72 kilometers) north of Jerusalem and seven miles (11.27 kilometers) southeast of the site where the city of Samaria was later built. Shechem was an important city in Israel under Saul, David, and Solomon, and was the main city in the kingdom of Israel after the kingdom was divided, but was later replaced by Samaria (see 1 Kings 16:23–24).

[391] Rehoboam's mother was Naamah, an Ammonite princess.

[392] For the background of Jeroboam and why Solomon sought his life, see story "142–Because You Have Broken My Covenant." That story provides essential background for this one.

[393] This is an interesting metaphor. The loins (the hips and lower abdomen) are usually associated with strength; thus the implication here is that Rehoboam would have greater strength (to control the people and place burdens upon them) in his little finger than Solomon had in his loins.

[394] The scorpions referred to here clearly have no allusion to the spider, but to a whip used for scourging. It is a figure of speech (see William Smith, *Dictionary of the Bible*, *GospeLink*, CD-ROM, s.v. "scorpion").

[395] See footnote 390.

ship and offer sacrifices without going to Jerusalem. So Jeroboam made two golden calves for the people of Israel to worship, and he said to the people, "Because it is too much for you to go up to Jerusalem to worship, I have made these golden calves. These are your gods that brought you up out of the land of Egypt."

Jeroboam set up his golden calves—one in the north of the kingdom at Dan and the other in the south of the kingdom at Beth-el. And he chose priests from the lowest classes of the people to officiate in the high places[396] that he created, disregarding the lineage of Levi and Aaron. He also established a new feast day on the fifteenth day of the eighth month—a day that he chose with his own imagination—and he offered sacrifices and burned incense to his golden calves on that day. Jeroboam was willing to do anything to prevent the children of Israel from returning to Jerusalem.[397] The result, however, was just the opposite of what he had intended, for those who refused to worship idols, along with the Levites and priests who had been displaced, all fled to King Rehoboam and the kingdom of Judah.[398]

144—A PROPHET COMES TO BETH-EL
(1 Kings 13)

One day as King Jeroboam of the kingdom of Israel stood by the altar in Beth-el to burn incense before his golden calf, a prophet who had been sent by Jehovah from the kingdom of Judah confronted him. The prophet prophesied against the altar in the name of Jehovah. "O altar, altar!" he cried, speaking to it as if it were alive. "Thus says Jehovah: a child shall be born of the house of David whose name will be Josiah, and he shall offer upon you the priests of the high places[399] that burn incense unto you, and men's bones shall he burn upon you."[400]

The prophet continued, speaking now to Jeroboam and all those who were present: "Jehovah shall give you this sign today," warned the prophet. "This altar will be torn down and the ashes that are upon it shall be poured out."

When Jeroboam heard these prophecies, he was upset. He stretched forth his hand from the altar and commanded his servants to seize the man. But, as he did so, his hand withered and he could not bring it back to his body. And, at the same time, the altar broke in two and the ashes were poured out—the very sign that the prophet had promised.

The prophet now had Jeroboam's attention, and Jeroboam said to him, "Pray for me that my hand may be restored." And, when the prophet prayed, the king's hand was restored as it had been before.

Jeroboam was impressed with this man of God from Judah. "Come home with me and refresh yourself," he said, "and I will give you a reward."

"If you were to give me half your house," replied the man of God, "I would not go with you. Neither will I eat bread nor drink water here in Beth-el, for thus was I charged by the word of God when he sent me here. I was also charged that I should return to Judah by a different way than that by which I came." And, having

---

[396] Before the temple was built, the children of Israel set up community centers for worship on tops of hills. These were called high places. It became common, especially in the later years of both kingdoms, for high places to also be set up as places for the worship of false gods, as Jeroboam did in Dan and Beth-el.

[397] These golden calves set up by King Jeroboam remained a barrier to the worship of Jehovah until Israel was finally taken captive by the Assyrians about 230 years later.

[398] See footnote 404 in story "145—Judah: Rehoboam's Kingdom."

[399] When the children of Israel came into the promised land, they set up community places of worship, including altars, on the tops of hills. These were called high places. Many of these altars were desecrated when Israel forsook Jehovah to worship false gods. Some high places, as appears to be the case here, were created specifically for the worship of false gods. Later, especially after the temple was built in Jerusalem, many of the leaders sought to get rid of these high places.

[400] The fulfillment of this prophecy more than 300 years later is told in story "189—King Josiah Fulfills the Prophecy" (see 2 Kings 23:15–20).

delivered his message, the prophet left Beth-el to return to Judah by another way.

At this same time there lived in Beth-el an old prophet whose sons came home and told him all that they had seen that day and the words that the prophet of Judah had spoken to Jeroboam. When the old prophet learned the road that the man had taken on his journey home, he set out after him.

When the old prophet of Beth-el found a man sitting under an oak tree, he asked, "Are you the man of God who came up from Judah?"

"I am," came the man's reply.

"Come home to Beth-el with me," said the old prophet, "and eat bread."

"I cannot return with you, nor can I eat bread or drink water in Beth-el," he said. "For Jehovah forbade it when he sent me there. And he told me also to return to my home by a different way than I came up."

Then the old man said to him, "I too am a prophet, just as you are, and an angel has told me to bring you back to my house that you may eat bread and drink water." And, in so saying, the old prophet did not lie.[401]

The prophet of Judah returned to Beth-el and ate and drank at the old prophet's house. But as they sat in the house, the word of Jehovah came to the old prophet and he said, "Jehovah has told me that because you have disobeyed his words and did not keep the commandment that he gave you, your carcass shall never come unto the sepulcher of your fathers."

The prophet of Judah was shaken by this announcement, for he had trusted the old man's words. But so it was that on his way home he was attacked and killed by a lion. The lion did not eat him, however, but stood by his body. Those who traveled along the road saw the man's body lying by the road, with the lion and the man's ass standing there beside it, and they brought word to the people of Beth-el of what they had seen.

When the old prophet heard the travelers' reports, he said, "It is the prophet of Judah who disobeyed the words of Jehovah. Surely Jehovah has delivered him to the lion, and the lion has slain him according to the word that Jehovah told me." Then the old prophet went out and brought the man's body back to Beth-el on his own beast.

Once back in Beth-el, he buried the man's body in his own grave. Then, as he mourned, he said to his sons, "When I am dead, bury me also in this sepulcher. Lay my bones beside his. For the saying that he cried

by the word of Jehovah against the altar and against all the houses of the high places shall surely be fulfilled."

Neither the words spoken to Jeroboam by the prophet from Judah, the withering of his hand, nor the breaking of the altar left a lasting impression on Jeroboam. He did not forsake his evil ways, continuing as before to worship his golden calves and to make the lowest classes of his people the priests of his high places.[402]

---

[401] The Joseph Smith Translation of the Bible reversed the meaning of this last sentence as it appears in the scripture by adding the word "not." It appears that, for some unexplained reason, Jehovah was testing his prophet from Judah.

[402] This is a troubling story in many ways. Perhaps some important details have been omitted from the story as it appears in the scriptures. One commentator made the following observations: "There are problems in the account of an 'old prophet' trying the integrity of the man of God from Judah, and the results seem unfair; but there is a general lesson: if one knows by revelation what he should do, he must not let anything dissuade him. There is precious little comfort in the honor the old prophet bestowed upon the dead corpse of the man of God from Judah" (Ellis T. Rasmussen, *A Latter-day Saint Commentary on the Old Testament* [Salt Lake City: Deseret Book Co., 1993], 289).

145–JUDAH: REHOBOAM'S KINGDOM

(1 Kings 14; 2 Chronicles 11–12)

When the prophet Shemaiah told Rehoboam that the division of Israel into two kingdoms was Jehovah's will, Rehoboam prevented his army from going to war against Jeroboam and the Northern Kingdom.[403] However, he labored diligently to build up the military strength of Judah. He fortified the strongholds of Judah and Benjamin and built fortified cities throughout the land. He also put military leaders over the cities and laid up great stores of food and weapons.

As the military strength of Rehoboam's kingdom increased, the strength of the kingdom also grew in other ways. When Jeroboam, in the Northern Kingdom, cast off the true bearers of the priesthood in favor of others, the priests and Levites from throughout the north fled to Judah and Jerusalem. Not only did the priests and Levites come to join King Rehoboam in Judah, but many others came also. Righteous Israelites fled the kingdom of Israel, and joined with the people of Judah and Benjamin because of their desire to offer sacrifices to Jehovah at the temple and not to Jeroboam's golden calves.[404]

Rehoboam walked in righteousness for three years, but when his kingdom became strong, he forsook Jehovah and took his people with him. They built high places[405] and groves[406] on every hill, and they began to worship idols. They were also given to the sexual perversions associated with the false gods that they worshipped.

In the fifth year of Rehoboam's reign, when the people were steeped in sin, Jehovah sent the Egyptians, under King Shishak, to conquer them. Many cities were taken, and when the armies of Egypt prepared to march into the city of Jerusalem, the prophet Shemaiah came to see Rehoboam and the princes of Judah. "Because you have forsaken Jehovah," Shemaiah said to them, "he has delivered you into the hands of Shishak."

After the Egyptians conquered Judah, the people humbled themselves in their distress and began to repent. And when Jehovah saw their repentance, he said, "I will not destroy them by the hands of Shishak, but they shall become Shishak's servants that they might know my service and the service of the kingdoms of the world."

So the people of Judah became servants to the Egyptians, and they lost to their Egyptian masters many of the treasures from both the temple and the king's palace.

Rehoboam, the son of Solomon, reigned seventeen years in Judah, doing evil because he did not prepare his heart to seek Jehovah. And there were continual wars between Judah and Israel.

---

[403] See story "143–Israel Divided."

[404] Information on these golden calves is also found in story "143–Israel Divided." It is interesting to note that the very thing that Jeroboam sought to prevent by placing his golden idols in Dan and Beth-el was the thing that this action caused. He lost many of his people—particularly the righteous people—to the kingdom of Judah.

[405] When the children of Israel came into the promised land, they set up community places of worship, including altars, on the tops of hills. These were called high places. Many of these altars were desecrated when Israel forsook Jehovah to worship false gods. Some high places, as shown here, were created specifically for the worship of false gods. Later, especially after the temple was built in Jerusalem, many of the leaders sought to get rid of these high places.

[406] Groves in the Old Testament are living trees or tree-like poles, set up as objects of worship. They were generally associated with fertility rites and sexual immorality. Groves were part of Baal worship and were symbolic of female fertility.

146−THE FALL OF JEROBOAM'S HOUSE FORETOLD

(1 Kings 14)

When King Jeroboam's son Abijah fell sick, Jeroboam sent his wife to Shiloh to find the prophet Ahijah. Because it was Ahijah who had earlier prophesied to Jeroboam that he would become king of Israel, Jeroboam thought that Ahijah might be able to tell him what would happen to the child. "Go in disguise that Ahijah may not know you," he told his wife, "and take with you ten loaves of bread, some cakes, and a cruse of honey."

While Jeroboam's wife was on the road to Shiloh, Jehovah spoke to Ahijah to tell him that the woman was coming. "Behold," said Jehovah, "the wife of Jeroboam is coming to ask a thing of you for her son, for he is sick." Then Jehovah told Ahijah that she was coming in disguise and what he should tell her.

Ahijah heard the sound of the woman's feet at his door, but he was blind with age and unable to see her. "Come in, wife of Jeroboam," he called. And when the woman came in, he said to her, "I am sorry that you pretend to be another, for Jehovah has instructed me to give you heavy tidings. Go tell Jeroboam that because Jehovah exalted him from among the people and tore the kingdom away from the house of David to give it to him, Jehovah expected much of him. But Jeroboam has done evil above all the kings that were before him. He has made other gods and molten images to provoke Jehovah to anger, and has cast Jehovah behind his back.

"Because of these sins, Jehovah will bring evil upon the house of Jeroboam and will cut off his male descendants. Jehovah will take away the remnant of the house of Jeroboam as a man takes away dung, until it is all gone. The dogs shall eat those of his house who die in the city, and the fowls of the air shall eat those who die in the field."

Ahijah went on: "Arise now and go home, and when your feet enter the city your son will die. All Israel will mourn for him and bury him, but he alone of Jeroboam's house will come to the grave, because in only him has Jehovah found some good.

"Jehovah will raise up a king over Israel who will cut off the house of Jeroboam. And, because of their groves,[407] the day will come when Jehovah will smite the children of Israel as a reed is shaken in the water, and he shall root them up out of this good land that he gave to their fathers and scatter them beyond the Euphrates River. Yea, Jehovah will give Israel up because of the sins of Jeroboam and because Jeroboam made Israel to sin."[408]

Jeroboam's wife departed from Ahijah's presence in despair because of his words. And when she came to her home in Tirzah,[409] the child Abijah died as she crossed the threshold. And when they buried the child, all Israel mourned, according to the words that Jehovah spoke through the prophet Ahijah.

---

[407] Groves in the Old Testament are living trees or tree-like poles, set up as objects of worship. They were generally associated with fertility rites and sexual immorality. Groves were part of Baal worship and were symbolic of female fertility.

[408] The sin of Jeroboam was related to the worship of the golden calves at Dan and Beth-el and the corruption of the priesthood. The fulfillment of this prophecy of the scattering of Israel is told in story "182−Assyria's Victory and Israel's Captivity."

[409] The scriptures do not tell when Tirzah replaced Shechem as the royal city of the kingdom of Israel. Obviously it was some time during the twenty-two year reign of Jeroboam. Tirzah was about eight or nine miles (about thirteen to fifteen kilometers) northeast of Shechem.

147—RIGHTEOUS KING ASA
(1 Kings 15; 2 Chronicles 13–16)

Eighteen years after Jehovah divided the kingdoms of Israel and Judah between Jeroboam and Rehoboam, Rehoboam died and his son Abijam[410] reigned over Judah for three years in his place. Abijam was the son of Rehoboam and Maachah, the daughter of Absalom.[411] And he was a wicked man who walked in the ways of his father.[412]

Upon Abijam's death, his son Asa was made king of Judah. Asa, who was a righteous king, ruled in Jerusalem for forty-one years. He removed his father's idols from the land and, though the high places[413] were not removed, Asa's heart was perfect before Jehovah all his days.

---

[410] In 2 Chronicles 13, the second king of Judah is called Abijah; while 1 Kings 15 gives his name as Abijam, the name used in this story. The difference between these two names is interesting. Abijah means "Jehovah is my father," and Abijam means "Yam [a Canaanite god of the sea] is my father."

[411] In 2 Chronicles 11:20 Absalom is named as the father of Abijah's (or Abijam's) mother (who was Rehoboam's wife). In 1 Kings 15:2 the father of Abijam's mother is called Abishalom, which is probably another author's version of Absalom. Note, also, that in 2 Chronicles 13:2, Abijah is said to be the son of Rehoboam and Michaiah, who was "the daughter of Uriel of Gibeah." It seems likely that Michaiah (or Maachah) was actually the granddaughter of Absalom (King David's ambitious son), through Absalom's daughter Tamar (see 2 Samuel 14:27).

[412] The two accounts of Abijam/Abijah as found in 1 Kings 15 and 2 Chronicles 13 are quite contradictory. While 1 Kings tells the story of a wicked man named Abijam who walked in the ways of his father Rehoboam, 2 Chronicles depicts a righteous and courageous warrior named Abijah who relied on Jehovah and led 400,000 chosen men of Judah in battle to defeat Jeroboam's armies. These brief accounts of the reign of Judah's second king are as different as the meanings of the two names (see footnote 410).

[413] When the children of Israel came into the promised land, they set up community places of worship, including altars, on the tops of hills. These were called high places. Many of the altars at the high places were desecrated when Israel forsook Jehovah to worship false gods. Some high places were created specifically for the worship of false gods. Later, especially after the temple was built in Jerusalem, many of the leaders sought to get rid of the high places.

The spirit of Jehovah came upon the prophet Azariah, the son of Obed, and he went to Asa to offer encouragement. "Jehovah is with you because you are with him," Azariah told Asa. "But if you forsake him, he will also forsake you."

Azariah went on to recount for King Asa the problems that had vexed the children of Israel through the years. "Israel has been without the Law and without a teaching priest for a long season," he said. "However, when the people of Israel have turned to the God of Israel in their troubles, they have found him. And when they have been disobedient, there has been no peace.

"Jehovah has caused wars, destruction, and adversity among the people when they have been disobedient. But he is pleased with you, Asa, and if you continue to be strong, your good works will be rewarded."

Asa took courage from the words of Azariah and continued working to remove the false gods from the land. He also renewed the altar of Jehovah on the porch in front of the temple. And in the third month of the fifteenth year of Asa's reign in Judah, he gathered all the people together in Jerusalem and offered a sacrifice to Jehovah of 700 oxen and 7,000 sheep. And that day the people of Judah made a covenant to seek Jehovah with all their hearts or be put to death. Gathered at Jerusalem on that occasion were not only the people of Judah and Benjamin, but also many people from Ephraim, Manasseh, and Simeon, who had fled to Judah because of their desire to be under King Asa's righteous rule.[414]

---

[414] This is not the end of King Asa's story. See story "148—Prophecies against Jeroboam and Baasha Fulfilled," for the account of how Asa displeased Jehovah by making an alliance with Syria against Israel rather than relying on Jehovah.

148–PROPHECIES AGAINST JEROBOAM AND BAASHA FULFILLED
(1 Kings 15–16; 2 Chronicles 16)

Two years after Asa became king in Judah, King Jeroboam of Israel died and was succeeded by his son Nadab. The reign of Nadab lasted just two years and was no improvement over the reign of his father. He too was a wicked man who did evil in Jehovah's sight, continuing his support of the golden calves at Beth-el and Dan.

A man named Baasha of the tribe of Issachar led a conspiracy against Nadab and ended Nadab's short reign, taking over the throne of Israel himself. Baasha's reign was marked by his destruction of the house of Jeroboam, fulfilling the prophecy of the prophet Ahijah.[415] There was not one person of the house of Jeroboam left living. But Baasha was also a wicked man; he too continued the tradition of evil in the kingdom of Israel and failed to remove the golden calves that Jeroboam had set up in Dan and Beth-el.

When Baasha led his army in battle against the army of King Asa of Judah, he captured the city of Ramah and attempted to build it up as a stronghold to keep the people of his kingdom from defecting to Judah. King Asa, however, made an alliance with Ben-hadad, king of Syria, which enabled Asa to thwart Baasha's plan. When the Syrian army captured several cities in northern Israel, Baasha abandoned Ramah. With Baasha gone, Asa and his people took the timbers and stones from Ramah and used them to build up Geba and Mizpah.

Jehovah sent the prophet Hanani to rebuke Asa for his alliance with Syria. Hanani explained the consequences of that decision. "Because you have relied on the king of Syria," said Hanani, "and not on Jehovah, the army of Syria has escaped out of your hands. When you relied on Jehovah you were blessed to win many battles, for Jehovah delivered your enemies into your hands. But because you acted foolishly in this thing, Judah shall have many wars with Syria."

And because Hanani's words angered King Asa, he put Hanani in stocks.

Then the word of Jehovah came to Jehu, the son of Hanani, telling him to go to Israel and prophesy against King Baasha. Jehu's message was not a happy one. "Though Jehovah exalted you from the dust and made you a prince over the people of Israel," Jehu said to Baasha, "you have walked in the ways of Jeroboam[416] and caused Israel to sin. Your course has made Jehovah angry and he has decreed against you. Behold, he will take away your posterity and the posterity of your house just as he did the house of Jeroboam. The dogs will eat those of your seed who die in the city, and the fowls of the air shall eat those who die in the field."

When Baasha died, after reigning in Israel for twenty-four years, his son Elah, still maintaining the golden calves in Dan and Beth-el, reigned in his father's place. Elah reigned for only one year before he was slain by Zimri, the captain of half his chariots. And, when Zimri took over the throne of Israel, he put to death all of Baasha's descendants.

Zimri, however, reigned for only seven days. He served just long enough to slay all the seed of Baasha, in fulfillment of Jehu's prophecy, then he too was removed from the throne. When the army of Israel rose up against him to make Omri their king, Zimri burned the king's palace in Tirzah with himself inside.

---

[415] See story "146–The Fall of Jeroboam's House Foretold."

[416] Walking in the ways of Jeroboam involved worshipping the golden calves that Jeroboam set up at Beth-el and Dan.

149—THE RIGHTEOUS REIGN OF JEHOSHAPHAT
(2 Chronicles 17)

When Asa died after reigning righteously as king of Judah for forty years, his son Jehoshaphat became king in his place. And Jehovah was with King Jehoshaphat because he was a righteous man like his father. Jehoshaphat built up the army of Judah that it might be strong to stand against the kingdom of Israel. He put troops in all the fortified cities of Judah and Benjamin and fortified those cities that his father Asa had taken from Ephraim.

Asa had been a righteous king and had destroyed the idols that were in the land, but he had not removed the high places[417] and the groves[418] out of Judah. But because Jehoshaphat's heart was lifted up in the ways of Jehovah, he was more determined than his father and was willing to take that step. Unfortunately, however, because the people's hearts were not prepared, the high places were not all removed.

When Jehoshaphat had reigned three years in Judah, he sent out five of his princes to teach the law of Jehovah to the people. And with the princes he sent nine Levites and two priests who took with them the book of the Law of Jehovah and read from it. Everything possible was done to help the people understand and keep their covenants with Jehovah.

Because of the righteousness of Jehoshaphat and the people of Judah, the fear of Jehovah was upon all the kingdoms in the lands round about, and they did not make war against Judah. In fact, the Philistines and the Arabians brought presents to Jehoshaphat so that he prospered and became very rich.

150—GREATER WICKEDNESS IN ISRAEL
(1 Kings 16)

Omri became king of Israel as the result of a military coup against Zimri, and, when Zimri took his own life by burning the king's palace,[419] the kingdom was divided into two factions—half followed Omri and half went after Tibni. This division of the kingdom, however, was short-lived, and Omri's followers won out. After reigning for six years in Tirzah, Omri bought a hill about ten miles (16.1 kilometers) west of Tirzah, for two talents of silver, where he built a new capital city and named it Samaria.

Omri was a wicked man; he, like those before him, refused to destroy the golden calves that Jeroboam had set up in Dan and Beth-el, and he continued to lead the kingdom of Israel to do wickedly. The scripture says that Omri "did worse than all [the kings] that were before him."

After reigning in Israel for twelve years, Omri died, leaving his son Ahab to be king. But, sadly, Ahab was even more wicked than his father. He continued to maintain the golden calves that Jeroboam had set up at Dan and Beth-el, but perhaps his biggest sin was his taking a wife from among the Zidonians. His wife Jezebel, a worshiper of Baal, was the daughter of Ethbaal, king of Zidonia.[420]

King Ahab openly worshipped Baal[421] and built an altar to honor him in a house of Baal that he erected in Samaria. Ahab also made a grove[422] and did more to provoke Jehovah to anger than all the kings of Israel who had reigned before him, including his wicked father Omri. And, as the king was wicked, so were the people.

---

[417] When the children of Israel came into the promised land, they set up community places of worship, including altars, on the tops of hills. These were called high places. Many of these altars were desecrated when Israel forsook Jehovah to worship false gods. Some high places were created specifically for the worship of false gods. Later, especially after the temple was built in Jerusalem, many of the leaders sought to get rid of these high places.

[418] Groves in the Old Testament are living trees or treelike poles, set up as objects of worship. They were generally associated with fertility rites and sexual immorality. Groves were part of Baal worship and were symbolic of female fertility.

---

[419] See story "148—Prophecies against Jeroboam and Baasha Fulfilled."

[420] Those whom the scriptures refer to as Zidonians, we know as Phoenicians

[421] Baal (plural form Baalim), the storm and fertility god, was symbolic of the male generative principle in nature. Baal worship was most common among the Zidonians or Phoenicians, but it seems that Baal's name (which means "lord") was used broadly in the Old Testament to refer to all heathen or foreign gods.

[422] Groves in the Old Testament were living trees or treelike poles, set up as objects of worship. They were generally associated with fertility rites and sexual immorality. Groves were part of Baal worship and were symbolic of female fertility.

151—THE CURSE OF JERICHO FULFILLED

(1 Kings 16)

When the children of Israel crossed the Jordan and entered the promised land, the first city that they captured was Jericho. The story of the unusual capture of the city by marching around it for seven days while blowing trumpets, and then shouting until the walls collapsed, is well known.[423] Perhaps less known is the curse that Jehovah—speaking through his servant Joshua—put on the man who would rebuild Jericho. The children of Israel, however, were well aware of that curse, and Jericho lay in ruins for about 530 years—until the days that King Ahab reigned in Israel.

The curse that Jehovah put on Jericho, as stated by Joshua, was that the man who would rise up to build the city of Jericho would "lay the foundation [of the city] in his firstborn, and [at the cost of] his youngest son shall he set up the gates of it."

The curse of Jericho was fulfilled when a man named Hiel came from Beth-el and rebuilt the city. When Hiel laid the city's foundation, he did so at the cost of the life of his firstborn son, Abiram. And when the city was built and Hiel set the gates, the life of his youngest son, Segub, was also lost.

152—YOUR BARREL OF MEAL SHALL NOT WASTE

(1 Kings 17)

In the days when wicked King Ahab reigned over the Northern Kingdom, a prophet called Elijah the Tishbite[424] came to him and said, "As Jehovah lives—whose servant I am—there shall be no dew or rain fall upon Israel during these years because of your wickedness."

Once Elijah's message had been delivered to the king, Jehovah instructed Elijah to hide himself at the brook Cherith, east of the Jordan. "There you shall drink of the brook," said Jehovah, "and I have commanded the ravens to feed you." And so the ravens brought Elijah bread and meat both morning and evening, and he drank water from the brook.

When the drought fell heavy upon the land and the brook dried up for lack of rain, Jehovah spoke again to Elijah and said, "Arise and go to Zarephath in Zidonia[425] and dwell there, for I have commanded a widow woman there to sustain you."

As Elijah approached the city gate and saw the widow gathering sticks, he called to her. "Fetch me a little water in a vessel that I may drink," he said. And as she started to go for the water, Elijah called to her again, "Bring me also a morsel of bread in your hand."

"My lord," replied the woman, "as Jehovah lives, I have no bread. I have only one handful of meal in a barrel and a little oil in a cruse. I am now gathering sticks that I may dress the oil and meal for my son and me, which we may eat and then die."

Elijah could see that the widow's situation was desperate and that she had given up all hope of surviving. "Fear not!" he said to her. "Go and do as you have said, but make a little cake for me first and bring it to me.

---

[424] There is some disagreement about the place whose natives were called Tishbites. One commentator had this to say on the subject: "The name naturally points to a place called Tishbeh, Tishbi, or rather perhaps Tesheb, as the residence of the prophet [Elijah]. Assuming that a town is alluded to as Elijah's native place, it is not necessary to infer that it was itself in Gilead, as many have imagined. The commentators and lexicographers, with few exceptions, adopt the name 'Tishbite' as referring to the place Thisbe in Naphtali" (William Smith, *Dictionary of the Bible*, *GospeLink*, CD-ROM, s.v. "Tishbite").

[425] Zarephath was in Zidonia, or what we call Phoenicia. In the New Testament this city was called Sarepta, which is the Greek form.

---

[423] The particulars of this dramatic event are told in story "75—The Fall of Jericho." It is based on Joshua, chapter 6.

After that, you may make one for yourself and your son, for your barrel of meal shall not waste. Neither shall the cruse of oil fail until the day Jehovah sends rain again upon the earth."

And when the woman did as Elijah told her, she and her son were able to eat for many days. For neither her barrel of meal nor her cruse of oil was ever empty.

While Elijah was living in the widow's loft, her son fell sick and died. The poor widow was devastated; first she had lost her husband and now her only son. Overcome with grief, she cried out, accusing Elijah. "What have I to do with you, you man of God?" she wailed. "Did you come here to bring my sins to remembrance and to slay my son?"

"Give me your son," said Elijah, ignoring the widow's insult. And he carried the boy's lifeless body up to his loft and laid it upon his own bed. Crying to Jehovah with all his heart, Elijah pleaded, "O Jehovah, my God, hast Thou also brought evil upon this poor widow by slaying her son?" He then stretched himself out on top of the child three times and cried again, "I pray Thee, O Jehovah, let this child's soul return to him."

Elijah restores the widow's son to life

Jehovah answered Elijah's pleadings, and the boy was restored to life. Then, bringing him back down to his mother, Elijah exclaimed, "See! Your son is now alive!"

"By this I know that you are a man of God," cried the woman, "and the word of Jehovah in your mouth is truth."

153—SHOWDOWN AT MOUNT CARMEL
(1 Kings 18)

The famine in Israel had reached its third year[426] and there was great suffering in the land since Elijah had used his priesthood powers to seal the heavens.[427] As the suffering became most severe, the word of Jehovah came to Elijah as he dwelt at the home of the widow of Zarephath. "Go show yourself to Ahab," said Jehovah, "and I will send rain upon the earth."

As Elijah traveled back toward Samaria he chanced to meet Obadiah, the governor of King Ahab's house. When Ahab's wife Jezebel had put to death all of Jehovah's prophets she could find, Obadiah, who was a God-fearing man, had hidden 100 prophets in caves and kept them alive with food and water. On the day Elijah met Obadiah, Obadiah was on an errand for Ahab. He and Ahab—at Ahab's bidding—had gone in different directions to seek grass for the horses and mules whose lives were threatened by the famine.

Obadiah recognized Elijah and fell on his face before him. "Are you the prophet Elijah?" he asked, just to be sure.

"I am," replied Elijah. "Arise now, and go tell King Ahab that I have come."

"Have I sinned that you should want me slain?" asked Obadiah. "If I go to my master with such a message he will surely kill me. For as Jehovah lives, there is no kingdom or nation to which he has not sent in search of you, and then he swore an oath against those who failed to find you. How can you now send me to tell him you are here? For as soon as I am gone from your sight, the Spirit of God will carry you away and Ahab will take my life."

Obadiah went on, seeking to establish his own reputation with Elijah. "I have been a servant of Jehovah from my youth," he explained, "and, as you may have heard, I hid 100 of Jehovah's prophets in caves and kept them alive when Jezebel sought to slay them."

Elijah assured Obadiah that he would not leave the area before Ahab arrived. "As Jehovah lives, whose servant I am" he said, "I will show myself to Ahab this day."

With that assurance, Obadiah found Ahab and brought him immediately to meet Elijah.

---

[426] The Epistle of James (James 5:17) says this drought lasted for three years and six months.
[427] See story "152—Your Barrel of Meal Shall Not Waste."

When Ahab saw Elijah, he asked him, "Are you not the man who has brought all this trouble to Israel?"

"I have brought no trouble to Israel," answered Elijah. "Israel's troubles were brought to them by you and your father's house when you forsook the commandments of Jehovah and followed Baalim."[428]

"Gather the people of Israel to Mount Carmel," Elijah continued, "and bring also the 450 prophets of Baal and 400 prophets of the groves[429] who eat at Jezebel's table." And so, in response to Elijah's instructions, Ahab gathered the people of Israel and all of Jezebel's prophets to Mount Carmel.

When the vast multitude had assembled from throughout the kingdom, Elijah addressed the people of Israel. "How long will you go back and forth between two opinions?" he asked them. "If Jehovah is God, follow him; but if Baal is God, then follow him."

The people stood silent.

Elijah went on: "I am the only remaining prophet of Jehovah in Israel, but Baal has here 450 prophets. Let us perform a test between Jehovah and Baal." Elijah then explained how the test would work. "Get two bullocks and let the prophets of Baal choose the one they want for their sacrifice," he instructed. "They will cut their bullock into pieces and lay it on wood, putting no fire under it. I will dress the other bullock and also lay it on wood without fire. The prophets of Baal will then call upon their gods to send fire to burn their sacrifice, and I will call upon Jehovah. And the God who answers by sending fire to burn the sacrifice, let him be your God."

And the people agreed that this was a fair test.

"Choose your bullock and dress it first," said Elijah to the prophets of Baal, "for there are many of you. Then call upon your gods to send fire."

When the sacrifice was prepared, the prophets of Baal called upon him from morning until noon, saying, "O Baal, hear us." And when there was no answer, they leaped up and down on the altar.

When noon had come and gone, Elijah began to mock them. "Cry louder!" he said, "For Baal is a god! Either he is talking, chasing someone, or away on a journey. Or is it possible that he is sleeping and must be awakened?"

And the prophets of Baal cried aloud and cut themselves with their knives and lancets—after the manner of their worship—until they were covered with their own blood. When the afternoon had passed and it was coming near time for the evening sacrifice, they prayed on, but still their prayers to Baal went unheeded.

Then Elijah called to the people of Israel and said, "Come near now to me." And, as they watched, Elijah took twelve stones—one for each of the tribes of Israel—and repaired the altar of Jehovah that had been broken down. Next Elijah dug a trench around the altar. Then he laid the wood in order, cut the bullock into pieces, and laid the pieces on top of the wood on the altar.

"Now," said he, "fill four barrels with water and pour the water on top of the sacrifice and the wood."

When the water had been poured as he requested, he had them fill the barrels and empty them two more times upon the wood and the sacrifice—making twelve barrels of water in all. The water flooded the altar and ran down to fill the trench.

When the time arrived for the evening sacrifice, Elijah was ready. He came near to the altar and prayed, saying, "O Lord Jehovah, God of Abraham, Isaac, and of Israel, let it be known this day that Thou art the God in Israel, that I am Thy servant, and that I have done all these things at Thy word. Hear me, O Jehovah, so that this people may know that Thou art *the* God and that Thou hast turned their hearts back again."

When Elijah had finished his prayer, the fire of Jehovah fell from heaven and consumed the sacrifice—as well as the wood, the stones, and the dust—and licked up the water that was in the trench. The people of Israel, when they saw what was done, fell on their faces to the earth and said, "Jehovah he is the God! Jehovah he is the God!"

Then Elijah took the prophets of Baal to the brook Kidron and slew them. Not one man of them escaped.

---

[428] Baal (plural form Baalim), the storm and fertility god, was symbolic of the male generative principle in nature. Baal worship was most common among the Zidonians or Phoenicians, the people to whom Ahab's wife Jezebel belonged.

[429] Groves in the Old Testament were living trees or treelike poles, set up as objects of worship. They were generally associated with fertility rites and sexual immorality. Groves were part of Baal worship and were symbolic of female fertility.

154—THE RAINS RETURN AND ELIJAH FLEES
(1 Kings 18–19)

The prophet Elijah had returned to Israel, bringing with him Jehovah's promise to end the drought, but rain had not yet come. After Jehovah had sent fire from heaven to consume Elijah's sacrifice on Mount Carmel and the prophets of Baal had been slain,[430] Elijah and his servant made their way to the top of the mountain, while King Ahab went to eat and drink.

Once on top of the mountain, Elijah cast himself upon the earth with his face between his knees. After he had prayed for a while, he said to his servant, "Go up and look toward the sea." And when the servant had looked, he returned to report that he saw nothing.

Elijah sent his servant up to look toward the sea seven times, praying each time in between. And when the servant returned after the seventh time, he said, "I see that a little cloud, about the size of a man's hand, has arisen out of the sea."

This was the answer that Elijah had been praying for. And he said to his servant, "Go tell Ahab to prepare his chariot and go quickly to Jezreel so that the rain does not stop him." And the servant went.

The clouds gathered quickly, the heavens grew black, and the rain began to fall. There was a great rain upon all the land. And as the rain began to fall, the hand of Jehovah was on Elijah. He girded his loins and ran to the city gate of Jezreel,[431] arriving before Ahab.

When King Ahab told Queen Jezebel all that Elijah had done on Mount Carmel and how he had slain the prophets of Baal at the brook Kidron, Jezebel was furious. She sent a messenger to Elijah saying, "So let the gods do to me, and more also, if I do not make your life as the life of one of the prophets of Baal by this time tomorrow."

When Elijah received Jezebel's threatening message, it was clear to him that he was no longer welcome in the kingdom of Israel. Taking his servant with him, he fled south into the kingdom of Judah and went a day's journey into the wilderness beyond Beersheba to call upon Jehovah.

---

[430] See story "153—Showdown at Mount Carmel."

[431] Though the capital of the kingdom of Israel at this time was Samaria, and had been since the reign of Ahab's father Omri, Ahab kept his chief residence in Jezreel. There was no doubt a temple of Baal there, where Jezebel's prophets served.

155—A STILL, SMALL VOICE
(1 Kings 19)

When the prophet Elijah fled from Israel to escape Queen Jezebel's wrath and her threat upon his life, he left his servant in Beersheba[432] and went a day's journey farther south into the wilderness. Elijah was discouraged because his efforts all seemed fruitless. As he sat down under a juniper tree, he prayed to Jehovah that he might die. And when he had finished praying, he lay down to sleep.

As Elijah slept, an angel touched him and commanded him to rise and eat. When he awoke and looked around, he saw a cake baking on the coals and cruse of water by his head. Elijah rose and ate, but once he had eaten, he lay down again and went back to sleep.

The angel came a second time and touched Elijah saying, "Arise and eat again, for the journey you must make is too great for you." Once more Elijah arose. He ate and drank and then, with the strength from what he had eaten, he went on to Mount Horeb,[433] where he fasted for forty days and forty nights.

When Elijah arrived at the mountain, still discouraged, he took shelter in a cave where he sought to hide himself and brood in his misery while he fasted. But as he sat in the darkness of the cave, his fasting finally complete, the voice of Jehovah came to him: "What are you doing here, Elijah?"

"I have been very zealous for Thee, Jehovah," answered Elijah, "but the children of Israel have forsaken Thy covenant. They have thrown down Thine altars and slain Thy prophets with the sword. Of all Thy prophets, I alone am left; and there are those who even now seek my life."

Jehovah, understanding Elijah's discouragement, commanded him to come out of his cave and stand upon the mountain. As Elijah stood there on Mount Horeb and Jehovah passed by him, he witnessed a mighty display of power. A great and strong wind rent the mountains and broke the rocks into pieces. But Jehovah was not in the wind. After the wind came an earthquake, but Jehovah was not in the earthquake. Af-

---

[432] Beersheba was the southernmost city of the kingdom of Judah.

[433] Mount Horeb is another name for Mount Sinai. This is the same mountain where Moses encountered the bush that burned without being consumed (see story "46—I Have Seen the Afflictions of My People") and where later, after coming out of Egypt, he fasted for forty days and forty nights and received God's law for the children of Israel and instructions for building the tabernacle.

ter the earthquake came fire, but Jehovah was not in the fire. Then, after the fire came a still small voice. When Elijah heard the voice, he wrapped his face in his mantle and stood in the entrance of the cave. And as he stood there, the voice of Jehovah spoke to him once again. "What are you doing here, Elijah?" he asked, just as he had before.

Because Jehovah's question was the same as before—and Elijah still did not completely understand—he answered as he had answered before. "I have been very zealous for Thee, Jehovah," replied Elijah, "but the children of Israel have forsaken Thy covenant. They have thrown down Thine altars and slain Thy prophets with the sword. Of all the prophets, I alone am left, and there are those who even now seek my life."

Upon hearing Elijah's response, Jehovah said to him, "Return to Damascus[434] and, when you come, anoint Hazael to be king of Syria, Jehu the son of Nimshi[435] to be king of Israel, and Elisha the son of Shaphat to be prophet of Israel in your place. He who escapes the sword of Hazael shall Jehu slay, and he who escapes the sword of Jehu shall Elisha slay."

Jehovah then spoke words of encouragement to Elijah. "Do not lose faith," he said, "for there are many in Israel who still love me; I have 7,000 souls there who have neither bowed to Baal nor kissed him."

When Elijah departed from Mount Horeb after his forty days of fasting and his communication with Jehovah, he was bolstered in his faith and was determined to serve Jehovah. As he walked, he came upon Elisha plowing in a field with eleven other men. Eleven yoke of oxen were before him, and Elisha's was the twelfth. When Elijah passed by Elisha and threw his mantle over him, Elisha left his oxen standing in the plowed furrow and ran after him. Elisha had recognized Elijah and knew that Elijah's mantle was a symbol of his power and authority. He considered this a call from God's prophet. "Wait," he called to Elijah. "Let me kiss my father and mother, then I will follow you."

"What have I done to you?" asked Elijah. "Go back." Elisha returned to his plow, but his determination to follow the prophet did not change. He butchered his oxen and boiled their flesh—using their yokes for the fire. And when he had given the ox flesh to the people to eat, he arose and followed Elijah.

---

[434] Damascus is the capital of Syria.
[435] Jehu was actually the grandson of Nimshi. His father was named Jehoshaphat. Story "172—The Beginning of the End for the House of Ahab" tells of Jehu becoming Israel's king. In the Hebrew language, any direct-line male ancestor might be identified as one's father. There was no distinction between generations.

156—KING AHAB DEFEATS SYRIA
(1 Kings 20)

Things did not look good for King Ahab and the kingdom of Israel. King Ben-hadad of Syria had come with a mighty army, invading the kingdom, and placed Samaria under siege.

From his camp, Ben-hadad sent men into Samaria with a message for Israel's king. "Thus says Ben-hadad," the Syrian messengers said to Ahab, "'Your silver and gold are mine, and so also are your wives and your children—even the goodliest. They are all mine.'"

Ahab was frightened both by Ben-hadad's threats and by the size of his army. "Surely I cannot prevail against this great army," he thought. So he sent a message back to Ben-hadad. "My lord the king," said Ahab's message, "may it be according to your word. I am yours and all that I have belongs to you."

After a short time, Ben-hadad's messengers came again to King Ahab, but with a different message: "Though I sent a message telling you to deliver to me your silver, your gold, your wives, and your children, I have now changed my mind. Instead, I will send my men to search your house and the houses of all your servants tomorrow at this time. My men will bring everything of value to me."

When King Ahab received this second message, he called his elders together and sought their counsel. "This man seeks mischief," he said, greatly understating the situation. "He first sent asking for my wives and children and for my silver and gold, and I did not deny his request. But now he plans to take everything that you have as well."

"You must not consent," cried the elders.

So Ahab told Ben-hadad's messengers that he would not consent to the latest request. "Tell your king that I will do all that he asked me at first," said Ahab, "but this last thing I will not do."

Ben-hadad liked to have his own way and did not take such refusals lightly, and he soon made his displeasure known. He immediately returned a message to Ahab. "May the gods do so to me and more also," said the message, "if the people who follow me are satisfied by handfuls of Samaria's dust."

Ahab answered the messengers boldly: "Tell your king that the man who puts on his armor to go to battle should not boast of his strength in the same way as the man who takes it off after the battle."

Ahab's brash response was enough for Ben-hadad. When he heard Ahab's answer—as he and his kings sat drinking in their shelters—he commanded that his army should attack Samaria.

At this same time a prophet came to King Ahab with a message. "Thus says Jehovah," said the prophet, "'I will deliver this great multitude of Syrians into your hands this day, and you shall know that I am Jehovah.'"

"By whom shall they be delivered?" asked Ahab.

"By the young men who are princes of the provinces of Israel," came the prophet's reply.

"And who shall order the battle?"

"You!"

So Ahab numbered his young princes and found that there were 232 of them. After that, he numbered all the people of Israel in the city, and found there were but 7,000. But, though their numbers were not great, when Ahab's army went out at noon as Jehovah commanded, they found Ben-hadad and the kings who were with him lying drunk in their shelters.

When the Syrian princes saw the men of Israel coming, they cried out to Ben-hadad, "Men have come out of Samaria against us!"

"Whether they come in peace or for war," shouted Ben-hadad, "take them alive!"

But, because Jehovah was with Ahab's tiny army that day, they slew every Syrian that they faced and sent the rest in full retreat. Ben-hadad managed to escape, riding on a horse behind another man, but the little army of Israelites had visited a great slaughter on the mighty Syrian army.

The prophet who had foretold Israel's victory over the Syrian army came again to King Ahab with further instructions from Jehovah. "Go strengthen yourself," said the prophet, "and mark my words well, for at the start of the new year the king of Syria will come against you again."

In the meantime, King Ben-hadad's servants convinced him that the Syrian army had been defeated by the Israelites only because the gods of Israel were the gods of the hills. "If we can fight them on the plain," they reasoned, "we will surely be stronger than they. If you will replace the kings with captains and go again with an army as large as the one you lost—horse for horse and chariot for chariot—Syria shall be stronger than Israel and shall prevail."

King Ben-hadad trusted his servants and did as they counseled, and, at the beginning of the next year, they went down to fight Israel on the plains near the city of Aphek.[436]

As the Syrians approached and the children of Israel went out to meet them in battle, the army of Israel was numbered again. And, compared to the Syrian hosts, the army of Israel was like two small flocks of young goats.

As the two armies were encamped preparing for the battle, a man of God came to King Ahab and told him what the Syrians had said about Jehovah being God of the hills but not of the valleys or plains. "Because of this," said the prophet to Ahab, "Jehovah will deliver this vast Syrian host into your hands. And by this you may know that Jehovah is God."

For six days the two sides prepared for war, and on the seventh day the battle began. On that day, the people of Israel killed 100,000 Syrian footmen. As the Syrian army was routed, those who managed to escape fled into the city of Aphek to hide, King Ben-hadad with them. But, as they hid against the city wall, the wall fell on 27,000 of them.

When the wall fell, Ben-hadad fled with his servants to the inner chamber of the city where his servants convinced him that they should dress in sackcloth, put ropes on their heads, and throw themselves on the mercy of King Ahab. "For," they said, "we have heard that the kings of Israel are merciful kings."

As King Ahab and his men entered the city of Aphek, Ben-hadad and his remaining men came out together dressed in sackcloth to meet their conquerors. But Ben-hadad could not be distinguished from the other men. The Syrians spoke to Ahab: "Your servant Ben-hadad says to tell you he is still alive and that he prays you will let him live."

"Is Ben-hadad alive?" asked Ahab, with surprise and excitement in his voice. "He is my brother! Go and bring him here!" This seemed a strange response from the king of Israel for the life of the man who had threatened, just one year earlier, to take away everything that he had and everything that his people had.

Ben-hadad, surprised to hear Ahab call him his brother, came forward from the crowd and made himself known. And Ahab brought him up into his chariot.

Ben-hadad was greatly humbled by Ahab's kindness to him. And he said, "The cities that my father took from your father I will restore to you, and you shall make trading centers for yourself in Damascus just as my father made in Samaria."

"If you will make that covenant," answered Ahab, "I will send you away." And when the covenant was made, King Ben-hadad and what remained of his army were set free to return to Syria.

At the same time this agreement was being made in Aphek, one of the prophets of Israel commanded a man to wound him. Once wounded, the prophet disguised himself with ashes on his face and waited by the way for King Ahab. And so it was that when Ahab passed by on his return to Samaria, the wounded prophet cried

---

[436] Aphek was a city on the military road from Syria to Israel, six miles (9.7 kilometers) east of the Sea of Chinnereth (or Sea of Galilee) (see William Smith, *Dictionary of the Bible*, *GospeLink*, CD-ROM, s.v. "Aphek").

out so that Ahab stopped. The prophet, unrecognized by the king, proceeded to tell this story: "As I went out into the midst of the battle, a man turned aside and brought one of the enemy to me, commanding me to keep the man for him. I agreed with the man that if the prisoner should escape, it would be my life for his life unless I paid him a talent of silver. Then, because I was busy here and there, the prisoner escaped."

"So, your judgment shall be your life," responded Ahab, "for you decided it yourself."

Once Ahab had given this answer, the prophet wiped the ashes from his face so that Ahab would recognize him. Then he said, "Thus says Jehovah: 'Because you have let a man of the enemy go out your hands whom I had appointed unto utter destruction, your life shall go for his life, and your people for his people.'"

And when Ahab heard this judgment, he returned to Samaria and to his house with great sadness.

157—NABOTH'S VINEYARD
(1 Kings 21)

Next to King Ahab's palace in Jezreel[437] was a beautiful vineyard belonging to a man named Naboth, which he had gained by inheritance. Ahab desired to have Naboth's vineyard for an herb garden, and he asked Naboth to give it to him. "If you will give it to me," Ahab told Naboth, "I will give you a better one. Or, if you prefer, I will pay you whatever money it is worth."

"Jehovah forbid me from doing so!" answered Naboth. "For I cannot give you my inheritance from my fathers."

Ahab was accustomed to having what he wanted, so he was displeased and dejected by Naboth's answer. He lay on his bed with his face to the wall and would not eat. When his wife Jezebel saw Ahab's great sadness, she asked, "Why is your spirit so sad that you will not eat?"

"Because I spoke to Naboth the Jezreelite about his vineyard," Ahab answered her, "and he will neither sell it to me for money nor take other land in exchange for it."

Jezebel was shocked that her husband would let such a thing deter him. After all, he was the king. "Do you not govern Israel?" she asked. "Arise, eat bread, and let your heart be merry. I will give you Naboth's vineyard."

Jezebel's plan for obtaining the vineyard was simple and devious. She wrote letters in Ahab's name, sealed them with Ahab's seal, and sent them to the elders and nobles of Samaria. Her letters contained this message: "Proclaim a fast among the people of Israel and seat Naboth the Jezreelite in a high position. Once he is seated, have two sons of Belial[438] come before him to bear witness against him, accusing him of blaspheming the names of God and the king. Then, with these accusations, take him out and stone him to death."

The elders and nobles, trusting that Jezebel had written the letters with the king's authority, did as they were requested. They proclaimed a fast and seated Naboth in a high position among the people. Then, according to Jezebel's instructions, they brought in the two worthless men to witness against Naboth in the

---

[437] Though the capital of the kingdom of Israel at this time was Samaria, and had been since the reign of Ahab's father Omri, Ahab had a palace in Jezreel and made it his chief residence.

[438] "Son of Belial" is a derisive term used many times in the scriptures. It simply means a worthless and lawless person.

presence of the people. And, when Naboth had been accused of cursing God and the king, they took him out and administered the punishment specified in the law of Moses—they stoned him to death,[439] both Naboth and his sons.[440]

When Jezebel received the news of Naboth's death, she said to Ahab, "Arise now and take possession of Naboth's vineyard that he refused to give you, for Naboth is now dead." And King Ahab went down to the vineyard and claimed it as his own.

And the word of Jehovah came to Elijah the Tishbite saying, "Go down to meet King Ahab in Naboth's vineyard, for he has gone to possess it. Ask the king if he has killed Naboth to take possession of his land. Then tell him that in the place where dogs licked up the blood of Naboth, they shall also lick up his blood."[441]

Ahab considered Elijah his enemy. So, when Elijah came and found King Ahab in Naboth's vineyard, Ahab said to him, "Have you found me, O my enemy?"

"Yes!" replied Elijah. "I have found you because you sold yourself to work evil in the sight of Jehovah." Then Elijah told King Ahab all that Jehovah had told him. "Behold," he said, "Jehovah will bring evil upon you and will cut off all your male posterity. Because you provoked Jehovah to anger and made Israel to sin, your house will be like the houses of Jeroboam, the son of Nebat, and Baasha, the son of Ahijah.[442] For the dogs shall eat him who dies of Ahab's family in the city, and he who dies in the field shall be eaten by the fowls of the air. And the dogs shall also eat your wife Jezebel by the walls of Jezreel."[443]

Although Ahab was wicked and selfish, he was not without feeling. Being greatly humbled by Elijah's rebuke, he tore his clothing, wore sackcloth against his flesh, and fasted. Then the word of Jehovah came to Elijah saying, "Because Ahab has humbled himself before me, I will not bring the promised evil upon his house in his days, but in the days of his son."

---

[439] See Leviticus 24:16.

[440] Although 1 Kings 21 says nothing about Naboth's sons, 2 Kings 9:26 indicates they were also stoned to death. The practice of killing the guilty party's descendants was common in ancient Israel. The benefit of this procedure was that there would be no one to come back later and complain of injustice.

[441] For the fulfillment of Elijah's prophecy, see story "158—King Ahab Is Slain in Battle."

[442] See story "148—Prophecies against Jeroboam and Baasha Fulfilled."

[443] The fulfillment of this prophecy against Queen Jezebel is told in story "172—The Beginning of the End for the House of Ahab."

158—KING AHAB IS SLAIN IN BATTLE

(1 Kings 22; 2 Chronicles 18)

King Jehoshaphat of Judah made an alliance with Ahab, the wicked king of Israel. After several years of reigning in Judah, Jehoshaphat went down from Jerusalem to Samaria to meet with Ahab and strengthen their alliance.

Ahab was pleased to welcome Jehoshaphat to his kingdom, for he felt he could persuade him to be his ally against Syria. When Jehoshaphat arrived, Ahab pressed him and asked, "Will you go up with me to Ramoth-gilead to fight against the Syrians? For they have occupied my land."

"Our peoples are as one," answered Jehoshaphat quickly. "If you go to war, we will go also."

Then Jehoshaphat began to have second thoughts about his hasty answer and said to Ahab, "Perhaps we should inquire of Jehovah first to see if he would have us go."

Seeking to assuage the feelings his visitor from Judah, Ahab called 400 of his prophets and asked them, "Should we go to Ramoth-gilead to battle against the Syrians, or should we forbear?"

"Go up," answered Ahab's prophets, "and Jehovah will deliver Ramoth-gilead into your hands."

The answer certainly sounded favorable, but Jehoshaphat had some concerns about Ahab's prophets; he knew that these were not prophets of God. "Is there not a prophet of Jehovah here in Israel," he asked, "that we might consult him about this matter?"

"There is one man," answered Ahab, "but I hate him. He has never prophesied anything good for me—but always evil. His name is Micaiah."

"We should summon him and see what he says," said Jehoshaphat.

When Micaiah was summoned and brought before them, the messenger who brought him instructed Micaiah to speak only good words to the king, like the other prophets.

"As Jehovah lives," responded Micaiah, "I will speak to him what Jehovah speaks to me."

As Micaiah was brought in to stand before the two kings, Ahab raised the issue. "Shall we go to Ramoth-gilead to battle the Syrians," he asked, "or shall we forbear?"

Micaiah spoke in jest, which was obvious to King Ahab. "You may go up," he said. "You will prosper and Jehovah will deliver Ramoth-gilead into your hands."

"How many times must I tell you to speak nothing but the truth to me when you speak in the name of Jehovah?" said Ahab with disgust.

Then Micaiah, speaking now in all seriousness, said, "I saw all Israel scattered on the mountains as sheep without a shepherd. And Jehovah said to me, 'These have no master. Let them return to their houses in peace.'"

Ahab, confused and angered by what Micaiah had said, asked Jehoshaphat, "Did I not tell you that he would prophesy evil against me rather than good?"

Then Micaiah continued: "I saw Jehovah sitting upon his throne and all the hosts of heaven standing by, on his right hand and on his left. And Jehovah said to them, 'Who will entice King Ahab of Israel that he may go up and fall at Ramoth-gilead?' And I saw that one spoke saying this and another spoke saying that. Then I saw a lying spirit come out and stand before them and say, 'I will entice him.' Then, when Jehovah asked him how he would do it, the lying spirit replied, 'I will be a lying spirit in the mouth of Ahab's prophets.' Then Jehovah said, 'You will entice him, and you will prevail. Go and do it, for all these have sinned against me.'"

Micaiah went on, now speaking directly to Ahab. "Jehovah has put a lying spirit in the mouths of your prophets and he has spoken evil against you," he said.

When the man who had brought in Micaiah heard this, he struck Micaiah on the cheek and asked, "Which way did the spirit of Jehovah go from me to speak to you?"

"You shall know the answer to your question on that day when you go into an inner chamber to hide yourself," replied Micaiah.

Ahab was now very angry. He ordered that Micaiah be taken before the governor of the city and before Joash, Ahab's son, that he might be punished for what he had said. "Put this man Micaiah into prison and feed him with the bread and water of affliction until I return in peace from Ramoth-gilead," instructed Ahab.

"May the people mark well," said Micaiah as he was led away. "If Ahab returns in peace, you shall know that Jehovah has not spoken to me."

So Ahab the king of Israel and Jehoshaphat the king of Judah went with their armies to Ramoth-gilead to battle the Syrians. And as they went, Ahab said to Jehoshaphat, "I will disguise myself when I go to the battle, but you shall put on your robes." Ahab had set Jehoshaphat up to fall in battle instead of himself. And thus they went to meet the Syrians.

The king of Syria, meanwhile, had commanded the captains of his chariots to fight only with the king of Israel. So, when they saw Jehoshaphat in his robes, they thought he was Ahab. But, when they surrounded Jeho-shaphat, he cried to Jehovah and was delivered, for Jehovah caused them to see that he was not Ahab and to leave him alone.

In the heat of the battle, a man of the Syrian army drew his bow and shot Ahab with an arrow, which pierced him between his armor and his breastplate. Ahab, badly wounded, commanded his chariot driver, "Turn and carry me out of the battle, for I am wounded."

But as the battle increased, Ahab, unable to resist the thrill of the fight, came back. And as the battle continued all that day, the wounded King Ahab propped himself up in his chariot to fight. And when the sun went down that evening, he died.

The body of King Ahab, the wicked king of Israel, was taken back to Samaria and buried there, and when they washed out his chariot in the pool of Samaria, the dogs licked up his blood, according to Elijah's prophecy.[444]

---

[444] This prophecy (which was a curse on Ahab) is told in story "157—Naboth's Vineyard." It is recorded in 1 Kings 21:19.

159—A MIRACULOUS VICTORY FOR JUDAH

(2 Chronicles 19–20)

Jehovah was not pleased that Jehoshaphat, the king of Judah, had joined forces with the wicked King Ahab, and he sent Jehu, the son of Hanani, to meet Jehoshaphat when he returned from Ahab's battle with the Syrians. "Is it good for you to help the ungodly and love them that hate Jehovah?" asked Jehu. "Because you have done this, Jehovah's wrath is upon you."

"But, though you have done this evil thing," Jehu continued, "there are good things found in you because you took the groves[445] out of the land and prepared your heart to seek God."

Jehoshaphat continued in his righteous ways. Being very diligent in the cause of righteousness, he went out among the people to teach them and bring them back to Jehovah. He set up judges from among the priests and Levites throughout the land. To those who were called as judges he said, "Take heed of what you do, for you judge not for man, but for God. Let the fear of Jehovah be upon you, for there is no iniquity with Jehovah, neither respect of persons or taking of bribes."

Because of Jehoshaphat's efforts, both Jehovah and the people of Judah loved him, and the people prospered. In their prosperity, they were the object of envy of other nations—the Ammonites, the Moabites, and the people of Mount Seir—who united their forces to come up against them to battle. When Jehoshaphat was told that a great multitude was approaching, he was afraid, but he followed the wisest course as he prepared to meet the invading army: he proclaimed a fast throughout all Judah and set his own heart to seek Jehovah.

As the people of Judah gathered to the temple from throughout the land, Jehoshaphat stood before them and prayed to Jehovah. "O Jehovah, God of our fathers," he pleaded. "Thou who art in the heavens and who rules over all the kingdoms of the heathen, in Thine hand is power and might so that none can withstand Thee. Thou art our God who did drive out the inhabitants of this land before Thy people Israel and gave it to the seed of Thy friend Abraham forever."

Jehoshaphat continued his prayer: "When evil comes upon us, we stand before this house, in Thy presence, and cry unto Thee that Thou wilt hear us and help us in our affliction. Now the children of Ammon, Moab, and Mount Seir—whom Thou would not let Israel invade when they came out of Egypt—are coming to cast us out of Thy possession. O God, let Thy judgments be upon them, for we have no might against their great army. Neither do we know what to do, but our eyes are upon Thee."

As all Judah stood at the temple, the Spirit of Jehovah rested upon a man named Jahaziel, the son of Zechariah, who stood in the midst of the congregation. Jahaziel spoke: "Hearken all you people of Judah and King Jehoshaphat. Jehovah has told me that Judah should not be afraid or dismayed because of the great multitude that now comes against them, for the battle is Jehovah's and not theirs."

Jahaziel went on as the Spirit rested upon him: "When you go down against them tomorrow, they will come up by the cliff of Ziz and you will find them at the end of the brook, before the wilderness of Jeruel. You shall not need to fight them; but shall stand still and see the salvation of Jehovah."

When Jehoshaphat and the people of Judah heard this, they bowed to the earth and worshipped Jehovah, and the Levites stood up to praise him with loud voices.

The next morning, as the people of Judah rose early and went into the wilderness of Tekoa,[446] Jehoshaphat said to them, "Hear me, O Judah and you inhabitants of Jerusalem. Believe in Jehovah and you will be established. Believe his prophets and you will prosper."

When King Jehoshaphat had consulted with his people, he appointed singers to sing praises to Jehovah, going out ahead of the army. And as the people of Judah began to sing and to praise, Jehovah set ambushes against their enemies, and caused them to fight each against the other. The people of Ammon and Moab battled the people of Mount Seir, and when the people of Mount Seir were destroyed, the Ammonites and the Moabites turned to destroy each other.

When the people of Judah finally approached the watchtower in the wilderness, they saw that their enemies were all lying dead upon the ground. None of them had escaped. And when Judah came to take the spoils of the fallen armies, they found an abundance of riches and precious jewels. The spoils were so great that they were three days in gathering them.

---

[445] Groves in the Old Testament were living trees or treelike poles, set up as objects of worship, and were generally associated with fertility rites and sexual immorality. The groves were part of Baal worship and were symbolic of female fertility.

---

[446] Tekoa was a town in the tribe of Judah on the range of hills rising near Hebron and stretching eastward toward the Dead Sea.

160—HE SHALL NOT COME DOWN FROM HIS BED

(2 Kings 1)

When King Ahab was dead, his son Ahaziah became king of Israel in his place. Ahaziah was a wicked man like his father before him, and caused Israel to worship false gods. He worshiped Baal like his mother and father and continued to maintain the golden calves that Jeroboam had set up in Dan and Beth-el.[447]

When Ahaziah had been king for only three years, he fell through a lattice in his upper chamber and was badly injured. Because of this injury, he sent messengers from Samaria to Ekron to inquire of the god Baal-zebub[448] as to whether he would die. Ahaziah's messengers never reached their destination, however, because the prophet Elijah was sent by the angel of Jehovah to meet them on the way.

When Elijah met the king's messengers, he asked them, "Is it because there is no God in Israel that you go to inquire of Baal-zebub, the god of Ekron? You must return and tell Ahaziah that because he has done this, Jehovah has decreed that he shall not come down from his bed, but shall surely die." His message delivered, Elijah turned and departed.

Much to King Ahaziah's surprise, his messengers did not go to Ekron, but returned immediately to Samaria and came to his bedside. "Why have you come back?" he asked them.

"There was a man who met us on the way," they explained. "He told us to return to the king who sent us and to tell him that—because he does not believe there is a God in Israel but sent to inquire of Baal-zebub—he shall not come down from his bed, but shall surely die."

"What did this man look like?" asked Ahaziah.

"He was a hairy man," said the messengers, "with a girdle of leather about his loins."

"The man was Elijah the Tishbite," said Ahaziah, recognizing the description. And Ahaziah sent out a captain with fifty men to find Elijah and bring him to Samaria. Ahaziah wanted nothing more than to put Elijah to death.

Ahaziah's men finally found Elijah sitting on top of a hill. And the captain said to him, "You, O man of God, the king has ordered you to come down to see him."

Elijah knew that his life would be worth nothing if he went with these men. "If I am a man of God, as you say," he replied, "let fire come down from heaven and consume you and your men." And fire came from heaven to consume them.

When the first group did not return, King Ahaziah sent another fifty men with the same message. But the same result followed, for these men were also consumed by fire from heaven when they ordered Elijah to come to see the king.

When the captain of the third fifty came to Elijah with his men, he had much more respect for Elijah than did those who came before him. He was well aware that the two groups of fifty who had been sent earlier had never returned; he knew that Elijah must be considered a dangerous man. He approached the prophet cautiously and fell to his knees before him. Pleading even for his life, he said, "O man of God, I beg of you, let my life and the lives of these fifty servants be precious in your sight. Let not fire come from heaven upon us as it did upon the others, but come down to see the king."

And the angel of Jehovah spoke to Elijah and said, "Go down with this man, and do not fear." So Elijah arose and went to Samaria to see King Ahaziah.

When Elijah came to King Ahaziah's bedchamber and saw him lying there, he delivered to him personally the message he had already heard. "Thus says Jehovah: 'Because you do not believe there is a God in Israel but sent messengers to inquire of Baal-zebub, the god of Ekron, you shall not come down from your bed but shall surely die.'"

And so it was that King Ahaziah died as Elijah had told him, and his brother Jehoram became king of Israel in his place.

---

[447] For the account of Jeroboam setting up the golden idols at Dan and Beth-el, see story "143—Israel Divided."

[448] Baal-zebub means "lord of the fly." This false god of the Philistines was worshipped especially in Ekron, the northernmost of the five cities belonging to the five princes of the Philistines. He was the god of both healing and disease.

161—I HAVE SEEN THE CHARIOT OF ISRAEL

(2 Kings 2)

Elijah's mission was fulfilled and Elisha had been chosen to be Jehovah's prophet in his place. Elijah had been told by Jehovah that he would be taken to heaven without tasting death, and the day had come, all too soon, when he and Elisha knew that Jehovah would take him. The two prophets went to Gilgal together, where Elijah instructed Elisha to remain while he went on to Beth-el, where Jehovah had sent him.

Elisha, however, declined to stay at Gilgal. "I will not leave you," he insisted.

And as the two prophets came to Beth-el, the sons of the prophets[449] who were in Beth-el came out from the city and said to Elisha, "Do you know that this is the day when Jehovah will take away your master?" They too knew what was going to happen that day.

"Yes, I know it," Elisha answered. "I know it all too well."

Then Elijah said to Elisha, "You must remain here in Beth-el, for Jehovah has now sent me to Jericho." But again Elisha refused to be left behind.[450]

As the two men of God approached Jericho, the same thing happened as at Beth-el. The sons of the prophets came out to ask Elisha if he knew that this was the day in which Jehovah would take his master. And, as he had done at Beth-el, Elisha assured them that he knew what was in store. Perhaps a bit impatiently, he said to them, "Now hold your peace."

Then Elijah turned again to his young companion, this time telling him that he should stay in Jericho because Jehovah had now sent him to the River Jordan. But Elisha still maintained his determination to remain with his master. "As Jehovah lives and as your soul lives," he insisted, "I will not leave you." And the two went on together to the Jordan.

As they stood by the Jordan, fifty men of the sons of the prophets watched from a distance while Elijah took off his mantle and folded it together. When he struck the waters of the river with the mantle, the waters divided and the two prophets passed through the middle of the river on dry ground.

As they stood on the opposite bank, Elijah spoke earnestly to his young associate. "Ask what you will of me," he said, "before I am taken from you."

"I will ask you only one thing," answered Elisha. He had thought this through very carefully long before. "I ask that a double portion of your spirit will be upon me."[451]

"You ask a hard thing," responded Elijah. "Nevertheless, if you are able to see me when I am taken up, you will know that your request has been granted. But if you do not see me, then it shall not be so."

As the two men of God went on, talking together, a chariot and horses of fire appeared between them, and Elijah was taken up into heaven with a whirlwind.[452] When Elisha realized that he had seen Elijah when he was taken up, he was overjoyed. He knew that his request for a double portion of Elijah's spirit had been granted. "My father! My father!" he cried. "I have seen the chariot and the horsemen of Israel!"

Elisha took hold of his own garment and tore it into two pieces. He then took up the mantle that had fallen from Elijah[453] and returned to the banks of the Jordan. When he struck the waters with Elijah's mantle, the waters parted before him so that he returned back over the river on dry ground.

Those who had been observing from a distance watched Elisha as he came toward them. When they saw him part the waters of the Jordan with Elijah's mantle, they exclaimed, "The spirit of Elijah has rested on Elisha."

When the men met Elisha, they were confused about what had happened. They bowed before him and said, "There are fifty of us—all strong men. Let us go now

---

[449] Those identified as sons of the prophets were, no doubt, faithful believers. Perhaps they were associated with one of the schools of the prophets such as had been established in Israel since the time of Samuel. Story "106—A Victim of Saul's Jealousy" tells of such a school at Naioth in Ramah where Samuel and David went when David was fleeing from King Saul.

[450] If one looks at a map and traces the travels of Elijah and Elisha that day—from Gilgal to Beth-el, and then from Beth-el back to Jericho—the route seems rather strange. The reason Jehovah had them follow this circuitous route is not explained.

[451] Under the laws of inheritance, the eldest son was the heir and received a double portion. It is apparent here that Elisha desired to be Elijah's spiritual heir.

[452] When Elijah was taken up into heaven, the change that he experienced is called translation. Translated beings do not become immortal, but are given power over death. When the purpose of their translation is fulfilled, they will die or—in most cases—be changed from mortality to immortality (i.e., resurrected) in the twinkling of an eye.

[453] Elisha's taking of Elijah's mantle is significant. He now possessed the mantle that Elijah had placed upon him symbolically when he first saw him plowing in the field (see story "155—A Still, Small Voice").

and search the wilderness for Elijah, for perhaps the Spirit of Jehovah has taken him up and cast him upon some mountain or in some valley."

Elisha, understanding the superstitions of these men, told them not to go. But when they persisted in their request, he finally agreed. However, after searching unsuccessfully for Elijah for three days, they gave up their search and returned to Jericho.

162—MOAB FALLS TO ISRAEL AND HER ALLIES
(2 Kings 3)

When King Ahaziah died from falling through a lattice,[454] his brother Jehoram became ruler of the Northern Kingdom. He was a wicked man, but not as wicked as his father and mother, Ahab and Jezebel, for Jehoram put away the image of Baal[455] that his father had made. The sin of Jeroboam, however, still prevailed throughout the kingdom of Israel, for the people still worshipped the golden calves that Jeroboam had set up at Dan and Beth-el.

The people of Moab[456] had been subservient to Israel under King Ahab, giving 100,000 lambs and 100,000 rams to Israel each year. When Moab decided to rebel, Jehoram united his forces with those of King Jehoshaphat of Judah and the king of Edom[457] to fight against Moab.

After circling for seven days to get on the other side of Moab, Israel and her allies found themselves in dire straits; they had no water. There was none—neither for them nor for the cattle they had brought with them. Jehoram became discouraged and resigned himself to defeat, thinking that their cause was surely lost. "Alas!" he lamented. "Jehovah has called these three kings together to deliver us all into the hands of Moab!"

King Jehoshaphat, however, was not ready to give up. He thought that perhaps Jehovah might still bless their cause and deliver them. "Is there not a prophet through whom we can seek Jehovah's assistance?" he asked.

And one of Jehoram's servants said, "Elisha the son of Shaphat lives near here."

Jehoshaphat was pleased. "Good!" he said. "I know that the word of Jehovah is with Elisha." And the three kings set out to see the prophet Elisha.

When they came before Elisha, he said to King Jehoram, "What have I to do with you? Go talk to the prophets of your father and mother."

---

[454] See story "160—He Shall Not Come Down from His Bed."

[455] Baal (plural form Baalim), the storm and fertility god, was symbolic of the male generative principle in nature. Baal worship was most common among the Zidonians or Phoenicians, the people to whom Ahab's wife Jezebel belonged.

[456] The Moabites were descended from Abraham's nephew Lot.

[457] The Edomites were descendants of Jacob's twin brother Esau.

"No!" responded Jehoram. "For Jehovah has called these three kings together to deliver us all into the hands of Moab."

Then Elisha said, "As Jehovah lives before whom I stand, were it not for the presence here of Jehoshaphat, the king of Judah, I would not look at you or give you any thought. However, because of Jehoshaphat, I ask that you bring a minstrel to play for me that I might seek the Spirit of Jehovah."

When the minstrel came and played for Elisha, the Spirit of Jehovah rested upon him and he prophesied. "Jehovah has said that he will make this valley full of ditches," said Elisha. "You shall see neither wind nor rain, yet this valley will be filled with water. Jehovah has told me that he will deliver the Moabites into your hands and will smite every fortified city and every choice city in Moab. You shall also fell every good tree, stop up all the wells of water, and mar every good piece of land with stones."

The next morning when the meat offering[458] was made in Israel's camp, water came flowing into the valley from the direction of Edom.

At the same time, when the Moabites learned that the kings of Edom, Judah, and Israel had come to fight against them, they gathered early in the morning with every man who could put on armor, and they stood at their border. As they waited, they saw the water come. And, as the sun shone upon the water, it looked as red as blood. "Look!" they cried. "It is blood! The men who have come to smite us have killed one another. Let us go and take the spoils."

But when the Moabites came to the camp of Israel, the Israelites were far from dead. They rose up and smote the people of Moab, driving them back into their own country. Then, as prophesied by Elisha, the united armies of Israel, Judah, and Moab beat down the cities and cast stones onto every good piece of land. They also felled the good trees and stopped up the wells of Moab.

When the king of Moab saw that he was losing the battle, he took 700 men and led them in an attempt to break through the ranks to the king of Edom—but his efforts failed. Finally, when he saw that all else had failed, he offered his eldest son as a burnt offering to his false gods upon the city wall.

And the armies of Israel, Judah, and Edom returned victorious to their own lands.

---

[458] Meat offerings are described in some detail in Leviticus, chapter 2. They could more properly be called meal offerings and were not always exactly alike. Usually they consisted of unleavened cakes or wafers made with fine flour and oil or of wafers anointed with oil.

163—THE WIDOW'S OIL
(2 Kings 4)

The widow of Obadiah,[459] the man who had been King Ahab's steward,[460] came to Elisha seeking his counsel. She explained her dilemma: "My husband feared Jehovah, but he is now dead and his creditor is threatening to take my two sons as bondsmen."

"How would you have me help you?" asked Elisha. "Tell me what you have in your house."

"I have nothing in my house except a pot of oil," replied the woman.

"Go then," said Elisha, "and borrow as many empty vessels as you can from your neighbors. Once you have them, go into your house and shut the door. Then you and your sons should take your pot of oil and pour it into all those vessels, and set each vessel aside when it is filled."

So, trusting Elisha's words, the woman went and did as he told her. She gathered empty vessels from her neighbors and then shut the door behind herself and her two sons. As the sons brought the vessels to her, she poured the oil, which flowed without interruption. When all the vessels were full, she said to her son, "Bring me another vessel."

"I cannot," replied the son, "for there are no more." And at that point the supply of oil ceased to increase.

Not knowing what to do next, the woman returned to Elisha and told him what had happened and how the vessels had all been filled. "Go!" he said to her. "Sell the oil to pay your debt, then you and your sons shall live on the rest."

---

[459] The scriptures do not identify this widow, but she is identified by Josephus (Flavius Josephus, *Antiquities of the Jews,* 9:4:2).

[460] See story "153—Showdown at Mount Carmel."

164—DEATH—THEN LIFE—
FOR THE PROMISED SON
(2 Kings 4)

As the prophet Elisha passed frequently through the village of Shunem,[461] he was blessed by the kindness of a woman of the city and her husband who took him in and fed him. After several of Elisha's visits, the woman told her husband that she thought the man they fed must be a holy man and that they ought to prepare a place for him to sleep when he passed through the village. So, they set up a small chamber with a bed, a table, a stool, and an oil cup[462] so that Elisha could use it as it might please him.

One day when Elisha and his servant Gehazi were in the chamber that the woman had prepared, he said to Gehazi, "Go ask this Shunammite woman what we can do to reward her for her kindness."

So Gehazi said to the woman, "You have been very kind to us and have shown great care. What would you have us do for you? Can we speak to the king in your behalf or to the captain of the army?"

"Oh no!" answered the woman. "That is of no interest to me, for I dwell here among my own people."

And when Gehazi reported his conversation to Elisha, Elisha said, "What then can we do for her?"

"There may be one thing," answered Gehazi. "For I see that she has no children and that her husband is old."

So Elisha called the woman and said to her, "About this season next year you shall embrace a son."

"Oh no, my lord," the woman answered with surprise. "Please do not deceive me!"

The woman, however, conceived and bore a son as Elisha had promised, and the child grew and was a great joy to his parents. Then one morning, while the boy was still young, he went out to be with his father in the field with the reapers. There in the field the lad fell sick and complained to his father of terrible pains in his head. So the father had one of the reapers carry him

back to his mother. And, as the mother held him on her knees, the young boy died.

In great sorrow, the mother took the lifeless body of her son and lay it on the bed in Elisha's chamber. She then shut the door and went out to her husband. "Send me one of the young men and one of the asses," she said, "that I may run to see the man of God." She did not tell him that their son was dead. But she saddled the ass and left with a servant for Mount Carmel to seek the prophet Elisha.

When Elisha saw the woman coming, he sent Gehazi to meet her and ask why she had come. But when Gehazi asked her concerning herself, her husband, and her son, she answered him only, "It is well."

When the woman came to Elisha, she caught hold of his feet, and Gehazi came near to push her away. But Elisha, sensing that the woman was deeply troubled, said, "Leave her alone. Her soul is vexed, but Jehovah has hidden from me the cause of her trouble."

Then the woman spoke. "Did I ask you to give me a son?" she cried. "Did I not tell you not to deceive me?" Elisha now understood the reason for the woman's coming and for her questions.

"Gird up your loins and take my staff in your hand," Elisha told Gehazi, "and go directly to Shunem. If you meet anyone along the way, do not stop to salute him, and if anyone salutes you, do not answer. And, when you get to Shunem, lay my staff upon the dead child's face."

"As Jehovah lives, and as your soul lives," said the mother, "I will go with you." And she arose to follow him. Gehazi went on ahead, with Elisha and the bereaved mother following behind.

When Gehazi reached the woman's house, he laid Elisha's staff on the dead child's face. When the child did not respond, however, Gehazi rushed back to meet Elisha and the mother. "The boy does not awaken!" he said.

Elisha was now deeply concerned. When he arrived at the house, he went into his bedchamber alone and closed the door. There, with just himself and the body of the dead child present, he knelt and prayed. After praying, he went up onto the bed and lay down on top of the child's body. He put his mouth upon the child's mouth, his eyes upon the child's eyes, and his hands upon the child's hands. And as he stretched himself out upon the body, the flesh began to grow warm. Then Elisha got down and walked back and forth in the room. Once more he went up to the bed and stretched himself out on top of the child. Then the child sneezed seven times and opened his eyes. Elisha's prayers had been answered.

Elisha, overjoyed that his prayers had been answered, called Gehazi and told him to bring the child's

---

[461] Shunem was a village in the Northern Kingdom, formerly in Issachar. It was located five miles (eight kilometers) south of Mount Tabor and three miles (4.8 kilometers) north of Jezreel. Those who lived there were called Shunammites. King David's nurse, Abishag, was a Shunammite (see story "138—Justice for His Father's Enemies").

[462] The scripture (2 Kings 4:10) says candlestick, but they had no candles. They burned olive oil in cup-like receptacles, using cloth for wicks.

mother. When she came into the chamber, Elisha said to her, "Take up your son!"

The woman fell at Elisha's feet, bowing herself to the ground in gratitude. Then, taking her son into her arms, she went out from Elisha's bedchamber.

165—MIRACLES AT GILGAL
(2 Kings 4)

When Elisha went to Gilgal, the sons of the prophets[463] who were there were suffering from the effects of a drought. As he sat with them, he sensed their hunger and said to his servant Gehazi, "Put on the great pot and boil some pottage[464] for these men." And Gehazi did so.

Then one of those present, seeking to be helpful, went out into the field and gathered a lap full of gourds from a wild vine. When the man returned, he shredded the gourds into the pottage.

When the pottage was well cooked, it was poured out for the men to eat. But, as they began to eat, one cried out, "O man of God, there is death in the pot!"[465] And none of them would eat it.

"Bring me some meal,"[466] said Elisha. When it was brought to him, Elisha put the meal into the pot and said, "Pour the pottage out now that the people may eat it." And when they ate the pottage, none of them was harmed.

Another man came and brought to Elisha twenty loaves of barley bread and a few full ears of corn still in the husk. "Give these also to the people that they may eat," said Elisha to the host.

"How can I set this small amount before 100 men?" asked the host. "It is not enough."

"Give it to them," said Elisha. "When they have eaten there shall be food left over, for thus has Jehovah said."

The food was prepared as instructed and set before the men to eat. And when they were filled, there was food left over, according to the word of Jehovah to Elisha.

---

[463] Those identified as sons of the prophets were, no doubt, associated with one of the schools of the prophets such as had been established in Israel since the time of Samuel. Story "106—A Victim of Saul's Jealousy" refers to such a school at Naioth in Ramah where David and Samuel went to live when David was fleeing from King Saul.

[464] Pottage is thick soup, usually made with lentils and containing both vegetables and meat.

[465] That is, it was poisonous.

[466] Meal is coarsely ground grain.

X

DIVIDED ISRAEL (PART II):

GOOD KINGS, BAD KINGS,

AND THE THREAT OF CAPTIVITY

166—THE HEALING OF NAAMAN

(2 Kings 5)

During those days when Jehoram, the son of Ahab, reigned over the kingdom of Israel at Samaria, there lived in Syria a very important man named Naaman. Naaman was greatly honored by the Syrian king, Ben-hadad II, and was one of those who accompanied the king when he went to worship at the house of Rimmon.[467] As captain of the Syrian army, Naaman had delivered Syria from her enemies. Though he was a great and honorable man and had many things in his favor, he had one very serious problem—he was a leper.

Living in Naaman's household was a young Hebrew girl who, though she had been captured and brought from Israel as a slave, had great love for her master. One day she said to her mistress, "I wish that God would allow my master to be in Israel with the prophet. For the prophet would heal his leprosy." And Naaman was told what the girl had said.

Word of the young girl's saying also came to the king. When he heard it, he called Naaman to him and said, "You must surely go down to Israel; I will send a letter with you to Israel's king."

The relationship between Israel and Syria was strained, to say the least. It had been only a few short years since King Jehoshaphat of Judah and King Ahab of Israel had joined their forces to battle against Syria when Syria had invaded Jabesh-gilead.[468] But both

Naaman and the king were willing to try almost anything that might heal Naaman's leprosy.

So Naaman departed for Israel with a large company, going south through Bashan, down the road east of the Lake of Chinnereth,[469] and across the Jordan to the city of Samaria. In addition to King Ben-hadad's letter of introduction to King Jehoram, Naaman also took with him ten talents of silver,[470] 600 pieces of gold, and ten changes of clothing. All of these were to be bestowed as gifts when Naaman's leprosy was healed.

Once in Samaria, Naaman and his company went directly to King Jehoram and presented the letter from King Ben-hadad. Jehoram was uneasy about the presence of this company of Syrians in his city, and he became even more uneasy when he read the letter. It said: "When this letter comes to you, King Jehoram, it will be in the hand of Naaman my servant. He has come to you that you may heal him of his leprosy."

Jehoram tore his clothing in anguish and cried, "Am I God that I can kill or make alive, that the king of Syria should send a man for me to heal of leprosy? Surely King Ben-hadad seeks only to start a quarrel with me."

When Elisha the prophet learned of Naaman's presence in Samaria and the anguish of King Jehoram, he sent a message to the king. "Why have you rent your clothing?" he asked. "Let the Syrian come to me that he may know there is a prophet in Israel."

So Naaman was directed to Elisha's house, and he stopped his horses and chariot at the door. But Elisha did not go out to meet Naaman. Instead, he sent his servant to deliver a very simple message: "Go and wash yourself in the River Jordan seven times and your flesh will come again to you and you will be clean."

When Naaman heard the message, he was livid. He said to those who were with him, "I thought that the man would surely come out of his house to see me. I thought he would stand by me and call on the name of Jehovah his God, strike his hand over the sore place, and heal the leper."

Naaman had his own ideas about how miracles should be wrought, and what he was experiencing certainly did not measure up. This was very unimpressive.

"Not only did the man of God fail to come out," said Naaman, "but he sent a mere servant to tell me to bathe in the Jordan. Are not the rivers of Damascus better than all the waters in Israel? May I not wash in

---

[467] Rimmon means "pomegranate." Its use here (2 Kings 5:18) is perhaps an abbreviation for Hadad-rimmon, Hadad being the sun god of the Syrians. Combining the sun god with the pomegranate, as Hadad-rimmon, would represent the sun god of the late summer, who ripens the pomegranate and other fruits (see William Smith, *Dictionary of the Bible*, *GospeLink*, CD-ROM, s.v. "Rimmon").

[468] See story "158—King Ahab Is Slain in Battle." A Jewish tradition at least as old as the time of Josephus, and which may very well be genuine, identifies Naaman as the archer whose arrow struck King Ahab with his mortal wound, and thus gave deliverance to Syria. The expression in 2 Kings 5:1: "because that by him the LORD had given deliverance to Syria," is interesting. Perhaps Naaman, in delivering his country, had not only slain a man who was the enemy to Syria but who was also an enemy to Jehovah (see William Smith, *Dictionary of the Bible*, *GospeLink*, CD-ROM, s.v. "Naaman").

[469] Or what we now know as the Sea of Galilee.

[470] A talent of silver was equivalent to 3,000 shekels and would have weighed slightly more than 75.5 pounds (34.29 kilograms). The ten talents of silver would have weighed 756 pounds (342.9 kilograms).

them and be clean?" So Naaman turned and went away in a rage. It was apparent that the only reasonable thing for him to do was to return to Damascus as quickly as possible. It was bad enough that he had to cross the Jordan on his way home. But wash himself in it?

Then one of Naaman's servants came near to him and offered wise counsel. "My father," said the servant, "if Israel's prophet had asked you to do some great thing, would you not have done it? How much better is it then that he should simply say, 'Wash and be clean'?"

Seeing the logic of his servant's words, Naaman humbled himself and went down and washed seven times in the Jordan, in accordance with Elisha's instructions. And on the seventh time, his flesh became again like the flesh of a child. The leper was clean!

Naaman the leper washes in the Jordan

Naaman returned immediately to Samaria to find Elisha. And as he stood before Elisha, he declared, "Now I know that there is no God in all the earth but in Israel. Now, therefore, please accept the gifts that I have brought."

"As Jehovah lives before whom I stand," said Elisha, "I will receive no gift." And when Naaman urged him to take the gifts, he still refused.

Then Naaman said, "Have your servants, then, give me as much of the soil of Israel as two mules can carry. For I will worship Jehovah on this soil in Syria. And, from this day forward, I will offer neither burnt offering nor sacrifice to any other god. And may Jehovah pardon me when I go with my king to the house of Rimmon when he goes to worship and leans upon my hand."

"Depart in peace," said Elisha.

This should have been the end of the story, but the situation took a tragic turn. Elisha's servant Gehazi was tempted to take advantage of Naaman's good will and enrich himself. He said to himself, "I will run after the Syrian and take a little of what he offered."

When Naaman saw Gehazi running after him, he stopped his chariot and stepped down to meet him. "Is all well?" inquired Naaman.

"Yes, all is well," Gehazi assured him, "but my master has sent me to you because two young men have just come from Mount Ephraim and he would like a talent of silver and two changes of clothing for each of them."

"It is a worthy cause," answered Naaman. "You should take two talents of silver for each of them." And he bound up two bags, each with two talents of silver and two changes of clothing, and he had two of his servants carry them back to Samaria for Gehazi.[471]

When Gehazi came to the tower, he relieved the men of their burdens and sent them back to Naaman. After he had put the bags into the house, he hurried in to see Elisha, hoping that his master had not noticed his absence.

"Where have you been?" Elisha quizzed him.

"Nowhere," Gehazi lied. Certainly he could get away with this.

But Elisha was well aware of what Gehazi had done. "Did your heart not go with you when the man of Syria turned from his chariot to meet you?" he asked. "Is it time to receive money and clothing and other gifts? Because of what you have done, Gehazi, the leprosy of Naaman shall cleave to you and to your seed forever."

And Gehazi went out from Elisha's presence a leper, as white as snow.

---

[471] Gehazi was given more than 300 pounds (136 kilograms) of silver by Naaman to take back for the "two young men" from Mount Ephraim.

167—THE FLOATING AX HEAD
(2 Kings 6)

The quarters where the sons of the prophets[472] were living became inadequate for their needs, so they asked Elisha if he would agree to their building new facilities and moving. "Let us go unto the Jordan and make a place for us there," they said to Elisha. "We will be able to cut the timber and build the place ourselves."

"You may go," said Elisha.

"Will you go with us?" one of them asked.

"I will go," he responded.

So all of them went down to the Jordan, where they commenced cutting wood for their new dwelling place. And as one man was felling a tree, the head of his ax came off and dropped into the river. He was greatly alarmed by the incident because the ax he was using was borrowed.

When he called out to Elisha, Elisha asked him where it had fallen. When the man had shown him the place where the ax head had fallen, Elisha cut a stick that he threw into the water in that place. And as soon as the stick was in the river, the ax head floated to the top of the water where it was easily retrieved.

---

[472] Those identified as sons of the prophets were, no doubt, associated with one of the schools of the prophets such as had been established in Israel since the time of Samuel. Story "106—A Victim of Saul's Jealousy" refers to such a school at Naioth in Ramah where David and Samuel went to live when David was fleeing from King Saul.

168—THOSE WHO ARE WITH US
(2 Kings 6)

Syria was a constant thorn in Israel's side. Once again King Ben-hadad II and his army came to war against Israel. But when Ben-hadad made a camp for his army, Jehovah told Elisha the location of the camp, and Elisha, in turn, passed the information along to Jehoram, the king of Israel. No matter where the Syrians camped, their encampment was attacked by Israel's army. And after Jehoram and his army had attacked the Syrian encampment several times, Ben-hadad became suspicious that there might be a traitor in his own camp who betrayed their location to Israel. "Show me," he said to his servants, "which one of us is for the king of Israel."

"It is none of us," replied one of the servants, "but Elisha the prophet. Elisha knows everything. He is able to tell Jehoram the words that you speak in your bedchamber."

"Find out where this man is, that I may send for him," demanded Ben-hadad. And in response to Ben-hadad's demand, it was revealed that Elisha was at Dothan.[473]

Ben-hadad, who—for the sake of his army's survival—was very serious about eliminating Elisha. He sent horses, chariots, and a great army to surround Dothan at night. And when Elisha's servant arose in the morning and saw the Syrian hosts surrounding them, he was filled with fear. "What shall we do?" he asked Elisha.

"Do not be afraid," answered Elisha. "Those who are with us are more than those who are with them." (15)

Then Elisha prayed, saying, "O Lord Jehovah, open the eyes of my servant that he may see." And when the eyes of the young servant were opened, he saw that the mountain was filled with horses and with chariots of fire all around Elisha.

When the Syrian host began to close in on him, Elisha prayed again. "O Lord Jehovah," he prayed, "smite these people with blindness." And the great army of Syrians was stricken with blindness in answer to Elisha's petition.

Elisha then went down and spoke to the sightless army. "This is not the way, neither is this the city you seek," he told them. "Follow me and I will lead you to the man you seek."

---

[473] Dothan, the place of Elisha's residence, was twelve miles (19.3 kilometers) north of the city of Samaria.

Elisha then led the blind Syrians to the city of Samaria, taking them inside the city walls. Once they were all inside the city, Elisha prayed again. "O Jehovah," he said, "open these men's eyes that they may see." And, when their eyes were opened, they saw that they were inside the city of Samaria and that the man who had led them there was Elisha.

When King Jehoram saw the Syrian army inside his city walls and completely within his control, he asked Elisha, "Shall I smite them?"

"Oh no," replied Elisha. "Would you smite those whom you have taken captive? Set food and water before them that they may eat and drink and then return to their master." So a bounteous meal was set before the Syrian army that day, and, when they had eaten, they were released to return to King Ben-hadad's camp.

169—BY THIS TIME TOMORROW

(2 Kings 6–7)

Life in Samaria had become extremely difficult. There was severe famine because Ben-hadad II of Syria and his army had besieged the city. Food had essentially run out and the people were desperate. They ate whatever they could find that might give nourishment, or at least fill their stomachs. Even the head of an ass sold for eight pieces of silver and a quarter cab of doves' dung[474] for five pieces of silver.

As King Jehoram walked on the broad wall of the city, he heard the cries of a frenzied woman: "Help me, O King!"

The king was distraught and wondered if they were all doomed to die. "If Jehovah does not help you, how is it possible that I can?" he asked the woman in frustration. "There is nothing either on the barn floor or in the winepress."

Then in a more rational tone, he questioned the woman further. "What is the cause of your distress?" he asked.

The woman's answer was shocking. It showed the depths of hopelessness to which the people of Samaria had sunk. "Another woman came to me," she explained, "and asked that I give my son that we might eat him. She said that we would eat my son that day and then eat her son the next day. So we boiled my son and ate him. But on the next day, when I asked that she give her son that we might eat him, she hid her son so that he could not be found."

When King Jehoram heard this revolting story, he tore his clothes and put sackcloth next to his skin. He

---

[474] A cab was an ancient Hebrew measure of slightly less than two quarts. It is not likely that doves' dung was actually eaten. William Smith cites various authorities to provide different possible explanations. One suggests that the item referred to is *cicer* or "chickpea," which the Arabs call *usnan*, and sometimes improperly "dove's dung" or "sparrow's dung." He says that some later authorities think it was the bulbous root of the star-of-Bethlehem (*Ornithogalum umbellatum*), a common edible root in Palestine (see William Smith, *Dictionary of the Bible*, *GospeLink*, CD-ROM, s.v. "dove's dung"). Edersheim and others suggest that doves' dung was the actual commodity, but that it was dried and used to make fires for cooking (see Alfred Edersheim, *Old Testament Bible History*, *GospeLink*, CD-ROM [Salt Lake City: Deseret Book Co., 2001], vol. VI, ch. 13).

knew the situation was desperate, but how could a mother—no matter what her state of mind—make a public appeal to the king for the second woman to keep her part of this evil bargain?

In his sorry state of mind, Jehoram was convinced that the prophet Elisha was somehow responsible for all of Israel's distress. And he felt that something should be done about it. In his anguish he said to the people, "May God do so to me and more also if Elisha the son of Shaphat does not give up his head today."

As Elisha sat in his place talking with the elders of Israel, the king sent a messenger to slay him. But before the man arrived, Elisha said to the elders, "You will soon see how the son of a murderer has sent a man to take my head. When that man comes in, shut the door and hold him here, for the feet of his master will not be far behind."

While Elisha yet spoke, the king's messenger arrived at the door, where the elders stopped him. Then the king came soon behind him, as Elisha had promised, and entered the house. As King Jehoram came in, he said to Elisha, "This evil is of Jehovah. Why should I wait any longer for him to give us relief?"

"You must not despair," responded Elisha. "Jehovah has told me that by this time tomorrow a measure of fine flour shall be sold at the gate of Samaria for a shekel, and two measures of barley shall also be sold for a shekel."

An aide who accompanied the king now spoke up, ridiculing all that Elisha had said. "Only if Jehovah should make windows in heaven could such a thing be," he said in disdain.

"You shall see it with your own eyes," said Elisha to the man, "but, because of your unbelief, you shall not partake of the bounty."

At the same time there were four lepers sitting at the city gate who talked among themselves. "Why do we just sit here and wait to die?" asked one. "If we enter the city we will die there from the famine, and if we sit here we will die also. Therefore, let us go out to the army of the Syrians. If the Syrians save our lives then we shall live, but if they kill us we shall but die." The lepers could see that the worst thing that the Syrians could do to them was take their lives, but they knew they would also die in the exercise of any other available option. So the men arose at twilight and went out to the Syrian camp.

When they arrived, they found the camp deserted. The horses and the asses were all still there—also the tents and all the goods—but not one living soul besides themselves.

Jehovah had caused the Syrian army to hear a great noise, a noise that sounded to them like horses and chariots and the marching of a great army. And, when they heard it, they said to one another, "The king of Israel has hired the kings of the Hittites and the Egyptians, and their armies are now coming upon us." And in their hysteria, the Syrians fled for their lives in the twilight, leaving everything behind.

The lepers did not know why the camp was deserted, but they were glad to see it empty. They went into one tent where they ate and drank, then carried out silver, gold, and clothing, which they hid. Then they returned and carried treasure out from a second tent. This was entirely too easy, and they began to be concerned. They said to each other: "What we are doing here is not good. This is indeed a day of good tidings and we are keeping it all to ourselves. If we wait here until morning, some mischief will surely befall us because of our selfishness. We must go and tell the king's household what we have found."

The four lepers hurried to the man who kept the city gate and said to him, "We went out to the camp of the Syrians and found no one there. But their horses and asses are there and their tents are still standing." And the gatekeeper gave this message to those who guarded the king's palace.

When King Jehoram heard the strange news, he feared that the Syrians were seeking to trick them and create a trap. Rising from his bed, he said to his servants, "Let me tell you what the Syrians are doing to us. Because they know we are hungry, they have gone out of their camp to hide in the field. Then, when we come out to loot their camp, they think to take us as prisoners and capture our city."

Then one of the servants spoke. "That may be so," he said, "but let us test them. Instead of all of us going out to loot the camp, first send five men with horses to discover the situation, for the Syrians are a great multitude."

Instead of five men with horses, King Jehoram sent out two chariots. And the charioteers followed the trail of the fleeing Syrians as far as the Jordan, finding the trail strewn with clothing and vessels that the army had dropped or cast aside in its hasty retreat.

When the men returned with their chariots and told the king what they had seen, all of Samaria went out to take spoils from the Syrian camp. And so it was that a measure of fine flour sold at the city gate for a shekel and two measures of barley for a shekel, just as Elisha had prophesied.

King Jehoram appointed the aide who had been with him in Elisha's house to take charge of the city gate, but the man was trampled by the rush of people. He died having seen the fulfillment of Elisha's prophecy with his own eyes but without partaking of the bounty.

170−THE MURDER OF BEN-HADAD
(2 Kings 8)

When Elisha the prophet journeyed to Damascus, King Ben-hadad II of Syria learned that he was there and sent Hazael to meet him with bounteous gifts. Ben-hadad did so because he was sick and wanted Hazael to ask Elisha if he would recover from his sickness. Ben-hadad was well aware of Elisha's powers because of previous experiences.[475]

When Hazael had asked Elisha the king's question, Elisha replied, "Tell your king that he may certainly recover from his disease. Nevertheless, Jehovah has shown me that he shall surely die." And when Elisha had said this, he looked very solemn and began to weep.

"Why do you weep?" asked Hazael.

"Because," replied Elisha, "Jehovah has shown me the evil that you will do to the children of Israel. I have seen that you will set their strongholds on fire, slay their young men with the sword, dash their children, and rip up the women who are with child."

"Am I a dog," asked Hazael, "that I should do such terrible things?"

"Jehovah has shown me that you shall become king of Syria," replied Elisha.[476]

When Hazael returned to his master, King Ben-hadad, he reported to the ailing king that Elisha had said that he could surely recover from his disease. Then, on the following day, Hazael spread a thick wet cloth over the sick king's face and caused him to die.

And when King Ben-hadad II was dead, Hazael was made king of Syria according to Elisha's prophecy.

---

[475] Among other things, Elisha had healed Ben-hadad's servant Naaman of leprosy (see story "166−The Healing of Naaman") and he had created serious problems for the Syrian army when they had attempted to invade Israel (see story "168−Those Who Are with Us").

[476] In 1 Kings 19:15, Jehovah told the prophet Elijah to go to Damascus and anoint Hazael to be king of Syria. The scriptures, however, do not indicate when or if that anointing ever took place. It appears that it probably did (see story "155−A Still, Small Voice").

171−THE WICKEDNESS OF JEHORAM
(2 Kings 8; 2 Chronicles 21)

Under the rule of Asa and Jehoshaphat, the kingdom of Judah was righteous and turned away from the worship of idols. That situation changed, however, when Jehoshaphat died and his eldest son Jehoram became king of Judah in his place.[477] Jehoram was quite a different man than his father. In fact, he was far more wicked than his counterpart by the same name in the kingdom of Israel. He seemed to have no inclination at all toward righteousness. One of his first official acts as king was to kill his six younger brothers with the sword. He also killed many of the princes of Judah.[478]

Perhaps Jehoram was the kind of man who might have been righteous under different circumstances, but when he married Athaliah, the daughter of King Ahab and Queen Jezebel of the kingdom of Israel, his evil nature had just the encouragement it needed to flourish. Jehoram brought the false gods of his wife's family into Judah and created high places[479] in the mountains. His wickedness caused all Judah to be unfaithful to Jehovah.

During Jehoram's wicked reign, he received a written message from the prophet Elijah that was very unsettling to him, but it did not cause him to repent. The message said that because Jehoram had departed from the ways of his fathers, Asa and Jehoshaphat, and had made the people of Judah serve the gods of Ahab, and because he had slain his brothers—who were much better men than he was—Jehovah would smite him with a sickness that would cause his bowels to fall out.

---

[477] This king is identified as Jehoram in 2 Chronicles 21, but in 2 Kings 8 he is called Joram. It should also be noted that 2 Kings 8 has his reign in the kingdom of Judah overlap part of the reign of his father Jehoshaphat rather than beginning at his father's death. In this story, I have followed the Chronicles account.

[478] Though the scripture (2 Chronicles 21:4) says that Jehoram killed many of the princes of Israel, that is not likely under the circumstances.

[479] When the children of Israel came into the promised land, they set up community places of worship, including altars, on the tops of hills. These were called high places. Many of these altars were desecrated when Israel forsook Jehovah to worship false gods. Later, especially after the temple was built in Jerusalem, many of the leaders sought to get rid of these high places. Some, as shown here, were especially created for the worship of false gods.

Jehovah also created other problems for Judah because of Jehoram's wickedness; he stirred up the Philistines and the Arabians against them and their king. When these peoples invaded Jerusalem, they not only carried away all that was valuable in the king's palace, but also the king's wives and his sons. The only one to escape was his youngest son Ahaziah.[480]

Elijah's prophecy concerning the disease in Jehoram's bowels was fulfilled to the letter. The disease was incurable and, after he had suffered for two years, his bowels fell out and he died.

Though Jehoram had reigned in Judah for eight years, there was no mourning for him in Judah when he died, and no spices were burned for him according to the usual custom at the death of a king. He was buried in the City of David but not in the sepulchers of the kings. And, when he was dead, his son Ahaziah—at the age of twenty-two[481]—became king of Judah.

172—THE BEGINNING OF THE END FOR THE HOUSE OF AHAB
(2 Kings 9; 2 Chronicles 22)

Ahaziah became king of Judah upon the death of his father Jehoram, but the quality of Ahaziah's reign was no better than his father's had been. He too walked in the ways of Ahab and promoted the sins of Israel in the kingdom of Judah. Yet Jehovah did not destroy Judah because of his promise to King David.[482]

King Ahaziah's mother was Athaliah, the daughter of King Ahab, so King Jehoram[483] of Israel was Ahaziah's uncle. And Judah was induced by Jehoram to join Israel in their war against King Hazael of Syria at Ramoth-gilead.

When King Jehoram was wounded in battle, he went to Jezreel to recover. And Ahaziah made the trip to Jezreel to visit his ailing uncle.

At this same time, the prophet Elisha sent a messenger—one of the sons of the prophets[484]—to Israel's battle headquarters at Ramoth-gilead. Elisha instructed the young man to take Jehu, the son of Jehoshaphat,[485] into an inner chamber and anoint him king of Israel. "And when you have anointed him," Elisha told the man, "open the door and flee."[486]

Jehu was a captain in King Jehoram's army, and when the young messenger came to Ramoth-gilead and

---

[480] In 2 Chronicles 21:17, Ahaziah is identified by the name Jehoahaz. In all other places he is called Ahaziah, as he is called in this story.

[481] 2 Chronicles 22:2 says that Ahaziah was forty-two years old when he began to reign in Judah, but that error was corrected by the Joseph Smith Translation to agree with 2 Kings 8:26. His father Jehoram was just forty years old at the time of his death (2 Chronicles 21:20).

[482] Jehovah's promise that the kingdom and house of David would be established forever is found in 2 Samuel 7:12–13, in 1 Chronicles 17:11–12, and in story "121—Your Son Shall Build My House."

[483] The scriptures sometimes refer to this king of Israel as Jehoram and sometimes as Joram. The name Jehoram has been used in all of these stories.

[484] Those identified as sons of the prophets were, no doubt, associated with one of the schools of the prophets such as had been established in Israel since the time of Samuel. Story "106—A Victim of Saul's Jealousy" refers to such a school at Naioth in Ramah.

[485] Note that Jehu's father Jehoshaphat is not the same man who was the righteous king of Judah. Jehoshaphat the king was the son of Asa, and all of his sons were slain by their brother Jehoram (see story "171—The Wickedness of Jehoram"). This Jehoshaphat, according to the scriptures, was the son of Nimshi.

[486] Jehovah had told the prophet Elijah on Mount Horeb that he was to go and anoint Jehu, the son of Nimshi (actually Nimshi's grandson), as king of Israel (see story "155—A Still, Small Voice"). There is no scriptural record of this anointing taking place.

found the captains sitting in council, he singled out Jehu from the group and took him into the house. Once in the house, he poured his box of oil upon Jehu's head and said to him, "Thus says Jehovah, God of Israel: 'I have anointed you to be king over the people of Jehovah, even over Israel. And you shall smite the house of Ahab, your master, that I may avenge the blood of my servants the prophets and the blood of all the servants of Jehovah who have died at the hands of Jezebel. For the whole house of Ahab shall perish. Indeed, I will make the house of Ahab like the house of Jeroboam and the house of Baasha.[487] The dogs shall eat Jezebel in Jezreel, and there shall be none to bury her.'"[488] His mission completed, the young prophet opened the door and fled, according to Elisha's charge.

When Jehu returned to his fellows, one of them spoke, asking, "Is everything well? Why did this mad fellow come for you?" And when Jehu told them that the young man had anointed him king of Israel, each man then took off his cloak and put it under Jehu at he top of the stairs. Then they blew their trumpets and shouted, "Jehu is king!"

Jehu and the other captains agreed that no one would go to Jezreel to tell King Jehoram what had happened before Jehu could go there himself—and that time soon came.

As Jehu and his men approached Jezreel in their chariots, the watchman on the tower of the city saw the company coming and told Jehoram. Jehoram sent a horseman out to meet them and ask if they came in peace.

When the horseman asked Jehu if he came in peace, Jehu replied, "What do you have to do with peace? Fall in behind me." And the horseman did.

When the watchman observed that the horseman was not returning but had joined the advancing party, a second horseman was sent. The result, however, was the same.

The watchman then said to Jehoram, "The horsemen you sent do not return and the man who leads this company appears to be Jehu, for he drives furiously." Jehoram, who had Ahaziah, the young king of Judah, with him, was now suspicious that something was amiss. The two kings quickly prepared their chariots and went out to meet the approaching troop. And they met them near the vineyard that had belonged to Naboth.[489]

"Have you come in peace, Jehu?" cried Jehoram.

"What peace can there be while the whoredoms and witchcraft of your mother are so many?" asked Jehu.

Great fear gripped the heart of Jehoram when he heard Jehu's mutinous reply, and he and Ahaziah both turned to flee from Jehu's treachery. As they retreated, Jehu drew his bow with full strength and shot an arrow into Jehoram's back. The arrow went through his heart, and he sank down in his chariot. As Jehoram fell, Jehu gave instructions to Bidkar, his captain. "Take up the body and cast it into Naboth's field," he said. "For remember how Jehovah laid the burden of Naboth's vineyard on Ahab when we rode in his army? And do you not remember also how Jehovah said to Ahab: 'Inasmuch as I have seen the blood of Naboth and his sons I will repay you in this plot'?"

When King Ahaziah saw what had happened to his uncle, King Jehoram, he fled past the garden house with Jehu in pursuit. And when Jehu gave instructions that Ahaziah should also be smitten, an arrow also struck him—and he died in Megiddo.[490] And Jehu and his men killed all those persons of the house of Ahab who served these two kings.

As Jehu and his men entered the city of Jezreel, Jezebel heard that he had come and looked out of her window. When Jehu looked up and saw Jezebel there, he called out, "Who is on my side?" And two or three eunuchs appeared immediately at the window behind her.

"Throw her down!" shouted Jehu to the eunuchs—and they did so. When Jezebel hit the ground, her blood splattered on the wall and on the horses. But Jehu and his men did not stop for her. Instead, they trod her body under their feet and under the hooves of their horses as they went on into the city to eat.

When Jehu and his troop had eaten and refreshed themselves, Jehu sent men to bury Jezebel. "Go see this cursed woman and bury her," he commanded, "for she is a king's daughter." But when the men returned to the place where Jezebel had fallen, they found only her

---

[487] Concerning the judgments that befell the houses of Jeroboam and Baasha, see story "148—Prophecies against Jeroboam and Baasha Fulfilled."

[488] This prophecy about Jezebel's death is a reiteration of a prophecy made earlier by Elijah. See 1 Kings 21:23 and story "157—Naboth's Vineyard."

[489] See story "157—Naboth's Vineyard."

[490] This account of Ahaziah's death is based on the account in 2 Kings 9. In 2 Chronicles 22:9 it says that Jehu "sought Ahaziah; and they [Jehu's men] caught him, (for he was hid in Samaria,) and brought him to Jehu: and when they had slain him, they buried him: Because, said they, he is the [grand]son of Jehoshaphat, who sought the LORD with all his heart."

skull, her feet, and the palms of her hands. She had been eaten by dogs, according to the prophecies.[491]

173−JEHU'S SACRIFICE TO BAAL

(2 Kings 10; 2 Chronicles 22)

Jehoram, king of Israel, and his nephew Ahaziah, king of Judah, were both dead, having been slain by Jehu. Queen Jezebel was also dead, and her body had been eaten by dogs in the streets of Jezreel. Elijah's prophecy concerning the destruction of King Ahab's family was well on its way to being fulfilled.[492]

Jehu was unrelenting in his pursuit of Ahab's descendants. Those who were responsible for the care of Ahab's seventy sons were afraid of Jehu and agreed to do whatever he asked of them. Thus, Jehu's instructions to them were fulfilled when they delivered the heads of all seventy to him in baskets at Jezreel. Jehu had his servants stack the heads of Ahab's sons overnight in two great heaps at the city gates. Then, in the morning, he went out and stood by them and said to the people, "You should observe that nothing that Jehovah has spoken concerning the house of Ahab will be left unfulfilled. For all that Jehovah promised by the mouth of his servant Elijah is now being fulfilled."

Jehu then proceeded to slay all that remained of the house of Ahab in Jezreel—not only Ahab's family but also his chief servants and his priests. When he was finished in Jezreel, he returned to Samaria, meeting and slaying on his way forty-two of Ahaziah's relatives who had not received word of Ahaziah's death and were traveling to Jezreel to see him.

En route to Samaria, Jehu also encountered Jehonadab the Rechabite[493] who had come to meet him.

---

[492] The prophecy concerning the destruction of Ahab's family (or house) is found in 1 Kings 21:17–24 and is recounted in story "157−Naboth's Vineyard"). It is also reiterated in 2 Kings 9:7–10 (see story "172−The Beginning of the End for the House of Ahab). The account of the deaths of these two wicked kings is found in story "172−The Beginning of the End for the House of Ahab."

[493] Jehonadab (or Jonadab, as the scriptures sometimes refer to him) was chief of the Rechabites, an Arab tribe that worshipped Jehovah. The house of Rechab is identified with a section of the Kenites, a Midianite tribe who came into Canaan with the Israelites but retained their nomadic habits. They worshipped Jehovah and were circumcised, though they were not looked upon as belonging to Israel and probably did not consider themselves bound by Mosaic law and ritual. The worship of Baal was offensive to them. They were not to drink wine, build houses, sow seed, or have vineyards. They

---

[491] See footnote 492 in story "173−Jehu's Sacrifice to Baal."

239

Jehonadab agreed to support Jehu in his campaign against the house of Ahab and the two men rode to Samaria together in Jehu's chariot. Once in Samaria, they united to slay all of Ahab's family who remained there.

With this accomplished, Jehu gathered the people of Samaria for a speech—a speech filled with subtlety and aimed at destroying all those who worshipped Baal.[494] "Ahab served Baal a little," Jehu told the gathered throng, "but Jehu will serve him much. I will show you how much if you will call to me all the prophets of Baal, all his servants, and all his priests. Let none of them be absent, for I have a great sacrifice to make to Baal; those who do not come shall be put to death." Jehu sent throughout all Israel, inviting the prophets and priests of Baal and every worshipper of Baal to a holy gathering in Samaria. And there was not one person in Israel who worshipped Baal that did not come.

The house of Baal was filled to capacity, and Jehu had the man in charge of the vestry provide sacred clothing for every person who came to worship. When all were gathered and properly clothed, Jehu and Jehonadab came into the house, before the vast congregation, and tested them one more time. "Search and make sure," they cried, "that none of the servants of Jehovah are here. This gathering is for only those who worship Baal."

When Jehu and Jehonadab went in to offer sacrifices and burnt offerings, they appointed eighty men outside to make sure that no one who was inside escaped. "If any of these men whom I have brought into your hands escapes," Jehu warned, "the life of him who allows the escape shall be taken."

When Jehu's sacrifice and burnt offering were ended, his plan was put into full effect as he commanded the guards and the captains to enter the house and slay all those who were there. When all the Baal worshippers were dead, Jehu's men next proceeded to burn all of the idols of Baal that were in the city. They broke down the image of Baal as well as the house of Baal. The worship of Baal was destroyed and banished out of Israel that day.

When Jehu had completed the destruction of the house of Ahab and all those who worshipped Baal, Jehovah spoke to him. "Because you have done that which is right in my eyes and have done unto the house of Ahab according to all that was in my heart," said Jehovah, "your children shall sit on Israel's throne to the fourth generation."[495]

Jehu reigned over Israel for twenty-eight years. But, though he ended the worship of Baal in the kingdom, Jehu still clung to the sins of Jeroboam and failed to walk according to God's laws. The golden calves set up by Jeroboam in Dan and Beth-el still remained in their places.[496]

---

were to dwell all their days in tents (see Jeremiah 35:6, 7). All of these things they did in an effort to retain their distinct tribal existence (see William Smith, *Dictionary of the Bible*, *GospeLink*, CD-ROM, s.v. "Re'chab").

[494] Baal (plural form Baalim), the storm and fertility god, was symbolic of the male generative principle in nature. Baal worship was most common among the Zidonians or Phoenicians, the people to whom Ahab's wife Jezebel belonged.

[495] The fulfillment of this four-generation prophecy is noted in story "180−The End of Israel Is in Sight."
[496] Story "143−Israel Divided" explains why King Jeroboam, the first king of divided Israel, set up the golden calves at Dan and Beth-el for the worship of his people.

174—FAREWELL TO ATHALIAH

(2 Kings 11; 2 Chronicles 22–23)

The house of Ahab and the worship of Baal[497] had both been eliminated from the kingdom of Israel—Jehu had seen to that[498]—but there were still serious problems in the kingdom of Judah. Athaliah, the mother of King Ahaziah and daughter of Ahab and Jezebel, was very much alive and making her presence felt.

When Athaliah learned of the death of her son Ahaziah, she acted quickly to have all of Ahaziah's sons—the royal heirs—killed, because she had her own plans for the kingdom of Judah. One son, however, a one-year-old child named Joash,[499] together with his nurse, was saved from Athaliah's murderous edict by Ahaziah's sister Jehosheba[500] and hidden in the temple for six years.

With the heirs to the throne out of the way, as Athaliah supposed, she usurped the throne for herself and reigned as queen of Judah. After six years, however, Jehoiada the priest devised a scheme with the priests and the army of Judah to overthrow Athaliah and crown young Joash as their king. Using as weapons the shields and spears of King David that were in the temple, the soldiers and the priests secured the temple, surrounded the boy, put the crown on his head, and gave him the Divine charge.[501] Then, when they had anointed Joash their king, they clapped their hands and shouted, "May the king live!"

When Athaliah heard the noise coming from the temple, she came to see the reason for the commotion. What she saw caught her completely by surprise. There was a young boy standing by the pillar of the temple where, according to custom, he was being made king. The princes and the trumpeters were by his side, the trumpets blowing and the people rejoicing in their new seven-year-old king.

"Treason! Treason!" screamed Athaliah as she tore her clothes and fled in fear for her life.

When Jehoiada the priest heard Athaliah's rantings and thus became aware of her presence, he commanded the captains and officers of the army to keep her between their ranks, to follow her out of the temple, and then to slay her with the sword. "But do not shed her blood in the temple," he cautioned them.

When Athaliah was outside the temple, she was slain in the horse gate of the king's palace. And all the people of the land went into the house of Baal that day, tearing down both the house and its altars, breaking the images of Baal into small pieces, and slaying the priest.

---

[497] Baal (plural form Baalim), the storm and fertility god, was symbolic of the male generative principle in nature. Baal worship was most common among the Zidonians or Phoenicians and was brought into the kingdom of Judah by Athaliah, the daughter of King Ahab of the kingdom of Israel and his Phoenician wife Jezebel.

[498] Much of Jehu's destruction of the family and descendants of Ahab is detailed in stories "172—The Beginning of the End for the House of Ahab" and "173—Jehu's Sacrifice to Baal." The completion of that destruction, in fulfillment of the prophecies, is told in this story.

[499] The scriptures give this young man's name variously as Joash and Jehoash. He is called Joash in this and subsequent stories.

[500] 2 Chronicles 22 calls this woman Jehoshabeath.

[501] The Divine charge to the kings is found in Deuteronomy 17:14–20. It reads as follows:

> 14 When thou art come unto the land which the LORD thy God giveth thee, and shalt possess it, and shalt dwell therein, and shalt say, I will set a king over me, like as all the nations that *are* about me;

> 15 Thou shalt in any wise set *him* king over thee, whom the LORD thy God shall choose: *one* from among thy brethren shalt thou set king over thee: thou mayest not set a stranger over thee, which *is* not thy brother.

> 16 But he shall not multiply horses to himself, nor cause the people to return to Egypt, to the end that he should multiply horses: forasmuch as the LORD hath said unto you, Ye shall henceforth return no more that way.

> 17 Neither shall he multiply wives to himself, that his heart turn not away: neither shall he greatly multiply to himself silver and gold.

> 18 And it shall be, when he sitteth upon the throne of his kingdom, that he shall write him a copy of this law in a book out of *that which is* before the priests the Levites:

> 19 And it shall be with him, and he shall read therein all the days of his life: that he may learn to fear the LORD his God, to keep all the words of this law and these statutes, to do them:

> 20 That his heart be not lifted up above his brethren, and that he turn not aside from the commandment, *to* the right hand, or *to* the left: to the end that he may prolong *his* days in his kingdom, he, and his children, in the midst of Israel.

As noted in story "142—Because You Have Broken My Covenant," it was Solomon's failure to keep this charge that led to his downfall. He multiplied to himself horses (i.e., military power), wives, and silver and gold.

Officers were appointed from among the priests and the Levites of Judah to be over the house of the Lord, and gatekeepers—or porters—were stationed there so that only those who were worthy could enter.

Young Joash was brought down to the king's palace that day to sit on the throne of the kings. And Jehoiada the priest swore a covenant between Jehovah, the king, and the people of Judah that they would be Jehovah's people.

175—KING JOASH FORSAKES JEHOVAH
(2 Kings 12; 2 Chronicles 24)

King Joash[502] was only seven years old when he began to reign in Judah at the overthrow and death of his grandmother Athaliah.[503] Under the guidance of Jehoiada the priest, Joash was a righteous king and was loved by his people. His great desire was to repair the temple and restore its vessels, because the sons of Athaliah had broken up the house of the Lord and taken its dedicated tools and vessels into the house of Baal.

Joash charged the priests and the Levites to go throughout the land and collect money for the temple repairs, but the process was very slow and Joash became discouraged. To expedite the collections, he commanded Jehoiada to make a chest, with a hole in the top, which he placed near the altar at the temple entrance, and called on the people to make their donations there.

Once the collection box was in place, Joash sent a proclamation throughout the land telling the people that they were being asked to make contributions for the temple just as Moses had requested of the children of Israel in the wilderness at Sinai.[504] The people rejoiced in this opportunity, and money for the temple was donated in great abundance. The money collected was given to the craftsmen to complete their work and, when the work was finished, Joash and Jehoiada used the surplus to make the tools and vessels required for temple service.[505]

Joash served faithfully and well while Jehoiada the priest was alive. But after Jehoiada's death, Joash was influenced by the princes of Judah to walk in strange paths. He departed from his worship in the house of the Lord to worship groves[506] and idols.

---

[502] The scriptures refer to this king as both Joash and Jehoash. For consistency, however, he is called Joash in all stories where he is mentioned.

[503] See story "174—Farewell to Athaliah."

[504] See story "59—The Tabernacle."

[505] The story at this point, where it says that they made vessels for use in the temple, is based on the account in 2 Chronicles 24. In 2 Kings 13 it says that no vessels were made and that the surplus money was given to the workmen. There are also other significant disagreements between these two accounts of King Joash's life.

[506] Groves in the Old Testament were living trees or treelike poles, set up as objects of worship, and were generally associated with fertility rites and sexual im-

When the people of Judah followed Joash's bad example and began also to fall away from the truth, Jehovah—in his great displeasure—sent prophets among them to testify of the truth. But the people of Judah would not hear them.

One such prophet was Zechariah,[507] the son of Jehoiada the priest. When the Spirit of Jehovah came upon Zechariah, he stood up in the midst of the people and called on them to repent. "Why do you break Jehovah's commandments?" he asked. "For in doing so you cannot prosper. Because you have forsaken Jehovah, he has also forsaken you."

Joash reached the low point of his reign when, in the court of the temple, he commanded the people to stone Zechariah. Unfortunately, Joash had a short memory and forgot the kindness that had been shown to him by Jehoiada the priest, Zechariah's father.

Near the end of the year when Zechariah was stoned, a small army of Syrians came against the city of Jerusalem, and Jehovah delivered Judah's much larger army into their hands. As the spoils of his victory, Hazael, the Syrian king, took all the treasures of the kings of Judah and the hallowed vessels and treasures of the temple. Joash was badly wounded in the battle and, as he lay on his sick bed, his servants conspired against him because of the blood of Zechariah. Joash was murdered in his bed after reigning in Judah for forty years.

176—THE ARROW OF JEHOVAH'S DELIVERANCE
(2 Kings 13)

In the twenty-third year of the reign of King Joash, son of Ahaziah, in the kingdom of Judah, King Jehu of Israel died, leaving the throne of the Northern Kingdom to his son Jehoahaz. Jehoahaz walked in the ways of Jeroboam[508] and did evil in the sight of Jehovah. Because Jehovah's anger was kindled against Jehoahaz and the kingdom of Israel for their wickedness, they were delivered into the hands of the Syrians and were greatly oppressed by King Hazael. The Syrian invasion was devastating. It left Jehoahaz's army with but fifty horsemen, ten chariots, and 10,000 footsoldiers. The Syrians beat down the people of Israel until they were like dust on the threshing floor.

Because of the oppression that Israel suffered at the hands of the Syrians, King Jehoahaz pleaded with Jehovah for deliverance. Jehovah answered Jehoahaz's prayers by sending a deliverer—but not during Jehoahaz's lifetime.

King Jehoahaz reigned in Israel for seventeen years, and when he died his son Jehoash[509] reigned in his place, having come to the throne in the thirty-seventh year of the reign of Joash, the son of Ahaziah, in Judah. King Jehoash followed in the pattern of wickedness that his father Jehoahaz had established.

During Jehoash's reign in Samaria, he fought against the kingdom of Judah and King Amaziah, the son of Joash. Jehoash was able to prevail over Judah and to cause great suffering in Jerusalem.[510]

The prophet Elisha was now a very old man. When he became sick, King Jehoash visited him and wept bitterly for the great prophet of God. "O my father, my father," cried Jehoash. "You are the chariot and the horsemen of Israel."

"Take your bow and your arrows," the aged prophet said to Jehoash.

---

morality. They were part of Baal worship and were symbolic of female fertility.

[507] Note that this prophet Zechariah, the son of Jehoiadah the priest lived much earlier than did the author of the book of Zechariah. It should also be noted that he is probably not the same Zechariah who is mentioned in story "178—Jeroboam's Success and Uzziah's Pride."

---

[508] He worshiped and maintained the golden calves that Jeroboam set up in Dan and Beth-el.

[509] The scriptures refer to this king of Israel as both Jehoash and Joash. This story, however, refers to him as Jehoash to give some distinction between him and the contemporaneous king of Judah who was also named Joash.

[510] A brief account of this battle with the kingdom of Judah and the events leading up to it is found in 2 Kings 14 and 2 Chronicles 25 (see story "177—Defeat on the Heels of Victory").

And when Jehoash had taken up his bow and removed several arrows from his quiver, Elisha continued: "Now put your hand on the bow as if to shoot it." And when Jehoash had done it, Elisha put his own hands on the bow on top of the king's hands.

"Now," said Elisha, "open the window toward the east."

And when the window lattice was removed, Elisha said, "Shoot an arrow!"[511]

When the arrow had been shot, Elisha then said, "That arrow is the arrow of Jehovah's deliverance of Israel from Syria. You shall smite the Syrians at Aphek until you have consumed them."

Elisha then gave further instructions to King Jehoash. "Take the arrows that remain in your hand and smite the ground with them," he said. And in response to these instructions, Jehoash struck the ground three times with the arrows in his hand.

Elisha was angry when Jehoash stopped striking the ground after only three times. "You should have struck five or six times," he exclaimed, "then you would be able to smite the Syrians until you consume them. But now you shall smite Syria but three times."

Jehovah was gracious to Israel and fulfilled the prophecy that Elisha had made to Jehoash. Though the people of Israel gave Jehovah great cause to mourn because they did not repent, he blessed them because of his covenant with Abraham, Isaac, and Jacob. Jehovah was not yet ready to cast the children of Israel out of his presence or to destroy them. Instead, he raised up Jehoash to deliver them from the hands of the Syrians.[512]

Upon the death of King Hazael, his son Ben-hadad III came to the Syrian throne, and Jehoash was able to prevail over Ben-hadad and his army. He defeated them three times and took back all the cities that King Hazael had captured during the reign of Jehoahaz. But, though Israel was delivered from her enemies, the people did not depart from the sins of Jeroboam, for they kept the golden calves in Beth-el and Dan and a grove[513] in Samaria. And Jehoash reigned in Samaria for sixteen years.

---

[511] The shooting of the arrow toward the east was symbolic because that was the direction of Syria.

[512] It appears that Jehoash and his son Jeroboam II were the deliverers that Jehovah raised up, as promised in 2 Kings 13:5. This story implies that if Jehoash had smitten the ground more times, he probably would have been able to complete the deliverance by himself.

[513] Groves in the Old Testament were living trees or treelike poles, set up as objects of worship, and were generally associated with fertility rites and sexual immorality. Groves were part of Baal worship and were symbolic of female fertility.

177—DEFEAT ON THE HEELS OF VICTORY
(2 Kings 14; 2 Chronicles 25)

In the second year after Jehoash became king of Israel, King Joash of Judah was slain by his servants in his own bed[514] and his son Amaziah inherited the throne of Judah. And King Amaziah slew the two men who murdered his father.

In many ways Amaziah was a good man in the beginning and he sought to be righteous, but he did not serve Jehovah with a perfect heart as King David had done. He failed to remove the high places from Judah and the people still used them as places of worship.[515]

As King Amaziah prepared his army for battle against the Edomites, he felt that his 300,000 choice men were not enough to assure his victory. To compensate and bolster the strength of his army, he hired 100,000 valiant men of Ephraim to join his forces. When he had done so, a man of God came to him and said, "Do not use these men of Ephraim in battle because Jehovah is not with Israel. If you use them to increase your strength for the battle, Jehovah will cause you to fall before your enemy, for he has power both to help and to cast down."

"If I do not take these men of Ephraim to battle with me," responded Amaziah, thinking of the dilemma in which he had placed himself, "what shall I do about the 100 talents of silver[516] that I have paid them?"

"The money is of no importance," replied the man of God. "Jehovah is able to give you much more than that." But when Amaziah dismissed the men of Ephraim from his service, they left in great anger, although they had been paid well for service they did not render.

---

[514] See story "175—King Joash Forsakes Jehovah."

[515] When the children of Israel came into the promised land, they set up community places of worship, including altars, on the tops of hills. These were called high places. Many of these altars were desecrated when Israel forsook Jehovah to worship false gods. After the temple was built in Jerusalem, many of the leaders sought to get rid of these high places as they tended to detract from the temple.

[516] A talent of silver weighed 3,000 shekels, or just more than 75.5 pounds (34.29 kilograms). Thus, 100 talents of silver would weigh about 7,560 pounds (3,429 kilograms), or nearly 3.8 tons (3.38 long tons or 3.43 metric tons).

Amaziah was successful in his war against Edom.[517] Jehovah blessed him and he was able to take their capital city of Selah, killing 20,000 men. But when Amaziah returned from the battle, he made a serious error. He brought with him the false gods of Edom and set them up where he could bow down to them and burn incense to them.

Amaziah's worship of false gods prompted Jehovah to send a prophet to call him to repentance. "Why have you sought after the gods of Edom?" asked the prophet. "Those gods could not deliver their own people out of your hands!"

Amaziah was greatly offended at the prophet's words. "Who has made you counsel to the king?" he asked the prophet. "Control your tongue!"

But the prophet spoke one last message to King Amaziah before he departed. "I will leave you," he said, "but I know this: God has determined to destroy you because you worship other gods and do not hearken to his counsel."

In the meantime, the soldiers of Ephraim—those whom Amaziah had earlier hired, then dismissed and sent home—attacked Judah, killing some 3,000 people and taking the spoils of battle. When Amaziah became aware of this unjust attack on his people, he challenged Jehoash and the kingdom of Israel to meet him in battle.

King Jehoash had no desire to fight Judah. He felt that Amaziah was overreacting—that Amaziah's quarrel was with the men of Ephraim and not with the whole kingdom of Israel. Hoping to calm the king of Judah and dissuade him from coming to battle, he sent Amaziah a message saying, "Your case is like that of the thistle who sent to the cedar in Lebanon asking for the cedar's daughter to marry his son. Then, when a wild beast came from Lebanon and trampled on the thistle, the thistle took vengeance on the cedar."

Jehoash's message continued: "Your heart lifts you up to boast because you have smitten the Edomites. But it would be better for you to stay home than to come to meddle with Israel and to fall, and all Judah fall with you."

King Joash's message to Amaziah went unheeded because it was Jehovah's will that he go to battle against Israel and be defeated—because he sought after the gods of Edom. As Amaziah attacked Israel and the battle ensued, Israel's army, under King Jehoash, defeated Judah soundly, inflicting great suffering and serious losses. The army of Israel broke down a large part of the wall of Jerusalem. They also took all the gold, the silver, and the sacred vessels from the temple and all the treasures of the king's palace. And many of the people of Judah were carried away as hostages.

And, because King Amaziah had turned away from Jehovah to worship the gods of Edom, a conspiracy arose against him in Jerusalem and he was finally slain at Lachish[518] after reigning in Judah for twenty-nine years.

_____

[517] The Edomites were descendants of Esau, the twin brother of Jacob. Though Israel and Edom were closely related, they seemed to share a mutual hatred.

[518] Lachish was a city lying south and west of Jerusalem. It had formerly been on the borders of Simeon and Judah, but was at this time part of the kingdom of Judah (see William Smith, *Dictionary of the Bible*, Gospe-Link, CD-ROM, s.v. "Lachish").

178—JEROBOAM'S SUCCESS AND UZZIAH'S PRIDE

(2 Kings 14–15; 2 Chronicles 26)

When Jehoash died, his son Jeroboam II came to the throne of Israel at Samaria. Jeroboam did evil in the sight of Jehovah and embraced the sins of the earlier king whose name he bore; the golden calves that had been set up for worship in Beth-el and Dan still remained.

Jeroboam, who reigned for forty-one years in Israel, was successful in liberating his people from the control of other countries. As his father Jehoash had smitten Syria, so did Jeroboam—but with far greater success. He was able to restore the borders of Israel from Hamath in upper Syria to the Dead Sea, as had been prophesied by the prophet Jonah, the son of Amittai.[519] Jehovah was aware of Israel's bitter afflictions and raised up Jeroboam, though not a righteous man, to be their deliverer.

In the twenty-seventh year of Jeroboam's reign over the Northern Kingdom, Uzziah[520]—at the age of sixteen—became king of Judah in place of his father Amaziah. Uzziah was a righteous man and did that which was right in the sight of Jehovah. He sought to follow Jehovah all the days of the prophet Zechariah.[521] Uzziah knew that Zechariah had knowledge of the visions of God, and Uzziah prospered as long as he followed him.

Uzziah assembled a great army, with 2,600 mighty men of valor and 307,500 footsoldiers. His army had much success against Judah's enemies, including the Philistines and the Arabians. He fortified Jerusalem and built towers both in the city and in the desert. Those whom he appointed to assist him and advise him were clever men who invented machines to shoot arrows and hurl great stones from his towers. Uzziah also bred cattle and dug many wells. He was an enterprising and prosperous king, and his fame spread as far as Egypt.

Because of Uzziah's successes, however, he came to suffer from a very serious affliction—pride! His heart became lifted up to his own destruction and he sinned against Jehovah. Although Uzziah had no priesthood authority, he believed that because he was the king he was entitled to do whatever he pleased. Thus, he took it upon himself to go into the temple to burn incense upon the temple altar.

Azariah the priest, along with eighty valiant priests, went into the temple after King Uzziah. There they confronted their king and told him, "This does not pertain to you, Uzziah. You have no authority to burn incense to Jehovah. This authority belongs only to those sons of Aaron who have been consecrated to do it. You must leave the sanctuary, for you have trespassed. And what you have done will bring you no honor before Jehovah."

Uzziah became very angry when challenged by the priests. But while he stood there in his anger—the censer in his hand—leprosy as white as snow rose up in his forehead. And as Azariah and the priests began to thrust him out, Uzziah himself hurried to leave the temple because Jehovah had smitten him.

King Uzziah was a leper for the rest of his life and lived in a separate house. He was separated from the house of the Lord and from the people of Judah, while his son Jotham acted as king in his behalf.

---

[519] We do not have the benefit of knowing specifically what Jonah prophesied, because this prophecy is not recorded in our scriptures. However, 2 Kings 14:25 refers to the prophecy's fulfillment. This, incidentally, is the same Jonah who would later be swallowed by a big fish.

[520] This king was called Uzziah in 2 Chronicles 26, but is identified as Azariah in 2 Kings 14 and 15. To avoid confusion, the name Uzziah is used in all of those stories where he is mentioned.

[521] Note that this prophet Zechariah lived much earlier than did the author of the book of Zechariah. It should also be noted that he is probably not the same Zechariah, the son of Jehoiada the priest, who was stoned by the authority of King Joash in 2 Chronicles 24:20–22. He was no doubt another prophet who lived at the time of King Uzziah's reign and should not be confused with either of the other prophets of the same name.

179–A LESSON FOR JONAH
(Jonah 1–4)

Nineveh, the capital city of Assyria, was a very wicked city, and Jonah, the son of Amittai, was not pleased when Jehovah called him to go there and preach the gospel. Thinking to escape Jehovah's call, Jonah fled to Joppa where he hoped to catch a ship to Tarshish.[522] Finding such a ship in port, he paid his fare and went on board, then went down deep into the ship's hold where he found a safe place to sleep.

Jehovah was fully aware of Jonah's intentions to avoid the call to Nineveh. He knew exactly where Jonah was. And, as the ship went out to sea, Jehovah sent a great wind upon the waters so that the ship was in danger of breaking up and sinking. The sailors became fearful of the tempest and threw their cargo overboard to lighten the ship's load, and each man cried unto his gods for deliverance. Meanwhile, Jonah lay fast asleep deep down inside the ship.

The ship's captain was angered because Jonah was sleeping while his crew members were praying for relief and fighting for their lives against the storm. He came down to Jonah's hiding place and awakened him. "What do you mean, O sleeper?" he asked angrily. "Arise and call upon your God to save us from a watery grave." Though the idea of praying had no appeal for a man who was trying to run away from Jehovah, Jonah made his way up to the main deck of the ship.

As the fury of the storm intensified, the crew decided to cast lots to discover who of those on board was to blame. And, when the lot fell upon Jonah, they confronted him. "Tell us the reason that this evil has come upon us," they demanded. "What is your occupation? Where have you come from? What is your country? And who are your people?" The questions came rapidly.

"I am a Hebrew," responded Jonah, "and I worship Jehovah, the God of heaven, who created both the sea and the dry land." When Jonah told them that he was fleeing from Jehovah's presence, the sailors were filled with great fear and concern.

"Why have you done this terrible thing?" they asked. "You have placed all of our lives in great jeopardy!" Then, seeking to take a practical approach to a very difficult problem, they asked Jonah, "Is there anything we can do to you that will calm the sea for us?"

"You can cast me into the sea," answered Jonah, for his heart was now also filled with fear. "I know that this tempest has come upon you because of me."

Jonah is cast overboard to quell the storm

The sailors were reluctant to throw Jonah overboard, even though they believed he had caused the storm. They rowed as hard as they could to bring the ship to land, but failed because of the storm's force. Not wanting to be responsible for Jonah's death, the sailors cried to Jehovah: "We beseech Thee, O Jehovah, let us not perish for this man's life. Neither lay upon us innocent blood, for Thou hast done as it pleased Thee."

Having thus prayed, the sailors reluctantly cast Jonah into the raging sea. As he went into the water, the storm ceased, and the sailors—being both alarmed and grateful—worshipped Jehovah, offering sacrifices to him and making solemn vows. Jonah, meanwhile, was swallowed by a great fish that Jehovah had prepared, and he remained in the belly of the fish.

Jonah was in great distress in the fish's belly and was moved to cry out to Jehovah, from whom he had sought to flee. "O Lord Jehovah!" he cried, "Thou hast cast me into the deep and into the midst of the seas. The floods have compassed me about and all Thy billows and Thy waves have passed over me. And though I have been cast out of Thy sight, I will yet look again toward Thy holy temple. And though I went to the bottoms of the mountains, yet Thou hast saved me from destruction. When my soul fainted within me, I remembered Thee, O Jehovah, and my prayer came up unto Thy holy temple."

Jonah continued his prayer, now even more fervently. "I know, O Lord Jehovah," he said "that those who follow after lying vanities forsake their own mercy. But I will sacrifice unto Thee with the voice of thanksgiving. I will pay that which I have vowed, for I know that salvation is from Thee!"

---

[522] According to *Bible Dictionary*, LDS-KJV, s.v. "Tarshish," this is probably Tartessus in Spain.

After three days and three nights, Jehovah caused the fish to vomit Jonah out upon dry land.

As Jonah recovered from his ordeal inside the fish, the voice of Jehovah came to him again and once more commanded him to go to Nineveh. "Arise and go to Nineveh, that great city," Jehovah said, "and preach to the people that which I commanded you."

Though Jonah still had some misgivings about preaching the gospel to a heathen people, he did as Jehovah commanded and took his journey to Nineveh.

Nineveh was a large city and it took three days for a man to walk from one end to the other. When Jonah had gone but one day's journey into the city, he began to cry repentance according to Jehovah's instructions. "Repent!" he warned them, "or Nineveh shall be overthrown in forty days."

Much to Jonah's surprise—and his dismay—the people of Nineveh listened to him and heeded his message. Turning their hearts to Jehovah, they proclaimed a fast and dressed in sackcloth and ashes—from the greatest to the least of them. Even the king of Nineveh took off his robes, covered himself with sackcloth, and sat in ashes. Then he published a decree throughout the city that none should eat or drink. "Let both man and beast be covered with sackcloth," the decree said, "and cry mightily to Jehovah. Yea, let every man turn from his evil ways and from the violence that is in his hands. For if we repent and turn unto Jehovah, who can tell but what he will turn his fierce anger away from us that we perish not?"

And when Jehovah saw that the people of Nineveh repented and turned from their evil works, he turned away the evil that he had prepared to bring upon them.

When Jonah learned that the city and the people would be spared the promised calamity because they had repented, he became angry. When he prayed to Jehovah he said, "Was this not what I said would happen before I fled for Tarshish? Was this not why I ran away? I knew that Thou art a merciful and gracious God. And because Thou art slow to anger and hast great kindness, I knew that Thou would revoke the calamity whether the people repented or not."

Jonah was very discouraged. He felt his efforts had been wasted on people whose lives were not worth the effort. "Take my life," he said to Jehovah, "for now it is better for me to die than to live."

"Does it do any good for you to be angry?" asked Jehovah.

Jonah did not answer Jehovah's question but left Nineveh in a huff. He built himself a small shelter on the side of the hill overlooking the city and sat under it in the shade. He decided he would wait there and see what might happen.

As Jonah sat in his little shelter, Jehovah caused a castor bean plant to come up in the night and grow over him, providing shade from the sun. Jonah was pleased with the plant, and day after day it gave him relief from some of his self-pity, as well as from the sun.

One night, however, Jehovah caused a worm to eat upon the stem of the plant, and next morning it withered and died. As the sun came up that morning, Jehovah also caused a burning east wind to blow upon Jonah. Life became very unpleasant and, as the sun beat down upon poor Jonah's head, he fainted and wished he could die. "Surely it is better to die than to live," he muttered in his misery.

In the midst of Jonah's misery, Jehovah spoke to him again, asking him another question: "Is it good for you to be angry with the castor bean plant, Jonah?"

"Yes it is!" responded Jonah, showing his irritation. "It is good for me to be angry—even unto death!" Poor Jonah could not let go of his self-pity.

Then Jehovah said to him: "You have had pity on the bean plant for which you did not labor and which you did not cause to grow. It came up in a night with no effort on your part, and it also perished in a night. As I perceive your reaction, you would rather save that bean plant than this city. But Nineveh is a great city in which there are more than six score thousand people[523] who cannot discern between their right hands and their left. Should I not have mercy on them and spare them?"

---

[523] A score is twenty, so six score thousand would be 120,000 people. We have no idea of the accuracy of this number. Bear in mind, however, that many of the numbers in the Old Testament are greatly exaggerated.

180—THE END OF ISRAEL
IS IN SIGHT
(2 Kings 15–16; Isaiah 7)

During the forty-one years[524] when Uzziah[525] reigned in Jerusalem as king of Judah, Israel—the kingdom to the north—had several kings, all of them wicked. Jeroboam II reigned for forty years, but once he was dead—in the thirty-eighth year of Uzziah's reign—a period of much more rapid turnover followed. And all of those who came to the throne during this period continued to walk in the ways of King Jeroboam I, maintaining the golden calves at Dan and Beth-el. Jeroboam II's son Zachariah succeeded him on Israel's throne but reigned for only six months. His wicked reign ended abruptly at the point of Shallum's sword, in front of all the people.

Zachariah's death ended the reign of Jehu's descendants, thus fulfilling Jehovah's promise that Jehu's descendants would sit on Israel's throne for four generations.[526]

Shallum, upon Zachariah's death, took over the kingly office, but his reign was even shorter than Zachariah's. He was slain by Menahem when he had been king for only one month. Menahem then became king in Shallum's place and reigned in wickedness for ten years.

During the reign of Menahem, the dreaded Assyrians—under King Pul—came into the land. To appease Pul and protect his own kingdom, Menahem gave him 1,000 talents of silver[527]—money that he extracted from the people of Israel by levying a tax of fifty shekels upon each man of wealth. Pul and his army left the land after receiving Menahem's payment, but only temporarily.

When Menahem died, his son Pekahiah took the throne of Israel and reigned for two years. His reign was cut short when one of his own servants, Pekah, the son of Remaliah, led a conspiracy and slew him.

Pekah—probably because of the alliance he made with Syria—was able to maintain the throne of Israel for twenty years. Pekah joined forces with Rezin, king of Syria, to battle King Ahaz and the kingdom of Judah, hoping to topple the government and set up a puppet king. However, it was not Jehovah's will that Judah be subdued.[528] He had promised David that only his descendants would sit upon the throne of Judah.[529]

The people of Israel also suffered great losses during Pekah's wicked reign. For the Assyrian army, under Tiglath-pileser,[530] returned and carried many of the people captive into Assyria. The captives were mostly from the lands of Gilead, Galilee, and Naphtali.[531] The armies of Tiglath-pileser also attacked Damascus, killing Rezin, and taking many of the Syrian people as captives into Assyria.

---

[524] The scriptures disagree about the length of King Uzziah's reign; 2 Kings 15:2 says he reigned for fifty-two years. These years do not add up, however, when they are matched against the reigns of the kings of Israel.

[525] This king was called Uzziah in 2 Chronicles 26, but is identified as Azariah in 2 Kings 14 and 15. To avoid confusion, the name Uzziah is used in all of those stories where he is mentioned.

[526] This promise, given by Jehovah to Jehu after he had destroyed the house of King Ahab and Baal worship in Israel, is found in 2 Kings 10:30 (see story "173—Jehu's Sacrifice to Baal") The four kings who were descendants of Jehu were Jehoahaz, Jehoash, Jeroboam II, and Zachariah.

[527] A talent of silver was equivalent to 3,000 shekels, or slightly more than 75.5 pounds. Thus 1,000 talents would be 75,600 pounds (34,292 kilograms), or nearly thirty-eight tons (33.75 long tons or 34.29 metric tons) of silver.

---

[528] For more on the hostilities between Judah and the kingdoms of Israel and Syria during the reign of Pekah see story "181—The Kings of Judah Forsake Jehovah."

[529] See story "121—Your Son Shall Build My House."

[530] Tiglath-pileser and Pul are believed by many scholars to be two different names for the same Assyrian king.

[531] This event was prophesied by the prophet Hosea when he wrote: "And it shall come to pass at that day, that I will break the bow of Israel in the valley of Jezreel (Hosea 1:5).

181–THE KINGS OF JUDAH FORSAKE JEHOVAH

(2 Kings 15–16; 2 Chronicles 27–28; Isaiah 7)

When King Uzziah[532] of Judah died, after reigning in Jerusalem for forty-one years,[533] his son Jotham reigned in his place. Jotham began his reign during the second year of Pekah's twenty-year reign in Samaria, though he had acted in his father's behalf much earlier than this because of his father's leprosy.[534]

Jotham did what was right in Jehovah's sight and maintained a steady course before him, but he did not enter the temple and he did nothing to curb the corruption among his people. Jotham, however, undertook the reconstruction of the city walls that were destroyed when the army of Israel under Jehoash attacked Jerusalem.[535] He also built cities in the mountains and castles and towers in the forests of Judah.

Jotham was successful in war. After defeating the Ammonites, he received tribute from them of 100 talents of silver, 10,000 measures of wheat, and 10,000 measures of barley each year for three years.

When death took Jotham after he had reigned for sixteen years, his son Ahaz became Judah's king. Ahaz, however, was quite a different man than his father. He was a wicked man who walked after the manner of the kings of Israel and made molten images for Baalim.[536] Ahaz avidly worshipped the heathen gods, even to offering his own children as burnt sacrifices. And he made sacrifices and burned incense to these false gods in the high places[537] of Judah.

Because of Ahaz's wickedness, Jehovah delivered him into the hands of Rezin, king of Syria and Pekah, king of Israel, who had combined their forces in an alliance against him. But, though Jehovah allowed Judah to suffer serious losses to these enemies, it was not Jehovah's will for Judah to be overcome.[538]

Jehovah sent the prophet Isaiah to see King Ahaz and tell him about the pending invasion of Syria and Israel and what would happen as a result. "Take heed and be quiet," Isaiah told Ahaz. "Do not be afraid of these two smoking firebrands[539]—King Rezin of Syria and King Pekah of Israel. Though they have taken evil counsel against you to establish a new king in your place, their counsel will not stand; neither will it come to pass. Within sixty-five years the kingdom of Israel will be broken and no longer be a people. Jehovah will make the land desolate by the hands of the king of Assyria and only a few survivors will remain."

The people of Judah suffered greatly at the hands of their attackers. Many were captured and taken to Damascus, and 120,000 of King Ahaz's valiant men fell by the sword in one day. Pekah's army also took great spoils from the land and carried 200,000 women and children captive to Samaria.

As Pekah's victorious army brought their captives to the city of Samaria, the prophet Oded met them at the gate. Oded stood before the army and spoke. "Jehovah has delivered these captives into your hands because he is angry with Judah," Oded said to them, "and you have

---

[532] This king was called Uzziah in 2 Chronicles 26, but is identified as Azariah in 2 Kings 14 and 15. To avoid confusion, the name Uzziah has been used in all of the stories where he is mentioned.

[533] The scriptures disagree about the length of King Uzziah's reigned; 2 Kings 15:2 says he reigned for fifty-two years. These years do not add up, however, when they are matched against the reigns of the kings of Israel.

[534] See story "178–Jeroboam's Success and Uzziah's Pride."

[535] See story "177–Defeat on the Heels of Victory."

[536] Baal (plural form Baalim), the storm and fertility god, was symbolic of the male generative principle in nature. Baal worship was most common among the Zidonians or Phoenicians and was brought into the kingdom of Judah by Athaliah, the daughter of King Ahab of the kingdom of Israel and his Phoenician wife Jezebel.

[537] When the children of Israel came into the promised land, they set up community places of worship, including altars, on the tops of hills. These were called high places. Many of these altars were desecrated when Israel forsook Jehovah to worship false gods. Later, especially after the temple was built in Jerusalem, many of the leaders sought to get rid of these high places. Unfortunately, the children of Israel always had a great inclination to worship false gods, and the existence of the high places often provided that opportunity.

[538] The prophet Isaiah says that Rezin and Remaliah's son (Pekah) wanted to install "the son of Tabeal"— probably a Syrian, judging from his father's name—as a puppet king in Judah (see Isaiah 7:6); but remember that Jehovah had promised King David that the throne of Judah would never be taken from his (David's) descendants (see story "121–Your Son Shall Build My House").

[539] A smoking firebrand is a stick that is taken out of the fire when it is burning. It starts to smoke when the fire is mostly gone out and there is very little fire (or power) left in it.

been able to slay the men of Judah because of a rage that reaches up to heaven. But before you make these captives your bondsmen, consider if you have not also committed sins against Jehovah. Hear me now and release these captives, for the fierce wrath of God is also upon you."

Some of the leaders of Ephraim also came forward and stood before Pekah's army. "We must not bring these captives in," they said, "for we have already offended God. To bring them in will only add more to our trespasses—which are already great—for Jehovah has fierce wrath against Israel."

The pleadings of Oded and the leaders of Ephraim had their desired affect. The armed men of Israel left their spoils and their captives before the princes and the congregation. The naked captives were clothed with the spoils, and they were all given food and drink. When the needs of the wounded had been satisfied, the captives were taken to Jericho where they were released to return to their families.

In addition to Judah's afflictions at the hands of Israel and Syria, King Ahaz and his people were also afflicted by attacks from the Edomites and the Philistines. Ahaz called upon Tilgath-pileser, king of Assyria, to come and help him meet these attacks, but the king would not help him. Though Tilgath-pileser came into the land with his army, he brought no help to the people—only problems and distress.

Ahaz was a confused and wicked man. He cut all the vessels of the temple into pieces and locked the temple doors. Instead of turning to Jehovah in his distress, he turned to the gods of the Syrians and made sacrifices to them. "Because these gods help the Syrians," he reasoned, "I will sacrifice to them that they may help me also." He built altars to the Syrian gods in every corner of Jerusalem and made high places to burn incense to them in every city of Judah. But the gods of the Syrians, instead of saving Ahaz, became the ruin of him and of all Judah.

182—ASSYRIA'S VICTORY AND ISRAEL'S CAPTIVITY
(2 Kings 17)

In the twelfth year of King Ahaz's reign in the kingdom of Judah, Hoshea conspired against King Pekah, slew him, and began to reign over the kingdom of Israel. Hoshea was not a righteous man,[540] but he was not as wicked as many of the kings of Israel who reigned before him.

During Hoshea's reign, the Assyrians invaded the land of Israel. Hoshea was made a servant to King Shalmaneser of Assyria and paid tribute to him year by year. But when Shalmaneser learned that Hoshea had sent messengers to King So of Egypt and had brought no gifts to the king of Assyria, he accused Hoshea of conspiracy with the Egyptians and threw him into prison.

Shalmaneser lay siege to Samaria and all of Israel for three years; then, in the ninth year of Hoshea's reign, Samaria was conquered and the people of Israel were carried away to Assyria. Once there, they were dispersed into Halah, Habor, Hara, and the cities of the Medes.[541]

All of these things befell the children of Israel because they had sinned against Jehovah and worshipped false gods. They had walked in the statutes of the heathen peoples whom Jehovah had cast out of the land before them. They had built high places[542] in all their cities, from the tower of the watchmen to the fortified city. They set up images and groves[543] on every high

---

[540] Just like every other king of Israel since the days when the unified kingdom was divided, Hoshea maintained the golden calves that King Jeroboam had set up for worship in Dan and Beth-el. This, probably more than any other factor, was the reason Jehovah caused Israel to be taken captive by the Assyrians.

[541] Media, which means "middle land," lay east of Assyria at the south end of the Caspian Sea.

[542] When the children of Israel came into the promised land, they set up community places of worship, including altars, on the tops of hills. These were called high places. Many of these altars were desecrated when Israel forsook Jehovah to worship false gods. Later, especially after the temple was built in Jerusalem, many of the leaders sought to get rid of these high places. Unfortunately, the children of Israel always had a great inclination to worship false gods, and the existence of the high places often provided that opportunity.

[543] Groves were living trees or treelike poles, set up as objects of worship, and were generally associated with

hill and under every green tree, where they burned incense to pagan gods. And, though Jehovah sent prophets and seers among them and warned them to keep his commandments according to the law he gave to their fathers, they hardened their necks. And, no matter what else, the people of Israel had continued to worship the two golden calves set up by Jeroboam at Beth-el and Dan.[544] They also made groves there, worshipped the hosts of heaven,[545] and served Baal.[546]

Jehovah was very angry with Israel because of these things, and removed them out of his sight. Except for a few scattered remnants, none of the people of the northern tribes, except those in the kingdom of Judah, were left in the land.

Once the people of Israel had been removed from the cities of Samaria, the king of Assyria sent in settlers from other places—from Babylon, Cuthah, Ava, Hamath, and Sepharvaim—to inhabit the land.[547] When lions came among the new settlers, the king of Assyria sent back one of the priests of Israel to dwell at Beth-el, that he might teach the new inhabitants the ways of the God of the land. Nevertheless, the peoples of every nation made their own gods and put them in the houses of the high places that the children of Israel had created. The people who came from Babylon made Succoth-benoth,[548] those from Cuth made Nergal,[549] those from

Hamath made Ashima,[550] the Avites made Nibhaz and Tartak,[551] and the Sepharvites burnt their children in fire to their gods Adrammelech and Anammelech.[552]

---

fertility rites and sexual immorality. The groves were part of Baal worship and were symbolic of female fertility.

[544] See story "143–Israel Divided."

[545] The hosts of heaven are the heavenly bodies—the sun, the moon, the planets, and the stars (see Genesis 2:1; Deuteronomy 4:19; 2 Kings 21:3, 5; 23:5).

[546] Baal (plural form Baalim), the storm and fertility god, was symbolic of the male generative principle in nature. Worship of Baal was most common among the Zidonians or Phoenicians and was brought into the kingdom of Israel by Jezebel, the Phoenician princess who became the wife of King Ahab.

[547] These peoples who were imported into the Northern Kingdom by the Assyrians, intermarried with the people of Israel who were not taken captive. It was the descendants of these mixed marriages—called Samaritans—who were looked down upon by the Jews and treated as an inferior race after the Jews returned from captivity and in the New Testament.

[548] There is some disagreement about the nature of the deity called Succoth-benoth. The term means "the tents of daughters." Some authorities say Succoth-benoth identifies the booths in which the daughters of the Babylonians prostituted themselves in honor of their idol. Others say it identifies small tabernacles containing images of female deities. Others say it refers to the

Chaldean goddess Zerbanit, the wife of Merodach, who was especially worshipped at Babylon (see William Smith, *Dictionary of the Bible*, *GospeLink*, CD-ROM, s.v. "Succoth-benoth").

[549] The location of Cuth (or Cuthah) is unknown. Some suggest that it was a city east of Babylon. Nergal means "hero." He was one of the chief Assyrian and Babylonian deities and seems to have corresponded closely to Mars. Some speculate that Nergal represents the deified Nimrod (see William Smith, *Dictionary of the Bible*, *GospeLink*, CD-ROM, s.v. "Cuth" and "Nergal").

[550] Hamath was a city in the northern part of Syria, controlled at this time by the Assyrians. Ashima is considered by some as being identical to Pan of the Greeks (see William Smith, *Dictionary of the Bible*, *GospeLink*, CD-ROM, s.v. "Hamath" and "Ashima").

[551] The location of Ava is not known. It is presumed to be the same as Ivah. Nibhaz means "the barker" and probably relates to a deity in the image of a dog or a man with the head of a dog. Evidence of such worship has been found in Syria. Tartak means "prince of darkness." Rabbinical tradition says that Tartak was worshipped under the form of an ass (see William Smith, *Dictionary of the Bible*, *GospeLink*, CD-ROM, s.v. "Ava," "Nibhaz," and "Tartak").

[552] Sepharvaim has been identified with the famous town of Sippara, north of Babylon on the Euphrates. The sun was the main object of worship there. Little is known of Adrammelech and Anammelech. However, some believe these twin gods represented the male and female powers of the sun. They appear to have been worshipped by rites similar to the rites of Molech, humans being sacrificed as burnt offerings (see William Smith, *Dictionary of the Bible*, *GospeLink*, CD-ROM, s.v. "Sepharvaim," "Adrammelech," and "Anammelech").

183—THE RENEWAL OF JUDAH'S RIGHTEOUSNESS

(2 Kings 18; 2 Chronicles 29–31)

In the third year of Hoshea's reign in Samaria, King Ahaz of Judah died and his son Hezekiah came to the throne. In striking contrast to his wicked father, Hezekiah was a very righteous king and walked faithfully in the ways of Jehovah.

At the very beginning of Hezekiah's reign, he repaired and reopen the doors of the temple so the people could return to worship Jehovah. He also brought in those priests and Levites that he could find and instructed them concerning their duties. He charged them to sanctify both themselves and the house of the Lord. "Carry out of this holy place all the filthiness that our fathers have brought into it," he told the assembled Levites, "for our fathers did evil in Jehovah's eyes, turning their backs on his house, shutting the doors, and putting out the lamps. They have burned no incense unto the God of Israel nor offered burnt offerings in the holy place.

"I know that God's wrath has been upon Judah and Jerusalem and, because of it, he has delivered our fathers into trouble, astonishment, and hissing. Even you have seen how our fathers fell by the sword and our wives and children were taken into captivity."

Hezekiah continued: "I now have it in my heart to make a covenant with Jehovah so that his fierce anger may be turned away from us. So I charge you, my sons, that you not be negligent, for Jehovah has chosen you to serve him, to minister unto him, and to burn incense in his holy house."

All the Levites who heard Hezekiah's charge arose and sought out their brethren. When they had sanctified themselves, according to his charge, they went in to cleanse the temple. The priests went into the inner part and carried all the impurities that they found out into the temple court. From there the Levites carried those impurities to the brook Kidron.[553] When they had labored for eight days, they reported to Hezekiah that the work he had charged them to do was finished.

The next day King Hezekiah rose early, gathered the rulers of the city, and went up to the temple where the priests made a burnt offering to Jehovah—a sin offering for all of Judah. Then the Levites came with their musical instruments. And as the singers sang and the trum-

peters blew their trumpets, the entire congregation bowed their heads and worshipped Jehovah until the burnt offerings were finished.

"Now that you have consecrated yourselves," said King Hezekiah to his people, "let those who are willing bring thank offerings to the temple."

The response to Hezekiah's suggestion was so great that the priests were unable to handle the offerings. The Levites were summoned to help them until the work was ended and until other priests could be sanctified. Because Jehovah had prepared the hearts of the people, the service of the temple was set in order.

Hezekiah also took the advice of his princes and the people of Judah to keep the Passover. He invited all of Israel and Judah—from Dan to Beersheba—to come up to Jerusalem to celebrate this holy feast. This was the first recorded celebration of the Passover since Joshua and the children of Israel celebrated it at Gilgal when they first entered the promised land.[554] It was decided, however, to celebrate the Passover in the second month rather than the first, as was specified by the law of Moses, because the priests had not yet sanctified themselves sufficiently and the first month was too soon for the people to gather to Jerusalem.

Couriers were sent out with letters to invite the people to Jerusalem for the Passover. The letters said: "Turn again to Jehovah, the God of Abraham, Isaac, and Jacob, you children of Israel, and he will return to the remnant that has escaped from the kings of Assyria. Do not be like your fathers and brethren who trespassed against Jehovah. Do not be stiffnecked, but yield yourselves to him. Enter his sanctuary to serve him so that his anger may turn away from you. For, if you will return to Jehovah, your brethren and your children will receive mercy from those who have taken them captive and will be brought again into this land. Jehovah is gracious and merciful, and he will not turn his face from you if you will return to him."

The letters were delivered to those who remained in Ephraim, Manasseh, and Zebulun, but the people mocked the couriers and laughed them to scorn. There were, however, some from Ephraim, Manasseh, Issachar, and Zebulun—those who humbled themselves—who came up to Jerusalem to celebrate the feast. The people of Judah flocked en masse to Jerusalem because Jehovah gave them one heart to follow his words.

Many who came to the Passover celebration, however, had not cleansed themselves according to the purification of the sanctuary as required by the law of Moses. Some also ate the Passover contrary to what was written in the Law. But Hezekiah, in his mercy and

---

[553] The Kidron (or Kedron) Valley seems to have been a place of impurity in the Old Testament. It was the location of the common cemetery of the city of Jerusalem.

[554] Mention of this Passover is found in story "74–The Captain of Jehovah's Army."

253

love for the people, pleaded with Jehovah to forgive them. And Jehovah answered Hezekiah's prayer and healed the people.

When the seven days of the feast were completed, the people decided to continue the feast for seven days more. Their joy was great because there had not been such a celebration in Jerusalem, for any occasion, since the days of King Solomon and the dedication of the temple.

When the people of Judah returned to their own places after the celebration, they broke their idolatrous symbols into pieces, cut down their groves,[555] and threw down all their high places[556] and altars. The people in Benjamin, Ephraim, and Manasseh did the same. In Jerusalem, King Hezekiah also broke down the false gods of the people and cut down their groves. And he broke into pieces the brass serpent that Moses had made in the wilderness,[557] because the children of Israel had been burning incense to it and worshipping it.

King Hezekiah did great works of righteousness and truth before Jehovah. And everything he did, he did with all his heart.

184—JUDAH'S ESCAPE FROM ASSYRIA'S GRASP

(2 Kings 18–19; 2 Chronicles 32; Isaiah 36–37)

Soon after righteous King Hezekiah had turned the hearts of Judah to Jehovah, King Sennacherib of Assyria marched into Judah with his armies. He encamped against the fortified cities and overcame them all, and then he lay siege against Jerusalem.

When prospects for Judah's survival began to look dismal, Hezekiah sent a message to Sennacherib asking what the price of tribute would be to purchase his departure. "For," he said, "I can bear whatever price you ask." In response, King Sennacherib demanded that Hezekiah pay him 300 talents of silver and thirty talents of gold.[558] To pay the requested ransom, Hezekiah took all the silver from the temple and the treasures from the king's palace. He also cut off the gold overlay from the temple doors and pillars and gave it all to Sennacherib. But, in spite of these generous gifts, the Assyrians did not leave the land. Sennacherib broke his word, and he and his army remained in the city of Lachish.

Hezekiah, realizing that Sennacherib's main objective was Jerusalem, made an alliance with Egypt for mutual support. He also stopped the waters of all the springs that were outside the city and of the upper watercourse of Gihon that ran through the middle of the land. He caused the waters of Gihon to flow into the pool of Siloam, inside the city, by way of a long tunnel chiseled through solid rock.[559] This would ensure that there would always be water in the city while the attacking army suffered from thirst. Hezekiah also raised the wall around the city up to the towers and built a

---

[555] Groves in the Old Testament were living trees or treelike poles, set up as objects of worship, and were generally associated with fertility rites and sexual immorality. The groves were part of Baal worship and were symbolic of female fertility.

[556] When the children of Israel came into the promised land, they set up community places of worship, including altars, on the tops of hills. These were called high places. Many of these altars were desecrated when Israel forsook Jehovah to worship false gods. Later, especially after the temple was built in Jerusalem, many of the leaders sought to get rid of these high places. Unfortunately, the children of Israel had a great inclination to worship false gods, and the existence of the high places often provided that opportunity.

[557] See story "67–The Brass Serpent" for the account of how Moses came to create it.

---

[558] A talent of silver was equivalent to 3,000 shekels, or just more that 75.5 pounds (34.29 kilograms). Thus, 300 talents of silver would be about 22,680 pounds (10,288 kilograms), or more than 11.3 tons (10.13 long tons or 10.29 metric tons). A talent of gold was equivalent to 10,000 shekels or 252 pounds (114.3 kilograms). Thus thirty talents of gold was 7,560 pounds (3429 kilograms) or nearly 3.8 tons (3.38 long tons or 3.43 metric tons).

[559] For an account of the digging of this tunnel, see *Bible Dictionary*, LDS-KJV, s.v. "Hezekiah's Tunnel." The tunnel still exists. The 1,700-foot tunnel followed an S-shaped course through the rock, rather than going in a straight line. This was reportedly done to avoid the graves of David and Solomon (see Werner Keller, *The Bible as History: What Archaeology Reveals about Scripture*, 2nd rev. ed. [New York: William Morrow and Co. Inc., 1981], 256–257).

second wall outside the first at the north end of the city to enclose the pool of Siloam. He repaired the millo[560] and made weapons and shields in great abundance.

When Hezekiah had done everything physically possible to prepare his people for war, he realized that no physical resources could save his people from the vast and powerful army of the Assyrians. The Assyrians had walked over one country after another—including the kingdom of Israel. When Hezekiah realized that the only way they could be saved from these dreaded invaders was to rely on Jehovah for assistance, he called his people together and tried to ease their fears. "Be strong and courageous," he told them. "Do not be afraid of the king of Assyria or of the multitude that is with him, for there are more with us than with him. He has only an arm of flesh with him, but we have our God Jehovah to help us and to fight our battles." And the people of Jerusalem trusted Hezekiah and relied on Jehovah as Hezekiah told them.

From Lachish, Sennacherib prepared again to strike Jerusalem, and he sent a great army to lay siege against the city. To convince the people to surrender, three men from the invading army—with Rab-shakeh as their spokesman—came to the city wall and stood by the ditch at the upper pool. Eliakim, Shebna, and Joah went out from the city to meet with them in behalf of King Hezekiah.

"Speak to Hezekiah for us," said Rab-shakeh, "and give him this message from Sennacherib. Tell him that his confidence is misplaced if he thinks he can rebel against the king of Assyria. He has trusted in Egypt to be his ally, but Egypt is like a bruised reed and cannot be trusted. If a man should lean on it, it will pierce his hand. And, if Hezekiah says he trusts in Jehovah, his actions do not show it. For he has taken down the high places and the altars and has commanded his people to worship only at the altar in Jerusalem."

Rab-shakeh continued: "If Hezekiah will surrender and give pledges to our master the king of Assyria, we will give him 2,000 horses. How then can he turn his face away from one captain of the least of our master's servants and trust in Egypt for chariots and horsemen?

"We have come up without Jehovah to destroy Jerusalem. In fact, Jehovah told us to come up against this land and destroy it."

Because Rab-shakeh had spoken so rudely, Eliakim, Shebna, and Joah requested that he speak to them in the

Syrian tongue rather than Hebrew so the people who stood guard on the city wall could not understand, but Rab-shakeh refused. He raised his voice higher and cried out to those on the wall, seeking to make them afraid. "Hear the words of the great king of Assyria," he shouted. "Thus says the king: 'Do not let Hezekiah deceive you, for he is powerless to deliver you out of our hands. Neither let him make you trust in Jehovah for deliverance, for Jehovah cannot deliver you from us.

"'It is best for you to make an agreement with me, along with a great gift, and then come out of your city. If you will do this, you shall eat the fruit of your own vines and fig trees and shall drink water from your own cisterns until the day that I come and take you away to another land—a land much like your own, a land of grain and wine, of bread and vineyards, of olive oil and honey. If you will do this, you may live. But do not listen to Hezekiah when he says that Jehovah will deliver you.

"'Have the gods of other nations delivered them from the hands of the Assyrians? Where are their gods now? If they could not deliver their peoples, how then can Jehovah deliver Jerusalem?'"

When the people heard Sennacherib's message, they said nothing, for Hezekiah had commanded them to give no answer.

When Eliakim, Shebna, and Joah returned to King Hezekiah with their clothes torn and told him the words of Rab-shakeh, Hezekiah also tore his clothing. Then he covered himself with sackcloth and went up to the temple. He was greatly distraught.

At the same time, however, Hezekiah sent Eliakim, Shebna, and the elders of the priests to find the prophet Isaiah. They were to tell Isaiah of the trouble now facing the people of Jerusalem. "This day is a day of trouble, of rebuke, and of blasphemy," the men said to Isaiah, "for Israel is come to be born and her mother does not have strength to bring her forth. Perhaps Jehovah has heard the words of Rab-shakeh, whom the king of Assyria has sent to dishonor us, and will condemn his blasphemous words. Please pray for the remnant of this people."

"Tell your master that he should not fear the words that you have heard," replied Isaiah, "even those words by which the servants of the Assyrian king have blasphemed Jehovah. For Jehovah will put a spirit in King Sennacherib of Assyria so that he will hear a report and return to his own land, where he will fall by the sword."

At this same time, things were not going well for King Sennacherib. He was having troubles of his own in conquering other cities. He was warring against Libnah, a fortified city near Lachish, but was not succeeding. And the king of Ethiopia was now also threatening

---

[560] Millo was a rampart or fortification of some type that existed in ancient Jerusalem. Both the name and the place seem to have been already in existence when King David conquered the city from the Jebusites (William Smith, *Dictionary of the Bible*, GospeLink, CD-ROM, s.v. "Millo").

to join the fight against him. Sennacherib needed desperately to succeed at Jerusalem, and it would certainly be best for him if Jerusalem could be frightened into surrendering without a fight.

Sennacherib sent messengers again to Hezekiah with a threatening letter. "Do not let this God in whom you trust deceive you and tell you that Jerusalem will not be delivered into my hands," said the letter. "You have heard how the kings of Assyria have destroyed all other lands and how the gods of those nations failed to deliver them. Thus shall it be with Jerusalem, and Jehovah cannot deliver you."

When Hezekiah had read Sennacherib's letter he was distraught. He went again to the temple and spread out the letter before Jehovah. Then he prayed, saying, "O Jehovah, God of Israel, bow down Thine ear to hear, and open Thine eyes to see. Hear the words that Sennacherib has sent to blaspheme Thee. Of a truth, O Jehovah, the kings of Assyria have destroyed the other nations. They have cast the gods of those nations into the fire, for their gods were not gods at all but the work of men's hands—wood and stone. Now, therefore, O Lord Jehovah, save us from the hands of Sennacherib that the kingdoms of the earth may know that Thou and Thou only art God."

When Jehovah spoke to Isaiah with regard to King Hezekiah's pleadings, Isaiah sent a message to Hezekiah. "Jehovah has heard your prayers against Sennacherib, king of Assyria," Isaiah assured him, "and will grant unto you according to your prayers. The virgin daughter of Zion[561] shall despise Sennacherib, laugh him to scorn, and shake her head at him—and this because Sennacherib has blasphemed Jehovah.

"Because the king of Assyria has exalted his own voice and lifted up his eyes against the Holy One of Israel, Jehovah's hook will be in his nose and Jehovah's bridle in his lips. He shall be turned back and return to Assyria in the way by which he came."

Isaiah's message to King Hezekiah continued: "The king of Assyria shall not enter Jerusalem. He shall not shoot one arrow there, come before it with his shield, or cast up a bank against it. For Jehovah will defend this city and save it for his own sake and for the sake of his servant David."

And so it was that night, as the Assyrian army slept, that the angel of Jehovah smote their camp and 185,000 men lay dead. And when Sennacherib received word of this great slaughter, he returned quickly to Nineveh, his capital city. And there, while worshipping in the house of his god Nisroch,[562] he was slain by two of his sons, according to Isaiah's prophecy.

---

[561] The virgin daughter of Zion spoken of here represents the unconquered people of Jerusalem.

[562] Nisroch means "the great eagle." This idol is identified with an eagle-headed human figure, which is one of the most prominent on the earliest Assyrian monuments. It was always represented as contending with and conquering a lion or a bull (see William Smith, *Dictionary of the Bible*, GospeLink, CD-ROM, s.v. "Nisroch").

185–FIFTEEN ADDITIONAL YEARS

(2 Kings 20; 2 Chronicles 32; Isaiah 38)

Before the Assyrian army lay siege against the city of Jerusalem, King Hezekiah lay sick in his bed with a boil. As he lay suffering, the prophet Isaiah came to him and said, "Set your house in order, Hezekiah, for Jehovah has said that you will die." Then Isaiah left.

When Hezekiah heard Isaiah prophesy of his death, he rolled over on his bed, turning his face to the wall, and prayed for his life. "O Jehovah," he pleaded, "remember now how I have walked before Thee in truth and with a perfect heart. For I have done that which is good in Thy sight." And Hezekiah wept bitterly.

Before Isaiah had departed out of the middle court of the king's palace, the word of Jehovah came to him again telling him to return to the king with a different message. "Tell Hezekiah that I have heard his prayer and seen his tears and that I will heal him," said Jehovah to Isaiah. "On the third day he shall go up to the temple, and I will add fifteen years to his life. Tell him also that I will deliver him and this city out of the hands of the Assyrians. For I Jehovah will defend Jerusalem for my own sake and for the sake of my servant David."

When Isaiah had delivered Jehovah's revised message to Hezekiah, he had the servants take a cake of pressed figs and lay it on the king's boil. Then Hezekiah looked at Isaiah and asked, "What shall be the sign that Jehovah will heal me and that I should go up to the house of the Lord on the third day?"

"This sign shall you have from Jehovah that he shall do the thing that he has spoken," answered Isaiah. "Would you have the shadow of the sun go forward ten degrees or back ten degrees?"

"It is a light thing for the shadow to go forward ten degrees," said the king. "Let the shadow go back ten degrees." And when Isaiah left the king's presence, he pleaded with Jehovah to give the promised sign.

And so it was that the shadow of the sun on the sundial went back ten degrees as a sign of Jehovah's pledge to King Hezekiah.

Though Jehovah blessed Hezekiah to lengthen his life, Hezekiah did not humble himself, and Jehovah's wrath came upon both him and the city of Jerusalem, being made manifest in the siege by the Assyrians. Jehovah's wrath was taken away, however, when Hezekiah repented of his pride.

186–JUDAH'S CAPTIVITY PROPHESIED

(2 Kings 20; Isaiah 39)

When Baladan, the king of Babylonia, heard of King Hezekiah's sickness, he instructed his son, Merodach-baladan, to send messengers to Jerusalem with letters and a gift for Hezekiah. And when the Babylonian messengers came, Hezekiah—being a gracious host—showed them all of his precious things and his treasures, for he had great wealth. There was nothing in Hezekiah's palace or in his kingdom that he did not show his visitors.

When the prophet Isaiah heard of Hezekiah's visitors, he asked Hezekiah, "Where did those men come from and what did they say to you?"

"They came from a far country, even from Babylon," answered Hezekiah.

"What have they seen in your house?"

"They have seen everything that is there," answered the king. "There are none of my treasures that I did not show them."

"Hear the word of Jehovah," said Isaiah. "The days will come that all that is in your palace and that which your fathers have laid up in store unto this day shall be carried into Babylon until there is nothing left. They will also take away your sons and make them eunuchs in the palace of the king of Babylon."

Upon hearing this prophetic warning from the Isaiah, Hezekiah gave a very strange reply. "The word of Jehovah that you have spoken is good," he said; "but is it not good for me to have peace and stability in my days?"

187–THE PROPHECY OF THE SEALED BOOK

(Isaiah 29, 2 Nephi 27)

The prophet Isaiah was greatly respected by King Hezekiah, and he was the chief adviser in Hezekiah's court. But, in spite of Hezekiah's righteousness, Isaiah foresaw the fall and captivity of the kingdom of Judah and made many prophecies concerning such. He also prophesied of Judah's return from captivity and named the man—King Cyrus of Persia—who would instigate both Judah's return to Jerusalem and the rebuilding of the temple.[563]

Isaiah used much symbolism in his writing and many of his prophecies are subject to more than one fulfillment. That is, they related to both ancient Judah (and Israel) as well as to a later time—either to the time of the Messiah's coming in the meridian of time, to the last days, or to both. Isaiah's prophecies, as they related to ancient Israel and Judah, were fulfilled anciently, and they either have been or will be fulfilled again.

Isaiah not only prophesied bad things against wayward Judah but also against those who caused problems for Jehovah's people. "All you nations that fight against Zion and distress her," he wrote, "will be as a dream of a night vision. You shall be as the hungry man who eats in his dream but then awakens and is still hungry, or as the thirsty man who drinks in his dream and then awakens and is still faint. All you who do iniquity should strengthen and support yourselves," he wrote, "for you will cry out in astonishment. You will be drunken but not with wine, and you will stagger but not because of strong drink. Jehovah has poured out the spirit of a deep sleep upon you because you have rejected his prophets. He has also covered your rulers and your seers because of your iniquity."

Isaiah continued, speaking now of the last days: "Jehovah will bring forth unto you the words of a book, even the words of them who have slumbered or who are long since dead. The book—which shall be sealed—will contain a revelation from God from the beginning of the world to its end. And because of the wickedness and abominations of the people in that day, the book and those things that are sealed in it will not be delivered to the people but shall be kept from them.

"The book, however, will be delivered to a man, and that man will deliver the words of the book—which are the words of those who have slumbered in the dust—unto another man. Then those same words of the book will be delivered by that other man to one who is learned saying, 'Read this, I pray of you,' and he will say, 'I cannot read it, for it is sealed.' But the book shall be delivered to him who is not learned saying, 'Read this, I pray of you,' and he will say, 'I am not learned.'"

"Wherefore," continued Isaiah, "because this people draw near to Jehovah with their mouths and honor him with their lips, but have removed their hearts far from him, he will proceed to do a marvelous work among them—even a marvelous work and a wonder. For the wisdom of their wise men shall perish and the understanding of their prudent men shall be hid. And in that day the deaf shall hear the words of the book and the eyes of the blind shall see out of obscurity and darkness. They also that erred in spirit shall understand, and they that murmured shall learn doctrine."

"That book," said Isaiah, "was sealed by the power of God because it reveals all things from the foundation of the world until its end. And the revelation shall be kept in the book and remain sealed until it is brought forth in God's due time. For the day will come that the words of the sealed book will be read upon the housetops, and they will be read by the power of the Messiah. And all things will be revealed unto mankind which ever have been among them and which ever will be, even unto the end of the earth."

---

[563] Isaiah 44:28–45:4 (see story "222–The Return of Judah's Exiles").

188–THE ABOMINATIONS OF KING MANASSEH

(2 Kings 21; 2 Chronicles 33; Jeremiah 15)

Upon the death of King Hezekiah, his twelve-year-old son Manasseh ascended to the throne of Judah. This son, who was born after Hezekiah's life was extended for fifteen years, was a very wicked man, and it would have been better for Judah if Hezekiah had died from his sickness.[564]

Manasseh's wickedness was soon reflected in the wickedness of his people. He returned to the worship of the false gods that his father had eliminated, and he again built up the high places[565] that his father had destroyed. In addition to making a grove,[566] he set up a graven image of the grove in the temple of God. Manasseh also erected altars to Baal, promoted the work of wizards in the land of Judah, and embraced familiar spirits.[567] But he reached the pinnacle of his wickedness when he offered his own son as a burnt offering to his heathen gods, just as King Ahaz had done earlier.[568]

The people of Judah became more wicked during the first part of Manasseh's fifty-five-year reign than any of the peoples whom Jehovah had expelled from the land when he gave it to the children of Israel. It was during this most unfavorable time that Jehovah sent prophets to warn the people of the dire consequences of their wicked ways.

---

[564] See story "185–Fifteen Additional Years" for the account of how Jehovah extended King Hezekiah's life.
[565] When the children of Israel came into the promised land, they set up community places of worship, including altars, on the tops of hills. These were called high places. Many of these altars were desecrated when Israel forsook Jehovah to worship false gods. Later, especially after the temple was built in Jerusalem, many of the leaders sought to get rid of these high places. Some high places, as shown here, were especially created for the worship of false gods.
[566] Groves in the Old Testament were living trees or treelike poles, set up as objects of worship, and were generally associated with fertility rites and sexual immorality. The groves were part of Baal worship and were symbolic of female fertility.
[567] Those who are said to seek after or embrace familiar spirits seek after revelation from sources that are not of God, especially from people or animals believed to be possessed by evil spirits.
[568] See story "181–The Kings of Judah Forsake Jehovah."

"Because Manasseh has done these abominations and has been more wicked than the Amorites who were before him," said Jehovah, "and because he has caused Judah to sin with his idols, I will bring such evil upon Jerusalem and Judah that the ears of those who hear it will tingle. I will bring upon Jerusalem the same judgments that I brought upon Samaria and the same heavy burdens that I brought upon the house of Ahab.

"I will wipe Jerusalem as a man wipes a dish—wiping it out and turning it upside down. I will forsake Judah, which alone remains of Jehovah's covenant people, and deliver them into the hands of their enemies—and all this because they have done evil in my sight since the day their fathers came out of Egypt. Manasseh has also shed much innocent blood, filling Jerusalem with blood from one end to the other."

Jehovah told the prophet Jeremiah that he would cause those who were left in Israel to be removed from their place and scattered into all the kingdoms of the earth because of King Manasseh's wickedness.

When Manasseh and the people of Judah refused to hearken to the words of the prophets, Jehovah again brought the Assyrian army against them. During the attack, King Manasseh was captured and taken to Assyria. The suffering he experienced in Assyria was great, and he was finally afflicted to such an extent that he humbled himself and sought Jehovah.

Jehovah, in his great mercy and his willingness to forgive, heard Manasseh's prayers and brought him back to Jerusalem. King Manasseh was a changed man because of the things he had suffered. He took away the strange gods, the altars, and the idols from the temple and cast them out of the city. He repaired the temple altar, offered sacrifices, and commanded the people of Judah to serve Jehovah. The people responded to Manasseh's pleadings and his example, and they repented as he had done. Though the priests continued to offer sacrifices in the high places, they offered them only to Jehovah.

After Manasseh's death, his son Amon reigned in Judah for two years. But because of Amon's wickedness, his servants conspired against him and slew him in his own house. He was not slain, however, before he had restored the carved images that his father had made and had worshipped those images.

XI

JUDAH'S CAPTIVITY:

THE PROPHECIES, THE SIEGE,

AND THE REALITY

189—KING JOSIAH FULFILLS THE PROPHECY

(2 Kings 22–23; 2 Chronicles 34–35)

With the untimely death of King Amon, his eight-year-old son Josiah became king, and the people of Judah put King Amon's servants to death because they had killed their king.[569] After his wicked father, Josiah was like a breath of fresh air; he walked righteously in the ways of King David and turned neither to the right nor to the left.

In the eighteenth year of Josiah's reign, he put forces into operation to repair the temple, with Hilkiah the high priest and Shaphan the scribe supervising the work. One day, while working in the temple, Hilkiah discovered the book of the Law that was given by Moses, and he gave it to Shaphan to read. When Shaphan had perused the pages of the book and realized what a great treasure it was, he reported Hilkiah's discovery to King Josiah and read parts of the book to him.

When Josiah heard the words of the book it was like a new revelation to him. He was stunned to realize that Judah had departed so drastically from the law that Moses had given them. He tore his clothes and called for his advisers: Hilkiah the priest, Achbor, Asahiah, Shaphan the scribe, and Ahikam the son of Shaphan. "Go and inquire of Jehovah for me and for this people concerning the words of this book," he directed them. "For I believe that the wrath of Jehovah is greatly kindled against us because our fathers have failed to keep the words of this book."

Seeking to obtain an answer from Jehovah, the five men went to Huldah the prophetess and made their inquiry. When Huldah had heard their report, she said, "Thus says Jehovah to the man who sent you: 'I will bring evil upon this place and upon its inhabitants—even all the words of the book that the king has read—because the children of Israel have forsaken me and have burned incense to other gods. My wrath is kindled and shall not be quenched.'"

"But," Huldah continued, "tell the king of Judah that, because his heart was tender and he did humble himself before Jehovah when he heard the words of the book, Jehovah has heard his prayers. He will go to his grave in peace and will not see the great evil that Jehovah will bring upon Jerusalem."

When King Josiah's advisers brought Huldah's message back to him, he gathered the elders of Judah and went up to the temple. And all the men of Judah and the inhabitants of Jerusalem went with them. There, as Josiah stood by the pillar in the temple, he read to them from the book of the Law. And when he had done so, he made a covenant with Jehovah, with all his heart and soul, to keep the commandments and statutes written in the book. And all the people of Jerusalem made that same covenant.

Josiah commanded Hilkiah and the priests to remove from the temple all the vessels that were made for Baal[570] and for the groves.[571] These he burned in the fields of Kidron, then carried the ashes to Beth-el. Josiah also removed the grove from the temple and took it to the brook Kidron where he burned it and stamped it into a fine powder. Then he cast the powder on the graves of the people.

King Josiah put down the idolatrous priests who had been ordained by the kings of Judah to burn incense in the high places[572] of Judah. He also put down those who burned incense to Baal and to all the hosts of heaven.[573] Every idolatrous practice, along with the altars and vessels that supported those practices, was eliminated from among the people as Josiah broke up their idols, cut down their groves, and filled their places with the bones of men. He also broke down the houses of the Sodomites near the temple where hangings for the groves were woven. He was unrelenting in his zeal to destroy those practices contrary to the Law and every physical thing that supported those forbidden practices.

---

[569] See story "188–The Abominations of King Manasseh."

[570] Baal (plural form Baalim), the storm and fertility god, was symbolic of the male generative principle in nature. Baal worship was most common among the Zidonians or Phoenicians and was brought into the kingdom of Judah by Athaliah, the daughter of King Ahab of the kingdom of Israel and his Phoenician wife Jezebel.

[571] Groves in the Old Testament were living trees or treelike poles, set up as objects of worship, and were generally associated with fertility rites and sexual immorality. The groves were part of Baal worship and were symbolic of female fertility.

[572] When the children of Israel came into the promised land, they set up community places of worship, including altars, on the tops of hills. These were called high places. Many of these altars were desecrated when Israel forsook Jehovah to worship false gods. Later, especially after the temple was built in Jerusalem, many of the leaders sought to get rid of these high places. Some high places, as shown here, were especially created for the worship of false gods.

[573] The hosts of heaven are the heavenly bodies—the sun, the moon, the planets, and the stars (see Genesis 2:1; Deuteronomy 4:19; 2 Kings 21:3, 5; 23:5).

Josiah did not limit his reform efforts to Judah only; he extended those efforts into the kingdom of Israel also. He went to the altar at the high place in Beth-el, where Jeroboam—more than 300 years before—had set up a golden calf for Israel to worship so they would not go up to Jerusalem.[574] And Josiah broke down that altar, along with the high place and the grove that were there.

Then, when he turned to leave, he saw the sepulchers on the side of the mountain and commanded that the bones be taken from those sepulchers and burned on the altar. Thus, Josiah fulfilled the prophecy that was made to King Jeroboam by the man of God from Judah.[575] But Josiah did not touch the sepulcher of the man of God who made the prophecy.

In Josiah's zeal for the book of the Law, he left Beth-el and went throughout all the Northern Kingdom destroying the high places, slaying the priests, and burning the bones of those priests upon their own altars. And when he returned to Jerusalem, he commanded the people to keep the Passover according to the instructions in the book of the Law.

There was no king like Josiah before him in Judah, for he turned to Jehovah with all his heart, his soul, and his might. Nor was there such a king after him. But, despite Josiah's righteousness and his zeal for the law, Jehovah's anger—which had been kindled by King Manasseh, Josiah's grandfather—was not turned away from Judah and Jerusalem. "I will remove Judah out of my sight just as I removed Israel," said Jehovah. "I will also cast off Jerusalem, my chosen city, as well as that house of which I said, My name shall be there."

When the Feast of the Passover was completed, Josiah sought to join forces with the king of Egypt, Pharaoh-necho, to fight against the dreaded Assyrians. But Necho resented Josiah's intrusion and advised him not to interfere. And when Josiah persisted, Necho slew him at Megiddo.[576]

With Josiah dead, his son Jehoahaz became king of Judah.

---

[574] See story "143–Israel Divided."

[575] This prophecy, as given in 1 Kings 13:2, is recounted in story "144–A Prophet Comes to Beth-el."

[576] As a result of information found on a fragment of cuneiform text in the British Museum, some historians believe that the scriptural account of this event is in error. The text in question says that the Egyptian army had gone to the aid of the Assyrians after the fall of Nineveh to the Babylonians. Josiah certainly had good reasons to not want anyone to aid his enemies, the Assyrians. But because of his zeal, he was slain by Pharaoh-necho. In spite of the assistance rendered by the Egyptians, Assyria never recovered and the Babylonians became the dominant political force in the area (see Werner Keller, *The Bible as History: What Archae-* *ology Reveals about Scripture*, 2nd rev. ed. [New York: William Morrow and Co. Inc., 1981], 274–275).

190–A PROPHET TO THE NATIONS

(Jeremiah 1–2)

In the thirteenth year of Josiah's reign in Judah, the word of Jehovah came to Jeremiah,[577] the son of Hilkiah the priest. "I knew you, Jeremiah, before you were formed in your mother's belly," said Jehovah. "And before you came forth out of her womb, I sanctified you and ordained you to be a prophet unto the nations."[578]

When Jeremiah protested that he was but a child and could not speak, Jehovah scolded him for so saying, then said, "You shall go wherever I send you and speak whatever I command you."

Then Jehovah touched Jeremiah's mouth and said, "I have put my words into your mouth and have set you over the nations—to root out, to pull down, to destroy, to throw down, to build, and to plant."

To help prepare him for the difficult mission that he had been given, Jehovah opened a vision to Jeremiah's view. First, Jeremiah was shown a shoot from an almond tree, which, Jehovah told him, was a sign that he would hasten the fulfillment of his words.[579] When Jehovah commanded Jeremiah to look a second time, he was shown a boiling pot facing toward the north. Concerning this pot, Jehovah said, "An evil will break forth out of the north upon all the inhabitants of this land. For I will call all the families of the kingdoms of the north, and they will set the thrones of their kings against the gates of Jerusalem, against the walls of Jerusalem, and against all the cities of Judah. My judgments shall come upon the people of Judah because of their wickedness—for they have forsaken me. They have burned incense unto other gods and have worshipped the works of their own hands. Yea, they have committed two evils: they have forsaken me, the fountain of living waters, and they have hewed for themselves cisterns—even broken cisterns[580]—that hold no water."[581]

Jehovah continued: "Gird up your loins now, Jeremiah. Arise and speak to these people all that I command you to speak. And if you fear the faces of the people or let them overwhelm you, I will confound you before them.

"But you shall be strong, for this day I have made you a fortified city, an iron pillar, and brass walls against the whole land, against the kings and princes of Judah, and against all the people of the land. Though they will fight against you, they will not prevail, for I am with you and will deliver you."

---

[577] The story line sequence is sometimes difficult to follow in the book of Jeremiah because the chapters do not seem to be arranged in proper sequence of time; thus the story jumps back and forth. Perhaps the best way to understand the book of Jeremiah is to group the chapters as they are grouped in the LDS-KJV *Bible Dictionary* (s.v. "Jeremiah"). The main groupings, as given there, are:

- Prophecies made during the reign of Josiah, chapters 1–6.
- Prophecies made during the reign of Jehoiakim, chapters 7–20.
- Prophecies made during the reign of Zedekiah, chapters 21–38.
- Jeremiah's history after the fall of Jerusalem, chapters 39–44.
- Prophecies against nations other than Judah (or Israel), chapters 46–51.
- Historical conclusion, chapter 52.

(See *Bible Dictionary*, LDS-KJV, s.v. "Jeremiah.")

[578] The many nations and kings to which Jeremiah was called to prophesy are named in Jeremiah 25:15–26. Note that "Jerusalem and the cities of Judah" were first on the list. Jeremiah's call to many nations was quite a contrast to the prophet Ezekiel's call, which was to the children of Israel only (see Ezekiel 2:3 and 3:4–6).

---

[579] The almond tree is the earliest tree to come into bloom in the land of Israel and thus was used as a symbol of haste.

[580] Or false prophets.

[581] Note that Jeremiah's call came five years before King Josiah's trusted servants found the book of the Law in the temple and he began his quest to restore the people of Judah to the true worship of Jehovah, as told in story "189–King Josiah Fulfills the Prophecy." Perhaps this accounts for Jehovah's harsh judgment of Judah's state of unrighteousness in this story, for Josiah certainly had turned things around.

191–AFTER THIS MANNER WILL I MAR THE PRIDE OF JUDAH

(Jeremiah 13)

The word of Jehovah came to the prophet Jeremiah saying, "Get a new linen girdle[582]—one that has never been put into water—and place it around your loins." And when Jeremiah had obeyed this first instruction, Jehovah spoke to him again: "Take now this girdle that is about your loins and go to Euphrates. There bury the girdle in a hole in a rock."

When many days had passed after Jeremiah had completed his assigned task, Jehovah spoke to him again, commanding him to return to Euphrates and retrieve his buried girdle. But when Jeremiah had retrieved the girdle from its hiding place, he saw that it was marred and good for nothing.

As Jeremiah looked at this now-worthless girdle that he had buried when it was new, the voice of Jehovah spoke to him again: "After this same manner will I mar the pride of Judah and the great pride of Jerusalem. For this evil people—who refuse to hear my words, who walk in the imagination of their hearts, who walk after and serve other gods—shall be even as this girdle.

"As a girdle cleaves to the loins of a man, so have I caused the whole house of Israel and the house of Judah to cleave to me that they might be my people and bear my name. And, though I caused them to receive my praise and my glory, they refused to hear me."

"Therefore," continued Jehovah, "tell them that Jehovah, the God of Israel, has said that every bottle shall be full of intoxicating wine. And, when they answer you that they already know this, tell them that Jehovah will fill all the inhabitants of this land—including their kings, their priests, and their prophets—with intoxication, as if they were bottles. Then tell them that I will dash them one against another, even the fathers against their sons. I will not pity, nor spare, nor have mercy on them—but I will destroy them. Tell them to listen and to be not proud, for I, Jehovah, have spoken.

"Tell them to give glory to me before I cause darkness and before their feet stumble upon the dark mountains. And while they wait for light, I will turn it into the shadow of death and make it gross darkness. And, if they will not hear it, my soul shall weep in secret places for their pride, and my eye shall weep sore and run down with tears because my flock is carried away captive."

Jehovah spoke to Jeremiah next concerning the rulers of Judah: "Tell the king and queen to humble themselves, for their principalities shall be brought down—even their crowns of glory. The cities of the south shall be shut up so that none shall open them, and all of Judah shall be carried away captive. Tell the king and queen also to look up and behold those who are coming from the north, for they shall carry away the flock that I have given them—yea, their beautiful flock.

"And if they ask in their hearts why these things have come upon them, tell them that their skirts have been discovered and their heels made bare because of the greatness of their iniquity.

"I will scatter their flock as the wind of the wilderness scatters the stubble. This is their lot and their portion from me because they have forgotten me and have trusted in falsehood. Woe unto Jerusalem, for I have seen her wickedness and her abominations.

"O, will she not repent and be made clean?"

---

[582] Girdles were highly prized in the Near East and were worn by both men and women. Some girdles were very decorative and others quite plain; they could be made either of leather or linen. They were sometimes embroidered with silk and even gold thread. An ornate girdle might also be studded with various kinds of gemstones. It was an important part of a soldier's battle dress and provided a place for a sword or dagger. Girding up ones loins was an essential preparation for battle. (see William Smith, *Dictionary of the Bible, GospeLink*, CD-ROM, s.v. "girdle").

192—THE POTTER AND HIS CLAY

(Jeremiah 18)

"Arise and go down to the potter's house," Jehovah said to Jeremiah, "and there I will cause you to hear my words." And when Jeremiah went and did as Jehovah required of him, he stood and watched as the potter worked clay upon his wheel. But when the vessel on the wheel was marred in the potter's hand, the potter threw it back and worked it again, molding and shaping it as it seemed good to him.

When Jeremiah had observed this process, Jehovah spoke to him as he had promised, but his words were addressed not to Jeremiah but to Judah and the house of Israel: "O house of Israel, can I not do with you as this potter? Behold, as the clay is in the potter's hands, so are you in my hands. If I speak against a nation or kingdom to pull it down or destroy it because of its wickedness, I will relent regarding that punishment if the people turn away from their evil. And if I speak concerning a nation or kingdom to build it up and establish it because of its righteousness, I will relent of the good that I thought to do if the people turn away and obey not my voice."[583]

Jehovah continued, now addressing his words to Jeremiah: "Go and speak to the men of Judah and the inhabitants of Jerusalem. Tell them that I frame evil against them and devise a device against them. But tell them also that if they will return from their evil ways and make their ways and their doings good, I will refrain from the evil that I have devised."

When Jeremiah went to the people and told them what Jehovah had said, they replied, "There is no hope. We will walk after our own devices and each of us will do the imaginations of his own heart."

Then Jehovah spoke again to the people through Jeremiah, saying, "Because my people have forgotten me, have burned incense to idols, and have stumbled from the ancient paths, their land shall become desolate and a perpetual hissing. And everyone who passes by shall be astonished and wag his head. I will scatter this people before their enemy as with an east wind. And I will show them my back instead of my face in the day of their calamity."

When the people heard Jehovah's message, they despised the messenger because they despised the message. "Come!" they said. "Let us devise devices[584] against Jeremiah, for the Law shall not perish from the priest, nor counsel from the wise, nor the word from the prophet. Let us smite this man with our tongues and give no heed to his words, for he prophesies only evil against us."

The people of Judah were beyond feeling and beyond repentance—though Jehovah still offered them the opportunity to repent. Though entrenched in wickedness, they were righteous in their own eyes. They had been adequately warned. But they, like the potter's clay, after it has been fashioned and fired, could not be reshaped, no matter how flawed.

---

[583] With regard to this demonstration of the potter and his clay, we find the following in *History of the Church*: "Elder Heber C. Kimball preached at the house of President Joseph Smith, on the parable in the 18th chapter of Jeremiah, of the clay in the hands of the potter, that when it marred in the hands of the potter it was cut off the wheel and then thrown back again into the mill, to go into the next batch, and was a vessel of dishonor; but all clay that formed well in the hands of the potter, and was pliable, was a vessel of honor; and thus it was with the human family, and ever will be: all that are pliable in the hands of God and are obedient to His commands, are vessels of honor, and God will receive them. President Joseph arose and said—'Brother Kimball has given you a true explanation of the parable' (HC 4:478)." (Quoted in Daniel H. Ludlow, *A Companion to Your Study of the Old Testament* [Salt Lake City: Deseret Book Co., 1981], 321–322)

---

[584] Or plans.

193—ONE MORE CHANCE
FOR JUDAH

(Jeremiah 26)

Jehovah was not through giving the people of Judah the opportunity to mend their ways. When King Josiah was dead and his son Jehoiakim ruled Judah,[585] Jehovah commanded Jeremiah to stand in the court of the temple and prophesy once more to all those who came to worship. "If they will hearken to your voice and turn from their evil ways," Jehovah told Jeremiah, "I will change my decree and will not cause evil to come upon them. But if they refuse to hearken to my prophets and repent, I will make this temple like Shiloh,[586] and this city shall be desolate and shall be a curse to all nations of the earth."

When Jeremiah had delivered Jehovah's unpopular message to the people and their priests, the people called for him to be put to death. And when the princes of Judah came to the temple from the king's palace, the priests and the people cried out to them, saying that Jeremiah was worthy of death.

Then Jeremiah, fearless before his accusers, rose up and spoke to the princes and all the people. "Jehovah sent me here to prophesy to this people all these words that you have heard," he said, "but if you will repent, he will turn away the evil that I have prophesied. And, though I am in your hands to do with me as seems good to you, know this for certain: if you put me to death, you will bring innocent blood both upon yourselves and upon this city."

King Jehoiakim was willing to put Jeremiah to death, but the princes of Judah were not ready to take that chance. "Wait," they cried to the people and the priests. "This man does not deserve to die, for he has spoken in the name of Jehovah." Though many other prophets had been slain for their prophecies against

Jerusalem, the princes—especially Ahikam, the son of Shaphan[587]—prevented Jeremiah's death at this time.

---

[585] Note that Jehoiakim did not become the king of Judah immediately after his father's death. King Josiah was actually succeeded by his son Jehoahaz, but Jehoahaz served for only three months before he was taken captive to Egypt. His brother Jehoiakim, previously known as Eliakim, took his place (see story "195—The Burning of the Book").

[586] This reference to the destruction of Shiloh is interesting, but the scriptures are otherwise silent on any great evil befalling Shiloh. Shiloh was the resting place of the tabernacle and the ark of the covenant—and thus the religious center of all Israel—until the ark was taken into battle and fell into the hands of the Philistines (see story "94—The Glory Departs from Israel).

[587] Shaphan and his son Ahikam were among the advisers to King Josiah just a few years earlier when the book of the Law was discovered in the temple and read to the people. Shaphan had been King Josiah's scribe (see story "189—King Josiah Fulfills the Prophecy").

194—AS THIS JUG IS BROKEN

(Jeremiah 19–20)

Jehovah spoke again to Jeremiah. "Get a potter's earthen jug," he said, "and take it to Tophet[588] in the valley of Hinnom. Take the elders of the people, the priests, and also the king of Judah there with you. When you are there, you will deliver my message to them, telling them that I will bring such evil upon the kings of Judah and the people of Jerusalem that it will make the ears of all who hear it tingle.

"My wrath is upon them because they have forsaken me and estranged this place. They have burned incense to other gods in this place and filled it with the blood of innocent people. They have also built up the high places of Baal to offer their sons as burnt offerings—which thing I did not command them; neither did such a thing come into my mind.

"Because of these things, the day will come when this place shall no more be called Tophet, nor the valley of the son of Hinnom, but the valley of slaughter. I will make void the counsel of Judah and Jerusalem in this place, and I will make them also fall by the sword before their enemies and by the hands of those who seek their lives. And I will give their carcasses to be meat for the fowls of heaven and the beasts of the earth."

Jehovah continued his dire promise for Tophet: "I will make this city desolate and a hissing. And everyone who passes by shall be astonished and hiss because of its plagues. I will cause the inhabitants to eat the flesh of their children. And every man shall eat the flesh of his friend because of the strictness of the siege by their enemies."

Jehovah told Jeremiah that, when he delivered this message to the people whom he would take with him to Tophet, he should break the potter's earthen jug in their sight and tell them the following: "Thus says Jehovah: as this jug is broken—because it is no longer pliable in the potter's hand—I will also break this people and this city so that they can never again be made whole. They shall be buried in Tophet until there are no places left to bury. The houses of Jerusalem and of the kings of Judah shall also be as Tophet, because of all those houses upon the roofs of which they have burned in-cense to the hosts of heaven[589] and poured out drink offerings to other gods."

When Jeremiah had delivered Jehovah's message at Tophet and had done all that Jehovah commanded him, he returned to Jerusalem. Once there, he stood in the court of the temple and said to the people, "Thus says Jehovah, the God of Israel: 'I will bring upon this city and all the towns of Judah all the evil that I have prophesied against them because they have hardened their necks and will not hear my words.'"

Pashur, the son of Immer the priest—who was also chief governor of the temple—was angry with Jeremiah for what he had said, and he put Jeremiah in stocks at the high gate of Benjamin near the temple. After spending a miserable night in stocks, Jeremiah was taken before Pashur.

Jeremiah spoke first. "Jehovah has not called your name Pashur," he said, "but Magor-missabib.[590] For thus says Jehovah: 'I will make you a terror to yourself and to all your friends. They shall fall by the swords of their enemies and your eyes shall behold it. For I will give all Judah into the hands of the king of Babylonia, and he shall carry them captive and slay them with the sword.'"

Jeremiah continued, still speaking for Jehovah to Pashur: "And I will deliver all the strength of this city, all its labors, and all its precious things—as well as the treasures of the kings of Judah—into the hands of Judah's enemies, who will carry them to Babylon. You, Pashur, and all who dwell in your house shall be taken into captivity. You will be carried to Babylon where you will die and be buried—you and your friends to whom you have prophesied your lies."

---

[588] Tophet is usually called Topheth in the scriptures. It was a place in the valley of Hinnom, southwest of Jerusalem, where human sacrifices were made to the Ammonite fire god Molech.

[589] The hosts of heaven are the heavenly bodies—the sun, the moon, the planets, and the stars (see Genesis 2:1; Deuteronomy 4:19; 2 Kings 21:3, 5; 23:5).

[590] The name Magor-missabib means "terror all around."

195—THE BURNING
OF THE BOOK

(2 Kings 23–24; 2 Chronicles 36; Jeremiah 21, 25, 36, 45)

When righteous King Josiah was dead, the people of Judah made his wicked son Jehoahaz king, but the reign of King Jehoahaz in Judah was very short. He was captured by Pharaoh-necho, the man responsible for Josiah's death,[591] and put into prison at Riblah in northern Syria. In the meantime, Necho extracted 100 talents of silver and one talent of gold as tribute from the land of Judah.[592]

With Jehoahaz in prison at Riblah, after reigning for only three months, Necho made Eliakim, Jehoahaz's brother, king. Eliakim was chosen because he feared Necho and was willing to do whatever Necho told him to do. Necho changed Eliakim's name to Jehoiakim[593] and took Jehoahaz to Egypt, where he eventually died.

During King Jehoiakim's eleven-year reign in Jerusalem, he taxed the people heavily to raise the tribute demanded by Pharaoh-necho. And because Jehoiakim did what was evil in Jehovah's sight, Jehovah allowed his troubles to continue.

In Jehoiakim's fourth year, Jehovah commanded Jeremiah to make a book[594] and write in it all the prophecies that he had made against Israel, Judah, and their neighboring nations since he was called to be a prophet twenty-three years earlier. "It may be," Jehovah told Jeremiah, "that the house of Judah will hear all the injury that I intend to do to them and return from their evil ways so that I can forgive them." In spite of Judah's long history of wickedness, Jehovah still had hope that the people of Judah would repent.

In response to Jehovah's instructions, Jeremiah called his scribe Baruch to write the prophecies as he dictated them. And when the book was finished, Jeremiah—because the king had put restraints upon him—commanded Baruch to go and read it to the people of Judah. "Read in the temple on the fasting day the words that you have written from my mouth," Jeremiah commanded Baruch. "Read in the ears of all Judah in all their cities, for the book contains the words of Jehovah unto them. Perhaps these prophecies will cause them to depart from their evil ways, for great is the anger and fury that Jehovah has pronounced against Judah." And Baruch went and did all that Jeremiah commanded him.

In King Jehoiakim's fifth year, as the people came to Jerusalem from all of Judah for the fasting day, Baruch stood in the higher court, at the entry of the new gate to the temple, and read from Jeremiah's prophecies so that all the people could hear him. When Michaiah, the grandson of the king's scribe, heard what Baruch was reading, he went and told the princes.

Being greatly alarmed by Michaiah's report, the princes sent for Baruch and requested that he come and read the book to them. And when they heard what Baruch read from Jeremiah's book, they knew that they must tell the king.

The princes spoke quietly to Baruch, warning him that both he and Jeremiah should hide and tell no one their hiding place. And though they sent Baruch away, they kept the book and hid it in the chamber of Elishama the scribe.

Filled with fear, the princes of Judah told King Jehoiakim of what Baruch had read, but they did not take the book to him.

"Bring me the book!" demanded the king. "Bring it here and read it to me." So the book was brought and, at King Jehoiakim's request, Jehudi read Jeremiah's prophecies to him one by one while all the princes of Judah listened.

When Jehudi had read part of the book, Jehoiakim took his penknife and cut that part from the book, throwing the severed portion into the fire that was burning on the hearth. When Jehudi had read more, the king also cut that part out of the book and burned it. This pattern continued until the entire book was read and all of it had been burned. Though some of the king's advisers had pleaded with him not to burn the book, their pleadings were ignored. The message of Jeremiah's prophecies was biting and poignant, but no one present

---

[591] The death of King Josiah at the hands of Pharaoh-necho of Egypt is told in story "189–King Josiah Fulfills the Prophecy" and in footnote 576. Following Josiah's death, the kingdom of Judah was subject to the conquering Egyptians and remained subservient to Egypt until both Egypt and Judah were conquered by the Babylonians. Most of the Jews had the erroneous notion that the Egyptians would save them from the Babylonians.

[592] A talent of silver weighed 3,000 shekels, or just more than 75.5 pounds (34.29 kilograms). Thus, 100 talents of silver would weigh about 7,560 pounds (3429 kilograms), or nearly 3.8 tons (3.38 long tons or 3.43 metric tons). A talent of gold weighed 10,000 shekels or about 252 pounds (114.3 kilograms).

[593] The significance of this name change is not clear, but the name Jehoiakim means "Jehovah raises him up" (*Bible Dictionary*, LDS-KJV, s.v. "Jehoiakim").

[594] This would not have been the kind of book that we know in modern times but was most likely a piece of parchment rolled up as a scroll.

showed signs of fear. It was as if, to them, the prophecies were nullified when the book was burned.

King Jehoiakim, now very angry, commanded that both Jeremiah and Baruch be captured and brought to him, but Jehovah had hid them where they could not be found.

Once more Jehovah spoke to Jeremiah, informing him that Jehoiakim had burned the book of prophecies. "But take another book," said Jehovah, "and write in it all those prophecies that were in the first. And when they are written, you shall tell Jehoiakim that—because he has burned your book, thinking to nullify my words—the king of Babylonia shall come and destroy this land, leaving neither man nor beast.

"Jehoiakim's issue shall not sit on David's throne, and his dead body shall be cast out to the heat in the day and to the frost in the night. I will punish him, his seed, and his servants for their iniquity, and I will bring upon them every evil that I have spoken against them. That which I have built I shall break down, and that which I have planted I shall pluck up—even this whole land."

Jeremiah obediently obtained another book and gave it to Baruch to write again the prophecies as they fell from Jeremiah's lips. The new book contained all that had been in the first, plus many more prophecies of similar portent. When it was finished, Jeremiah went forth to prophesy and to deliver to Jehoiakim the message that Jehovah had given him. He told the people plainly that the Babylonians would come against Judah and her inhabitants to destroy them. "Behold, Jehovah will take your voice of mirth and gladness from you," said Jeremiah. "He will also take away your bride and your bridegroom, and you will serve the king of Babylonia for seventy years."

Life had been hard—though not unbearable—for King Jehoiakim and the people of Judah under the tyranny of the Egyptians. And, just when things seemed to be improving, King Nebuchadnezzar of Babylonia invaded the land of Judah, bound Jehoiakim in chains, and took him captive to Babylon. Nebuchadnezzar also took with him to Babylon the vessels of the temple and put them in his own temple, but Jerusalem had not yet fallen and the people of Judah still believed that they would prevail.

196—JUDAH ON THE BRINK OF DESTRUCTION
(2 Kings 24; 2 Chronicles 36; 1 Nephi 1)

When Jehoiakim, the son of Josiah, was taken to Babylon in chains,[595] his eight-year-old son, Jehoiachin[596] became king of Judah. At the end of the year, however—after reigning for just three months and ten days—Jehoiachin was also taken to Babylon, and King Nebuchadnezzar appointed Mattaniah—another of Josiah's sons—as king over Judah.[597] And Nebuchadnezzar changed Mattaniah's name to Zedekiah.[598]

King Zedekiah, like his brothers Jehoahaz and Jehoiakim, was a wicked man and refused to be humble, in spite of the afflictions heaped upon him. He would not listen to the prophets who foretold Judah's destruction and captivity, even though Jerusalem lay in a state of siege.

When Zedekiah sent messengers to the prophet Jeremiah asking Jeremiah to inquire of Jehovah in his behalf and to seek deliverance, Jeremiah's response was not favorable to the king. "Thus shall you say to Zedekiah," Jeremiah told the king's messengers, "Jehovah, the God of Israel, will turn back the weapons that are in the hands of Judah, which you use to fight against Babylonia[599] and the Chaldeans.[600] He will bring your own weapons against you into the midst of this city.

---

[595] See story "195—The Burning of the Book."

[596] In various places in the scriptures, Jehoiachin is also called Coniah, Joachin, and Jeconiah.

[597] Because Jehoiakim burned Jeremiah's book of prophecies, Jehovah, through Jeremiah, promised that Jehoiakim's issue would not sit on David's throne. This is the fulfillment of that promise (see story "195—The Burning of the Book").

[598] The significance of this name change is unknown. However, the name Zedekiah means "the right of Jehovah" (see "The King James Bible with Strong's Dictionary," *The HTML Bible* [2004], < http://www.sacrednamebible.com/kjvstrongs/index2.htm >).

[599] Though there is some variation of usage in the scriptures, the country was Babylonia and the city was Babylon. In these stories, there has been an attempt to use the proper designations.

[600] The Chaldeans (or the Chaldees) were the most prominent tribe in the country of Babylonia at the time of the captivity. This title was frequently used in the scriptures to refer to the people of Babylonia.

"Jehovah himself will fight against you in fury, with an outstretched hand and a strong arm. He will smite the inhabitants of Jerusalem that they shall die of a great pestilence. He will then deliver Zedekiah and those who do not die from pestilence and famine into the hands of the king of Babylonia. He will not spare them but will smite them with the edge of the sword, showing neither pity nor mercy."

Jeremiah's dire prophecy continued: "Tell the people of Jerusalem that Jehovah will deliver those who are in the city to death by the sword, by famine, and by pestilence unless they surrender to the Chaldeans. If they will surrender, they shall live—though their lives shall be unto Nebuchadnezzar as the lives of those who are prey. For Jehovah has set his face against Jerusalem for evil and he will give it into the hands of the king of Babylonia, who shall burn the city with fire." This message was certainly not encouraging to the king, nor did it serve to improve his opinion of Jeremiah.

But, in spite of Jeremiah's grim message, neither Zedekiah nor the people of Judah would humble themselves. They continued to worship their heathen idols and to pollute the house of the Lord. They mocked Jehovah's messengers and despised their words, abusing and misusing them until Jehovah's wrath rose up against them and there was no remedy.

In the first year of Zedekiah's reign in Judah, a prophet named Lehi was among those who warned the people of Jerusalem of their impending destruction and Babylonian captivity, declaring the words that Jehovah had told him. But the Jews rejected Lehi and sought to take his life, just as they had rejected Jeremiah's and the other prophets.[601]

The stiffnecked Jews still listened to the ranting and lying of their false prophets and clung doggedly to their misguided belief that Egypt would save them from their Babylonian tormentors. The stage was set for the kingdom of Judah to feel the full power of God's wrath.

197—HANANIAH
(Jeremiah 27–28)

At the beginning of King Jehoiakim's reign in Judah, the Lord commanded Jeremiah to make bonds and yokes and wear them on his neck as he prophesied concerning the captivity and destruction that were to come upon Judah and her neighbors at the hands of the Babylonians. Jeremiah not only prophesied of these terrible events, but also warned the people against the false prophets who uttered promises of peace and of freedom from the Babylonians.

In the fifth month of the first year of Zedekiah's reign, a man named Hananiah, the son of Azur, came to Jeremiah in the temple before the priests and all the people. Claiming to be inspired of God, Hananiah began to prophesy concerning the fate of Judah.

"Thus says the Lord Jehovah," said Hananiah. "'I have broken the yoke of the king of Babylonia. Within two years I will bring again into this place all the vessels of the house of the Lord that Nebuchadnezzar has taken away and carried to Babylon.'"

Hananiah continued, still speaking—as he said—in behalf of Jehovah, "And I will bring again to this place Jehoiachin,[602] the son of Jehoiakim king of Judah, with all the captives of Judah that went to Babylon, for I will break the yoke of the king of Babylonia."

Jeremiah could not let this go unchallenged. When he heard Hananiah's prophecy, he stood up in the presence of the priests and the people to answer him. "Amen!" he said to Hananiah. "May the Lord Jehovah bring to pass all that you have spoken."

But then Jeremiah's mood became more serious. "Nevertheless," he continued, "listen carefully to the words that I will speak into your ears. The prophets of old who were before us prophesied both against many countries and against great kingdoms, telling of wars, of evil, and of pestilence. But there is a test by which the truth of any prophecy may be known. That test is this: if a prophet prophesies of peace, and the word of the prophet comes to pass, then it shall be known that Jehovah has sent him."

When Jeremiah had spoken, Hananiah lifted the yoke from Jeremiah's neck and broke it. "Thus says Jehovah," said Hananiah. "'As I have broken this yoke, even so will I break the yoke of Nebuchadnezzar from

---

[601] See 1 Nephi 1 in the Book of Mormon for a discussion of Lehi's experience when he sought to warn the Jews of their destruction and captivity.

[602] In this scripture (Jeremiah 28) the name Jeconiah is used. I have used the name Jehoiachin in this story for consistency. He is the young man who served as king of Judah for three months and ten days after the death of his father before being taken captive to Babylon (see story "196—Judah on the Brink of Destruction").

the neck of all nations within the space of two full years.'" And, when Jeremiah heard this strange prophecy from Hananiah, he did not respond but went his way in disgust.

Then the word of Jehovah came to Jeremiah: "Return and tell Hananiah that though he has broken a wooden yoke, I have put an iron yoke upon the neck of all these nations that they may serve King Nebuchadnezzar. Tell Hananiah that not only will the people of these nations serve King Nebuchadnezzar, but I have also given him the beasts of the field."

In obedience to Jehovah, Jeremiah went back to the temple, where he found Hananiah and delivered Jehovah's message. Then he said, "Hear me now, Hananiah. Because Jehovah has not sent you and you have caused this people to trust in a lie, he will cast you from the face of the earth. You shall die this very year because you have taught rebellion against Jehovah."

And, according to Jeremiah's word, Hananiah died in the seventh month of the year.

198—JEREMIAH'S IMPRISONMENT
(Jeremiah 37, 32, 38)[603]

The Egyptians were anxious to protect their interests in the land of Judah and sent their army to deter the Chaldeans.[604] When the Egyptian army came into the land, the Chaldeans, who had besieged the city, withdrew, but the situation in Jerusalem was still difficult. And, as life became progressively more difficult for the people of Judah, King Zedekiah sent messengers to the prophet Jeremiah asking that he pray in behalf of the people.

As Jeremiah considered the king's request, Jehovah spoke to him and said, "Have these messengers tell King Zedekiah that this army that has come to help him will abandon him and return to Egypt and—when they are gone—the Chaldeans will come again. Tell the king not to be deceived into thinking that the Chaldeans will depart, for they will not. Even if Zedekiah should smite their whole army and only wounded men remain, they will rise up and burn Jerusalem."

When the Babylonians abandoned their siege of Jerusalem because of their fear of the Egyptians, Jeremiah also left Jerusalem and went to the land of Benjamin. He felt it was best to leave Jerusalem because his words had brought him nothing but trouble. Going to Benjamin, however, did not protect him from the wrath of the people as he had hoped. When he came to Benjamin, a man named Irijah confronted him at the gate. "You have deserted your own people to embrace the Chaldeans," Irijah accused him.

"That is not true!" Jeremiah insisted, "for I have spoken only that which Jehovah has told me." But Irijah was not convinced. He delivered Jeremiah to the princes, who promptly beat him and imprisoned him in the house of Jonathan the scribe.

When Jeremiah had been imprisoned for many days, King Zedekiah had him brought secretly to Jerusalem so he could question him. "Is there any word from Jehovah?" Zedekiah asked the prophet.

"There is," replied Jeremiah. "Jehovah says that you shall be delivered into the hands of the king of Babylonia."

---

[603] See footnote 577 in story "190—A Prophet to the Nations."

[604] The Chaldeans (or Chaldees) were the most prominent tribe in the country of Babylonia at the time of the captivity. This title was frequently used in the scriptures to refer to the people of Babylonia.

Then Jeremiah changed the subject. "What is my offense against you or against this people that I have been put into prison? And where are your prophets now who swore that the Chaldeans would not come against you or against this land? But if you must keep me in prison, I pray of you, O my lord the king, do not send me back to Jonathan's house, lest I should die there."

And King Zedekiah, taking pity on Jeremiah, put him in the prison court at Jerusalem. There he received a piece of bread each day until there was no bread left in the city.

While in prison, Jeremiah continued to prophesy, renewing his message to Zedekiah that he would be delivered into the hands of the Chaldeans. "You will speak with the king of Babylonia mouth to mouth and your eyes shall behold his," said Jeremiah. "He will lead you to Babylon where you will remain. Jehovah has also declared that all who remain in this city will die—either by the sword, by famine, or by pestilence. If you fight against the Babylonians you shall not prosper, for only those who surrender shall live."

While Jeremiah was languishing in the prison court, Jehovah told him that his cousin Hanameel would come and request him to buy a field. And, just as Jehovah had said, Hanameel soon came and told Jeremiah of a field in Anathoth[605] that he had a right to redeem.[606]

When the redemption was complete and the deed delivered, Jeremiah gave the papers to his scribe Baruch for safekeeping. "Take the deed and the evidence of my purchase," he told Baruch, "and seal them in a earthen vessel where they will be preserved. Though Jerusalem will be given into the hands of the Chaldeans, Jehovah has told me that my purchase of this land will be a sign that the houses and vineyards that he gave to our fathers shall again be possessed by this people. And though the wrath of Jehovah is now poured out upon them for their disobedience, he will also bring them back from their captivity. For nothing is too hard for Jehovah."

Because of Jeremiah's many prophecies concerning the success of the Babylonians, the Jews hated him. The princes of Judah pleaded with King Zedekiah to put him to death. "This man weakens the hands of our men of war," they complained to the king, "as well as the hands of all the people. He seeks our hurt and not our welfare."

Zedekiah gave in to the princes' protests. "Jeremiah is in your hands to do with as you wish," he told them, "for I cannot prevail against you."

With these words of permission from Zedekiah, the princes did not kill Jeremiah outright but let him down with ropes into the dungeon of Malchiah beneath the prison court. The dungeon was filled with miry mud, and there was neither water to drink nor food to eat; death would be an early visitor.

And, except for the actions of an Ethiopian eunuch named Ebed-melech who served in the king's palace, Jeremiah would have perished in the dungeon. But Ebed-melech intervened with King Zedekiah in Jeremiah's behalf. "These men have done evil," he said to Zedekiah. "They have put the prophet Jeremiah into the dungeon, where he will perish from hunger."

Responding to Ebed-melech's pleadings, Zedekiah commanded Ebed-melech to take thirty men and rescue the prophet. And thus Jeremiah was delivered from the pit and confined once more in the prison court.

The siege of Jerusalem by the Chaldeans was wearing hard on Judah's king, and he sent once more for Jeremiah—this time to meet him at the third entry of the temple. "I will ask you but one question," said the king to Jeremiah, "and I insist that you hide nothing from me when you answer."

"You put me in a difficult position," responded Jeremiah. "If I tell you the truth you will put me to death, and if I give you counsel you will not listen."

So Zedekiah swore an oath. "As Jehovah lives who made us," said Zedekiah, "I will not put you to death, neither will I give you into the hands of those men who seek your life."

Trusting the king's word, Jeremiah gave his reply: "If you will go out and surrender yourself to the king of the Babylonians, you and your family will be allowed to live and Jerusalem will not be burned. But if you will not do it, this great city will be given into the hands of Chaldeans. They will burn the city and you shall not escape."

Zedekiah was perplexed by Jeremiah message. "I am afraid of the Jews who have deserted to the Chaldeans," he said. "I fear that they will deliver me into the hands of the Chaldeans and I will be mistreated."

"They shall not deliver you," Jeremiah promised. "If you will obey the voice of Jehovah, you shall live. But, if you refuse to go forth, Jehovah has shown me that you will cause this city to be burned. You will not escape, and the women and children of your house will be brought forth to the Babylonian princes."

---

[605] Anathoth was a city in Benjamin that belonged to the priests. It was about three miles (4.8 kilometers) from Jerusalem.

[606] A person with the right of redemption could prevent property from going to any other claimant by purchasing it. The property involved was property that had belonged to an ancestor or close family member who had died. The closest relative had the right of redemption ahead of all others. This allowed property that could not be inherited because of an encumbrance, to be redeemed and remain in the family.

King Zedekiah wanted to believe Jeremiah, but Jeremiah never seemed to tell him what he wanted to hear. Though he was not completely convinced that Jeremiah's words were true, he was still careful. "Let no man know what we have discussed," he told Jeremiah, "and you shall not die. If the princes should hear that I have talked to you on this matter, they will not hesitate to put you to death. So, when they ask about this conversation, tell them that you pleaded with me not to return you to the house of Jonathan the scribe."

And so it was that when the princes of Judah asked Jeremiah about his conversation with the king, he told them as the king had said, and they remained ignorant of what had taken place. Thus, Jeremiah remained in the prison court until the day Jerusalem was taken by the Chaldeans.

199—A WATCHMAN TO THE HOUSE OF ISRAEL
(Ezekiel 1–5, 18)

Ezekiel was the son of Buzi the priest and a descendant of Zadok, who served as high priest in the days of King David. He was one of those men who had been taken captive by the armies of King Nebuchadnezzar of Babylonia prior to the fall of Jerusalem. In the fifth year of King Jehoiachin's captivity,[607] Ezekiel was living among the Hebrew exiles at the river Chebar.[608] It was here that Jehovah first spoke to him, showing him heavenly visions and calling him to his prophetic ministry.

Ezekiel was shown a vision in which he saw a mighty whirlwind coming out of the north, with a great cloud and a fire that burned continuously. In the whirlwind was the chariot-throne of God, which was nearly impossible to describe, yet Ezekiel attempted to do so. The chariot-throne, he said, was suspended on marvelous wheels by four identical creatures—which Ezekiel later identified as cherubim[609]—each creature having four faces and four wings. "And over their heads," he said, "was the likeness of a throne that had the appearance of a sapphire stone. And upon the throne sat a being who appeared in the likeness of a man."

Ezekiel then described the glory of Jehovah that emanated from the throne. He said it was like fire and like the rainbow that is in the cloud on a rainy day.

"Stand upon your feet, son of man," said Jehovah, speaking to Ezekiel from his throne. And the Spirit entered Ezekiel and stood him up upon his feet. Then Jehovah spoke: "I will send you to the children of Israel,[610] a rebellious nation of impudent and stubborn

---

[607] This would have been about 592 BC—still five years before the fall of Jerusalem (see story "196—Judah on the Brink of Destruction"). Jehoiachin was brought out of prison in Babylon by King Evil-merodach and placed in authority over all of the other kings that had been taken to Babylon (see Jeremiah 52:31–34).

[608] The river Chebar is believed by many to be the Royal Canal of King Nebuchadnezzar, which was dug—probably by the captive Jews—to join the Tigris and Euphates Rivers.

[609] See Ezekiel 10. A cherub is a figure that represents a heavenly creature, the exact form of which is unknown. The plural form is cherubim. Ezekiel's description of a cherub here may be as good as any we have.

[610] The call of Ezekiel to the children of Israel only was in contrast to the call of the prophet Jeremiah, who was

children. Whether they will listen to you or not, they shall know that there has been a prophet among them. You must speak to them the words that I give you, although they will refuse to hear you.

"Eat that which I will give you," Jehovah instructed Ezekiel. And a hand came forth holding a scroll, which was then spread out before him to show that there was writing on both sides. And words of lamentation, mourning, and woe were written upon the scroll.

"Eat this scroll," said Jehovah, "then go and speak to the house of Israel." When Ezekiel ate the scroll it was sweet in his mouth and it filled his belly and his bowels with the word of Jehovah.

"Go now," said Jehovah, "and speak my words to these people. And though they will not hearken to your voice, do not fear them."

Jehovah sent Ezekiel first to those Jews already in captivity, and he went to teach those who were at Tel-abib.[611] Ezekiel sat among the people of Tel-abib and taught them for seven days. And, when the seven days had passed, Jehovah spoke to him again saying, "I have made you a watchman to the house of Israel. Therefore hear my words and give Judah a warning from me. If I say that the wicked will die and you do not warn them, their blood will be on your hands. And if those who have been warned do not turn from their wickedness, you will have delivered your soul.

"Also, if those who are righteous turn away from their righteousness, I will lay a stumbling block before them and they will die. If they die in their sins and you did not warn them, their blood will be on your hands. Nevertheless, if you warn them and they do not sin, they shall live because they were warned and you will have delivered your soul."

Then Jehovah, speaking rhetorically, asked, "Have I any pleasure when the wicked die rather than repent of their sinful ways?" Then, answering his own question with both compassion and pleading, he said, "Why will you die, O house of Israel? I have no pleasure in your death. Cast away your transgressions and make you a new heart and a new spirit. Yeah, turn yourselves and live."

Jehovah next sent Ezekiel to preach to those who were on the plain. But as Ezekiel went, Jehovah seemed to change his mind and spoke to him again: "Do not go to these people for they will put bands upon you. Go instead and shut yourself in your own house, for I will

cause your tongue to cleave to the roof of your mouth among this people because of their rebellion. You shall be dumb before them and shall not be their reprover. But when I would speak to them, I will open your mouth and will say 'Thus says Jehovah.' Then let those hear you who will hear. And let those who will not hear you forbear, for they are a rebellious house."

Jehovah instructed Ezekiel to make a demonstration of the siege and the taking of Jerusalem by her enemies. He was to first make a small model of the city on a tile, then use this model to demonstrate an attack against the city. "Set up also a camp against it and fortifications, then build up an embankment and set battering rams against it round about. When you have done this, take an iron pan and set it up for a wall of iron between you and the city and lay siege against it. This demonstration will be a sign to the house of Israel."

Jehovah then told Ezekiel to give a second sign to the people, to go along with the first, by lying on his sides—first on his left side for 390 days, and then on his right side for forty days.[612] "And according to the number of days," said Jehovah, "you will bear the iniquity of this people. Each day will represent one year, for it has been 390 years since the kingdom of Israel was split into two kingdoms. And it has been forty years since great wickedness came to the kingdom of Judah.[613]

"As you lie on your side, your face shall be set toward the siege of Jerusalem. Your arm shall be uncovered, and you shall prophesy against it. And I will lay bands upon you so that you do not turn from one side to the other until you have ended the days of your siege."

Jehovah then told Ezekiel concerning a third sign that he was to give of the fate of the people of Jerusalem. "Make bread of mixed grains and, according to the number of days that you are lying on your sides, you shall eat twenty shekels' weight of this bread each day, and nothing else.[614] You shall also drink a sixth part of a hin of water each day,[615] and your bread shall be baked by burning the dung of man."

When Ezekiel protested the use of human dung, Jehovah allowed him to use cow dung in its place, but emphasized that it would not be so among the Jews during the siege of Jerusalem.

---

called as a prophet to many nations (see Jeremiah 25:15–26 and story "190–A Prophet to the Nations").
[611] Tel-abib (which means "corn hill") was a city on the river Chebar. Its exact location is unknown (see William Smith, *Dictionary of the Bible*, GospeLink, CD-ROM, s.v. "Tel-abib").

[612] It is not clear how Ezekiel was able to lie on his side for this length of time. Apparently some symbolism here has not been explained.
[613] The date forty years earlier would have been near the end of King Josiah's reign in Judah.
[614] The grains for each day's ration would weight about one-half pound (226.8 grams).
[615] This was about one quart of water (.95 liters).

The fourth sign specified by Jehovah required Ezekiel to shave off his hair and divide it into three equal piles. "The first pile you shall burn in the city when the days of the siege are fulfilled," said Jehovah. "The second pile you shall smite with a sharp knife, and the third you shall scatter in the wind. You shall also take a small amount of your hair and bind it in your skirts—then take this part again and cast it into the midst of the fire. From such will the fire come forth unto all the house of Israel."

Jehovah continued: "I have set Jerusalem in the midst of the nations that are round about her. And because she has changed my judgments into wickedness and refused to walk in my statutes, I will execute my judgments in her midst in the sight of the nations. Because of her abominations, I will do to her what I have never done before and will never do again. Therefore shall the fathers eat their sons in the midst of her. The sons shall also eat their fathers, and I will scatter her whole remnant to the winds. A third part shall be consumed with pestilence and famine, a third part will fall by the sword, and a third part I will scatter into all the winds and will draw out a sword after them.

"I will make Israel a waste and a reproach among the nations. I will make her also a reproach and a taunt, an instruction and astonishment unto all nations when I execute my judgments against her. She will suffer with famine, with evil beasts, with pestilence, and with the sword. For I Jehovah have spoken it."

200—JUDAH, THE HARLOT WIFE
(Ezekiel 6–16)

The prophet Ezekiel made his home among the Jewish exiles in Tel-abib on the River Chebar and went forth prophesying to the people of Judah as Jehovah commanded him. His mission was to prophesy against the kingdom of Judah and the stiffnecked Jewish people. "Tell them," Jehovah said, "that I will shortly pour out my fury upon them, that I will judge them according to their ways, and that I will repay them for their abominations."

Jehovah gave Ezekiel a vision of Jerusalem that he might see for himself the wickedness of the people. He was shown the works that they did in their secret places when they though that Jehovah could not see them. He was also shown that, even in the temple, the people of Judah bowed down and worshipped the sun.

He saw in his vision a man with a writer's inkhorn that Jehovah sent out to mark the foreheads of those few who were righteous so that they might be spared. And when Ezekiel saw the destruction of the wicked and the scattering of those who were left, he mourned for them.

When Jehovah told Ezekiel to rebuke the false prophets of Israel, he did so. "Woe unto you foolish prophets who follow your own spirits and have seen nothing," he told them. "You have prophesied in vain. Though Jehovah has not sent you, your prophecies have made others hope. Woe also unto you women who prophesy from your own hearts and follow magical arts," he said. "You have made the hearts of the righteous sad and strengthened the hands of the wicked by promising them life.

"As a vine in the forest of trees is cut down and used for fuel, so Jehovah will burn the inhabitants of Jerusalem. He will set his face against them and when they come forth out of one fire, another fire will devour them."

Jehovah gave Ezekiel this parable, which Ezekiel told to the people: "Your father, O house of Judah, is the Amorite, and your mother the Hittite.[616] But when you were young and tender your father and mother had no regard for you and cast you away into the field. When I found you there, I cared for you and saved you from death. I nurtured you carefully and, when you

---

[616] This parable, which names the Amorites and the Hittites as the father and mother of Judah, was given because Judah, though in the promised land, was worshipping the gods of the heathens.

were grown, I made you my wife and made a covenant with you. However, you trusted in your own beauty and had no respect for me. You became like a harlot because of your renown and poured out your fornications on every one that passed by. You also took the jewels, the gold, and the silver that I gave you and used them to make images of men, before which you set my oil and my incense. And to those images you have offered the fine flour, oil, and honey with which I fed you. And you have taken the sons and daughters that you have borne unto me and offered them as sacrifices.

"You also committed fornication with your neighbors the Egyptians and the Assyrians, and multiplied your fornication in the land of Canaan unto Chaldea,[617] turning to them rather than to me, and still you were not satisfied. Yet, in all this, you have not been as the true harlot—for you have scorned any payment for your favors. In fact, you have been like the wife who goes in to strangers in preference to her husband, and then, instead of receiving gifts from them, scorns their gifts and offers a reward to them.

"Your elder sister is Samaria and your younger sister Sodom. And though they were sinful, you have not walked after their ways. You have been more corrupt than they. Even your younger sister Sodom and Sodom's daughters[618] did not sin as you and your daughters have sinned.

"Nevertheless," Jehovah continued his parable, "I will remember the covenant that I made with you in the days of your youth, and will establish an everlasting covenant with you. When you remember your ways and are ashamed, you shall receive your sisters—both the elder and the younger—for I will give them to you as daughters, though not by the covenant. In that day I will establish my covenant with you and you shall know that I am God.

"And though I shall cast you afar off among the heathen and scatter your people among the countries, yet will I be to you as a refuge in those countries where you go. And I will gather you from among the people where you have been scattered and give you the land of Israel. I will also give you one heart and put into you a new spirit. I will take your stony heart out of you and give you a heart of flesh, that you may walk in my stat-utes and keep my ordinances. You will be my people and I will be your God."

But the people of Judah gave no heed to Ezekiel when he told them these things.

---

[617] The Chaldeans (or the Chaldees) were the most prominent tribe in the country of Babylonia at the time of the captivity. This title was generally used in the scriptures to refer to the people of Babylonia.

[618] The daughters of Sodom in Ezekiel's parable are the Moabites and Ammonites, those peoples who were descendants of Lot, whom Jehovah delivered from Sodom when the city was destroyed.

201−TWO EAGLES, THE CEDAR TREE, AND THE VINE
(Ezekiel 17)

Jehovah gave the prophet Ezekiel a parable, in the form of a riddle, and sent him to tell it to the people of Judah. "There was a great eagle," said Jehovah, "that came into Lebanon, where he cut off and carried away the highest branch of the cedar tree—along with the young twigs of the tree's highest branch. He carried them into the land of traders, where he set them up in the city of merchants. The eagle also took the seed of the land and planted it, as a willow tree, in a fruitful field by great waters. But the seed of the willow tree grew and became a low, spreading vine instead of a tree, bringing forth branches and sprigs. And its branches and roots turned toward the great eagle.

"Then, when the vine was flourishing, another great eagle came into Lebanon. And when the second eagle came, the vine bent its roots toward this new eagle and sent out branches toward him to get water from the furrows of his plantation—even though it was already planted in good soil and by great waters."

When Jehovah finished his parable, he asked Ezekiel, "Shall this vine prosper? Shall the first eagle not pull up the roots of it and cut off its fruit so that it withers? And shall it not utterly wither when the east wind touches it?"

Then Jehovah answered his own questions: "It shall wither in the very furrows where it grew.

"Go now and tell this parable to this rebellious house, even the house of Judah," said Jehovah to Ezekiel, "and tell them what it means. The king of Babylonia [the first great eagle] has come to Jerusalem [Lebanon] and has taken King Zedekiah [the highest branch] of the Jews [the cedar tree]. The king's seed and his princes [the young twigs] were also led away to Babylonia [the land of traders]. Remind the Jews that the king of Babylonia has made a covenant with the king of Judah and that the king of Babylonia has also taken away the mighty of the land that Judah might have no power to lift himself up [hence, the low-growing vine]. But, by keeping the covenant, Judah could stand and prosper. Nevertheless, the king of Judah has rebelled and sent his ambassadors into Egypt [the second eagle] that the Pharaoh might send horses and armies to assist him."

And then Jehovah asked, "Shall the kingdom of Judah prosper in its deceit? Shall they who do such things escape? Or shall the king of Judah win deliverance by breaking his covenant?

"As I live, surely in the place where the king lives who made Zedekiah king of Judah, and whose covenant Zedekiah has failed to keep—surely in the midst of that place shall the king of Judah die. And Pharaoh, with his mighty army and great company—though they come and cast up mounds and built forts—will not be able to save him.

"Because the king of Judah broke his covenant with the king of Babylonia, he shall not escape. And in breaking that covenant, the king of Judah has also despised my oath and broken my covenant, and I will bring judgments upon his head. I will spread my net upon him and he will be taken in my snare. I will bring him to Babylon and contend with him there for his trespasses against me. All his fugitives shall fall by the sword and they who remain shall be scattered to the winds. And you shall know that I Jehovah have spoken it."

Jehovah then continued his parable: "I will also take the highest branch [King Zedekiah] of the high cedar [the Jews] and will cut off from the top of his young twigs a tender one. And I will plant that tender twig upon a high and eminent mountain where it shall bear fruit and become a goodly cedar.[619] Fowl of every wing shall dwell under it, and the trees of the field shall know that I Jehovah have brought down the high tree and exalted the low tree. They shall know that I have dried up the green tree and made the dry tree to flourish."

---

[619] The "tender one" that was taken from the top of King Zedekiah's "young twigs" and who became a "goodly cedar" on a "high and eminent mountain" is said by some scholars to be Zedekiah's youngest son Mulek who was brought by Jehovah to the Americas with a group of exiles (see footnote 634 in story "208−The Fall of Jerusalem").

202–WHY WILL YOU DIE, O ISRAEL?

(Ezekiel 18)

As Jehovah talked to Ezekiel about the instructions he was to give to the disobedient Jews, he told him that he should stop using a certain proverb that had become common among the people.

"What do you mean," Jehovah asked him, "when you say that the fathers have eaten sour grapes and their children's teeth are set on edge? As I live, you shall no more use this proverb in Israel. For all souls are mine—both those of the fathers and those of the children—and the soul who sins is the soul who shall die. If a man has walked in my statutes, kept my judgments, and dealt truly, he is a just man and he shall live."[620]

Jehovah then told Ezekiel what he should say to the people of Judah. "Tell these people," he said, "that if a wicked man begets a son and the son sees all of the father's sins but does not do them, that son shall not die for the iniquity of his father. But the father, because he did what was not good among the people, he shall die for his own iniquity.

"I, Jehovah, take no pleasure in the death of those who die. So why will you die, O Israel?" And because I will judge each man according to his own ways, the righteous man who turns aside from his righteous ways shall die, and the wicked man who turns from his wicked ways shall live. Therefore, O wayward Israel, turn yourself and cast your transgressions away from you that you might make yourself a new heart and a new spirit and live."

---

[620] Jehovah gave this same instruction concerning the proverb of the sour grapes to the prophet Jeremiah (see Jeremiah 31:29–30).

203–YOU SHALL NOT MOURN FOR HER

(Ezekiel 24)

On the tenth day of the ninth month of the ninth year of the reign of Nebuchadnezzar, king of Babylonia, Jehovah spoke to his prophet Ezekiel. "Mark this day and write it down," Jehovah told him, "for on this day Babylonia has set himself against Jerusalem. Babylonia is as a fire that shall consume Judah in her filthiness. And because Judah has ignored my chastenings and my reproofs, I have now caused my fury to come upon her. I will not spare her nor go back."

Then Jehovah said to Ezekiel, "I will take away your wife, the desire of your eyes, with one stroke. But you shall not mourn for her nor shed one tear. Put your turban on your head and your shoes on your feet. But do not cover your lips like the leper, and do not eat the bread of men."

Jehovah's instructions were hard for Ezekiel, but when his wife died that same evening, he did as Jehovah commanded him.

When the Jewish exiles at Tel-abib saw that Ezekiel did not mourn his wife's death, they questioned him. "What is the meaning of this?" they asked him. "What does it mean to us that you do not mourn?"

"I do not mourn for her because of instructions that Jehovah has given me," answered Ezekiel. "He told me that I should not mourn for her as a sign to you and to the people of Judah. For he said to me, 'I will defile my holy temple—even the excellency of your strength and the desire of your eyes. And the sons and daughters of this people, they who are left at Jerusalem, shall also fall by the sword.'"

Ezekiel continued: "Because I am a sign to you, Jehovah has told me that you are also to do as I have done. You shall put your turbans on your heads and your shoes on your feet and shall not mourn nor weep for yourselves. You shall, however, pine for your iniquities and shall mourn for one another.

"When word comes to you, from the mouths of those who escape, concerning the destruction of your sons and your daughters and of Jerusalem's captivity, you shall know that Jehovah is God. You shall open your mouths to those who have escaped, speaking to them and mourning for them. And in that day, when you do not mourn for your own terrible losses, you shall be a sign unto them, and they shall also know that Jehovah is God."[621]

---

[621] The idea here is that Jehovah did not want the people to focus on the terrible tragedy that had befallen

204—I WILL SAVE MY FLOCK

(Ezekiel 34, 36, 37)

"Tell the shepherds of Israel," said Jehovah to Ezekiel, "that they are being punished because they have not fed their flock but have fed themselves instead. Though they eat the fat and clothe themselves with wool, they do not feed their flock. They have ruled the flock with cruelty for they have not strengthened those who are diseased nor healed those who are sick. They have not bound up that which was broken, brought again those who were driven away, nor sought for those who were lost. The flock is scattered because there has been no shepherd, and it has become meat for the beasts of the field."

When Ezekiel received this message from Jehovah, he went to the leaders of Judah and said, "As I live, you shepherds of Israel, Jehovah is against you and will require the flock at your hands. He will cause you to cease from feeding the flocks and, in the latter days, he will be their shepherd. For, as a shepherd seeks out his flock in the day that he is among those that are scattered, so will Jehovah seek out his sheep and deliver them from all places where they were scattered on the dark and cloudy day. Yea, he will gather them from the far countries and bring them to their own land to feed them upon the mountains of Israel, by the rivers, and in all those places of the country where they live. He will feed them in good pastures and will cause them to lie down and rest."

Ezekiel continued: "Thus says Jehovah: 'As for you, my flock, I will judge between one sheep and another and will save my flock that they may no more be prey for the heathen. I will set one shepherd over them in that day—even my servant David—and he shall feed them.[622] I Jehovah will be their God and my servant David will be a prince among them.

"'I will make an everlasting covenant of peace with them, and I will multiply them and set my sanctuary in their midst forever. I will make a good planting place for them that they may be consumed no more with hunger in the land. And they shall know that I am with them and that they are my people. They are the flock of my pasture, and I am their God.'

"Jehovah will take Judah from among the heathen," Ezekiel explained to the leaders of Judah, "gathering them out of all countries and bringing them back to their own land. The mountains of Israel shall shoot forth branches and yield fruit for them. Jehovah will multiply men upon Israel's mountains, the cities shall be inhabited, and the waste places built up. But Jehovah will not bring the people of Judah back for their own sakes, but for the sake of his holy name, which they have profaned.

"And in that day he will cleanse Judah, with clean water, from all her filthiness and her idols. He will put his Spirit in the people, causing them to walk in his statutes and keep his judgments. They shall dwell in the

---

them but to go on with hope for the future. In response to this, one commentator wrote: "If the contents of chapter 24 [of Ezekiel] all pertain to the same day, the wife of Ezekiel died the very day the 'king of Babylon [Nebuchadnezzar]' started his siege against Jerusalem. (Compare Ezek. 24:1–2, 18 with 2 Kgs. 25:1–2.) Ezekiel was commanded by the Lord [Jehovah] not to mourn the passing of his wife ('the desire of thine eyes') as an example to the Israelites that they were not to mourn unduly their temporary state of siege and captivity. The Lord [Jehovah] promised Israel through his prophets Jeremiah (Jer. 25:12; 2 Chr. 36:21) and Zechariah (Zech. 1:12; 7:5) that if they endured the captivity well he would deliver them in about seventy years. (See also Dan. 9:2, 24.)" (Daniel H. Ludlow, *A Companion to Your Study of the Old Testament* [Salt Lake City: Deseret Book Co., 1981], 338)

[622] There are many prophecies in the ancient scriptures concerning a great leader named David whom Jehovah would raise up in the last days as a shepherd to gathered Israel (see Jeremiah 23:5; 30:9; 33:15–26; Psalms 89:3–4; Isaiah 55:3–4; and Ezekiel 34:24; 37:22–25). Daniel H. Ludlow, quoting the Prophet Joseph Smith, wrote the following concerning modern references to this shepherd: "Prophets of this dispensation have also spoken and prophesied concerning the spiritual giant named David who will come forth in the last days to be a blessing to gathered Judah. Just three months before his martyrdom, the Prophet Joseph Smith taught concerning this David: 'The throne and kingdom of David is to be taken from him and given to another by the name of David in the last days, raised up out of his lineage.' (TPJS, page 339.)" (Daniel H. Ludlow, *A Companion to Your Study of the Old Testament* [Salt Lake City: Deseret Book Co., 1981], 339.) Some claim that this latter-day leader of Judah and Israel will be the Savior himself—sitting on the throne of David—during his millennial reign. This may be the correct interpretation, but that does not seem likely, in light of the wording used in Ezekiel 34:24: "And I the LORD [i.e., Jehovah] will be their God, *and my servant David* a prince among them; I the LORD [i.e., Jehovah] have spoken it" (emphasis added). However, when the prophecy is fulfilled, we shall all know the answer. Until then, it is not a matter that should trouble us.

land that he gave to their fathers and shall increase like a flock. And as flocks fill Jerusalem at the solemn feast, so shall the waste cities of Judah be filled with flocks of men, and they shall know that he is Jehovah."

205—CAN THESE BONES LIVE?

(Ezekiel 37)

The hand of Jehovah rested upon Ezekiel and carried him in the spirit into the midst of a valley filled with bones. And, as he looked around, he saw that the bones were very dry. Then Jehovah spoke to him asking, "Can these bones live?"

"Thou knowest," answered Ezekiel.

Then Jehovah commanded Ezekiel to prophesy to the bones. "Tell these dry bones to hear the word of Jehovah," he said. "Tell them that I will lay sinews and flesh upon them and will cover them with skin. Tell them also that I will cause breath to come into them and that they shall live and know that I am Jehovah."

When Ezekiel prophesied to the dry bones as Jehovah had commanded him, the bones shook and came together, bone to bone. Then, as Ezekiel watched, sinews and flesh came upon them and skin covered them—but there was no breath in them.

"Prophesy to the wind," said Jehovah. "For I have commanded breath to come from the four winds to breathe upon these who were slain, that they may live." And when Ezekiel prophesied as Jehovah commanded him, breath came into the bodies and they stood upon their feet as a great army.

Then Jehovah explained to Ezekiel, "These bones are the whole house of Israel. They say that their bones are dried and that they have no hope. But behold, I will open the graves of my people and bring them forth into the land of Israel. I will put my Spirit into them that they may live, and I will place them in their own land. Then shall they know that I Jehovah have spoken it and have performed it."[623]

---

[623] Ezekiel 37 is more than just a vision of the resurrection—though it is that. In this vision Jehovah showed the prophet Ezekiel the resurrection as a similitude of the total and complete restoration of Israel in the last days, even though they have lost hope.

206–THE TWO SHALL
BE ONE
(Ezekiel 37)

When Jehovah had assured Ezekiel that the restoration of Israel to her inheritance in the last days was certain, he spoke to him once more saying, "Take one stick[624] and write upon that stick for Judah and for the children of Israel who are his companions. Then take another stick—the stick of Ephraim—and write upon that stick for Joseph and for all of the children of Israel who are his companions. When you have written on both sticks, join them one to the other and they shall become one in your hand.[625]

"When the children of your people ask you what you mean by these two sticks, tell them that God will take the stick of Joseph which is in the hand of Ephraim and in the hands of the tribes of Israel his fellows and will put it with the stick of Judah and make them one stick. These two stick shall be one in your hand, and these two sticks upon which you write shall be in your hand before their eyes."

Jehovah continued, "Then shall you say also to the children of your people that God has said thus to you: 'I will take the children of Israel from among the heathen, where they have gone—both Judah and Ephraim[626]—and will gather them on every side. I will bring them into their own land and will make them one nation upon the mountains of Israel. They shall no more be two nations or two kingdoms, but one king shall be king to them all. I will cleanse them from their idols and their transgressions. They shall be my people, I will be their God, and my servant David shall be their king.'"[627]

---

[624] Or a wooden writing tablet.

[625] Latter-day prophets have interpreted this prophecy to refer to the Bible (the stick of Judah) and the Book of Mormon (the stick of Joseph or stick of Ephraim). In Doctrine and Covenants 27:5, the Lord speaks of "Moroni, whom I have sent unto you to reveal the Book of Mormon…[and] to whom I have committed the keys of the record of the stick of Ephraim." One may wonder why it is called the stick of Ephraim rather than the stick of Manasseh, but remember that both tribes, Ephraim and Manasseh, were present in the Book of Mormon civilizations. The term, "stick of Joseph," which Jehovah mentions to Ezekiel first, seems to be more accurate—especially when he talks about the "stick of Joseph, which is in the hands of Ephraim, and the tribes of Israel his fellows" (Ezekiel 37:19). This seems fitting when we consider that Ephraim is the lineage of the majority of the members of The Church of Jesus Christ of Latter-day Saints in our day, and that the Book of Mormon is primarily in their hands. Also note that some scholars have interpreted this prophecy as another statement of the prophecy that follows it—interpreting the two sticks as being two nations or two kingdoms—Judah and Ephraim (Israel)—coming together as one in the latter days. Because many prophecies of the scriptures can be fulfilled more than once or in more than one way, this interpretation might also be correct.

---

[626] It is important to remember, when reading this prophecy, that the kingdom of Israel was often called Ephraim because Ephraim was the dominant tribe.

[627] See footnote 622 in story "204–I Will Save My Flock."

207—WATER FROM UNDER THE TEMPLE

(Ezekiel 38–48)

The prophet Ezekiel was privileged to see many of the events of the latter days in vision and he foretold many events that would precede the Savior's Second Coming. He learned from Jehovah that, after the house of Israel has been gathered back to the promised land and has embraced the gospel, a vast army will come from the north to fight against them. This terrible army will be led by Gog, from the land of Magog.

Ezekiel also learned that these invaders will fail in their purpose because Jehovah will stand against them, sending a great earthquake that will throw down mountains and cause great walls to crumble to the ground. He will also send pestilence and a great storm of hailstones, fire, and brimstone to consume the enemy. The casualties will be so great that it will take the children of Israel seven months to bury the dead of this invading army, and they will gather no firewood for seven years while they burn the weapons of those who have fallen.

Jehovah then took Ezekiel and set him upon a high mountain in the land of Israel, where he showed him a vision of a great city.[628] As Ezekiel beheld the city, a man who looked to be made of brass came to him with a line of flax and a measuring stick the length of a reed[629] in his hand. The man stood at the gate of the city and commanded Ezekiel to observe carefully and then to declare to the house of Israel all that he would see.

The man then proceeded to show Ezekiel the city and all of its gates in great detail as he took the measurements of them. He also showed him a temple in the city, together with its form and measurements. He showed him the inside of the temple in complex detail, with its forms and measurements, including the sanctuary or holy of holies.

When Ezekiel had seen the details of the temple, his guide took him to the city's east gate where he beheld the glory of Jehovah, the God of Israel. And he heard Jehovah's voice speaking to him like the noise of many waters, and he saw the earth shine with Jehovah's glory.

"Behold the place of my throne," said Jehovah, "and the place of the soles of my feet. This is where I will dwell in the midst of the children of Israel forever, and the house of Israel shall defile my holy name no more—neither they nor their kings." And Ezekiel bowed down with his face to the ground.

"Show this temple to the house of Israel and let them measure its pattern," said Jehovah to Ezekiel. "If they are ashamed of the iniquities that they have done, then show them the form of the house and the fashion of it. Show them the comings in and the forms thereof and all the ordinances and the laws. Write all these things in their sight that they may keep the ordinances of my house."

Jehovah then told Ezekiel that a priest of the lineage of Zadok[630] would make a burnt offering—a young bullock for a sin offering—on the altar of the temple that day. Other offerings were also specified for seven days. And many other things did Ezekiel both see and hear.

Then, when Ezekiel's brass guide brought him back to the east door of the temple, he saw that water came out from under the temple threshold on the east side. He saw that the water originated under the right side of the temple on the south side of the altar. Then the guide measured out 1,000 cubits from the temple and took Ezekiel through the water—and it was up to his ankles. He measured another 1,000 cubits and took Ezekiel though the waters again—and it was up to his knees. After another 1,000 cubits the water came up to his loins, and when the next 1,000 cubits after that were measured, he was unable to cross the water because it was a mighty river.

The guide then took Ezekiel along the bank of the river where he saw many trees growing on both sides. And he said to Ezekiel, "These waters issue out toward the east country and go down to the desert and into the Dead Sea. They will heal the waters of the sea, and everything that moves—wherever the river goes—shall live."[631]

---

[628] The city Ezekiel saw was Jerusalem.

[629] A reed was an ancient Hebrew linear measurement equal to about six cubits, or about nine feet (2.74 meters). It is not clear what the line of flax was for, but it probably had something to do with taking measurements also.

---

[630] Zadok was the high priest in the days of King David.

[631] Though I have no doubt that this prophecy of water flowing from under the Lord's temple in Jerusalem will be literally fulfilled in due time, I also believe that there is a symbolic fulfillment of this prophecy at every temple of the Lord. Living water flows out of every temple through blessings, ordinances, and covenants, giving both life and healing to all that it touches. The depth of the water depends on how often we avail ourselves of its benefit.

208–THE FALL OF JERUSALEM

(2 Kings 25; Jeremiah 39–40)

In the ninth year of the reign of Zedekiah in the kingdom of Judah, King Nebuchadnezzar of Babylonia came against Jerusalem with all his army,[632] and the city was under siege until the eleventh year. Because of the siege there was sore famine in the land and great suffering because of the scarcity of food.

When the Babylonians finally broke into the city, King Zedekiah, along with Judah's men of war, fled during the night by way of the king's garden and the gate between the two walls. They were pursued by the Chaldeans,[633] however, and King Zedekiah was overtaken on the plains of Jericho. Upon his capture, Zedekiah was taken before King Nebuchadnezzar at Riblah to be judged. His eyes were put out and he was taken to Babylon in brass chains. Zedekiah's sons were slain, with the exception of Mulek, who escaped with several others and was brought by the hand of Jehovah to the Americas, where his people eventually became part of the Nephite nation.[634]

When Nebuzar-adan, the captain of the Babylonian guard, came into Jerusalem, he burned the temple and the entire city. The army of Chaldeans that was with him also broke down the city walls. The brass pillars of the temple, the ornate bases for the lavers, and the brazen baptismal font were all broken into pieces. The pots, the shovels, the snuffers, the spoons, and the vessels of brass that were used for the temple rites were all taken away. The devastation was great, and all who were left in the city surrendered and were taken to Babylon. Only the poor were left behind to be vinedressers and husbandmen of the land. And Nebuchad-

nezzar named Gedaliah to be governor over those who remained.

The prophet Jeremiah, because he was in prison in Jerusalem, was among those taken captive. But the king gave Nebuzar-adan a special charge concerning Jeremiah's welfare. "Take him and look well to him," said King Nebuchadnezzar. "Do unto him as he shall tell you."

Jeremiah was taken in chains with the other captives on their way to Babylon. When they came to Ramah, however, Nebuzar-adan said to him, "I will loose you this day from your chains and you may go wherever you like. If you choose to come with me to Babylon, I will take good care of you. But if it does not suit you to come with me, you may stay here. Or you may to go back to Gedaliah, whom the king has made governor over the cities of Judah, and dwell with him if you choose to do so. You are free to go wherever it is convenient for you." When Nebuzar-adan had given Jeremiah food and money to sustain him, Jeremiah went to Mizpah, where he dwelt with the people who were under the care of Gedaliah.

Gedaliah the governor sent out messengers to tell the Jews who had been scattered that they could return to the land of Judah. "Do not be afraid to serve the Chaldeans," he told them. "If you come here to dwell in the land and will serve the king of Babylonia, it will be well with you. As for me," he said, "I must dwell at Mizpah to serve the Chaldeans who will come to us, but you may go wherever you choose to gather wine, summer fruits, and oil and put them in your vessels."

When the Jews who were among the Moabites, the Ammonites, the Edomites, and all other countries learned that the king of Babylonia had left a remnant of Judah and had made Gedaliah governor, many of them returned to the land and gathered wine and summer fruits in abundance.

---

[632] The Babylonians, under Nabopolassar, had overthrown the Assyrian Empire in 625 BC and had become the most powerful force in the area. That position was solidified when the Babylonians defeated the Egyptians in 605 BC in a battle at Carchemish. Nabopolassar's son Nebuchadnezzar, who led the battle against the Egyptians, succeeded to the throne upon his father's death in 604 BC. For background, see story "211–The Babylonian and Persian Empires."

[633] The Chaldeans (or Chaldees) were the most prominent tribe in the country of Babylonia at the time of the captivity. This title was generally used in the scriptures to refer to the people of Babylonia.

[634] Pertinent references from the Book of Mormon relating to Mulek and his people include Omni 1:14–15; Mosiah 25:2; and Helaman 6:10, 8:21.

209—JUDAH'S REMNANT FLEES TO EGYPT

(Jeremiah 40–43)

When the king of Babylonia made Gedaliah governor over those who remained in the kingdom of Judah, Gedaliah set up his headquarters at Mizpah. Among those who came to Mizpah and joined themselves with Gedaliah were remnants of Judah's army that had escaped and had been scattered during the siege and at the time the city fell.

Two leaders of these military men were Ishmael, the son of Nethaniah, and Johanan, the son of Kareah. As time went on, Johanan became aware that Ishmael was involved in a conspiracy with King Baalis of the Ammorites to assassinate Gedaliah. But when he warned Gedaliah of the plot, Gedaliah—trusting soul that he was—did not believe Johanan. Johanan plead with Gedaliah to let him slay Ishmael secretly, lest he be killed and all the gathered Jews be scattered again. But Gedaliah said to him, "You shall not do this terrible thing. Surely you have spoken falsely of Ishmael."

Unfortunately, Johanan was right about Ishmael. And so it was that when Ishmael came with ten of his men as guests in Gedaliah's house, he murdered Gedaliah while they sat at a feast. Not only was Gedaliah killed, but also all those who were with him in his house—both the Jewish attendants and the Babylonian guards—so that no one else knew of the crime for several days.

Ishmael and his cohorts also butchered a company that had come from Shechem, Shiloh, and Samaria to bring incense and offerings for the temple, when they pretended to take these visitors to see Gedaliah. When Ishmael's men had thrown the bodies of their victims into a pit, they took all the people of Mizpah captive—including the prophet Jeremiah, Jeremiah's scribe Baruch, and the daughters of King Zedekiah—and departed with them for the land of the Ammonites.

Johanan, upon hearing of the evil that was done by Ishmael at Mizpah, took all the captains of the forces of Judah who were with him and went in pursuit of the outlaws and their prisoners, overtaking them as they were encamped by the pools at Gibeon. When the prisoners saw Johanan and his men coming, they were greatly relieved and turned back to join them. Ishmael and eight of his men, however, managed to escape to the Ammonites.

The captives liberated, Johanan took all those who were with him to Chimham, near Bethlehem, in preparation for taking them to Egypt. Now that Gedaliah, Nebuchadnezzar's handpicked governor, was dead, they were afraid to return to Mizpah or to remain any-where in the land of Judah. The people could only imagine what measures King Nebuchadnezzar might take against them.

As this little remnant of Judah prepared for their journey to Egypt, Johanan and his captains came to Jeremiah and asked him to intercede with Jehovah in behalf of the people. "Pray unto Jehovah for us," they pleaded, "even for all this remnant, to show us the way we may walk and the thing we must do."

"I will pray as you have asked," answered Jeremiah, "and whatever Jehovah tells me, I will tell it to you."

"As Jehovah is a true and faithful witness between us," the captains responded, "we will do whatever he tells us through you. Whether it seems good or evil, we will obey the voice of Jehovah."

After ten days had passed, the word of Jehovah came to Jeremiah, and he called together Johanan, the captains, and all the people to give them Jehovah's answer. "Jehovah has told me that if you will stay here in this land," said Jeremiah, "he will build you up and not pull you down; he will plant you and not pluck you up. Jehovah has said that you should not fear the king of Babylonia, for he is with you to deliver you from the king's hand."

Jeremiah continued: "However, if you choose to disobey the voice of Jehovah and go instead into Egypt, the sword you fear will overtake you there. The famine of which you were afraid shall also overtake you and you shall die there. No one who sets his face to go into Egypt shall escape the evil that Jehovah will bring upon him. And as his anger has been poured out upon the inhabitants of Jerusalem, so shall his fury be poured out upon all those who go into Egypt. Such shall die there—by the sword, by famine, and by pestilence—and shall never again see this place."

These instructions from Jehovah were contrary to what the people and their leaders had wanted to hear, for they had set their hearts on Egypt. They were also suspicious of Jeremiah because he had opposed the Egyptians and favored the Babylonians as the best hope for Judah's safety during the dark days of the siege before Jerusalem was destroyed.

Thus Johanan and all the proud men began to accuse Jeremiah: "You have spoken falsely, Jeremiah. Jehovah did not tell you that we should not go to Egypt, but your servant Baruch has set you against us. You only seek to deliver us into the hands of the Chaldeans that they may put us to death and carry us captive."

So, in complete disregard for the word of Jehovah that they had so earnestly sought and pledged to obey, the remnant of Judah went into Egypt and dwelt in

Tahpanhes.[635] And Jeremiah, his servant Baruch, and the daughters of King Zedekiah were all taken to Egypt with them.

Once they were in Egypt, the word of Jehovah came to Jeremiah again saying, "Take great stones in the sight of all the men of Judah and hide them in the clay of the brick kiln at the entry of Pharaoh's palace. And as you do so, tell the men of Judah that I will bring my servant Nebuchadnezzar,[636] and set his throne upon these stones."

Jehovah continued: "King Nebuchadnezzar will spread his royal pavilion over these great stones and will smite the land of Egypt. He will deliver such as are for death to death, such as are for captivity to captivity, and such as are for the sword to the sword. He will kindle a fire in the houses of the gods of Egypt; he will break the images of the Egyptian gods and will burn their houses. Yea, he shall clothe himself with the land of Egypt as a shepherd puts on his garment. Then he shall depart in peace."

And as Jeremiah hid the great stones in the brick kiln, according to Jehovah's instructions, he delivered Jehovah's fateful message to the men of Judah.

---

[635] Tahpanhes was evidently a town in Lower (i.e., northern) Egypt, near the eastern border (see William Smith, *Dictionary of the Bible*, *GospeLink*, CD-ROM, s.v. "Tahpanhes").

[636] Jehovah referred to Nebuchadnezzar as "my servant" not because he was a righteous man, but because, as a wicked man, he was an instrument in Jehovah's hands to smite Judah (and others). It seems to be Jehovah's normal method of operation to use the wicked to destroy the wicked. In a similar vein, the book of Habakkuk also prophesied that the Chaldeans would be used by Jehovah to do a dreadful and terrible work in the land of Judah. Jehovah said that he would raise up "the Chaldeans, that bitter and hasty nation," to overrun the land of Judah and take the people captive (see Habakkuk 1:5–11).

210—WE WILL BURN INCENSE TO THE QUEEN OF HEAVEN
(Jeremiah 44)

Things were not going well for the Jews who had gone to Egypt after the murder of Gedaliah, the man whom King Nebuchadnezzar had made governor of Judah's remnant.[637] The people were still caught up in the same idolatrous practices that had led to the destruction of Jerusalem and the captivity of Judah in Babylon.

It was in this difficult situation that Jehovah spoke to the prophet Jeremiah in Egypt concerning them, and Jeremiah carried Jehovah's message to the people. "Thus says Jehovah, the God of Israel," said Jeremiah. "'You have seen all the evil that I brought upon Jerusalem and the cities of Judah. They lie in desolation today because of their wickedness. I was provoked to anger when the people of Judah burned incense to gods they did not know. And though I sent my prophets to warn them, they did not hearken or incline their ears to turn from their wickedness.'"

Jeremiah continued, still speaking the words of Jehovah: "Though you are well aware of the great destruction that came upon the people of Judah, you continue to provoke me by burning incense to other gods. Have you forgotten the wickedness of your fathers, the wickedness of the kings of Judah and their wives, and your own wickedness that you committed in the land of Judah and in the streets of Jerusalem? You are not humbled, even unto this day. Neither have you feared me nor obeyed my law.

"I will set my face against you for evil and will cut off all Judah. I will take this remnant that set its face to come into Egypt, and they shall all fall here in this land, consumed by sword and famine. They shall be an astonishment, a curse, and a reproach, for I will punish them as I have punished Jerusalem. None shall escape to return to the land of their fathers."

The people were angry at Jehovah's message that Jeremiah had delivered to them, and they rejected it. They were upset because they felt justified in the things of which they were accused. "We will not hearken to the words you have spoken," they replied to Jeremiah, "but will fulfill the vows that we have made and do those things that we have spoken. We will burn incense to the queen of heaven and pour out drink offerings to her as we have done before, as our fathers have done,

---

[637] See story "209—Judah's Remnant Flees to Egypt" for the account of Gedaliah's death and the circumstances that then led the people to go to Egypt.

and as our kings and princes did before us in Judah and in the streets of Jerusalem. We know that we were blessed with abundant food, that we were all well, and that no evil came upon us when we did these things. But when we stopped these practices, we wanted for all these things and were consumed by the sword and by famine."

Jeremiah, frustrated by the people's stiff necks and self-righteousness, spoke again. "It was because of the incense that you, your fathers, your kings, and your princes burned in Judah and in the streets of Jerusalem," he said, "that Jehovah could no longer forebear. It is because of these abominations that your land is desolate today. And it is because you have sinned against Jehovah—neither obeying his voice nor walking in his laws and statutes—that you now suffer this great evil."

And then to all the people, both men and women, Jeremiah said, "Hear the word of Jehovah, all Judah that are in the land of Egypt. You have spoken with your mouths and borne witness with your hands that you will perform all your vows unto the queen of heaven, burn incense unto her, and pour out your drink offerings to her. And now, because of this, Jehovah has sworn by his great name that his name shall be spoken no more by the mouth of any man of Judah in the land of Egypt. He will watch over them for evil and not for good. And all you of Judah who are here in Egypt shall be consumed by the sword and by famine till none is left. And though a few may escape to return to the land of Judah, all the remnant of Judah who have come here shall know whose words will stand—mine or theirs."

"Jehovah will give you these signs," Jeremiah continued. "He will punish you in this place, that you may know that his words will stand against you for evil. And he will deliver Pharaoh-hophra, king of Egypt, into the hands of those who seek his life. Even as Jehovah gave King Zedekiah into the hands of Nebuchadnezzar, king of Babylonia, so will Pharaoh-hophra be delivered into Nebuchadnezzar's hands."[638]

---

[638] The scriptures do not tell the fulfillment of Jeremiah's prophecy against the Pharaoh and the idolatrous remnant of Judah in Egypt. However, Josephus says that "... on the fifth year after the destruction of Jerusalem, which was the twenty-third of the reign of Nebuchadnezzar, he made an expedition against Celesyria; and when he had possessed himself of it, he made war against the Ammonites and Moabites; and when he had brought all these nations under subjection, he fell upon Egypt, in order to overthrow it; and he slew the king that then reigned and set up another; and he took those Jews that were there captives, and led them away to Babylon" (Flavius Josephus, *Antiquities of the Jews*, 10:9:7).

XII

THE CAPTIVITY OF JUDAH,

THE RETURN, AND BEYOND

211—THE BABYLONIAN AND PERSIAN EMPIRES

(This brief account is included here to provide perspective to the stories that are associated with Judah's captivity. It is based on information found in Dictionary of the Bible *by William Smith,* Illustrated Bible Dictionary *by M.M. Easton, and the Bible Dictionary in the Latter-day Saint Edition of the King James Version of the Bible. Much information came also from the scriptures themselves, especially Ezekiel 29—30 and Daniel 4.)*

Babylonia existed long before the captivity of Judah, but did not become a major power until 606 BC when Nabopolassar, the viceroy of Babylon, made himself king; destroyed the city of Nineveh, the Assyrian capital; and declared Babylonia to be independent. When Nabopolassar died in 604 BC, his son Nebuchadnezzar came to the throne in his father's place. This was one year after Nebuchadnezzar had led the Babylonian army in defeating Pharaoh-necho and the Egyptians.

Nebuchadnezzar attacked Judah many times and conquered the entire kingdom except for the city of Jerusalem. Seeking that final objective, he lay siege against the city of Jerusalem in 598 BC. His siege succeeded in 587 BC when his army destroyed the city, burned the temple, and took the people of Judah captive to Babylon.

In 585 BC, Tyre, in Phoenicia, also fell before the Babylonian assault. Egypt, however, was a different story. Though Egypt was attacked and brought into submission by the Babylonians, the army of Nebuchadnezzar departed with the treasures of the land and left the people to govern themselves. Many of the Egyptians, however, were scattered into other countries, as Ezekiel had prophesied.[639] The remnant of Judah that had come to Egypt for safety was sorely afflicted. All were either slain or carried captive to Babylon.[640]

After his attacks on Egypt, Nebuchadnezzar concerned himself less with empire building than he did with enhancing the city of Babylon with the spoils of his conquests. He rebuilt the temple of Bel[641] and strengthened the city's fortifications. He beautified the existing city and added a new area in which he built a magnificent new palace with its famed hanging gardens. During the last part of Nebuchadnezzar's life, he suffered from mental illness for seven years, but was then restored to health.[642] When he died in 561 BC, after reigning for forty-three years, his son Evil-merodach came to the throne. Evil-merodach was murdered two years later by his brother-in-law Neriglissar, who then occupied the throne. Neriglissar is believed to be the man identified as Nergal-sharezer,[643] a captain of the King's guard at the time of the destruction of Jerusalem. His reign over the Babylonians was also brief, lasting only until 556 BC.

Nabonidus, who married Nitocris (who was both Neriglissar's widow and Nebuchadnezzar's daughter) was the last king of Babylonia. His son Belshazzar served with him as prince regent and was associated with his father on the throne when the Persians, under Cyrus, conquered the Babylonian Empire. The Babylonians were conquered with relative ease with the help of both the Babylonian people and the captive Jews. The brutality of the Babylonians provided ample incentive for the Jews and the Chaldeans[644] to assist the Persian conquest. Cyrus and the Persians were always kind to the Jews.

With the fall of the Babylonian Empire, the Persians had control of all areas that had previously belonged to the Assyrian Empire, and much more.

The relationship between the Persians and the Medes is also significant in the story of Judah's captivity. When the Persians conquered King Astyages and Media in 550 BC, the rulers appointed some of the Medes to responsible positions in their government. Perhaps this is because Cyrus the Persian was Astyages's grandson, being the son of his daughter Mandane.[645]

The Persians chose Achmetha, the Median capital, as their own capital city,[646] and it remained such until the Persian capital was moved to Shushan (in the land

---

[639] See Ezekiel 30:20–26.

[640] See the prophecy concerning this in story "210—We Will Burn Incense to the Queen of Heaven."

[641] The Babylonian god Bel is identical to Baal. Baal, the storm and fertility god, was symbolic of the male generative principle in nature.

[642] See story "215–The Great Tree."

[643] He is mentioned only twice in the scriptures—Jeremiah 39:3 and 39:13.

[644] The Chaldeans (or the Chaldees) were the most prominent tribe in the country of Babylonia at the time of the captivity. This title was generally used in the scriptures to refer to the people of Babylonia.

[645] The story is much more complicated than this brief account. For more information, see Werner Keller, *The Bible as History: What Archaeology Reveals about Scripture*, 2nd rev. ed. (New York: William Morrow and Co. Inc., 1981), 297–298.

[646] Achmetha was called Ecbatana by the classical writers. It was located on the site of the modern Iranian city of Hamadan.

that had previously been Elam).[647] The Persians' approach to governing actually united the two empires, and the kingdom is often referred to as the kingdom of the Medes and Persians.

After the Babylonians were conquered, Darius the Mede was made ruler over the area that included the city of Babylon—serving for but one year—until Cyrus himself became king over the entire Persian Empire.

212–THE PREPARATION OF DANIEL
(Daniel 1)

Jehoiakim had been king of Judah for just three years when Nebuchadnezzar came to the throne of Babylonia.[648] In that same year—the year before Jehoiakim burned Jeremiah's prophecies[649]—Nebuchadnezzar's army attacked Jerusalem. The Babylonians did not prevail but, in the aftermath of that attack, they carried off part of the sacred vessels of the temple and took some of the mighty men and chief officers of Judah captive to Shinar.[650]

The master of Nebuchadnezzar's eunuchs chose very carefully those men who were taken—all according to the king's criteria. All were well-favored men without blemish. And they were skillful in all wisdom and in their understanding of science. They were also men with potential to learn the Chaldean language and serve in the king's palace. Among these captives were four young Jews named Daniel, Hananiah, Mishael, and Azariah, whose names were changed by the Babylonians to Belteshazzar, Shadrach, Meshach, and Abednego.[651]

The Jewish captives were well cared for. Part of the plan for their training was to feed them a special diet of the king's meat and wine for three years, after which they would stand personally before the king. Daniel and his three young friends, however, were not happy with the king's diet because it was contrary to the Jewish dietary laws. They were determined not to defile themselves with the portions of meat and wine that were given to them, and they made their desires know to the prince of the Eunuchs.

The prince of the Eunuchs was partial to Daniel, for God had brought Daniel into his favor, but he was concerned about this request. "I fear the king," the prince

---

[647] Shushan (or Susa) was originally the capital of Elam, an area named for Shem's son. It was later part of the Assyrian Empire. At the time of Daniel, Shushan lay in the Babylonian province of Elam. The conquest of Babylon by Cyrus transferred Shushan to Persia, and before long it became the Persian capital and the chief place of the king's residence, probably during the reign of Darius (see William Smith, *Dictionary of the Bible*, *GospeLink*, CD-ROM, s.v. "Shushan").

[648] This would have been about 604 BC.

[649] See story "195–The Burning of the Book."

[650] Shinar was in the alluvial plain, between the Tigris and Euphrates rivers, where the rivers emptied into the Persian Gulf. The name, however, was sometimes—as here—used as an equivalent for Babylonia, which included that area. The place called Shinar here is, no doubt, the city of Babylon.

[651] Belteshazzar means "favored by Bel (or Baal)." Shadrach means "the great scribe." Meshach means "guest of a king." Abednego means "servant of Nego." Nego is probably the same as Nebo, a Chaldean deity identified with the planet Mercury. (The name Nebuchadnezzar means "may Nebo protect the crown.")

told the young Jews, "for he has personally chosen your meat and drink. What if he should see that your faces are less healthy than the faces of the other Jews of your age? That would endanger my head to the king."

Daniel, not wanting to put the man's life at risk, devised a plan and presented it to the steward who was over him and his friends. "Prove us for ten days," he urged. "Let us eat only pulse[652] and drink only water for that time. Then look at our faces and compare them with the faces of those who eat the king's diet. You may then deal with us according to what you see." And the steward consented to the ten-day test.

When the ten days had passed, the comparison was made. And when the steward saw that the faces of Daniel and his three friends were fairer and fatter than all those who ate the king's meat, it was agreed that the four young men would not be required to eat the king's meat and drink his wine. And the steward gave them pulse for their diet from that day on.

Jehovah gave these four young men the ability to excel in all matters of learning and wisdom, and Daniel also had understanding of visions and dreams. Thus, at the end of the three years when the captives were brought to stand before King Nebuchadnezzar for approval, there were no others among all of the Jews like Daniel, Shadrach, Meshach, and Abednego.[653] In everything that the king inquired of them, he found that they were ten times better than were all the magicians and astrologers in his kingdom. Because of his superior skills, Daniel was assigned as a wise man in the king's court and served there until the reign of Cyrus the Persian.

213—YOU BEHELD A GREAT IMAGE
(Daniel 2)

In the second year of his reign in Babylonia, king Nebuchadnezzar had a dream.[654] The dream troubled him so that he was unable to sleep, and he called for his wise men and magicians to help him understand what he had dreamed. "I had a dream," he told them, "and my spirit is troubled to know what it means."

"Tell us your dream," responded the wise men, "and we will tell you the interpretation."

"No," replied Nebuchadnezzar. "Though the dream is sure with me, I will not tell it.[655] You must tell me both the dream and its interpretation or you shall be slain and your houses turned into dunghills. However, if you can tell me the dream and its interpretation, I will give you both gifts and great honors."

Because this seemed like a strange request to the king's wise men, they said to him again, "If you tell us the dream, we will give the interpretation."

"If you cannot reveal my dream, there is but one decree for you—and that is death," responded the king, holding his ground. "You spend all your time seeking your own advantage by preparing lying and corrupt words to speak before me, always hoping to change your circumstances. But now you must prove yourselves by telling my dream. Only then will I know that I can trust your interpretation."

The wise men were disturbed that the king would put them to such a test. "There is not a man on earth who can tell you your dream," they protested. "No

---

[652] Pulse consists of the edible seeds of beans, lentils, peas, and other leguminous plants.

[653] The names of Daniel's three friends used here are their Chaldean names and not the Hebrew names used in this scripture. These names are used in this story because they are the names most familiar to us.

---

[654] The timing of this story does not fully agree with the events told in Daniel 1 (see story "212—The Preparation of Daniel"). That chapter states that Daniel was taken captive during the first year of King Nebuchadnezzar's reign. Chapter 1 also says that these young men were in training for three years before they became wise men in the king's court. From the context in Daniel 2, it would appear that King Nebuchadnezzar had this dream while Daniel and his friends were still in training. From the substance of this account, such does not seem likely.

[655] The wording in the King James Version suggests that King Nebuchadnezzar did not remember his dream, but from other sources it appears that this understanding is incorrect. The Persian word *azda*, which was used here, means "sure." The king, by asking his wise men to tell him what the dream was, apparently wanted to test them to see if they were telling him only what they thought he wanted to hear or if he could trust their interpretations.

other king would ask such a thing of his wise men. Only the gods, whose dwellings are not with flesh, could know your dream."

Nebuchadnezzar was furious. And, in his anger, he ordered the immediate destruction of all the wise men who served him. As the decree was to be fulfilled, Daniel and his friends, though they had not been present when the king gave his command, were also sought.

When Daniel learned what had happened, he spoke to Arioch, the captain of the guard, who was responsible for carrying out the order. "Why was the king's decree made in such haste?" he asked. "Perhaps I can tell the king his dream if I have more time."

When Arioch told the king what Daniel had said, Daniel was taken before the king to state his case. "Give me more time," Daniel pleaded with Nebuchadnezzar, "and I will tell you both your dream and its interpretation."

When Nebuchadnezzar agreed to the requested delay, Daniel returned to his house and told his friends—Shadrach, Meshach, and Abednego—all that had occurred. He pleaded with them to pray that Jehovah would reveal the dream to him so that they and the rest of the wise men might not perish.

In response to the prayers of these four faithful young Jews, both the dream and its interpretation were made known to Daniel in a night vision. And Daniel blessed God and offered thanks. "Blessed be the name of God forever and ever, for wisdom and might are his," exclaimed Daniel. "He changes the times and the seasons. He removes kings and sets up kings. He gives wisdom to the wise and knowledge to those who know understanding. He reveals deep and secret things. He knows what is in the darkness, and the light dwells in him. I thank Thee and praise Thee, O Thou God of my fathers, Thou who has given me wisdom and might and has made known to me the king's dream as we desired of Thee."

Daniel hurried to report to Arioch, who had been charged to carry out the king's decree. "Do not destroy the wise men of Babylonia," said Daniel, "but take me before the king; I am prepared to tell him his dream."

The two men went together before King Nebuchadnezzar, and Arioch said, "This man of the captives of Judah has come to make known your dream and its interpretation."

"Are you able to tell both the dream and its interpretation?" the king asked.

Daniel answered boldly: "Though the wise men and magicians cannot show you that which you demanded of them, there is a God in heaven who reveals secrets and who has made known to you what shall be in the latter days. He has also revealed your dream to me so that I might show the interpretation. As these thoughts came to you upon you bed, God revealed to you secrets of what shall happen hereafter. But, as for me, these secrets were not revealed to me for any wisdom that I have, but only that I might give you the interpretation."

Daniel then rehearsed for King Nebuchadnezzar all that he had seen in his dream. "You beheld a great image," said Daniel. "And this image, with superior brightness and terrifying aspect, stood before you. His head was of fine gold, his breast and arms of silver, his belly and thighs of brass, his legs of iron, and his feet part of iron and part of clay. You also saw a great stone that was cut from the mountain without human hands, which struck the image on his feet—even his feet of iron and clay—and broke them into pieces. You saw then that the iron, the clay, the brass, the silver, and the gold were all broken into pieces together and became like chaff on the summer threshing floor. Then you saw the wind carry them away so that they could not be found. And the stone that smote the image rolled forth until it became a great mountain and filled the whole earth. This was your dream!" The king was amazed.

Daniel then went on to give King Nebuchadnezzar the interpretation of his dream. "You, O King, are a king of kings," said Daniel, "and the God of heaven has given you a kingdom, power, strength, and glory. Wherever the children of men dwell, God has given the beasts of the field and fowls of heaven into your hands and has made you ruler over them. You are the head of gold.

"Another kingdom—a kingdom of silver—will arise after you. It will be inferior to you. And it will be followed by a third kingdom of brass that will bear rule over all the earth. The fourth kingdom will be strong as iron, because iron breaks all things into pieces and subdues them. And, as iron breaks all the others, so shall it bruise and break into pieces itself."

Daniel went on: "And, as you saw the feet and toes to be part of potters' clay and part of iron, the kingdom shall be divided—but there shall be in it the strength of iron, for you saw the iron mixed with miry clay. And as the toes were part of iron and part of clay, the kingdom shall be partly strong and partly broken. The iron and miry clay will mingle themselves with the seed of men, but they will not cleave to each other—even as iron docs not mix with clay. And, in the days of these kings, the God of heaven will set up a kingdom that will never be destroyed. This kingdom shall not be left to another people, but will break into pieces and consume all these other kingdoms and will stand forever.

"And as you saw that the stone was cut out of the mountain without human hands and broke the iron, the brass, the clay, the silver, and the gold into pieces, the great God has made it known to you what shall come to pass hereafter. Your dream is certain and its interpretation is sure."

When the king heard Daniel's report of the dream and its interpretation, he fell on his face and worshipped Daniel, and he commanded that a sacrifice should be made to him. "Surely your God is a God of gods, a Lord of kings, and a revealer of secrets!" he cried.

Then the king made Daniel ruler over the province of Babylon and chief over those who governed the wise men. And, at Daniel's request, King Nebuchadnezzar appointed Shadrach, Meshach, and Abednego to administer the affairs of the province while Daniel remained in the king's court.

214—WE CANNOT SERVE YOUR GODS
(Daniel 3)

King Nebuchadnezzar created a giant image of gold on the plain of Dura, in the province of Babylon, and commanded that all the people should bow down and worship it. The image stood sixty cubits high and was six cubits wide.[656] To celebrate the building of this wonderful image and to dedicate it, the king called all the prominent people and rulers of his empire to come to Babylon.

As the people stood before the great image at the dedication, a herald cried out, "You are commanded—all you people, nations, and languages—that whenever you hear the sound of any musical instrument[657] playing, you must fall down and worship the golden image that the king has set up. And whoever does not fall down and worship this golden image shall be cast that same hour into the midst of a fiery furnace." And when the people heard the musical instruments, they all bowed down before the image.

As the ceremonies progressed, certain Chaldeans[658] came to the king to inform him that some of the Jewish captives had not obeyed his command. "O King," they said, seeking to win his favor, "you have made a decree that every man who hears the musical instruments, as you have said, shall fall down and worship the golden image or be cast into the fiery furnace. We thought you would want to know, however, that certain Jews—men whom you have set in places of authority in Babylon—have no regard for you. For these men do not bow down and serve your gods or worship the golden image. They are Shadrach, Meshach, and Abednego."

The information had the effect with Nebuchadnezzar that the Chaldeans had hoped for. He flew into a rage and commanded that the three young Jews be brought before him at once. "Is it true that you do not serve my gods or worship the golden image that I have

---

[656] This massive golden image would have been about ninety feet (27.43 meters) tall and nine feet (2.74 meters) wide.

[657] The specific musical instruments that were named in the scriptures were "the cornet, flute, harp, sackbut, psaltery, dulcimer, and all kinds of musick" (see Daniel 3:5).

[658] The Chaldeans (or the Chaldees) were the most prominent tribe in the country of Babylonia. This title was generally used in the scriptures to refer to the people of Babylonia at the time of the captivity.

set up?" he asked them. And the young Jews assured him that the accusations were true.

Then, because of his great admiration for the three men, Nebuchadnezzar offered them a chance to make amends. "You may still redeem yourselves if you are ready to fall down and worship when you hear the music," he said. "But, if not, you must be cast this same hour into the midst of a burning furnace. Then what God is there who can deliver you?"

The three young Jews considered carefully what they might say to the king. They knew that Jehovah had commanded them to worship no other gods but him, and they were willing to die—if need be—to obey that commandment. "The God whom we serve is able to deliver us from your fiery furnace," they answered the king, "and, if it is his will to do so, he shall deliver us out of your hands. Yet, even if he will not deliver us, we will not serve your gods or worship the golden image."

Nebuchadnezzar had expected that Shadrach, Meshach, and Abednego would relent and bow before the massive image, and their stubbornness made him more angry than before. He was now determined that these three young Jews would not humiliate him before his whole kingdom by refusing to obey his decree. He commanded that the furnace be heated to a temperature seven times hotter than usual and that these young Jewish rebels be thrown into the fire.

When Shadrach, Meshach, and Abednego had been bound securely, they were cast into the midst of the fiery furnace. So hot was the furnace that the men who cast them in were overcome and died from the heat as the three young Jews fell down into the midst of the roaring flames.

As the king watched, a look of amazement came upon his face. He arose and spoke to his counselors. "Did we not cast three men bound into the fire?" he asked.

"Yes, three," they assured him, "and they were bound."

"But lo," said King Nebuchadnezzar, "I see four men in the midst of the fire, loosed and walking around unhurt. And the form of the fourth man is like the Son of God."

Then the king approached the mouth of the furnace and called, "Shadrach, Meshach, and Abednego, you servants of the Most High God, come forth!" And the young men came forth from the fire at King Nebuchadnezzar's command.

All those present saw the men come out of the fire. They saw also that the fire had no power over their bodies and that not even their hair had been singed. And they saw that their clothing was undamaged and did not have even the smell of the fire.

"Blessed be the God of Shadrach, Meshach, and Abednego!" said King Nebuchadnezzar. "For he sent his holy angel and delivered these his servants who trusted in him. They were successful in defying my decree when they yielded their bodies to be burned rather than worship any god except their own God. I therefore make a new decree that every people, nation, and language that speaks anything amiss against the God of Shadrach, Meshach, and Abednego shall be cut to pieces and their houses made into dunghills. For there is no other God that can deliver after this manner."[659]

And King Nebuchadnezzar promoted the three young Jewish captives to higher positions in the province of Babylon.

The young Hebrews and a heavenly visitor in the fiery furnace

---

[659] It should not be assumed that King Nebuchadnezzar was instantly converted to the God of Israel and or that he abandoned all other gods. In matters of worship, Nebuchadnezzar was very broad minded and had room in his life for many gods.

215—THE GREAT TREE
(Daniel 4)

One night, King Nebuchadnezzar of Babylonia had a dream that filled his heart with fear. Seeking to understand the meaning of his dream, he brought all the wise men of his kingdom before him to tell him the interpretation.

The king recounted his dream to them in detail. "I saw a tree in the midst of the earth," he said, "and it was a tree of great height. The tree grew and was strong, and when it finally reached to heaven it could be seen from the ends of the earth. The tree's leaves were fair and its fruit abundant, so that it provided food for all—both man and beast. The beasts of the field came under the tree both for shelter and shade and to eat of its fruit. The fowls of heaven lived in its branches and also ate the fruit.

"I then saw a holy being—a watcher—come down from heaven and give orders for the tree to be cut down. 'Hew down the tree, cut off its branches, shake off its leaves, and scatter its fruit,' the watcher instructed. Then the watcher said, 'Let the beasts get away from under him and fowls out of his branches. Only the stump shall be left, and he shall be bound with bands of iron and brass in the tender grass where he will be wet with the dews of heaven. His lot shall be with the beasts in the grass of the earth. The tree's heart will be changed from the heart of a man to the heart of a beast, and then seven years will pass over him.'

"Finally," said King Nebuchadnezzar, "the watcher ended his message by saying that these events were brought about by an order from the holy ones so that those who live on the earth may know that the Most High rules in the affairs of men—that by these events men may know that God gives power to whomever he will and that he sets the humblest of men to rule over the kingdoms of the earth."

When the wise men of Babylon had listened carefully to the dream, but were unable to give an interpretation, King Nebuchadnezzar sent for Daniel, the young Jewish captive whom he had placed in authority over the wise men in his kingdom.[660] "Because the spirit of the holy gods is in you and no secrets trouble you," the king said to Daniel, "I know you can tell me the meaning of my dream." Then he repeated the entire dream for Daniel just as he had told it to the others.

Daniel was perplexed by what he heard—but not because he did not understand—and he said nothing for an hour. King Nebuchadnezzar finally broke the silence. "Let neither the dream nor its interpretation trouble you," he said, giving Daniel reassurance.

Daniel had great concern about what he was going to tell the king, and he chose his words carefully. "My lord," he said, "your dream favors those who hate you, and its interpretation favors your enemies. The great tree in your dream is you. You have grown strong and your greatness has increased and reached to heaven. Your dominion has extended to the ends of the earth.

"The words spoken by the watcher," Daniel continued, "will be fulfilled by decree of the Most High. You will be cut down, leaving only a stump, and you will be bound with bands of iron and brass in the tender grass. You will be driven from among men to have a portion with the beasts, and you will dwell with them. You will eat grass like an ox and shall be wet with the dews of heaven until seven years pass over you and you know that the Most High rules in the kingdoms of men and gives those kingdoms to whomever he will. Then, because it was commanded that your stump be left, the kingdom shall be restored to you once you have learned that the heavens rule."

Then Daniel pleaded with the King Nebuchadnezzar. "Accept my counsel and break off your sins by doing righteousness," he said. "Cease your iniquities by showing mercy to the poor. For if you will do these things, your prosperity will be long." Because King Nebuchadnezzar did not believe Daniel, he ignored his counsel and refused to acknowledge the hand of God in the affairs of men.

But then, when twelve months had passed since the dream, a voice came to him from heaven saying, "O King Nebuchadnezzar, your kingdom is departed from you. You shall be driven from among men and dwell with the beasts of the field. You shall eat grass like an ox, and seven years shall pass over you until you learn that the Most High rules in the kingdoms of men and gives power to whomever he will."

All that was shown to King Nebuchadnezzar in his dream of the great tree came upon him in that same hour. He became mad and was driven from among men. He ate grass like an ox, and his body was wet with the dews of heaven, till his hair had grown like eagles' feathers and his nails like the claws of a bird.

Then, at the end of seven years, King Nebuchadnezzar lifted up his eyes to heaven and his understanding and reason returned to him. He gave praise and honor to the Most High and was established once more in his kingdom. He became greater than before because he honored God and acknowledged that all God's works are truth, that his ways are just, and that he is able to humble those who walk in pride.

---

[660] See story "213—You Beheld a Great Image."

216−AN EVERLASTING KINGDOM

(Daniel 7)

In the first year[661] of Belshazzar's reign in the kingdom of Babylonia,[662] the prophet Daniel had a dream in which he saw four great beasts come up out of the turbulent sea. The first beast was like a lion with the wings of an eagle. And, as Daniel watched, the wings of this beast were plucked out. He also saw that the beast was lifted up from the earth and made to stand on its hind legs like a man and that it was given a man's heart.

The second beast that Daniel saw was like a bear. When it raised itself up on one side, it had three ribs in its mouth. And Daniel heard a voice speak to this beast saying, "Arise and devour much flesh."

The third beast was like a four-headed leopard with four wings like those of a bird on its back, and it was given power to rule.

The fourth beast, which was dreadful, terrible, and very strong, was different from all the others; it was like nothing that Daniel had ever seen. It had great iron teeth, with which it broke into pieces and devoured whatever it encountered. Then, if there was anything left, it trampled the rest under its feet. This beast also had ten horns. As Daniel observed the beast's horns, he saw another, smaller horn come up in the middle of the others and pluck out three of the other horns by their roots. This little horn had eyes like a man and a mouth with which it spoke great things.

The scene of Daniel's dream then changed. He saw that the thrones of the kings of the earth were all destroyed and that Adam, the Ancient of Days, was seated upon a fiery throne with wheels like fire. Adam was clothed in a white garment and his hair was as white as pure wool. A fiery stream came forth from before him and a great gathering of people—ten thousand times ten thousand—stood before him, and a thousand thousands

ministered unto him. Daniel then saw that the judgment of the earth was set and that the books were opened.[663]

The dream then returned to the terrible ten-horned beast and its little horn that spoke great words. And Daniel saw that, because of the words that the little horn spoke, the beast was slain and its body given to the burning flame that issued from before the Ancient of Days. Daniel also saw that the other beasts had their dominion taken away, but that their lives were prolonged for a season.

Next, Daniel saw the Son of God, the Great Jehovah, ascending from the clouds of heaven in all his glory and coming to the Ancient of Days. And, as the Son of God stood before Father Adam, Adam delivered to him glory, power, and dominion over all peoples and nations of the earth. Daniel also saw that the dominion of the Son of God was everlasting and could never be destroyed or taken from him.

While still in his dream, Daniel's spirit was troubled because he did not understand the meaning of what he saw. But he came near to an angel that was standing by and asked for an explanation.

"The four great beasts are four kings who will arise in the earth,"[664] explained the angel, "but the Saints of God shall take the kingdom away from these kings and possess it forever." Then, concerning the fourth beast, the angel told Daniel that the little horn would make war with the Saints of God and prevail against them until the time when the Ancient of Days would come. But when the Ancient of Days comes, judgment will be given to the Saints and they shall possess the kingdom.

"The fourth beast is the fourth kingdom upon the earth. This kingdom will be different from all other kingdoms and will devour the whole earth. It will tread down the earth and break it into pieces. The ten horns are ten kings who shall arise, and the little horn is yet another king. He is different from the others and shall subdue three of them, speak great words against the Most High, and wear out the Saints. He will think to

---

[661] Daniel was no longer a young man. This dream was fifty years after he and his friends were taken captive and brought to Babylon.

[662] Note that in this story (and in other stories where Belshazzar is mentioned) I have not referred to him as the king, even though he is called King Belshazzar in the King James Version of the Bible. As prince regent, he was actually second in authority to his father Nabonidus and shared in the powers of the crown (see story "211−The Babylonian and Persian Empires").

[663] This great gathering at which Adam, the Ancient of Days, will preside and to which the Savior will come and receive all the keys from Adam is the council that will be held at Adam-ondi-Ahman prior to the Second Coming (see Doctrine and Covenants 116:1 and story "7−A Prince over Them Forever"; see also Doctrine and Covenants 27:11).

[664] The interpretation of this dream is the same as in the dream that Daniel interpreted for King Nebuchadnezzar, the Babylonian king, in Daniel 2 (see story "213−You Beheld a Great Image"). The lion represents the Babylonians, the bear represents the Persians, the leopard represents the Grecians (or Macedonians), and the terrible diverse beast represents the Romans.

change times and laws, and both times and laws will be given into his hands until a time and times and the dividing of time.[665] But then the judgment of God will take away the little horn's dominion, consume it, and destroy it.

"Then shall the kingdom of the Most High—with all its dominion, its power, and its greatness—be given to the Saints. For the kingdom of the Most High is an everlasting kingdom, and all other dominions shall serve the Most High and obey him."

Daniel was troubled by this strange dream, but he kept it in his heart.

---

[665] According to some scholars: "A 'time' equals one year, 'times' equal two years, and a 'half' [or the dividing of time] equals half a year, based on the Hebrew calendar of thirty days per month. The total time is three and one-half years. A wicked king will blaspheme God and persecute the Saints for this time period." (Donald W. Parry and Jay A. Parry, *Understanding the Book of Revelation* [Salt Lake City: Deseret Book Co., 1998], 137). The aforementioned authors attribute this interpretation to an article by Reed C. Durham entitled "Revelation: The Plainest Book Ever Written." (*New Era*, May 1973, 21–27). How literal an interpretation can be given to this is unknown. Some say that this time period is the time from the Apostasy until the Restoration and that the three and one-half years are actually 1,260 days (based on the Hebrew's lunar calendar with its thirty-day months) and that the days represent years. Realize, also, that this prophecy may not relate to our day at all, but perhaps to the approximate three and one-half year period of the persecution of the Jews by Antiochus Epiphanes, the king of Syria, prior to the rededication of the temple, between 168–67 to 164–63 BC (see Richard D. Draper, *Opening the Seven Seals: The Visions of John the Revelator* [Salt Lake City: Deseret Book Co., 1991], 121). Any time used in trying to find the correct interpretation could probably be better spent in other pursuits.

217—THE TIME OF THIS VISION IS THE TIME OF THE END
(Daniel 8)

Two years after Daniel's dream of the four beasts,[666] he had another dream. In this later dream he stood in the city of Shushan[667] by the river Ulai, and when he looked up he saw a ram with two horns. One horn was higher on the ram's head than the other, and Daniel saw that the higher horn grew in last. The ram was guarding the way to the west, the north, and the south, and he pushed with great power so that no other beast might be superior to him. Because there were none who could overcome him, the powerful ram could do as he wished. And Daniel saw that the ram became great.

As Daniel stood in awe at the power of the ram, a he-goat with a remarkable horn between his eyes came out of the west, not touching the ground. The he-goat attacked the ram with great fury, breaking both of the ram's horns. With his horns broken, the ram had no power to stand before the goat and was thus thrown to the ground and trampled upon.

The he-goat grew very strong, but when he was at his strongest, his remarkable horn was broken. And when that great horn was broken, four less significant horns came up in its place—one toward each of the four winds of heaven.

As time passed, a little horn grew out of one of the four, and that little horn, as it grew, became very strong toward the east. The little horn had great power, even against the hosts of heaven,[668] and it cast some of the stars to the ground and stamped on them. The little horn also magnified himself against the prince of the host of

---

[666] See story "216—An Everlasting Kingdom."

[667] Shushan (or Susa) was originally the capital of Elam, an area named for Shem's son. It was later part of the Assyrian Empire. At the time of Daniel, Shushan belonged to the Babylonians and was in the province of Elam. The conquest of Babylon by Cyrus transferred Shushan to Persia and, before long, it became the Persian capital and chief place of the king's residence, probably during the reign of Darius (see William Smith, *Dictionary of the Bible*, *GospeLink*, CD-ROM, s.v. "Shushan").

[668] The hosts of heaven are the heavenly bodies—the sun, the moon, the planets, and the stars (see Genesis 2:1; Deuteronomy 4:19; 2 Kings 21:3, 5; 23:5).

Jehovah.[669] He took away the daily sacrifice and cast down and defiled the place of the sanctuary. The little horn was given power to oppose the daily sacrifice because of the transgressions of the people. In all things the little horn was very prosperous.

Daniel then heard two Saints speaking, and one of them said to the other: "How long shall this vision last concerning the daily sacrifice and this transgression of desolation wherein both the sanctuary and the hosts of heaven are trodden under foot?"

The other Saint replied to the question, but spoke directly to Daniel as he did so: "It shall last for 2,300 days, then the sanctuary shall be cleansed."[670]

When Daniel had seen the vision and sought to know its meaning, he saw what appeared to be a man standing before him. And as he looked at this personage, he heard a voice call to him from between the banks of the Ulai, saying that the personage before him was the angel Gabriel[671] and that Gabriel would help him understand the vision.

When Gabriel came near, Daniel fell on his face because he was afraid. Gabriel then spoke to him and said, "You must understand, O son of man, that the time of this vision is the time of the end."

As Gabriel spoke, Daniel was in a deep sleep with his face toward the ground, but Gabriel touched him and set him upright. "Behold," said Gabriel, "I will make you to know what shall be at the last end of the indignation, for the end will come at the appointed time."

Gabriel continued—now explaining the details of the dream: "The ram and its two horns are the kings of Media and Persia.[672] The rough he-goat is the kingdom of Grecia, and the great horn between his eyes is the first king of Grecia.[673] Now as you saw that the horn was broken and four other horns stood up in its place, four kingdoms shall arise out of that nation but will lack the power of the first.

"In the latter time of their kingdom, when transgressors have come into full prosperity, a king of fierce countenance and with an understanding for riddles shall arise. The power of this king will be mighty, but his power will not be his own. He will prosper and will destroy both those who are mighty and those who are holy. And because of his policies, deceit will prosper. He will magnify himself in his own heart and destroy many in a time of peace. He will also stand up against the Prince of princes but, when he does so, he shall be broken into pieces without hands."

Gabriel then concluded his explanation to Daniel by saying: "The vision you have seen is true, but you must not speak of it because its fulfillment will be many days hereafter." And Daniel was perplexed because he still did not understand the vision.

---

[669] According to Daniel 10:21, the prince of the host of Jehovah was Michael (or Adam).

[670] No attempt has been made to explain or interpret the meaning of the time period that is given here. That information has not been revealed and, apparently, it is not essential for us to understand it.

[671] The Prophet Joseph Smith said that Gabriel is the patriarch Noah (*History of the Church*, 3:386).

[672] The kings were Darius the Mede and Cyrus the Persian (see story "211−The Babylonian and Persian Empires"). It is interesting to note that Daniel had this dream before the fall of Babylonia to the Medes and Persians.

[673] Grecia was Macedonia, and the remarkable king was Alexander the Great. When Alexander died at the age of thirty-two, the kingdom was divided among four of his generals.

218—THE HANDWRITING ON THE WALL
(Daniel 5)

It had been sixty-seven years since Daniel and his friends had been brought to Babylon as captives from the land of Judah. Daniel still served in the court of the king, but he was now an old man and few remembered his earlier deeds. King Nebuchadnezzar was long since dead, and a son-in-law named Nabonidus sat on the throne of the Babylonian kingdom. Ruling with Nabonidus was his son Belshazzar, the prince regent and second in command.[674]

Belshazzar made a great feast for 1,000 of the lords of the kingdom, along with their wives and concubines. During the feast he served wine to his guests from the gold and silver vessels that his grandfather Nebuchadnezzar[675] had extracted from the temple in Jerusalem. And while they drank from these sacred vessels, they praised the false gods that they had made with their own hands.

As Belshazzar's feast progressed, part of a man's hand appeared and wrote with its finger, in an unknown language, on the palace wall. And as Belshazzar looked up, he saw the hand and the writing. So troubling and frightening was this vision to him that the joints of his hips became loose and his knees began to knock together.

Belshazzar called for the wise men of the city to come in and see the writing. "Whoever can give me the interpretation of this strange writing," he promised them, "shall be clothed with scarlet, have a gold chain placed around his neck, and become the third ruler in the kingdom." But none of the wise men of Babylon could tell Belshazzar what the writing meant.

When the queen[676] saw Belshazzar's anguish, she said, "Do not let your thoughts trouble you or your countenance be changed because of this strange writing. There is a man in the kingdom who has the spirit of the holy gods who, in the days of your grandfather, interpreted dreams and showed forth his understanding. He had the wisdom of the gods in interpreting dreams and dissolving doubts. This man is Daniel, whom the king named Belteshazzar and made him master of the magicians and of all the wise men. Let Daniel be called and he will give you the interpretation."

When Daniel was summoned before Belshazzar, Belshazzar questioned him. "Are you that Daniel who was brought captive from Judah by my grandfather?" asked Belshazzar.

"I am," answered Daniel.

"I have heard that you have the spirit of the gods in you, as well as light, understanding, and excellent wisdom," said Belshazzar. "My wise men have been brought in that they might read this writing that you see on the wall and tell me its meaning, but they could not do it. If you can tell me what this writing means, you shall be clothed with scarlet, a gold chain shall be placed around your neck, and you shall be the third ruler in the kingdom."

"You may keep your gifts and give your rewards to another," answered Daniel, "yet I will read the writing and make known its interpretation.

"The Most High God gave Nebuchadnezzar a kingdom with majesty, glory, and honor. Because of the majesty that God gave him, all people, nations, and languages trembled and feared before him, for he had the power of life and death over them. But when your grandfather hardened his heart with pride, he was removed from his throne and his glory was taken from him. He was driven from among men and his heart made like that of the beast. He dwelt with wild asses, fed on grass like an ox, and his body was wet with dew until he knew that the Most High God rules in the kingdoms of men and appoints whomever he will as their kings.

"And you, O Belshazzar, have not humbled your heart even though you knew all this. You have lifted yourself up against Jehovah and have brought the vessels of his temple before you to be used for the praising of gods that are made by men's hands. You have not glorified that God in whose hands is your very breath and who watches over all that you do. Because of your

---

[674] Note that this story (and other stories in which Belshazzar is mentioned) does not refer to him as the king, even though he is called King Belshazzar in the King James Version of the Bible. As prince regent, he was actually second in authority to his father Nabonidus and shared in the powers of the crown (see story "211—The Babylonian and Persian Empires").

[675] The scriptural text refers to Nebuchadnezzar as Belshazzar's father, but he was really his grandfather. In the Hebrew and Chaldean languages, the same word was used for all male ancestors in the direct line and did not distinguish by generation as we do. (The same was also true of female ancestors.) This story uses *grandfather*, which is the correct relationship.

[676] It is not clear here whether the queen was Belshazzar's mother or his wife. She seems to have a better memory of Daniel's earlier deeds than does Belshazzar, so it is likely that she is his mother, Nebuchadnezzar's daughter.

deeds, this hand was sent from him to write upon your wall.

"This is what was written: 'Mene, mene, tekel, upharsin.'

"And this is the interpretation: *Mene* means that God has numbered your kingdom and finished it. *Tekel* means that you are weighed in the balance and found wanting. And *upharsin*[677] means that your kingdom is divided and given to the Medes and the Persians."[678]

And when Belshazzar heard Daniel's interpretation of the writing, he commanded that Daniel should be clothed in scarlet, with a gold chain around his neck, and that he should be made third ruler in the kingdom. But Belshazzar was slain that night when Darius the Mede took the kingdom.

219—INTO THE LIONS' DEN
(Daniel 6)

After the fall of Babylonia to the Medes and Persians, Daniel, the Jewish captive, was highly favored by King Darius the Mede. And, although Daniel was now a very old man, he was appointed to be the highest of three presidents to whom all the princes in the province rendered their accounts. And the king, because of Daniel's ability and his great loyalty, thought to set him over the whole realm. However, it did not seem proper to the princes and the other presidents for a Jew to have such a high post, and they sought for a way to bring Daniel down.

Because Daniel was circumspect and faithful in all his dealings, his detractors could find neither fault nor error in anything that he did. They could see that their only opportunity to remove Daniel from his position related to his devotion to the laws of God.

After careful scheming, these men went to King Darius and said, "All the leaders of the land have consulted together to establish a royal statute. The statute we propose would make a firm decree that whoever asks a petition of any god or any man—except you, O King, during the next thirty days, shall be cast into the lions' den. We urge you, O King, to sign this decree so that it cannot be changed, for this is according to the laws of the Medes and Persians."

King Darius's ego was bolstered by the idea and he signed the decree without understanding its full implications.

Though Daniel learned of the king's decree, he did not alter his behavior. He went into his bedchamber three times each day, just as he had always done, and opened the window toward Jerusalem.[679] Then he knelt down and prayed to thank God for his blessings.

---

[677] Verse 27 of Daniel 5 gives the interpretation of the word *peres* rather than *upharsin*. This was changed to give consistency to the story.

[678] The message was written in Aramaic. A literal translation of *mene, mene, tekel, upharsin* would be "numbered, numbered, weighed, divided." Though most any one could interpret the words of this message, the inspiration of God was essential for one to understand their meaning.

[679] The idea of praying toward Jerusalem and the temple comes from Solomon's prayer at the temple's dedication. He prayed that when the people went out to battle or were otherwise prevented from going to the temple, they should "pray unto the LORD toward the city which thou hast chosen, and toward the house that I have built for thy name" (1 Kings 8:44). President Wilford Woodruff expressed this same idea when he dedicated the Salt Lake Temple (see James E. Talmage, *The House of the Lord* [Salt Lake City: Deseret Book Co. 1968], 142). The very idea of praying toward the temple is symbolic. Much more important than the physical direction one faces when praying is the attitude of facing the temple spiritually. "To face the temple, which is the spiritual representation of the House of God, suggests that one turns his heart to the Lord and the cove-

The men, knowing of Daniel's devotion to God and of his daily routine, came together and found him praying at his window. Then they promptly reported their findings to the king. "Have you not signed a decree that any man who asks a petition of any god or any man except you, O King, within thirty days, shall be cast into the lions' den?"

"I have," replied Darius. "And that decree is unalterable according to the laws of the Medes and Persians."

"It is a sad thing," replied the men, feigning concern, "that Daniel has no regard for you or for your decree. He yet makes petitions to his God three times a day."

King Darius was distraught when heard this bitter message, because of his devotion to Daniel. He sought until sundown to find a way that Daniel might be spared. But the men persisted. "It is a sad thing," they said again, "but you know that no decree or statute signed by the king may be changed."

King Darius, having no other choice than to obey his own decree, commanded that Daniel be cast into the lions' den. But as Daniel came, the king spoke to him saying, "Your God whom you serve continually will deliver you."

Daniel's life is preserved in the lion's den

Once Daniel was inside, a stone was placed over the mouth of the den and the king sealed it with his own signet and with the signet of his lords so that no one could release Daniel without it being known.

King Darius did not sleep that night but spent the night in prayer and fasting for Daniel. When morning finally came, he rose early and went in haste to the lions' den. Once there, he removed the stone and cried with a loud voice: "O Daniel, servant of the living God, was your God able to deliver you from the lions?"

And to the king's great relief, Daniel's voice came back to him. "O King," said Daniel, "may you live forever. My God sent his angel to shut the lions' mouths that they have not hurt me. And this because innocence was found in me and because I have done you no hurt."

King Darius commanded his men to take Daniel up out of the den, and they all saw that he had suffered no injuries because he believed in his God. Then the king commanded that those men who had accused Daniel should themselves be cast into the lions' den, along with their wives and their children.[680]

And the king sent out a new unalterable decree that in every dominion of his kingdom men should tremble and fear before the God of Daniel, the living God, who is steadfast forever. "For," said he, "Daniel's God delivers and rescues. He works signs and wonders in heaven and on earth, and he has delivered Daniel from the power of the lions."

And Daniel continued to prosper in Babylon both during the reign of Darius and that of Cyrus the Persian.

---

nants made in the temples to be more like him." (*Old Testament: 1 Kings–Malachi [Student Manual, Religion 302]*, 2nd ed. [Salt Lake City: The Church of Jesus Christ of Latter-day Saints, 1982], 303.)

---

[680] It was not uncommon, when the punishment of death was meted out, for wives and children to also be slain with the offenders. This practice ensured that the matter was resolved forever and would never be raised again by future generations.

220–HE SHALL CONFIRM HIS COVENANT

(Daniel 9)

During the year that Darius the Mede ruled in the province of Babylon,[681] Daniel learned from the books available to him that the prophet Jeremiah had foretold that Judah's captivity and the desolation of Jerusalem would last for seventy years. When Daniel realized that the seventy years were nearly gone, he wondered if somehow the new government in the land might facilitate the return of his people to their homeland. With this possibility in mind, Daniel dressed himself in sackcloth and ashes and fasted and prayed mightily for his people.

In his prayer, Daniel first confessed the sins of Israel. "We have done wickedly," he said. "We have rebelled by departing from Thy judgments and precepts, and we have failed to hearken to Thy prophets. Righteousness belongs to Thee, O Lord, and shame belongs to us, the men of Israel, who have been scattered for our trespasses. But, though we have rebelled against Thee and Thou hast brought this curse of captivity upon us, I know that Thou art merciful and forgiving.

"When all the evils that were written in the law of Moses came upon us to turn us from our iniquities, we still failed to respond to Thy voice. Yet Thou art righteous and, because of Thy righteousness, I beseech Thee to turn away Thine anger both from us and from Jerusalem. Cause Thy face to shine upon Thy sanctuary—which now lies desolate—for Thine own sake. Incline Thine ear and open Thine eyes to see our desolation and the desolation of the city that is called by Thy name.

"I do not present these supplications because of our righteousness," Daniel continued. "But because of Thy great mercies and for Thine own sake do I plead. Yea, I plead that Thou wilt not delay the restoration of Thy city and Thy people."

As Daniel poured out his heart in humble prayer, confessing the sins of Israel and pleading for forgiveness, the angel Gabriel[682] came to him and touched him. "O Daniel," said the angel, "because you are greatly loved, I have been commanded to give you skill to understand this matter and to consider Jeremiah's vision. Jehovah has determined that his people and his holy city must suffer for seventy weeks to pay for their transgressions, to make a reconciliation for their iniquity, and to bring in everlasting righteousness—even to seal up Jeremiah's vision and prophecy and to anoint the Most Holy.

"Sixty-nine weeks shall also pass from the time when the commandment is given to restore and build Jerusalem until the time of the Messiah, the Prince. But the streets of Jerusalem shall be built again. Her walls shall also be rebuilt, though in troubled times.

"You should also know, Daniel, that the Messiah himself shall be cut off after sixty two weeks—but not for himself. And at the appointed time, the people of the prince who comes will destroy the city and the sanctuary. The end thereof shall be with a flood, and there shall be desolations until the end of the war."[683]

Gabriel went on, speaking again of the Messiah. "He shall confirm his covenant with many for one week," said Gabriel, "and in the midst of that week he shall cause sacrifice and offering to cease as they are known under the law of Moses. Then a covering of abominations shall make both the city and the people desolate until the end."

---

[681] Darius the Mede reigned for only one year before Cyrus became King over all the Persian Empire (see story "211–The Babylonian and Persian Empires").

[682] The Prophet Joseph Smith said that Gabriel is the patriarch Noah (*History of the Church*, 3:386).

[683] From the scriptures it is clear that Daniel foresaw the return of Israel from captivity, the future coming of the Messiah, and the destruction of Jerusalem by the Romans under Titus, though the time references given are obscure.

221—ANOTHER VISION OF JUDAH'S FUTURE

(Daniel 10–12)

Daniel sought to draw closer to Jehovah during the third year of the reign of King Cyrus of Persia.[684] He was in a very serious mood for three full weeks because he had set himself to gain understanding and to humble himself before God. He ate no desirable foods or meat and drank no wine during the entire time. Then, on the twenty-fourth day of the first month, as Daniel stood on the banks of the Tigris River, he looked up and saw a vision of Jehovah. Jehovah was dressed in a linen robe with a girdle of fine gold about his loins. His body had the brilliance of beryl, his face was like lightning, his eyes like lamps of fire, his arms and feet like polished brass, and his voice like the voice of a multitude. Because Daniel saw Jehovah in vision, those others who were present did not see him. And, when the earth began to shake, the others fled, leaving Daniel alone. And, as the vision continued, Daniel's strength completely left him.

As Daniel lay prostrate, his face upon the ground in a deep sleep, an angel touched him and lifted him to his hands and knees. Then Jehovah spoke.

"O Daniel, my greatly beloved," said Jehovah, "understand the words that I speak, and stand upright." And Daniel stood upright, trembling.

Jehovah continued: "Fear not, Daniel, for from the first day that you set your heart to understand and to humble yourself before me, your words have been heard, and I have now come because of your words. I have come to give you understanding of what shall befall your people in the latter days. And that which you shall see in vision shall cover many days."

When Daniel again prostrated himself upon the ground and could not speak, an angel came and touched his lips. Then Daniel opened his mouth and spoke to Jehovah. "Because of this vision my sorrows are turned upon me," he said. "I have lost my strength and have no breath. How then can I talk with Thee?"

Then another angel came and touched Daniel's lips and Jehovah said to him, "O you who are greatly loved, be strong."

"Speak to me now," responded Daniel, "for you have strengthened me."

"Do you know why I have come to you?" Jehovah asked. Then, without waiting for Daniel's reply, he went on. "I shall now go forth and fight against the prince of Persia, and when I have gone forth the prince of Grecia shall come. But there is none except Michael your prince[685] who supports me in these things.

"Though I strengthened Darius the Mede in his first year," Jehovah continued, "I will now show you the truth. Three kings will stand in Persia. And then shall a fourth king, far richer than the kings of Persia, arise in the kingdom of Grecia.[686] This mighty king will rule with great authority by the power that comes from his riches, and he shall do whatever he pleases. But when he has stood up, his kingdom shall be broken and divided into four kingdoms, according to the winds of heaven. The kingdom will not be given to this king's posterity; nor will it continue with the same power as that by which this mighty king ruled.

"When the kingdom is divided, the king of the south will be strong,[687] but one of his princes will be even stronger than he and will have a great dominion. But after many years, these two—the king of the south and his prince—will join forces. The daughter of the king shall then go to the king of the north[688] to make an alliance. Her efforts will fail, however, and so will her father and those who support him.

"When this king has failed, a new king shall arise in the south out of a branch of the roots of the first king's daughter. He shall come with his army and shall prevail over the king of the north. He will carry captives from the north into Egypt, as well as their idols and precious treasures. In his power he shall separate himself from the king of the north.

"When the sons of the king of the south become stirred up, they will assemble a multitude of great armies. The king of the north, however, will also be stirred up. He and his armies will overflow into the

---

[684] This was about 536 BC. Cyrus was the son of Ahazuerus.

[685] The prince Michael is Adam (see Doctrine and Covenants 27:11).

[686] Grecia was Macedonia and the great king spoken of was Alexander the Great.

[687] This kingdom of the south was based in Egypt. Ptolemy I (called Ptolemy Soter), who had been one of Alexander's generals was the king. See also footnote 688.

[688] This kingdom of the north was centered in Syria. The first king of the north was Seleucus I, the Macedonian general who founded the Seleucid dynasty. After that, there is much vagueness and uncertainty in Daniel's narrative. You will want to look at the chronology tables in the *Bible Dictionary*, LDS-KJV, s.v. "Chronology," pages 639 to 645. In the battles between the kings of the north and the kings of the south, the people of Judah were essentially pawns caught in the middle. At various times, Palestine belonged to both of these kingdoms.

south, but will then return to their own fortress. The king of the south will be angry because of the intrusion by the king of the north and go to war against him. Though the king of the north will meet him with a great multitude, the king of the south will prevail and many ten thousands of the multitude of the north shall be slain.

"The king of the north shall return after many years with an even greater army and great riches. Though others will fight against the king of the south and fail, the king of the south will not be strong enough to withstand the king of the north. The fortified cities of the south will be captured and the king of the north will be able to do whatever he pleases. When no one is able to stand against him, he shall stand in the glorious land and consume it.

"With his great power, the king of the north will set his face to enter into the south with the strength of his whole kingdom, and he shall do so. Once he has conquered the kingdom of the south, he shall turn his face to the isles of the sea and shall also subdue many of them. However, one of the princes of the north will take the evil reward offered to him by his king and turn it against his benefactor.

"The king of the north will next turn his face to return to the fort of his own land, but he shall stumble and fall. And when he cannot be found, a tax collector will stand up in his place. After a few days, however, a depraved and evil man will obtain the kingdom by flattery and deceit.[689] This evil man shall become strong though only a few people support him, and his wickedness will exceed that of all the kings before him. He shall loot the land and mistreat the people, and when he goes to battle against the king of the south, he shall defeat the king of the south with cunning and contrived schemes.

"The hearts of both of these kings shall be inclined to do mischief, and they shall speak lies at the same table. Their mischief, however, shall not prosper because the ends of both will come at their appointed times. When the evil king of the north returns to his own land with his great riches, his heart will be set against the holy covenant. Then, when he goes again to the south, the ships of Chittim[690] will come against him and he shall return home with indignation against the holy covenant. Through secret communications with those who have forsaken the covenant, he shall pollute the holy temple, take away the daily sacrifice, and put into place the abomination that makes desolate.[691]

"The people who betray the covenant and fight against it shall be corrupted by flatteries, but those who know God will be strong and do great works. Those who understand shall instruct many, yet they shall fall by the sword for many days—as well as by flame, captivity, and spoil. When those who understand fall, they shall receive little help, but many will cleave to them with flatteries. Some of these will also fall, and their fall will be a test and trial to the others, purging them and making them white, even until the time of the end,[692] for the appointed time will not yet have come.

"The wicked king of the north who fights against the covenant will be free to do whatever he pleases and will exalt himself above God. He will prosper until the cup of God's wrath is full, for everything that he decides he will do. He will regard neither the God of his fathers nor the desire of women but will magnify himself above all. He will honor the god of forces with his many possessions, as well as a god that his fathers did not know. In his strongholds he will honor that unknown god with gold and silver, with precious stones, and with pleasant things. He will also divide the land for his own gain and make his friends the rulers.

"At the time of the end, the king of the south shall push at this wicked king, and the king of the north shall come against him like a whirlwind with chariots, horsemen, and many ships. Yet the evil king will continue to enter countries to conquer them and then move on. He shall enter the glorious land, and many countries—including Egypt—shall be overthrown. Edom, Moab, and Ammon, however, will be spared. He shall have power over the treasures of Egypt, and the Libyans and the Ethiopians shall march with him. When tidings from the east and the north trouble him, he shall go forth with great fury to destroy all things. He shall plant his palace between the seas in the glorious holy

---

[689] This evil and depraved king of the north was no doubt Antiochus Epiphanes. He meted out great indignities and sufferings upon the people of Judah, essentially trying to destroy everything that was Jewish (see *Bible Dictionary*, LDS-KJV, s.v. "Antiochus Epiphanes").

[690] Chittim was what we now call the isle of Cyprus.

---

[691] This is one of many Old Testament prophecies that was to be fulfilled twice. In the New Testament (Matthew 24:15) and in the Pearl of Great Price (JS—Matthew 1:12, 32), this (these) future event (events) is (are) referred to as the "abomination of desolation." In the Doctrine and Covenants, where the latter-day fulfillment is prophesied, the term "desolation of abomination" is used (84:117; 88:84–85). An excellent discussion of the subject is found in *Bible Dictionary*, LDS-KJV, s.v. "Abomination of Desolation."

[692] The end that this prophecy is looking toward seems to be the destruction of Jerusalem by Titus and the Romans in AD 70. But, see also footnote 691.

mountain; yet he too will meet his end and there will be none to help him.

"This shall be a time of great trouble among the Jews, such a time as there never has been since there was a Jewish nation. And at this time of great trouble, Michael the great prince will stand up in behalf of the people, and every one whose name is found written in the book of life shall be delivered. Many who sleep in the dust of the earth shall awaken, some to eternal life and some to shame and everlasting contempt. The wise will shine as the brightness of the firmament and those who turn many to righteousness shall be like the stars forever. There are many who shall run to and fro, and knowledge shall increase."

And when Daniel was shown all these things and they were written in the book, he was commanded to seal the book until the time of the end.

Daniel then looked up and saw two men, one on either side of the river. One of the men spoke to Jehovah, who was standing upon the waters of the river. "How long," he asked, "shall it be till the end of these wonders?"

And Jehovah held up his hands to heaven, swearing by Him Who Lives Forever, and answered, "It shall be for a time, times, and a half.[693] And when he has spread the power of the holy people abroad in the earth, all of these things shall be finished."

Daniel heard all of this, but he did not understand. "O Lord Jehovah," he questioned, "what shall be the end of these things?"

"Go your way, Daniel," Jehovah answered him, "for the words are closed up and sealed until the time of the end. Many shall be purified and many shall be tried, but the wicked shall not understand. Those who are wise, however, will understand. And from the time that the daily sacrifice shall be taken away until the abomination of desolation is set up, there shall be 1,290 days. But blessed is he who waits for 1,335 days. Now go your way until the end comes. For after your rest you shall stand in your own place at the end of these days."[694]

---

[693] See footnote 665 in story "216–An Everlasting Kingdom."

[694] Like the prophet Daniel, we do not understand all things—only those that we need to understand. For example, no attempt is made to explain or interpret the meaning of the time periods that are given here. That information has not been revealed and, apparently, it is not essential for us to understand it. We will need further revelation before we can understand the meanings of all these things. It will come when we need it and when we merit it.

222–THE RETURN OF JUDAH'S EXILES

(Ezra 1–4; Nehemiah 7, Isaiah 44, 45)

In the first year of the reign of King Cyrus of Persia in what had previously been the Babylonian Empire,[695] Jehovah stirred up Cyrus's spirit to fulfill the words that had been spoken by the prophets. One of those prophets, Jeremiah, had prophesied that Israel would serve the king of Babylon for seventy years.[696] Isaiah also made important prophecies more than 100 years earlier. He prophesied that the Babylonian Empire would fall[697] and that Cyrus would order the rebuilding of Jerusalem and the temple.[698]

The manner in which the Persians dealt with the peoples they conquered—unlike the cruel Babylonians—was to let the captive peoples return to their homelands if they desired to go, but those who returned

---

[695] The first year of Cyrus, as stated here, would have been the year he began ruling over the area that had been Babylonia, 538 BC. He began reigning in Persia twenty years earlier.

[696] See Jeremiah 25:12 and story "196–Judah on the Brink of Destruction."

[697] See Isaiah 13:1–22 and 48:14.

[698] Isaiah's prophecy concerning Cyrus is as follows: "[Thus the LORD]…saith of Cyrus, He is my shepherd, and shall perform all my pleasure: even saying to Jerusalem, Thou shalt be built; and to the temple, Thy foundation shall be laid. Thus saith the LORD to his anointed, to Cyrus, whose right hand I have holden, to subdue nations before him; and I will loose the loins of kings, to open before him the two leaved gates; and the gates shall not be shut. I will go before thee, and make the crooked places straight: I will break in pieces the gates of brass, and cut in sunder the bars of iron: And I will give thee the treasures of darkness, and hidden riches of secret places, that thou mayest know that I, the LORD, which call thee by thy name, am the God of Israel. For Jacob my servant's sake, and Israel mine elect, I have even called thee by thy name: I have surnamed thee, though thou hast not known me." (Isaiah 44:28–45:4) According to Josephus, when Cyrus read Isaiah's prophecies "and admired the divine power, an earnest desire and ambition seized upon him to fulfill what was so written." (Flavius Josephus, *Antiquities of the Jews,* 11:1:1–2, as quoted by Ellis T. Rasmussen, *A Latter-day Saint Commentary on the Old Testament* [Salt Lake City: Deseret Book Co., 1993], 367.) Isaiah also referred to Cyrus in 41:2, 25 and 47:2, but he did not name him.

still remained under the authority and rule of the Persians.

As Jehovah's spirit moved upon Cyrus, he made a proclamation and sent it throughout the land. The proclamation said, "Jehovah, the God of heaven, has given me all the kingdoms of the earth and has charged me to build him a house at Jerusalem, which is in Judah. If any of you are of this people, may your God be with him and let you go up to Jerusalem and build the house of the God of Israel, for he is *the* God. And whoever of his people are in any place of exile, let the men of that place help them with silver and gold, with goods, and with beasts, in addition to their freewill offerings for the house of God."

Cyrus also brought out the vessels of the temple that King Nebuchadnezzar had taken from Jerusalem many years before to put in his pagan temple in Babylon. Cyrus put these vessels into the hands of Zerubbabel,[699] the prince of Judah, to return them to Jerusalem.

In response to Cyrus's decree, the people filled the hands of those who were going up to Jerusalem with precious gifts to benefit their work. These gifts were all carried up to Jerusalem, along with the vessels from the temple. Those who made the journey under the leadership of Zerubbabel and the ten men who labored with him were numbered at 42,360, plus 7,337 servants and 200 singers.[700] Once in Judah, they returned to those cities from which they, their parents, or their grandparents had come.

In the seventh month, once the people were well settled in their own cities, they gathered at Jerusalem where the priests and Zerubbabel's men had built an altar to Jehovah, according to the law of Moses. The priests made burnt offerings for the people both morning and evening every day, and they kept all the rites and feast days prescribed by the Law.

In the second year after their coming, once they had gathered the necessary materials for construction, the foundation of the temple was laid. At the laying of the foundation, the priests in their sacred clothing rejoiced with trumpets and the Levites rejoiced with cymbals. The people sang together to praise and give thanks to Jehovah, and all of them joined in a great shout of rejoicing.[701]

The old men among those priests and Levites who were present—those who had seen and remembered Solomon's temple—wept and shouted for joy to think that they had lived to see again the foundation of this great house. And so great was the noise, those present could not discern between the joyous shouts and the weeping.

The people who lived in Samaria—the descendants of the remnants who were left and the colonists who were settled there by the Assyrians when the ten tribes were taken away[702]—soon became aware that the Jews had returned to rebuild their temple. These people of Samaria came to Zerubbabel and asked if they could help with the work. "Let us build with you," they pleaded, "for we also worship your God and have offered sacrifices to him from the days when our fathers were brought here."

"It cannot be allowed," responded Zerubbabel and the chief fathers. "You may have nothing to do with the building of a house to our God, for we were commanded by King Cyrus to build it ourselves."[703]

Offended because they were denied participation, the peoples of Samaria did all they could both to discourage the people of Judah and to thwart their work. Their opposition continued from the reign of Cyrus

---

[699] In some places in the book of Ezra, Zerubbabel is referred to by the Persian or Chaldean name of Sheshbazzar. He was at the head of those who went up to Jerusalem to build the temple. He was the grandson of Jehoiachin, the penultimate king of Judah before the destruction of Jerusalem and the Babylonian captivity. The fact that Zerubbabel was given a Persian name suggests that he, like Daniel, was in the king's service.

[700] The number of singers given in Ezra 2:64–65 (200) is somewhat smaller than the number given in Nehemiah 7:66–67 (245). The other numbers agree.

[701] This was, no doubt, something very similar to (if not the same as) the "Hosannah" shout given by the members of The Church of Jesus Christ of Latter-day Saints in connection with temple dedications and other special occasions.

[702] See story "182–Assyria's Victory and Israel's Captivity."

[703] The sincerity of the Samaritans in offering to help build the temple is hard to read. Ezra 4:1 refers to them as "the adversaries of Judah and Benjamin." One commentator made this observation: "It is difficult to know whether the 'people of the land' really wanted to seek the Lord or were 'adversaries of Judah' from the beginning and had selfish motives. They were descendants of people who lived there when the ten tribes were taken away by Assyria and replaced by other peoples brought in from many nations, who intermixed both blood and faith with the remnant Israelites (2 Kings 17)." (Ellis T. Rasmussen, *A Latter-day Saint Commentary on the Old Testament* [Salt Lake City: Deseret Book Co., 1993], 369.) If they were not adversaries before this incident, they certainly were afterwards, continually interrupting the work on the temple. The first interruption lasted for fifteen years.

until the reign of King Darius.[704] They hired counselors against the Jews to hinder their work. They also wrote letters to the Persian kings—first to Ahasuerus and then to Artaxerxes.[705]

One letter to King Artaxerxes alleged that the Jews were building a rebellious city. "If this city is built and its walls are set up," said the letter, "the Jews will stop paying tribute and will destroy the revenue of the kings. Not only are we dependent on the king's revenues, we do not wish to see the king dishonored. These Jews are moved to sedition as they were in old times, which is the very reason this city was destroyed."

The Samaritans' letter to Artaxerxes had the desired effect in Persia and produced the desired response. Artaxerxes, convinced that trouble was brewing in Jerusalem, sent a hasty reply. "I have read your letter and have learned from my records that Jerusalem in old times was prone to rebellion against those who were their kings. I have learned, in fact, that they also had their own mighty kings who ruled over countries beyond the river, exacting tribute and taxes from other peoples. Command these men to cease their work until you receive further word from me."

Armed now with the king's letter, the Samaritans went up to Jerusalem and, by force, halted all work by the Jews both on the city and on the temple.

---

[704] This is not Darius the Mede who was placed in authority over the city of Babylon when the Persians first conquered the Babylonians. Any connection between the two is unlikely (see story "211—The Babylonian and Persian Empires").

[705] The kings of Persia who ruled during the time included in this story were, in order, Cyrus, Ahasuerus, Artaxerxes, and Darius. The man called Ahasuerus is known in history as Cambyses and may have been Cyrus's son. Artaxerxes (the king involved in this story) is known in history as Smedis. He was an impostor who pretended to be the brother of Cambyses. He usurped the throne in 522 BC and reigned for just five months. Darius, the son of Hystaspes, conspired with six Persian chiefs and dethroned the impostor Smedis. He restored the favorable policies of Cyrus.

223—KING DARIUS SUPPORTS THE TEMPLE PROJECT
(Ezra 5–6, Haggai 1–2)

Once Darius had deposed the impostor Artaxerxes from the throne of Persia,[706] the people of Judah resumed their labors on the temple and on the city of Jerusalem, much to the displeasure of their Samaritan neighbors. And the prophets Haggai and Zechariah prophesied among the Jews and were counted among those who labored on the temple. It was, in fact, because of the urging of Haggai that the work of building the temple was resumed.[707]

In the second year of King Darius, as the people were content to do nothing because they believed that the time had not yet come for the temple to be built, Jehovah spoke to Haggai. Jehovah's pointed message was addressed to Zerubbabel, Joshua the priest, and the people of Judah. "Is this the time for you to dwell in paneled houses," asked Jehovah, "while my house lies waste?"

"Consider your ways, you people of Judah," Jehovah continued, "for because you have failed to build my house, you have not prospered. You have sown much and brought forth little. You eat but are not filled. You drink but are not satisfied. You clothe yourselves but you cannot keep warm. The wages you earn are put into a bag filled with holes. And I have brought a drought upon the land because you have failed to build my house.

"Go to the mountains and bring wood to build my house. And when you build it, I will take pleasure in it and be glorified."

When the prophet Haggai spoke Jehovah's words to Zerubbabel and the people of Judah, their hearts were stirred up to commence once more their work on the house of the Lord.

The following month, Jehovah once again gave Haggai a message for Zerubbabel. "Be strong," he said, "and according to the word that I covenanted with this people as they came out of Egypt,[708] even so my Spirit remains among them, and they need not fear. In a little

---

[706] See footnote 705 in story "222—The Return of Judah's Exiles."

[707] The halt in the construction of the temple by the returning exiles is explained in story "222—The Return of Judah's Exiles."

[708] This reference to Israel coming out of Egypt does not relate to any recent event in Jewish history, but to the days of Moses.

while I will shake the heavens, the earth, the sea, and the dry land. And when I shake the nations, the Desire of All Nations shall come. Then will I fill this house with glory, and the glory of this latter house shall be greater than the glory of the former. And I will give peace in this place."

A man named Tatnai was appointed by the Persians as governor over all the territory west of the Euphrates River and, as work on the temple resumed, Tatnai came to Jerusalem and saw what was happening. He became deeply concerned when he saw the people laboring so diligently to build the temple and the city, and he made inquiry. "Who commanded you to build this house and to make these walls?" he asked the elders. "What are the names of the men responsible?" With the information that Tatnai obtained, he sent a letter to King Darius seeking further instructions. But work on the temple did not stop.

Tatnai's letter to Darius contained much detail. "We went up to the province of Judea," he wrote, "and saw them building a house of the great God with stones and timbers—and their work is prospering. We asked the elders of Judah who commanded them to build this house and to make these walls, and we also asked for the names of those who are chief among them. They answered that they are servants of God and are rebuilding a house that was built many years ago by a great king of Israel. They claim that their fathers provoked the God of Heaven to wrath and that he gave them into the hands of King Nebuchadnezzar, the Chaldean,[709] who destroyed the house and carried the people captive into Babylon.

"They now claim that King Cyrus, in the first year of his reign, issued a decree for them to build this house of God. They say also that Cyrus returned to them the vessels of gold and silver that Nebuchadnezzar took from their temple to place in his temple at Babylon. Their claim is that Cyrus delivered these vessels into the hands of one Zerubbabel, whom Cyrus had made governor, to carry them back to Jerusalem. They also say that they returned here to lay the foundation of this house and have been laboring to build it since that time—but it is not yet completed."

Tatnai's letter to Darius concluded: "Now, if it seems good to you, let a search be made in the records of the king's treasure house in Babylon to see if King Cyrus actually made such a decree. Then let us know what to do."

When King Darius had read Tatnai's letter, he ordered that the records of Babylonia be searched for any evidence that Cyrus had issued the decree to which the Jews laid claim. And, after diligent search, a copy of Darius's decree was discovered in the palace at Achmetha in the province of Media.[710] Not only did they find the decree requiring the temple to be built, but also Cyrus's order that the gold and silver vessels taken from the temple in Jerusalem by King Nebuchadnezzar should be returned for placement in the new house of the Lord and that the expense of building the temple should be paid by the king's house.

With Cyrus's long-forgotten decrees in his hand, Darius instructed Tatnai and his companions that they should not interfere with the construction work. He also ordered that the tribute money collected in Tatnai's province be used to pay the expenses of the builders so that work might not be hindered. And, on top of all that, Darius offered to provide animals for sacrifice in the temple when it was finished, as well as wheat, salt, wine, and oil.

In another decree, Darius said that if anyone altered his words, timber would be pulled down from that person's house and set up so that he could be hanged on it, and his house would be made a dunghill. "And now," the decree went on, "may the God of Heaven destroy all kings and peoples who put forth their hands to alter or destroy this house at Jerusalem. This is my decree. Now let it be done with speed."

With this support from King Darius, the work went forward with dispatch, and the temple was soon finished, according to God's commandment.

The temple was completed in the month of Adar—the twelfth month of the Jewish calendar—in the sixth year of the reign of Darius. It was dedicated, and the priests and Levites performed the service required of them, as written in the book of Moses.

And on the fourteenth day of the first month of the seventh year, the people of Judah and all those who had separated themselves from the abominations of their heathen neighbors kept the Passover and observed the seven-day feast of unleavened bread with great joy.

---

[709] The Chaldeans (or Chaldees) were the most prominent tribe in the country of Babylonia during the captivity. This title was generally used in the scriptures to refer to the people of Babylonia.

[710] When the Persians conquered Media, they chose Achmetha, the Median capital city, as their capital, and it remained such until the Persian capital was moved to Shushan (see story "211–The Babylonian and Persian Empires"). The classical writers called this city (i.e., Achmetha) Ecbatana. It was located on the site of the modern Iranian city of Hamadan.

224—FOR SUCH A TIME AS THIS
(Esther 1–10)

During his reign over Persia and Media, King Ahasuerus[711] had dominion over 127 provinces from India to Ethiopia,[712] including all of the Middle Eastern countries. In the third year of Ahasuerus's reign, he made a 180-day feast for the nobles and princes of his provinces. And King Ahasuerus showed them all the wealth of his kingdom. After that feast was completed, he gave a seven-day feast for the people of Shushan. And, at the same time, Queen Vashti gave a great feast for the women of the royal house.

On the final day of the king's feast, when he had drunk too much wine, he ordered his chamberlains to bring Queen Vashti to him that he might show off her beauty, for she was very fair. The queen, however, was offended by the request and refused to come,[713] which left King Ahasuerus embarrassed and angry.

After the king had brooded over his humiliation, he called his wise men and counseled with them what should be done to Queen Vashti for her disobedience to the king. Memucan, one of the seven princes of Persia, gave his opinion. "The queen has done wrong not only to the king," he reasoned, "but to all the princes and peoples in the kingdom. Once her disobedience becomes known, all women will disobey their husbands. And, just as she refused to come when summoned by the king, likewise—when they have heard—so shall the ladies of Persia and Media do to the king's princes."

"If it pleases the king," Memucan continued, "let him issue a royal decree, written among the laws of the Persians and the Medes so that it cannot be altered, that Vashti may come no more before the king and that the king will give her royal estate to one better than she. When this decree has been published throughout the empire, all wives—whether great or small—will honor their husbands."

Memucan's suggestion pleased the king and his princes, and a letter was sent throughout the kingdom, giving notice of the king's decree, so that every man would be supported as ruler of his own house.

When this was done, the king's servants counseled him to appoint officers in all the provinces to seek out fair young virgins and send them to Shushan for the king to choose a new queen from among them. The king agreed.

Living in Shushan was a Jew of the tribe of Benjamin named Mordecai, who was brought from Jerusalem by King Nebuchadnezzar at the time of the captivity. Mordecai had reared his young cousin Hadassah—whom the Persians called Esther—as his own daughter, for her parents were both deceased. And when the fair virgins were brought to the king's palace, the beautiful young Esther was among them, but she told no one that she was a Jew.

Esther was given seven maidens from the king's palace to attend her and she began her purification according to Persian customs. She and her maidens were more pleasing to King Ahasuerus than all the others from the very beginning and, because of this, they were given the best place in the house of the women. And Mordecai walked daily in front of the court of the women's house to learn of Esther's status.

When the twelve months required for purification were past, the maidens were called to appear before the king, one each day. And each young woman took with her whatever she desired to take. After a maiden had gone before the king, she was sent next day to the house of the concubines, never again to come before him. However, if the king was pleased with her, he honored her by calling her by her name.

When it came Esther's turn to go before the king, she pleased the king more than all the other virgins, and he placed the crown upon her head. The king then sent word to the provinces that he had chosen a new queen and he made a great feast to honor her. He also gave her many precious gifts such as a king would give but, true to Mordecai's instructions, Esther still told no one that she was a Jew.

When the virgins were gathered together for a second time, Mordecai sat in the king's gate,[714] where he

---

[711] The identity of the king, as given here, is believed to be incorrect. Most Bible scholars think that the king involved was actually Xerxes (the Great), son of Darius. The reason for the error is unknown, but it may be because the account was written some time later.

[712] The Hebrews called Ethiopia Cush. It lay to the south of Egypt, and embraced, in its most extended sense, modern Nubia, Sennaar, Kordofan, and northern Abyssinia (see William Smith, *Dictionary of the Bible*, *GospeLink*, CD-ROM, s.v. "Ethiopia").

[713] According to Josephus, Vashti refused to respond to the king's request "out of regard for the laws of the Persians, which forbid the wives to be seen by strangers" (Flavius Josephus, *The Antiquities of the Jews*, 11:6:1). Certainly this was a righteous woman who, in her rebuff of the king, was willing to risk her position for her religious standards.

[714] The king's gate, where Mordecai sat, is believed to have been a hall about 100 feet (30.5 meters) square (see William Smith, *Dictionary of the Bible*, *GospeLink*, CD-ROM, s.v. "king's gate").

overheard two of the chamberlains who kept the king's gate plot against the king's life. Mordecai informed Esther of what he had heard, and Esther passed the message on to King Ahasuerus in Mordecai's name. When the matter was investigated and found to be true, both men were hanged and the whole matter was noted in the king's record book.

With the new queen chosen and the conspirators dead, King Ahasuerus went on to other business. His first official act was to promote Haman the Agagite,[715] a man whom he greatly admired. Haman was made superior to all the princes of the kingdom, and the king commanded that everyone should bow down before Haman in the king's gate.

Mordecai the Jew, however, did not bow to Haman. And when the servants pressed Mordecai to know why he disobeyed the king's command, Mordecai told them he was a Jew. "I have no disrespect for Haman," said Mordecai, "but the Jews bow only before God."[716]

The king's servants reported to Haman that Mordecai refused to honor him. And when Haman himself saw that it was so and learned that Mordecai was a Jew, he became very angry. He reasoned in his mind that not only Mordecai should be punished, but all Jews in the kingdom. It would be best, he thought, if they could be destroyed. And, being a very superstitious man, Haman cast lots,[717] beginning in the first month and continuing until the twelfth, to determine the best time of year to act against the Jews.

When the proper time had been chosen, according to Haman's superstitions, he spoke to the king. "There is a certain group of people in your kingdom," said Haman to the king, "whose laws are different from the laws of all other peoples. Because they do not obey your laws, it is not good for you to tolerate them. If it pleases the king to let these people be destroyed, I will pay 10,000 talents of silver into your treasury."[718]

---

[715] The Jews believe that Haman was a descendant of Agag, the Amalekite king mentioned in 1 Samuel 15 (see William Smith, *Dictionary of the Bible*, *Gospe-Link*, CD-ROM, s.v. "Haman").

[716] Interestingly, there are no direct references to God in the book of Esther, but his influence is implied throughout.

[717] The scripture says that Haman "cast Pur," which means he cast lots (Esther 3:7).

[718] A talent of silver was equivalent to 3,000 shekels or just more that 75.5 pounds (34.29 kilograms). Thus, 1,000 talents of silver would be 75,600 pounds (34,290 kilograms) or 37.8 tons (33.75 long tons or 34.29 metric tons) of silver. It is not stated where Haman intended to get the silver he promised to the king. But it appears likely that he intended to take it as spoils from

Haman did not identify the offending people to King Ahasuerus, but his apparent concern for the welfare of the kingdom pleased the king; he gave his consent for their destruction. The king then took the ring from his own hand and put it on Haman. "Because of your love for me and for the kingdom," he said, "I will give the silver that you have promised into your own hands that you may use it to benefit the people of the kingdom in whatever way you think best."

The king called his scribes on the thirteenth day of the first month and they wrote to the governors of the provinces all that Haman commanded them. They wrote in the king's name, and Haman sealed it with the king's own ring.

Haman's decree was very clear: "You shall destroy, kill, and cause to perish all Jews, both young and old, little children and women, in one day—on the thirteenth day of Adar, the twelfth month. And you shall also take the spoils of them. A copy of this decree is to be published among the people so that they may prepare for that day." And so the decree went out, hastened by the king's commandment. The fate of the Jews was sealed.

When Haman's decree was announced in Shushan, the city was deeply troubled. When Mordecai learned what had happened he rent his clothes, put on sackcloth and ashes, and went out into the midst of the city, where he cried with loud and bitter weeping. He came before the king's gate but was not allowed to enter wearing sackcloth.

When Esther's maids and chamberlains told her of Mordecai's weeping and wailing in the city, she too became grieved, though she did not yet know of the decree. When she sent clothing to Mordecai that he might remove his sackcloth, he would not receive it.

Sensing that something was seriously wrong, Esther sent a chamberlain to Mordecai to discover the problem. When the man found him in the street beyond the king's gate, Mordecai explained all that had happened, and gave the chamberlain a copy of Haman's decree. Mordecai then charged Queen Esther, through her chamberlain, to go in to King Ahasuerus and ask him to intervene in behalf of her people.

When Esther received Mordecai's message, she was very fearful about what he had asked her to do, and she sent the chamberlain to explain her dilemma to Mordecai. She explained that all the king's servants and the people of the provinces knew that whoever comes in to

---

the Jews when they were destroyed. If the edict of the king applied to the entire kingdom, as appears to be the case, it would have also included the province of Judea. And the treasures of the temple in Jerusalem would have been fair game.

the king in his inner court, who has not been summoned by the king, is put to death, according to the Law.[719] Only if the king holds out his golden scepter—giving the interloper a royal pardon—may that person live. And then she said, "I have not been called to go in unto the king in the last thirty days."

Mordecai understood Esther's concern, but he pointed out to her that she would not escape Haman's dreadful decree, even in the king's own palace. "I know that if you do nothing to save your people," he said, "relief will come from another source, but you and your father's house will be destroyed. And who knows but what Jehovah has brought you to the kingdom for such a time as this?"

When Esther had pondered her cousin's message, she sent back her answer. "Gather all the Jews who are in Shushan and fast for me," she said. "Tell them to neither eat nor drink for three days and nights. My maidens and I will also fast—then I will go in unto the king. And if I perish, I perish."

Mordecai was relieved by Esther's response, and he went and did as she commanded him, calling on all the Jews in Shushan to fast for Queen Esther.

On the third day of Esther's fast, she put on her royal clothing and stood near to the king's palace, in the inner court. And as the king sat on his throne near the gate, he saw Esther standing in the court. Her prayers were answered when the king held out his golden scepter to her, and she came in and touched the top of the scepter.[720]

---

719 Such a law was necessary in a society where the king lived in constant fear of assassins, as was the case here. There were always plots against the king's life, and coming into his court without being summoned was a sentence of death—automatically. A pardon could be granted to the intruder only by the king extending his scepter. And certainly there were no guarantees—not even for the queen.

720 Josephus tells the story somewhat differently. He says that when Esther came into the king's presence "her joints failed her immediately, out of the dread she was in, and she fell down sideways in a swoon: but the king changed his mind...and was concerned for his wife, lest her fear should bring some very evil thing upon her, and he leaped from his throne, and took her in his arms, and recovered her, by embracing her, and speaking comfortably to her, exhorting her to be of good cheer, and not to suspect anything that was sad on account of her coming to him without being called, because that law was made for subjects, but that she, who was a queen, as well as he a king, might be entirely secure: and as he said this, he put the scepter into her hand, and laid his rod upon her neck on account of

"What will you have me do for you, Queen Esther?" asked the king. "Whatever you request, it shall be given to you—even unto half my kingdom."

Esther answered carefully. "If it seems good to you, O King," she replied, "let the king and Haman come today to a banquet that I have prepared." The king consented, and Haman was invited to Esther's banquet.

At the banquet, the king repeated his pledge to grant Esther's request, even unto half his kingdom. But Esther answered him much as she had before. "Let the king and Haman come to the banquet that I shall prepare for them tomorrow," she replied, "and then I will tell you my request."

Haman rejoiced all that day for the great honor of dining with the king and queen. But his day was ruined when Mordecai refused to bow to him in the king's gate. And though Haman was filled with anger, he restrained himself and did not react.

Once Haman was home, he called his wife and friends to tell them of all his great riches and what an honorable man he was in the king's eyes. "And besides all that," he boasted, "Queen Esther is preparing a banquet tomorrow for only the king and me."

Haman then suddenly became very serious. "But all these honors are of little value to me," he said, "as long as I see Mordecai the Jew sitting at the king's gate."

"Your problem can be easily solved," Haman's friends assured him, "because of your great influence with the king. Build a gallows fifty cubits high,[721] and then speak to the king tomorrow that Mordecai may be hanged on it. Then you can go merrily to your banquet with the king." And Haman gave orders for the gallows to be built immediately.

That night, when the king was unable to sleep, he asked for his record book to be brought and read to him. When the servants read how Mordecai had exposed the plot against his life by the two gatekeepers, he asked, "What honor was given to Mordecai for saving my life?" And he was told him that nothing had been done.

As the servants finished reading, Haman entered the outer court of the king's palace, having come to ask about hanging Mordecai on his newly constructed gallows. When the king saw Haman, he invited him in. "What shall be done," the king asked Haman, "for the man whom the king wishes to honor?"

Haman, thinking in his prideful heart that it was he who would be honored, replied, "Let this man be dressed in the king's own clothing and the king's crown

---

the law; and so freed her from her fear" (Flavius Josephus, *The Antiquities of the Jews*, 11:6:9).

721 This would be a very high gallows—about seventy-five feet (22.9 meters).

upon his head. Then let him ride through the streets of the city upon the king's horse, with one of the king's most noble princes going before him to proclaim to the people that this man is the man the king delights to honor."

King Ahasuerus, being greatly pleased with Haman's suggestion, said, "Make haste, Haman. Take my clothing and my horse and do to Mordecai the Jew as you have said. Let nothing fail of all that you have spoken." So, in obedience to the king's command, Haman dressed Mordecai in the king's apparel, put him on the king's horse, and led him through the streets of Shushan proclaiming that Mordecai was the man whom the king delighted to honor. Nothing could have been more humiliating to Haman than this.

When the procession ended, Mordecai returned to his place in the king's gate and Haman to his own house—but with his head covered in humiliation. When Haman told his wife and friends what had happened, they replied, "If this Mordecai is a Jew, you shall not prevail against him, but shall surely fall before him."

As Haman and his friends talked, the king's chamberlain came to take Haman to Queen Esther's banquet.

When the king, Haman, and Esther were gathered for their private feast, the king again asked Esther, "What is your petition, my queen? It shall be granted to you, even to half of my kingdom."

Esther spoke carefully. "If I have found favor in your sight, O King," she said, "and if it pleases you, let my life be given me and also the lives of my people. For we have been sold, my people and I, to be destroyed, to be slain, and to perish. You should know, however, that if we had been sold as bondsmen, I would hold my tongue, for that would not have damaged the king's interests."

King Ahasuerus was astonished and angry by what Esther had just told him. "Who is responsible for this?" he asked. "Who dares to presume in his heart to do such a thing?"

"The enemy," replied Esther, "is this wicked Haman." And Haman sat by, listening in great fear.

Rising in his wrath, King Ahasuerus went out from the banquet into the palace garden. Meanwhile, Haman stood up and began to plead with Queen Esther to spare his life. It was not difficult for him to foresee the evil that the king had determined against him.

When the king returned from the garden, he saw that Haman had fallen onto the Queen's bed as he pleaded with her for his life. "Will you also force the queen before me in my own house?" he asked.

As the king spoke, his servants took hold of Haman and covered his face. Then one of the chamberlains said to the king, "There is a gallows fifty cubits high standing at Haman's house, which Haman built to hang Mordecai."

"Hang Haman on his own gallows!" ordered King Ahasuerus.

So that day Haman was hanged on the gallows he had built for Mordecai, and the king's anger was pacified. King Ahasuerus gave Haman's house to Queen Esther. And when Esther told the king that Mordecai was her cousin and had raised her as his own child, Mordecai was brought before the king. The king gave Mordecai his ring, and Esther made him the ruler over her house.

There was, however, one more problem that needed to be resolved, and Queen Esther fell weeping at the king's feet to seek this one more favor. When the king held out his golden scepter and bid her to rise, she said to him, "If it pleases the king and if I have found favor in your sight, let a decree be written to reverse the letters devised by Haman the Agagite, in which he commanded the destruction of all Jews. For I cannot endure to see this great evil come upon my people."

King Ahasuerus commanded Mordecai to prepare a new decree. "Write for the Jews as it pleases you," he said. "Write it in my name and seal it with my ring, and that which you write, no man can reverse."

So Mordecai drafted a new decree to be sent to the provinces. It read: "The Jews in every city are to gather themselves together and stand for their lives, to destroy, to slay, and to cause to perish all those in the provinces who would assault them." And on the thirteenth day of Adar, the twelfth month—that same day which Haman had named for the destruction of the Jews—Mordecai's decree was enforced as a commandment of the king.

The fourteenth and fifteenth days of the twelfth month were decreed by Mordecai—and confirmed by Queen Esther—to be remembered yearly, from generation to generation, as the Festival of Purim in remembrance of how Queen Esther saved the Jews from destruction.[722]

---

[722] Purim is also known as the Festival of Lots. The name Purim came from the word *pur*, which means "lots." It was called this because Haman cast pur to decide the day of the Jews' destruction. Purim is still celebrated and the book of Esther is read as part of the celebration. Everyone hisses and boos whenever Haman's name is read. They also eat triangular cookies that represent Haman's three-cornered hat.

225–EZRA BRINGS MORE EXILES
(Ezra 7–8)

The year was now 458 BC. Eighty long years had passed since Zerubbabel responded to the decree of Cyrus and brought the willing Jews back to Jerusalem to rebuild the temple. And King Darius, who had issued a new decree that allowed the temple to be finished,[723] was long since deceased and had been replaced by his son Xerxes—called Xerxes the Great.[724] King Xerxes was also now dead, and his son Artaxerxes was in his seventh year as king of Persia.

Ezra the priest, whose claim to the priesthood came through Aaron's son Eleazar, requested a commission from King Artaxerxes to lead more of the exiled Jews to Jerusalem. When King Artaxerxes agreed to Ezra's request, he gave Ezra a letter of authorization to carry with him. The king also authorized Ezra to take all the silver and gold that could be collected as a freewill offering to buy animals for sacrifice in the temple and for other temple-related uses.

Artaxerxes issued a decree to the treasurers of all provinces west of the Euphrates, directing them to give Ezra whatever he requested—up to 100 talents of silver,[725] 100 measures of wheat,[726] 100 baths of wine, 100 baths of oil,[727] and salt to whatever amount might be required.

"Whatever is commanded by the God of heaven," said the king, "let it be diligently done for the house of the Lord, lest there should be wrath against the realm of the king and his sons."

King Artaxerxes assigned Ezra to appoint magistrates and judges in the land of Judah and to teach these men their duties. The king also issued a decree that the priests, the Levites, the singers, the doorkeepers (or porters), the Nethinims[728]—all those who were the ministers of the temple—should be exempt from paying any toll, tribute, or custom.

In Ezra's company of exiles were 1,754 men, plus women and children. As they prepared to depart from Babylon, they gathered at the river of Ahava, where they fasted to humble themselves for their journey.

Ezra gave the gold, silver, and other treasures to twelve trusted men and charged these men to carry them safely. Everything was weighed and counted before the journey, then weighed and counted again when they arrived in Jerusalem, for the value of the treasure was great—650 talents of silver, 100 talents of gold, plus gold and silver basins and other precious vessels.

The trip from Babylon to Jerusalem took Ezra and his party five months. And, though the journey was long and hard, Jehovah was with them and protected them from enemies and robbers along the way. When they finally arrived in Jerusalem they offered burnt offerings to Jehovah in gratitude for their blessings.

---

[723] See story "223–King Darius Supports the Temple Project."

[724] Xerxes the Great is believed to be the same king who is identified as Ahasuerus in the book of Esther (see story "224–For Such a Time as This").

[725] A talent of silver was equivalent to 3,000 shekels, or just more that 75.5 pounds (34.29 kilograms). Thus, 100 talents of silver would be about 7,560 pounds (3,429 kilograms) or nearly 3.8 tons (3.38 long tons or 3.43 metric tons) of silver.

[726] A *measure* was equivalent to a *cor* (liquid or dry). It was equal to ten baths, or approximately eighty-five U.S. gallons (313 liters). A *bath* (liquid) is said to be about 8.5 U.S. gallons (31.3 liters). One hundred measures would be about 8,500 gallons or 1,062.5 bushels.

[727] A *bath* is believed to be about 8.5 U.S. gallons (31.3 liters). Thus, 100 baths (whether wine or oil) would be about 830 U.S. gallons (3,142 liters or about 691 imperial gallons).

---

[728] Nethenims were those assigned to do the rougher, more menial work of the temple, thus enabling the Levites to take a higher position as the religious representatives and instructors of the people. Nethenims had served in the temple since the days of King David (see William Smith, *Dictionary of the Bible*, GospeLink, CD-ROM, s.v. "Nethinims").

226—MARRIAGES TO UNBELIEVERS

(Ezra 9–10; Nehemiah 8)

When Ezra arrived in Jerusalem with his company of exiles from Babylon,[729] he met with the princes of Judah. They told him how the returned Jewish exiles were now intermarrying with the other peoples of the land, a practice that Jehovah had strictly forbidden. Ezra was so shocked when he learned of this disgraceful practice that he tore his clothing and pulled out his hair.

As time approached for the evening sacrifice that day, Ezra fell to his knees and called on Jehovah for an answer. "I am ashamed to lift my face to Thee, O God," he cried. "For the iniquities and trespasses of this people have multiplied unto the heavens. Since the days of our fathers, we have been in a great trespass, and we have been punished for our iniquities. Because of our iniquities Thou hast delivered us into the hands of the kings of the lands, to the sword, to captivity, and to shame, as it is this day.

"Yet, in spite of our sins, Thou hast also shown us Thy grace. For Thou hast restored us from bondage and left us a remnant. Thou hast never forsaken us, even when we were bondsmen, and Thou didst extend mercy to us through the eyes of the kings of Persia that we might return to restore Thy holy house."

Ezra continued: "What can we say after all this? For we have forsaken Thy commandments and partaken of the iniquities of our neighbors. We have taken the daughters of the land to marry our sons and their sons to marry our daughters. And after all that we have suffered for our evil deeds, we know that Thou hast punished us far less than our sins deserve and hast given us such deliverance as this. Yet, here we are, again breaking Thy commandments and intermarrying with the people of these abominations.

"I am amazed that Thou hast not been so angry with us that we were consumed and left no remnant. Though Thou hast been righteous and freed us from captivity, we are unworthy to stand before Thee because of our trespasses."

The people were assembled when Ezra finished praying, and they wept bitterly for their sins. As they wept, Shechaniah the son of Jehiel spoke for the group. "We have sinned against God by taking wives of the peoples of this land," he confessed. "Yet there is hope in Israel, for we will covenant to put away all these wives and their children, according to the counsel of

Jehovah. And to those who tremble at this commandment of our God, let it be done to them according to the Law."

Ezra arose and made all those present swear an oath that they would do according to the words of Shechaniah. But Ezra was still discouraged because of the great sins of the returned exiles, and he mourned for them with fasting and prayer.

Because of the oath that the people had made, the priests and the elders sent a proclamation throughout the land requesting the men of Judah to come up to Jerusalem within three days. He told them that those who did not come within that time would forfeit their property and be cut off from the congregation.

When the people arrived in Jerusalem, they assembled in a rainstorm in the street before the temple. They were trembling, both because of their fear and because of the rain. Ezra the priest arose and spoke to the multitude.

"You have sorely transgressed by taking strange wives," Ezra told them, "and have thus increased the trespasses of Israel. You must now confess this sin to God and do his pleasure by separating yourselves from these wives and from the people of this land."

"As you have said to us, so will we do," the people answered Ezra as with one voice.

When this vow was made, those who were spokesmen for the people spoke. "This is not an easy thing," they said. "It cannot be done quickly, for there are many who have sinned. Also, we are not able to stand here long because of the rain. Let the rulers of the congregation stand now, and then let those who have taken strange wives come by appointment before the judges and the elders till all have appeared." And so it was done according to their request.

When the offenders had all appeared before the elders and judges at their appointed times, the people gathered again—this time in the street before the water gate. They said that they wanted to keep the Law but were not sure of all that the Law required of them. They requested that Ezra bring out the book containing the law of Moses and read it to them.

When the book was brought, the people stood and listened as Ezra read, desiring to understand the Law and to know what Jehovah required. Ezra read from morning until midday. And he also explained what he read.

As the people understood the words of the Law, they wept for joy. And Ezra said to them, "Weep not and mourn not, for this day is holy unto Jehovah. Go your ways and do not sorrow, for the joy of Jehovah is your strength. Eat the fat, drink the sweet, and share what you have also with those who have not."

---

[729] See story "225 Ezra Brings More Exiles."

Ezra read to the people from the book of the Law and explained his readings to them throughout each day of the Feast of the Tabernacles, which Judah now celebrated because of what they had learned from Ezra's reading.

227—LET US RISE UP AND BUILD

(Nehemiah 1–7)

Though the temple had been rebuilt and dedicated in Jerusalem by the returning exiles from Babylon, under the benevolent decrees of Cyrus and Darius, the city walls had never been rebuilt. This failure to build was due primarily to the antagonism and interference of others in the area. Those most difficult to deal with were the people who settled in Samaria after the Assyrians took the Northern Kingdom into captivity.[730]

In 445 BC, the twentieth year of the reign of King Artaxerxes in the Persian Empire, a Jew named Nehemiah held the high office of cupbearer to the king at the palace in Shushan.[731] Some men came to Shushan from Jerusalem that year and told Nehemiah about the sorry state of Jews who had returned from captivity. "The remnant that returned is in great affliction and reproach," they reported to Nehemiah. "The walls of Jerusalem are also broken down and the city gates have been burned."

Nehemiah wept for the hardships of his people, fasting and praying for many days. "These are Thy servants and Thy people, O Lord," he prayed. "Let Thine ear be attentive to their prayers as they desire to honor Thy name. And please prosper me also and grant me mercy in the sight of the king."

As Nehemiah performed his duties, King Artaxerxes noticed that his countenance was sad, and the king asked him, "Why are you sad when you are not sick? There must certainly be sorrow in your heart."

Nehemiah was frightened by the king's inquiry. "Let the king live forever," he answered hesitantly. "Why should I not be sad when the city of my fathers' sepulchers lies waste and the city gates have been burned with fire?"

---

[730] See story "182—Assyria's Victory and Israel's Captivity."

[731] Shushan (or Susa) was originally the capital of Elam, an area named for Shem's son. Later it was part of the Assyrian Empire. At the time of Daniel, Shushan was in the possession of the Babylonians and was in the province of Elam (see Daniel 8:2). The conquest of Babylon by Cyrus transferred Shushan to Persia; it was not long before it became the Persian capital and the chief place of the king's residence, probably during the reign of Darius (see William Smith, *Dictionary of the Bible*, *GospeLink*, CD-ROM, s.v. "Shushan").

King Artaxerxes was sympathetic to what Nehemiah was telling him. "What do you wish me to do?" he asked.

This was the opportunity that Nehemiah had prayed for. "If it pleases you and if I have found favor in your sight," he said, choosing his words carefully, "I would have you send me to Judah, to the city of my fathers, that I may rebuild it."

"When will you go and how long will you be gone?" asked the king, responding favorably to Nehemiah's petition. And Nehemiah gave him a time.

Then Nehemiah said to King Artaxerxes, "If it pleases you, give me letters to the governors west of the Euphrates, that I may have safe passage through their lands—and also a letter to the keeper of the forest, that he will give me timber for the city's many gates."

In a short time Nehemiah was on his way to Jerusalem with the desired letters from the king, as well as a letter appointing him governor of Judea. The king also sent horsemen and captains from his army to accompany Nehemiah and protect him on his journey.

When Nehemiah first arrived in Jerusalem, he told no one why he had come. But when he had been in the city three days, he went out by night to survey the city walls to see the extent of the damage. When he returned from surveying the desolation, he spoke to the Jewish leaders. "You see how Jerusalem lies in waste and the gates are burned with fire," he said. "Come now, let us build up the walls of our city that we are no longer a disgrace."

And when Nehemiah told the Jewish leaders of the words of King Artaxerxes—how he was appointed governor of Judea and had been charged to rebuild the city walls—and how the hand of Jehovah had brought him to Jerusalem, they were excited. "Let us rise up and build!" they cried.

The rebuilding of the city walls was not without opposition, however. Nehemiah's plan was certainly not popular with the governors of the surrounding territories. Chief among the opponents were Sanballat the Horonite,[732] Tobiah the Ammonite, and Geshem the Arabian. When these men heard of Nehemiah's plan, they despised the Jews and laughed them to scorn. They were not pleased that anyone should come to promote the welfare of Judah. "Will you rebel against the king?" they asked Nehemiah.

Nehemiah answered his detractors that Jehovah would prosper his servants. "We will arise and build," he said, "for we have the king's blessing. And because you have no portion, no right, and no memorial in the city of Jerusalem, you have no right to tell us what we can do."

The work of building was divided so that different groups of men were assigned to rebuild different portions of the wall. The entire wall was being rebuilt at the same time, and the work went rapidly.

Sanballat, however, was not willing to let the matter rest. In his determination to stop the work, he mocked the workers and spoke out against their work to the Samaritan army. "What will these Jews do?" he asked. "Will they fortify themselves with stones from rubbish heaps?"

Tobiah also mocked the Jewish builders and made sarcastic comments. "The quality of the work is poor," he said. "If a fox were to go up on this wall that they are building, the fox's weight would break it down." But work on the wall continued despite the opposition.

When Sanballat and those who listened to his rantings saw that the city walls continued to rise, they determined to do battle against Jerusalem, but Nehemiah and his workers offered their prayers to Jehovah and set men to keep watch over the city both day and night.

As fear and fatigue increased and the project slowed, Nehemiah spoke to his people to encourage them. "Do not fear our enemies," he told them. "Trust in Jehovah, who is great and revered, then fight for your brethren, your sons, your daughters, your wives, and your houses."

Once Judah's enemies discovered that Nehemiah and his workers knew of their plot and that God had brought their evil counsel to naught, the workers were able to return to their labors with renewed energy. From that time forth, half the men worked on the wall while the other half stood guard. Every man labored, as it were, with one hand, while holding his weapon in the other. Those with homes outside Jerusalem no longer left the city at night. They labored on the wall by day and stood guard by night, and none of the laborers took off their clothes except to wash them.

Nehemiah warned the people, because the wall was large and the workers were widely scattered, that when the trumpet sounded, they should assemble quickly to the sound. They were assured that Jehovah would fight for them if it became necessary to fight.[733]

When Sanballat, Tobiah, and Geshem learned that there were no longer breaches in the city wall, they requested Nehemiah to come out to meet them at a vil-

---

[732] Sanballat was a Moabite who was in authority in Samaria.

[733] In addition to the problems caused by Judah's enemies during the construction of the city wall, there were also internal problems that hindered the work. These problems and Nehemiah's solution are discussed in story "228—Should You Not Walk in the Fear of God?"

lage on the plain of Ono. Nehemiah understood, however, that the motive of these men was to lure him out of the city to do him harm. Thus, he responded to their message saying, "I will not come because I am doing a great work. Why should my work cease while I go to see you?"

Four times Nehemiah's detractors sent their invitation, and four times he gave the same reply. On the fifth time, Sanballat's servant came with an open letter in his hand. The letter said, "It has been reported that the Jews seek to rebel against King Artaxerxes and that you are building this wall so that you can be king. It is also reported that you have appointed prophets who are preaching that you will be king in Judah. If you will not come now and counsel with us, we will report this matter to the king."

Nehemiah was furious at such accusations. He knew that this was no more than blackmail, and he sent a quick reply: "There are no such things done. You have only imagined them in your hearts."

The devious opposition continued. Shemaiah, who had been a faithful helper, also came to Nehemiah, prophesying that his life was in danger. "Hide in the temple," he urged Nehemiah, "so your enemies cannot murder you in the night."

"Should a man such as I flee?" Nehemiah asked Shemaiah. "Who indeed is my enemy that a man such as I would go into the temple to save his life? I will not go!"

Then Nehemiah perceived that Jehovah had not sent Shemaiah but that Sanballat and Tobiah had hired him. They sought to use Shemaiah to make him afraid for his life so that they might give an evil report.

But in spite of the myriad distractions and the efforts of Judah's enemies to thwart the work, the city walls were eventually finished and the gates were hung. This was the cause of great distress for Sanballat and his heathen friends, for they perceived that completion of the walls was the work of Jehovah.

Because there were but few inhabitants in Jerusalem, Nehemiah gave his brother Hanani charge over the city with careful instructions about opening and closing the gates and how the gates should be controlled. Then, as he had promised, Nehemiah returned to Persia to his position as cupbearer in the house of Artaxerxes.

228–SHOULD YOU NOT WALK IN THE FEAR OF GOD?
(Nehemiah 5)

In addition to the problems caused by their annoying neighbors during the time the wall of Jerusalem was being rebuilt,[734] the returned Jewish exiles also had problems within their own community. Many complained against their brethren because those who had substance—the nobles of Judah—were bringing their neighbors into bondage. Because of the famine, many people mortgaged their lands and their houses to the nobles so that they could buy grain. Still others borrowed money from them to pay the king's tribute, using their lands and houses as security. "Yet, now," they said, "we are left with no money and have no power to redeem our property."

Nehemiah was angry when he learned of these problems. He rebuked those nobles and the rulers who were responsible. "We redeemed our brethren the Jews who were sold to the heathen," Nehemiah told them, "yet now you turn around and sell your own brethren.

"Should you not walk in the fear of God," asked Nehemiah, "because of the reproach of the heathen, our enemies?" But when the nobles heard Nehemiah's accusations, no one dared to answer him.

"You must cease collecting usury," Nehemiah continued, "and restore the land to those from whom it was taken—also their vineyards, their oliveyards, and their houses. You must also restore to your brethren the money, the grain, the wine, and the oil that you have exacted from them."

When the guilty Jewish nobles had made an oath to restore that which they had taken unrighteously, Nehemiah shook the lap of his garment and said, "So may God shake out every man from his house and from his labor who fails to fulfill this promise."

"Amen," cried the people. And they praised Jehovah and kept their promise.

Nehemiah then rehearsed for the people his record of service during the twelve years he had been governor of Judea. "I have never eaten the governor's bread nor taken anything from the people for the service I have given," he said. He also told how he fed 150 Jews at his own table and gave freely to those in need while devoting his full time and energy to building the city wall.

---

[734] See story "227–Let Us Rise Up and Build."

229-JUDAH STRUGGLES TO BE OBEDIENT

(Nehemiah 9-13)

When the people of Judah who had returned from exile in Babylon heard Ezra read to them from the book of the Law, they fasted and confessed their sins, dressing in sackcloth and covering themselves with dirt.[735] They acknowledged that the judgments that Jehovah had poured out upon them were fair because they had failed to abide by the Law, though given repeated opportunities to do so.

"But now," they pledged to Jehovah, "we are Thy servants this day and will continue to be faithful servants in the land that Thou didst give to our fathers. Though we have been blessed with great abundance in this land, it now yields its bounty to benefit the kings who rule over us. We are in great distress because of our sins, for these kings have dominion over all that we own, as well as our bodies. And, O Jehovah, because of our afflictions, we make a sure covenant with Thee—a covenant that we are willing to put into writing and upon which the Levites may put their seal."[736]

The people—from the governor Nehemiah to the last man of Israel who had understanding—swore an oath that a curse should come upon them if they did not walk according to God's law and keep all his commandments, judgments, and statutes.

They covenanted that they would not give their daughters to the peoples of the land in marriage nor marry the daughters of those people.

They covenanted that they would keep the Sabbath, neither buying nor selling on that holy day.

They covenanted also to observe the sabbatical year[737] and cease being unfair to their debtors.

They covenanted to pay willingly the money required to supply the daily offerings in the temple[738] and to bring the firstfruits of all they produced to the Levites as a tithe, thus providing for the needs of those who served in the house of the Lord.

The city of Jerusalem was large, but the population was small. The rulers of the people lived in the city of Jerusalem, while the rest of the people lived in their own ancestral cities. Thus, it was decided that every tenth man with his family should move to Jerusalem that there might be more people available for the city's defense. Lots were cast to determine who would come. There were also some who volunteered and went to live in Jerusalem without being called. And the people blessed them for their willingness to sacrifice.

When the newly rebuilt walls of the city were dedicated, the Levites from throughout the land were brought in to provide music. And the priests and Levites purified themselves—as well as the people, the gates, and the city wall. For the dedication, the people of Judah were divided into two large companies that went up to give thanks in the temple. There they offered great sacrifices and the whole city rejoiced.

On the day of dedication, the people listened as Ezra read to them from the book of Moses that the Ammonites and the Moabites were to be banned from the congregation of God because their fathers failed to assist the children of Israel in the wilderness and hired Balaam to curse them.[739] And, in obedience to what they heard read in the Law, all those who were not of Israel were separated from Judah that day.

Though Nehemiah went back to Persia as he had promised King Artaxerxes,[740] he could not stay away; he soon returned to Jerusalem. And though things seemed to be going well when he left, the situation deteriorated rapidly in his absence. The hearts of the people were right before God and they wanted to be obedient, but they seemed unable to resist the temptations that so readily presented themselves.

While Nehemiah was in Persia, Eliashib the high priest made an alliance with Tobiah the Ammonite, because of Tobiah's connections to Shechaniah.[741] Living quarters were prepared for Tobiah within the courts of the temple. Unfortunately, these accommodations for Tobiah displaced the storage of the temple vessels and

---

[735] See Story "226-Marriages to Unbelievers."

[736] There is an overlap between the events of this story and the end of story "227-Let Us Rise Up and Build." Though the end of that story has Nehemiah returning to Persia, most of the events in this story took place before Nehemiah left on that journey. He was obviously present for the events in Nehemiah 12, as shown by his personal references in verses 38 and 40.

[737] The sabbatical year is explained in Leviticus 25. Under the law of Moses, every seventh year was a sabbatical year. In that year the land was to rest. The ground was not plowed, no crops were planted or harvested, and no fruit was taken from the trees or the vines. The children of Israel were also to forgive all debts owed to them by other Israelites.

[738] See Numbers 28:1–8.

[739] See Deuteronomy 23:3–5 and story "68-The Curse of Balaam."

[740] See story "227-Let Us Rise Up and Build."

[741] Shechaniah was the head of a priestly family who returned from the captivity with Zerubbabel (see Nehemiah 12:3).

sent the Levites and singers who worked in the temple out of the city to fend for themselves.

When Nehemiah returned and saw what had happened, he was irate. He threw all of Tobiah's belongings out of the chamber, and returned the vessels of the temple to their proper place.

Nehemiah next questioned the city's rulers about the Levites and singers who had been sent away. "Why has the house of God been forsaken?" he asked them. And when the Levites had been brought back to their proper place from the temple, the people brought their tithes of grain, wine, and oil to the temple storehouse.

Nehemiah also observed that other serious problems had crept in among the people during his absence. Many of the people were not keeping the Sabbath, and some were again marrying the daughters of their hea

then neighbors, the peoples of Ashdod,[742] Ammon, and Moab.[743] As a result of these marriages, half the children of those who married the daughters of Ashdod spoke the language of the Philistines. Even one of the grandsons of Eliashib the high priest was the son-in-law of Sanballat the Horonite, the man who caused such great misery for the people while the city walls were being rebuilt.[744]

Just as he had done before his return to Persia, Nehemiah again ordered that the gates of Jerusalem be closed on the Sabbath so that no goods could be brought in and sold. He also worked to cleanse the people of Judah from the foreigners who were living among them.

---

[742] Ashdod was one of the five unified cities of the Philistines. The others were Ashkelon, Ekron, Gath, and Gaza.

[743] The peoples of Ammon and Moab were descendants of Abraham's nephew Lot.

[744] See story "227−Let Us Rise Up and Build."

MAPS*

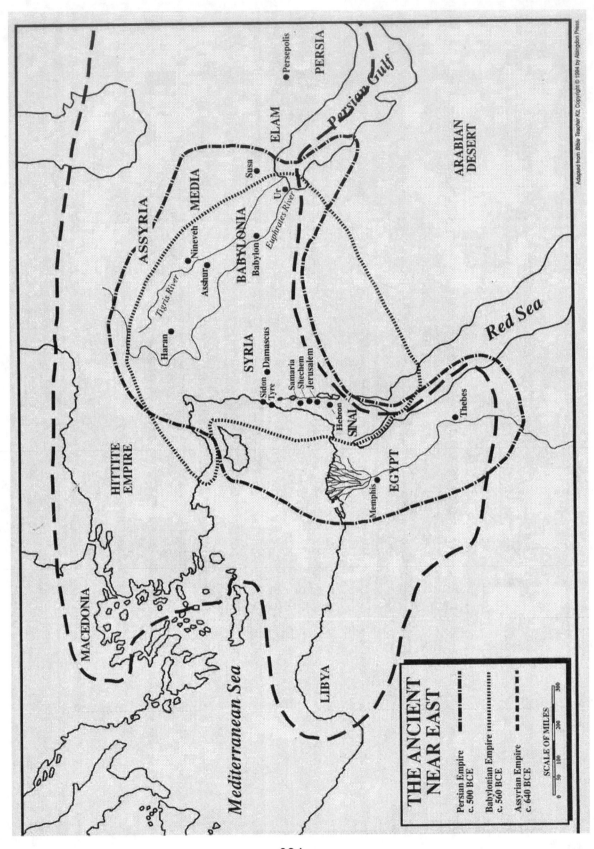

THE ANCIENT
NEAR EAST

Persian Empire
c. 500 BCE

Babylonian Empire
c. 560 BCE

Assyrian Empire
c. 640 BCE

SCALE OF MILES
0   50 100   200   300

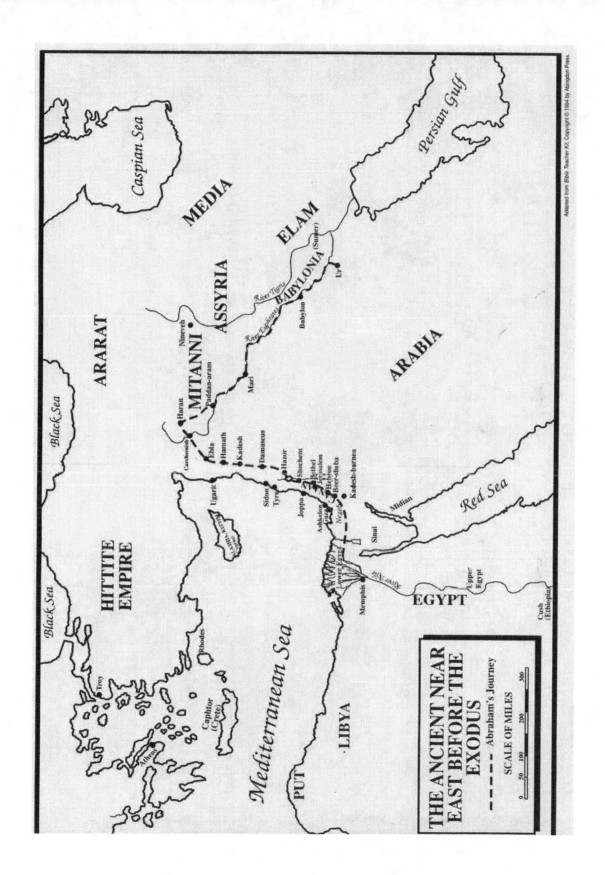

THE ANCIENT NEAR
EAST BEFORE THE
EXODUS

— — — Abraham's Journey

SCALE OF MILES

0   50 100   200   300

325

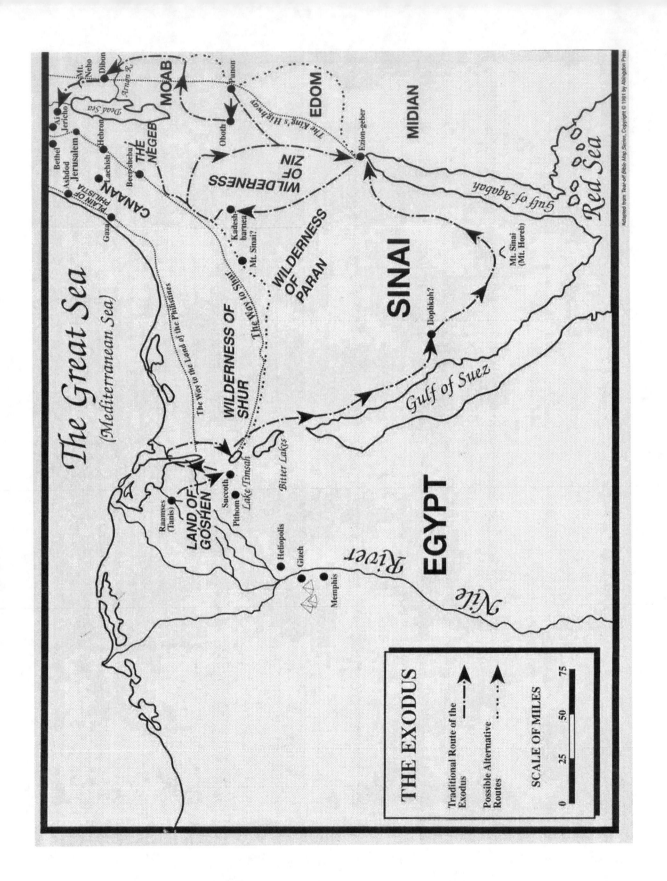

THE EXODUS

Traditional Route of the Exodus

Possible Alternative Routes

SCALE OF MILES

0   25   50   75

326

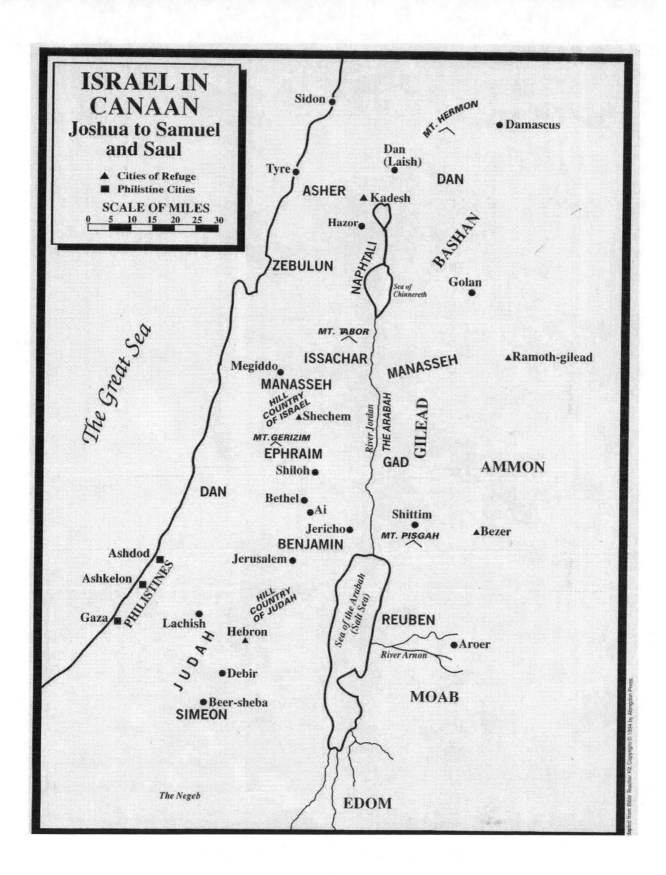

ISRAEL IN CANAAN

Joshua to Samuel and Saul

▲ Cities of Refuge
■ Philistine Cities

SCALE OF MILES

0   5   10 15 20 25 30

Sidon

MT. HERMON

• Damascus

Dan
(Laish)

DAN

Tyre

ASHER

▲ Kadesh

Hazor

BASHAN

ZEBULUN

NAPHTALI

Sea of
Chinnereth

Golan

MT. TABOR

ISSACHAR

MANASSEH

▲ Ramoth-gilead

Megiddo

MANASSEH

HILL
COUNTRY
OF ISRAEL

River Jordan

THE ARABAH

GILEAD

▲ Shechem

MT. GERIZIM

EPHRAIM

GAD

AMMON

Shiloh

DAN

Bethel

Ai

Shittim

Jericho

MT. PISGAH

▲ Bezer

BENJAMIN

Ashdod

Jerusalem

Ashkelon

PHILISTINES

HILL
COUNTRY
OF JUDAH

Sea of the Arabah
(Salt Sea)

REUBEN

Gaza

Lachish

Hebron

JUDAH

Aroer

River Arnon

Debir

Beer-sheba

SIMEON

MOAB

The Negeb

EDOM

The Great Sea

327

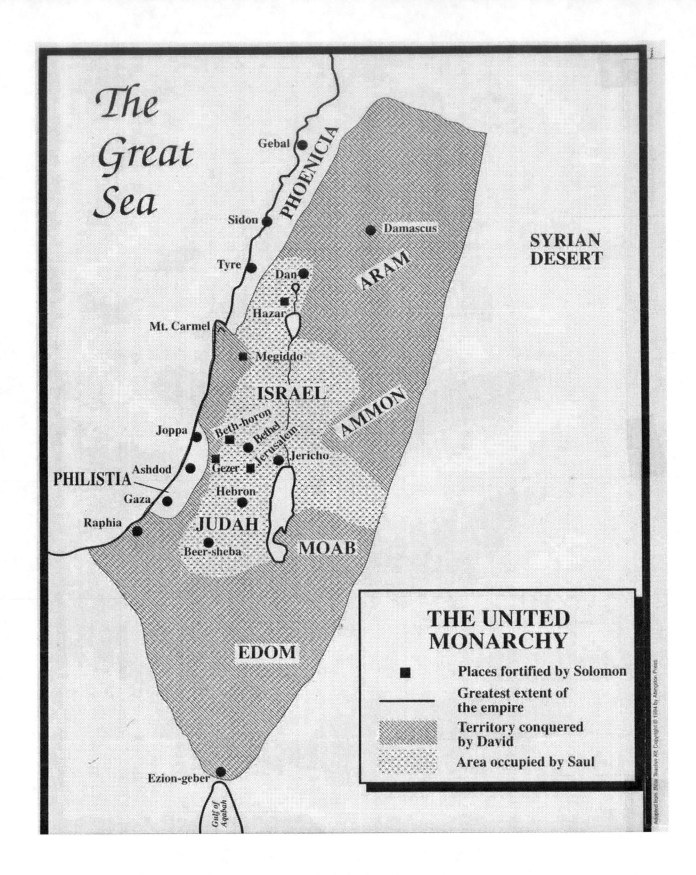

The Great Sea

PHOENICIA

SYRIAN DESERT

Gebal

Sidon

Tyre

Damascus

ARAM

Dan

Hazar

Mt. Carmel

Megiddo

ISRAEL

AMMON

Joppa

Beth-horon

Bethel

Jerusalem

Jericho

Ashdod

Gezer

PHILISTIA

Gaza

Hebron

Raphia

JUDAH

MOAB

Beer-sheba

EDOM

Ezion-geber

Gulf of Aqabah

THE UNITED MONARCHY

■ Places fortified by Solomon

Greatest extent of the empire

Territory conquered by David

Area occupied by Saul

328

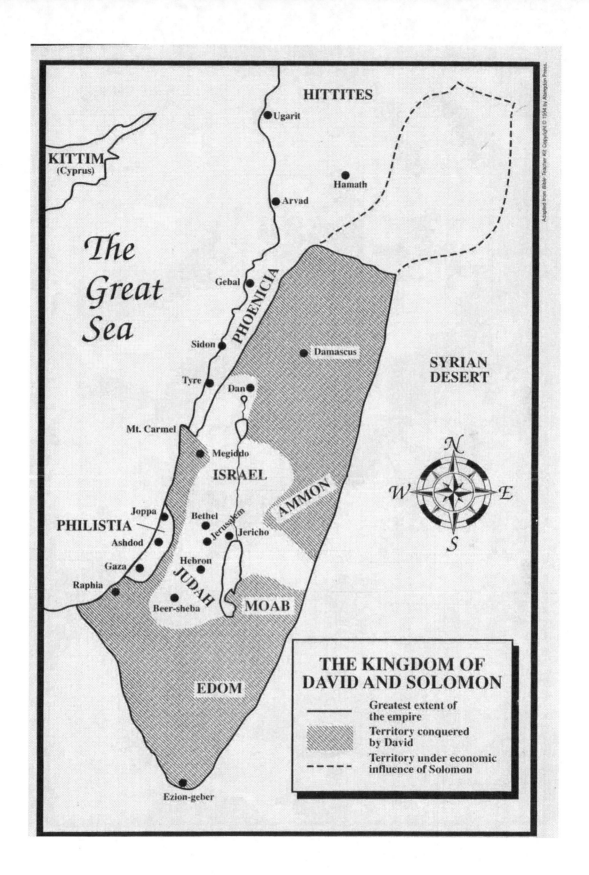

KITTIM
(Cyprus)

HITTITES

Ugarit

Hamath

Arvad

The Great Sea

Gebal

PHOENICIA

SYRIAN
DESERT

Sidon

Damascus

Tyre

Dan

Mt. Carmel

Megiddo

ISRAEL

AMMON

Joppa

Bethel

PHILISTIA

Jerusalem

Jericho

Ashdod

Gaza

Hebron

JUDAH

Beer-sheba

MOAB

Raphia

EDOM

THE KINGDOM OF DAVID AND SOLOMON

———— Greatest extent of the empire

Territory conquered by David

– – – Territory under economic influence of Solomon

Ezion-geber

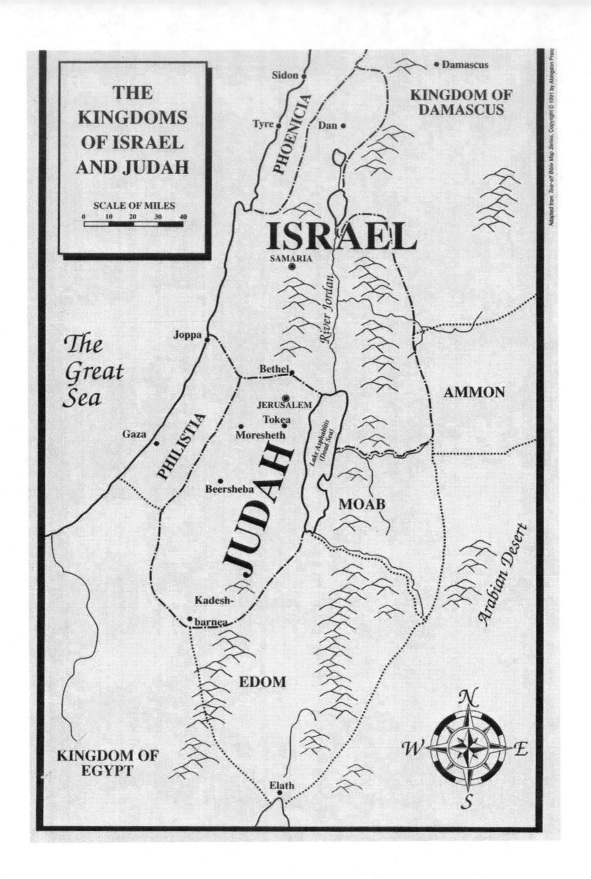

THE KINGDOMS OF ISRAEL AND JUDAH

SCALE OF MILES

0 10 20 30 40

The Great Sea

ISRAEL

SAMARIA

River Jordan

PHOENICIA

Sidon

Tyre

Dan

• Damascus

KINGDOM OF DAMASCUS

Joppa

Bethel

JERUSALEM

Tokea

Moresheth

Gaza

PHILISTIA

JUDAH

Beersheba

Lake Asphaltitis (Dead Sea)

AMMON

MOAB

Kadesh-barnea

EDOM

Arabian Desert

KINGDOM OF EGYPT

Elath

N
W   E
S

PRONUNCIATION GUIDE

The phonetic system in this guide is used to represent the sounds in the names, places, and unfamiliar words that are found in these stories. This system was developed by Net Ministries (http://netministries.org/bbasics/bbasics.htm) and is used here with their permission. Like all phonetic systems, this system gives the sound for each syllable in each word. The system does not require the use of special symbols and markings but uses only the letters of the alphabet. In the examples below, the pronunciation of each sound is shown by the use of common words containing that sound.

When using this pronunciation guide, remember that we are not always using ancient pronunciations. We frequently use more familiar modern versions. We admit that many of the pronunciations given here are nowhere near the original pronunciations but are given here as suggestions and for purposes of consistency. Most, however, are based on respected opinions.

Vowel Sounds:

- EE – eat, beet, neat
- IH – bit, hit
- AY – ace, hey, day
- EH – bread, Fred, Ted
- A – cat, sat
- AH – car, far
- AW – law, saw
- O – home, coat
- OU – book, took, hook
- OO – moon, spoon
- UH – cut, nut, love
- ER – bird, heard
- EHR – air, tear, fair
- AI – ice, nice, fly
- AU – out, shout, down
- OI – boy, coin

Consonant Sounds:

Consonants sound as the letter normally sounds, with these exceptions:

- G – (hard G) gun, lug
- TSH – church, chance, cheep
- ZH – garage, mirage, lodge

Syllable Emphasis

The syllable on which to put the emphasis is shown in CAPITAL LETTERS.

Aaron	EHR-uhn
Abarim	AB-ah-rim
Abednego	ah-BEHD-nee-go
Abel	AY-b'l
Abel Beth-maachah	AY-b'l-behth-MAH-ah-kah
Abiah	ah-BAI-ah
Abiathar	ah-BAI-ah-thahr
Abigail	AB-ih-gayl
Abihu	ah-BAI-hyoo
Abijah	ah-BAI-jah
Abijam	ah-BAI-j'm
Abimelech	ah-BIHM-eh-lehk
Abinadab	ah-BIHN-ah-dab
Abiram	ah-BAI-r'm
Abishag	AB-ihsh-ag
Abishai	ah-BIHSH-ay-ai
Abishalom	ah-BIHSH-ah-lahm
Abner	AB-n'r
Abraham	AY-brah-ham
Abram	AY-bruhm
Absalom	AB-sah-l'm
Abyssinia	ab-ih-SIHN-ee-ah
acacia	ah-KAY-shah
Achan	AY-k'n
Achbor	AHK-bor
Achish	AY-kihsh
Achmetha	AHK-mehth-ah
Adah	AY-dah
Adam	AD-uhm
Adam-ondi-Ahman	AD-uhm-awn-dai-AH-muhn
Adar	AY-dahr
Admah	AD-mah
Adonai	AH-duhn-ai
Adonijah	ad-o-NAI-jah
Adrammelech	ah-DRAM-eh-lehk
Adullum	AD-yoo-l'm
Agag	AY-gag
Agagite	AY-gag-ait
Ahab	AY-hab
Ahasuerus	ay-HAZ-yoo-EHR-uhs
Ahava	ah-HAHV-ah
Ahaz	AY-haz
	or ah-HAHZ
Ahaziah	ay-haz-AI-yah
Ahijah	ah-HAI-jah
Ahikam	ah-HAI-kuhm
Ahio	ah-HAI-o
Ahimaaz	ah-HIHM-uh-az
Ahimelech	ah-HIHM-eh-lehk
Ahithophel	ah-HIHTH-o-fehl
Ahinoam	ah-HIHN-o-uhm
Aholiab	ah-HO-lee-ab
Ai	AY-ai
Ajalon	AJ-uh-lawn

332

Alexander	al-ehk-ZAN-d'r
Amalek	AM-ah-lehk
Amalekite	uh-MAL-eh-kait
Amasa	AM-uh-suh
Amaziah	am-uh-ZAI-ah
Amittai	ah-MIHT-ay-ai
Ammah	ah-MAH
Ammon	AM-uhn
Ammonite	AM-uh-nait
Amnon	AM-nohn
Amon	ah-MON
Amorite	AM-or-ait
Amram	AM-r'm
Anak	AN-uhk
Anammelech	ah-NAM-eh-lehk
Anathoth	AN-uh-thawth
Aphek	AY-fehk
Arabian	ah-RAY-bee-uhn
Aramaic	ehr-uh-MAY-ihk
Ararat	EHR-uh-rat
Araunah	ah-RAW-nah
Arbah	ahr-BAH
Arioch	AHR-ee-ahk
Arnon	AHR-nahn
Artaxerxes	ahr-tah-ZERK-seez
Asa	AY-suh
Asahel	AHS-ah-hehl
Asahiah	ay-suh-HAI-ah
Asenath	ah-SEHN-uhth
Ashdod	ASH-dawd
Asher	ASH-uhr
Asherah	ASH-uhr-ah
Ashima	ASH-ih-mah
Ashkclon	ASH-keh-lawn
Ashtaroth	ASH-tuh-rahth
Ashtoreth	ASII-to-rehth
Assyria	uh-SIHR-ee-ah
Assyrian	uh-SIHR-ee-uhn
Astarte	ahs-TAHR-tay
Astyages	ahs-tai-AZH-ehs
Athaliah	ath-ah-LAI-ah
Ava	AY-vah
Avite	AY-vait
Azariah	az-ah-RAI-ah
Baal	bah-AHL
Baal-berith	bah-AHL-BEE-r'th
Baal-hazor	bah-AHL-HAY-zor
Baalim	bah-AHL-ihm
Baalis	bah-AHL-ihs
Baal-peor	bah-AHL pee-OR
Baal-zebub	bah-AHL-zee-buhb
Baasha	bah-AHSH-ah
Babel	BAY-buhl
Babylon	BAB-ih-lahn

Babylonia	bab-ih-LO-nee-ah
Babylonian	bab-ih-LO-nee-uhn
Bahurim	bah-hoo-REEM
Balaam	BAY-luhm
Baladan	BAL-ah-dan
Balak	BAHL-ahk
Barak	bah-RAHK
Baruch	bah-ROOK
Barzillai	bahr-ZIHL-ay-ai
Bashan…	bay-SHAHN
Bashemath	BASH-eh-math
Bathsheba	bath-SHEE-bah
Beeroth	bee-EHR-oth
Beersheba	bee-er-SHAY-bah
Bel	BEHL
Bela	BEE-lah
Belial	BEE-lee-uhl
Belshazzar	behl-SHAZ-uhr
Belteshazzar	behl-teh-SHAZ-uhr
Benaiah	behn-AY-yah
Ben-hadad	ben-HAY-dahd
Benjamin	BEHN-juh-mihn
Benjamite	BEHN-juh-mait
Benoni	beh-NON-ee
Besor	BEE-sor
Beth-barah	behth-bah-RAW
Beth-el	behth-EHL
Beth-horon	behth-HOR-uhn
Bethlehem	BEHTH-leh-hehm
Bethlehem-judah	BEHTH-leh-hehm-JOO-dah
Beth-shan	behth-SHAN
Beth-shean	behth-SHEE-ahn
Beth-shemesh	behth-SHEHM-ehsh
Bethuel	BEHTH-yoo-ehl
Bezaleel	behz-AL-ee-ehl
Bidkar	BIHD-kahr
Bilhah	BIHL-hah
Boaz	BO-az
Buzi	BOO-zee
Cain	KAYN
Cainan	KAYN-uhn
Caleb	KAY-lehb
Cambyses	kam-BAI-seez
Canaan	KAYN-uhn
Canaanite	KAYN-uhn-ait
Carmel	kahr-MEHL
Carmi	KAHR-mee
Chaldean	kahl-DEE-uhn
Chaldees	kahl-DEEZ
Chebar	kee-BAHR
Chedorlaomer	kehd-ohr-lay-O-muhr
Chemosh	KEE-mosh
Chephirah	keh-FAI-rah
Cherith	KEE-rihth

334

Cherithite	KEE-rihth-ait
Chilion	KIHL-ee-ahn
Chimham	KIHM-huhm
Chinnereth	KIHN-eh-rehth
Coniah	ko-NAI-ah
coriander	kor-ee-AN-duhr
Cush	KOUSH
Cushi	KOUSH-ai
Cushite	KOUSH-ait
Cuth	KOOTH
Cuthah	koo-THAH
Cyrus	SAI-r's
Dagon	DAY-guhn
Damascus	duh-MAS-kuhs
Dan	DAN
Daniel	DAN-yuhl
Danite	DAN-ait
Darius	dah-RAI-uhs
Dathan	DAY-thuhn
David	DAY-vihd
Deborah	DEHB-o-rah
Delilah	dee-LAI-lah
Dinah	DAI-nah
Doeg	DO-ehg
Dothan	DO-thuhn
Dura	DOU-rah
Ebal	EE-buhl
Ebed-melech	EE-behd-MEE-lehk
Ebenezer	ehb-eh-NEE-zuhr
Ecbatana	ehk-bah-TAH-nuh
Eden	EE-duhn
Edom	EE-duhm
Edomite	EE-duhm-ait
Eglon	EHG-lahn
Egypt	EE-jihpt
Egyptian	EE-jihp-tshuhn
Ehud	AY-hood
Ekron	EHK-rahn
Elah	EE-lah
Elam	EE-luhm
El-Beth-el	ehl-behth-EHL
Eldad	EHL-dad
Eleazar	ehl-ee-AY-z'r
El-elohe-Israel	ehl-eh-LO-hay-IHZ-rehl
Eli	EE-lai
Eliakim	ehl-AI-uh-kihm
Eliashib	ehl-AI-uh-shihb
Eliezer	ehl-ih-EE-z'r
Elihu	ehl-AI-hyoo
Elijah	ehl-AI-jah
Elimelech	ehl-LIHM-eh-lehk
Eliphaz	EHL-ih-fahz
Elisha	ehl-AI-shah
Elishama	ehl-IHSH-uh-muh

Elkanah	ehl-KAY-nah
El Shaddai	ehl-shah-DAI
emerod	EHM-eh-rahd
Endor	EHN-dor
Engedi	ehn-GEHD-ee
Enoch	EE-nawk
Enos	EE-nuhs
ephah	EE-fah
ephod	EE-fahd
Ephraim	EE-fr'm
Ephraimite	EE-fr'm-ait
Ephrath	EHF-ruhth
Er	ER
Esau	EE-saw
Esek	EE-sehk
Esther	EHS-t'r
Etam	EE-tuhm
Ethbaal	ehth-BAH-ahl
Ethiopia	eeth-ee-OP-ee-ah
Ethiopian	eeth-ee-OP-ee-uhn
Euphrates	yoo-FRAY-teez
Eve	EEV
Evil-merodach	EE-vihl-meh-RO-dahk
Ezekiel	eh-ZEE-kee-ehl
Ezel	EE-zehl
Ezra	EHZ-rah
Gaal	gay-AHL
Gabriel	GAY-bree-ehl
Gad	GAD
Galeed	GAL-ee-ehd
Galilee	gal-ih-LEE
Gath	GATH
Gaza	GAH-zah
Gazer	GAH-z'r
Geba	GEE-bah
Gedaliah	gehd-ah-LAI-ah
Gehazi	geh-HAH-zee
Gerar	gee-RAHR
Gerizim	GEHR-ih-zihm
Gershom	GUHR-shuhm
Gershon	GUHR-shahn
Geshem	GEH-shehm
Geshur	GEH-shuhr
Gibeah	GIHB-ee-ah
Gibeon	GIHB-ee-ahn
Gibeonite	GIHB-ee-ahn-ait
Gihon	GAI-hahn
Gilboa	gihl-BO-ah
Gilead	GIHL-ee-uhd
Gileadite	GIHL-ee-uhd-ait
Gilgal	GIHL-gal
Giloh	GAI-lo
Gilonite	GAI-lo-nait
Gittite	GIHT-ait

Goliath	go-LAI-uhth
Gomorrah	go-MOR-ah
Goshen	GO-shuhn
Grecia	GREE-shuh
Habor	HAY-b'r
Hachilah	HAK-ih-lah
Hadassah	hah-DAHS-ah
Hagar	HAY-gahr
Haggai	HAG-ay-ai
Haggith	HAG-ihth
Halah	HAY-lah
Ham	HAM
Haman	HAY-muhn
Hamath	HAY-muhth
Hamor	HAY-m'r
Hanameel	hah-NAM-ee-ehl
Hanani	hah-NAHN-ee
Hananiah	han-ah-NAI-ah
Hannah	HAN-ah
Haran	hah-RAHN
Havilah	HAV-ih-lah
Hazael	HAW-zah-ehl
Hazeroth	hah-ZEE-rahth
Heber	HEE-b'r
Hebrew	HEE-broo
Hebron	HEHB-rahn
Heliopolis	hee-lee-AHP-o-lihs
Hezekiah	hehz-eh-KAI-ah
Hiel	HAI-uhl
Hilkiah	hihl-KAI-ah
Hinnom	HIHN-uhm
Hirah	HAI-rah
Hiram	HAI-ruhm
Hittite	HIHT-ait
Hivite	HIHV-ait
Hobah	HO-bah
Hophni	HAHF-nee
Hor	HOR
Horeb	HOR-ehb
Horonite	HOR-o-nait
Hoshea	ho-SHEE-ah
Huldah	HUHL-dah
Hur	HUHR
Hushai	HOO-shah-ai
Hyksos	HIHK-sos
hyssop	HIHS-uhp
Hystaspes	hihs-TAHS-pehs
Immer	IHM-uhr
Irad	AI-rad
Iranian	ih-RAY-nee-uhn
Irijah	ih-RAI-jah
Isaac	AI-z'k
Isaiah	ai-ZAY-ah
Ishbak	IHSH-bahk

337

Ishbosheth	IHSH-bo-shehth
Ishmael	IHSH-muhl
Ishmaelite	IHSH-muhl-ait
Ishtar	IHSH-tahr
Israel	IHZ-ruhl
Israelite	IHZ-ruhl-ait
Issachar	IHS-ah-kahr
Ithamar	IHTH-ah-mahr
Ittai	IHT-ah-ai
Ivah	AI-vah
Jabal	jay-BAHL
Jabbok	JAHB-uhk
Jabesh	JAY-behsh
Jabesh-gilead	JAY-behsh-GIHL-ee-ahd
Jachim	jah-KEEM
Jabin	JAY-bihn
Jacob	JAY-k'b
Jael	JAY-ehl
Jahaziel	jah-HAY-zee-ehl
Japheth	JAY-fehth
Jared	JEHR-uhd
Jebusite	JEHB-hyoo-sait
Jeconiah	jehk-o-NAI-ah
Jedidiah	jehd-ih-DAI-ah
Jegarsahadutha	jeh-GAHR-sah-hah-DOO-thah
Jehiel	jeh-HAI-ehl
Jehoahaz	jeh-HO-ah-haz
Jehoash	jeh-HO-ash
Jehoiachin	jeh-HOI-ah-kihn
Jehoiada	jeh-HOI-ah-dah
Jehoiakim	jeh-HOI-ah-kihm
Jehonadab	jeh-HO-nah-dab
Jehoram	jeh-HOR-uhm
Jehoshabeath	jeh-HAHSH-ah-bee-uth
Jehoshaphat	jeh-HAHSH-ah-fat
Jehosheba	jeh-HAHSH-eh-bah
Jehovah	jeh-HO-vah
Jehovah-jireh	jeh-HO-vah-JAI-reh
Jehovah-nissi	jeh-HO-vah-NIHS-ee
Jehovah-shalom	jeh-HO-vah-shah-LOM
Jehu	JAY-hyoo
Jehudi	jeh-HOO-dai
Jemima	jeh-MAI-mah
Jephthah	JEHF-thah
Jeremiah	jehr-eh-MAI-ah
Jericho	JEHR-ih-ko
Jeroboam	jehr-o-BO-am
Jerubbaal	jeh-ROO-bah-ahl
Jeruel	JEHR-hyoo-ehl
Jerusalem	jeh-ROO-sah-lehm
Jesse	JEHS-ee
Jethro	JEHTH-ro
Jezebel	JEHZ-eh-behl
Jezreel	JEHZ-ree-ehl

Jezreelite	JEHZ-ree-ul-ait
Jezreelitess	JEHZ-ree-ehl-ai-tehs
Joab	JO-ab
Joachin	JO-ah-kihn
Joah	JO-ah
Joash	JO-ash
Job	JOB
Jochebed	JOK-eh-behd
Joel	JO-ehl
Johanan	jo-HAN-uhn
Jokshan	JOK-shahn
Jonadab	JO-nah-dab
Jonah	JO-nah
Jonathan	JAHN-uh-th'n
Joppa	JAHP-ah
Joram	JOR-uhm
Jordan	JOR-d'n
Joseph	JO-sehf
Joshua	JAHSH-you-uh
Josiah	jo-SAI-ah
Jotham	JO-thuhm
Jubal	JOO-buhl
Judah	JOO-dah
Judea	jou-DEE-ah
Judith	JOO-dihth
Juttah	JUHT-ah
Kadesh	KAY-dehsh
Kareah	kah-REE-ah
Kedesh	KEE-dehsh
Kedron	KEHD-r'n
Keilah	KEE-lah
Kenite	KEHN-ait
Keren-happuch	KEHR-uhn-HAP-uhk
Keturah	keh-TOUR-ah
Kezia	kehz-AI-uh
Khudur-lagamar	KOU-door-LAY-gah-mahr
Kibroth-hattaavah	KIHB-rahth-hah-TAY-ah-vuh
Kidron	KIHD-ruhn
Kirjath-jearim	KIHR-jath-jee-AHR-ihm
Kish	KIHSH
Kishon	KEE-shahn
Kohath	KO-hath
Kolob	KO-lahb
Korah	kor-AH
Kordofan	KOR-do-fan
Laban	LAY-b'n
Lachish	LAY-kihsh
Laish	LAY-ihsh
Lamech	LAY-mehk
Leah	LEE-ah
Lebanon	LEHB-uh-nawn
Lehi	LEE-hai
Levi	LEE-vai
Levite	LEE-vait

339

Libnah	LIHB-nah
Lodebar	LO-duh-bahr
Lot	LAWT
Lucifer	LOO-sih-fer
Luz	LUHZ
Maachah	mah-AH-kah
Macedonia	mas-eh-DO-nee-ah
Machir	may-KIHR
Magor-missabib	MAY-gor-MIHS-uh-bihb
Mahalaleel	mah-HAH-lah-lee'l
Mahanaim	mah-hah-NAY-ihm
Mahlon	MAHL-uhn
Mahonri Moriancumer	mah-HAHN-rai-mor-ee-AN-kuh-m'r
Malchishua	mal-KIHSH-you-uh
Mamre	MAHM-ray
Manasseh	mah-NAS-uh
Mandane	MAN-dayn
Maon	MAY-awn
Manoah	mah-NO-ah
Mara	MEHR-ah
Marah	mahr-AH
Massah	mah-SAH
Matri	MAHT-ree
Mattaniah	mat-ah-NAI-ah
Medad	MEE-dad
Medan	MEE-dan
Mede	MEED
Media	MEE-dee-ah
Megiddo	meh-GEE-do
Mehujael	mee-HOO-dzah-ehl
Melchi-shua	MEHL-kee-SHOO-ah
Melchizedek	mehl-KIHZ-eh-dehk
Mene	MEE-nee
Memucan	meh-MOO-k'n
Menahem	MEHN-ah-hehm
Mephibosheth	meh-FIHB-o-shehth
Merab	MEHR-uhb
Merari	meh-RAHR-ee
Meribah	MEHR-ih-bah
Merodach-baladan	meh-RO-dak-BAL-uh-dahn
Meshach	MEE-shak
Mesopotamia	mehs-o-pah-TAY-mee-uh
Messiah	meh-SAI-ah
Methusael	meh-THOO-sah-ehl
Methuselah	meh-THOO-zuh-luh
Micah	MAI-kuh
Micaiah	mai-KAY-yah
Michael	MAI-kuhl
Michaiah	mai-KAY-yah
Michal	mee-KAHL
Michmash	MIHK-mash
Midian	MIHD-ee-uhn
Midianite	MIHD-ee-uhn-ait
Migdol	MIHG-dahl

Milcah	MIHL-kah
Millo	MIHL-o
Miriam	MIHR-ee-uhm
Mishael	MIHSH-ay-ehl
Mizpah	MIHZ-pah
Mizpeh	MIHZ-peh
Moab	MO-ab
Moabite	MO-ah-bait
Moabitess	MO-ah-BAIT-ehs
Molech	MOL-ehk
Mordecai	MOR-deh-kai
Moreh	MOR-uh
Moriah	mor-AI-uh
Moroni	mor-O-nai
Moses	MO-zuhz
Mulek	MYOO-lehk
Naamah	nay-AH-mah
Naaman	NAY-ah-muhn
Nabal	nay-BAHL
Nabonidus	na-BON-ih-d's
Nabopolassar	NA-bo-po-LAHS-uhr
Naboth	NAY-bawth
Nachon	NAY-kahn
Nadab	NAY-dab
Nahash	NAY-hash
Nahor	NAY-hor
Naioth	NAY-ahth
Naomi	nay-O-mee
Naphtali	NAF-tah-lee
Nathan	NAY-thuhn
Nazarite	NAZ-ah-rait
Nebat	NEE-baht
Nebo	NEE-bo
Nebuchadnezzar	nehb-yoo-kad-NEHZ-uhr
Nebuzar-adan	nehb-yoo-zahr-AY-d'n
Nehemiah	nee-hehm-AI-uh
Nergal	NEHR-gahl
Nergal-sharezer	NEHR-gahl-shahr-EEZ-uhr
Neriglissar	nehr-IHG-lih-sahr
Nethaniah	nehth-ah-NAI-ah
Nethinim	NEHTH-eh-nihm
Nibhaz	NIHB-hahz
Nile	NAIL
Nimrod	NIHM-rahd
Nimshi	NIHM-shee
Nineveh	NIHN-uh-vuh
Nisroch	NEES-rawk
Nitocris	nai-TOK-rihs
Noah	NO-ah
Nob	NAHB
Nod	NAHD
Nubia	NOO-bee-ah
Nun	NUHN
Obadiah	o-bah-DAI-ah

Obed	O-behd
Obed-edom	O-behd-EE-duhm
Oded	O-dehd
Omri	OM-ree
On	AHN
Onan	O-n'n
Ophrah	OF-ruh
Ornan	OR-n'n
Orpah	OR-pah
Othniel	OTH-nee-ehl
Padan-aram	pay-DAHN-ehr-AHM
Palestine	PAL-ehs-tain
Paran	pah-RAHN
Pashur	pah SHUHR
Pekah	pee-KAH
Pekahiah	peek-ah-HAI-ah
Pelethite	PEHL-eh-thait
Pelusiac	pehl-OO-see-ak
Peniel	PEHN-ee-ehl
Peninnah	peh-NIHN-uh
Penuel	pen-YOO-ehl
Perdition	per-DIHSH-uhn
Peres	pee-REEZ
Perizzite	PEHR-ih-zait
Persia	PUHR-zhuh
Persian	PUHR-zh'n
Pethor	PEE-thor
Phaltiel	FAHL-tee-ehl
Pharaoh	FEHR-o
Pharaoh-necho	FEHR-o-NEH-ko
Pharez	FEHR-ehz
Philistine	FIHL-ihs-teen
Phinehas	FIHN-ee-uhs
Phoenicia	feh-NEESH-ah
Phoenician	feh-NEESH-uhn
Phurah	FYOUR-ah
Pithom	PAI-th'm
Potiphar	PAHT-ih-f'r
Potipherah	pah-tih-FEHR-ah
Pul	PUHL
Purim	POUR-ihm
Raamses	ray-AHM-seez
Rab-shakeh	RAB-shak-eh
Rachel	RAY-tshuhl
Raguel	RAG-yoo-ehl
Rahab	RAY-hab
Ramah	rah-MAH
Rameses	RAM-eh-seez
Ramoth-gilead	RAY-mahth-GIHL-ee-ad
Rebekah	reh-BEHK-ah
Rechabite	REHK-ah-bait
Rehoboam	ray-ho-BO-uhm
Rehoboth	ray-HO-b'th
Remaliah	rehm-ah-LAI-yuh

342

Rephaim	REHF-ah-ihm
Rephidim	REHF-ih-dihm
Reuben	ROO-b'n
Reuel	ROO-ehl
Rezin	REE-zihn
Riblah	RIHB-lah
Rimmon	RIHM-uhn
Rimmon-hadad	RIHM-uhn-HAY-dahd
Rizpah	RIHZ-pah
Ruth	ROOTH
Salem	SAY-lehm
Samaria	suh-MEHR-ee-ah
Samaritan	suh-MEHR-ih-t'n
Samson	SAM-s'n
Samuel	SAM-yoo-uhl
Sanballat	san-BAH-l't
Sarah	SEHR-ah
Sarai	sah-RAI
Sarepta	sah-REHP-tah
Satan	SAY-t'n
Saul	SAHL
Segub	SEE-guhb
Seir	SEE-ihr
Seirath	SEE-ih-rath
Selah	see-LAW
Sennaar	SEHN-ay-ahr
Sennacherib	seh-NAK-uh-rihb
Sepharvaim	sehf-ahr-VAY-ihm
Sepharvite	SEHF-ahr-vait
Seth	SEHTH
Shadrach	SHAY-drak
Shalmanezer	shal-mah-NEE-z'r
Shammah	sham-AH
Shaphan	SHAY-fuhn
Shaphat	shay-FAHT
Shebah	SHAY-bah
Shebna	SHEHB-nah
Shechaniah	shehk-ah-NAI-ah
Shechem	SHEH-k'm
Shelah	shee-LAH
Shem	SHEHM
Shemaiah	sheh-MAY-ah
Sheshbazzar	shehsh-BAZ-uhr
Shibboleth	SHIHB-o-lehth
Shiloh	SHAI-lo
Shilonite	SHAI-lo-nait
Shimea	SHIHM-ee-ah
Shimei	SHIHM-ee-ai
Shinar	shee-NAHR
Shishak	SHEE-shak
Shittim	shih-TEEM
Shobab	SHO-bab
shofar	sho-FAHR
Shuah	SHOO-ah

Shunammite	SHOO-nam-ait
Shunem	SHOO-n'm
Shur	SHOOR
Shushan	SHOO-shawn
Sibboleth	SIHB-o-lehth
Sihon	SAI-hon
Siloam	sih-LO-ahm
Simeon	SIHM-ee-uhn
Sin	SIHN
Sinai	SAI-nai
Sippara	SIHP-ahr-ah
Sisera	SIHS-uhr-uh
Sitnah	SIHT-nah
Smedis	SMEHD-ihs
So	SO
Sochoh	SO-ko
Sodom	SAH-d'm
Solomon	SAHL-o-m'n
Sorek	SOR-ehk
Succoth	SOOK-oth
Succoth-benoth	SOOK-oth-BEE-nahth
Susa	SOO-suh
Syria	SIHR-ee-ah
Syrian	SIHR-ee-uhn
Tabeal	TAB-ee-ahl
Taberah	TAB-uhr-uh
Tabor	tay-BOR
Tahpanhes	TAH-pan-heez
Tamar	tay-MAHR
Tarshish	TAHR-shihsh
Tartak	TAHR-tak
Tatnai	TAT-nah-ai
Tekel	TEE-kehl
Tekoa	teh-KO-ah
Tel-abib	TEL-ah-beeb
Terah	teh-RAH
teraphim	TEHR-ah-fihm
Thebez	THEE-behz
Thummim	THUHM-ihm
Tibni	TIHB-nai
Tiglath-pileser	TIHG-lath-pih-LEE-z'r
Tigris	TAI-grihs
Timnath	TIHM-nath
Timnite	TIHM-nait
Tirzah	TIHR-zuh
Tishbite	TIHSH-bait
Tobiah	to-BAI-ah
Tophet	TO-feht
Tubal-cain	TOO-b'l-kayn
Tyre	TAI-uhr
Ulai	YOO-lah-ai
Upharsin	yoo-FAHR-sihn
Ur	UHR

Uriah	you-RAI-ah
Uriel	YOUR-ee-ehl
Urim	YOOR-uhm
Uzzah	UHZ-ah
Uzziah	yoo-ZAI-ah
Vashti	VASH-tee
Xerxes	ZERK-seez
Yahweh	YAH-weh
Zachariah	zak-ah-RAI-ah
Zadok	ZAY-dahk
Zaphnath-paaneah	ZAF-n'th-PAY-ah-NEE-uh
Zarah	ZEHR-ah
Zarephath	ZEHR-uh-fath
Zeboiim	zeh-BOI-ihm
Zebul	ZEE-buhl
Zebulun	ZEHB-yoo-l'n
Zechariah	zehk-ah-RAI-ah
Zedekiah	zehd-uh-KAI-ah
Zelzah	ZEHL-zah
Zerbanit	zer-BAN-iht
Zerubbabel	zeh-ROO-buh-b'l
Zeruiah	zehr-oo-AI-yah
Ziba	ZAI-buh
Zidon	ZAI-d'n
Zidonia	zih-DO-nee-ah
Zidonian	zih-DO-nee-yuhn
Ziklag	ZIHK-lahg
Zillah	ZIHL-uh
Zilpah	ZIHL-pah
Zimran	ZIHM-rahn
Zimri	ZIHM-ree
Zin	ZIHN
Zion	ZAI-uhn
Ziph	ZIHF
Zipporah	zih-POR-ah
Ziz	ZIHZ
Zoar	ZO-ahr
Zophar	zo-FAHR
Zorah	ZOR ah
Zuph	ZUHF

BIBLIOGRAPHY

In addition to the scriptures themselves and the study aids contained in the Latter-day Saint editions of the scriptures, the following sources were used to varying degrees in the preparation and writing of this book. Information derived from these sources is primarily contained within the footnotes, where it is used to provide background information relating to the stories.

Draper, Richard D. *Opening the Seven Seals: The Visions of John the Revelator.* Salt Lake City: Deseret Book Co., 1991.

Edersheim, Alfred. *Old Testament Bible History. GospeLink,* CD-ROM. Salt Lake City: Deseret Book Co., 2001.

Fletcher, Allen J. *Two Articles on the Facsimiles of the Book of Abraham.* 2nd ed. Sterling, Alberta, Canada: the author, 1999.

Josephus, Flavius. *The Works of Josephus.* New updated edition. Translated by William Whiston. Peabody, Massachusetts: Hendrickson Publishers Inc., 1987.

Journal of Discourses, 26 vols. London: Latter-day Saints' Book Depot, 1854–86.

Keller, Werner, *The Bible as History: What Archaeology Reveals about Scripture.* 2nd rev. ed. New York: William Morrow and Co. Inc., 1981.

Ludlow, Daniel H. *A Companion to Your Study of the Old Testament.* Salt Lake City: Deseret Book Co., 1981.

Ludlow, Victor. *Unlocking the Old Testament.* Salt Lake City: Deseret Book Co., 1981.

Nibley, Hugh. *Abraham in Egypt.* Salt Lake City: Deseret Book Co., 1981.

_____. *Teachings of the Book of Mormon.* Semester 2. Transcript of lectures presented to an Honors Book of Mormon class at Brigham Young University, Provo, Utah,1988–90.

Old Testament: 1 Kings–Malachi [Student Manual, Religion 302]. 2nd ed. Salt Lake City: The Church of Jesus Christ of Latter-day Saints, 1982.

Parry, Donald W. and Jay A. Parry, *Understanding the Book of Revelation.* Salt Lake City: Deseret Book Co., 1998.

Rasmussen, Ellis T. *A Latter-day Saint Commentary on the Old Testament.* Salt Lake City: Deseret Book Co., 1993.

Smith, Joseph. *History of The Church of Jesus Christ of Latter-day Saints.* 7 vols. Introduction and notes by B. H. Roberts. Salt Lake City: Deseret Book Co., 1948.

Smith, Joseph Fielding. *Answers to Gospel Questions.* 5 vols. Salt Lake City: Deseret Book Co., 1957–1966.

Smith, William. *Dictionary of the Bible. GospeLink,* CD-ROM. Salt Lake City: Deseret Book Co., 2001.

Sperry, Sydney B. *Book of Mormon Compendium.* Salt Lake City: Bookcraft, 1968.

Talmage, James E. *The House of the Lord.* Salt Lake City: Deseret Book Co., 1968.

Tate, Charles D., Jr., and Monte S. Nyman. *Alma, the Testimony of the Word.* Provo, Utah: BYU Religious Studies Center, 1992.

Taylor, John. *Mediation and Atonement.* Salt Lake City: Deseret News Co., 1882.

Webster, Noah . *An American Dictionary of the English Language,* 1828 edition. GospeLink, CD-ROM. Salt Lake City: Deseret Book Co., 2001.

NAME INDEX

The entries in this index refer to story numbers rather than page numbers.

David's army against Absalom, 130; restrained again from slaying Shimei, 131; sent after Sheba when Amasa delays, 132

Abishalom, *Father of Abijam's mother (probably Absalom),* 147 (fn. 411)

Abner, *Saul's captain,* fails to detect David's incursion into Saul's camp, 111; supports Ishbosheth as king after Saul's death, 117; fights with Joab's men and slays Asahel, 118; accused of adultery by Ishbosheth, 117; negotiates with David to unite two kingdoms, 117; slain by Joab and Abishai, honored after death by David, 117

Abraham (Abram), *Patriarch, prophet,* noble and great one in pre-earth council, 1; blessed for righteousness, given priesthood, 10; saved by Jehovah from being sacrificial offering, 10; promised he would be father of many nations, 10; moves to Haran, at Jehovah's instruction, due to famine, takes Lot, 11; leaves Haran, goes through Canaan worshipping and building altars, then to Egypt, 11; returns to Canaan, gives Lot choice of lands, 11; moves to plain of Mamre in Hebron, 11; Abrahamic covenant given, 12; Jehovah teaches him order of worlds, 13; tells Egyptians that Sarai is his sister, 13; rescues Lot, pays tithes to Melchizedek, 14; has son Ishmael by Hagar, 15; Abram becomes Abraham, promised a son by Sarah, told to name him Isaac, 16; entertains three holy men, 16; holy men promise Sodom will be spared if ten righteous found there, 17; in Gerar, tells Abimelech Sarah is sister, 18; has son Isaac, sends Hagar and Ishmael away, 19; commanded to offer Isaac as sacrifice, then spared, 20; buries Sarah at Hebron, 21; sends servant to find wife for Isaac, 21; marries Keturah and has six sons, 22; dies, buried at Hebron, 22

Abram, see Abraham

Absalom, *David's son,* plots revenge for sister Tamar, slays Amnon, flees 125; returns from exile, reunites with David, 126; lays plan to overthrow David, 127; lies with David's concubines for all to see, 129; accepts Hushai's counsel over Ahithophel's, 129; slain in battle against David's army, David sorrows for, 130

Achan, slain for taking spoils from Jericho, 76

Achbor, adviser to King Josiah, 189

Achish, *Philistine king,* thinks David is mad, refuses to see him, 108; gives Ziklag to David, makes David his bodyguard, 112; recruits David and his men to fight against Saul but is vetoed by other Philistine leaders, 114

Adah, *Lamech's wife,* gives birth to twins, Jabal and Jubal, rebels against Lamech when he tells her his secret, 5

Adam, *Patriarch, first man,* created and placed in garden, 3; refuses forbidden fruit, partakes after Eve, becomes mortal, driven from garden, 3; rejoices in fall, 3; suffers heartache because of Cain killing Abel, has another son, Seth, 4; ordains Enoch to priesthood, 6; at Adam-ondi-Ahman, 7; seen by Daniel on fiery throne, 216; prince of host of Jehovah in Daniel's dream, 217 (fn. 689)

Adonai (Lord), name used instead of Jehovah, 2 (fn. 5)

Adonijah, *David's son,* conspires to be king, holds feast, plan thwarted when Solomon anointed, 136; seeks favor of Solomon through Bathsheba, slain because of his request, 138

Adrammelech, *false god,* 182 (fn. 552)

Agag, *Amalekite king,* captured by Saul, slain by Samuel, 102

Ahab, *king of Israel, Omri's son,* marries Zidonian princess Jezebel, 150; cursed with drought because of wickedness, 151; his prophets of Baal fail to bring fire from heaven, 152; tells Jezebel that her priests have been slain, 153; Jehovah gives him victory over Syrians, he frees Ben-hadad contrary to Jehovah's will, 156; covets, then takes, Naboth's vineyard, 157; curse placed on him and his seed, 157; joins with Jehoshaphat to fight Syrians, slain in battle, 158; succeeded by son Ahaziah, 160

Ahasuerus, *Persian king* to whom Esther is queen (according to Bible), 224 (fn. 711); see also Xerxes

Ahaz, *king of Judah, son of Jotham,* replaces father, 181; suffers great losses to Israel and Syria because of wickedness, many people carried captive to Samaria, 181; offers his children as burnt sacrifices, 181; Isaiah warns him of invasion, promises he will not be killed, 181; closes temple and worships false gods, 181; kings of Israel and Syria fail in attempt to replace him because it is contrary to against Jehovah's will, 180; dies, succeeded by son Hezekiah, 183

Ahaziah, *king of Israel, Ahab's son,* injured by fall through lattice, sends messengers to inquire of false gods, 160; sent warning by Elijah for rejecting Jehovah, told he will die, 160; efforts to capture Elijah and put him to death fail, 160; dies, succeeded by brother Jehoram, 160, 162

Ahaziah, *king of Judah,* only son of King Jehoram not taken captive by Philistines and Arabians, 171; mother is King Ahab's daughter Athaliah, 171; succeeds father, brings sins of Israel to Judah, 172; joins Israel's war against Syria, 172; goes to Jezreel to visit wounded uncle, Jehoram, king of Israel, 172; he and Jehoram slain by Jehu, 172; succeeded by Athaliah, 174

Ahijah, *prophet,* prophesies to Jeroboam that he will be king, 142; prophesies death of Jeroboam's son Abijah and fall of Jeroboam's house, 146

Ahijah, *father of Baasha,* 157

Ahikam, *Shaphan's son,* adviser to King Josiah of Judah, 189; helps preserve Jeremiah's life, 193

Ahio, *son of Abinadab the priest,* drove cart, with brother Uzzah, to bring the ark of the covenant to Jerusalem, 119

Ahimaaz, *son of Zadok the priest,* returns to Jerusalem with his father, 127; he and Jonathan deliver Hushai's message to David, 129; delivers message of Absalom's death to David, 130

Ahimelech, *priest of Nob,* gives Goliath's sword to David when he is fleeing from Saul, 108; he and 85 priests slain by Doeg, at Saul's request, for aiding David, 108

Ahithophel, *David's adviser, grandfather of Bathsheba,* joins Absalom's conspiracy to overthrow David, 127; David prays that his counsel to Absalom will be turned to foolishness, 127; counsels Absalom to lie with David's concubines, 129; his counsel for defeating David rejected in favor of Hushai's, 129; takes his own life, 129

Ahinoam, *Jezreelitess, David's wife,* flees with him to Gath, 112

Aholiab, *artisan from Dan,* prepared by Jehovah to build tabernacle, 56, 59

Alexander the Great, seen in Daniel's dream as a great

horn between the eyes of rough he-goat, 217 (fn. 671); seen in dream as king far richer than the kings of Persia, 221 (fn. 686)

Amalekites, attack Israelites in the wilderness, defeated by Moses holding up staff, 53; Israel's spies find them in south of promised land, 64; joins with Moab to subdue and bind Israel, 79; Saul disobeys Jehovah's instruction to completely destroy them, 102; wretched spirit tells Saul that, because he failed to destroy them, Jehovah will tear kingdom from him, 113; burn Ziklag, David pursues and destroys them, 114

Amasa, *David's nephew, captain of Absalom's army of Israel,* defeated by David's army, 130; appointed captain by David in Joab's place, 131; slain by Joab, 132

Amaziah, *king of Judah, son of Joash,* defeated by Jehoash of Israel, 176; slays men who murdered his father, 177; hires 100,000 Ephraimites to fight against Edom, sends them home when warned by prophet, 177; defeats Edomites and brings home their gods, 177; goes to war with Israel because of unjust attack by Ephraim, sorely defeated, 177; slain by conspiracy because he rejected Jehovah, 177

Ammonites, *descendants of Lot,* 17; enslave Israel through alliance with Moab and Amalek, 79; Jephthah's help sought to stop invasion of, defeated by Jephthah in their unjust cause, 83; invade Jabesh-gilead and promise peace at price of every man's right eye, defeated by Saul's and Samuel's army, 99; David's army, under Joab, goes to war against them when gesture of goodwill is repaid with insult, 123; Uriah the Hittite slain in battle against fortified city of, 123; prophet Nathan accuses David of killing Uriah with sword of, 124; assist David and his army in exile, 130; Solomon takes wives of, worships their gods, 142; come with Moabites and people of Mt. Seir to conquer Judah, destroy each other, 159; defeated by King Jotham of Judah, 181; Jews who are among, come to join Gedaliah in Judah, 208; Johanan and eight men escape to land of, after killing Gedaliah, 209; to be overthrown by king of the north (Daniel's dream), 221; banned from congregation of Judah because their fathers did not help Israel in wilderness, 229

Amnon, *David's son,* abuses his sister Tamar, killed by Absalom, 125

Amon, *king of Judah, Manasseh's son,* slain by ser-

Amorites, assist in rescue of Lot, 14; Israel's spies find then in mountains of promised land, 64; make war against Israel in wilderness, defeated, 68; Israel humbled by defeat at Ai at hands of, 76; Joshua asks Israel to choose between Jehovah and gods of, 78; Israel worships gods of, 79; Midianites overrun land because Israel worships gods of, 81; Jehovah promises to bring heavy judgments on Judah, because King Manasseh is more wicked than, 188; Judah called daughter of (in allegory), 200

Amram, *Moses' father, grandson of Levi*, 44

Anak, *giants*, Israel's spies find them in promised land, 64; Jehovah promises to drive them out, 78

Anammelech, *false god*, 182 (fn. 552)

Araunah, *Jebusite*, David builds altar on his threshing floor, he offers oxen and wood for sacrifice, 134; temple built on site of his threshing floor, 141

Arioch, *captain of King Nebuchadnezzar's guard*, intermediary between Daniel and king, 213

Artaxerxes (also called Smedis), *Persian impostor king*, Samaritans hire counselors to write letters to him against Jews, building of temple stopped, 222; deposed by Darius, 223

Artaxerxes, *Persian king, son of Xerxes*, commissions Ezra the priest to lead exiled Jews to Jerusalem and appoint magistrates and judges, 225; commissions Nehemiah to be governor of Judea and rebuild walls of Jerusalem, 227

Asa, *king of Judah, son of Abijam*, serves righteously, 147; makes alliance with Syria to defend against Israel, 148; rebuked by prophet Hanani for joining with Syria, puts Hanani in stocks, 148; dies, 149

Asahel, *David's nephew, brother of Joab and Abishai*, pursues Abner until Abner slays him, 118; death avenged by his brothers, 117

Asahiah, *adviser to King Josiah* of Judah, 189

Asenath, *daughter of Potipherah, priest of On*, becomes Joseph's wife, 38; has sons Manasseh and Ephraim, 40

Asher, *son of Jacob and Zilpah*, 28; blessed by Jacob,

Asherah, *false goddess*, description of, Gideon destroys grove of, 81; 81 (fn. 191)

Ashima, *false god*, worshipped by people of Hamath, 182

Ashtaroth, *false goddess, plural form of Ashtoreth*, q.v.

Ashtoreth, *false goddess*, worshipped by Israel, along with Baal, 79; description of, 81 (fn. 191); Israel forsakes, at Samuel's urging, 96; Saul's head and his armor put in house of, 115; Solomon worships, 142

Astyages, *Median king, Cyrus's grandfather*, conquered by Persians in 550 BC, 211

Athaliah, *daughter of Ahab and Jezebel*, marries Jehoram, king of Judah, 171; mother of Ahaziah, king of Judah, and sister of Jehoram, king of Israel, 172; becomes ruler of Judah on Ahaziah's death after slaying his children, 174; slain, replaced by Joash, 175

Azariah, *prophet, Obed's son*, offers encouragement to King Asa, 147

Azariah, *priest*, rebukes King Uzziah for performing temple rites without authority, 178

Azariah (Uzziah, king of Judah), 180 (fn. 525)

Azariah (Abednego), 212

Baal, *false god*, daughters of Moab entice men of Israel to worship, 69; worshipped by Israel during time of judges, 81; Gideon obeys command to tear down altar of, 81; description of, 81 (fn. 191); Israel forsakes, at Samuel's urging, 96; Ahab's wife Jezebel worships, 150; Elijah challenges prophets of, at Mt. Carmel, then slays prophets, 153; Elijah challenges Israel to follow either Jehovah or Baal, 153; Jezebel threatens Elijah's life for killing prophets of, 154; Still 7,000 souls in Israel who do not bow to, 155; King Ahaziah, Ahab's son, worships, 160; King Jehoram puts away image of, made by his father Ahab, 162; King Jehu of Israel destroys all followers of, 173; people of Judah destroy house of, and slay priest, 174; King Joash restores temple vessels taken for house of, 175; King Ahaz of Judah makes molten images of, offers his children as sacrifices, 181; King Manasseh of Judah erects altars to, offers his son as sacrifice, 188; King Josiah of Judah commands that vessels of be removed from temple, puts down those who burn incense to, 189; Jeremiah prophesies against those who worship, 194

Baal-berith, men of Shechem hide and are burned in house of, 82

Baalis, *Ammorite king*, joins conspiracy to slay Gedaliah, 209

Baal-peor, *false god*, Moab women entice men of Israel to worship, 69

Baal-zebub, *false god*, King Ahaziah sends servants to seek help from, 160

Baasha, *king of Israel*, slays Nadab to become king, 148; destroys house of Jeroboam, 148; leads army against Judah, captures Ramah, 148; defeated by Judah, with Syria's help, 148; cursed by prophet Jehu for his wickedness, 148; dies, succeeded by son Elah, 148; Zimri destroys all seed of, fulfilling curse, 148

Babylonians, defeat Sodom and Gomorrah in battle near Dead Sea, 14; King Hezekiah shows his treasures to, 186; Jeremiah prophesies that, will come against Judah's inhabitants and destroy them, 195; Jews believe that Egypt will save them from, 196; Jeremiah wears bonds and yokes as he prophesies captivity and destruction of Judah by, 197; false prophet Hananiah prophesies delivery from, 197; Jeremiah tells King Zedekiah that if he fights against, he will not prosper, 198; Jerusalem falls to, 208; background of the empire, 211; also called Chaldeans or Chaldees, 211; take captives and carry off temple vessels, 212; fall to Persia, 218; Isaiah earlier prophesied of their fall, 222; see also Chaldeans

Balaam, *false prophet*, when called by Balak to curse Israel, blesses them instead, 68

Baladan, *Babylonian king*, sends emissaries to King Hezekiah, 186

Balak, *Moabite king*, fears Israel and hires Balaam to curse them, 68

Barak, *captain of Deborah's army*, defeats Canaanites, 80

Baruch, *Jeremiah's scribe*, writes Jeremiah's prophecies and reads them to people of Judah, 195; Jeremiah gives deed to him for safekeeping, 198; taken into Egypt with Judah's remnant, 209

Barzillai, *Gileadite*, befriends David in exile, 137

Bashemath, *Esau's wife*, 25

Bathsheba, *wife of Uriah the Hittite*, conceives child by David, 123; mourns Uriah's death, marries David, 123; David comforts her when child dies, she has son Solomon, 124; granddaughter of Ahithophel, 129; warns David of Adonijah's plot to become king, 136; asks favor of Solomon in Adonijah's behalf, 138

Belshazzar, *prince regent of Babylonia, King Nabonidus's son*, 211; hosts great feast, sees handwriting on wall, 218; gets Daniel to interpret handwriting, 218

Belteshazzar (Daniel), 212, 218

Benaiah, *mighty man of David, Jehoiadah's son*, not invited to Adonijah's feast, part of party to Gihon to make Solomon king, 136; sent by Solomon to kill David's enemies, 138; slays Joab, becomes Solomon's captain in Joab's place, 138

Ben-hadad I, *Syrian king*, joins with King Asa of Judah to fight King Baasha and Israel, 148; invades Israel with mighty threats, but defeated (twice) by King Ahab, 156; his life preserved by Ahab against Jehovah's will, 156

Ben-hadad II, *Syrian king*, sends Naaman to Samaria to be healed of leprosy, 166; his army struck blind when sent to capture Elisha, 168; lays siege to Samaria, causes great suffering, 169; his army abandons siege and flees because of great noise, Israel spared, 169; murdered by Hazael, who then becomes king, 170

Ben-hadad III, *Syrian king, Hazael's son*, defeated by King Jehoash of Israel, cities taken back, 176

Benjamin, *son of Jacob and Rachel*, Rachel dies at birth of, 34; brought to Egypt by brothers to save Simeon, reunited with Joseph, 39; blessed by Jacob, 41

Benoni (Benjamin), 34

Bethuel, *Nahor's son*, gives daughter Rebekah to be Isaac's wife, 21

Bezaleel, *artisan of Judah* prepared by Jehovah to build tabernacle, 56, 59

Bidkar, *King Jehu's captain*, assists in slaying of Jehoram and Ahaziah, 172

Bildad, *friend of Job*, 43

Bilhah, *Rachel's handmaiden*, 27; given to Jacob by Rachel to bear him children, bears sons Dan and Naphtali, 28; meets Esau, 32

Boaz, *prosperous Bethlehemite*, takes Ruth to wife by right as first husband's kinsman, 90

Cain, *Adam's son*, makes secret oath with Satan and slays Abel, cursed, 4; his posterity, 5

Cainan, *Patriarch, Enos's son*, at Adam-ondi-Ahman, 7

Caleb, *spy from tribe of Judah*, gives faithful report, nearly stoned, 64; promised he will enter promised land, 64; still living at time of preparation to enter promised land, 70; given inheritance, 78; ancestor of Nabal, 80

Cambyses (Ahasuerus), 222 (fn. 705)

Canaanites, explanation of, 21 (fn. 52); Isaac counsels Jacob not to seek wife among, 26; Judah's wife is one of, 36; Jehovah promises Moses land of, 51; spies sent into land of, punished because of bad report, 64; Israel attacked by, Jehovah gives Israel victory, 67; Moses tells why Israelites are chosen people rather than they, 71; Joshua sends spies to Jericho in land of, 72; Israel feared by, 74; Israel conquers land of, makes no allies, 78; Israel worships gods of, 79; Israel in bondage to, delivered by Deborah and Barak, 80

Chaldeans (Chaldees), Abraham lived among, Egyptian influence great, 10; stole Job's camels, 43; will use Judah's own weapons against them, 196; Jeremiah says people of Jerusalem will die unless they surrender to, 196; Egyptians will bring armies to deter, but will fail, 198; King Zedekiah and others captured by, 208; they name Gedaliah governor of those left, 208; Jeremiah tells those left that, if they remain in the land, they will not be harmed by, 209; also called Babylonians, 211; people of, and Jews assist Persians in conquering Babylonia, 211; well-favored Jewish captives to be taught language of, 212; Shadrach, Meshach, and Abednego inspire jealousy in, 214; letter to Darius tells of Jews' earlier defeat and captivity by, 223; see also Babylonians

Chedorlaomer, *king of Elam*, makes war against cities of plains, captures Lot, 14

Chemosh, *false god of Moabites*, worshipped by Solomon, 142

Chilion, *son of Elimelech and Naomi, husband of Orpah*, dies in Moab, 90

Coniah (Jehoiachin), 196 (fn. 596)

Cushi, *messenger*, sent to tell David of Absalom's death, arrives second, 130

Cyrus, *Persian king*, named in Isaiah's prophecy as one who would instigate return of Jews and rebuilding of temple, 187; conquers Babylonian Empire, 211; grandson of Astyages, the Median king, 211; Daniel serves in king's court in Babylon until time of, 212; orders rebuilding of Jerusalem and temple, returns temple vessels to Zerubbabel, 222; Tatnai gets verification from Darius that temple rebuilding was authorized by, 223

Dagon, *false god*, feast in house of, spoiled by Samson, 87; Philistines put ark of covenant in house of, 95

Dan, *son of Jacob and Bilhah*, born, 28; blessed by Jacob, 41

Daniel, *prophet*, taken captive, given special training to serve in king's palace, along with Shadrach, Meshach, Abednego, and others, 212; tells king's dream of great image, interprets dream, 213; interprets king's dream of great tree, 215; has dream with many beasts, interpreted by angel, 216; has vision of a ram and a he-goat with many horns, 217; interprets writing on wall for Belshazzar, 218; prays contrary to law, preserved when cast into lions' den, 219; pleads with Jehovah for captive Judah, 220; told by angel Gabriel that Judah will be restored and Messiah will come, 220; has another vision of Judah's future, but much not understood, 221

Darius, *the Mede*, ruler of Babylon after fall to Persians, served one year, 211, 218; his law causes Daniel to be thrown to lions, prays for Daniel's deliverance, 219

Darius, *Persian king*, local opposition to temple rebuilding continues through reign of, 222; deposes impostor king, Artaxerxes, 223; finds record of Cyrus's decree, gives added support to temple project, 223

Dathan, rebels against priesthood authority in wilderness, slain by Jehovah, 65

David, *king of Israel, Jesse's son, descendant of Boaz and Ruth*, 90; anointed king, 103; plays harp for Saul, 104; slays Goliath, 105; lives with Saul, who becomes jealous because of people's love for, 106; Saul seeks to have him killed in battle, 106; marries Saul's daughter Michal, she saves his life, 106; has strong bond of friendship with Saul's son Jonathan, 107; warned by Jonathan to flee for his life, 107; hides from Saul in various places, gains army of 400 men, 108; takes in Abimelech's son Abiathar after Saul has priests slain, 108; has chance to slay Saul as he sleeps in cave, refuses, 109; offended by Nabal, kept from slaying him by Abigail, 110; marries Abigail after Nabal's death, 110; has second chance to slay Saul, still declines, 111; goes to live with Philistines to escape Saul, 112; becomes bodyguard for Philistine King Achish, 112; not allowed to serve in Philistine army to fight Saul, 114; returns to Ziklag, finds city burned and families gone, 114; destroys raiders and rescue families, 114; informed of Saul's and Jonathan's deaths, slays messenger who claims he killed Saul, 116; returns to Hebron, made king of Judah only, 117; becomes king of all Israel upon death of Ishbosheth, 117; mourns death of Abner, slays those who killed Ishbosheth, 117; conquers Jerusalem and brings ark of covenant there, 119; has falling out with Michal, 120; told he will not build temple because he is man of war, 121; honors Jonathan's son Mephibosheth, 122; covets Uriah's wife and commits adultery, has Uriah killed in war, 123; chastened by prophet Nathan, 124; his child by Bathsheba dies, has son Solomon, 124; tricked by son Amnon, 125; has Absalom brought back from exile in Geshur, reconciles, 126; deceived by Absalom, who seeks to depose him, flees from Jerusalem, 127; goes beyond Jordan to Menahem with those who followed him from Jerusalem, 128; his plan to defeat counsel of Ahithophel is carried out by Hushai, 129; his army prevails over Absalom, he mourns Absalom's death, 130; returns triumphant to Jerusalem, forgives those who opposed him, 131; sends army to defeat Sheba the Benjamite, 132; to abate famine he seeks to rectify Saul's slaying of Gibeonites, 133; brings bones of Saul and Jonathan to land of Benjamin, 133; his counting of Judah and Israel brings plague that kills 70,000, 134; offers sacrifice, fire from heaven comes to altar, 134; gathers materials for temple, 135; makes Solomon king to thwart Adonijah, 136; gives Solomon instructions on being king, requests that he deal with enemies, 137; kept warm in old age by Abishag, 138; dies, buried, 137; his enemies dealt with by Solomon, 138

David, *latter-day king*, will feed flock and be prince over them, 204; will be king over people of Judah, Jehovah will be their God, 206

Deborah, *judge of Israel*, frees Israel from Canaanite bondage with Barak as captain, 80

Delilah, *Philistine woman*, causes defeat of Samson, 87

Dinah, *daughter of Jacob and Leah*, born, 28; violated by Shechem, violation avenged by her brothers, 33

Doeg, *Edomite, Saul's chief herdsman*, sees David with Abimelech at Nob, 108; reports this to Saul, slays priests at Saul's command, 108

Ebed-melech, *Ethiopian eunuch*, saves Jeremiah's life, 198

Edomites, *descendants of Esau*, refuse to let Israel pass through their lands, 66; Israel skirts the land of, 67; Solomon takes wives from among, 142; join with Jeroboam, king of Israel, and Jehoshaphat, king of Judah, to fight Moab, victorious, 162; King Ahaziah of Judah fights against, he prevails but brings back their false gods, 177; King Ahaz and Judah attacked by, and many other nations, Assyria invited to Judah's rescue, 181; Jews among them join Gedaliah in Judah, 208

Eglon, *Moabite king*, slain by Ehud, 79

Egyptians, had great influence on Chaldeans, their gods worshipped by Abraham's family and others at Ur, 10; taught by Abraham, 13; welcome Jacob and his family to Goshen, 39; mourn Jacob's death, 41; Israelites feared by, 44; placed heavy burdens on Israelites, 45; Jehovah promises to deliver Israel from, 46; Moses instructed to tell people that Jehovah will deliver them from, 48, 49; suffer severe plagues because Pharaoh will not let Israel go, 49; their firstborn are smitten and die, eager to have Israel leave, 50; give departing Israelites gold, silver, and jewels, 50; follow Israel into wilderness and drown in Red Sea, 51; Israel promised they would not have the diseases of, 52; conquer Judah in fifth year of Rehoboam, take many temple treasures, 145; Syrian army flees for fear of, 169; Assyrians accuse King Hoshea of conspiracy with them, imprison him, 182; send army to deter Chaldeans in Judah, 198; (allegory) harlot Judah commits fornication with, 200; mistakenly counted on by Judah to deliver them from Babylonians, 209; defeated by Nebuchadnezzar and Babylonians, 211

Ehud, *Benjamite judge in Israel*, slays King Eglon, frees Israel from Moab, 79

Elah, *king of Israel, son of Baasha*, slain after one-year reign, 148

El Shaddai, *name for God*, 31

Eldad, *elder of Israel*, praised by Moses for prophesying, 62

Eleazar, *Aaron's son*, Jehovah calls him, his father, and his brothers to be priests, 56; he, Ithamar, and Aaron left alone as priests after deaths of Abihu and Nadab, 61; is trumpeter with Ithamar, 62; becomes presiding priest after Aaron's death, 66

Eleazar, *priest, son of Abinadab*, presides over ark of covenant twenty years at Kirjath-jearim, 95

Eli, *priest and judge in Israel*, sees Hannah praying, tells her she will find God's grace, 91; receives Samuel to raise, 91; warned by man of God because he cannot control wicked sons, 92; tells Samuel that Jehovah is calling him, 93; dies when he learns that the ark is gone and his sons are dead, 94

Eliab, *Jesse's eldest son*, not to become king of Israel, 103; at battlefront when David slays Goliath, 105

Eliakim, *King Hezekiah's agent*, meets, along with others, with Sennacherib's agents, then is sent to find Isaiah, 184

Eliakim (Jehoiakim, king of Judah), 195

Eliashib, *high priest*, allows Tobiah to move into temple courts, 229

Eliezer, *Abram's steward*, son born to, 15

Eliezer, *Moses' son*, leaves for Egypt with family, 48; joins Moses in wilderness, 54

Elihu, questions Job and friends, 43

Elijah, *Tishbite, prophet*, seals heavens to stop rain and dew, 152; is fed by ravens, 152; goes to Zarephath, miraculously provides food for widow, raises her son from dead, 152; returns to Samaria, challenges people to worship either Jehovah or Baal, calls fire from heaven, 153; restores rain, threatened by Jezebel,

154; visited by angel in wilderness and sent to Mt. Horeb, 155; has vision of power but discovers Jehovah is in still, small voice, 155; finds Elisha, joined by him, 155; warns and curses King Ahab in Naboth's vineyard, 157; his prophecy concerning death of King Ahab fulfilled, 158; prophesies to King Ahaziah that he will not recover from his fall, 160; prophesies that King Jehoram's bowels will fall out, 171; taken to heaven in chariot of fire, his mantle taken by Elisha, 161; his prophecy concerning Jezebel's death fulfilled, 173

Elimelech, *Naomi's husband*, takes family from Bethlehem to Moab, dies there, 90

Eliphaz, *friend of Job*, 43

Elisha, *prophet*, leaves plowing to follow Elijah, 155; sees Elijah taken into heaven, takes his mantle, 161; his help is sought by kings of Judah, Israel, and Edom who are fighting against Syria, 162; turns widow's pot of oil into many vessels full, 163; promises Shunammite woman a son, restores the son to life when he dies, 164; his miracles provide food at Gilgal, 165; heals Naaman's leprosy, gives leprosy to his servant Gehazi, 166; causes ax head to float, 167; causes Syrian army to go blind, feeds them and sends them home, 168; prophesies that city under siege (Samaria) would have abundance, 169; foretells murder of King Ben-hadad II by Hazael, 170; sends messenger to anoint Jehu king of Israel, 172; has King Jehoash shoot arrows as a sign of Israel's deliverance from Syria, 176

Elishama, *scribe*, hides book of Jeremiah's prophecies, 195

Elkanah, *Samuel's father, Levite*, he and wives offer yearly sacrifices at Shiloh, 91; blessed by Eli that Hannah will have more children, 93

Enoch, *Cain's son*, 5

Enoch, *Patriarch, prophet, founder of City of Zion*, loves Jehovah and serves righteously, eventually translated with his city, 6; at council at Adam-ondi-Ahman, prophecies of Adam written in Book of, 7; righteous people before flood caught up to be with, 8; rainbow set in clouds as token of Jehovah's covenant with, 8

Enos, *Patriarch, Seth's son*, at council at Adam-ondi-Ahman, 7

Ephraim, *Joseph's second son*, adopted by Jacob as his own son and given blessing of first son, 40; his children seen by Joseph to third generation, 42

Er, *first of Judah's three sons by Canaanite wife*, slain by Jehovah because of wickedness, 36

Esau, *Isaac's first son, Jacob's twin*, sells birthright to Jacob, 23; takes two Hittite women as wives, 25; Jacob tricks Isaac to get the blessing belonging to, 25; hates Jacob and plans to kill him, 25; Jacob, returning home, sends letter to, 31; cordial reunion with Jacob, 32; Isaac dies and is buried by Jacob and, 34

Esther, *orphan Jewess of captivity*, becomes queen of Persia because of beauty, saves Jews from destruction, 224

Ethbaal, *Zidonian king, Jezebel's father*, 150

Ethiopian woman, Moses marries, 63

Eve, *first woman*, created and given to Adam, 3; gives in to Lucifer, eats forbidden fruit, convinces Adam to eat, 3; she and Adam become mortal and are expelled from garden, 3; has sons Cain and Abel, grieves when Cain slays Abel, has son Seth, 4

Evil-merodach, *Nebuchadnezzar's son, Babylonian king*, gives King Jehoiachin of Judah authority over other captive kings in Babylon, 199 (fn. 607); succeeds father in 561 BC, murdered two years later, 211

Ezekiel, *priest, prophet of Judah, descendant of Zadok*, called as prophet to house of Israel while a captive in Babylonia, receives signs to give to people, 199; compares wayward Judah to harlot wife but promises that Jehovah will remember his covenant with her in last days, 200; gives parable comparing Babylonia and Egypt to two great eagles and Jews to cedar tree, 201; to tell Judah that judgment is meted to each person according to his own works, 202; told not to mourn for his wife's death as sign to Judah not to weep for their own sorrow but to have hope for future, 203; warns shepherds of Israel they will be punished for not feeding flock, but Judah will be cleansed in last days, 204; tells people that Judah, though apparently dead, will be restored in last days, 205; prophesies that sticks of Judah and Joseph will become as one, 206; sees in vision temple being rebuilt, water issuing from under threshold to heal and give life, 207

Ezra, *priest, descendant of Eleazar*, commissioned to lead Jewish exiles back to Jerusalem, 225; calls returned Jewish exiles to repentance for taking wives of unbelievers, reads to people from law of Moses, 226; his reading requires separation of believing Ammonites and Moabites from congregation of Jews, 229

Gaal, challenges leadership of Abimelech at Shechem, challenged by Zebul and is defeated, 82

Gabriel, *angel*, appears to Daniel to explain his vision of Israel's future, 217; appears to Daniel to assure him of Jehovah's love and to give understanding, 220

Gad, *son of Jacob and Zilpah*, born, 28; blessed by Jacob, 41

Gad, *prophet*, advises David to leave cave above Adullam, 108; gives David choice of punishment for counting men of Israel, 134; commands David to build altar to stop plague, 134

Gedaliah, *governor of those remaining in Judah after fall of Jerusalem*, appointed governor, sends out word for those scattered to come back, 208; murdered by Johanan, 209

Gehazi, *Elisha's servant*, intermediary between Elisha and Shunammite woman, 164; prepares food at Gilgal, 165; intermediary between Elisha and Naaman, 166; stricken with leprosy because he seeks personal benefit from Naaman, 166

Gershom, *Moses' son*, leaves for Egypt with family, 48; joins Moses in wilderness, 54; his son Jonathan is priest to Micah, then to Danites, 88

Gershon, *one of Levi's three sons*, 61

Geshem, *Arabian*, nemesis to Jews returning from Babylon, 227

Gibeonites, trick Joshua and elders into making covenant of peace, 77; Israel makes no allies except with, 78; seven descendants of Saul slain to appease, 133

Gog, *head of army from Magog*, to lose battle against house of Israel, 207

Gideon, *judge in Israel, Joash's son*, called by angel to lead Israel against Midianites, 81; destroys altar of Baal, 81; asks for and receives signs about validity of his calling, 81; gathers army, then instructed to send all but 300 home so Jehovah's power can be manifest, 81; goes with Phurah to eavesdrop on Midianites, 81; puts army of Midianites to flight, 81; has many wives and seventy sons, 82

Gileadites, seek leadership of Jephthah to fight Ammonites, 83; slay Ephraimites who attack them for unjust cause, 84; give succor to David during exile, 130; taken captive by Assyrians, 180

Goliath, *giant of Gath*, challenges army of Israel, slain by David, 105

Hadassah (Esther), 224

Hagar, *Abram's concubine, mother of Ishmael*, sent away when she treats Sarai harshly, returns, 15; sent away again with Ishmael, preserved by angel showing her water, 19

Haggai, *prophet*, urges resumption of work on temple, labors personally, 223

Haggith, *David's wife, Adonijah's mother*, supports son's attempt to usurp throne of Israel, 136

Ham, *Noah's son*, saved on ark, 8; his grandson Nimrod is leader of tower builders, 9

Haman, *Agagite*, seeks destruction of Jews in Persian Empire, destroyed himself, 224

Hamor, *Shechem's father*, petitions Jacob for Dinah to be Shechem's wife, 33

Hanameel, *Jeremiah's cousin*, brings word of land available for redemption, 198

Hanani, *prophet of Judah*, rebukes King Asa for alliance with Syria, put in stocks, 148

Hanani, *overseer of Jerusalem*, given charge by Nehemiah, 227

Hananiah, *false prophet in Judah*, falsely prophesies that Judah will be victorious over the Babylonians, rebuked by Jeremiah, dies, 197

Hananiah (Shadrach) 212

Hannah, *Elkanah's wife, Samuel's mother*, prays to have a child, blessed by Eli, 91; has son Samuel, gives him to Jehovah in Eli's care, 91; blessed with more children, 93

Haran, *Abram's (Abraham's) brother*, dies from famine in Ur, his son Lot goes with Abram, 10

Hazael, *Syrian king*, Elijah told to anoint him king of Syria, 155; murders Ben-hadad II, becomes king, 170; at war with Israel (Jehoram) and Judah (Ahaziah), 172; leads small army to victory over Judah, 175; Israel delivered into his hands and greatly oppressed because of their wickedness, 176; dies, 176

Heber the Kenite, tells Sisera that Deborah's army had gone to Mt. Tabor, 80; his wife slays Sisera, 80

Hezekiah, *king of Judah, son of Ahaz*, reopens temple, reinstitutes Passover, reigns in righteousness, 183; stands up to Assyrian invasion and siege, makes alliance with Egypt, angel of death visits Assyrian army, 184; Is given additional fifteen years of life, 185; shows all treasures to Babylonian visitors, 186; dies 188

Hiel, rebuilds Jericho, his sons die, 151

Hilkiah, *high priest, Jeremiah's father*, finds book of Law in temple, 189

Hirah, *Judah's friend*, 36

Hiram, *king of Tyre*, provides cedar wood and laborers for temple, 119, 141 (fn. 371)

Hittites, Esau marries two women of, 25; Israel's spies find them in mountains of promised land, 64; Solomon takes wives from among, 142; Syrian army flees for fear of, 169; called mother of harlot Israel (allegory), 200

Hivites, Israel worships gods of, 79

Hophni, *Eli's son, priest, wicked man*, Eli warned to correct him but does not, 92; he and brother Phinehas take ark of covenant to battlefront, slain in battle, 94

Hoshea, *king of Israel*, slays King Pekah and becomes king, 182; made a servant to Assyrians, Samaria is conquered and people are taken captive, 182

Huldah, *prophetess*, King Josiah sends five men to seek her counsel, she gives good report, 189

Hur, he and Aaron lift Moses' arms during Amalekite battle, 53; he and Aaron to handle problems while Moses in mount, 56; returns to main camp when

Moses does not come from the mountain, 57

Hushai, *David's friend,* sent by David to discredit counsel of Ahithophel before Absalom, 127; wins Absalom's trust and discredits Ahithophel, 129

Hystaspes, *Persian prince of Anshan, Darius's father,* conspires in overthrow of Artaxerxes the impostor, 222 (fn. 705)

Irad, *Cain's grandson, Enoch's son,* slain by Lamech, 5

Irijah, *man of Benjamin,* puts Jeremiah in jail, 198

Isaac, *Patriarch, son of Abraham and Sarah,* Jehovah tells Abraham that Isaac is the name for his son, covenant to be established through him, 16; mocking of, by Ishmael causes Hagar and Ishmael to be sent away, 19; Abraham commanded to offer, as sacrifice, restrained, 20; servant goes to Haran and finds wife for, 21; Keturah's sons sent away from, 22; his twin sons, Esau and Jacob are born to Rebekah, 23; redigs Abraham's wells in Gerar, envied and rejected, 24; tricked into giving Esau's blessing to Jacob, 25; sends Jacob to house of Laban, 26; dies, buried by Esau and Jacob, 34

Isaiah, *prophet,* sent to warn King Ahaz of coming invasion of Judah by Israel and Syria, 184; King Hezekiah sends elders to seek counsel of, 184; promises King Hezekiah fifteen more years of life, 185; reproves Hezekiah for showing riches to Babylonians, 186; prophesies of sealed book to come forth in last days, 187; prophesies concerning Cyrus, 222

Ishbak, *son of Abraham and Keturah,* 22

Ishbosheth, *Saul's son,* becomes king of Israel after Saul's death, 117; David's men, under Joab, fight with his men, under Abner, 118; murdered by two of his captains, David laments death of, then slays his murderers, 117

Ishmael, *son of Abraham and Hagar,* born and named, 15; not birthright son, 16; sent away with Hagar when he mocks Isaac, preserved in wilderness by angel, 19; to become father of great nation, takes Egyptian wife, 19

Ishmael, *Nethaniah's son, military leader,* warns Gedaliah of Johanan's plot to kill him, not believed, 209

Ishmaelites, Joseph's brothers sell him to, 35; sell Joseph to Potiphar, 35, 37

Ishtar, *false goddess of Greeks and Romans,* 79 (fn. 185)

Israel, Jacob's name changed to, 31

Issachar, *son of Jacob and Leah,* born, 28; blessed by Jacob, 41

Ithamar, *Aaron's son,* Jehovah calls him, his father, and his brothers to be priests, 56; he, Eleazar, and Aaron left alone as priests after deaths of Abihu and Nadab, 61; is trumpeter with Eleazar, 62

Ittai, *Gittite,* commands third of David's army against Absalom, 130

Jabal, *Lamech's son,* 5

Jabin, *Canaanite king,* defeated by Deborah and Barak, 80

Jacob, *Patriarch, prophet,* born, 23; buys Esau's birthright, 23; receives Esau's blessing, 25; life threatened by Esau, 25; dreams of ladder to heaven, 26; meets Rachel and her family, works for Laban, 27; has twelve children by four wives at Padan-aram, 28; prospers in Laban's service, 29; leaves Padan-aram secretly, makes peace covenant with Laban, 30; wrestles with angel (Jehovah), is named Israel, 31; reunites with Esau on good terms, 32; his sons kill Shechem, 33; son Benjamin is born, Rachel dies, 34; he and Esau bury Isaac, 34; shows favoritism to Joseph, crushed by report of Joseph's death, 35; sends sons to Egypt for grain, 39; rejoices to find Joseph alive, goes to live in Egypt, 39; blesses Ephraim and Manasseh, 40; blesses his sons, 41; dies in Egypt, buried in Hebron, 41

Jael, *wife of Heber the Kenite,* slays Sisera with nail through head, 80

Jahaziel, *Zechariah's son,* prophesies that Jehovah will fight battle for Judah, 159

Japheth, *Noah's son,* saved on ark, 8

Jared, *Patriarch, Mahalaleel's son, Enoch's father,* taught ways of God to Enoch, 6; at Adam-ondi-Ahman, 7

Jared, *Book of Mormon prophet,* his language, and that of his friends and family, preserved at tower, led to promised land, 9

359

Jebusites, *former inhabitants of Jerusalem*, Israel's spies find them in mountains of promised land, 64; conquered by King David, 119

Jeconiah (Jehoiachin, king of Judah), 196 (fn. 596); false prophecy concerning, 197

Jedidiah (Solomon), 124

Jehoahaz (Azariah, king of Judah), 171 (fn. 480)

Jehoahaz, *king of Israel, Jehu's son*, Israel is delivered into hands of Syria because of his wickedness, prays for deliverance, deliverance comes, but not soon, 176

Jehoahaz, *king of Judah, Josiah's son*, succeeds father on throne, 189; imprisoned at Riplah by Pharaoh-necho, 195

Jehoash, *king of Israel, Jehoahaz's son*, fights against Judah and causes great suffering, 176; shoots three arrows toward Syria, as Elisha's directs, prevails over Syria three times, 176; challenged, then attacked, by King Amaziah of Judah, he prevails, 177; dies, succeeded by son Jeroboam II, 178

Jehoiachin, *king of Judah, Jehoiakim's son*, becomes king at age eight, taken captive to Babylon, 196

Jehoiada, *priest*, devises plot, then overthrows Athalilah and installs Joash as king of Judah, 174; mentors young Joash 175

Jehoiakim, *king of Judah, Josiah's son*, wishes to kill Jeremiah, overruled by princes, 193; succeeds brother Jehoahaz, name changed from Eliakim, 195; burns Jeremiah's prophecies, 195; taken captive to Babylon, 195; brother of King Zedekiah, 196

Jehonadab, *Rechabite*, helps Jehu destroy Baal worshippers, 173

Jehoram, *king of Israel, Ahab's son*, succeeds brother Ahaziah, 160, 162; prevails, with Judah and Edom, in war against Moab, 162; visited by Naaman with request for healing, 166; gets military intelligence about Syrians from Elisha, 168; blames Elisha for Syria's siege of Samaria, 169

Jehoram, *king of Judah, Jehoshaphat's son*, succeeds father to throne, marries Athaliah, daughter of Ahab, 171; Elijah prophesies that his bowels will fall out, prophecy fulfilled, 171; succeeded by son Ahaziah,

Jehoshabeath (Jehosheba), 174 (fn. 500)

Jehoshaphat, *king of Judah, Asa's son*, succeeds father, is greatly renowned, teaches people law of Moses, 149; joins with King Ahab of Judah to fight Syria, 158; his alliance with Ahab displeases Jehovah, 159; Jehovah gives him victory over Judah's invaders without fighting, 159; prevails, with Israel and Edom, in war against Moab, 162; dies, succeeded by son Jehoram, 171

Jehosheba, *Jehoram's daughter and Ahaziah's sister*, saves young Joash from death sentence of Athaliah, 174

Jehu, *prophet, Hanani's son*, criticizes Jehoshaphat for allying with King Ahab of Israel, 159

Jehu, *king of Israel*, Elijah told to anoint, king of Israel, 155; young man sent by Elisha anoints him king, 172; goes to Jezreel where he slays Jehoram, Ahaziah, and Jezebel, 172; slays all Baal worshippers in Israel, 173; dies, succeeded by son Jehoahaz, 175

Jehudi, reads Jeremiah's prophecies to King Jehoiakim, 195

Jemima, *Job's daughter*, 43

Jephthah, *judge in Israel*, leads people of Gilead to defeat Ammonites in battle, 83; sacrifices his daughter because of oath, 83; fights Ephraimites who come to destroy him because he went to battle without them, 84

Jeremiah, *prophet, son of Hilkiah the priest*, condemns Israel for King Manasseh's wickedness, 188; called as prophet to all nations, 190; shown by Jehovah, using a girdle as a type, how Judah would be marred, 191; shown by Jehovah that man is as clay in potter's hands, 192; people want to kill him when he tells of coming judgments, saved by princes, 193; foretells judgments coming to Tophet, put in stocks, 194; his prophecies are read to King Jehoiakim who burns them, 195; King Zedekiah and people of Judah refuse to believe his message, 196; prophesies death of false prophet Hananiah, 197; warns Jews that Egypt will not save them, imprisoned, predicts captivity of Zedekiah unless he surrenders to Chaldeans, 198; released, after fall of Jerusalem, and joins with Gedaliah, 208; refugees do not believe his prophecy and take him to Egypt, 209; prophesies destruction of

fense, 106; when unable to dissuade Saul, shoots arrows to warn David, sends him away, 107; visits David in woods to lend support, 109; killed in battle, along with father and two brothers, 115; news of death comes to David, 116; his bones returned to land of his fathers, 133

Jonathan, *son of Abiathar the priest*, returns to Jerusalem with his father as David flees, 127; Hushai's message delivered to David by Ahimaaz and, 129; brings news to Adonijah that Solomon has been anointed king, 136

Joram (Jehoram, son of King Jehoshaphat), 171 (fns. 460, 466)

Joseph, *son of Jacob and Rachel*, born, 28; put in rear of company with his mother when Jacob meets Esau, 32; his dreams upset his family, 35; sold to Ishmaelite traders, taken to Egypt, 35; becomes trusted overseer of Potiphar's house, rejects advances of Potiphar's wife and goes to prison, 37; interpretation of dreams gets him out of prison to interpret Pharaoh's dream, 38; made ruler of Egypt to prepare for famine, 38; his brothers come to Egypt for grain, he brings them and his father to live in Egypt, 39; blessed by Jacob, 41; buries father in Hebron, 41; makes prophecies of Moses delivering Israel from Egypt and of a latter-day seer named Joseph, 42; makes brethren swear to carry his coffin out of Egypt when they are delivered, 42; dies, 42; his bones are carried out of Egypt, 51; his bones are buried at Shechem, 78

Joshua, *Nun's son, prophet*, takes chosen army to fight Amalekites, 53; goes into mount with Moses, waits halfway up, 56; returns to camp with Moses to find Israel worshipping golden calf, 57; criticizes Eldad and Medad for prophesying, 62; serves as spy from tribe of Ephraim, gives faithful report, nearly stoned, 64; promised he will enter promised land, 64; named to be Moses' successor, given priesthood, 70; becomes leader of Israel after mourning for Moses is over, 71; receives instructions from Jehovah, sends spies to Jericho, 72; takes Israel over Jordan on dry ground, 73; encounters captain of Jehovah's army, 74; leads Israel in capturing and destroying Jericho, 75; his army fails at Ai because someone took spoils at Jericho, he identifies the man, 76; believes Gibeonites' story and makes peace covenant with them, 77; leads Israel in conquering peoples of Canaan, gives land inheritance to each tribe, 78; challenges Israel to choose between false gods and Jehovah, 8

Joshua, *priest*, assistant to Zerubbabel in rebuilding temple, 123

Josiah, *king of Judah, Amon's son*, his works prophesied to Jeroboam by prophet of Judah at Beth-el, 144; when book of Law is found during temple repairs, he fears for his people who have not followed the law, 189; reads law to the people, burns idols and destroys altars, fulfilling earlier prophecy, reinstitutes Passover, 189; slain by Pharaoh-necho, 189

Jotham, *Gideon's youngest son*, he alone of the sixty-eight sons of Gideon escapes assassination by his brother Abimelech, tells people of Shechem parable of the trees and the thistle, 82

Jotham, *king of Judah, Uzziah's son, Ahaz's father*, acted as king in his father's behalf when father stricken with leprosy, 178, 181; undertakes rebuilding of Jerusalem walls, builds other cities, defeats Ammonites, 181; dies, succeeded by Ahaz, 181

Jubal, *Lamech's son*, 5

Judah, *son of Jacob and Leah*, born, 28; convinces brothers to sell Joseph to Ishmaelites, 35; has twin sons by daughter-in-law Tamar after death of two eldest sons, 36; convinces Jacob to send Benjamin to Egypt with them, 39; offers to take punishment instead of Benjamin for "stolen" silver cup, 39; blessed by Jacob, 41

Judith, *Esau's wife, Hittite*, 25

Kenites, origin of, 80 (fn. 188), warned to separate from Amalekites before battle, 102

Keren-happuch, *Job's daughter*, 43

Keturah, *Abraham's wife*, 22

Kezia, *Job's daughter*, 43

Khudur-lagamar (Chedorlaomer), 14 (fn. 32)

Kish, *Saul's father*, Saul's and Jonathan's bones buried in his sepulcher, 133

Kishon, *Levi's son, Moses' grandfather*, his descendants chosen to serve in tabernacle, numbered, 61

Kohath, *one of Levi's three sons*, 61

Korah, *Levite*, rebels against priesthood authority in

wilderness, slain, 65

Laban, *Bethuel's son, Rebekah's brother, Leah and Rachel's father*, entertains Abraham's servant, agrees his sister Rebekah should marry Isaac, 21; Rebekah proposes that Jacob go and live with him, 25; Isaac tells Jacob to go to his house to seek a wife, 26; Jacob is brought by Rachel to house of, stays there, 27; gives his daughters to be Jacob's wives for fourteen years' labor, 27; makes agreement for Jacob's service with cattle as compensation, continually changes the terms, 29; when his relationship with Jacob becomes strained, Jacob and his family leave secretly, 30; follows Jacob, makes peace covenant with him, 30

Lamech, *Methusael's son, descendant of Cain*, kills Irad, makes covenant with Satan, tells secret to his wives, cursed and cast out, 5

Leah, *Laban's older daughter*, given to Jacob as wife instead of Rachel, 27; receives Zilpah as handmaid, 27; bears six sons and one daughter, gives Zilpah to be Joseph's wife, 28; feels Laban has been unfair, agrees to leave Padan-aram, 29; meets Esau, 32; buried at Hebron with Jacob's parents and grandparents, 41

Lehi, *Book of Mormon prophet*, his preaching to Jews is rejected, 196

Levi, *son of Jacob and Leah*, born, 28; he and Simeon murder people of Shechem for Dinah's honor, 33; blessed by Jacob, 41

Levites, *descendants of Levi*, called to assist priests in tabernacle, 61; belong to Jehovah in place of firstborn, 61; descendants of each of Levi's three sons counted, given specific duties, 61; no inheritance of land, to be sustained with tithes, 61; carry tabernacle and ark of covenant in wilderness, 62; given forty-eight cities in promised land, 70; receive ark of covenant back from Philistines, 95; leave Jerusalem with fleeing David, 127; David teaches Solomon how to organize them, 135; Jeroboam disregards their lineage and they flee to Judah, 143, 145; sent by Jehoshaphat to teach Judah the Law of Jehovah, 149; Jehoshaphat makes them judges over the people, 159; praise Jehovah for delivering Judah from her enemies, 159; Jehoiadah appoints them as gatekeepers (porters) at temple, 174; Joash has them collect money for temple repairs, 175; Hezekiah instructs them in their duties, 183; carry impurities out of temple to brook Kidron, 183; play musical instruments and help priest with sacrifices, 183; after return from Babylon, play cymbals as foundation of reconstructed temple is laid, those who remember former temple shout for joy, 222; perform required service after temple is completed, 223; King Artaxerxes exempts them from tolls, tributes, and customs, 225; displaced by Tobiah and sent out of temple, 229; when brought back to temple by Nehemiah, Jews covenant to pay tithes to support them, 229; provide music when city walls are dedicated, purify themselves, 229

Lot, *Haran's son, Abraham's nephew*, goes with Abraham from Ur to live in Haran, 10; goes with Abraham to Egypt, 13; given choice of lands by Abraham, chooses Sodom and fertile plain of Jordan, 11; is rescued by Abraham from Babylonian captors, 14; delivered from Sodom before its destruction, 17; becomes father of Moabites and Ammonites, 17

Lucifer, offers to be Savior, 1; rebels when his offer is rejected, cast out of heaven with followers, becomes Satan, 1; tempts Adam and Eve, 3; Adam's children love him more than God, 4; Cain swears secret oath to him that he will murder to get gain, 4; Lamech makes covenant with him to preserve his secret, 5; his power is rampant in land after City of Zion is gone, 6; Abraham sees him being cast out of heaven, 13; he is allowed by Jehovah to smite and tempt Job, 43; pretends to be God, commands Moses to worship him, 47; David yields to him, counts Israel, 134

Maachah (Michaiah), 147 (fn. 411)

Magor-missabib, name given by Jeremiah to Pashur, 194

Mahalaleel, *Patriarch, Cainan's son, Jared's father*, at council at Adam-ondi-Ahman, 7

Mahlon, *son of Elimelech and Naomi, Ruth's first husband*, dies in Moab, 90

Mahonri Moriancumer, see Moriancumer

Malchishua, *Saul's son*, dies in battle, 115

Manasseh, *Joseph's eldest son*, Jacob adopts as own son and gives him blessing of second son, 40; Joseph sees his children to third generation, 42

Manasseh, *king of Judah, Hezekiah's son*, born after father's life is extended, becomes king when twelve years old, reigns fifty-five years, 188; Assyrian army

363

is brought against Judah because of his wickedness, more wicked than any other king, 188; taken captive to Assyria, repents and returns, 188; his wickedness assures Judah's captivity, 189

Manoah, *Samson's father*, he and barren wife visited by angel, promised son who would begin to deliver Israel, 85; he disapproves Samson's choice of wife, 86

Mara, name that Naomi calls herself, meaning "bitter" or "very sad," 90

Matri, *ancestor of King Saul*, 98

Mattaniah (Zedekiah), name changed by King Nebuchadnezzar, 196

Medad, *elder of Israel*, praised by Moses for prophesying, 62

Medan, *son of Abraham and Keturah*, 22

Medes, conquered by Persians, two empires combined, 211; Daniel reads writing on wall telling of fall of Babylonia to Persians and, 218; laws unalterable if signed by king, 219

Mehujael, *Irad's son, descendant of Cain*, 5

Melchi-shua (Malchishua), 115

Melchizedek, *great high priest*, ordains Abraham to priesthood, 10; administers bread and wine to Abraham and companions when returning from battle of kings, 14; Abraham pays tithing to, 14

Memucan, *one of seven Persian princes*, suggests that King Ahasuerus remove Queen Vashti and choose new queen so wives will obey husbands, 224

Menahem, *king of Israel*, murders Shallum and becomes king, 180; Assyrians invade Israel during his reign, he levies tax to pay tribute, 180; dies, son Pekahiah succeeds him as king, 180

Mephibosheth, *lame son of Jonathan*, honored by David in reverence to his friend, Ziba and his sons appointed to care for his land, 122; Ziba tells David that he wants to be king, 128; comes out to meet David when he returns to Jerusalem, says Ziba lied, 131; spared when Gibeonites ask to hang up seven of Saul's descendants, 133

Merab, *Saul's eldest daughter*, offered to David as a

wife, then given to another, 106; her five sons given to Gibeonites to be hanged up in Gibeah, 133

Merari, *one of Levi's three sons*, 61

Merodach-baladan, *son of King Baladan of Babylonia*, his messengers are shown all treasures of Hezekiah's kingdom, 186

Meshach, *Jewish captive in Babylon*, with Daniel, Shadrach, and Abednego, in special training program in Babylon, prospers on special diet, 212; prays for Daniel to interpret king's dream, rewarded with administrative office, 213; refuses to bow before golden idol, thrown into fiery furnace, 214

Methusael, *Mehujael's son, Cain's descendant*, 5

Methuselah, *Patriarch, Enoch's son, Lamech's father*, at council at Adam-ondi-Ahman, 7

Micah, hires Moses' grandson Jonathan to be his priest, loses him to Danites, 88

Micaiah, *prophet of Israel*, foretells Ahab's defeat by the Syrians, 158

Michael (Adam), honored at council at Adam-ondi-Ahman, 7; supports Jehovah in defeat of Persians by Grecia, 221; at time of great trouble among Jews, he shall stand up in behalf of the people, 221; see also Adam

Michaiah (or Maachah), *wife of Rehoboam, granddaughter of Absalom, Abijam's mother*, 147 (fn. 411)

Michaiah, *grandson of King Jehoiakim's scribe*, hears Baruch reading Jeremiah's prophecies and tells princes of Judah, 195

Michal, *Saul's daughter*, Saul tries to use her as bait to cause David's death, she becomes David's wife, 106; saves David when Saul seeks to kill him, 106; she and Jonathan only members of Saul's household not seeking David's life, 107; taken from David by Saul and given to Phaltiel, 112 (fn. 268), 117 (fn. 290); David requests Abner to get her back from Phaltiel as condition for uniting kingdoms, she is returned, 117; sees David dance before ark of covenant, hates him and is spurned by him, 120

Midian, *son of Abraham and Keturah*, 22

Midianites, Moses goes to land of, 45; lead Israelites to

sin, 69; defeated by Gideon, 81; Kenites a tribe of, 102 (fn. 243)

Milcah, *Nahor's wife and Bethuel's mother*, 21

Miriam, *Moses' sister*, watches over baby Moses' basket among reeds, gets her mother to nurse baby for princess, 44; plays timbrels (drums) and dances as Israel celebrates, 52; is called to account for speaking against Moses, stricken with leprosy, 63

Mishael (Meshach), 212

Moabites, *descendants of Lot,* 17; have great fear of Israelites in wilderness, 68; hold Israel in bondage until freed by Ehud, 79; Elimelech and Naomi go to live among, 90; Solomon takes wives from among, worships their gods, 142; come with Ammonites and people of Mt. Seir to conquer Judah, destroy each other, 159; fall to Israel, Judah, and Edom after Elisha's blessing, 162; Jews among them join Gedaliah in Judah, 208; banned from congregation of Jews because their fathers failed to help Israel in wilderness, 229

Molech, *false god of Ammonites*, Solomon worships, 142

Mordecai, *Esther's cousin*, supports her efforts and encourages her to use her position to save her people, is honored with high position, 224

Moriancumer, *brother of Jared,* in Book of Mormon, 9 (fn. 25)

Moroni, *Book of Mormon prophet*, 206 (fn. 625)

Moses, *son of Amram and Jochebed*, born when Hebrew baby boys were to be killed, placed in basket at river's edge, claimed by Pharaoh's daughter who has Jochebed raise him, 44; schooled in Pharaoh's court, named Moses, 44; kills Egyptian taskmaster, flees to Midian, 45; taken in by Jethro for helping daughters at well, 45; tends Jethro's sheep and marries his daughter Zipporah, 45; ordained to priesthood, 45; called by Jehovah from burning bush to free Israel, 46; is shown signs by Jehovah and given his brother Aaron to assist him, 46; sees glorious visions, has confrontation with Satan, he wins, sees another glorious vision, 47; takes his family to Egypt, meets Aaron on the way, 48; meets with elders of Israel and shows signs, then with Pharaoh, who refuses to let Israel go, 48; when Pharaoh declines to let Israel go, Moses brings plagues, 49; brings final plague of death to firstborn of Egypt while Israel is passed over, departs Egypt with his people, 50; takes Israel across Red Sea on dry land, Pharaoh's army drowns, 51; makes bitter water sweet, gives meat and manna to Israel, 52; brings water from rock at Horeb, 52; attacked by Amalekites, sends army to fight them, prevails when hands and rod are raised, 53; counseled by Jethro to delegate responsibility, 54; called by Jehovah to go up into Mt. Sinai, 55; instructed by Jehovah to prepare the people to meet him on third day, leads them to base of mountain, then goes to summit, warning people not to go onto mountain, 55; takes Aaron with him to mountain top, receives Ten Commandments, instructs the people then returns to mountain for more instructions, 55; commanded to bring Aaron, two of Aaron's sons, and seventy elders to the mountain, they see Jehovah, 56; he goes into mountain for forty days with Joshua, receives Jehovah's law on stone tablets, 56; returns from mountain to find Israel worshipping golden calf, breaks the tablets, grinds up calf, has Levites slay the unrepentant, 57; hews new stone tablets, returns to mountain, Ten Commandments and lesser law written on the tablets, 58; veils his face as he teaches people because of brilliance, 58; instructs people on building tabernacle and ark of covenant, they build them, 59; anoints Aaron, sons, and tabernacle, dresses them in sacred clothing, talks to Jehovah face-to-face in door of tabernacle, 60; pleads for Jehovah to forgive his people and go before them into promised land, 60; told that Levites are Jehovah's in place of firstborn and will assist priests, 61; makes two silver trumpets to be blown by Eleazar and Ithamar to communicate with people, 62; goes to Jehovah in frustration for ungrateful people, asks to be killed and relieved of his misery, request denied, 62; questions Jehovah when he promises meat, 62; teaches elders to help him govern people, tells Joshua not to criticize prophesying of Eldad and Medad, 62; criticized openly by Aaron and Miriam for marrying Ethiopian woman, they are punished—Miriam with leprosy, 63; sends spies into Canaan, Israel to spend forty years in wilderness because of spies' bad report, 64; refutes those who question priesthood authority, instigators slain by Jehovah, plague kills many more, 65; gets rod from head of each tribe, puts them together in tabernacle, Aaron's rod has budded, bloomed, and yielded almonds by next day, 65; he and Aaron offend Jehovah by not following instructions: strikes rock twice to bring forth water, rather than speaking to it, told they will not enter promised land, 66; takes Aaron and Eleazar into mountain, where he removes Aaron's sacred clothing and puts it on Eleazar, Aaron dies, 66; puts brass serpent on pole to heal serpent bites,

67; has judges slay Israelites who worship Baal-peor, 69; counts each tribe in preparation for entering promised land, 70; requests Jehovah to name his replacement, Joshua chosen and ordained, 70; rehearses experiences in wilderness, clarifies law, and gives final instructions, warns about kings and prophesies of Christ, 71; tells Joshua and elders that he knows the people will turn from commandments and corrupt themselves after his death, 71; pronounces last blessing on Israel, 71; goes onto mountain and views promised land, 71; is taken into heaven without tasting death, 71

Mulek, *King Zedekiah's son*, escapes from Babylonians, brought by hand of Jehovah to Americas, 208

Naamah, *daughter of Lamech and Zilla, descendant of Cain*, 5

Naamah, *Ammonite princess, wife of Solomon, and mother of Rehoboam*, 143 (fn. 391)

Naaman, *captain of Syrian army*, healed of leprosy by following Elisha's instructions to bathe seven times in Jordan, 166

Nabal, *descendant of Caleb, Abigail's husband*, offends David and his men, saved by Abigail's gifts and pleadings, 110; dies, Abigail marries David, 110

Nabonidus, *last king of Babylonia*, marries Nitocris, is Belshazzar's father, 211, 218

Nabopolassar, *Nebuchadnezzar's father*, viceroy of Babylon, makes himself king and overthrows Assyrian empire, dies 604 BC, 211

Naboth, stoned to death and vineyard taken from him by Jezebel because he refused to sell to Ahab, 157; sons also killed, 172

Nachon, owned threshing floor where ox stumbled while taking ark of covenant to Jerusalem, 119

Nadab, *Aaron's son*, goes out, with others, to meet Jehovah at Mt. Sinai, 56; Jehovah calls him, his father, and his brothers to be priests, 56; slain by Jehovah, with brother Abihu, for using strange fire, 61

Nadab, *king of Israel, son of Jeroboam*, reigns two years in wickedness, 148; killed by Baasha, 148

Nahash, *Ammonite king*, invades Jabesh-gilead, provides first victory for King Saul, 99

Nahor, *Abraham's brother*, 10; has wife Milcah and son Bethuel, 21

Naomi, *Elimelech's wife, Ruth's mother-in-law*, returns to Bethlehem when husband and sons die in Moab, brings Ruth, 90

Naphtali, *son of Jacob and Bilhah*, born, 28; blessed by Jacob, 41

Nathan, *prophet*, encourages David for his desire to build temple, retracts when Jehovah gives different message, 121; tells David parable of ewe lamb, pronounces curse, 124; when not invited to Adonijah's feast, he and Bathsheba advise David of the insurrection, 136; he and Zadok anoint Solomon as king, 136

Nathan, son of David and Bathsheba, 124 (fn. 308)

Nebuchadnezzar, *king of Babylon, Nabopolassar's son*, conquers Egypt in 605 BC, comes to throne in 604 BC when father dies, 211; takes Daniel and other mighty men of Judah captive, puts them in training to serve in his palace, 212; his dream of a great image interpreted by Daniel, 213; invades Judah, takes King Jehoiakim captive to Babylon, takes temple vessels to Babylon, 195; appoints Mattaniah king of Judah and changes his name to Zedekiah, 196; throws Shadrach, Meshach, and Abednego into fiery furnace for refusing to worship giant image, 214; conquers all of Judah except Jerusalem, lays siege to Jerusalem, 211; Jeremiah tells Zedekiah that if he will serve him, he will be spared, 196; false prophet Hananiah prophesies defeat of, 197; Ezekiel is captive of, 199; lays siege against Jerusalem in ninth year of Zedekiah's reign, city falls in eleventh year, 208; captures Zedekiah and puts out his eyes, kills his sons, takes him to Babylon in chains, 208; names Gedaliah governor of remnant not taken captive, 208; remnant goes to Egypt after Gedaliah's murder because they fear him, 209; his conquest of Egypt prophesied by Jeremiah, 209; Jeremiah prophesies that Pharaoh will be delivered into his hands, 210; conquers Egypt, scatters people, then leaves, 211; he is less concerned with building empire after attacking Egypt, concentrates on building Babylon, 211; his dream of great tree interpreted by Daniel, 215; suffers mental illness for seven years, 211; dies in 561 BC, succeeded by son Evil-merodach, 211

Nebuzar-adan, *captain of Babylonian guard*, burns temple and city of Jerusalem, 208

Nehemiah, *cupbearer in palace of King Artaxerxes of Persia*, made governor of Judea by king, sent to Jerusalem with charge to rebuild city walls, 227; tells Jews of his assignment and rallies them to rebuild the walls, task completed in spite of opposition, 227; returns to Jerusalem to find many problems, rebukes nobles who hold poorer brethren in bondage, 228; serves twelve years without compensation, feeds 150 Jews at own table, gives freely to those in need, devotes full time and energy to building walls, 228; swears oath, along with the people, to keep God's laws or be cursed, 229; gives Hanani charge over city and control of gates, returns to Persia, 227; comes back from Persia, throws Tobiah out of temple, restores temple vessels and Levites whom Tobiah had displaced, 229; commits people to keep Sabbath and put away heathen wives, 229

Nergal, *false god of people from Cuth* who settled in Samaria after Israel's capture by Assyrians, 182 (fn. 549)

Nergal-sharezer (Neriglissar), 212

Neriglissar, *Babylonian king, Nebuchadnezzar's son-in-law* because of his marriage to Nitocris, murders Evil-merodach and takes throne, dies 556 BC, 211

Niblaz, *false god of Avites* who settle in Samaria after Israel is captured by Assyrians, 182 (fn. 551)

Nimrod, *Ham's grandson, mighty hunter*, leader of people of Shinar who build city and Tower of Babel, 9; 182 (fn. 549)

Nisroch, *false god of Assyrians*, 184

Nitocris, *daughter of Nebuchadnezzar, wife of Neriglissar, then wife of Nabonidus*, 211

Noah, *Patriarch, prophet, son of Lamech*, builds ark at Jehovah's command, he, his family, and animal species are saved from flood, 8; convinces Jehovah to make covenant to never again destroy the earth by flood, 8

Obadiah, *God-fearing governor of King Ahab's house*, hides 110 prophets to save them from Jezebel, 153; meets Elijah returning from Zarephath, summons Ahab, 153; his widow blessed by Elisha to multiply oil and pay her debts, 163

Obed, *Boaz and Ruth's son, Jesse's father, and David's grandfather*, born, 90

Obed-edom, *Gittite*, ark of covenant taken to house of, when Uzzah is stricken, 119

Oded, *prophet*, meets Pekah's victorious army with captive people of Judah, pleads for their release, 181

Omri, *king of Israel, Ahab's father*, when army rises up to make him king, King Zimri burns himself in king's palace, 148; prevails over Tibni to unite divided kingdom, 150; moves Israel's capitol from Tirzah to Samaria, 150; dies, succeeded by Ahab, 150

Onan, *second of Judah's three sons by Canaanite wife*, refused to have children by Tamar that would be counted seed of his brother Er, slain by Jehovah, 36

Ornan (Araunah), 134 (fn. 343)

Orpah, *Naomi's daughter-in-law, Chilion's widow*, stays in Moab, 90

Othniel, *judge in Israel, Caleb's nephew*, frees Israel from bondage to Mesopotamia, 79

Pashur, *son of Immer the priest, chief governor of temple*, puts Jeremiah in stocks for speaking against Judah, 194; Jeremiah prophesies that he will die in Babylon, 194

Pekah, *Remaliah's son, king of Israel*, slays King Pekahiah, takes throne, 180; joins with King Rezin of Syria to defeat Judah and replace King Ahaz, they fail, 180; Judah devastated by his invading army, but does not fall, 181; many people taken captive by Assyrians during his reign, 180

Pekahiah, *king of Israel, Menahem's son*, succeeds father, killed by his servant Pekah, 180

Peninnah, *Elkanah's wife*, has sons and daughters, torments childless Hannah, 91

Persians, conquer Medes in 550 BC, then conquer Babylonians, 211; in Daniel's dream, the ram and its two horns are kings of Medes and, 217; decrees signed by their kings are unalterable, 219; are to have three kings, then be conquered by richer king, 221; allow captive peoples to return to homelands, 222; empire has 127 provinces from India to Ethiopia, 224

Phaltiel, *Michal's other husband*, Michal taken from David by Saul and given to, 112 (fn. 268), 117 (fn. 290); Michal taken from him and returned to David,

gathers army to fight against Jeroboam but constrained by prophet Shemaiah because Jehovah has divided Israel, 143, 145; builds up Judah's military strength, 145; he and his people became wicked, Jehovah sends Egypt to conquer them, 145; has continual wars with Israel during his seventeenth year, 145

Remaliah, *King Pekah's father*, 180

Reuben, *eldest son of Jacob and Leah*, born, 28; suggests that Joseph be cast into pit rather than killed, 35; planned to return Joseph to father, not present when Joseph is sold, 35; pleads with Jacob to let Benjamin go to Egypt, 39; blessed by Jacob, 41

Reuel (Jethro), 45 (fn. 108)

Rezin, *Syrian king*, joins with King Pekah and Israel to defeat Judah and set up puppet king, 180; Jehovah delivers King Ahaz into hands of, 181; killed when Assyrians conquer Syria, 180

Rizpah, *Saul's concubine*, Ishbosheth accuses Abner of adultery with, 117; her two sons given to Gibeonites, 133; keeps vigil to keep birds and beasts away from her sons' bodies, 133

Ruth, *Moabitess, Naomi's daughter-in-law*, her husband Mahlon dies, she goes with Naomi to Bethlehem, gleans in fields of Boaz, marries him, 90

Samson, *Nazarite, judge in Israel*, birth and mission foretold to parents by angel, 85; marriage to Philistine woman is of Jehovah to create rift, 86; events arising from marriage cause him to wreak havoc and take many Philistine lives, 86; Delilah induces him to reveal source of strength, is taken captive by Philistines, 86; causes collapse of house of Dagon killing many Philistines, 86

Samuel, *Levite, judge, priest, and prophet, son of Elkanah and Hannah*, born to barren mother as result of Eli's blessing, 91; taken to temple and given to Jehovah as child, 91; raised by Eli the priest, 91, 92; Jehovah talks to him by night about judgment to come on Eli because of wicked sons, 92; leads Israel in victory over Philistines at Mizpeh, 96; Israel petitions him to give them a king, he tells them problems this would bring, 97; anoints Saul king of Israel, first privately, then before all Israel, 98; goes with Saul's army to fight Ammonites at Jabesh-gilead, anoints him again at Gilgal, 99; rebukes Saul for offering burnt offering at Gilgal, 100; sends Saul to destroy Amalekites, 102; tells Saul that he and his seed are

no longer accepted of Jehovah, to be taken from throne, because he disobeyed, 102; slays Agag, Ammonite king, 102; anoints David king of Israel, 103; David, fleeing from Saul, finds him at Ramah, 106; dies, 110

Sanballat, *Moabite in authority in Samaria*, actively opposes rebuilding Jerusalem's walls, plots to lure Nehemiah out of city and kill him, 227; his daughter marries grandson of Eliashib the high priest, 229

Sarah (Sarai), *Abraham's wife, Isaac's mother*, goes with Abram from Ur to Haran, 10; goes with Abram from Haran into Canaan, 11; tells Egyptians she is Abram's sister as instructed by Jehovah, 13; barren, gives handmaid Hagar to be Abram's wife, 15; is despised by Hagar and is compelled to send her away, 15; name changed from Sarai to Sarah, 16; promised a son in her old age, to be named Isaac, 16; presents herself to Abimelech as Abraham's sister, told by Abimelech not to worry about Abraham being killed because of her, 18; Isaac born to, sends Hagar and Ishmael away, 19; dies, buried in cave at Hebron, 21

Sarai, see Sarah

Satan, see Lucifer

Saul, *first king of Israel, Benjamite, son of Kish*, anointed by Samuel to be king while searching for father's asses, 98; hides when called to be anointed before all Israel at Mizpeh, 98; leads army in defeat of Ammonites at Jabesh-gilead, goes to Gilgal and is anointed again, 99; offers sacrifice that should have been offered by Samuel, is rebuked severely, 100; sent to destroy Amalekites, brings back King Agag and animals for sacrifice, kingdom taken from him and his seed, 102; Jehovah rebukes Samuel because he mourns for, 103; Spirit leaves him and is replaced by evil spirit, brings David to play harp for him, 104; convinced that David has faith needed to overcome Goliath, he sends David to battle, 105; takes David into household and makes him armorbearer, becomes jealous and tries to kill him by various means, 106; becomes angry with Jonathan and tries to kill him for defending David, 107; has Doeg the Edomite kill Abimelech and all priests at Nob for helping David, 108; pursues David relentlessly, his life is spared by David when he finds him asleep in cave at Engedi, 109; while he sleeps in camp at Hachilah, David and Abishai take his spear and water cruse, but David still declines to kill him, 111; stops seeking David when David goes to Gath, 112; he goes to a witch when war pending and he has no answers from Jehovah, requests her to bring up Samuel, the spirit foretells his death, 113; he and three sons slain in battle with Philistines at Mt. Gilboa, 115; his head and armor put in house of Ashtoreth, his body and sons' bodies hung on wall at Beth-shean, bones retrieved and buried at Jabesh-gilead, 115; David receives word of his death from young man who claims to have killed him, David has young man slain, 116

Segub, *Heil's son*, loses life when gate is set at rebuilt Jericho, 151

Sennacherib, *Assyrian king*, invades Judah, overcomes all cities, except Jerusalem, lays siege to Jerusalem demanding tribute and making threats, when his army is stricken and dies in one night, he returns to Nineveh, 184

Seth, *Adam's son*, born, looks like Adam except for age, obeys God and offers acceptable sacrifice, 4

Shadrach, *Jewish captive in Babylon*, with Daniel, Meshach, and Abednego, in special training program in Babylon, prospers on special diet, 212; prays for Daniel to interpret king's dream, rewarded with administrative office, 213; refuses to bow before golden idol, thrown into fiery furnace, 21

Shalmanezer, *Assyrian king*, invades Israel and makes King Hoshea a servant, exacts tribute, puts Hoshea in prison upon learning that he sent messengers to Egypt but brought no gifts to him, conquers Samaria and the kingdom of Israel, carries people captive to Assyria, 182

Shammah, *Jesse's third son*, not chosen king of Israel, 103; at battlefront when David slays Goliath, 105

Shaphan, *scribe*, he and Hilkiah the high priest assigned by King Josiah to supervise temple cleanup, book of Law is found, he reads it and reports it to Josiah, is sent, with others, to prophetess Huldah to ask about the book, 189

Shebna, *King Hezekiah's agent*, meets, along with others, with Sennacherib's agents, then is sent to find Isaiah, 184

Shechaniah, *head of priestly family and spokesman for returned Jews*, agrees that Jews will covenant to put away heathen wives and children, all take oath to do as he says, 226; has connection with Tobiah the Ammonite, 229

Shechem, *son of Hamor, prince of Shechem*, desires Dinah to be his wife, slain by Levi and Simeon for defiling their sister Dinah, 33

Shelah, *third of Judah's three sons by Canaanite wife*, is to marry his brothers' wife Tamar after he comes of age, but Judah fails to follow through, 36

Shem, *Noah's son*, saved on ark, 8; is ancestor of Abraham, 10

Shemaiah, *prophet of Judah*, warns Rehoboam not to fight against Jeroboam because division of Israel is Jehovah's will, 143, 145; tells Rehoboam that Egypt conquered Judah because Judah has forsaken Jehovah, 145

Shemaiah, *traitor to returning Jews*, hired by Sanballat and Tobiah, tells Nehemiah that his life is in danger and that he should hide in temple, 227

Sheshbazzar (Zerubbabel) 222 (fn. 699)

Shimea, *son of David and Bathsheba*, 124 (fn. 308)

Shimei, *Benjamite*, curses David as he flees from Absalom, 128; comes to welcome David returning from exile, admits his error, 131; David charges Solomon to bring his gray head down to grave with blood, 137; is allowed to dwell in Jerusalem with agreement to never leave city, slain when he leaves seeking servants who went to Gath, 138

Shishak, *Egyptian king*, conquers Judah in days of Rehoboam because Judah had forsaken Jehovah, 145

Shobab, *son of David and Bathsheba*, 124 (fn. 308)

Shuah, *son of Abraham and Keturah*, 22

Simeon, *son of Jacob and Leah*, born, 28; he and Levi murder people of Shechem for Dinah's honor, 33; held hostage in Egypt by Joseph, 39; blessed by Jacob, 41

Sisera, *captain of Canaanite army occupying Israel*, defeated by Deborah and Barak, slain by Jael, 80

Smedis (Artaxerxes, the impostor king), 222 (fn. 705)

So, *Egyptian king*, gifts sent to him by King Hoshea of Israel, 182

Solomon, *king of Israel, son of David and Bathsheba*,

born, 124; Jehovah names him as the one who will build temple, David gathers materials and makes preparations, 135; anointed king, at David's direction, to thwart Adonijah's attempt to become king, 136; charged by David to deal with David's enemies, 137; deals with Adonijah and David's enemies, 138; asks Jehovah for wisdom, is blessed with wisdom and riches, 139; instructs that child be divided to end women's dispute, 140; builds and dedicates temple, 141; gains great riches, takes many wives, forsakes Jehovah for false gods of his wives, 142; Jehovah tells him that the kingdom will be given to his servant, 142; dies, succeeded by son Rehoboam, 143

Tamar, *Judah's daughter-in-law*, left widow without children by Judah's sons, when Judah fails to give her his youngest son she plays harlot, conceives twins by Judah, 36

Tamar, *David's daughter*, seduced by half-brother Amnon, wrong is avenged by Absalom, 125

Tamar, *Absalom's daughter*, 147 (fn. 411)

Tartak, *false god of Avites*, 182

Tatnai, *Persian governor*, writes letter to King Darius when he sees temple being rebuilt to confirm that work was authorized by Cyrus, 223

Terah, *Abraham's father*, worships false gods, seeks to sacrifice Abraham, repents during famine and goes with Abraham to Nahor, dies there, 10

Tibni, *king over half of Northern Kingdom*, loses kingdom to Omri, 150

Tiglath-pileser, *Assyrian king*, believed by some to be Pul (q.v.), takes first people of Israel and many Syrians captive to Assyria, 180

Tobiah, *Ammonite*, opponent to rebuilding Jerusalem's walls, mocks builders, seeks Nehemiah's life, 227; makes alliance with Eliashib and establishes living quarters in temple, 229; evicted from temple by Nehemiah, 229

Tubal-cain, *son of Lamech and Zillah, descendant of Cain*, 5

Uriah the Hittite, *husband of Bathsheba and one of David's mighty men*, murdered by David with swords of the Ammonites, 123; account of his murder told to David in parable form by Nathan, 124

Uzzah, *son of Abinadab the priest*, steadies ark of covenant, struck dead, 119

Uzziah, *king of Judah, Amaziah's son*, is righteous and successful in war, 178; goes into temple and offers sacrifice without authority, stricken with leprosy, son Jotham acts for him, 178; dies, replaced by son Jotham, 181

Vashti, *Persian queen*, refuses to display her beauty at King Ahasuerus's feast, is dethroned, 224

Widow of Zarephath, Elijah promises that her oil and meal will not run out, she sustains Elijah during drought, he raises her son from dead, 152

Xerxes (the Great), Persian king, *Darius's son, Artaxerxes' father*, 211; believed to be king in story of Esther, rather than Ahasuerus, 224 (fn. 711)

Zachariah, *king of Israel, Jeroboam II's son*, succeeds father, reigns six months in wickedness, slain, succeeded by Shallum, 180

Zadok, *priest*, leaves Jerusalem with David, sent back with Abiathar and their sons, 127; relays Hushai's message to David via his son Ahimaaz, 129; not invited to Adonijah's feast, sent to Gihon by David, he and prophet Nathan anoint Solomon king of Israel, 136; Solomon appoints him in Abiathar's place, 138; ancestor of prophet Ezekiel, 199; one of his descendants will make burnt offering in temple in last days, 207

Zaphnath-paaneah (Joseph), Egyptian name given to him by Pharaoh, 38

Zarah, *twin son (with Pharez) of Judah and Tamar*, 36

Zebul, *ruler of Shechem*, sides with Abimelech against Gaal, warns Abimelech and challenges Gaal, 82

Zebulun, *son of Jacob and Leah*, born, 28; blessed by Jacob, 41

Zechariah, *prophet, son of Jehoiada the priest, Jahaziel's father*, 159; prophesies and calls Judah to repentance, stoned by command of King Joash, 175

Zechariah, *prophet*, mentor to king Uzziah, 178

Zechariah, *prophet, son of Berechiah*, prophesies among Jews, works on rebuilding of temple of

SUBJECT INDEX

The entries in this index refer to story numbers rather than page numbers.

golden calves of Jeroboam, 143, 144, 145, 148, 150, 160, 162, 173, 176, 178, 180, 182, 189
gratitude, 3, 8, 21, 52, 96, 110, 164, 179, 225
great image, dream of, 213
grove(s), 81, 146, 149, 150, 153, 159, 175, 176, 182, 183, 188, 189
guilt, feelings of, 39, 41, 43
handwriting on wall, 218
hard-heartedness, 48, 49, 51
hatred, 6, 15, 21, 24, 25, 35, 41, 48, 82, 83, 86, 120, 125, 129, 130, 131, 158, 198, see also *contempt*
heaven, hosts of, 156, 182, 189, 194, 217
high place(s), 98, 139, 142, 143, 144, 145, 147, 149, 171, 177, 181, 182, 183, 184, 188, 189, 194
holiness, 46, 55, 56, 61, 65, 71, 74, 221
holy men, 16, 17, 92, 144, 156, 177, see also *prophets, unnamed*
holy of holies, 56, 94, 141, 207
homosexuality, 17
hope, 19, 43, 98, 152, 192, 205, 226
hosts of heaven, 156, 182, 189, 194, 217
house of the Lord, see *tabernacle* and *temple*
human sacrifice, 10, 162, 181, 188, 194
humility, 26, 46, 56, 58, 63, 87, 98, 106, 110, 145, 156, 157, 166, 183, 185, 188, 189, 215, 220, 221, 225
idol worship, see *false gods*
image, great, dream of, 213
immorality, see *sexual immorality*
imprisonment of Jeremiah, 198
incense, burning improperly, 61, 65
incense, burning to Jehovah, 56, 183
incense, burning to false gods, 143, 144, 177, 178, 181, 182, 189, 192, 210
ingratitude, 4, 29, 30, 52, 57, 62, 65, 179
Israel, a chosen people, 46, 71
Israel, delivered from Egypt, 48, 49, 50
Israel, divided into two kingdoms, 142, 143
Israel, in Egypt, 39, 40, 41, 42, 44, 46, 48, 49, 50
jealousy, 4, 35, 106, 107, 109
Jericho, curse of, 75, 151
Jerusalem, conquering of, 119
Jerusalem, fall of, 208
Jordan, parting of, 73, 61
Judah's future, seen in vision, 217, 220, 221
judgments of God, 4, 43, 48, 49, 50, 57, 69, 119, 135, 141, 156, 159, 188, 190, 199, 201, 202, 204, 216, 220, 229
justice, 43, 127, 138
kindness, 18, 21, 24, 32, 33, 41, 45, 90, 102, 108, 110, 122, 137, 139, 143, 156, 164, 175, 179, 211
kings, desire of Israel to have, 97
kings, righteous, go astray, 100, 102, 123, 142, 175, 178
language confounded, 9

last days, prophecies concerning restoration of Israel and Judah in, 200, 204, 205, 206, 207, 216, 217
laws, to govern Israel, 54, 55, 58, 71, 72, 76, 78, 90, 149, 226, 229
Levites, chosen by Jehovah, 61, 183
lineage, of Savior, 36, 41
lions' den, Daniel in, 219
love of God, 1, 2, 6
love, family, 32, 39, 41, 48, 54
love, parental, 4, 16, 19, 20, 21, 25, 39
loyalty, 29, 35, 37, 38, 39, 68, 90, 117, 123, 127, 129, 219
Lucifer, see *Satan*
man of God, see *holy men* and *prophets, unnamed*
man, each, responsible for own sins, 202
man, preeminence of, 2
man, spirit child of God, 2
manna 52, 62, 74
mantle, Elijah's, 155, 161
marriage to unbelievers, 8, 21, 25, 33, 36, 78, 79, 86, 142, 150, 171, 226, 229
marriage, 3, 21, 22, 27, 33, 38, 45
mercy seat, 56, 94, 141
mercy, 32, 58, 60, 121, 139, 156, 179, 183, 188, 220, 215, 226, 227
miracles, 49, 51, 52, 53, 66, 67, 78, 95, 134, 154, 165, 166, 167, 168, 169, 185
mortal probation, 1
mortality, 3
most holy place, 56, see also *holy of holies*
mourning, 4, 8, 35, 36, 41, 43, 64, 66, 71, 102, 110, 116, 123, 144, 146, 200, 203, 226
murmuring, 51, 52, 63, 64, 65, 67, 77, 187
names, changes of, made by God, 16, 31
names, changes of, made by men, 38, 81, 195, 196, 212, 224
neighbors, relationships with, 14, 24, 33, 48, 49, 50, 55, 69, 85, 96, 223, 226, 228, 229
night visions, see *dreams*
Noah's ark, 8
oaths, see *covenants*
obedience and its fruits, 1, 3, 4, 6, 7, 8, 10, 12, 13, 15, 20, 21, 24, 25, 46, 52, 55, 99, 139, 142, 144, 198
offerings, see *sacrifices and offerings*
opposition, 1, 12, 101, 222, 227
parables, 82, 124, 200, 201
parent, fails to correct unrighteous children, 92
passover, 50, 74, 183, 189, 192, 204, 223
patience, 24, 43, 57
patriarchal blessings, 7, 25, 40, 41
persecution, 43, 44, 48, 49, 53
Persians and Medes, Babylonians defeated by, 211, 216, 217, 218, 221
Persians and Medes, defeated by Grecia, 216, 217, 221

376

sealed book, prophecy of, 187
Second Coming, 7, 207
secret oaths, 4, 5
seer, latter-day, 42
seers, 6, 42, 98, 182, 187
self mastery, 23, 110
service, 1, 25, 27, 28, 29, 30, 32, 37, 61, 78, 223, 228
sexual immorality, 17, 33, 36, 37, 69, 87, 89, 92, 123, 129
shame, 33, 36, 63, 74, 125, 131, 200, 207, 221, 226
Shiloh, religious center, site of tabernacle, 78, 88, 89, 91, 92
siege, 109, 132, 156, 182, 184, 185, 196, 198, 199, 208, 211
signs, 46, 48, 49, 50, 51, 56, 64, 65, 73, 81, 98, 101, 144, 185, 190, 198, 199, 203, 210
sin of Jeroboam, 143, 144, 145, 148, 150, 160, 162, 173, 176, 178, 180, 182, 189
sins, each person responsible for own, 202
Sodom, 11, 14, 17
sorrow, 3, 19, 20, 25, 35, 39, 44, 46, 89, 91, 116, 126, 130, 131, 134, 156, 164, 221, 227
spiritual death, 1, 3
stars and planets, order of, 13
stars and planets, vision of, 47
sticks of Judah and Joseph, 42, 206
still, small voice, 155
stone tablets, 56, 58
stone, pillars of, 26, 30, 34, 56
stoning, death by, 55, 76, 157, 175
suffering for righteousness, 4, 7, 10, 24, 37, 38,43, 106, 198, 214
suicide, 150
sundial, turned back, 185
Syria, defeated by Assyria, 180
Syria, Israel's alliances with, 180, 181
Syria, Israel's battles with, 123, 156, 158, 168, 169, 172, 176, 178
Syria, Judah's alliances with, 148
Syria, Judah's battles with, 158, 172, 175, 180, 181
tabernacle, 56, 59, 91, 92, see also *temple*
temple, David not to build, 121
temple, dedication, 141
temple, in last days, 207, 221
temple, rebuilding of, 187, 222, 223, 225, 226, 227, 229
temple, Solomon's 121, 135, 139, 141, 143, 147, 159, 174, 175, 178, 179, 181, 183, 185, 188, 189, 193, 194, 195, 196, 197, 198, 200, 203, 208, 209, see also *tabernacle*
temple, treasures removed, 145, 175, 177, 184, 197, 212, 218, 222
temple, vessels desecrated, 175, 177, 181, 195, 208, 212, 218, 229

temple, Zerubbabel's, 187, 222, 223, 225, 226, 227, 229
temptation, 1, 2, 3, 4, 37, 47, 54, 166, 229
Ten Commandments, 55, 58
testimony, 6, 43
theft, 30, 39, 43, 76, 88, 92
time, God's, 13
tithing, 14, 26, 61, 229
Tower of Babel, 9
transgression, 3, 55, 101, 102, 142, 199, 202, 206, 217, 220, 226
translated beings, 6, 71, 161
tree, dream of great, 215
tree of knowledge of good and evil, 3
tree of life, 3
trials, 20, 43, 128, 155, 169, 182, 196, 198, 208, 224, 227, 229
trust, 20, 37, 38, 43, 163, 184, 213, 227
trusting in falsehood, 82, 86, 144, 156, 197, 200, 209
unity of husband and wife, 3, 13, 18, 19, 24, 30, 34, 106
unkindness, 5, 15, 19, 24, 35, 43, 44, 48, 82, 88, 106, 108, 109, 110, 128, 143, 157, 170, 175, 198, 227, 228
unrepentant sinners, 5, 8, 33, 58, 65, 82, 89, 92, 197
unrighteousness, 4, 5, 6, 8, 9, 17, 36, 80, 92, 97, 142
unrighteousness, fruits of, 82, 94, 100, 102, 138, 142, 148, 153, 160, 171, 172, 173, 174, 177,178, 182, 188, 208, 210, 215, 218, 219
Urim and Thummim, 13, 70, 113
valley of dry bones, 205
victory, with Jehovah's help, 6, 14, 53, 67, 79, 80, 81, 83, 96, 99, 101, 109, 114, 130, 132, 156, 162, 168, 172, 176, 177, 178, 189, 194, 227 see also *defeat, with Jehovah's intervention*
victory, without war, 34, 51, 75, 105, 159, 169, 184
vineyard, Naboth's, 157, 172
visions, 6, 47, 56, 63, 68, 158, 161, 168, 170, 190, 199, 200, 207, 212, 217, 218, 221, see also *dreams, prophecies,* and *revelations*
wall, handwriting on, 218
walls, of Jerusalem rebuilt, 181, 220, 222, 223, 227
War in Heaven, 1, 2
washing of priests, 56, 59
watchers, 215
watchman, to Israel, 199
water, bitter made sweet, 52
water, from a rock, 52, 66
water, from under temple, 207
wickedness, see *unrighteousness*
wisdom, a gift from God, 43, 47, 135, 139, 140, 212, 213, 218
witch, Saul seeks guidance from, 113
women, childless, blessed with children, 16, 19, 23, 28, 91
world, vision of, 47

ABOUT THE AUTHOR

Val D. Greenwood was born and raised in Utah and is a lifelong member of The Church of Jesus Christ of Latter-day Saints. He graduated from Brigham Young University in 1962 with a bachelor of science degree in journalism, and from the University of Idaho in 1974 with a Juris Doctor degree. Before his retirement in 1999, he worked for the Church for thirty-seven years. His assignments included being a researcher and writer in the Genealogical Department (now Family History Department) and a faculty member at Ricks College (now Brigham Young University—Idaho). He worked for more than nineteen years in the Temple Department and was a director in that department for fifteen years. He has been a lifelong student of the scriptures and has taught LDS Institute classes in Salt Lake City, Utah; Moscow, Idaho; and

Santa Barbara, California; as well as religion classes at Ricks College. He has also taught at BYU Education Weeks in Provo and in Idaho.

Mr. Greenwood is the author of *The Researcher's Guide to American Genealogy*, first published in 1973 and in its third edition since 2000. This book is now considered a classic and is the standard work in the field. He has also written articles for Church magazines as well as genealogical articles.

As a young man, he filled a mission for The Church of Jesus Christ of Latter-day Saints in Canada and has also served as a high councilor, bishop, and patriarch. Together with his first wife, he served a two-year mission for the Church Educational System in Santa Barbara. He has been a sealer in the Jordan River Utah Temple for more than twenty years and also serves as a volunteer assistant temple recorder.

Mr. Greenwood lives in Riverton, Utah, with his wife, Patricia (Patty) Tanner Greenwood, whom he married in 2004. (His first wife, Margaret [Peggy] Turner Greenwood, passed away in early 2003 from cancer.) He has three daughters, a stepdaughter, and two stepsons. He and Patty have twenty-two grandchildren between them.

Email: howoften@valgreenwood.com

Web Site: http://newviewoldtestament.com